BORIS WILSON

A TIME OF INNOCENCE

For Pauline, Adrian, Nigel and Virginia

BORIS WILSON

A TIME OF INNOCENCE

*For my dear friend
Louise Betz Silman
from
Boris Wilson november 1991*

...As much as I ever did, more than I ever did, I believe in
Liberalism. But there was a rosy time of innocence when I
believed in Liberals.

*GK Chesterton
Orthodoxy, 1908*

Murray Coombes Publisher
IN ASSOCIATION WITH

RANDOM CENTURY
SOUTH AFRICA (PTY) LTD.

First published in 1991 by
Murray Coombes, Publisher,
in association with
Random Century South Africa (Pty) Ltd
PO Box 337
Bergvlei
2012 South Africa

ISBN 0 947024 37 9

Typeset and repro by Adcolour

Printed by Robprint

ACKNOWLEDGEMENTS

I was in a murderous mood about South African publishers until Andrew Meyer of Random Century read my manuscript; he enjoyed it and said he wanted it published.

He introduced me to our co-publisher, my editor Murray Coombes, and we immediately found rapport. Murray is a delightful person, easy to work with, highly competent and in a large measure responsible that *A Time of Innocence* is in the bookshops.

I am fortunate that three former editors of *The Rand Daily Mail*, Laurence Gandar, Raymond Louw (now editor and publisher of the influential Southern Africa Report), and Allister Sparks (author of *The Mind of South Africa*), all encouraged me for the eight years that it took me to write this book.

To Laurence Gandar in particular I owe a special debt of gratitude for critically reading the final draft, and for his valuable advice.

Dr Brian Hackland lent me his massive thesis on the Progressive Party 1959-81, with some of his original papers, and gave me permission to use whatever data I needed.

My wife, Pauline, painstakingly read the manuscript and made many helpful corrections; my sister, Ethel Gordon, let me off the family hook after reading it with a "positive response".

Jack Bleiman, a founder Progressive now in London, let me scrutinise his records, and read an early draft. Dr Van Zyl Slabbert had critical comments on the last chapters which I welcomed. Tom Weldon, editor at William Heineman in London, after reading an early version, urged me to get it published in South Africa.

My thanks to my only known surviving relative, Ruth Tobin, in New York, who withstood my arguments about my father's origins and gave me important background as a result of her researches into the family tree.

I must especially thank Jock Leyden of the *Natal Daily News*, one of South Africa's famous political cartoonists, whom I met while I was in Parliament, and who years ago gave me the originals of the cartoons he drew of me.

Thanks also to *The Star* newspaper in Johannesburg, who were very helpful in locating photographs for the book, and for giving me permission to use them.

Finally, to the intrepid class of 1959, my United Party colleagues who stepped with me into the political unknown, into the new world of the Progressive Party; to them and to all the many unsung members of the Party, I say a sincere "Thank you".

I salute all my critics and adversaries, of whom there have been so many, who shared my political experiences, enriched my life and ultimately made it all worthwhile.

ACKNOWLEDGMENTS

AUTHOR'S NOTE

Looking back on a life in South Africa, one realises how diverse and complex we whites have made our country. The social environment has changed from the age of the slow, horse drawn cart and the Model T Ford of the 1920s to the frenetic modernity of the 1990s, with its supermarkets, fast cars and television.

Not so with the country's built-in racial problems. They stayed relatively static in a white-dominated limbo until the Nationalists arrived in 1948, putting on pressures to legalise apartheid in the hope that it would leave the whites in perpetual domination and blacks, coloureds and Indians in bondage, under the guise of separate development.

In February 1990 the apartheid dream collapsed, destroyed by its Nationalist founders. A start was made to clear the political debris that tainted and cluttered South African society so that the infrastructure of the new South Africa could be erected.

The decade ahead is going to be a testing time for everyone, whether they live in the squalid squatter camps of Crossroads in the Cape, the unrest fields of Natal, the wide stretches of the Karoo, or the high-walled and protected wealthy homes of Sandton in the Transvaal.

Will our multiracial descendants be able to find the elusive consensus to rectify the unforgiveable mistakes we whites made in governing of South Africa without ever bringing in the blacks, coloureds and Indians to share power with us?

A Time of Innocence does not pretend to provide academic answers to South Africa's problems – that was never the intention when I started to write my autobiography eight years ago.

Looking back over the years of my political life was a necessary catharsis. I relived the most profound influence my father had on me, and to whom this book is an act of homage. He was a man of no public importance whatsoever, a stateless alien, who struggled hard to find solutions to the world's problems and failed to solve many of his own. But his determination in the face of extremely adverse circumstances made its mark indelibly on me.

My father's social and philosophical views may occasionally have been somewhat bizarre, but his concern for the oppressed led me inevitably to liberal politics. I realised very early on that South African society was becoming increasingly brutalised and diseased, developing in ways which were completely unacceptable to anyone who regarded himself as humanist, egalitarian and liberal. It led me to affirm my faith in liberalism in South Africa, but to question the political credibility of some of its leading liberals.

I expect that some of my political friends and opponents who read this book will disagree with my opinions and conclusions. If so, those disagreements may well mirror the rough road that FW de Klerk and Nelson Mandela have to walk before they find the pathway to the promised land of the new South Africa somewhere in the mists of the future.

Boris Wilson
July 1991

THE MARKET

All humans are alike to me
Whether black, yellow, brown or white
Whether young, old – a he or a she
All are the same humans with equal rights.
                                    Samuel Wilson, 1949

"Go away Jew-boy" – almost at the beginning of my life and one of the first things I can remember.

I was four years old, playing on the unmade sandy pavement fronting the tin-roofed semi-detached next to our house. I stood there terrified, unable to move, staring at the vitriolic face of the man, our angry neighbour. He had rushed out of his front door waving his arms, yelling at me, telling me to go away from the pavement in front of his house.

I do not recall all that happened. I know that I suddenly fled, crying, running into our house, into the arms of my father. Somehow, between sobs, I told him what had happened.

My father had been sitting in his usual place, drinking his Russian tea and lemon, sweetened with a few teaspoons of homemade black cherry jam.

He took me by the hand and we went outside. The neighbour, a tall spare man, was still on his veranda. I was petrified as I heard my father angrily threatening the bigger man with a physical and violent end. Father placed me firmly on the pavement outside the neighbour's house, told me to play where I liked and to ignore the neighbour.

This was the first and earliest recollection I have of my father's determination to stand up against injustice and racial intolerance. There was widespread anti-semitism after extensive Jewish immigration to South Africa in the 1920s and 1930s, fueled by Dr Daniel Malan's notorious Quota Act. This Act was intended to limit the number of Jews entering the Union. I was aware of this, as a small boy, through the many letters my father wrote to the press on the subject.

In the early 1920s we lived in Hunter Street in Bellevue, a lower-middle-class suburb of Johannesburg. Our house was typical of those opposite the local Scout and Recreation hall in which was my nursery school.

Hunter Street was like many of the streets of Johannesburg as I knew it over the next few years. Most roads were untarred, rutted and sandy, often full of droppings from the horses who pulled various carts over them. Roads were awful in winter because cold winds swirled the loose sand of the street with the dust from the mine dumps to the south of the town.

Semi-detached were interspersed with superior-looking single-storey detached houses. Practically every one had a corrugated galvanised-iron roof which clattered terribly when the frequent summer highveld hailstorms came down in uncontrolled ferocity.

Traffic was mostly horse-drawn, but I still have images of the Model-T Fords riding majestically over the ruts and bumps of the roads.

In the next street to the south was the local tram service to Observatory. Large, nondescript, noisy trams trundled and jerked their way in fits and starts down narrow Rockey Street to the terminus.

I have two earlier recollections.

The first is of a fat middle-aged black woman, a servant, holding me in her arms with my eldest sister Hannah at her side, waiting on the pavement outside our house for my father to come home. She had a smiling oval face and wore a *doek* on her head. The second is of my father and mother framed in the doorway of my room where, from my cot, I was yelling and crying as a result of a nightmare.

2

I was born in February 1917 in Hillbrow, a suburb perched on one of the many hills that make up Johannesburg.

I often went to see the small semi-detached house in Jager Street, but about ten years ago when I went to take a photograph of it, it was gone. In its place was a towering block of those concrete flats which now proliferate in the area.

My father and mother met in Johannesburg as immigrants from Eastern Europe. They were introduced to each other by her relations who wanted her off their hands. For many years we were never sure where Father came from – we always believed it was near Moscow – because he spoke and wrote Russian fluently. I finally found out, years after he died, that he did indeed come from a small town called Dubrovna near Moscow. However, in October 1990, while I was visiting Moscow, I failed to find Dubrovna. No one was able to tell me if there had ever been such a town.

My father left us with these mysteries about his origins and personal history; he probably had his own convincing reasons for this silence, so that we can only speculate about who he really was and what he had done.

But the reason that he came to South Africa was made clear in a play he wrote, based on his experiences on a ship sailing from Australia to England via the Cape. According to Father, he was on his way to England when he was put off the boat in Cape Town by the captain.

It appears that, during the voyage, my father had violent disagreements and arguments with a priest about religion and the church, and whether God existed; so bad was the atmosphere on board that the captain decided, for safety's sake, to put my father ashore in Cape Town.

One can imagine the scene at the docks in Cape Town: immigration, police and customs officials waiting for the ship to tie up, and Father being escorted down the ramp into the arms of authority, with hundreds of gawking passengers lining the rails.

The play, *The Extremists*, is about a priest, a young man called Lova, and the theological arguments they had. It seems, then, that it was not Father's intention to come to South Africa at all; he was an "accidental" immigrant. Knowing him as I did, this is not an implausible scenario, and this is in fact the story of his arrival in South Africa.

What is a complete blank, however, is what happened to him after he left the United States – sometime in 1908 or 1909 – for Australia via Fiji. He must have lived in Australia for two or three years before setting out on this uncompleted journey to England. He never talked about this period – where he lived, what he did, why he left. He might well have been deported from Australia, which may account for the captain's drastic decision to expel him from the ship in Cape Town.

Samuel, my father, was a stocky man, well-built, with a strongly modelled face and a stern serious expression. He always wore a hat; and his clothes, which were well-tailored, nevertheless hung loosely on him.

My mother Sonya, considerably younger than Father, was a school teacher from Suwalki, a small town in what is today north-eastern Poland. She was as tall as him, slender, with beautiful long black hair, a lovely face with smiling dark eyes.

In 1914, when they married, my father had already stopped pushing his barrow of fruit around the streets of Johannnesburg, and was a stallholder at the old Market Square in the centre of Johannesburg, behind the Town Hall.

Johannesburg, in the centre of the Witwatersrand – the Ridge of White Waters – is today a city of low hills competing with fast-disappearing yellow goldmine dumps. The metropolitan area extends east and west for about fifty kilometres in both directions and includes a number of smaller towns and cities. This is the wealthy *eGoli*, the greatest gold-mining area in the world.

We lived north of the main railway line which bisected the town. Our homes were always in the same suburbs; Bellevue and Yeoville, which we knew intimately because we moved frequently as social and economic circumstances dictated; and as the family grew in size. There were five children. Hannah was the eldest a year older than me, Leon a year younger, followed by Ethel six years later. Finally Max, the youngest who arrived six years after Ethel. Max's birth lead to a serious crisis in Mother's life.

Often our houses were too small and we moved. On the other, hand we also moved because of the serious effects of the great Depression of the early 1930s and the struggles my father had to pay for such basic items as the monthly rent. He never had enough money to buy a house. On the contrary, we were evicted several times because he could not pay the rent.

I always knew my father as a poor man, who worked hard and struggled for a living. It was only in his latter years that he managed to own his house and had enough money to retire, long after most men retired, at the age of seventy-four.

He never squandered or spent money on things not needed for our family's survival, except that he frequented a bookseller's shop run by a very fat friend, Fanny Klennerman, a Trotskyist and freethinking socialist. Over the years he built up a library of books in politics, philosophy and poetry. He would delve into these books almost every day of his life, when he came home from the market. He would annotate the pages with his comments – both approving and disapproving the arguments.

Years later I realised that although his background was hidden from us, he must have had some valuable educational training, or at least some strong intellectual stimulus. He bought and read philosophical books ranging from Plato to Schopenhauer, Nietzsche, Bertrand Russell and poets like Shelley, Byron and Tennyson.

During his lifetime he worked very hard and with devotion, to keep his family fed, clothed and educated as he saw fit. He was an angry man, a martinet. In fact, I have never met an angrier man. His commands had to be obeyed. He decided what we should do and how we should behave. As a result we were witnesses to the frequent bitter rows between our parents, which became part of our daily lives.

I can now understand some of the reasons for these parental rows – many were due to my father's unpredictable, terrible tempers. Often the fights were triggered by minor incidents, on trivial family matters – like the evening meal not ready on time, or a casual remark by Mother, to which my father objected.

However, there were serious causes too. During the late 1920s, in the Depression, we were so poor that the only hope for Father was to appeal for help from my mother's wealthier cousins who lived nearby. I know about this because he took me with him.

I heard him plead for financial help standing at the front door of my mother's cousin's house without being invited inside, with his pleas for help refused. When we got home, Father went for Mother in a rage, blaming her for his failure to get help.

I was six years old at the time. Although we were really too young to understand the complexities of our parents' marital problems, there was a cumulative and important effect on our emotional and mental development, with even more serious family disruptions yet to come.

Father was the dominant personality – decisive, hurtful, brutal and frightening – especially when he was angry. My mother was gentle, forgetful and totally unable to withstand his verbal onslaughts, which too often ended in a physical assault – a slap or a punch in the face. It also happened to us as children. We were careful not to incur his wrath, when we knew he was tired after a long day at the Market, especially when business was bad, or when our parents fought.

I began to realise how unusual my father was when I visited friends and saw how nicely their mothers and fathers treated each other – and their children.

Father used to tell us about small incidents of his childhood in Russia, like swimming the Volga River, or stealing cucumbers from a neighbour's vegetable garden. We had a lovely silver samovar in our living room and he told us that his family had several of them in his home town.

He was secretive about his early youth and his family – who his parents were and whether he had brothers and sisters. He once told me that his grandfather had been a rabbi, and that I was named after him. Other than these meagre clues, there was almost nothing. He did say that he had been sentenced to four years in a Siberian prison by the Russian Czar for his role in an army rebellion, but he managed to escape making his way to Vladivostok in the east, with graphic descriptions of how he outwitted the wolves in the Siberian snow. He came to New York to join a younger brother. At Ellis Island the immigration authorities named him Samuel Wilson, a name which he adopted.

We never knew his real Russian name, nor did my mother ever tell us what it was. It is possible that she never knew it, because he seems to have arrived in South Africa as Samuel Wilson. It was only during my Moscow visit in 1990 that I discovered some possibilities which will be examined later.

His first job in New York was serving iced water at mealtimes and clearing tables in a restaurant. Then he was a clothes presser. Later he went to Denver, Colorado, selling apples in the streets from a barrow. Once he was part of Rosa Luxembourg's entourage when she visited America on a speaking tour (so he said).

I never learnt directly from my father what prompted him to leave Russia. His claim that he was an escaped military prisoner – even in the circumstances of the time – lacks credibility.

In February 1929, when I was twelve, he dictated a poem to me, which he had written in a small black notebook he always carried:

I AM NOT LONGING FOR MY HOME

I am not longing for my home
Not because it was not a home
Like a child there born
And to her as a mother insworn
I am not longing anymore for her
Not because her ruler was a born vampire
And was sitting calmly smiling as a mimic
After the blood was streaming in the streets
I am not longing for my sweet home
Not because the green fields were done
By slaves enslaved to dukes alone
Only for their pleasure under a rulers gun
I am not longing for my home
Not because my soul was there run down
And Siberian roads in deep snow
In heavy chains I had to cut, like with a saw
I am not longing for my beautiful home
Not because of the bugs in Siberian prisons I won
And cockroaches in my soup were overdone
And the doctors were saying "it is good for you my son"
I am not longing for my home sweet home
Not because in nineteen hundred and six I had to run
Through wilderness where wolves were screaming
And night by night my steps were spied on
But I am longing for no home

5

Because the feeling of longing creates a sodom
And every spot in the world's surrounding is my home
Until the last moment – as a true son.

The poem was written in the self-taught English my father had picked up from the people he spoke to every day and the newspapers and books he read. This poem suggests that the little he told us about his Siberian prison could be true, and why he seemed to have so little longing for his native land.

Later, my cousins in New York gave other reasons why Father was sent to a Siberian prison. Although he never told us in detail why he was imprisoned in Siberia it is possible that the answer may be found in some writings of his in Cyrillic script, which are in my possession. I hope that a translation and interpretation – not an easy matter for so arcane a manuscript – will help solve some of the problems about my father's identity.

This poem, as with much of his poetry, revealed early on how cynical and stateless he always felt. It explains why he refused to apply for South African citizenship and a passport. He remained, as far as South Africa was concerned, an alien and a stateless person until he died.

It was only when my brothers and sisters were much older that we learnt more about his past. Because of the close contact I had with him, he began to tell me things which, when related to much of what he wrote, built up the character of the man. As I grew older and the details of his personal life unfolded I was able to reconstruct something of his past.

Many other images of our turbulent family life remain. In 1922 we lived in Becker Street, Bellevue at the corner of Bezuidenhout Street, next to a shop owned by a Chinese grocer and his family.

I have a vivid picture of running up Bezuidenhout Hill, calling my mother to look at a small aeroplane which was dropping red objects in the distance. My mother ran after me, somewhat distraught, and bundled me into the house because those "red things" were bombs being dropped on the striking 1922 gold miners several miles away, in Fordsburg. I was five years old and General Smuts was dealing with the 1922 rebellion!

Some while later my youngest sister Ethel was born at our house in Becker Street amidst a great deal of commotion. Father confined us to our beds. Water was boiled on an old black coal stove; the midwife seemed to be all over the house.

Father was constantly shouting to keep us quiet as we huddled beneath our blankets. My mother screamed out frequently with the pain of childbirth, which mounted to a crescendo. Suddenly there was a new sound – the cries of the new baby – my sister Ethel had arrived.

From Becker Street I went to primary school in nearby Observatory after having gone to a small kindergarten for a year.

By now I was six years old.

I was puzzled when the school principal questioned my mother about my first name – Benny – telling my mother that it was probably a shortened form of Benjamin. My mother agreed to this suggestion and so I became Benjamin Wilson, the "son of good fortune".

In those days the school principal did not ask for birth certificates. If she had, it would have saved a lot of trouble later in my political career.

Becker Street was like all the other built-up streets of detached and semi-detached houses. It was conveniently situated near the top of the hill and from there it was great fun to ride precariously down to Rockey Street on our home-made carts and drag them up again.

From our hill we could see and hear the trams travelling noisily down Rockey Street in the valley below. On the other side of the hill, to the south, lay the business centre of sprawling Johannesburg, with buildings of no more than three or four storeys in height contrasting with the golden mine-dumps surrounding them, and to the east and west as far as the eye could see. The black mine headgears always fascinated me and I was determined one day to get close enough to them to watch the large wheels revolving in the highveld sunlight.

The only other memory of the Becker Street of the time is of a tough family of brothers who really frightened me. I met two of them at school; menacingly they were called Forkey and Knifey.

Years later, an older brother who had a scar on his face, punched me on the nose one afternoon after school because he said I was trying to steal his girlfriend.

My father used to waken very early in the morning, usually about 4 am. He moved quietly about the house so as not to disturb us. If I was awake, I would hear the front door close as he left to walk to the tramstop in Raleigh Street, or get a lift to the Newtown Market, near Fordsburg. He could not afford a car. He gave up his bicycle in 1919 after he was knocked down by a horse and cart which caused serious injury to one ear.

In later years when we again lived north of Rockey Street across the valley in Dunbar Street, he used to walk to the old tram terminus at Yeoville; from there he would be given a lift by John Bell, a wholesale fruiterer who owned a large Buick. Sometimes he stopped one of the large green buses packed with blacks from the segregated township of Alexandra, on Louis Botha Avenue, the main road to Pretoria. For a sixpenny fare, he had standing room in the front, next to the white driver. My father, I am sure, was the only white man in Johannesburg who went to work in a bus for blacks. When I started to help him at the Market, in 1925, at the age of eight, I too rode in the big green buses with him, filled with the steamy, pungent smell of black people packed like sardines. I cannot remember why my father took me to the market as his helper at this early age, but that is when it happened.

I helped my father at the Market for about nine years until I was seventeen, on every Saturday, and every school holiday. On only one occasion was I unable to go to the Market, a story which will be related below. Other than that, my life had a regular pattern. It was accepted by the family and my school friends that I had a job at the Market when I was not at school.

Father and I used to arrive at the Market between 5.30 and 6.00 am, often in the pitch dark, especially in winter. My father's stall was in the centre of the cavernous building which was at least three hundred yards or more from end to end. I always had an eerie feeling as we entered the east entrance at the small flower section. It was always dark – beyond it one heard the noisy black porters and saw their shapeless figures under bright arc-lights that made the further reaches of the building seem even gloomier. The only shops open at that hour were on the sides of of the Market – some butchers and a tea-room.

Most of the stalls belonging to the sellers of fruit and vegetables, who were mainly Lebanese or Syrian, were not yet open for business. The main activity was at the wholesale market which was beyond Father's fruit stall, under the balcony where vocal black porters were bringing in fruit and vegetables in boxes and baskets from the goods trains lined up outside. As the porters moved about the wholesale market, they whistled, sang, yelled, swore and sometimes fought with each other, making a great clattering noise as their wheelbarrows were pushed over the cold stone floor. Many were itinerants earning a few shillings a day to buy food.

In the winter months the Market was as icy as a tomb. No matter how one dressed to keep warm, it became a battle against the bitterly cold winds and mine dust rushing through the numerous open steel gates on either side. It was so cold at times that it became an effort to work, with hands frozen stiff, huddled in a thick coat and with a scarf wound tightly around my neck.

Our stall was amongst a small group of retail traders who were also mostly Lebanese or Syrian. Our next door neighbour was Joe Nikolas, a marvellous, smiling old Turk, who always welcomed me as if I was his son, even when he and Father did not speak to each other. This occurred from time to time because there were always disputes over where fruit could be placed or when customers were enticed away from the adjacent stall. But there was generally a warm camaraderie, because everyone was engaged in trying to make enough money to survive in the difficult times of the Depression.

Between the flower section at the east entrance and our stall, were the vegetable retailers. On the north side there was a small group of Chinese vegetable growers who sold their own produce –crates of fresh crispy lettuce piled high in old banana boxes, cabbages, celery and exciting red or black radishes. Opposite the Chinese stalls was a long row of shops which included two large butcher shops always full of the bloody carcasses of beef and lamb; interspersed were shops selling eggs, butter, several kinds of polonies and delicatessen.

Several grocers had shops. The largest one belonged to Mr Jankelowitz, a fat, waddling immigrant. Bags of nuts, dried fruits, beans and other edibles, were on display outside his shop. When he and his assistants were inside the shop I would help myself to a few "samples". My father did not have his own telephone so I was a frequent visitor to Jankelowitz's shop.

Jankelowitz was an amiable man. When Father did not have money to pay for the groceries he needed for the family, Jankelowitz would take fruit in lieu of cash. Further down from the grocery shop was the tea-room with its hot enticing coffee aroma, from where we got our daily tray of coffee and toast. Next door to the tea-room was the fish-shop; the entrance to the small Indian Market was at the end of the row of shops. It was segregated from the main Market. The traders had exotic and strange names like Khan, Patel, Moosa and Dadabhai. They sold all the tropical fruits: bananas, pineapples and eastern foodstuffs, curries and spices.

By contrast the Wholesale Market was large. I used to wander over on the flimsiest pretext, between the toweringly high stacks of boxes of yellow-green pawpaws from the Lowveld, the trays of hard pear-shaped avocados, the thousands of bags of oranges and lemons, and the mountains of pineapples which every year, when in season, were dumped right next to our stall.

To separate the retailers from the Wholesale Market were two rows of large steel tables where the egg and butter farmers and their agents sold their produce.

From outside we could hear the hissing noises of the giant steam railway locomotives as they came and went with their large fruit and vegetable trucks from all over South Africa.

Sometimes, when Father was away, I would sneak across the railway bridge to wander about the open onion and potato market on the other side of the railway line, which had a totally different atmosphere to the fruit and vegetable market.

Running the full length of the Market, on the south side, was a long loading platform where all the dray carts, trucks and cars could directly load or unload fruit and vegetables. Beyond this rushed the trams, their bells clanging, from the western suburbs of Fordsburg and Newlands. Across the street was the huge Market Square, filled on Fridays and Saturdays with a multiracial mass of humanity – cars, horses, carts, manure and trucks. Hovering over all this were the four enormous water-cooling towers of the municipal power station continuously spewing large clouds of steam and gases into the atmosphere.

Today the Market is closed and silent. Market Square is lifeless and empty. The trams are gone, the tracks removed. The Indian Market is now the Market Theatre trying to capture the old spirit of the Patels and the Dadabhais. The Africana Museum is moving into much of the old building from its present home in the Johannesburg Library on Market Square.

Our stall was small. When Father had money to buy lots of fruit to sell, it was always piled high with boxes of fruit of all kinds, bags of oranges, lemons and grapefruit and fruits changing with the seasons of the year. Early in November the peaches, pears, apples and plums would arrive from local orchards, in baskets which were returned to farmers; or in wooden trays from the Cape Province.

December brought large baskets of black grapes from the Cape, followed by luscious mangoes from the Eastern Transvaal. Father employed Charlie as his main helper. He was a smiling Tswana, a black man who lived illegally in a backyard in nearby Fordsburg. His family remained somewhere in the western Transvaal as squatters on a Boer farm; he visited them once a year.

Charlie and I would get the stall ready for the day's selling. Father would put on his white coat, his hat still firmly on his head, and would go off to the Wholesale Market to see what fruit had arrived during the night. He would decide what to buy when the auctions began. Quite often he was able to buy fruit out of hand by negotiation, especially when there was a glut, which sometimes occurred in the summer. He would then send a porter with the fruit to our stall, or Charlie would go and fetch it. I always enjoyed opening the boxes and baskets to see what Father had bought. I would then tastefully design and arrange an attractive multicoloured display of fruit on our stall.

The fruit arrangements were like a painting which was always new because of the changing types of seasonal fruit. In order to accommodate smaller buyers I would often repack fruit into smaller baskets.

Saturdays were the days I liked best, because it was always busy and I had regular customers who started coming at about 7 am. They would seek me out because they found Father difficult. He could be rude to them and hated people who fingered the fruit before buying, because most people did not know how to handle fruit without causing damage. He did relent, however, with special customers and offer them fruit to taste as an inducement to buy. Sometimes when he was angry with a customer he would curse them in Russian, which they did not understand. Often they walked off in disgust and vowed never to return to buy from him. Happily, some had short memories.

The hours would pass, my pockets would get full of money, and I would periodically go to Father to give him the money I had accumulated. As I grew older I grew bolder. Copying other stallholders, I would stand at the corner of our stall and shout to passers-by to come and buy our fruit.

My mother went to the Market to help during the week. Most days she left early in order to attend to the household chores. It was sad to see how Father's temper sometimes got the better of him, when he did not like something Mother had done.

He would shout and hurl abuse at her. She would weep. Sometimes she walked away and came back later without saying a word, or she went home. It used to make me very sad.

I realised, more than my brothers and sisters, why rows took place. In many cases they originated in the Market.

A few years after I started working in the Market, my younger brother Leon joined me. He hated the Market and used every pretext to get away to go to a bioscope, play football or cricket (to which he was addicted), without my father knowing. Max, the youngest, followed years later. At various times both my sisters were roped in to help – they all hated the Market. My stay there was the longest – I found life at the Market stimulating despite Father's temper. I also wanted to help him – we were very poor.

As I now see it, apart from enjoying the atmosphere of the Market, I learnt a great deal about people, their habits, reactions and temperaments, particularly under the constant pressure of volatile situations in the Market. I recognised the adult world of human beings who were all physically different; and how race and colour in South Africa determined whether one was a "have" or a "have-not".

At the same time, I was taught the rudiments of running a business and the meaning and importance of money. It helped me to understand and relate to Father's struggle to make ends meet and to satisfy our family's barest needs. The depression was an ever-present reality and survival for all of us was uppermost in Father's mind.

Nothing was static at the Market. Every minute was different. When we were busy the pressure was intense. Tempers were often stretched to the limit, with unpredictable consequences. Fights would break out between customers and stallholders, people would shout "Stop thief!" Arguments, sometimes ending in fisticuffs, would take place at auctions between buyers who thought they had been the successful bidders for parcels of fruit. It was not surprising that the Market matured and influenced me as much as my father did. For this I am grateful to both – as they were indivisibly linked in a unique set of circumstances.

The Market itself was a polyglot of sallow looking Syrians and Lebanese together with a small number of Jewish stallholders and shopkeepers. Amongst the fruit and vegetable agents there were more Afrikaners, probably due to their connections with the farming community.

I made many friends amongst the older Syrians and Lebanese. Sometimes when my father was having an argument somewhere in the Market with another trader or a Municipal Inspector, they would call me to fetch Father away. Often, when business was quiet, they would talk to me about their own lives, why they came to South Africa and how they missed their families in the Middle East.

Despite my youth and lack of experience, I was always appalled at the amount of fruit that rotted and was thrown away when there were gluts in the Market. I wondered why the fruit could not be given instead to the poor – whites, blacks and coloureds – who came to the Market daily and who lived in the depressed areas like nearby Vrededorp and Fordsburg.

On Saturdays a number of black, white and coloured neighbourhood boys from Vrededorp and Fordsburg, all poverty-stricken (and about my age) used to look for jobs carrying purchases for people who shopped at the stalls and shops. For this they earned their "tickey" (three pence) or a sixpence. I befriended some of them, often making one my Saturday assistant both at the stall and to help my customers with their fruit to their cars. At the end of the day I always gave them fruit to take home to their families.

By the time I was twelve years old I was able to manage the stall on my own. On Saturdays, knowing that Father was tired, I would urge him to go home in the early afternoon. I liked being alone with Charlie. I would rearrange the fruit display, bearing in mind the instructions Father always gave me about the necessity to sell fruit that would not last the weekend. I looked forward to my regular Saturday afternoon customers.

If things were slow, and there were not too many people in the Market, I would try and attract them to our stall by shouting out my special offers.

11

This often happened because wholesalers would on Saturdays approach my father with special low-priced offers of fruit which they wanted off their hands at the weekend. Father was always prepared to take the chance that he would sell the fruit. However it usually fell to me to find ways and means of getting rid of the boxes of peaches for one shilling and sixpence or bags of oranges at only a shilling a bag.

At times even old Joe Nikolas would get fed-up with me and my voice: "Benny, it's enough." He would turn his back on me. Nevertheless, I had to get rid of the fruit. I knew that there were people who specially came on Saturday afternoons to get these bargains. It was like a competition for me. My goal was to take more money, if I could, in the afternoon than we did in the morning. Sometimes I succeeded.

Late on winter afternoons, the Market grew progressively darker and colder. Charlie and I would close up the stall. I would pay him his week's wages and send him off with as much fruit as he could carry. Then I would hurry home by tram to Father with my pockets bulging with notes and silver. Quite often Charlie and I were the last to leave the Market. By the time we reached the exit only one steel gate would be open with the night inspector and his bundle of keys waiting to lock up.

On Saturdays Father usually hired a horse-drawn draycart and filled it with all sorts of fruit, especially the overripe soft varieties, which he sent to our house. The family survived on this for the week.

There were times at the Market when business was terribly bad. Fruit was not sold and rotted. Charlie and I would spend hours repacking boxes, crates and bags before we could go home on a Saturday. Monday was a notoriously poor day, so by Tuesday many boxes of fruit had to be thrown away and Father would lose money. This fuelled his labile temper – he suffered much at the Market because he could not control the daily events that affected him. As a result he was often involved in arguments which led to fights. Many of the traders were wary of him. He was fearless and did not let anyone intimidate him. The Market Inspectors kept their distance even when they were forced to draw his attention to an infringement of the by-laws.

The severity of the Depression in 1929 and the early 1930s twice made him bankrupt. The problems at home and his unhappy relationship with my mother did not improve matters. Often he would arrive home from a long day at the Market with all the money he owned in one of his pockets; it could be as little as a few shillings. He carried on his business by getting credit from a few wholesalers who trusted him. I rarely asked him for pocket-money for working at the Market. When I needed some he was generous.

I hated it when he came home exhausted, bad-tempered and tired.

I knew what caused his moods – and I dreaded the atmosphere that would follow at home. Many of the rows that he had with Mother occurred on these days.

The Market had become an integral part of my life. I never challenged my father's reasons for taking me there to help him. I enjoyed the vitality of the place, the contact with different people. It was an adult world, completely different from my weekday school environment. I loved school, but could never savour it fully because my father forbade us to take part in organised games after school hours. We were instructed to come directly home.

During the week he invariably came home between 3.00 and 4.00 pm. If we were not there, we had to concoct good reasons for being late, particularly if we had disobeyed him by playing football or cricket. Our shoes would be inspected to see if they were scuffed from football. The important thing was to get a brush to clean and polish our shoes. Of course, there were times when we were caught, with disastrous consequences.

In Dunbar Street, where we lived in 1930, the semi-detached house had a convenient side lane. Both Leon and I would creep up the lane, open the sash window of our bedroom, quietly climb in, and if Father was home take out our books and start doing our homework. We hoped to give the impression we had been home a long time.

These subterfuges did not always work, because he had checked whether we were home when he arrived. If he was resting when we got home we breathed sighs of relief – the problem was solved.

It was only recently that I discovered why Father prohibited games; the reasons were in the numerous letters he had written to the Johannesburg newspapers. As children we could never understand his motives when all our school friends were encouraged to participate in sport.

In the late 1920s or early 1930s he took part in a newspaper controversy on "Sport and Children" which appeared in the letter columns of *The Rand Daily Mail*.

"Sir," he wrote, "I have always held the opinion that cricket, boxing and football are dangerous. Our children would be much happier and more developed mentally if these games did not figure in the school curriculum. Sport becomes a mania with children. They forget about the real needs of their lives such as mathematics and science. If the plays of Bernard Shaw or Shakespeare were produced at the City Hall would people spend their last few shillings to see them . . .?"

He never relented about sport. It was a hard cross to bear. At the time he wrote this letter I was acting as his scribe, but I did not recall this letter. So many were written over the years it is not surprising that I don't remember them all.

Father always tried to put his theories into practice. As a result Leon and I became clandestine sportsmen at school, often winning prizes because of our prowess, but we could never openly enjoy our successes. It was all, sadly, a secret.

I do not exactly recall when I began acting as my father's scribe. It may have been some time after I brought him a poem I had written, when I was eight or nine years old.

Away from the Market my father was a different person. When he relaxed, he would spend most of his time reading and writing. He amassed a large library over the years and would often buy a book when he could least afford it.

Much of it was over my head, especially when he wrote letters to newspapers. He was always quoting from his books, so at a tender age I learned about the great philosophers. It did not stop there. The world of politicians and revolutionaries – Lenin, Stalin, Trotsky, the Bolsheviks, Mensheviks; they all came up over the years. Political activists – Proudhon and Rosa Luxembourg were explained to me – as were the writings of Karl Marx, Engels, Plato and Socrates who were followed by Shakespeare.

The poets Shelley and Byron were his favourites. All became everyday names to me. Often Father would ask me to read out aloud a poem by Shelley or a sonnet by Shakespeare.

These "scribe" sessions took place around the only table we possessed, in the diningroom. In the afternoons this became the writing room. There my father sat, with his five-shilling spectacles, bought from the C-to-C Bazaars, perched on the edge of his nose. With a pencil in his hand, our work would begin. In spite of not being able to enjoy games after school or playing with my friends, I was introduced to a fascinating new world through my father's intellectual interests.

I was his link between the rigors of the Market and the turbulence at home. He needed me. His English vocabulary was limited and his grammar poor. He could write the language, but as his verse and his surviving letters show, his ability was rather less than rudimentary.

But his mind was alive and enormously creative. Looking back, I am surprised that during those formative school years I was of such help to him. It was a unique partnership between father and son in very stressful times, forged at our diningroom table.

Father was always very serious. As soon as he came home, he would eat and rest for a while. Then he would send for me, either to write a poem, or to dictate a letter to a newspaper. The words came slowly, but were clearly chosen with as much care as he could give. I would write in block letters what he dictated. He would often command me to stop and to read back what I had written. If he was satisfied we would continue.

Poetry was his first love. He wrote phonetically, relating the words to poetic rhythms. When he could not spell a word he would look it up in a dictionary. He used poetry not only to express what he found beautiful, but to express own his beliefs on religious philosophical and political matters. These first poems were soon followed by the newspaper letters, at least once a week, mostly published with corrections.

The letter columns of *The Star* and *The Rand Daily Mail* were frequent vehicles for his trenchant attacks on politicians and matters of the day. He attacked the "hypocrisy" of the Church and conflicts within it; commented on the unjust society in which we lived; he was intensely anti-war and was a great moralist. He regarded the newspaper columns as a weapon to be used to improve the lot of mankind.

On many occasions his newspaper letters warned about the impending atrocities and the dangers of Hitler and the Nazis. The list of subjects was formidable – the headlines to the letters are self-explanatory: "Campaign Against War; Hitler No Friend of Christianity; Religion Is Not a School Subject; Communism and Fascism; The Pass Laws; No Democracy in Russia; Christianity and Militarism."

It was a wide spectrum of issues of the day and included Market problems, about which he was an expert.

In addition, he never failed to write poems to me, my brothers and sisters on our birthdays. It was not unusual for him to dictate my birthday poem to me which I then had to read back to him!

Although Hannah and Leon were old enough to do this work, they were not involved as long as I was available. They were secretly very happy at this arrangement. It left them free to do what they wanted and it kept my father occupied for several hours a day. Father's preoccupation with writing and poetry was a blessing in disguise for the family.

He never met the newspaper editors in his time, but the signature Samuel Wilson must have given them grey hairs on more than a few occasions because of his outspoken views.

I completely filled a duplicate-paged book of his poetry which took a number of years. On the frontispiece, in his own handwriting, he wrote the following legend: "Poems of the Truth about the World's Lies".

Father's magnum opus is the play (*The Extremists*, mentioned earlier) which he dictated to me when I was twelve years old. I treasure the original manuscript which was also written in a duplicate book. I cannot recall how long it took to complete.

My father was strongly antagonistic to the Church. Our home was anti-religious. We never received religious instruction nor were we allowed to visit a place of worship. Mother was forbidden to teach us about religion, which caused her great distress because she believed in God. We were Jewish, but there was no teaching of Judaism. Our upbringing excluded all Jewish religious beliefs and customs. There were no ceremonial Friday night dinners with the family; we never knew anything about synagogues where Jews worshipped. We were a household without any religious beliefs. I never had a Barmitzvah – the official rite of passage to manhood which Jewish boys perform at thirteen – nor did my brothers. It was only from the mocking of the other Jewish boys at school that I learned that our family life was different from theirs.

I was sent to school on Jewish holidays; at Athlone High School, predominantly Jewish and co-educational, the boys complained about me. I was the only Jewish boy at school on those days. I was embarrassed at first, but I soon hardened to the derisory *poyer* (heathen) flung at me when my classmates returned to school.

The only kind of religious discussion in our house was criticism of the Church; in speech, poems and articles to the newspapers and listening to Father's lectures at the dinner table – with my mother silent.

One incident stands out in my memory. I was seven years old. It was 1924 and a Saturday morning. I was walking down the pavement of a street near our house in Yeoville, past the small detached homes, dressed in a white shirt and short trousers with *takkies* (tennis shoes) on, no socks and no hat or cap, happily bouncing a tennis ball as I went along.

As I passed the Isaacson's house on the corner of Webb Street, the twins, who were in my class at school, came out dressed as if they were going to a wedding – two boys about my age, in dark suit, caps on their heads and each carrying a small bible.

Scarves were loosely hanging around their necks.

"Hullo!" I exclaimed. "Where are you going to, all dressed up – it's not school today. Let's play somewhere."

They were horrified.

One of them said: "Benny, you should be ashamed of yourself. It's *Shabat*. You should be going to *shul* (synagogue) with us."

I looked at them with surprise.

"What is *shul*? What is *Shabat*?"

"What, you don't know what *shul* is? Then come with us and we will show you."

I followed them down the street, still bouncing my ball and chattering along like any seven-year-old schoolboy.

We came to a large red brick building with several domes. The twins entered by a side-door, beckoning me to follow. It was dark, and I could hardly see ahead. Then we entered into a well-lit high-domed hall and I could hear and see people singing and chanting. In front of me were some old men dressed in strange shawls and scarfs. Candles were burning and there were colourful objects, which I had never seen before, behind them. Around me were men all wearing hats or small caps.

Suddenly there was silence. People were looking at me. I was standing in the middle of the *shul* – the Berea Synagogue – with a ball in my hand, bewildered. I looked around for the Isaacson twins but they were nowhere to be seen.

Before I knew what to do, I saw a line of old men advancing towards me, hands stretched out, as if they were trying to scoop me out of the *shul*. I turned tail in the face of this phalanx and fled through the main entrance of the synagogue whose religious service I had brought to a standstill.

Clutching my ball, I ran until I was exhausted.

I never told my father of this incident. But, as a result, I never entered a synagogue or any other place of worship for almost two decades, and then only to attend the wedding of a university friend.

I never forgot this incident, because it reflected the powerful influence Father had on me and my development.

How did I feel about my father and the way he used up my schoolboy's time at home and the Market?

I do not recall that I resented it. There must have been times when I rebelled, but these times do not stand out from the past. They are shadows. I derived pleasure and satisfaction from what most children would regard as an imposition.

I had a great love for my father. I realised, however imperfectly, that he had something to tell and teach me. He took me into his volatile adult world.

16

As I grew older, I admired him because he struggled hard to keep the family together when my mother was no longer with us. He worked long hours, fed us, educated us and tried to make intellectuals of us.

Obviously, subjects that interested him – literary, political, philosophical and artistic – plus the art of being satirical and critical, must have greatly influenced me as I grew older. I may not have seen it at the time, but the hours of dictation in my father's company, listening to him expounding his intellectual and artistic views, left a subliminal imprint and had some bearing on my adult behaviour.

My father was unsuccessful in influencing my brothers and sisters to the same degree. Years later he formed a love-hate relationship with Max, my youngest brother, when I was no longer at home. Hannah, my oldest sister, was very musical. He encouraged her to play the piano, despite our chronic shortage of money. Somehow we always had a Steinway or Bluthner "baby-grand" piano struggling for space in our congested living room which also functioned as diningroom, study and finally Hanah's piano practice room.

There were several occasions when I came home from school to find Hannah in tears because the piano had disappeared while she was at school. It had been repossessed by the hire-purchase company because Father was unable to keep up the monthly payments. This did not defeat him. Invariably, a few days later, a new piano would arrive, bought once more on hire-purchase. Hannah was able to continue with her music lessons, developing into a fine pianist.

My father's musical appreciation was at a high level. He would often instruct Hannah to play music for him that he liked. Our discordant family home was often filled with the soothing sounds of Beethoven, Mozart, Chopin and popular music of the day, such as "In a Persian Market". One afternoon Mother took Hannah and me to the old Standard Theatre in town to see a performance of the "Dying Swan" danced by the famous Pavlova when she visited South Africa – I remember my mother crying at the moving and beautiful portrayal by the ballerina.

One day, when I was about six years old, Father came home from the Market with a small box of water-colours, a brush and some paper. Later that afternoon, as the sun was setting, he took me to the front of the house in Jolly Street, and pointing to the spectacular highveld sunset he commanded me to paint it.

It was the first painting I ever did "in the field". I never knew how or why he had concluded that I had a talent for painting. I have had it all my life – he was right. I became so keen that I asked to go to the Art School which I had heard about through our school's art teacher. He agreed for a while to let me attend a Saturday class. However, this ended after a few lessons because he could not spare me from the Market.

An alternative time was offered by the principal of the Art School, a "life" class on a Monday evening with adults and the older students. This was a blessing in disguise because I was then taught by leading South African artists like Sydney Carter, who made his name as one of the country's finest landscape painters. I formed a lifelong friendship with with a young student much older than me, a judge's registrar who was in this Monday class. His name was Walter Battiss. He took Leon and me on our first painting expedition to Nancefield, by train, some miles west of Johannesburg amongst the mine-dumps and the early segregated black townships. Battiss encouraged me to paint landscapes. Through him I met several painters whom he admired – like Erich Meyer. Battiss became one of South Africa's most famous painters.

For years, at every opportunity, I wandered in the open spaces and low hills of Mountain View near our house painting landscapes, including a view of Bezuidenhout's Farm house, one of the pioneer homes of Johannesburg. I still take my "oils" and a canvas along; I have painted all over the world in my travels abroad.

One morning the Headmaster of Athlone High School called me to the platform during assembly. He told the school that I had won a national poster competition, open to all schools on the subject of "Stopping Veld Fires ".

3

My father was a frustrated politician. Although he constantly criticised and analysed the political scene in South Africa through his poems and letters, and in lectures to us, the only activity which resembled politics which he attended was an open-air Sunday evening meeting held on the Town Hall steps at about 6 pm.

It was like Speaker's Corner in London's Hyde Park. He would join a small crowd of "regulars", socialists, trade-unionists and freethinkers to hear a man called Dunbar haranguing them on the problems of South Africa or developments in Russia.

Dunbar was a trade unionist, a professed socialist who came to South Africa from Scotland. Father did not ask me whether I liked to go to Dunbar's meetings – he took me. He got involved in the arguments which often became heated, generating real excitement. These meetings had a great effect on me. By coincidence, years later on the very same spot I helped to organise public protest meetings against the Nationalist Party's attack on the constitution, held by the Opposition United Party of which I was then a supporter.

As a child I was fascinated by Dunbar's meetings. They encouraged me in later years to join the school debating society, which I regret was used at times as a cover-up for participating in school sports. Surreptitiously over the years I played football, eventually for the school's First Team.

I ran in athletic competitions with commendable success. I was not a great shot, but in my final year I won the the school shooting trophy, much to every one's surprise.

Another thing I had to be secretive about was that as Head of House, I was in charge of cadet training. We won the competition for the first time in years. I had a very difficult time hiding my cadet uniform at home, but there was no option. I had to arrive at school fully dressed for cadets on Friday mornings.

My brother Leon was not so careful. My father found his cadet cap, cut it to shreds and gave him a thrashing for attending cadets. Father was so anti-militaristic that even school cadets were forbidden.

Our dilemma was that we could not avoid it. I knew that if Father applied for exemptions for us, there would be a terrible row at school. Leon and I had to resort to subterfuge to cover up our illegal activities – at which we became quite expert.

One incident is worth recounting.

In 1931 I was the left fullback for the under-14 football team. We won the semifinal against a stronger team from St John's College late one Friday afternoon. The final was to be played the next day at the old Wanderers ground, just north of Park Station near the centre of Johannesburg. Our opponents were St George's Home, who had a good reputation. Our school had never won the cup.

But the next day was Saturday and I had to be at the Market to help my father.

I wrestled with my conscience. Should I tell my father and ask for permission to play? I knew he would not only forbid it, but we would end up in an awful row, with him in a rage.

I decided that I was going to play. Not only was it the final of the under-14 competition, but our match was one of the curtain-raisers to a great sporting event. Motherwell of Scotland were playing against Transvaal for the first time. As a bonus after our match, we were to be given lunch and seats to watch the great game.

All my team-mates were excited by the prospect. I was in despair.

At the same time I did not want to let Father down at the Market, especially on a Saturday. I knew how he relied on my help. Many of my special customers would not deal with him. If they did not see me they would go away.

I knew that Father would come to my room to wake me at about 4.30 on Saturday morning, when I would quickly dress and walk with him to the bus-stop to go to the Market. Somehow, I managed to wake up before he came to my room. I spent several minutes rubbing my forehead hard with both hands, then feeling it to check whether it was warmer than the rest of my face. I was very tense, and listened for his approaching footsteps.

As soon as I heard him, I started rubbing hard again.

"Benny, wake up. It's time to go to the Market."

"Daddy, I'm sick. Feel my forehead."

He put his hand to my head.

"Are you sure you're sick? "

"Yes Daddy, I feel hot."

He felt my forehead again, hesitated and then said:

"Well, you'd better stay in bed. I must go, I don't want to miss my bus and be late for the Market. It's Saturday."

I heard the front door close a few minutes later, as he left the still-dark house. I breathed a sigh of relief. I would be playing in the final.

I still hear the deafening cheers coming from the packed stands of the old Wanderers Stadium on the edge of town, as our Athlone under-14 team, in their green and gold jerseys, ran on to the field at noon. The St George's Home boys looked much smaller than us, but they turned out to be quicker and better players. The ball seemed as heavy as lead when it came my way; the field seemed enormous compared to the grounds on which had played. I found the constant roar from the crowd disconcerting. We lost the match by one goal to nil.

I can remember having a quick shower, changing my clothes, and giving my football clothes to our diminutive goalkeeper, Stompie Rosen, to take home to his house.

"Ben, where are you going? Why aren't you staying for lunch and the main match?"

"Stompie, I've got to go. My Dad's expecting me at the Market."

Telling him to say nothing to anyone if he was asked why I was not watching the big match, I left the dressing rooms after we had showered and dressed, and started running as soon as I got out of the Wanderers. I ran through the long tunnel under the railway lines, dodging in and out of the hundreds of football fans who were still making their way to the Wanderers to see Motherwell play. I rushed along Bree Street, past the Old Kazerne goods yard and the large steamy facade of the Imperial Cold Storage. At last I reached the Market, exhausted. My heart was pounding and singing.

I had played in the final, although we lost the match. It was worth it, even though I never saw Motherwell play.

Father was surprised to see me.

"Daddy, I feel a lot better – my headache went away. You can go home – I'll look after things with Charlie."

I never told him about the under-14 final on the day that Motherwell played their first match in South Africa.

4

The Market dominated and influenced my life in a profound way. And then there was the force of my father's powerful dominating presence, which left its mark on my own personality, character and outlook on life.

A small boy goes to school all week. He is guided by teachers over the years, building up his knowledge. But he gains little experience of what life is really like until he leaves his school.

For me there was not only the consequence of my relationship with Father. The Market itself, because of its vitality and volatility, left indelible impressions which have lasted through my whole life.

As a child I was forced to come to grips with many of the problems which most meet only in adult life. Sometimes I was embroiled in situations of which I would never have been a part, if I had not been taken to the Market by my father.

The Market, although an amorphous mass of people that changed every day, had a personality of its own – one could sense and smell it. It was full of colour and shape – it made sounds one recognised and it engulfed all those who were forced to spend their days there.

It was physically enormous. I always felt I was entering a metropolis, full of surprises. Every Saturday and school holiday there seemed like a carnival. Not only did the people change, but the four seasons of the year shifted the kaleidoscope of fruits and vegetables with their rich exotic scents and aromas.

One could tell where the orange section was, or where the peaches and plums were stacked in the wholesale market, or where the pineapples were unloaded, from their heady, mouthwatering perfumes.

Then again there were so many different races in the Market: Syrians, Indians, Jews, Lebanese, Afrikaners, Zulus, Tswanas, Xhosas – white, pink, brown, almost-black, yellow and sallow.

It taught me that while people were different in colour, smell and dress, they were all the human beings about which Father had been telling me through his poetry and his letters to the newspapers.

They were all involved in the struggle for survival. It was easy to distinguish a Syrian from a Jew or an Indian or an Afrikaner.

As far as Natives (blacks) were concerned, they were the workers who kept the Market going. They worked long hours. Many were malnourished, poorly dressed and poorly paid.

The Market taught me, as a child, how badly blacks were treated by whites; early evidence in my life of the unequal character of South African society. This has exerted a great influence on my own social and political attitudes throughout my life.

At the Market my father was in close daily contact with the local bureaucrats – the Market Master and his Inspectors – who were responsible for its administration. Unfortunately the Inspectors seemed always to be harassing my father for breaking the Municipal by-laws, mostly to do with the way he stored fruit near our small stall. Often when he bought a large consignment of fruit there would be no place to store it until late in the day when selling had stopped and the stall repacked.

There were many arguments between the Inspectors and Father. He was contemptuous of them. Sometimes when he had a row with them, his angry voice could be heard all over the Market. The other traders would stand around giving moral support, saying little. Although, on many occasions, he fought for their rights if he thought a by-law was bad, it was he who was summonsed to appear in court, and who often ended up paying an admission of guilt fine.

Father never gave up fighting the municipal by-laws at the Market, most of which he thought were bad, drawing attention to them in his letters to newspapers. It did not help his cause and he was in a constant state of war with authority.

More often than not he defended himself in court.

Sometimes he went to court with his solicitor, other times alone. Once he succeeded in proving one of the Market by-laws *ultra vires*.

A short time before retiring from the Market, after a noisy row, he chased the Market Master out of the building at the point of the revolver which he always carried in his back pocket. The Market Master, for some inexplicable reason, never had him charged for threatening behaviour.

At one of his last appearances in court the following dialogue took place:

The Magistrate: "Mr Wilson, how many times have you been convicted for breaking the municipal by-laws of the Johannesburg Newtown Market?"

Father: "I don't know, Your Worship."

Magistrate: "Mr Wilson, I will tell you. Seventy-two times. I have come to the conclusion that I cannot find you guilty, because there must be something wrong with the by-laws if you have been brought before the courts so many times."

Father at last felt his long-standing fight against the bureaucrats had been vindicated.

I suspect my father got his own back on the Market officials through his letter-writing and public criticism. He likened the running of the Market to any system of dictatorship, to which he was opposed.

He objected repeatedly to racial discrimination against the Indian traders at the Market and fought for them in the newspaper columns. My interest in the Indian market was different. I loved the small Indian Market, stuck like a knob at the one end of the main Market. There were only about twenty fruit stalls in the hexagonal building, built somewhat like an arena without seats. It was always crowded, and overhung with the scent of ripe bananas, pineapples and aromatic Indian spices.

One day in 1925, soon after I had started going to the market, Father told me to look after our stall. He had just received a telephone call from the Rand Club, (his main customer for years) to find some ripe spotted bananas for the Prince of Wales (later King Edward VIII) who was visiting South Africa and staying at the Rand Club. He found them at the Indian market and every few days it became my job to find the spotted bananas.

During the Prince's stay all the school children of Johannesburg were invited to see him at a gathering at the Milner Park showgrounds. Needless to say I had the warm superior glow associated with the smell of ripe spotted bananas as the Prince of Wales walked past me.

22

ure in the Alien's Registra-
Certificate of Samuel
son.

An early picture of my father, probably taken in Russia.

My mother, Sonya, in 1915.

Observatory School – unchanged in 1990.

My Std IV class in 1928. I am next to Mr Osborne, second row from the front.

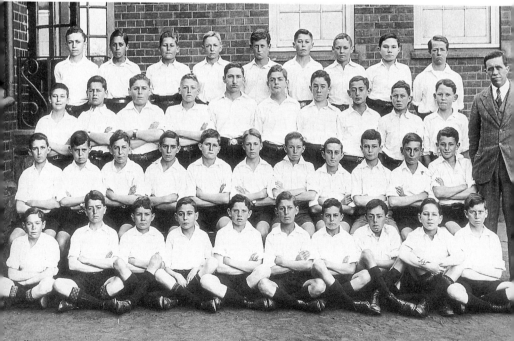

I was in standard five at Yeoville School in 1929, which was to prove an eventful year for our family. We lived in Jolly Street, near the Water Tower, on one of the hills overlooking the centre of the town and and its distant yellow mine-dumps.

At home we were going through a bad period of rows between Mother and Father. There were many angry outbursts, shouting and screaming from Father often ending in a crescendo, with Mother in tears. One night at dinner he was castigating Mother who was weeping. Suddenly Father, with a mighty heave, lifted up the table. For a moment it was suspended in space. Then plates, food and cutlery were thrown to the floor.

The four small children around the table were terrified. Father was beside himself, yelling and swearing in Russian. Mother was shocked and petrified. We wept in fear. I think the row was over something my mother had done at the Market that day; when he came home all Father's pent-up wrath and anger exploded.

The rows at the dinner table were in marked contrast to the silence that prevailed when we were eating fish.

Eating fish was a ritual at dinner. We often had fish, because it was cheap and fresh. Father would buy a whole one at the Market Fish Shop, bring it home and cook it himself. Usually it was a large river carp, or "line-fish" from the coast. We were forbidden to speak until we had finished eating. He did not want us to choke on fishbones, so prevalent in river fish.

If one of us inadvertently spoke, the speaker would receive a sudden smack in the face as a reminder.

Father's sudden outbursts of rage were inconsistent with his great opposition to all forms of social and political violence. There must have been some profound unhappiness, or some unnamed disorder, which caused him to lose control of himself so completely that he assaulted us and my mother.

It is clear that although he philosophised about the world's morals and ethics, he had other standards at home. Possibly he theorised that family discipline was somehow different from the great issues.

Some time in 1929, when I was twelve, it became evident to all of us that my mother was breaking down under the great strains imposed on her by Father, the Market and looking after us.

It got to the point where we often heard her threaten to end her life by committing suicide. She said she would drink Lysol of which there was always a supply in the house.

We were very upset, pleading with her not to do so. I do not recall that any one of us spoke to my Father about it – we feared him – nor was there any one else to whom we could turn.

Ethel, my youngest sister, was six years old and not yet at school. Hannah and I told her not to leave Mother alone or let her out of sight while we were away at school. Above all we warned Ethel to stop her if she tried to drink anything out of a bottle.

I now marvel that, not only were we aware as small children, of her suicide threats and deep depression, but we evolved a plan to stop her taking her life. It all depended on six-year-old Ethel's watchdog powers. In our naive way we thought we could stop Mother's suicide attempt. We did not tell Father because we feared him. We had this innocent childish trust that our small six-year-old sister would protect Mother while we were at school and so prevent the threatening tragedy. But it was not to be.

Late one morning at school, the arithmetic lesson was interrupted by a messenger who told the teacher that the headmaster wanted to see me in his office.

I was anxious. What was wrong?

"Sir, you sent for me."

The kindly Mr Jack peered at me over his half-spectacles, and in his pronounced Scottish accent wasted no time.

"Benny, something has happened at home – you must go there now. Off you go."

"Thank you, sir."

No one had come to fetch me – we did not own a car, nor did we even have a telephone at home.

I ran all the way up Cavendish Road, up the other steep streets to our house in Jolly Street, sick with fear and apprehension. As I entered our house I saw two policemen in blue. Father was in the lounge, red-eyed, as if he had been weeping. I do not recall seeing my sisters or Leon. A sense of panic overcame me.

Where was my mother? Where was Ethel?

Mother had drunk the Lysol at Mrs Miller's house nearby, in the garden, in front of Ethel, who was powerless to stop her. Ethel had the presence of mind to call Mrs Miller who immediately forced milk down Mother's throat and summoned the ambulance and police.

Later, Ethel managed to tell us what had happened. She and Mother walked to the Miller's garden, where she watched my Mother take a bottle out of her handbag, remove the cork, drink the contents, scream and fall to the ground.

My Mother survived – but with severe throat strictures. Father, after a few days, refused to have her back home. He said he could never forgive her for what she had done. As far as he was concerned she was now the responsibility of her relatives.

Unfortunately, they did not want her either. After a few weeks, unknown to us, Father signed the necessary papers committing her to the mental hospital in Pretoria.

Ethel was deeply affected by the event, more so than the rest of us, as she had witnessed it. My father would not allow us to visit Mother, but the forty-mile journey to Pretoria was in any case beyond the capacity of five small children. No one would dare to incur the wrath of Father. It was many years before any of the children saw my mother again.

Recently paging through the book of my father's poems, I found what could be some further light on my parents unhappy marriage, and Mother's attempted suicide.

In September 1927 he dictated a poem which I transcribed:

> My wife is ready for someone,
> He must be a very handsome one
> I don't know if he is dark or fair
> I hope he will get the right share
> She has taken off the piano cover
> Her house looks briskly all over
> Her dear God
> Help her once
> To stick to her friend
> And that would free my heart and soul
> Just like from its harness –
> An enslaved mule.

Was Father jealous of my mother? Did my mother have a liaison with some man? Was my father looking for a way to break up his marriage? These are questions that will never be answered, but further clues to their unsatisfactory relationship are provided in the poem he wrote dedicated to Ethel in 1928:

> To you my child I am opening the truth,
> About your mother's brutal root
> You came against your mother's will to the world
> My sweetest dearest little girl
> Your mother was doing away with you
> While it was only the start of you
> She had taken the doctor's advice –
> But it was not very nice.
> I had a bitter struggle through you,
> With your absent minded mother too
> She never played guilty yet
> She was never sorry about your fate.

Perhaps there were things about my mother's character that we were too young to understand. Father was the dominant personality and many of the marital conflicts were judged by his actions alone.

It is clear that he loved his family and wanted all his children with him. He could have sent us all to an orphanage instead of maintaining us as a family unit during our formative years.

Judging by the sentiments expressed in his poems, Mother did not want Max and Ethel; not because she did not want children, but because she was mentally worn out and on the road to a breakdown, a direct result of the

25

terrible distress of her life with my father.

Max's arrival was the last straw. It added depressive fuel to her mental instability. She could not cope with another child and simply collapsed. The attempted suicide was her way out. This is a well-known reaction after childbirth. A child can be rejected by the mother, when involutional melancholia sets in.

What is especially tragic is that fifty-two years later Max, who became devoted to my mother later on, took his own life by an overdose.

So, Father was left alone to care for five children. Max was the youngest at two months.

What was Father going to do? We heard with trepidation that we might be sent to an orphanage. Near us was the Nazareth Home for children, with its high walls. I often watched the children and the nuns. The thought of being abandoned there was terrifying.

Father again went to Mother's relations for help. Again they refused to assist him as they held him responsible for her suicide attempt.

I should have known that it was not in my father's character to break his family up by sending us to an orphanage.

But I was too young to work things out. We were all involved in the harsh reality of the recent tragedy. We wanted, despite everything, to remain at home with our father, whatever his faults, because he was at least familiar.

My father was a survivor. He did not give in easily. He loved his children, obviously wanting them to succeed in life, especially in the intellectual and artistic fields. He recognised, in Hannah and me, evidence of some of these talents. Although there was very little money, he did his best to develop them. Above all, he wanted a home to come back to at the end of a long day at the Market, even though he was not particularly skilled in dealing with the family's domestic problems.

So he kept us together – a family without its mother. The first few months were very difficult. Father was away all day at the Market and it was through the help and support of our black servant, the surrogate head of the household, who saw that we were fed, sent off to school with our sandwiches, supervised our baths at night, and prepared evening meals, that we managed.

We knew that my father was trying to employ a housekeeper. Through the agencies and newspaper advertisements he secured living-in women who looked after us. Soon some of the women were living with my father. Some we liked, others we detested. Until Ida came along. Ida was much younger – blonde, short and fat, and full of humour. She became a substitute mother, and like my mother, worked in the Market. She remained with Father until he died in 1955.

Some of us liked her. My sisters had reservations. I liked Ida.

She was kind, hard-working and an excellent cook. She was better able to cope with my father's awful tempers and dominant ways. It says a great deal for her fortitude that my father's outbursts did not drive her away at an early stage. She was not as sensitive as my mother and was certainly much tougher.

26

I cannot recall how Ida arrived at our home, but it must have been in response to one of Father's advertisements. Why he took her in is a puzzle, because she was his intellectual antithesis and by comparison uneducated.

My father never stopped supporting the family to the best of his ability. He did what was best for us. He was so pedantic and opinionated that his instructions had to be carried out, even when it was patently obvious that he was mistaken or wrong. I am certain that he later regretted this attitude to his family.

His innermost thoughts run like strands through the poems which he wrote to us, and to others. I always felt I understood him better than the rest of the family because of my association with him at the Market, where I saw the other sides of his behaviour. I always felt there was a special bond between us because of my role as the scribe.

As the years passed I could see that my father had changed. The shock of my mother's attempted suicide had obviously affected him. I was better able to make a value judgement, because of his writings. I also saw it in his general demeanour at the Market, which was not generally known to the rest of the family.

6

On my eighth birthday he wrote a poem to me, dictating it a few years later:

> You are eight years of age,
> You have not passed the childhood stage
> I hope you will not remain childish forever
> You will open your eyes to be clever
> You will try to learn as much as you can
> With your tongue and your pen
> You will not miss a drop of science
> Without intention of lies
> You will keep right to the truth
> Standing up for humanity
> From sunrise to sunset
> That must become your human fate.

My tongue and my pen! Was this prophetic or was it just the fond imagination of this extraordinarily strong-willed man, Leoned Open-hearted, as he sometimes signed his writings?

He was always generous in his praise when he looked at one of my paintings, which he insisted on seeing. Since it was he who initially instructed me to paint, he commanded me to create and devise a cartoon for him on the "world's poverty" for a short poem he had written. He was so pleased with it that I had to add the poem to the cartoon as the legend describing it. He then framed it. I still have it today.

In June 1929 he fell ill. The doctor said he had to go to Durban to convalesce; to take a holiday. Fortunately it was school holidays. Instead of closing the business which he was contemplating, I persuaded him to let me run it. Although I was only twelve years old I knew I could manage the business.

He arranged with a Market friend and agent, Joe Sarembock, an immigrant like Father, to send me a selection of fruit daily that he thought I needed for selling.

Father went off to recuperate in Natal with one of his customers because he got a lift by road. I was left to my own devices.

Every day I rose early, making my way in the cold winter's morning to the Yeoville terminus – then by bus or the first tram. I followed Father's routine, inspecting the wholesale market to see what fruit had come in during the night.

So while my school friends, whose families could afford it, were enjoying their holidays at the seaside, I was enjoying a different kind of break. I had never seen the sea, but that never bothered me. I revelled in my responsibility at the Market – the buying, the selling and the negotiation with the customers – and, with old Charlie's help, I had a great feeling of achievement.

The days fled by. Our regular customers were very kind to the small boy with curly hair. I specially enjoyed dealing with Father's own customers, like the conservatively-dressed and kindly Mr Hesselberg of the Rand Club. I was constantly having to make decisions. When I was in doubt I would rush off to the wholesale market and find Joe Sarembock. I soon plucked up courage to buy my own fruit and bid at the auctions. The auctioneers, who knew me, saw that I got my share of the fruit.

My father came back a month later, looking very healthy. Some months later, in November 1929, I was once again called to the headmaster's office during a lesson. This time Mr Jack came to the classroom and called me out. As we walked to his office, he put his arm on my shoulder. He was a dour Scotsman, or so it seemed. I was in awe of him, particularly when he stood on the platform at assembly, thundering at the silent children: "Can you stand the strain?"

This early morning scene greatly impressed me, and it was not until years later that I really understood the impact of Mr Jack's message.

As we walked to the office, I knew there was something wrong again. I was already sick with apprehension.

He sat down behind his desk and peered at me from behind his glasses.

"Benny, something has happened to your father at the Market. I want you to go as quickly as you can, by tram. Here is a sixpence for the fare – you know how to get there."

28

I stifled a sob. I rushed across the empty school hall to the Raleigh Street tram stop at the shops in Yeoville, passing the cinema where I had spent many a happy hour.

Normally I would dally at the posters at the "bioscope" to see if there was a new film featuring my boyhood hero Douglas Fairbanks Senior, whom I had recently seen in *The Black Pirate*. All I could think of that day was my father and the Market. Why was the tram so long in coming?

The tram was our main means of transport. When the huge, red, lumbering, noisy tram did arrive, I was on it in a flash, rushing to my favourite seat on the front balcony. From there I had a good view as we clanged and shuddered to town, swaying drunkenly, stopping and starting to pick up and set down passengers, guided by the shining steel rails embedded in the grey tarmac.

Going down Twist Street hill, was an alarming experience. The driver was always jamming on his brakes and ringing his bell, and stopping with a jerk that often catapulted us out of our seats.

At the Town Hall I boarded another for the Market. The cavernous hall was almost empty. It was near midday in the middle of the week, so there were not many buyers. From the direction of our stall I could hear a mumble of voices. When I reached it I was confronted by dozens of Lebanese, Syrians, blacks and some Market Inspectors – but my father was missing.

My spirits sank. There were lots of voices, all coming at me in a confused babble.

Where was Father? He was nowhere to be seen. What had happened?

Then out of this noisy disorder and the crowd in front of our stall, came old Joe Sarembock. Taking me aside and in a very quiet voice he told me that my father was in the nearby Fordsburg police station cells. He had stabbed a man in the stomach after a row that morning. I was aghast. Why, why had he done this awful thing?

Sarembock told me the story. Father had bought the first consignment of the new season's black cherries, which were individually packed in small boxes. He was offering these for sale when a Syrian or Lebanese shopkeeper from Jeppe inspected them, asked the price and then decided to sample the cherries. As a result he spoilt the careful packing of the cherries. Father asked him to pay for the box of cherries and take it away.

The shopkeeper refused. A row ensued. They started pushing each other around. My father fell to the ground. He managed to struggle to his feet, and while people were trying to separate them, the shopkeeper dropped to the floor. He had been stabbed in the abdomen. The police and an ambulance were called. My father was taken away in a Black Maria to the Fordsburg cells. Before he left he told Sarembock to contact me at school.

The police never found the knife. It had been spirited away by his friends at the Market.

I listened, transfixed, to Joe Sarembock's story of the event.

"Benny," he said, "your father wants to see you right away, so hurry off. I will look after the stall and get Charlie to close it up. I'll see you when you get back."

29

I could hardly see – I was holding back my tears.

"Have you got money for the tram? "

"No, Mr Sarembock."

He gave me a few pence and I rushed away.

I remember going to the Fordsburg Police Station, about a five minute tram-ride away. The gaol was at the back. At the charge office I asked a policeman if I could see my father. He took me by the hand, down a corridor, unlocked a door and there was my father, sitting in a corner at the back of a dark cell, with his hat still on his head and in his white market coat.

"Mr Wilson, your son is here."

My father looked as if he was one of Cezanne's ceramic-like paintings of a man in his hat sitting in the half-light of the cell, not moving.

"Daddy, what can I do ?"

In an unusually quiet voice he spoke.

"Go back, Benny, to the Market. Try and get me ten pounds for bail. Ask Joe Sarembock, if he has got it. If not ask . . ." He gave me the names of a number of stallholders and agents whom he knew.

Times were bad and he did not have any money on him.

I ran all the way back to the Market. What was going to happen to my father? Was he going to be gaoled for a long time? Did he really do it? What would we do? Would I have to leave school to look after the business? As I crossed the busy streets of Newtown these thoughts tumbled through my mind. Breathless, I arrived back at the Market. The stall was deserted. Old Charlie was there.

"Charlie, where is Mr Sarembock?"

"There, Baas Benny, by the orange bags." He pointed to the wholesale section.

I found him amongst the high piles of orange pockets. I reported on the conversation in the police cells. Could he lend me the ten pounds to bail Father out of gaol? He said that he could not let me have the money, as all he had with him was needed to pay the Market Master the following day for purchases he had already made.

I pleaded with him to let me have ten pounds, assuring him that we would repay it in time for him to meet his commitments. He agreed.

Elated and tightly clutching the ten pounds, I rushed back to the Fordsburg Police station.

I stood at the high desk in the Charge Office.

"Sir, I have my father's bail," I told the policeman in charge.

I placed the ten pounds on the counter.

The policeman slowly wrote out the receipt, which he gave me. Then he went to the cells, returning a few minutes later with my father.

"Benny . . ." Father started to say. His voice faltered.

We rode back in a tram, silent, rapt in our own thoughts. He held my hand.

That evening *The Star* carried a report of the stabbing. A few months later my Father appeared in court. As the knife was never found, the magistrate said that although the police could not prove that Father had stabbed the shopkeeper, there was strong circumstantial evidence that he had done so. He found Father guilty, fining him twenty-five pounds or three months gaol.

7

The following year, 1930, we moved house again. This time it was to the northern side of the valley, in Dunbar Street, near the corner of Bezuidenhout Street, which ran from the Water Tower in the south, past Becker Street and the Chinaman's shop, across Rockey Street and up past Dunbar Street disappearing over the brow of the hill in the distant north of Bellevue.

Jolly Street was left behind us with its sad memories. It was here, at 93a Dunbar Street, another semi-detached house, that Ida moved in on what turned out to be a permanent basis.

The Depression was having a marked effect on our lives. Earning a living was a real struggle for my father. Despite his daily preoccupation with tough conditions at the Market, he was very much concerned with what we were doing at school. Almost every day we had to report to him.

Were we doing well? Why were we home late? Had we done our homework? Did Hannah practise on the piano?

I had a long walk of about four miles to school. We were now much further away because of the move. Father could not afford to give me bus fare. He also refused to let me ride a bicycle. So I had to walk all the way to Bezuidenhout Valley, around the Curve, and through Observatory to school. Athlone High was a co-educational school, mostly of Jewish children from Doornfontein, the "Brooklyn" of Johannesburg.

It saw me through adolescence. The social contact with girls in the class was valuable. I always wanted to take a lead in school activities and was involved in the dramatic society, precocious enough to produce plays, although I had never had training. I had an enjoyable relationship with some of my teachers; I think they knew, or suspected, what our home circumstances were.

I put down much of my good association with the teachers to the adult company I had at the Market.

I continued my clandestine sport, especially football and athletics, using the fact that art class sessions took place after school. It was easy, too, to create a few non-existent sessions whenever a football match or sport fixture involved me.

Allan Holland, the headmaster, was a slightly-built grey-haired man whom I regarded as a father-figure of another kind. He took a special interest in me, often giving me special jobs to do. His deputy, Mrs Emily Norgarb, was a tough woman, or so it seemed to me and others at school.

Once or twice I came into conflict with her, especially over my artwork which she criticised. On the other hand, our English teacher Miss Cohen, a satirical and witty spinster, made the English classes alive and she liked my paintings and encouraged my art.

One afternoon she asked to see me in her classroom.

"Benny," she said, "I like your painting of the trees which is displayed in the Art Exhibition – will you sell it to me for a pound?"

I was flattered, but to her consternation refused to sell it to her, as it was one of my best paintings.

"Miss Cohen," I replied, " I will take two pounds for it."

I remember with shame how her face fell. She turned away. I think she never forgave me for this. I now realise Miss Cohen was a casualty of the influence that money had on me – thanks to the Market.

Dear Miss Cohen, wherever you are, I have always regretted my arrogance. I would love to have given you some of my paintings.

My sister Hannah used to call me a conceited "swank" whenever she was angry with me. How right she must have been!

Of course it was the Market in me speaking. Most things in my life in those early days were related to bargaining and measured in financial terms because of the constant battle for survival.

The Market's wide influence revealed itself in other ways. In 1933, the year before I matriculated, living conditions were still bad. The Depression continued. My father could not afford to buy the school books which I needed for matriculation study. I was very worried. The solution came to me during the school holidays. I had been browsing around some second-hand book shops after the Market one day, and noticed that there were many second-hand school books, which were on the prescribed list of books for the 1934 matriculation examination.

I hurried to the school and saw the secretary who gave me a list of the prescribed books. There was Shakespeare's *Julius Caesar* and two other books which I no longer recall. I then spent the next few weeks of the school holidays visiting all the second-hand booksellers in Johannesburg, buying up all the copies of the prescribed books which my school friends would need.

At the commencement of the new school term, I sold all the books to the boys and girls of the matriculation class, who regarded my action as a favour. It saved them hunting through Johannesburg's second-hand book-shops looking for books. That is how I made enough money to pay for all my matriculation set works in my final year at school.

I received so many orders for books that I went back to the second-hand booksellers – there were no books left. One bookseller was angry with me because I did not tell him, when I bought up his stock, that they were prescribed books. He forbade me to enter his shop again. That did not worry me. I had my books, and my father did not have to pay for them.

Life was very full during my last year at Athlone. I was busy at school and spent every Saturday and school holiday at the Market. I seemed to be living in a world of my own, removed from my brothers and sisters.

As we grew up we realised that Father never gave any of us sex education, nor did he ever mention it. It was not taught at school.

In the 1930s sex, as a school subject, was taboo. I learnt about the mysteries of sex from my school friends, and from the coy portrayals of the early "talkies" at the cinema. Although our school was co-educational, it was up to the pupils as boys and girls to find their own way through social and physical relations – if they existed.

I became an avid reader of the daily newspapers. This was a direct consequence of the numerous letters my father wrote to them on current affairs. I became fascinated, in the early 1930s, with the alarming and threatening political events which were setting Europe afire.

Hitler was taking over in Germany. Russia was struggling with one of its five-year plans. South Africa was trying to get over the effects of the Depression by going off the gold standard. Jewish refugees were coming to South Africa, fleeing from the Nazis.

Father concentrated a great deal on Fascism, writing innumerable letters on it and related subjects to the newspapers, warning readers of the dangers it posed to mankind. If Hitler and Mussolini were allowed to continue, democracy was in serious trouble. There is no doubt that his prognosis regarding Fascism and its effects on the world was accurate.

Even as a child I was aware of the unequal relationship between white and black in South Africa. I saw it in operation in the Market and at home where we relied on black labour. Like almost all white South Africans we had a "boy" or "girl" in the backyard, a "native" adult living in miserable conditions considered the acceptable norm by whites.

The "boy" or "girl" did all the menial tasks in the house; the cleaning, washing, scrubbing, ironing and cooked the family meals. Once a year the servant went off to his or her rural home to visit their family, returning a few weeks later to work for the white "baas" and "madam" so that the family would have money to survive in the poverty-stricken native reserves. Most whites knew nothing about their servant's backgrounds, where they came from, or whether what they earned was adequate for their needs.

There were no laws to protect black domestic workers – they could be engaged and dismissed at will; and paid a pittance.

Often, in the early hours of the morning, one might hear a commotion in the backyard. The police would be raiding the premises to check whether the black servant had a right to be there, if there were illegal blacks staying there; or if there was a "shebeen" operated by the servant, who may have been brewing or selling "kaffir beer". As often as not one's servant would be taken away to be charged on some minor offence because the urban areas laws were wide reaching.

A major consequence of black servants running our home was that, as children, we forged strong bonds with them; as we grew older we became very attached to them. They were part of our extended family.

I remember Tom, a large smiling man, who made life very enjoyable. Often, while I was very young, when I came back from school he would help me set up an old banana crate in our overcrowded yard. He would then put a seat in it, construct a kind of steering wheel and a gear lever, and pick me up and put me in this large crate.

My imagination then took over. I was now driving the large orange-coloured Lion Bus that passed our house several times a day. I would sit there, turning the wheel, changing gear and making all the noises of the bus on its journey to and from the centre of Johannesburg to its terminus in Observatory.

Tom, big, black and smiling would roar with laughter.

"Stop, Basie," he would shout as if he was a passenger stopping the Lion Bus. "I want to go to town."

I would take his imaginary fare, and he would pretend to climb in, and we would drive away.

The reality of it, which neither of us cared about, was that he was not allowed in the Lion Bus at all – he was black, and it was a whites-only bus!

The Lion Bus on our road made a real impression on me. At the time we lived in Isipingo Street, near Becker Street, and I always marvelled at this huge bus as it came past our house. I recall the day my mother told us that the bus service was to begin. I was about seven, and we waited outside our house for this huge orange monster to appear.

When it eventually arrived people came out of their houses and cheered, because it meant there was no longer a need to walk all the way to Raleigh Street to catch the tram.

Jeremiah, was another "native boy" who lived with us for several years. Father relied on him a great deal when there was no one to look after us. Jeremiah fed us, made our school sandwiches and had us properly dressed for school, although he had never been to one.

He had a wonderful sense of humour – we were very attached to him. At the time Max was small and needed constant attention. Jeremiah used to wash and feed him and take him for outings in his pram.

He was Max's black "foster-mother". One day he disappeared and we never found out what happened to him.

And then there was old Charlie, my father's right hand man at the Market. I never knew much about his background, but he led the life my father did. He never complained even when my father lost his temper which was often enough. He was a workhorse; loading, unloading, carrying boxes of fruit all day. No one ever met his family in all the years he worked for Father, because they lived segregated in a "Native Reserve" hundreds of miles away. Like all the other blacks employed by us, once a year he went to visit his family, returning after a few weeks ready for another year of hard labour at the Market.

The blacks were always with us. They were accepted from the earliest age as inferior people who did the worst jobs, to be rebuked at will, to be given the handouts. The way they were treated depended very much on the attitude of the employer.

We learnt nothing at school to change our attitudes to blacks either. In fact, we learnt that as whites we were superior beings. Blacks only appeared in our history books when the Zulu or Xhosa battles occurred or the

Afrikaner Voortrekkers fought them when they left the Cape during the 1830s. In our history books they were always represented as primitive savages, the hewers of wood and the carriers of water; heathens, to be kept in their place by the civilised white man.

My school debating society often discussed matters relating to "Natives" (blacks) and "Europeans" (whites), in which I made my views known. Why were whites always richer then blacks? Why did we as whites always employ the blacks – and not the other way round? Why were there no proper schools, no families living in the towns? There were dozens of answers – all founded on colour prejudice. Everyone accepted the master and servant relationship as the norm.

As a reflection of the times there were very few letters by Father on the subject of white-black relationships. His letters were full of references and quotations from the philosophers like Nietzsche or Locke about the rights of human beings, but little on the problems of colour and race in South Africa. Apartheid as we know it today existed in a "paternal" way. Nevertheless it was very much there. It lacked the statutory backing the Nationalists gave it after they came into power in 1948, but it was very real just the same.

8

Matriculation year meant decisions on my future. Much as I liked the Market and the things it taught me about selling, and handling money, I did not relish the thought of of a business career with my father in the Market – this was furthest from my thoughts.

My main desire was to get to university, although I was not clear what vocation or profession I wanted to follow. The problem was how to get there, since there was no money.

It was difficult to come to a decision. Life was unsettling at home. Father was dictatorial – it was not easy to discuss issues with him and there was no one else in the family to whom I could speak.

As a school prefect I was friendly with a young teacher who had recently married. In long discussions with him and talks with Walter Battiss, who was then doing a teaching course, I decided that the only way I would ever get to Witwatersrand University would be by studying education, because I could then get a bursary.

Our chronically unstable family home did not help either. As we got older and more independent we also asserted our views. Life without Mother had taken its toll. Daily disagreements with Father switched to us, mostly Hannah and Leon. He was demanding too much from us – too restrictive about our free time.

For example, if we wanted to go to a school concert or a function held at night, we had a hard struggle to get his permission to attend. The vexed question of his restrictions on sport were never accepted by us. We did not mind when we were younger, but we objected more and more as we grew older, especially to the indiscriminate punishments. His beatings were sometimes carried out in a frenetic way, more like an assault than a simple chastisement.

There was another factor. Father always carried a revolver. This gun put the fear of God into us, because he was always threatening to use it, although he never did so at home.

Hannah now objected more and more to Father's intolerance. She was always very emotional about the loss of Mother from our home. She often wept, saying she wanted to go and see her, but that was impossible.

One day, when she was in standard eight at school, she left home after a disagreement with Father. We did not know where she lived, but she did go to school every day. For a few days my Father ignored her absence, then he got worried. Finally, Hannah was back home. However, her "running away" episodes became more frequent, once lasting for weeks. Leon, diminutive and keeping much to himself, was no great scholar, hating the Market, the jobs Father gave him from time to time and strenuously opposing Father's anti-sport policy.

At the age of fourteen, he persuaded my father to let him leave school and find a job. Much to my surprise Father agreed.

Through some school friends Leon got work at an engineering firm, in their spares department. In no time he acquired a small motor bike, of which he was very proud. It was bought from his own savings and cost five pounds.

One day when Father was in one of his hyperactive phases of anger, he went outside and in a few minutes slashed the tyres of Leon's motor bike to pieces.

"Dad," Leon cried, " why have you done this to me?" He was distraught. A few days later he left the house with his belongings and his motor bike. He never returned home.

He lived with friends, and carried on with his job, until World War II broke out. He joined the signal corps and was soon made an officer.

When Hannah and Leon left home, it was clear that the family unit was breaking up, not because they were growing older, but of the accumulative effect of living with Father.

My father never, to my knowledge, reported disappearances from our home, because he did not want to be involved with the police.

I was not greatly affected by what was happening and busy studying for my matriculation examination. I was used to Father's idiosyncrasies and habits and his constant threats. I developed a sense of resignation about events which I knew I could not influence. It was a case of the environment at home taking a back-seat while I got on with my own ambitions.

At school I was the vice-head prefect and head of York House, I enjoyed what I regarded as a special relationship with some of the teachers, and was often invited to their homes. Some of my own problems at home were solved in talks with them.

The matriculation year was a busy one, and in many ways I was sad that school days were soon ending.

A few months before writing the examinations, we were asked to bring our birth certificates to school to confirm our names and birth date. My father told me to go to the Registrar of Births and Deaths at the old Post Office in town to get a copy of my birth certificate.

I presented myself to the clerk who dealt with the matter. I gave him my name and date of birth and he went to the strongroom and returned in a few minutes with a large book, which he started paging through.

I waited patiently.

"What did you say your name is?"

"Benjamin Wilson."

"Your father and mother's name?"

"Samuel and Sonya Wilson. "

He looked up at me and beckoned.

I went to his desk and as I stood beside him his finger slowly pointed out the entry in the register.

The name in the register was Bores not Benjamin. The rest of the entry was correct. Born 1 February 1917. Father Samuel Wilson, mother Sonya Wilson. Address 6 b Jager Street Hillbrow Johannesburg.

"Well, what have you got to say to that?"

Momentarily nonplussed, I was unable to reply.

"I really don't know. I've always been called Benny – I'll have to ask my father – he should know. Isn't my name spelt wrong, if it is my name, shouldn't it be spelt with an 'i' – Boris?"

"No, it is clearly spelt in the register with an 'e' before the 's'."

The clerk wrote out the certificate, I paid him the sixpenny fee and all the way home in the tram I puzzled about my name.

Father was resting when I got home. When he woke I showed him the birth certificate and asked for an explanation.

"Yes, Benny," he said, "your name is Boris. We always called you Benny because you were our first son."

"But Dad, how do you spell Boris?"

He thought a moment, then he spelt it out slowly. "B-O-R", then he hesitated, and went on "E-S".

"But Dad, shouldn't it be Boris with an 'i' before the 's'?"

He answered quite firmly "No."

So just as I was about to leave school I learnt that my name was really Bores, when all the time everyone knew me as Benjamin.

The next day I gave my birth certificate to my teacher and she asked me if I was sure it was correct. I told her about my Father's recollection. She laughed.

"It's a very nice, unusual name "

So I decided I liked my real name Bores better than Benjamin and henceforth I would use it and make it known to everyone, causing some hilarity amongst my school friends, many of whom thought for years afterwards that I had changed my name.

A few months later, early one Saturday morning, the matriculation results were published in *The Rand Daily Mail*. Father and I were standing in the semi-dark at the Yeoville terminus waiting for John Bell to come by with his car to pick us up to take us to the Market. The newspaper "boy" arrived with the papers, just as John Bell's Buick drove up.

I hurriedly scanned the lists and to my joy discovered I had passed. "Dad, I've passed." I shouted with joy.

Some of the regulars waiting at the bus stop crowded around congratulating me as they heard me shout the news to my father.

His response was a disappointingly laconic question.

"Did you get a first class?"

"No – Dad, I didn't . . ."

"Well, I expected you to . . ."

My joy was momentarily shattered with disappointment. Was that all my father had to say?

We rode in John Bell's car to the Market. During the journey I told him that I passed Matric. He too congratulated me. Father again repeated his assertion that I should have got a first. John Bell, keeping his eyes glued to the busy Louis Botha Avenue with its early morning traffic from Alexandra township scolded my father.

"Wilson," he said, "you should be ashamed of yourself. Your son deserves congratulations from you. Look what he has done for you at the Market. What would you have done without his help?"

Father said nothing. I was still very hurt.

I knew my father well. I should not have been surprised by his reaction. Incidents like this made me realise that although there was a strong emotional and intellectual link between us, I knew in my heart of hearts that I had to escape from his dominance. I did not see myself succumbing to his fixed ideas on morals and ethics, which he forced on all of us. I wanted to create my own way of life and be completely independent; to fulfill my own emotional, intellectual and artistic needs, and not to be just a rubber stamp in his image.

I loved the Market and all it represented. But I could see what it had done to my father, how he was completely trapped by it. He would only leave its embrace when he died or retired.

He still had family responsibilities that kept him slaving away in a social environment that made him the complicated person he was – father, philosopher, poet, political critic, martinet and anarchist.

My father had trained me to think for myself. Out of this grew my strong desire for independence, moving away from the narrow confines of his beliefs. It also helped me to perceive something of the tragedy of his marriage and why it failed.

In a poem he wrote:

> I have lost my human heart long ago
> Through the lot of the five of you
> By undertaking such a task in life
> Of a struggle, and your mother as a wife . . .

In 1928 he wrote a poem to me, which I did not fully understand at the time, while Mother was still with us:

> All the chains are broken in my life
> No children will keep me, no wife,
> All strivings and hopes are buried
> My wrong step; I got married.

Perhaps he wrote it hoping that I would one day comprehend the import of his unhappy cry, caught in his unsatisfactory marriage, caught at the Market and caught by the ties of his five children. I do not know whether my mother ever saw this poem because he had little communication with her. I do not recall him ever discussing his poetry or writings with her.

9

It was now January 1935, and time for me to plan my career. If I was to get to university the only way would be through teaching, and the bursary it provided. Father was not enthusiastic at all, but I explained it would cost him nothing and I would still help him at the Market.

I had no other career in mind. I certainly did not want to go into business, least of all to end up in the Market. I had no difficulty in getting the bursary and started lectures at university doing an Arts course with additional classes at the Teacher's College.

University life enthralled me. I could not wait to get there every day, but on Saturdays I still went to the Market to help Father.

"Wits" University is built on a hill in Braamfontein, spilling down to the Parktown border. Southwards it looks over the centre of Johannesburg, with the old Kazerne railway marshalling yards then in the foreground. To the left were the emerging high-rise buildings of the city's centre. To the east, the west and the south were the large bright-yellow and ochre goldmine dumps and their slimes dams, with their fascinating tall headgears, all disappearing into the highveld haze.

I often stood behind the Main Block of the campus admiring the view, promising myself that I would one day paint the vista. I eventually did.

To the north was the wooded suburb of Parktown, dotted with the stone houses designed by Sir Herbert Baker. To the left was the Milner Park Showgrounds, where I had seen the Prince of Wales.

Mornings at University were full of lectures. Much time, too, was spent sitting beneath the tall Doric columns of the imposing Main Block, on the famous university "steps". There we relaxed with friends talking about issues that rose from studies, personal problems, or just watching the world go by. The "steps" gave one a great personal sense of freedom, epitomising what the university meant to me in my fresher days. The "steps" was the great open air forum for student meetings, where the most contentious affairs were hotly debated.

Many new friends were made at University – including many who became well-known in public life. One first-year student impressed me. She was a quiet, dark-haired girl who sat close to me in the English class. We often went to tea together or relaxed on the steps in the sunshine. Her name was Ruth First.

One day at the "steps", in a deep discussion with one of the senior students, I mentioned that I was interested in politics.

He invited me to a private discussion group that met at the home of Julius Lewin, the lecturer in Native Law and Administration, who lived nearby.

Julius Lewin encouraged us to argue amongst ourselves about the basic problems of South African politics, a topic on which he was an acknowledged expert. I took a great liking to him and we became lifelong friends. He was a small man, always conservatively dressed, with a firm voice and conversationally to the point. He had a delightful dry sense of humour.

Lewin became one of South Africa's leading liberal academics, noted for his writings and political perception, especially his opposition to apartheid after the Nationalists won power. He was involved in many organisations in the field of race relations. As a constitutional lawyer, he wrote for the media and appeared on public platforms. In later years he was a member of the Defence and Aid Committee, a group formed by lawyers to assist political opponents of apartheid who fell foul of the Nationalist government.

He was shocked to the core when his home and university offices were raided by the security police. For some time he and others had been harassed by the authorities. He grew dispirited and decided to leave South Africa for Britain during the 1960s.

Under his influence, my basic knowledge of politics developed. The weekly gatherings taught me how to think clearly and marshall my thoughts. I knew that I had to learn as much as I could about South Africa's racial system, which, before the official advent of apartheid, was as socially and economically discriminatory as anything which was to come.

My mind was receptive. For years my father had drummed into me the injustices of our social system, in general terms, to explain what was "good" and what was "bad". As a small boy I had witnessed many examples of the white man's hatefulness to the black man.

It was not unexpected that the university and Julius Lewin, in no time, began to wean me away from the overpowering effects of Father's doctrines, his political philosophies and his solutions for South Africa and the world's problems.

This became significant at home. It reflected itself in growing discord between Father and me – not only in our opinions but in other, personal, ways.

Father could not get used to the idea that I was no longer a schoolboy. For example, he could not understand that functions and meetings at university took place at night. He would refuse permission to attend meetings in the evening which often lead to bitterness, acrimony and at times a shouting-match.

This did not deter me from extracurricular activities. Within a few months I was greatly integrated into university life.

But the specific requirements of the teaching syllabus began to bother me. I was frustrated because I could not study subjects of my choice such as politics and philosophy – the teaching subjects such as English and Geography did not interest me. It was like school all over again. Student societies like the Debating Union or the Socialist Party did not fulfill my political and philosophical needs.

Unexpectedly, I achieved university notoriety through attending the annual Fresher's Hat Dress debate. Subjects were selected out of a hat and the "fresher" concerned had to extemporise on the subject for five minutes, after which the University Registrar, who was the judge, selected the best speaker.

I decided to speak at the debate, but there was a problem. To my consternation, on the morning of the day the debate was due to be held, I learnt that I could only speak if I wore a dress suit with black tie, neither of which I owned, nor could I afford to hire. I did not even have a friend who could lend one to me.

On the "steps" I sought out the Debating Society secretary, John O'Meara. I explained my problem and asked if I could speak in ordinary dress. He was adamant that I couldn't participate unless I wore a dress suit and was "properly dressed".

I told my story to Gideon Chagy, a well-known senior student. Gideon advised me that proper university dress was an undergraduate gown – not a dress suit.

"Boris," he said, "if you want to speak, borrow a gown and go to the meeting. Good luck."

That evening, at 8 pm, in a borrowed gown, I sat high up in the middle of the lecture room amongst an audience with a number of "freshers" in dress suits and black ties.

HC Nicholas, chairman of the society, leader of the student Conservative Party, who years later became a judge, opened the proceedings by introducing the University Registrar (both resplendent in dress suits and black ties) who was to adjudicate.

When Nicholas completed his welcome and the first speaker was called to draw the subject out of the hat, I rose at the back of the hall.

With my heart thumping and in the loudest voice I could muster, I interrupted the proceedings on a point of order.

Nicholas and the Registrar gaped at me. I also remember everyone turning round to look at this impudent disrupter. I could scarcely get the words out of my mouth.

"Mr Chairman, it is with trepidation that I raise my point of order. This morning when I spoke to the secretary of the Debating Society telling him I could not afford to buy or rent a dress suit and black tie, he told me that I could not speak tonight unless I was 'properly dressed'. Well, Mr Chairman, to my knowledge at the great universities of Oxford and Cambridge proper evening dress is the official academic dress, a university gown, which I am now wearing – I consider that I am properly dressed for the debate."

Some students cheered and clapped. I continued to speak until I'd had my five minutes while Nicholas remained frozen in the chair and the Registrar seemed amused.

So ended my first and only speech to the debating society.

Shaking with tension I gathered up my gown and strode down the stairs without looking to left or right, out of the meeting – to wild applause from most of the students present.

A week later the university newspaper, UMPA, appeared with a main article entitled "The Hat Dress Debate" in which the case "for" and "against" dress suits and black ties was thrashed out by Nicholas, and Chagy who defended my stand but advised me to "relax Hildegarde, relax " an expression attributed to a visiting singer in Johannesburg at the time.

10

By May 1935 I decided I could no longer continue with my teaching subjects, and would talk to the principal of the Teacher's Training College about alternatives.

One Friday afternoon I asked to see him. He was a heavily-built, dour, perpetually angry Scotsman who never minced his words.

"Yes, Mr Wilson, what is it about?"

"Professor MacGregor," I began, "I want to change one of my teaching subjects, from English to Art. I have concluded that I will never make a good teacher of English. I love painting; I always have – so at this early stage I would like to change to an Art course."

He was quick to reply.

"Art is not a major subject for anyone at this college and I cannot allow it."

"Professor, but . . ."

He cut me short.

"That is all I have to say. There can be no further discussion about it."

I was stung by his reply.

"If that is the position," I angrily retorted, "then I will have to consider giving up teaching."

"In that case you will pay back the bursary money already advanced to you."

There was no more to say. I left him glaring at me. Although I had not expected to be manoeuvred into saying what I did say, I was glad I'd done it. I was unhappy about remaining on at the college under false pretences. I was certain I did not want to be a teacher.

I spent an agonising weekend thinking about what I had done. I decided I was right to leave teaching. I had chosen teaching only because of the bursary and the university opportunity.

I do not recall telling Father of my decision, but in a matter of days a sequence of events occurred which made my departure from the training college and university inevitable.

Unknown to the university authorities I had for some weeks been going to Fine Arts lectures given by Rex Martienssen, a young architect who invited me to attend his course. I was attracted to Martienssen because of his warm personality and his genuine interest in my problems. He was a short, fair-haired man with a pipe and Balkan Sobranie tobacco always at hand. He was acknowledged as a leading personality in the modern architectural movement in South Africa.

He had travelled widely overseas, and spoke knowledgeably about painters and places that were only names in books to me – Giotto, Leonardo Da Vinci – Florence, Venice and London. He opened doors to another world and treated me like an equal. In retrospect, my decision to leave teaching must have been stimulated by Rex, since he suggested that because of my interest in Art perhaps architecture was the course to pursue.

After the weekend I told him that I had left teaching. He told me he would do all he could to help me, but I should bear in mind the problem of financing the architecture course which was lengthy and expensive.

He invited me to visit his home in Forest Town so that I could talk to other students and architects. As a result I confirmed my decision to switch to architecture, assuming that I could raise the fees. This visit helped cement my friendship with Rex, a unique civilised man.

At his home there were original pictures on the wall by Bracque, Le Corbusier the famous French modern architect, Leger and many prints by the Impressionists – Van Gogh, Cezanne and others.

I felt I was now able to resolve my problems and would talk to my father about the developments of the past week – Rex had come up with the idea that I could do the architectural course part-time.

Although, technically, I had left teaching, I was still at university. It was now a question of getting a job or finding enough money to see me through a six-year architectural course.

By coincidence that week there was a debate on whether "abortion was a crime or not". I and some friends decided we would attend it, since at the time the question of abortion was a an avant-garde issue. In 1935 it was socially taboo to openly discuss this subject. It was illegal in South Africa, although many abortions were secretly carried out in backrooms by midwives and others, often with disastrous results.

Relations with my father were deteriorating by the day because he was constantly interfering with my activities at the university. I was in open rebellion about his domineering ways – I was at a stage where I believed it was necessary for me to be free to sort out my own life without my father dictating every move.

· The position at home was becoming untenable. Hannah and Leon had left after several disagreements. Almost every evening my father would get rid of his own frustrations and disappointments on me. I was the only victim he could find at home.

On the night of the abortion debate I slipped away from the house early and spent a hilarious and argumentative evening at the university. There were so many students present that the venue had, at the last minute, to be moved to a larger lecture room. The debate did not start until much later and finished well after 11 pm.

As soon as it ended I rushed up Ameshoff Street hill and managed to catch the last tram to Yeoville terminus, racing back to the house through the darkened streets.

I was out of breath when I reached home – there was still a light on. I crept down the lane, quietly pushed open the sash window of my bedroom and heaved myself in, as I had done many times before.

At that moment the light was switched on in my room. Father stood there in the doorway, in his open-necked shirt, braces and baggy trousers. His sparse hair was tousled – he had a grim look.

"Where've you been? Why are you so late?"

He grabbed me by the hand and dragged me along the passage to the diningroom. We stood between Hannah's piano and the oak dining table.

I wrenched my hand away.

"Dad, I have been to the university. There was a debate on abortion."

I was fearful and trembling. I had a premonition that something bad was going to happen.

"Abortion, abortion, what has it to do with you? I don't believe you, you have been out with a girl."

"Dad . . ."

Before I could finish the sentence, he struck me in the face with an open hand – a searing cut. In a moment I was no longer his son, but fighting for my life. I hit him back. He staggered and then came at me with both hands. I struggled with him. The tears were streaming down my cheeks. We grappled like all-in wrestlers.

Suddenly we stopped and stood there staring at each other.

He looked at me in a kind of daze, slowly turned his back on me and went to his bedroom and closed the door.

I just stood, for a moment. I was shaking all over and weeping. I went to my room. I sat on my bed, numb and in a state of shock.

Without any clear idea of what to do, I rolled up the blanket on my bed, a heavy woollen dark-blue one I had slept under for most of my youth. I took the only money I had in the world, a sixpence from my bedside drawer, tucked the blanket under my arm and silently crept out of the window into the lane and the dark night.

I ran up Dunbar Street without stopping, past the darkened houses, until I reached the Yeoville tram lines. I rested outside my old primary school.

I was out of breath, and asked myself: "Where am I going, what am I to do?"

There seemed to be no answer. It was after midnight. No trams running and only an occasional car passed.

I decided I would go to High Street in Berea, about a mile away along the tram route to town, past the Yeoville shops and try to wake up my old school and university friend Manny Sidley. This was easy – his room faced the pavement. All I had to do was to tap on his window as I had done many times before.

There were no lights on at the Sidley's house when I reached it. I quietly tapped at Manny's window.

"Manny, Manny, wake up – it's me, Boris."

I tapped again. I heard movement in the room, the light came on and there was Manny, half-asleep, standing by the window. He opened it. I whispered to him what had happened. He told me to meet him in the backyard. When he came out in his pyjamas, he had a pillow and a blanket.

"Boris," he said, "I don't want to waken my father and mother. Come with me to the garden and you can sleep on the bench under the portico."

I followed him.

We put his blanket on the long garden bench for me to lie on. We would discuss the matter in the morning.

I lay down on the bench covering myself with my blanket. In the cool of the night I stared at the clear sky and the stars trying to find some coherence in my thoughts.

I was still tense and could not stop shaking. This added to my miseries because the bench was slatted and uncomfortable.

The night seemed endless. I slept in fits and starts until the autumn dawn and the Highveld cold finally woke me completely.

Early in the morning Manny came to talk to me. I repeated what had happened at home.

He understood. He knew what our home was like.

"Boris, what are you going to do?"

"Manny, I have to go away, I can't stay here any more. I have never been to Durban, but I imagine the best place for me is as far away from my father as possible. I can't take it any longer. Can you lend me some money for a train ticket to Durban? I will get a job there and send the money back to you."

He told me to come in and have breakfast, which would not cause any special comment because I had often done so in the past.

He was a late riser; I was used to getting up early.

If we had an early lecture, it was the rule for me to hustle him along out of bed and bath and then either watch him eating his breakfast or join him. It was not necessary to tell his family why I was there on that fateful morning.

He lent me some money which we hoped was enough to get me to Durban. It was one pound ten shillings for the ticket with an extra ten shillings for food and other expenses.

He thought it was a great idea to go to Durban and wished me luck.

I caught a tram to Park Station in the centre of Johannesburg at the north end of Eloff Street, carrying my blanket.

My mood changed. I was tired, depressed and exhausted.

At the station, I bought my Durban ticket, and was sitting in a second-class compartment waiting for the train to go, when I realised I had no food with me. I could not afford to buy a meal on the train, nor could I pay for a bed. At least I could stretch out on the bunk. My own blanket would keep me warm and I hoped I would get some much-needed sleep.

There was about half an hour before the train left. I rushed from the train, up the stairs, through the old concourse with its Pierneef paintings high on the walls.

Once outside, I crossed a busy Eloff Street into the nearest "Greek" shop to buy some fruit which would be sufficient for my journey into the unknown.

Clasping my parcel of fruit, I hurried back to Platform 16 where the Durban train was standing, now full with passengers and friends and relatives saying their goodbyes.

Just as was about to enter my carriage I heard a voice.

"Hullo, Boris, where are you off to?"

It was George Coetzee, a fair-haired, slightly plump architectural student I had recently met through Rex Martienssen at the University.

For a moment I hesitated. Then, uncontrollably, it all poured out I told him what had happened and why I was going away.

He listened carefully.

"Boris, don't rush away. You're doing the wrong thing. Stay here and think things over. You may well feel differently about everything in a matter of days."

As I was weighing up his words of advice the announcement that the train was due to leave boomed out.

"George," I hesitated, "George, I have nowhere to go. What will I do? I've already got my ticket and the train will soon leave."

He took me by the arm.

"Don't go, get your things off, quickly. You can go to my room and sleep. I'm going away for the weekend. Running away will not solve your problems."

He gave me a push.

"Go on, get your baggage."

That did it. He was right. I rushed into the carriage, grabbed my smelly old blanket and got off the train as it was starting to move on its four hundred mile journey to Durban.

George stood there with his hands in his pockets.

"You've done the right thing, Boris."

I looked at him, somewhat bewildered and then at the dirty red-brown train steaming and hissing its way out of Park Station.

George told me where he lived, gave me the key of his room and we walked slowly out of the station.

I went back to the railway ticket office and got a refund on my ticket.

George hurried away. For a few minutes I stood outside the station collecting my thoughts.

I was confused – but the die was cast. It may have been a very important coincidence that I met George Coetzee, whom I hardly knew, and that he stopped me from going to Durban.

I was too tired to worry any more.

I took a tram to Doornfontein, walking to the house where he rented a room. I opened the door and fell into his unmade bed.

I slept for the rest of the day, until about 6 pm.

I cleaned myself up and decided I would go to Rex Martienssen's home. The atmosphere there was just what I needed. Rex's house was simply and artistically furnished. For the first time in days I relaxed in another world, discussing architectural trends, art in general to a background of music from a portable gramophone which we periodically wound up by hand. Out of its "His Master's Voice" horn came the resonant voices of the Mills Brothers or Cab Calloway with "California – Here I Come" and other 1930 hits.

That evening's experience at Rex's, the people there, the ambience, made me realise that there was another world waiting for me – there was no need to run away.

In the early hours of the morning I told Rex what had happened. He offered to help me sort out my future. After breakfast I returned to George's room, much happier, and fell into a deep sleep.

One thing was certain. I was not going back to my father, the problems at home and the Market.

I spent the rest of the weekend deciding what to do.

First I had to find a a place to live, then a job. I could not continue at University full-time, but would try and convert to a part-time course, if this was possible.

On mature reflection, becoming an architect was out. I had slim chances of raising the fees. The most likely course, if I could manage it, would be an Arts one in Politics and Philosophy.

By Monday I had evolved a plan of action.

I saw my Professor of English at the university. He recommended I see the editor of the evening newspaper *The Star* to discuss whether I was suitable as a trainee journalist. I was trying to find work in a field that suited my general interests.

I saw the editor the following day. He seemed a tired old man who gave me no encouragement whatsoever to be a journalist.

I left him somewhat deflated. As I was walking past the General Mining Company's offices in nearby Sauer Street, I met a schoolfriend from Yeoville Primary School, George Berry, whom I had not seen for years.

George told me he worked on a goldmine and liked it. I asked him if he knew where I could find a job in a hurry. He told me to see a Mr van der Merwe on the sixth floor, because there was a job vacant on one of the group's mines.

He went off. For a few minutes I pondered whether I should go up, because working on a goldmine was the last thing I wanted to do. On the other hand if there was job, it might give me time to look around and I would be earning some money.

I went up in the lift, and was ushered into Mr van der Merwe's office. He was going through a pile of letters.

"I have come about the job you are advertising – George Berry sent me here."

Thin, balding and from behind thick glasses came a smile.

"Well, I'm afraid you're too late. All the applications had to be in by yesterday. I'm going through them now, to make my decision."

"Won't you consider me?"

I was in luck. For some reason he questioned me. I told him that I was compelled for family reasons to leave university and support myself. While he was listening he kept going through the papers on his desk. Then he pushed a form over to me.

"Fill it in – while I go through these applications."

I did so. I told him I would telephone him with my address later that day. He said that he would advise me of the outcome in a day or two.

After I left Mr Van der Merwe I bought *The Star* and scanned the "Rooms To Let" classified column. Amongst several offers there was one that interested me. From a nearby public telephone I rang the advertiser, who told me there was a room available for a young man, at three pounds a month, which included all board and washing. I was invited to inspect the room that afternoon.

I found 4 Pretoria Street in Hillbrow, near the rambling buildings of the old General Hospital, about a hundred yards from the huge Old Fort, Johannesburg's prison, on the adjacent Hospital Hill where Pretoria Street ends.

Pretoria Street was full of a variety of small shops frequented by the young people who lived in boarding houses who needed cheap meals and entertainment. It was becoming the Chelsea of Johannesburg. South of it the trams noisily turned the corner into Kotze Street after a struggle up the steep Twist Street hill, on their journey to Yeoville and Observatory.

Number 4 Pretoria Street was at the dead-end, next to the Fort. It was a small single-storey bungalow house, built in the early days, typical of Johannesburg's less-affluent suburbs; red galvanised tin roof, with a small neatly kept garden behind a hedge and a small lawn with shrubs at the back, overshadowed by the sloping grassed walls of the sinister prison.

I knocked at the front door. A well-dressed middle-aged man asked me to come inside.

The house was comfortably furnished. The living-room had several sofas and easy chairs. Off this room were the bedrooms of the four men who lived there – the house was a bachelor's home.

I was shown a small neat room, and invited to discuss the terms. For the three pounds a month, as the advertisement indicated, I would get all my meals, the washing done, and the room cleaned daily. I saw the smiling Malay housekeeper who did all the work. She greeted me warmly as I was shown around.

I agreed to take the room and to move in that evening with my few possessions. I turned up at eight o'clock and met some of the other men who shared the house.

I was too preoccupied to notice much about my new home – I was elated that I had found what appeared to be a very suitable place. Now all I needed was a job.

The only interview I'd had was for the mining job. The idea of working on a mine depressed me. I didn't really have a chance anyway. There seemed to be many applications for it – I was sure that I would not get it.

I spent the following day criss-crossing the streets of central Johannesburg with its never-ending stream of horses, carts, cars and petrol fumes. I eagerly bought *The Star* when it appeared on the streets that afternoon to see what jobs were on offer.

I arrived back at my new home exhausted, dispirited, having made no progress, to be given a message that Mr Van der Merwe of General Mining had telephoned asking to see me the next morning.

I spent a restless night wondering whether I would take the job if he offered it to me. I came to the conclusion that I would be foolish not to do so. I had to start somewhere and I needed money to pay my rent.

The next day, I sat before Mr Van der Merwe. There was only one application on his desk and I could see it was mine.

"I have given you the job, Wilson. You must go out to the mine immediately. It's the CMR, on the Old Main Reef Road. You take a bus which starts around the corner from here in Commissioner Street. It takes about half-an-hour to get there."

I was stunned. I had got the job despite my late application over the many others who had wanted it. I realised I knew nothing about mining. In my excitement that I'd found work I did not pay full attention to Mr Van der Merwe's description of what this job was like.

I was to be a clerk in the statistics office of the Consolidated Main Reef Gold Mining Company, one of the earliest mines founded on the Witwatersrand by the gold-mining pioneers. The secretary, Mr Catto, would give me the details when I reached the mine.

My starting salary was five pounds a month with no transport allowance.

The CMR mine was near a small mining town called Roodepoort to the west of Johannesburg. I left Mr Van der Merwe, my mind in a whirl, to find the bus terminus. I had the first shock, when I was asked to pay five shillings for the weekly return ticket. This meant one pound a month leaving me four pounds to pay for my new lodgings and other expenses.

We passed through the old suburb of Mayfair with its rows of corrugated iron-roofed houses reaching Old Main Reef Road that wound its way to Roodepoort between the yellow-ochred mine dumps and their busy headgears. I was worrying how I would manage on the pound that was left from my salary to pay for everything else I needed. Where was the money to come from for my clothes, entertainment and the rest of my living expenses?

Before the bus reached the CMR mine, I had made up my mind that I would speak to the mine secretary, explaining that I could not come out on five pounds a month, and ask him whether it was possible to increase it.

The old CMR mine was like all the goldmines on the Witwatersrand. The mine offices were housed in dirty, tired, corrugated-iron buildings over which the huge headgear towered. Its enormous wheels carried the cables of the "skips" in which the miners and the gold ore were hauled from the bowels of the earth.

I found the mine secretary, Mr Catto in his office. He was a sour-looking man, semi-bald with spectacles, wearing a waistcoat. His worn shiny jacket was hanging on a hook behind him.

He looked across at me over masses of papers, several telephones, files and a half-full cup of tea. He said little.

He filled in the contract I was to sign. As he handed it to me he described the work I was to do. I was to go to the minehead below the headgear, every hour of the day. At a special telephone there, I would receive reports from miners thousands of feet below me with statistics relating to the hourly production of gold ore as it was being mined. In addition I had to note the urgent requests from the underground workers for supplies. To fill in my time between listening for the telephone calls I had to count the thousands of wooden poles that were stacked in piles below the rusty headgear.

I swallowed hard at this job description. Inwardly I was asking myself how I had taken this job without really investigating what it was all about. I was very undecided at that point as to whether I was doing the right thing or not.

I could not come out on the salary. I desperately needed the job and the best plan was to tell Mr Catto there and then.

"Mr Catto, before I sign this contract, I must tell you that I cannot come out on five pounds a month."

I briefly explained why, telling him when I accepted the job, I was not told that I would have to spend a pound a month on transport, a fifth of my month's pay.

"I need at least seven pounds ten shillings a month."

He exploded.

"Why did you take the job – there were dozens of applications for it? Why didn't you tell Mr Van der Merwe that the salary was too low – we could have given the job to someone else."

"I didn't know until I reached the bus terminus to buy the weekly ticket how expensive it was. It bothered me all the way here. I thought it best to tell you now. It was never my intention to mislead you."

He stared at me through his glasses, took a sip of his tea and coughed. "Do you want the job?"

"Yes, Mr Catto."

He gritted his teeth, thought a moment and then said:

"Well, its against the rules, but I'll see that your salary is seven pounds ten shillings."

He took back the contract from me, altered the salary and handed it back to me for signature.

I was too excited to read it properly. I had got an increase of fifty per cent before I started. The extra sum, in those days, of two pounds ten shillings was large. It was going to make all the difference to me in supporting myself.

Before signing the contract I noticed I was subject to twenty-four hours notice – I had expected a monthly contract.

Mr Catto then sent for another clerk, who immediately took me out to the minehead after being shown around the statistics office and meeting some of the other men working there.

I was shown the all-important telephone and taken around the piles and piles of timber that I was to count.

For two days, I rose early, walked into town, with lunch sandwiches in a packet. The long bus ride to the stark dirty atmosphere of the old CMR mine followed. The first move was to the telephone at the shaft head to receive the messages from the unknown miner.

I never understood for a moment what the messages meant. I felt odd in that I was speaking to someone thousands of feet below me whom I would never meet or recognise. I would then rush back to the office to give the details to another clerk who would act on them while I entered the details as given to me in a large book.

Counting the timber was to me a mindless waste of my time. I came to the conclusion I had to find more interesting work. The next job had to be in something more congenial, in Johannesburg. That evening, back at Pretoria Street, I was talking to Edmund, one of the young men who lived in the house, whose room was next to mine about my disappointment over the CMR job.

Edmund was a very lively person who worked in Johannesburg. He was about ten years older than me. In the little time that I knew him I realised that he drank far too much. As our rooms were next to each other I got to know him better than the others in the house. Edmund said he would make enquiries for me about a job.

The next day when I came home from the CMR, Edmund told me that he had spoken to one of the men who lived in our house, whom I had not

51

yet met, who would see me later that evening about my possibilities of a job as an insurance clerk in a large company in Johannesburg.

After dinner I was introduced to a tall fair-haired man whose name was Orford. He told me that there was a vacancy immediately available at the Norwich Union Assurance Company. If possible, I should see a Mr Clymo of the Marine department the following day.

Luckily the mine office day finishes early. I was able to get to Johannesburg in time to see Mr Clymo at the Norwich Union, whose offices were by coincidence next to General Mining's.

As it was late in the day there was no one else there when I was interviewed by Mr Clymo, a short man wearing dark tortoise-shell glasses, who told me there was a job in the marine insurance department as a clerk. He pointed to one of the desks in the large office which I would use if I was suitable.

"Do you think you would like the work in the marine section?"

"I think so."

"In view of Mr Orford's introduction the job is yours."

"Thank you, Mr Clymo."

"Be here on Monday morning at eight o'clock – your salary will be seven pounds ten shillings a month."

I could not get to the CMR offices the next day quickly enough. I walked into Mr Catto's office and told him that I was giving him twenty-four hours notice, because I had found a job in Johannesburg at the same salary and that I did not wish to make a career on a mine.

I thought he was going to explode again. He was about to say something, but instead picked up my contract which was still on his desk and read it.

He never spoke to me again. I left the CMR mine the next evening.

I began to take in my new situation. In the space of a week my life had dramatically changed. I had broken with my father, left home and University, and found two jobs. I had lodgings in little house with some men I did not know, in a new atmosphere which allowed me to relax for the first time. I did not know what my future was going to be – it was very early days. But I knew, as I sat sunbathing in the garden with the others, that it was the beginning of a new life.

There was no contact with my family. I did not miss them – nor did I feel like seeing them. I did not know where Hannah was staying but I knew where Leon was to be found and where he worked.

On Monday I arrived early at the Norwich Union offices. I was introduced to some of the clerks learning that my predecessor was a 17-year-old young golfer, by name Bobby Locke.

He was being sponsored in his golf by the mining magnate Norbert Erleigh, who thus gave Locke the chance to become a world famous golfer.

I walked to work and back every day, which I enjoyed. The route was down Hospital Hill to Joubert Park, through this green patch between the large buildings of the town and the congestion of Hospital Hill and Hillbrow. I would cross the railway bridge at Park Station and walk through the busy streets of Johannesburg to the financial and mining offices south of the town.

Once again I realised after a few weeks that being an insurance clerk was the same kind of monotonous job as mining – both were dull vocations for me. I spent all day, sometimes Saturdays included, once on a Sunday morning, writing out marine declarations relating to shipments of goods to and from obscure ports in Portuguese East Africa with tantalising names like Beira and Inhambane, which I had never heard of, but nevertheless a meaningless exercise.

I could not remain in this job. I would start looking for work that really suited me once I made up my mind what I wanted to do.

A thought that kept recurring was that my training at the Market with my father had made me a good salesman. Perhaps this was the field I should explore.

I decided there was no rush to move. I would settle down in Pretoria Street, which I was enjoying, and when I had become certain that I wanted a salesman's job I would look for one.

The house in Pretoria Street was very well run – my new-found friends were kind to me. Through them I was made a member of the Johannesburg Repertory Players and found satisfaction in amateur theatricals.

I was out a lot at night seeing my friends at the university, savouring and enjoying the life style of the Johannesburg of the mid-1930s; and especially the new freedom. I hardly ever took part in the activities of 4 Pretoria Street – I did not feel I had much in common with the men whom lived there.

At weekends I noticed that the living room was crowded with young men, friends of the other boarders who seemed to spend most of their time sitting around, drinking and conversing which did not interest me much.

I paid no attention to the occasional compliment thrown at me when I passed through the room, by one or other of the boarders declining most of the invitations to sit with them and join the throng.

My main conversations were with Edmund with whom I had a rapport. One day after I had been there about two months I was ill with a bad dose of influenza, so I stayed home for the day.

I had nothing to read so I went into Edmund's room to find a book because he had several shelves full. On his desk lay *Sexual Inversion* written by an author I had never heard of – Havelock Ellis.

I took the book, went back to my room, lay on my bed and paged through it. I read for several hours. By the time late afternoon had come, I realised with a shock that I must be living in a house of homosexual men.

I knew nothing about homosexualism – until I had read Havelock Ellis's book that day. My first reaction was to take my few belongings and leave as quickly as I could.

I calmed down and returned the book to Edmund's desk. I decided to speak to him when he came home that evening. I was worried about the implications of living in this house if all the men in it were homosexual.

There had been some incidents which I had not understood, but which I had ignored. I now realised the extent of my ignorance of homosexuality.

I recalled that when I had gone to the offices of the Registrar of Births and Deaths to get my birth certificate, the clerk, a fair-haired young man, had stroked the back of my leg as he paged through the large book seeking my birth date. At the time it had meant nothing to me. To my surprise, this young man was one of the regular Sunday visitors to Pretoria Street. It was he who suggested I join the Repertory Players.

On another occasion when I was passing through the livingroom crowded with men, one of them called out to me: "Boris you've got nice hips." The others had laughed. I was embarrassed, but again did not pay much attention to the remark.

I remembered also that there had been odd things that I had noticed but dismissed as irrelevant. Some of the boarders were very fussy about their hair. One had his hair regularly "set"; another had his hair dyed. Some men used facial make up. Once there was a heated argument between two of the boarders in the bedroom they shared. The next morning I saw that one was in tears and clearly upset.

That evening after dinner, I went into Edmund's room.

"Edmund, I borrowed a book from your room this morning, I hope you don't mind. I've returned it. It's the one by Havelock Ellis called *Sexual Inversion*. Can I ask you a question – I don't want to upset you?"

Edmund smiled.

"Are you a homosexual, and are all the men here homosexuals?"

He had a whisky in his hand, took up the book looked at it, and with a little laugh replied.

"Yes, Boris, I've been waiting several weeks for you to ask me that question. In fact, I purposely left the book on my desk knowing you were home today. I hoped that you might look at it."

We talked for a long time in his room. He told me that he and the other men had come to the conclusion I was not homosexual. After I had been there a few days they decided they liked me, and were prepared to let me stay with them because of my problems. They had hoped that their advertisement would have attracted someone who shared their inclinations.

Edmund was very frank with me. He assured me that there was no question of my being involved or molested. He hoped I would stay on and not be frightened or disturbed by what I had discovered.

The next morning, however, I had made up my mind that I would leave as soon as I could find alternative lodgings. The notion of living with homosexuals revolted me. Staying on in that environment was impossible, in spite of the warm and friendly way I had been treated.

I was attracted to women and I did not want to get embroiled in male relationships where there were risks of sexual involvement.

The Johannesburg Market. The wholesale section is in the foreground. My father's stall was just to the left of the balcony clock.

King George Street, Johannesburg, in the 1920s. The building on the right is where United Party divisional meetings were held from 1954.

My brother Len in the western desert,
1941, after he escaped from Tobruk.

Max, alias Desmond J Leaney, aged
illegally in the South African Navy.
signed it "Max".

My brothers and sisters with me at my house in Parktown, Johannesburg, 1955.

11

That weekend I started looking for a new place to live. I remembered that at the university, in the main lobby of the Arts Block, there were always advertisements offering accommodation to students who wished to live near the university.

There was no question of my going back home. I had not only temporarily shut my father out of my life, but also the rest of my family. I had to sort my future out and decide what I would do with my life. I was still unclear what career I would follow – I needed plenty of time to find inspiration or motivation about a vocation or a profession.

It was early days. All I wanted to do at that moment was to get away from 4 Pretoria Street before it became a problem.

I scanned the few accommodation notices on the Arts Block notice board. There was one which interested me. It offered a room in a private house in Loch Avenue, Parktown West, a lovely old suburb of Johannesburg near the university, full of trees and old houses built of granite, some of them designed by the ubiquitous Sir Herbert Baker – architect to the rich and famous.

I decided to go to Loch Avenue without delay.

That afternoon at about 4 pm I walked up its long drive to the veranda of the large single-storey house, surrounded by leafy jacaranda trees not yet in bloom.

The door opened to my knock. The lady who stood there looked like a middle-aged ballerina, with sleek black hair ending in a bun. In her left hand, which she held up as if she was posing for a photograph, she had a cigarette in a long ivory holder with smoke curling lazily from it. She asked me what I wanted.

"Madam", I said, "I've come in response to your notice on the main board of the Arts Block at the university offering accommodation to a male student. Is it still available?"

She laughed.

"You're about three months too late," she said in a very Afrikaans accent. "I put up that notice a long time ago. I only have one student at a time and she has been here since the term began. I'm sorry there is nothing else available."

I apologised for bothering her and was leaving, when she called me back.

"You've come all this way – it's tea time – would you like to join me?"

"Thank you very much."

She invited me into the long, beautifully-furnished livingroom with old Cape Dutch stinkwood antiques and paintings by Pierneef and Erich Mayer on the walls, which I recognised.

Over tea she asked me questions about myself and why I was looking for lodgings at this time of the year.

I told her of my problem at Pretoria Street, and eventually a little about recent events. The longer I stayed, the more I felt drawn to her. She seemed to be genuinely interested in my story, and was an extraordinarily intelligent person who was worth getting to know. We talked over for a long while, over innumerable cups of tea.

As I was leaving she said: "You can come and stay here."

I was overwhelmed.

"Do you really mean it ?"

"I never say anything I don't mean."

That is how I became the second boarder at Poppy B's home in Loch Avenue.

I left Pretoria Street a few days later. With limited belongings I moved into the much larger room that was to be my new home.

Across the passage was Mary's room; she was about four years older than me and I recognised her as one of the junior lecturers in the department of Geography at the university.

Poppy B and I enjoyed conversing with each other. I told her my family history and how I had fared since I left home.

She was very interested in my plans and agreed that I should leave the insurance world and get a salesman's position if I could find one. When I expressed my disappointment at leaving university, she was supportive when I said that I had made an appointment to see Iuan Glyn-Thomas, the Registrar, whom I had met at the Left Book Club, about continuing my BA degree on a part-time basis.

Glyn-Thomas listened to why I had left university, and my ideas on a part-time BA degree at Wits. He suggested that I should contact the University of South Africa which ran extramural courses. It would cost me much less, take only a year longer to get a my BA and I could study in my own time at home.

I followed his advice and wrote immediately.

Once more I was in a settled home environment, quite different from my father's house in Dunbar Street, or the menage at 4 Pretoria Street.

Poppy B was always ready to listen when I wanted to talk about my future. Art, literature, South African politics and history loomed large in our discussions and I looked forward to coming home to Loch Avenue at the end of a day's work.

I was still writing marine insurance declarations, hating it more and more. I took every opportunity to apply for suitable jobs. One advertisement called for a young man to sell "famous brand-name chocolates and sweets – transport provided". I was summoned to an interview. The manager, a pleasant man with a marked side flexion of his neck, told me that they wanted an aggressive young man to sell their "famous Clarnico chocolates" throughout the Witwatersrand.

I got the job. The transport, to my surprise, was not a motor car as I had expected, but a powerful blue and white Norton motor cycle and sidecar, the latter to carry my chocolate samples. I was to begin as soon as I had given notice to Norwich Union Insurance.

I had to learn, with some urgency, how to ride a motor cycle and get a license, no mean task, since it was a giant of a machine, with a tremendously powerful, gleaming engine. I wondered what my father would have said had he known that I had accepted a job riding a motor cycle, since he had so savagely mutilated Lion's bike.

Poppy B was thrilled that I was making the change. She was even more pleased that I'd made the decision to start the extra-mural Arts degree course. The University of South Africa informed me that they would accept my late entry and I would write my first year examinations in November 1935. If I passed I would not have lost a whole year.

Rex Martienssen was pleased too. He was disappointed that I could not carry out my intention to become an architect; he hoped that, some time in the future when I had become financially independent, I would do a part-time architectural course.

For my BA degree I decided to take a gamble. Although it was near the mid-year, I would study three subjects. I had some knowledge of two: Geography, which Mary said she would help me with at home; and Fine Arts which was not demanding, it was literally the matriculation syllabus all over again. English was the third subject.

I could not afford the written lectures offered by the University of South Africa. Instead I bought the recommended books second-hand and used the university library to study on my own – when I had the time.

So I started a regimen that I kept going for four years. I would wake early, between 5 and 6 am, study for two hours at my desk working through the syllabus, then work a full day selling Clarnico chocolates on my Norton bike. I would be home by 6 pm ready to study again.

I became a workaholic. I had a tremendous urge to prove to myself, my father and the people who were interested in me that I could overcome the odds against me. At the same time I was avid for the knowledge I was taking in, despite the fact that I was working alone without the benefit of university tutorials.

I would study for an hour or so before dinner, then back to work afterwards until I was really tired. Poppy would invite me to the livingroom for some tea and a snack. It was then that our dialogues would begin. She was a lonely woman who wanted to talk about South Africa and her own life. From her I learnt about the bitter background of Afrikaner nationalism and its politics; why hatred had arisen between Afrikaans- and English-speakers in our country, from the earliest time of the occupation of South Africa by the British.

The defeat of the Afrikaners in the Boer War had left scars that Poppy would never forget. As a small child, she and her mother were interned by the British in the concentration camps, which created an abiding hatred of the English and their institutions. I was horrified to find how vehement this hatred was to the extent that she was determined to exact her revenge at some time in the future.

Her marriage to a leading Johannesburg dentist had ended in a divorce. She was very disappointed because her only son, who was a little younger than me, was not interested in the things she valued most and loved. He was an out and out extrovert and caused her emotional distress. It seemed as if she was transferring frustrated motherly love to me.

She needed someone to look after, someone in tune with her intellectual needs and emotions, and I seemed to be that person. Despite my refusal to accept her prejudiced, dogmatic views about English-speaking South Africans and their history *vis-à-vis* the Afrikaner struggle, our friendship matured. I could reject her extreme views and retain my independence. I disappointed her about a few things. I was a member of the Left Book Club of which she totally disapproved. Most times when I came home late she would be waiting for me, and we would talk for an hour or so.

Sometimes when she or I could not sleep we would talk into the early hours of the morning. They were important moments in my life. I also needed someone who would listen to me; for years I had been my father's captive audience of one. With Poppy I could speak my mind.

12

Later in the year my examination results came out. I opened the letter and *mirabile dictu*, I had passed all my subjects. The first person I told the good news to was Poppy, who was delighted. She insisted on giving me a present of some money to spend on myself.

Because of her confidence in me, she was frank about her innermost feelings. I realised why she was a lonely woman, why her marriage had failed and why the British concentration camps in the Boer War, that sordid event in South Africa's history, had turned her into an ultraconservative Nationalist Afrikaner. Her family was intimately concerned in the struggle of the Afrikaners to rid themselves of the British yoke. They had not only established a name in South African politics since Union in 1910, but their political links could be traced back to the Voortrekker movement of 1836.

Often after I'd gone to bed, come home late, or was studying, Poppy would be listening to a "wireless" in her bedroom. At first I paid no attention to it, but became interested when I heard German voices speaking English. She was listening to the special broadcasts from Zeesen's short-wave station in Hitler's Germany, beamed to South Africa to the conservative Afrikaners whose aim was to establish the all-white Afrikaner republic.

The Nazis encouraged the Afrikaners to rebellion. They were helped in these vitriolic broadcasts by a coterie of young Afrikaners who knew how to appeal to *die volk*, the people.

From all I knew about Poppy, I had to admit that she could be a Nazi supporter. Later I found out that she was a member of the *Ossewa Brandwag* (Oxwagon Sentinel), an organisation set up to bring about a republic and who believed that a Nazi victory would help them to achieve this. During World War II, the OB carried out acts of sabotage against Smuts's war effort.

Did she play an active role in the OB to overthrow the government of South Africa? The evidence suggested that she could have been involved.

Once again there was a moral dilemma. Was it reason enough for me to leave Poppy and her very satisfactory home, because her political beliefs were wholly opposed to mine? Could I continue to live with someone who wanted the Nazis to triumph in the fight against democracy?

I wrestled with my conscience. I concluded that it was none of my business. She was not harming me. I liked her and staying at her house meant a great deal to me. Were her beliefs not her private affair?

So I suppressed my scruples, but I could not avoid the knowledge that she was being indoctrinated by the late-night broadcasts from Germany. She was constantly vitriolic about the British, but she was not the only Afrikaner to speak of them in this fashion. I forced myself to avoid arguments with her on a personal basis, despite my dislike of her regular anti-British tirades and her open declaration of support for Hitler and the Nazis.

In those days we knew nothing about the German holocaust. I had been brought up by my father to abhor the inhuman character of Fascism – if it was not destroyed it would destroy the world.

I found it tragic that an extraordinary lovely person like Poppy could identify herself with the Nazis who systematically killed and tortured people, persecuted Jews, Christians and anyone else who opposed them in the Europe of the 1930s.

I tried to be pragmatic in dealing with her. I decided to stay at Loch Avenue, live with the situation and see how it developed.

In the 1930s, I was very interested in international politics, especially in what was happening in the Fascist countries of Germany, Italy and the turbulence in Spain. Meetings of the Left Book Club helped me to understand what was going on in these dictatorships.

I have never forgotten how the rise of the Blackshirts in Italy shocked me. I was staring out of the window from my desk at the insurance company and saw *The Star* poster with one word on it: "WAR". I rushed outside to buy the paper and read that Mussolini's troops had invaded Ethiopia.

From my earliest "scribe" days, my father wrote letters to the newspapers on the rise of Hitler and Mussolini. Many letters contained warnings to western democracies to stop the Fascists in Germany and Italy, because they were intent on world domination.

The German broadcasts to which Poppy listened reminded me of a letter Father had written to the editor of *The Rand Daily Mail:*

"I hope that the hypocrisy of Nazi politics will not sink very deeply into the minds of those South Africans to whom Herr Hitler is paying the compliment that they are the representatives of the German race in South Africa. That is only a political bluff! Herr Hitler is in need of their sympathy and help . . . Last year the *Kreutzzeitung* of Berlin said of South West Africa: 'The Fatherland will thus raise the defenders of civilisation who will not intermarry with the Boers and the natives. The present and the future belong to the racially pure, not to crossbreeds'."

At that time South Africa was admitting (to strenuous objections from right wing Nationalists) Jews who were fleeing from Germany. I heard from some of them at first-hand what conditions were like in Nazi Germany.

Therefore, for totally different reasons, I started to listen to Zeesen myself – the transmissions were powerful and "Lord Haw Haw", the British traitor led the indoctrination in his familiarly sarcastic voice.

After hearing what he had to say I could readily understand how Nationalist fervour was inflamed and the Ossewa Brandwag and Poppy became easy converts.

13

I was enjoying my new job selling Clarnico chocolates. I soon got used to the powerful Norton motor bike. I often detached the side-car when doing my Witwatersrand runs from Springs in the east to Randfontein in the west, if I did not need to carry my samples to show to the many "Greek" shops on whom I called.

I must have known every "Greek" shop on the Witwatersrand. Their owners were swarthy people like the Lebanese and Syrians of the Market – mostly uneducated, speaking poor English, working long hours from early morning until late at night. They were kind to me. I think they liked me as much as I liked them.

From the early resistance to Clarnico, which had lost most of its market on the Reef before I took over, I had in a space of twelve weeks put Clarnico back on the shelves of most of the Greek cafes on the Witwatersrand with over 120 new customers. It was obvious that selling was a forte of mine and I should capitalise on it.

I was earning ten pounds a month with a small sales commission and I was at last able to save some money.

I had had no contact with my father. My conscience bothered me so I sent him three pounds a month – Leon told me things were bad both at home and the Market. Father was having a struggle to make ends meet.

Leon was happy in his job. Hannah was working and paying for her piano lessons. Ida was helping Father at the Market. Max, the youngest, was still at home but continuing to play truant from school.

In 1936 I started studying for my second year of the BA course, with subjects I always wanted to read – Politics, Psychology and Social Anthropology. My association with the Left Book Club was invaluable because it made up for the discussion I missed by not attending university seminars, especially on current international politics. The meetings gave me additional perspective on Mussolini's role in Africa, the importance of the powerful Hitler-Mussolini Axis and the disturbing role that Britain's government was playing which eventually lead to the fateful Munich crisis.

In pre-war Johannesburg, long before the Nationalists came to power, centres of liberal discussion like the Left Book Club helped to clarify my thinking. I met Trade Unionists, Labour Party members, refugees from Hitler and visiting writers and politicians. In the 1930s neither the Communist Party its satellites nor its fellow-travellers like the Congress of Democrats were banned.

Extreme left wing political movements did not interest me. I knew little about them and the role they played in South Africa. Much of my political outlook stemmed from my father and his views.

At a Left Book Club meeting I met Lionel Bernstein, "Rusty" to his friends, a year younger than me, fair-haired, angular features with a strong chin, an architectural student. I was impressed by his political knowledge. As a result I regularly visited his home, where he held frequent meetings discussing the theories of Lenin, Marx and Engels; the only background knowledge I had about these gentlemen came from my father in his poetry and newspaper letters.

Rusty Bernstein taught me more about Marx and Lenin than my father did, extrapolating their political importance in terms of the activities of the Labour Party. Under his influence I started struggling through Marx's *Das Kapital*. One evening he suggested that I should join the Labour Party, of which he was a member, and take an interest in the practical politics of socialism in South Africa. My problem was that I did not want active politics to interfere with my studies and I had little time to spare. He convinced me, however, that it would help me in my studies and would give me a practical insight into politics of South Africa.

Persuaded, I joined the Labour Party as a member of the Berea-Yeoville Branch, attending meetings in an old house close to 4 Pretoria Street. Before long I became the treasurer.

By the summer of 1936 I was fully occupied. I sold chocolates during the day, studied in the early mornings and evenings. I disciplined myself to wake early and worked late when not involved in political meetings.

I felt secure and happy at Poppy B's. For some time she had been urging me to see my father. Under her influence and prompting I went to see him at his new home in Sydenham, having been away for a year. The meeting was not as traumatic as I had expected. He was calm, wanted to know all about my activities, gave me lunch which he had prepared. It was a happy reconciliation.

The break had made a great difference to our relationship. He made me promise to come and see him again, asking me if I would come and take some dictation from him which he sorely missed. The only one who could help him was Max, but Father told me that he was very unreliable and never at home. I agreed to be the scribe again, but only at weekends.

He never mentioned my mother – neither did I. I recall, however, that I was beginning to think more and more about her. I felt guilty that now, as

I was independent, I had made no moves to see her at Pretoria. I heard that Hannah had visited her, at a very emotional meeting, but as my mother was an advanced psychotic, she was incoherent. Hannah had been very upset by the visit.

For reasons I could not explain, I made no move to see my mother despite the fact that I felt guilty, and no longer needed my father's permission.

There were very heavy rainstorms in summer of 1936, with frightening thunder and lightning, often with huge hailstones. Twice, while I was riding the Norton on the East Rand on the main road between the old mine dumps, I was caught by the sudden downpours and completely drenched.

I complained to the manager of Hill and Everett urging that they get me a car. I was now mostly on the road because of the large number of customers I had, and being caught in the rain was no fun.

I had built up Clarnico to one of the largest-selling sweet ranges on the Witwatersrand, and felt sure that having achieved this the company would let me have a car.

I also could not stand the terrible dust storms on the Reef, especially in the winter months. The mine dumps were the cause of the blinding dust which covered everything. Riding a motor bike in a duststorm was as bad as being drenched in a rainstorm, and I disliked both experiences.

The manager, who was sympathetic, said he would consult the head office in Cape Town. Several weeks went by without an answer. The delay simply increased my frustration and hardened my resolve that if they did not give me a car I would look for another job and leave.

One evening, returning home down the University hill in a heavy rainstorm, the Norton went into a skid. In a moment of panic I applied the brakes, which I learnt afterwards was the wrong thing to do. In an instant the heavy Norton with the engine roaring, started to slide down the hill, falling on its side with me underneath. The Norton and I travelled like this for about fifty yards in a headlong rush. It was terrifying – I thought I would be killed. Remarkably we came to a sudden stop at the kerbside. How I survived I do not know, because all around me cars swerved to avoid me and my motor bike. Some motorists got out of their cars and lifted the Norton off me. Miraculously, although I was cut and bruised, my clothes in tatters, I suffered no serious injury.

The next morning I went to the Clarnico office, to learn from the manager that head office had refused my request for a car.

"Well, that's that," I told him. "Here's my notice. I'm leaving the job. However much I like it, I am not prepared to risk my life selling chocolates. I've had enough."

The manager spent a fruitless hour trying to convince me that I had a great future with Clarnico if only I would be patient.

Once again I was looking for a job. Selling was what I most liked, especially if a commission went with it. I liked to earn more than a basic salary, if it was possible.

The next day, riding in a car with Manny Sidley, one of his brothers asked me if I was a good salesman.

"I can sell anything," I confidently answered, speaking with the wealth of experience of fruit at the Market and Clarnico chocolates!

"Could you sell radio sets?"

For a moment I hesitated.

"What are radio sets?" I asked. "I know what a wireless is and a crystal set, but not a radio set."

I instantly remembered the small crystal set I had built at Dunbar Street, which cost about ninepence, and the struggles I had to get broadcasts from the early South African Broadcasting Company, which was then owned by the Schlesinger family.

"Come and meet my father," invited Manny's brother.

We were going to the Sidley's house anyway. There was the old man, short and bent, in his shirtsleeves pouring over papers, glasses perched on the edge of his nose. He didn't waste time.

"Well, Boris, you can sell radio?" asked Old Man Sidley in his guttural German accent.

Before I could explain that I didn't know the difference between wireless and radio, he seemed to assume I'd taken the job.

"How much are you earning now?"

"With my commission, about twelve pounds ten a month."

"Well, twelve pounds ten shillings is a lot of money to start. I'll pay you the same if you can begin soon. You will be the sales manager of our new radio company – yes?"

I could not believe it. I was only eighteen – I knew nothing about a sales manager's function but made a quick decision.

"Yes, Mr Sidley, I can start right away, I've just given notice where I work."

I told him about the Norton, the disasters and how I nearly lost my life. His response satisfied me.

"You will have a company car – there will be a lot of travel."

It was only then that details of the job emerged. The Sidleys, who owned a large chemical factory, had decided to pioneer the manufacture of radio in South Africa. It was housed in part of their existing plant under the control of the eldest son, an inventive engineer. The radio company was called Mars Manufacturing. More about the venture, the type of radio to be made and what was expected from me would come when I met the Chief Engineer, Horace Dainty. A few nights later I went to a boarding house in the vicinity of Pretoria Street to meet him.

14

Horace Dainty was a young man about my age. He was more solidly built than I was, taller and sported a small moustache. So the chief engineer of the company was nineteen and the sales manager eighteen.

He was very self-possessed. During the course of the evening he told me about his personal background. He had been orphaned at the age of thirteen, and had literally looked after himself ever since. He had been apprenticed to a firm which was engaged in development in the early stages of electronics. By studying at night he had become an expert in radio technology, which was the modern name for "wireless". The invention of the battery eliminator converted wireless sets to mains operation. This was a tremendous step forward in the mid-1930s.

Next to Horace's bed was the first radio set I had ever seen with valves. Patiently, he went through its design, telling me about Marconi's work, explaining the various components, much beyond my understanding. Dainty's radio had no connection whatsoever with the primitive crystal set in my bedroom at home.

What he was telling me was quite foreign to a mind entirely given to artistic and philosophical matters, but he succeeded in giving me a rough idea of what it was all about.

Horace was already working at Mars Manufacturing, set in among the mine dumps south of Johannesburg next to the Robinson Deep mine. He had reached the stage where design of the radio set was complete.

He was training several white women as operatives to do the delicate work of manufacturing the chasses. Production would soon commence. It would be the first radio set built in South Africa – my job was to put it on the market.

The Mars Manufacturing Company was wholly owned by the Sidleys. Apart from Horace and me, there were three young men, technical assistants, and Botha Mabuza a young black man, a general factotum who did the cleaning, made the tea and ran the errands.

Our manufacturing team included an expatriate Polish cabinet-maker called Kronik who was in charge of the cabinet-making unit. On my first day I learnt the radio was to be called "Viking".

There were no cabinet designs, no promotional material, no leaflets and no marketing plans. There was no trade mark for Viking. I was expected to attend to these matters as part of the job.

It was a challenging beginning – I knew nothing about the radio business or to what extent a market existed. I had been thrown into the deep end by the Sidleys and told to get on with it!

First things came first. I drew up some designs for the trade mark "Viking" – a strong Nordic head with the logo "radio" running through it. Everyone liked it, so it was adopted as the emblem for Viking and the promotional literature to follow.

No cabinet designs existed for Viking – none of us liked Kronik's ideas.

Undaunted by the challenge and my lack of experience I spent a night drawing cabinet designs, incorporating an electric gramophone unit. There were limitations. Our cabinet works had no machinery for making rounded corners – everything had to be squared or rectangular. My designs once again met with approval. With minor modifications, Kronik was able to use them.

"Viking Radio" pioneered the assembly of a complicated radio unit in South Africa, and the standing cabinet models were new because of the built-in electrically-operated gramophone player.

When I look back on the way we set about planning, producing and marketing "Viking" I am astonished at the audacity of the project. We did it on a shoestring, with little help from the Sidleys who financed it. It was very exciting.

My new Opel Kadett car became my second home. During the course of the year I travelled the length and breadth of South Africa seeking dealers who would venture into selling radio – especially a South African-made receiver which was unknown. They were mostly general dealers still in the era of "His Masters Voice" hand-wound gramophones and small imported table "wireless" sets. The big Viking scared them. The sample I carried was in two large versions, one walnut the other in bird's eye maple. I found the dealers wary and Viking Radio a hard sell.

Johannesburg was a very difficult town in which to launch Viking. I soon found I would have to break into business sectors other than the general dealers if I was to have success with Viking. I was despondent. Few radios were sold. Most dealers knew nothing about radio. There had to be a way of establishing the market. But how? I had an idea that if I could induce one of the motor distributors to branch out into radio, existing radio dealers might follow the lead and start buying radio. A genial car salesman, Graham Morley of Williams Hunt, the Chevrolet distributors, introduced me to their sales manager Al Du Quette.

I proposed that he should open a special department selling Viking. He agreed, providing I supplied the radio on "sale or return". I had a struggle to induce Old Man Sidley to agree, but he did. In return, Williams Hunt allocated part of their main display windows in Eloff Street to Viking, supported by advertisements in the newspapers. Even if they did not sell many the publicity was worth the effort.

Then I had a stroke of luck. Two directors of Williams Hunt bought a Viking each for personal use. The news got around and gradually the sets started selling. Dealers who were sceptical came to inspect Hunt's show-room. One of my problems was a logistic one. In order to get sales I offered to do the first demonstrations for the dealers in customers' homes – the Vikings were so advanced they did not properly understand how to operate them. This gave me less time for my other activities especially my studies – but one way and another I managed.

On my trips I took my books with me. In small country hotels in the dorps, I would burn the midnight oil reading JS Mill or the *Philosophical Theory of the State* by Bosanquet.

I had become firm friends with Horace Dainty who, for his age, was a unique and extraordinary engineer. He managed the factory with precision and good control, devoting himself day and night to Viking.

For nearly a year we worked hard. I had sold nearly thousand Vikings – in retrospect this was an unexpected achievement, since I knew nothing about the fledgling radio market.

The Sidleys never told us whether the company was making money or not – we presumed it was beginning to show profits otherwise we would have heard from them.

One day, Horace looking distressed and miserable, told me that he was fed-up because he could not come out on the salary of twelve pounds ten shillings, which we were both being paid.

He said he did not know how to approach Old Man Sidley about an increase. I told him I had been thinking about it as well, and I was not frightened to speak to him for both of us, since I'd had some experience in this respect.

I went to see Mr Sidley at his house, because he hardly ever came to the factories which were under the control of his sons. As usual he was in his shirtsleeves, immersed in paperwork.

"Mr Sidley, Horace and I can't come out on our present salary. We both get twelve pounds ten shillings a month. Although you promised us a share of the profits we have heard nothing from you, nor have we seen any financial statements. Horace is an orphan, we have both worked very hard day and night – we need to earn more money now."

He was not very sympathetic. Looking straight at me he said:

"Things are tough, Boris. We have put a lot of money into the factory – it needs a lot more. We will have to sell many more sets to make it pay. I can only afford an increase to fifteen pounds a month – that's the best I can do."

I recalled my meeting with Mr Catto at the CMR mine.

"Mr Sidley, we cannot take less than twenty-five pounds a month. Otherwise I'm afraid we will both leave."

Old Man Sidley looked as if he was going to burst. His lips twitched, he fiddled with his papers on his desk – his face blanched.

I waited for the onslaught, but it never came only a heavy silence. Then he spoke.

"Boris," he said slowly, "I will give you both twenty-five pounds a month from the first of next month."

I could hardly contain my elation as I raced back to the factory to tell Horace the news of my success. He didn't believe it at first. In the mid-1930s a salary of twenty-five pounds a month was a fortune.

We decided as it was Easter in a few days we would celebrate by taking a holiday together in Durban where Horace had spent much of his childhood.

I'd never had a holiday in my life. The idea of Durban and the sea was very attractive. The problem was how to get there and back during the Easter weekend of 1936.

We solved it by suggesting to one of our salesman, who owned an old Riley tourer, that the three of us should go to Durban in his car and share expenses.

The next hurdle to overcome was to tell Old Man Sidley that we were going to Durban, leaving late on Thursday evening and returning on Easter Monday, in good time for work on Tuesday.

Mr Sidley was very upset that we were going, pointing out that if anything happened to us there would be no one to look after the factory. He appealed to us to give up the idea of the two key personnel being out of Johannesburg at the same time.

We discussed the matter with one of the sons, deciding that we would go, certain that nothing could delay our safe return.

I was excited as we packed our bags into the small green Riley tourer. On Thursday we left for Durban as soon as we could. On the outskirts of the town we joined the main untarred Durban road in the company of hundreds of other weekend motorists and motor cyclists who were on the annual Easter rush to Durban, four hundred miles away.

Our first "upset" came very soon – the weather suddenly changed. It started raining heavily. The untarred road became slippery and muddy. Despite windscreen-wipers, visibility became worse because of their inefficiency. It was getting colder by the minute. Two and a half hours later we reached our first "platteland" town, on the banks of Vaal River at the Orange Free State border.

Dozens of cars were ahead of us. To our chagrin we learnt that the swollen brown Vaal River had flooded over the bridge into the town, stopping all traffic in both directions. In high spirits, we treated the delay with contempt and took the opportunity to put a makeshift cover over the right rear window of the Riley which had broken and was letting in cold air. Eventually, after an hour's wait, the swollen river subsided enough for cars to cross the bridge. We passed through Standerton much later than planned. Night was upon us. A short while afterwards it began to snow, heavily. Despite the repair to the window we were freezing because the Riley's heating system was non-existent. None of us had brought thick coats. Who would have thought that it would snow at Easter?

All we wanted to do was get to Durban for the long weekend as quickly as possible. Excited by the idea of the holiday, we had ignored the possible vagaries of Easter weather.

As the snow increased, our progress became slower. It got so bad we reluctantly decided to turn back to Johannesburg. Eventually we found ourselves once more in Standerton with another surprise in store – we could not cross the bridge because the Vaal River had risen again during the night with traffic held up again on both sides of the river.

We fortified ourselves with coffee. After much talk, we decided that we should once again go south and try to reach Durban. The drive then became a nightmare, with more disasters to follow. The snow came down heavily; the windscreen wiper failed; the car hardly moved, struggling in the snow. Where were we? No one knew.

Suddenly we smelled burning. In a few minutes the car filled with acrid smoke. Stopping in the blinding snow, we opened the bonnet. To our horror the engine was on fire. Like madmen the three of us desperately scooped handfuls of snow, threw them on to the engine and eventually the fire was out.

Exhausted and wet we clambered back into the car. Unbelievably, the engine started. We shouted our heads off with delight. On we went, very slowly, growing stiff with cold. Suddenly the car refused to move – it was tilted at an alarming angle in the snow. It was obvious – we were off the road and in a ditch!

There were now no options left. It was in the early hours of the morning, the night was black, the snow was falling, no cars were passing, and we did not know where on earth we were.

We huddled together in the car, periodically blocking the hole in the window to stop the snow and cold coming in. We sang, we talked, we laughed. We knew that we were very close to a railway line, because a train came steaming slowly by, hissing and blinding us with its powerful lights.

The hours passed. Fitfully, we tried to sleep, always with one of us starting the engine every ten minutes. Horace was worried that it would freeze and not start again. That would have been total disaster.

Morning! The panorama of whiteness that greeted us was blinding. I had never seen a proper fall of snow before. As it became lighter, our surroundings took shape.

We had driven the car on to a fence protecting the main railway line to Durban, well off the Durban road which we could not see. On our left, several hundred yards away, we made out the huts of a Zulu village. We could see a few old men and women wrapped in colourful blankets walking about in the snow.

Horace, who was a fluent Zulu speaker, made his way to the huts and came back with three men, who, in a short while, to the accompaniment of singing, lifted the Riley out of its snowy grave.

We thanked the Zulu men, and gave them some of our food and money. It was now Saturday morning. The clouds were suddenly gone, the weather improved and our morale revived.

By agreement, we continued our way to Durban. A few hours later we reached Estcourt, a small country town, where we had a memorable breakfast of bacon and eggs at the Estcourt Hotel.

Much fortified we drove on, very slowly, because of the volume of traffic and the poor state of the road. We had more hair-raising escapes in the midlands of Natal. In the rain at Curries Post I nearly turned the car over on the wet and muddy road. Going down the hill, I braked and lost control. The car spun around three times before stabilising – I thought it was overturning, but it remained upright.

On Easter Monday, the day we should have been on our way back to Johannesburg we reached the outskirts of Durban, exhausted. We were so pleased to be there we gave no thought to Old Man Sidley, his problems, and the Viking Radio factory. Happily we drove to the seafront. I remembered a fragment of one of my father's poems:

"I saw the sea, a day of sunshine . . . the turbulent waves with a silver brush . . . in a lightening rush."

I was overcome by its vastness and beauty and savoured the soft white sands of Durban beach, in my bare feet, for the first time in my life at eighteen.

We spent Easter Monday in Durban, deciding to leave the next day for Johannesburg. We were dead tired and needed one decent night's sleep. The Riley was in bad shape – there were no garages open, but we could not get back in it without the repairs, which could only be done the next day. I agreed that I would try and hitch a lift back to Johannesburg – the others could follow a day later.

We sent a telegram to the Sidleys telling them of our misfortune, hoping that they would understand.

I managed the lift, reaching Johannesburg on Wednesday to find Old Man Sidley in a huge rage. He said he always knew we would not get back in time. To make things worse, Horace and the Riley took a further two days to return, because it constantly broke down *en route* despite the repair.

The shock came about a week later. Horace and I were called in to a meeting with all the Sidleys. They announced the closure of the Viking Radio factory.

It was a bitter blow in view of the hard work we had put in. It was also clear that if the factory was to succeed the Sidley's would have to find additional capital, which they were unwilling to do.

15

Thus began a new chapter in my life. Once again I was facing new decisions about my future. It was the middle of 1936. The newspapers and the radio were full of the war in Ethiopia and carried reports daily of the activities of the Fascist dictators, Hitler and Mussolini. Poppy B was avidly listening to the propaganda and anti-South African broadcasts from Zeesen.

My father, who I was now seeing regularly, warned in *The Star* and *The Rand Daily Mail* of the consequences of Fascism through his numerous letters. The South African government led by General Hertzog took a major step along the road to apartheid by removing the already limited franchise rights of blacks on the Common Roll – voting rights which they had secured when South Africa became a Union in 1910 – and which were entrenched in the constitution. The Hertzog government, as a quid pro quo, increased the area of land occupied by Natives (blacks) to 13 per cent of the total through the Native Trust Land Act of 1936.

Through my activity in the Berea-Yeoville branch of the Labour Party, I was nominated to the National Executive of the Party which pleased my branch committee. I was keeping up my studies with difficulty. My routine of waking up early to swot was gruelling.

I found time to do some writing. A short descriptive piece accepted by *The Sunday Times* earned me my first journalism cheque of fifteen shillings and gave great pleasure to Poppy and my father.

My friendship with Rex Martienssen developed – I had become one of a regular group which met at his house. In these meetings I learnt about the writings of Wyndham Lewis, Isherwood, Auden and a great deal about modern architecture. Most of all, I enjoyed firsthand accounts from Rex who had recently met Fernand Leger the French modernist painter, Corbusier the famous architect and others, which stimulated my growing interest in contemporary art.

My life was very full. I was determined to be successful in my business career. I regretted the fact that I was not full-time at university. However, I made up for this by attending meetings and discussions at night whenever I was able. My intellectual and artistic needs always remained important to me. I wore a porkpie hat, coloured shirts, tweed jackets and imitated Rex by smoking Balkan Sobranie tobacco.

I had met a lot of people through selling Viking, but had very little in common with them. I had visited many at night when helping my dealers to sell the Vikings. Wealthy white Johannesburg homes during 1936 vividly demonstrated how whites and blacks lived separate lives – the blacks always in the backyards, the easy acceptance by the whites that adult black men were "boys" and adult black women were "girls".

I realised that much of my life style would change as the result of the closure of the Viking radio factory. The Sidleys came to me with a proposal that if I would sell their instruments and radio equipment, they would pay me an additional commission. I accepted and induced one of our competitors, Pilot Radio and Tube Company to buy all our instruments. Harry Hampson, the senior partner who negotiated the purchase of the equipment from me, asked, as he was handing the cheque over in his office:

"What are you going to do, now that we have bought all the equipment?"

"I'm looking for a job."

"Well, we like you. Would you like to work for us? I can offer you a position as assistant manager?"

Harry Hampson intrigued me. Despite his age he was very active. I enjoyed doing business with him. The prospects seemed good, and as I liked the atmosphere at Pilot I decided that I had little to lose in joining them. I accepted the post of assistant manager to Roderick Garden, with whom I developed a firm friendship. I wondered how I would get on, because all the staff were older than my nineteen years.

In a matter of a few weeks, having got rid of all the equipment we had a sad farewell at Viking. Horace went to Durban to join a radio parts business. I started at Pilot Radio.

I soon realised the work there lacked the glamour and excitement of Viking, where every sale was an event. However, there were advantages. My life was more organised – I no longer travelled the countryside.

I was able to concentrate on my studies, spending more time on other activities, especially politics and stage designs for the Johannesburg Repertory Players in amateur theatricals.

At Pilot I became friendly with two older salesmen – Mike Kruger, a short, pudgy man with little charisma who spent most of his day at a desk in the showroom, attending to retail sales. His main claim to fame was that he spent his nights logging distant radio short-wave stations on Pilot sets. Almost every week Pilot would advertise another "achievement" by Mike Kruger. For example, he heard the South African expedition in the Antarctic and a short-wave station in Chile. Both "achievements" were then advertised in the newspapers. In 1937, South Africans were becoming interested in short-wave radio and Pilot capitalised on Kruger's prowess to bring customers into the showroom.

Claude Townsend, a close friend of Kruger's, was quite different. He was a large jovial man, always smiling, full of jokes and smoked continuously. Although not employed by Pilot, he also used their showroom to bring in his customers and sell sets from which he made his living.

At the end of the working day at Pilot, if I was not studying, much of my spare time would be spent in political work. The Berea-Yeoville Branch was becoming the most active unit in the Labour Party and rapidly increasing its membership, through regular political discussions, sending resolutions to provincial congresses, and attempting to influence the National Executive in its trade union policy and attitude to non-white workers.

The branch was a mixture of students, trade unionists and left wing intellectuals, most of whom I gradually got to know. Rusty Bernstein was still my main political mentor. I have rarely been in a branch of a political party that exercised such a powerful influence, out of all proportion to its numerical strength.

We often issued press statements in the name of the Labour Party giving the impression that what we published was the official view of the party.

Our branch regarded the National Executive as "right wing". Everything pointed to a confrontation with the NEC because of our public statements. They were embarrassed by us, and often politically wrong-footed. The crises were becoming more frequent.

I was never consulted by the senior members of the branch whenever these controversial statements were issued. It was thus difficult for me to know who was in the right or the wrong in the looming confrontation.

Matters suddenly came to a head. The National Executive of the Labour Party called an urgent meeting of its members. After a closed session it issued a statement expelling the Berea-Yeoville Branch, accusing it of being a Communist Party cell. It invited non-Communists in the branch to rejoin the Labour Party's head-office branch.

I was stunned. I could not make out why Rusty Bernstein had not told me about the Communist Party of which I knew nothing. At a hastily called meeting of the expelled branch I spoke to Rusty.

"Is this all true – or is it a frame-up by the NEC?"

"Yes, Boris it's true. I never told you because I had not made up my mind whether you would become closer to the CP or not. At this stage our main concern was to get your support and help in radicalising the Labour Party."

I still could not believe that that most of the members of the disbanded branch were Communists, not Labour Party enthusiasts like myself.

The list of expelled branch members included people who then openly became known members of the Communist Party. Most fled the country years later or were involved in various treason trials like Rivonia. Some received heavy prison sentences when the Nationalist government banned the Communist Party.

Rusty, to whom I was greatly attached, eventually fled South Africa, during the Rivonia Trial, with his wife Hilda Watts. They were both out on bail at the time.

There was no doubt that our branch was a leading Communist Party cell. The names of the Communist party members read like a Who's Who of the SACP. Prominent activists were Jack Hodgson, Rita Gampel, and Michael Harmel. Many of them were subsequently incarcerated by the Nationalist government.

My political future was in the balance.

At that time there was only one thing to do. I was not interested in the Communist Party or its doctrines. My father had over the years condemned the Stalinites. At heart I was really a social democrat and a liberal as a result of my political studies. I rejoined the Labour Party. I found that I was the only expelled member of the Berea-Yeoville Branch to do so. Nevertheless, I was sorry to lose contact with Rusty and some of CP members. They had political courage and taught me a great deal about the South African race relations scene.

In a sense it was a political blessing in disguise. Being a member of the NEC, friendly with its leadership, I was able to evaluate its leaders at first hand. They were a mixed bag of "pink intellectuals" from the northern suburbs of Johannesburg and Trade Unionists like Alex Hepple, Ben Weinbren of the Laundry Workers Union, who were closer to the Communists, and right-wingers like Jimmy Briggs of the Engineers Union.

In the Labour Party the "pink intellectuals" like Richard Feldman, a wealthy tobacconist, were forerunners of the liberals who participated in anti-Nationalist political activity. Although they expressed concern for the "native" in his deprived economic state, like their successors in later years, the political parties who opposed the Nationalists and apartheid, they had little or no contact with black people or organisations.

The Labour Party had no black members; nor did it extend its activities, with few exceptions, to black trade unionists.

The Labour Party published its own newspaper *Forward*, with a small circulation. It was poorly edited and printed, but it served as a useful indicator of Labour Party activity.

I was the youngest member of the NEC. Its meetings were dominated by trade-unionists. Although the Labour Party had six MPs in Parliament, its impact on the political scene was minimal. It was restricted in what it could do by the trade unionists who held the whip hand at party congresses because of the card vote system.

These unions were small, with little influence on either the large conservative unions like the right wing mine-workers who in any event did not belong to the LP, or the emerging unregistered black unions. The most powerful affiliated union was the all-women Garment Workers Union, whose general secretary was Solly Sachs. His card vote, with those of Ben Weinbren's Laundry Workers and Jimmy Briggs's Engineers, was where the real power lay in the LP.

By the time I joined the Labour Party, its political influence in South Africa had greatly diminished. It was only through the electoral agreements with Hertzog, Smuts and later the United Party that it was able to keep a parliamentary presence. When these links were broken, the LP died.

Nevertheless, it was for me a very fruitful and useful training ground especially since I was on the National Executive. Compared to Sachs and Weinbren on the one hand and Briggs the chairman, I was a "centrist". This drew me towards two interesting older members of the NEC, Dr Tom Osborn a physiologist at the Medical School and Margaret Mackenzie his friend. Political discussions with them improved my understanding and knowledge of international and local events.

16

South Africa was far removed from European turbulence caused by Hitler and Mussolini. It was involved with its own political problems. From 1936 there was great pressure on the South African Fusion government of Hertzog and Smuts to modify and reverse the liberal and middle-of-the-road policies of the past. Parliament in 1936 had taken the disastrous step of removing blacks from the Common Roll, denying rights to Indians and coloureds. Anti-semitism was becoming more prominent because dispossessed Jews were fleeing from Nazi atrocities to South Africa. This put pressure on the government to stop Jewish immigration.

The highly secretive *Broederbond*, an Afrikaner ultra-right wing society was a political force. On the extreme left Communists were active amongst "Natives", stirring up opposition to the entrenched white privilege and demanding greater participation.

Every day I learnt more about these problems of our white-dominated black society. The Labour Party, weak as it was, provided vital political background knowledge to my strong interest in the changing South African scene of the 1930s.

My father convinced me at an early age that all men were equal irrespective of colour, in the eyes of society and the law. It was natural, in gravitating to the Labour Party (especially when events in South Africa and Europe were undergoing great changes), that I would take a liberal-progressive stance on human problems of the day. Party politics, because of my need to discuss political ideas and theories, became the ideal vehicle to make up for the lack of university tutorials. In many respects, politics was far more valuable because it dealt with current realities.

The advent of Victor Gollancz's Left Book Club in South Africa had made a great difference to my political life. There I met all shades of left wing opinion, with discussions at meetings full of verve. For a few shillings in those days one could buy Left Book Club publications on the important political subjects of the the time. This was backed up by the impact speakers made, especially when analysing the crisis in Europe that lead to World War II.

The members of the Club came from a wide spectrum of Johannesburg society – a mixture of professional and white-collar workers. Some of the most active and energetic participants were Communists I knew from my membership in the LP and there is no doubt that despite their attempts to steer discussions their way, their presence enlivened the atmosphere and educated all the members.

17

A year had passed since I joined Pilot Radio. It was the base that allowed me to carry out all my other activities. It was already 1937. I was restless – I wanted to leave business and go back to university. Politics, the arts, literature, friends like Rex Martienssen and his group and my urge to write were pressurising me to change. I began to question what I was doing at Pilot. I wanted something more interesting, where I earned more money. I also had personal reasons to make a change.

I wanted to break away from Poppy. She was becoming, in many ways, possessive of my time. I objected to her very strong right wing views, especially her support of Hitler's Nazis; I didn't want an open conflict with her on this issue.

I was approached by Emmanuel (Manny) Bradlow, whose family furniture business was a customer of Pilot Radio about a job in Bulawayo, Southern Rhodesia, as their salesman and personal assistant to Manny, who was the managing director. He was a Cambridge law graduate whose task was to open and manage the new branch.

I decided to accept the offer although I had never been to Rhodesia. I was impressed with Bradlow. There was the chance that I would achieve my objective, earn much more money, and go back to university in the foreseeable future.

I packed my bags, took all my books and went off to Bulawayo.

Bradlow had arranged accommodation for me at the rambling old Grand Hotel, where he lived, in the centre of the town.

We had to set up Bradlow's branch from scratch, an interesting exercise since I had already had one experience in South Africa with Viking. Bradlows furniture store was a much more organised affair. We worked hard all day and ate our meals together at night.

There was not a great deal else to do in Bulawayo, a quiet colonial town, of slow pace and wide streets. I managed to see the Victoria Falls one weekend making my first flight ever over it in a small Gypsy Moth biplane which was an exciting experience.

I was saving money because I worked hard, earning a salary with commission on sales. My yearning to get back to university and politics never left me – I felt out of it. I managed to find plenty of time for my studies at night, which was my only real diversion.

Manny Bradlow was my sole source of "intellectual" conversation. Seeing him at work and dinner became too much. In some ways our relationship was being strained. We both felt we were in the wrong place at the wrong time. We were frustrated academics in business together. Nevertheless, Bulawayo was very useful. It gave me the chance to assess where I was going.

One morning I saw an advertisement in the *Bulawayo Chronicle* calling for applications for the Elsie Ballot Scholarship, which offered three years study at Cambridge. I looked hard and long at the advertisement and wondered whether I was mad at even entertaining the idea of applying for the scholarship. As Manny was a Cambridge graduate I decided to ask his advice.

He could not have been more helpful in encouraging me to apply. Shortly thereafter, on a visit to Johannesburg, I obtained the application forms and talked to Rex Martienssen who was enthusiastic. He and a friend wrote supportive statements on my behalf which were included in my application.

To my surprise, I was short-listed for an interview. Bradlow was delighted and I flew to the selection meeting in Johannesburg. While waiting for my turn to see the selectors I learnt that six candidates had been short-listed and I was the youngest.

Waiting for the result was tense. I was called in again to see the selection committee before the results were made known.

Mr Justice Greenberg, well-known in Johannesburg, was in the Chair.

"Mr Wilson, we have seriously considered your application. If circumstances had been different we would have awarded you one of the scholarships to Cambridge which we believe you deserve."

My disappointment was obvious, but I waited for him to finish.

"We have decided that two other candidates have preference over you, because they already have their Bachelor's degrees. You still have to get yours. We have no doubt that by this time next year you should have your degree. We are taking the unusual step of inviting you to apply again next year and hope you will do so."

The door to Cambridge was not closed. I was determined to finish my studies and apply again the following year.

I returned to Bulawayo, unsettled and homesick for Johannesburg. To Manny Bradlow's disappointment I resigned and with seventy-five pounds saved made my way back to Poppy B's. She was glad to have me back at Loch Avenue. Pilot Radio offered me my me my old job back at a higher salary and the Labour Party invited me back to the head office branch.

18

My father gave me a disturbing account of Max, who was then nine years old. The headmaster of King Edward's Primary School was constantly asking to see Father about Max's behaviour. He did not concentrate on his schoolwork, kept upsetting the other boys in class and was a general nuisance. Most serious, however, was his truancy. This upset my father a great deal. He could not understand that he had a small motherless child on his hands who had serious problems of insecurity and behavioural disturbance.

Father and Ida were in a cleft stick. Both were fully occupied at the Market during the mornings. They had to rely on the "boy", the black servant who took Max to school daily into the schoolgrounds, with no guarantee that he remained at school.

Max would disappear a short while later. No one knew what he did or where he went. At first he used to come home at night. Then for days he would be missing. Father got very worried and both Leon and I were asked to find him, and bring him back home.

How on earth were we to find him? I remembered that Max used to tell me that he stole money from Father when he sneaked away from school. In the centre of Johannesburg there were "cafe bioscopes". The sixpenny admission included the film, tea, coffee, cold drink and a sandwich or chips. Max would sit for hours in the darkened cinema, drinking his lemonade, munching chips, his eyes glued to Tom Mix or Buster Keaton on the screen.

Max told me that when he started to play truant, he was scared that Father would thrash him, so he spent nights in the school washroom or toilets. At one point he disappeared for over three weeks. The headmaster and Father could do nothing to stop Max.

Father was distraught by Max's behaviour. He eventually told the local police about the problem – they were not helpful. The school principal gave up. It was now Father's problem.

Leon and I decided we had better do something about Max.

For several weeks we met daily in the centre of Johannesburg and systematically did the rounds of the cafe bios. These were situated in basements or first floors of old buildings in President or Pritchard Streets near the City Hall. If the cinema had two entrances we would each take one, waiting there until our eyes were accustomed to the darkness so we could make out the shapes of people sitting absorbed in the flickering screen.

If Max was in the bioscope he was easily identifiable. Small and fat, he sat well down in the seat in a characteristic way. Having signalled to each other, Len and I would creep down the aisles in the dark, trying not to disturb the moviegoers. Having reached his row we would then try and attract his attention.

Quite often he ignored us. We would then have to raise our voices, provoking a chorus of dissent from the audience. In the end, he would come out.

We would take the scruffy little boy by the hand to the nearest tram and make our way home. Father would lose his temper with Max. He would be beaten in front of us. There was little we could do about that, although we pleaded with Father to reason with Max.

Max's truancy got so bad that the headmaster told Father to take him away from King Edward's.

Father gave up. He said he could no longer look after Max. He said Max was like his mother, completely uncontrollable. In one of his moods of cutting cynicism and sarcasm, Father said that since I was now supporting myself I should take over the responsibility for Max's education and upkeep.

This reaction from my father hurt me. I felt he was doing me a great injustice and removing himself from the situation which was all of his own making. He was largely responsible for the tragedies in his marriage and breakdown in our family life.

Leon and I talked the situation over, concluding that the only solution was to send Max to a boarding school. We managed to get Father's co-operation. We told him that we would pay our share if Max was sent to a boarding school about twenty miles from Johannesburg.

This did not last long. Max started disappearing again, managing to get back, on one or two occasions, to his old haunts – the cafe bioscopes.

We were at our wit's end. We then decided there was only one thing to do. Max had to be sent to a boarding school as far away from Johannesburg as possible, because apart from anything else my father still refused to look after him. In retrospect it was an extraordinary decision by a parent, but we knew my father.

We realised that he had his own problems running a household and his business at the Market.

There was no alternative but to find a school. We chose St Mark's at Mbabane in Swaziland, hundreds of miles away.

Fortunately, they were able to take Max as a boarder. We had a problem in trying to get him there. We did not trust him alone on the train. Leon owned an old Austin 10 tourer and we decided that we would, one weekend, take him by road.

The journey was unbelievable, outdoing my first trip to Durban. It poured down as only a heavy Transvaal highveld storm can, and hailed as if the heavens were bent on destroying us. The dirt road to Swaziland down the escarpment was a quagmire through mountain passes. We often stopped to let the storm abate or push the water-logged car out of mud. Eventually we arrived at St Mark's after travelling through the night.

We think Max secretly enjoyed the journey. After paying the first term's, fees we left him in the headmaster's care.

All was well for some weeks. We thought that Max had settled down. However the dreaded telephone call came – Max had disappeared.

Naturally, we were upset to learn that he had run away. There was nothing we could do from Johannesburg. The Swaziland police were alerted by the headmaster. A few days later Max was found on the main road near the Transvaal border, and brought back to school by the police.

Max's disappearances started soon thereafter. The school urgently advised us to take him away. They said he could not be controlled nor would he settle down in Swaziland. In short, nothing had been achieved by sending him to St Mark's.

Father relented and took Max back. He tried methods which we knew were doomed to failure – giving him extra pocket money, letting him go to the local bioscope once a week and trying to take a greater interest, tightening his control over his behaviour. Max, however defeated all my father's efforts.

He was back at school, continuing to play truant. I cannot remember how many schools he went to. As he grew older he became more astute – I felt I was perpetually engaged as the official "finder" of Max for my father.

On one occasion, I found Max at one of the cafe bios. I dragged him out, and put him into my small car. As I was driving to Father's house, Max opened the door at a traffic light and jumped out. In an instant I was after him. He was then a well-built boy, but still fat. I was lithe and fast and caught up with him.

I was so angry that I lashed out at him and hit him on the jaw. He fell down, "out for the count".

Years later, when I looked at Max, I realised that the shape of his jawbone had changed – it was irregular. I am sure that my loss of temper resulted in a minor fracture to Max's jaw.

In the circumstances, I suppose Father did his best to educate and bring Max up, but Max had learnt how to exist on his own.

He was not interested in school. By the age of thirteen, as far as he was concerned, he no longer needed to go to school.

Like me, he used to go to the Market and help. It was only in this way that Father was able to keep an eye over him for most of the day. Max was a very good salesman, which in later life helped him to make and lose a great deal of money. He was extraordinarily strong-willed, like Father. He was an innovator in many ways. He was able at a tender age to hold his own with adults.

He could keep things to himself. He never disclosed what he did when he played truant. Somehow he had no difficulty in finding money to spend hours seeing films over and over again in the cafe bioscopes of the 1930s. I often wondered who the unknown people were to whom Max went. He must have had places and people to go to. He could not have survived the life style he had created without assistance.

Max never knew his mother. This must have had a profound effect on him, which we as children never realised. Coupling this with the environment of our home and my father's inflexible attitudes and strong personality, Max's rebellious life was the only way in which he could express his own strong personality, individualism and loss of his mother.

Were there others in his life in the shadows?

No one will ever know because Max is dead. He committed suicide, after a stormy life, years later.

19

After I returned to Johannesburg, I resolved not to work for others to earn my living. I had learnt much about business since the Market days. I knew that if I had the chance, I could run my own business. I also reminded myself that I never intended to be in business, but knew that it was the only way I could earn a living and afford to do everything else. The dream of university was still in the lap of the gods. The reality was that I had to keep myself – the sooner I had my own business the better it would be for me. I was adequately trained for it – so I thought.

My early days in the Market, selling Clarnico chocolates on the road, establishing Viking Radio, selling furniture in Bulawayo and my experience with Pilot strengthened my resolve.

Then, of course, there is the interesting phenomenon of the unexpected. After I returned to Pilot, Mike Kruger and Claude Townsend confided to me that they had formed a company to import radio sets from Britain.

Claude was going to leave Pilot to run the operation from the sixth floor of nearby Greaterman's Building. They wanted to set up their own business before it was too late. Would I like to join their new enterprise?

It did not take me long to decide that I would resign at the end of 1938 and join Townsend at the beginning of 1939. It was a condition of the partnership that I would buy out Mike Kruger's share for seventy-five pounds. During the course of our discussions Mike changed his mind about leaving Pilot. He indicated he would consider leaving Pilot when we had established the business. This change of mind did not worry me unduly because I did not believe that he really wanted to leave Pilot. As far as I was concerned it was going to be a battle for Claude Townsend and me to keep our heads above water.

In many ways it was the worst possible time to take such a step; 1938 was a year of uncertainty and serious foreboding in Europe. Hitler was very much on the march. Munich had taken place. The war clouds were heavy on the horizons.

I understood the unstable political conditions better than either Mike or Claude. Such was our zeal, however, that I took seventy-five pounds from the money I had saved in Bulawayo and bought Mike's fifty per cent of the shareholding in CH Townsend and Company on 17 November 1938.

To Pilot's surprise, I gave notice of my resignation. There was no turning back. The die had been cast.

I'd arranged to start in the business on 2 January 1939 and I could not wait for it to come.

I am astonished, now, at the ease with which I made decisions to change jobs; launching myself into an unknown business at a time when South Africa was in a recession.

I was still working for my BA degree and had not given up the idea of sending in my application for the Elsie Ballot Scholarship later in the year, obviously keeping my options wide open. I decided that if I did take up the scholarship, I might induce Mike Kruger to take my place in the company.

My studies had gone well. Despite the fact that I had changed jobs and made the return trip to Bradlows in Rhodesia, only my final examinations remained to be written. I had three major subjects left, Political Philosophy, Psychology and Social Anthropology.

I was finally rewarded for my years of effort by passing and getting my Bachelor of Arts degree. Poppy was excited, I was over the moon and my father showed great pleasure at my success.

My proposed move to the new business was now made easier because my studies were behind me. I would be able to devote all my spare time to developing the business.

On 2 January 1939, I took the lift to the sixth floor of Greaterman's Building in the centre of Johannesburg, around the corner from the City Hall steps, where the trade unionist Dunbar held court on Sunday nights when I was a small boy.

CH Townsend and Company had three offices, a small showroom empty of any stock, a second occupied by a young secretary, and in the third office the shirt-sleeved Claude Townsend, smiling and smoking his habitual cigarette.

I walked in just after 8.30.

"Good morning, Claude, I'm here."

"Sit down – make yourself comfortable."

I took off my jacket, loosened my tie, and sat down opposite him.

"How are things going Claude?"

He hesitated.

"Not very well, Boris."

"Why, what's the trouble? I'm all ready to get going and find the customers."

"I'm afraid we have nothing to sell."

For a moment I was nonplussed.

"What do you mean nothing to sell? What happened to the seventy-five pounds I paid for my shares which you were going to use for the radio sets coming from England?"

He smiled at me. Claude always smiled in a benign way. He inhaled deeply, carefully stubbed out his cigarette and blew out the smoke.

"Boris, we don't have the money – that's all."

"But Claude, what have you done with it? I gave you the money in November because you told me the sets were on their way and the money was going to be used for payment of the first shipment."

The penny dropped. There were no radio sets in the showroom as I had noticed when I came in.

What had he done with the money?

Claude told me that he found selling goods he didn't have very difficult, and he said he wasn't used to wholesale selling. He had used the money to keep himself above water.

He told me the sets were due any day. He had kept going by selling the occasional radio set to retail customers which he bought from Pilot.

The conversation got heated. Claude kept smoking and putting out the cigarettes, but despite all my questioning I failed to find out what he had done with the money. In fact, there was little more than a few pounds left in the business.

I realised after two hours of frustrating discussion that I was in an impossible situation. I had given up my secure job with Pilot, and Claude Townsend had squandered the capital of the company, amounting to £150, and could not say what had happened to the money. It was obvious that the business such as it was, could not sustain both of us because it was insolvent. One of us had to go.

I stood firm. I decided there and then that it had to be Claude. I accused him of failing to tell me about his problems before I resigned from Pilot.

"You have to go Claude. We cannot both stay in the business – it will never support us both. You must sell me your 50 per cent holding for a nominal sum, which I will work out now."

I didn't give him any time to argue. I think he knew there was no way out.

"OK, Boris, I'll agree to that. I'm going back to Pilot."

I examined the books, which had luckily been written up, and calculated that his share was worth a little over thirty-nine pounds. But as he had overdrawn considerably more than that, he accepted the figure as satisfactory, and I drew up an agreement which we both signed.

By eleven o'clock that morning Claude Townsend with his usual smile, said goodbye to me and left the business. I sat there trying to recover my composure; the sole owner of an insolvent company, no money, no stock to sell and twelve radio sets due from overseas which had to be paid for before I could get them. Ninety-six pounds was needed for the shipment and I did not have a clue as to where the money was going to come from.

I was not shedding tears for Claude. I knew what he would do. He would talk Pilot into giving him his former job back, and that is exactly what he did. I sat there on that January morning in 1939, nearly twenty-two years old, having completed my first business takeover before I had started to work in the company. I had no idea how I was going to survive.

For about an hour, I painstakingly went through the ledger and the entries which had been neatly written up by the bookkeeper, a member of Pilot's staff who looked after the books in her spare time. I went to see the bank and the agents who serviced the sets already sold, explaining I had taken over the company.

I wondered how I was going to manage to pay for the twelve Cossor radios coming from England. Claude had ordered these through a shipping house called WA Sparrow Ltd of London, whose local representative in Johannesburg was a Mr Whiting.

I decided the best thing to do was to telephone Mr Whiting, and to ask for an urgent appointment to discuss the matter of payment for the sets.

I saw Mr Whiting later that afternoon at his nearby office. He was a very large man, with a ruddy complexion who towered over me, dissecting with his piercing blue eyes.

I told him the story. I was the new owner of the business and I needed his help.

I could see Mr Whiting struggling to control himself.

"You want me to give you credit on this first shipment? I have never dealt with you and I don't know you. Mr Townsend told me he would pay cash for the shipment and on the strength of his word I imported them for him. Now you say he's gone. Apart from this I took a lot of trouble to arrange the sole franchise for him with Cossor for South Africa."

"Mr Whiting, I've been caught in this unhappy state of affairs just as you have. I didn't expect to be talking to you today. Townsend is the one whom you must shout at – not me. I need those sets, but I cannot pay you cash. I promise if you draw a ninety day bill on me I will meet it on due date."

He threw up his hands.

"What guarantees can you give me that you will meet the bill? I don't want those radios, I don't know the first thing about them and I am not a distributor."

He stopped talking and we looked at each other in silence. Then he spoke:

"Wilson, have you got faith in what you are doing?"

I did not hesitate.

"Of course – I would not be here if I had any doubts in my mind."

"All right, I will give you the credit terms but don't let me down."

I walked out of his office with a lighter heart, and I vowed to forget what happened that morning with Claude Townsend. Instead I set out to sell the twelve Cossor radios before they arrived.

I realised that I needed a general assistant. I managed to find Botha, the black man who worked for me at Viking. He knew a lot about the radio business and he joined me as my right hand man. It was he who received the sets when they arrived a few weeks later and who proudly unpacked and checked each one.

I was out all day looking for business, visiting prospective clients. Slowly, dealers began to order the Cossors. In order to sell one of the sets for a dealer, (who became a close friend of mine), I drove him forty miles to Pretoria with the Cossor in the back of the car, to demonstrate it to his customer. We sold it, at the retail price of nineteen pounds, and he paid me the trade price of fourteen pounds.

As a result of this success Alec Steel, the dealer, then bought another Cossor for his stock.

In a matter of a few weeks after the sets arrived I had sold them all, and Mr Whiting agreed to order a further shipment for me.

I was on the road to establishing my business, which was now called CH Townsend and Wilson (Pty) Ltd.

In the middle of the year, when the applications for the Elsie Ballot Scholarship became due, I realised that if I was successful I would have to face the dilemma of choosing between my new business and a university career at Cambridge in England.

The decision was really made for me. I had no partner in the fledgling business. If I got the scholarship I would have to wind up the business and leave South Africa for three years.

The other factor was the menacing look of international events and the immediate future in Europe. Chamberlain's peace moves were in tatters. Hitler had marched into Austria and Czechoslovakia. The war in Spain had ended with Franco the victor. Mussolini was sitting astride Ethiopia. Hitler's Nazis and their race theories had powerful effects on a large section of the Afrikaner Nationalists in South Africa under their leader Dr Malan. He accused the Jews of being responsible for an increasingly serious black-white situation saying that they were responsible for the poor economic state of the country.

The advent of the lunatic right wing fringe of Nationalists lead to the establishment of the Greyshirts, who emulated their Blackshirt masters in Germany by goose-stepping and intimidation.

They encouraged blacks to boycott Jewish traders, who were accused of exploiting everyone. The Labour Party in which I was again active was losing ground and political significance. Nevertheless, it served its purpose. It allowed me independence of thought and a political home for my radical leanings.

Smuts and Hertzog were in an uneasy coalition. The object of the fusion between the nationalist Afrikaners who supported Hertzog, the English-speaking South Africans and a minority of Afrikaners who followed Smuts, was ostensibly to unite white South Africa. It led, however, to the historically important split in the Nationalist movement, which, whilst gaining control of white trade unions, were consolidating on a base (which we did not know then) to become the Nationalist's stepping-stone to the 1948 election success and the establishment of the future apartheid state of South Africa.

There was a small political party of English-speaking Dominionites who were in favour of strong ties with Britain – but they were like the Labour Party – losing ground in the South African scene.

All told, it was a politically turbulent and indecisive period. It was clear that my own financial and economic survival was important. At the same time I was maturing and looking at my future in a more pragmatic way. I had to be realistic too. The business was making headway, I was enjoying the freedom of owning my own business and was prepared to work every day as long as was necessary. I could take part in politics, write and paint. I even managed to keep up amateur theatricals turning my attention to stage design, creating the decor for *Six Characters in Search of an Author* by Pirandello, which was produced by the famous German director Leontine Sagan for the Johannesburg Repertory Players.

By the middle of of 1939 I reached the target set for me in the contract with Cossor, to sell three hundred sets in the first year, which would then automatically give me a three-year sole distribution franchise in South Africa. I wrote to Cossor that I had fulfilled my side of the agreement asking them to confirm the new three-year agreement.

I was astonished to get a cable back from Sir Louis Sterling, the chairman of Cossor stating that they would give me the new contract, providing I guaranteed them markedly increased quantities every year.

This was never in the original contract. In anger, I went to see Whiting, who now regarded me as somewhat of a "golden boy" since I was giving him a lot of business and meeting his drafts. He arranged for me to see Laurie Harrison, the British Trade Commissioner, to whom I told my story.

After contacting Cossor, Harrison told me not to waste my time, and suggested I find another radio agency in England.

It was ironic, because if this had occurred a few months earlier I may well have said "to hell with business", closed up Townsend and Wilson, applied for the Elsie Ballot Scholarship and gone off to Cambridge.

I had seen some British radio sets in Johannesburg called Ekco, made by EK Cole Ltd, of Southend. I tested them and asked Harrison to get the Board of Trade in Britain to get me the sole franchise. In a matter of weeks it was a reality, with no strings attached. The first shipment was on its way.

Then came the shattering news that war was inevitable. On 3 September 1939 I was driving my car listening to its radio. The sombre voice of Neville Chamberlain, mixed with crackling interference, announced that Britain had declared war on Hitler's Germany.

This produced an immediate political crisis in South Africa. Hertzog and the Nationalists did not want to go to war against the Germans, nor did they want to be seen to be on the side of the British colonialists. Smuts, the great supporter of the British, bowed instantly to the views of his English-speaking followers in South Africa. Parliament was recalled. Smuts and Hertzog split over the war issue.

Smuts became the Prime Minister of a coalition which included the Labour Party and South Africa entered the war on the side of the British.

Because of the internal problems and vociferous opposition of the Nationalist faction, "joining up" to fight the Fascists was voluntary. Conscription would have caused civil war between the whites, English and Afrikaans, and between "loyal" Afrikaners and the Afrikaners of the "volk".

During the first few weeks of World War II, whilst everyone was trying to assess what it all meant, Smuts interning anyone who might pose a threat to the security of the State. The prevailing view in the English-speaking community was that the Nazis had to be fought and smashed.

I had no difficulty in selling the few radio sets I had in stock. Then I received a cable from Ekco which said that, as they were turning their efforts to wartime production, no more domestic radio sets would be made. They offered me six hundred sets for immediate shipment, and there would be no more for the duration of the war.

Six hundred sets involved approximately forty thousand pounds, which was a fortune. I had never dealt with such large sums before. I called on Whiting. He agreed to recommend to London that payment be made over an extended period. The Ekco radios were shipped while the sea-lanes to South Africa were still open.

I knew that I would have a supply of radios for some time, provided I rationed the receivers when they arrived. Meanwhile I had other things to sort out as a result of the war.

My Cambridge ambitions were obviously not to be fulfilled. Even if I was granted the scholarship, I would not be able to go overseas to study, nor could I leave the business. The best I could do was to continue to study part-time for an honours degree.

Of more direct importance were the problems that faced the country. South Africans were split in their loyalties. Many Afrikaners who were opposed to Jan Smuts openly supported Germany. Some felt that it would be possible to negotiate a favourable deal with Hitler on South West Africa.

The organisations on the Nationalist "lunatic" fringe like the Greyshirts and Ossewa Brandwag were driven underground by Smuts, who banned them and incarcerated their leaders in concentration camps. They were trying to sabotage Smuts's war effort politically and physically with the bombing of essential services.

In my small world, Poppy B became more noisily vocal in her condemnation of Smuts and his determination to involve South Africa in the war against Germany which, at that early stage, had not yet developed greatly in western Europe.

One evening I came home to find her in tears.

"What's wrong?" I asked.

"Rost has joined the air force."

Rost was her only son. He had "joined up" to fight the Nazis. This was, for her, the unspeakable disaster. Poppy B, the lifelong die-hard Nationalist, who hated the British because of what they had done in the Boer War to her family, had been humiliated by her only son.

He had joined the Smuts camp, the British, against her heroic Nazis. She was sure that they would would win the war.

I was of little help to her in her grief. I did not want to criticise her openly, because she had been very kind to me. On the other hand, I could not sympathise with her. My feelings for her were ambivalent. I was grateful for her care and warmth towards me; but I also detested her support for the Nazis, the Ossewa Brandwag and the daily diet of race hatred poured out by Zeesen to ultra-right wing Nationalists.

The effect of Rost's action on her was traumatic. She looked haggard, thinner than ever and smoked incessantly. Her depression pervaded Loch Avenue. Conversation virtually ceased.

In one sense, I must have been some kind of a comfort to her, because, although my views on the Third Reich were diametrically opposed to hers, she knew I was a pacifist at heart. My father's strong opinions on the subject of war as a means of settling national differences, the stupidity of using violence to stop violence, had helped to define my thinking.

There was no conscription in South Africa. Smuts did not dare to bring it in. He knew that he would have had civil war and disobedience had he tried to legalise it, with open rebellion from Afrikaner youth, and the right wing Nationalists.

War psychosis had gripped English-speaking South Africa. Smuts's actions gave those in South Africa who supported the war effort a conviction that they had a special role.

South Africa's involvement ran like a sword of fire through many families, splitting their loyalties. Fathers did not speak to sons, brothers hated brothers, the closest family ties were broken. Afrikaners hated Afrikaners.

It was clear from Poppy's experience that a new phase of bitterness had been created in South Africa that would be indelibly tattooed on the sunburnt skins of South Africans and cause the enmity to last for a long time after the war ended.

Smuts's enemies were mainly his own kith and kin, the nationalist Afrikaners for whose cause he had fought over the years. At the same time, his relations with the English-speaking voters were maintained at the highest pitch. He was the one Afrikaner they loved. For them, he was the focus that allowed the whites to at least pretend to some semblance of unity. He was an international statesman who strutted around the war-torn West and gave them security and comfort.

It was a strange situation in that the white population was split on the war issue, while the blacks were largely, with some notable exceptions, excluded. Apart from increasing involvement in South Africa's new wartime industries, thousands of blacks, coloureds and Indians volunteered to serve in the military.

From my viewpoint as a member of the Labour Party, it was clear that when the war ended, so would the coalition with Smuts's United Party. I knew, as did others on the National Executive, that we would never win an election seat on our own again.

Trade Unionists who supported the LP had declined in numbers. Many white workers were so well off, or had joined the armed forces, that there was little in the way of grassroots support, and the black trade unionists had no vote, and were not interested.

The business demanded my full attention. Imported radio sets had stopped arriving after the last shipments in early 1940 and I could no longer continue supplying the retail trade. I rented a shop in Plein Street next to St Mary's Cathedral, formed another company called Sound-Electric, and sold Ekco radio direct to the public. Most of the sales were to residents from nearby Hospital Hill and Hillbrow. This meant that I was often out at night demonstrating the radio sets in flats and homes, which interfered with my university tutorials for an MA degree and my political activities.

The two most important matters to me were my studies and the business. Politics was resolving itself, as the war went on during the early "phony period", into whether one was for or against the war effort. I was neutral. Although I detested Hitler and the Nazis, I could not support the violence of modern warfare as the sole means of destroying the evils of twentieth-century Fascism.

On the Labour Party's National Executive I found that Tom Osborn, Margaret McKenzie and I were often the only opposition to left wing trade unions who used the party for their own political purposes. The "intellectuals" of the LP came from the wealthy northern suburbs of Johannesburg.

It seemed so inappropriate, in the luxurious homes of Houghton, to be discussing the plight of white and black workers in the South African economy. These workers lived in the poverty-stricken suburbs and townships around Johannesburg; the city depended upon them for its labour and we all knew that the most we would ever do was talk.

We had the same kind of situation at the University. There I got to know a group of younger students who also lived in the wealthy northern suburbs of Johannesburg. They regarded themselves as "socialists".

They saw the solution to South Africa's emerging racial problems in simplistic "socialist" terms. They tended to look down on me because of my association with the Labour Party. Their political leader was Senator Basner, a well-known Native Representative. In the early 1940s, under his leadership, they founded the Socialist Party. It made little impact on the political scene – it was really little more than a "talking shop" as far as national politics was concerned.

However, it was one of the few socialist organisations which was inspired by some of its members to do very valuable practical work. A night school for illiterate black workers was started in an old dilapidated and disused church in Diagonal Street. It was near the bus terminus for the black townships and the Indian business quarter in Johannesburg. I knew this area well from my days at the Market. Father used to buy fruit from John Bell, whose business was off Diagonal Street.

Twice a week the students and I would go to the old church at night and teach adult black workers who had never been to school. Most of the lessons were on basic reading and writing. I, however, decided to teach Geography.

It was stimulating teaching these "raw" Zulu men, who were cleaners, street sweepers and labourers. Their disbelief was undisguised when I explained to them, with simple models, that the world was round and not flat. I had to demonstrate over and over again how the earth moved around the sun, and how night and day came about.

Often, a few days later when I wanted to teach new aspects, I would be asked to explain again the concept of night and day and why the world was not flat.

How we managed to teach in this poorly lit church without proper equipment was astonishing. There were at least five classes crammed into its inadequate space, so that we just had to get used to the noise and the babble. Eventually we started a second school for adult workers, but this time we managed to find a sympathetic headmaster at the Polly Street School, who let us use proper classrooms at night where we had the luxury of separate classrooms, desks and blackboards. I believe we were the founders of night schools for adult black education in Johannesburg.

When the Nationalists came to power they closed the night schools; they suspected that the schools were a cover for black subversion, because several political organisations followed our lead.

20

Late in 1941 I began to realise that selling radio sets, despite the fact that I had my own business, was doing nothing for me intellectually. I was much happier when I was involved in politics or the university. I became very interested in the questions of poverty, social deprivation, and the reasons for ill-health of individuals and population groups. By attending political meetings, and being embroiled in party organisation without being a professional expert in these social problems I was stimulated to know more about solutions to these issues.

The knowledge I had theoretically gained from my political philosophy studies was always fresh in my mind, but often, when seeking a solution for a current social problem, the matter had to be handed over to the experts. I came to the conclusion that I had already had enough political experience and it was time to consider whether I should go the whole hog and become professionally proficient in one of the social sciences or in medicine.

I felt the need to do something more than talking at meetings, something more specific and worthwhile.

One night I came home at about eleven o'clock. Poppy was still up. She made me a cup of coffee and we started talking about my future.

"Poppy, I'm totally frustrated. I'm running my own business, which I never intended to set up. I've got an Arts degree. I'm active in the Labour Party. I'm not satisfied that the Honours course is really what I want to do, or will be of any practical use. I feel I want to learn more about the way people react to the social and medical pressures of society and the problems they face at home. What I'm trying to say is that I want to get away from philosophising get properly involved. I think I can do this by studying medicine."

"Boris," she replied in her most careful voice, "I've always thought you would make a good doctor. You're interested in people and politics. You've already studied Psychology and Anthropology, and you've had a more varied experience of life than most people of your age that I know. So, if you are clear in your mind, think seriously about studying medicine. But it's a full time course. How will you overcome that problem? The business needs you as well and has to pay for your studies."

How to do it? What were the pitfalls, the alternatives and advantages? We spoke talked until the early hours of the morning, drinking numerous cups of coffee, while Poppy's cigarette butts piled up in the ash tray.

Just before we finally retired, the answer to the business problem came to me. I would speak to Mike Kruger, still at Pilot Radio. He had recently told me he was unhappy at his job. My problems would be solved if Mike joined me as a partner and took over day-to-day running of the business.

"Poppy, I am sure that I could do the medical course during the day and attend to management and control of the business in the evening. Mike Kruger, who likes dealing with the public, can sell the radios and run the shop. Of course, I have to see if I can get into the Medical School – I'll see Iuan Glyn-Thomas tomorrow at the university. If I'm accepted, I'll talk to Kruger."

The next day I went to see the Registrar of the University. Iuan was a small man with smooth dark hair, who wore glasses, had a lovely smile and a lilting Welsh voice. The previous time I saw him about my career he advised me to study for my BA extramurally. Once more I was consulting him about my future.

"Are you sure you can manage both medicine and business? Most people have a struggle just to get through medicine – never mind doing other things. The course lasts six years. You are twenty-four now, and if I can get you a place you will be over thirty when you finish – quite an old man!"

"I can do it, Iuan. When you advised me to study on my own for my BA, I battled for four years and qualified. I'm satisfied that however long it takes me, and however hard it is, I will succeed. As far as the business is concerned, I think I can get a friend of mine to take over the selling to the public. I can pay my own fees. I won't let you down if you can get me in."

"Boris, of course I will help you. I will speak to the Dean of the Medical Faculty about a place for you next year. Good luck to you. But what about your politics? Will you give it up – at least for some years?"

89

"Yes, the Labour Party will have to go into cold storage, and take a back seat. Thank you for having faith in me."

I walked through the corridors of the Main Block a very happy young man.

Back at the shop at Plein Street, I telephoned Mike Kruger and asked him to meet me that evening.

Mike smoked incessantly, never exercised and still spent most of his time selling radio sets, through listening to and logging distant radio stations all over the world. Short-wave radio as a means of communication was beginning to come into its own, and the war in Europe and the Far East made it imperative for many South Africans to own a short-wave radio, creating a large demand.

Mike listened to broadcasts of world events and often reported on them before the local newspapers. He would telephone to tell them of some event thousands of miles away which he had picked up on his Pilot short-wave set and of which they had not yet received news. He was well-known to the public and this made him the expert to consult if one was buying a new radio.

It was obvious that he would be an ideal person to run the shop during the day dealing with the public while I studied medicine.

I put my proposal to Mike.

"If you join me, I will let you have fifty per cent of the business, a full partnership, and it will cost you five hundred pounds. I have done a quick calculation of the net worth of the business and it is more than a thousand pounds. In view of the fact that I need as much time during the day to attend the university and medical school, I am prepared to forego any goodwill in the price, and you can pay your five hundred pounds out of future profits over the next few years. Your job will be to attend to all the retail selling in the shop and outside demonstrations. I will look after the day-to-day administration, correspondence and be responsible for all planning and overseas matters. Well – what do you think ?"

Mike was silent, puffing away at his cigarette. He asked me a few questions. Then he put out his hand.

"OK, Boris, it's a deal." We shook hands.

21

The next day I telephoned Glyn-Thomas and told him I could start in January 1942. He was delighted, as was my father when I told him the news. Poppy showered me with congratulations. I think it meant a lot to her, because of her disappointment about Rost and the South African Air Force.

Mike Kruger joined me a month later. We did a lot of preliminary organising to make sure that my absence during most of the day would be a practical proposition and not disruptive in the business.

One day I came home to find Poppy in tears. When I managed to calm her she told me that Rost had been shot down in a raid over Yugoslavia and was presumed killed-in-action.

"I told him not to join up. I said he would be killed in the Air Force. I knew that something like this would happen. Smuts has killed my son. They did this to my family in the Boer War." There was little of comfort I could say to her.

After this episode she changed. She became uncommunicative and morose. The lively Poppy, with her flashes of wit and laughter, her diatribes against the British, her secret listening to Nazi broadcasts and her warm feelings towards me just faded away. The atmosphere in the house was of gloom and deep depression. It affected me greatly. I had looked forward to a tranquil home environment; I expected to have more than enough problems at the business and the medical school.

I was faced with a painful decision. It was clear that I was not in control of the situation and the best thing to do was to find another place to live. After I told Poppy of my decision, she became even more aloof.

I found a flat near my old school in Yeoville, which would give me peace and quiet for study. I continued to see Poppy periodically, but our relationship had changed. She felt the loss of her son very deeply; the affection she had shown me, as a sort of substitute, become a reproach.

Later in 1942 I heard she was ill with cancer of the throat or lungs. I never saw her again. I was told she had given up all desire to live and she died, a lonely sad woman.

The first year medical course was held at the main university and not at the medical school. I had a big job on my hands because I was never any good at Physics and Chemistry and had to start from scratch competing with most students who had just matriculated.

I had just turned twenty-five, and was one of a small group of mature students in the large first year class. I had become friendly with another older student, Leslie Weiner, whom I met in the first Physics practical in the laboratory. He was a short man, always smiling, walked with a limp, stuttered badly at times and had the most wonderful sense of humour.

Leslie was a motor car parts salesman who had worked and scrimped for years in order to study medicine, and finally made it. He was witty and often wrote poems and limericks about life at the university to amuse us. We got to know each other well. He was very helpful in that when I had to dash off to the business and miss part of a lecture, or if I was late, he would have notes for me or could tell me what had transpired.

The first year passed almost unbelievably quickly. It was a job getting to grips with scientific subjects, but I was determined not to let them defeat me. It meant starting early in the morning, some days rushing off to business first and then the university, or the university first and then the business mid-morning. Back at the university until lunchtime, then to the office for a session with Mike, deal with correspondence, place orders, do credit control and then rush back to the afternoon classes which in the first year were mostly practicals.

While the other students played games, or relaxed, I was at the office. At the end of the day, I would get back to my flat and start writing up notes, read and swot.

Often I would go to Leslie's house to get some notes or discuss chemistry and physics with him, which he found easy to understand.

By keeping a tight control on my activities, I survived the tremendous schedule of business and study. The shop was well-managed by Mike. We were paying our expenses and rationing our supplies of radio sets.

While the first year of Medicine was at the university, the rest of the course was at the Medical School, near to the Fort and Pretoria Street where I had earlier lived. Being at the University gave me the chance to sample some student life. Although I had dropped out of party politics, I felt that I should participate in some extracurricular activity. I decided to stand for the Student's Representative Council, was elected, and at one of the meetings learnt that the university newspaper had no editor.

I volunteered to take it on, encouraged by friends who seemed to think I would somehow manage the extra work.

Leslie nearly had a fit.

"Boris, are you mad?"

"No, I'm not involved in politics and I need some mental stimulation – even if it is university politics."

"What do you know about newspapers?"

"I'll find out."

I did.

The "newspaper" was embryonic; it had very little real form. I perused earlier copies and decided that I would coerce some students from other faculties to take on certain jobs, including Leslie, whom I appointed English Editor. Johan van Deventer, a dental student in first year, became Afrikaans Editor. I became the Editor-in-Chief.

I revamped the layout and made *WU's Views*, as it was called, look like a miniature newspaper with the main editorial on the front page. There was a column I wrote headed "If I Had My Way," in which I told the University what I would do on all sorts of issues.

My first editorial on a current national problem "Soil Erosion", evoked an enthusiastic response from Glyn-Thomas who congratulated me on the "first professional newspaper" the University had seen. Naturally I was delighted. We had a great deal of fun somehow getting the paper out. It was always a rush getting copy together, and editorial meetings were often hilarious shouting matches. The night before it was printed I would take all the copy to the printer, sometimes accompanied by Leslie and Johan. We would correct it on the slabs. I would be responsible for the layout; I would make changes, which I enjoyed because it allowed me to use my artistic abilities. The newspaper was a growing success and copies were sold out in a few hours at the University.

20th CENTURY
Now Showing:
"The Pied Piper"
with MONTY WOOLLEY
RODDY McDOWALL
Anne Baxter.
20th Century Masterpiece.

20th CENTURY
Now Showing:
"The Pied Piper"
with MONTY WOOLLEY
RODDY McDOWALL
Anne Baxter
20th Century Masterpiece.

WU'S VIEWS

Official Newspaper of the Students of University of Witwatersrand
VOLUME VII. No. 2.
THURSDAY,
APRIL 8th, 1943

Amptelike Nuus-blad van die Studente van Universiteit Witwatersrand.

PRICE ONE PENNY.

OUR "YELLOW" LETTER

Arthur G. Barlow, Esq.,
Editor, "Arthur Barlow's Weekly,"
Sometime Editor "Sunday Express,"
Sometime Member of Parliament,
Sometime Member of Every Political Party in South Africa,
Aspiring Candidate for Hospital Hill.

Dear Arthur G.,

We know that imitation is the sincerest form of flattery, but, you see, we mean to flatter you. You yourself admit to being the finest journalist in South Africa, and who are we to say you are not? But even had you not told us of this fact, we should yet have placed you amongst the best in the land. For you are a great journalist, Arthur G. — of that there is not the slightest doubt.

Other persons and newspapers condemned by you have crept into their "funkholes," and heroically ignored you. We, however, are creeping out of ours (which you have thought fit to publicise), and are writing you one of your own great, warm, personal letters, in order that some reply should be made to one of the most vitriolic and stupid attacks that has ever appeared in the South African press. And from the pen of a man of your calibre, dear Arthur G.! What a pity!

You are a well known South African. You have shown the ability in the past to take it on the chin, and to be capable of starting all over again from scratch. You have, on occasion, disclosed scandalous situations. In your loftier moments you have without doubt fought for the underdog. As old readers of your paper, (yes, "funks" though we are, and notwithstanding our university education, we can still appreciate a good journalist when we see one) it satisfies the sadist in one, you know. And surely, thought we, Mr. Arthur G. Barlow would not make statements unless he had facts to back them up. And then came your devastating article, hurling fire and brimstone on our University, on us students, and on us personally. And NOT ONE FACT to back you up! . . . It makes one think, doesn't it?

Will you give your readers the following FACTS, dear Arthur:—
(a) The number of Afrikaner students at the University, who are dead against the war effort. Notwithstanding our disagreement with them on their policy, you can certainly not class them as "funks."
(b) The number of students medically unfit for war service.
(c) The number of students who have brothers or fathers in the army, and whose parents are determined to have at least one member of the family decently prepared for the post-war world.
(d) The number of students under the age of 18 at the University.
(e) The number of students who had already begun their studies before 1939 and who were asked by the authorities to refrain from joining up until they had qualified.
(e) The number of students who, during the last 4 years, have joined the army immediately after obtaining their degrees.

Yes, you are a good journalist, Arthur G. There comes a time, however, in a man's life when he does make mistakes. Sometimes he makes them because of his kow-towing to public opinion, and he has then to keep up the pretence.

You know what we are driving at. You have made a mistake. You have gloated, from your high horse, over our "funkhole" University — not all universities, of course, just ours. ("But," we hear a little voice say, "You are the only university crying out against the rise in fees." "Yes," we answer sweetly, "'tis true. But we are also the only university in S.A. whose fees have been raised!") You are still smarting, like a naughty little child, from the rebuff you received last year, when our Principal banned a talk of yours at our "funkhole." We don't say that we agreed with that decision, but why take it out on us — and on your unsuspecting public?

Now about your allegations. Is our University a "funkhole"? What FACTS have you given your readers to substantiate your big, openhearted and patriotic declarations?

None whatsoever, dear Arthur G. You see, your kind of case is not based on fact. It is the type of outcry that led to this terrible World War II, the kind of shouting that in the first place led the youth of 1914-1918 to their doom, and now again you are typifying that same generation that bluffed the young men and women throughout the world into the jaws of Death. Your type of person, with its "catch-phrases" and white feathers. You know as well as we do that this war was not inevitable. The youth of today did not create this war. They did not want it. Your generation, with its money lust, was the arch-criminal.

Now that the war is on us, we agree that it must be won — and the peace thereafter must be won too. And to state, as you do in so many words, that the closing of the universities will contribute to this end, is, my dear Arthur, just so much balderdash.

You see, we cannot expect you to see things as we do. You stand for no principles — and if you do, you manage to hide them with the utmost efficiency. Our principles are clear. We know why this war is being fought. We know, too, that unless something is done about it, the sacrifices of our friends and fathers and brothers will have been in vain. (Yes, dear Arthur G., you would probably be very surprised at the number of us who have brothers and fathers in the army.) We know too, that Chiang Kai-Sack keeps 4,000 students at the university of bombed Chungking, because he understands that he cannot build his new China without their aid. Prime Minister Curtin is no fool either. To the Australian people he recently said: "There must continue the adequate training of men and women in Medicine, Dentistry, Engineering and Chemistry. Education is now more than ever the responsibility of the State." Britain's universities are functioning at full blast; so are Canada's and America's. Stalin

(*Continued on back page*)

DRAMATIC LAST-MINUTE DEVELOPMENTS

PRINCIPAL ISSUES STATEMENT

THIS issue of "Wu's Views" had already gone to press, when news was communicated to the Presidents of the S.R.C. and S.M.C. by the Editor of Wu's Views, of the Principal's decision to inform the students of the activity that was taking place behind the scenes.

There has been no time for editorial comment. We wish to state however that we fully subscribe to the plan of action as placed before the students yesterday, and we are convinced that in the long run, the University will get its much needed grant, and fees will be reduced.

We wish to pay tribute to Mr. Raikes and the Council, and Mr. I. Glyn Thomas for the work they have done. We wish to pay tribute too, to the solidarity with which the Medical Students and Milner Park students supported their leaders.

This is the text of Mr. H. R. Raikes's statement:

(1) The Government grant was to all intents and purposes stabilised in 1930 when it reached £98,545. It is now £100,000.
(2) Since then the number of students has risen by about 70 per cent, and since students fees on the old basis only equalled 44 per cent. of total cost (new basis 47 per cent.) it is evident that a deficit is very likely.
(3) Till about three to four years ago, the Council managed to control the deficit. It is however now out of hand and further income is essential.
(4) The Council has requested the Minister to appoint a Commission into the finance of the University. It is probable that the commission will be appointed.
(5) The calling of evidence is a matter for the Commission, but I will ask it to hear the evidence of students. I cannot guarantee that my request will be agreed to.

(Signed) H. R. RAIKES.
5th April, 1943.

N.U.S.A.S.

LATEST BULLETIN

IT is officially announced that N.U.S.A.S. has not yet awakened from the profound slumber into which it fell two or three years ago. Its doctors advise that in order to divert the attention of the Angel of Death when he comes its way, its name be altered to the "Notorious Union of Sleepers and Snorers". . . Or perhaps some Princess Charming might be available who, with a glamorous kiss here and a gluteal kick there, might inspire N.U.S.A.S. to rise from its sick-bed and make its existence justifiable.

Is there a Princess Charming amongst you?

If I had my way . . .

I'd start a night-school for misguided public men like Arthur G. Barlow.

★

I'd provide free University education for the poorer classes.

★

I'd find the sneakthief who steals books at the Medical School and expel him.

★

I wouldn't admit a student to University unless he promised to take part in student activities.

★

I'd remove the Johannesburg Fort from Hospital Hill, and build a new Medical School with decent air-conditioned lecture theatres and student amenities.

★

I'd allow students the use of the University swimming bath during weekends.

★

I'd divorce the post of Minister of Education, from that of Finance on the grounds of malicious desertion; it's an unholy alliance anyway.

★

And I'd think twice about giving either portfolio to the present holder.

CHEMICAL ENGINEERING SOCIETY is holding a

FILM EVENING

on WEDNESDAY, APRIL 14th, at 8.15 p.m. in GREAT HALL.
Admission 1 -.
In aid of War Funds.

As editor, I had to have dealings with the University Principal, Humphry Raikes. When we had a crisis about University fees in 1943, I was inevitably involved in keeping students and Raikes abreast of developments. I found time to speak at Great Hall meetings and acted as mediator in resolving the impasse between the Principal and the SRC by producing a special issue of *WU's Views* setting out the facts for students and staff.

The saddest thing I had to do was to write an obituary about Rex Martienssen, who had died suddenly at the age of 37, while on an officer's course at the Military Headquarters, Roberts Heights, Pretoria. It was vacation time. He had gone on the army course more for relaxation than anything else since it was expected that university staff and students should do their bit for the war effort. Apparently he felt unwell and was admitted to the military hospital. His death was not only a loss to the University and his close friends, but there is no doubt that South Africa lost a great leader in the development of modern architecture exemplified by his interest in the Bauhaus School and le Corbusier.

It was a deep personal loss – Rex had been a tower of strength to me when I needed help and advice.

Also in that first year, I organised a student conference on Nutrition and Public Health over a six week period. This incurred the displeasure of senior students at the Medical School, who took umbrage at the fact that an unknown first-year student had the temerity to organise such a conference. This reaction was unexpected. It was not well attended. I added insult to injury by publishing the discussions in *WU's Views* in a series called "Medical Systems of the World", which included the "Doctor in Society" and "Organised Medicine for South Africa".

Although I was absorbed in the nitty-gritty of the first year course, I had to extract political satisfaction from university life and satisfy my urge to write and influence events and people – or at least to do something politically constructive. This was one of the reasons that I had taken up medicine in the first place.

There were some unexpected incidents.

A month before the first year examinations I was very perturbed by the fact, as was Leslie, that our Physics Practical results in electricity were always inaccurate. These experiments took place on Friday afternoons. I was bored because I did not really understand or like Physics. On the other hand, Leslie was most meticulous with the experiments, and enjoyed them. Friday was usually a busy day at the shop, and after about twenty minutes I would say to Leslie, "I'm off to the shop, you carry on and I'll get the results from you at the weekend."

It seemed to be mainly our electrical experiments which were always incorrect – we could never get them right and the laboratory staff were mystified. I was always in the laboratory when the main part of the work was done.

Leslie, a good physicist, was most upset. In turn, I was worried whether I would pass the Physics examinations even if our results were correct, because it was the one subject I could not grasp.

One Friday afternoon as I was leaving our laboratory desk for the shop I heard Leslie call me back. I walked through the double row of desks with their galvanometers and electrical apparatus.

Leslie was shouting: "Eureka! Eureka!"

I thought he'd gone mad.

"Leslie, what the hell's going on?"

"Boris, stand still where you are. Don't move."

I did not understand what was happening. He was concentrating on the galvanometer.

"Now," he instructed, "walk past me and stop when I say so."

I followed his instructions.

"Stop," came the next command. Then: "Turn around and come back past me." This performance went on for a few minutes. I was completely mystified. He called me over to his side of the desk, and told me what he had discovered.

As I was saying goodbye to him and walking away from the galvanometer, he was looking at it and recording a result. The needle suddenly started to move in my direction, and the further I moved the more it altered its position. When he shouted "Stop", it stopped registering. When I moved again it registered anew and went in the opposite direction when I retraced my steps.

The galvanometer needle was being influenced by my body. This had distorted all our electrical experiment results. We looked at each other in amazement. Leslie grinned with the pleasure of discovery. The other students around us had become absorbed in what was going on.

"Boris," said Leslie, "your steel jacket has been upsetting all the experiments, and we never realised it."

I was astonished. I had completely forgotten I had been compelled, for three months, to wear a steel jacket and a corset under my clothing. The steel brace, supported by the corset, was to force my back to remain as straight as possible.

Earlier in the year, I had been carried off a golf course because of "sciatic pain" down my left leg, which had been bothering me for about a year. An orthopaedic surgeon had diagnosed Marie Strumpel disease, then considered the forerunner of a spinal disease called Ankylosing Spondilitis. This affected the vertebral column and progressively moved from the sacro-iliac joints in the hip, up the spinal column to the neck, eventually stiffening the spine with serious deformities.

In the days before this disease was clinically understood, sufferers ended up with a fixed flexed spine so that it could not straighten and were forced to walk in this position for the rest of their lives.

The steel jacket I wore during the day helped to keep the vertebral column upright. I learnt to live with this disability – it did not stop me having an active life at the university and in business. I suffered from constant aches and pains but I put up with this because there were many other things more important than back pain and the inconvenience of a steel brace.

Leslie and I discussed this important discovery. In the first place it explained why all Leslie's painstaking work was inaccurate and Dr Halliday, the Physics lecturer, had to be told. Secondly, it raised the question as to whether I could do the Electricity practical examination wearing my steel jacket.

We found Dr Halliday in the laboratory. Leslie explained to him what he had discovered about our poor results in the experiments.

Dr Halliday's reaction was a hearty laugh.

"Boris," he said, "I'm sorry to have to tell you that you will not be able to do the practical examination in Electricity. Of course the other two questions, on Heat and Weights, have to be answered. I presume missing Electricity won't upset you too much."

I think Dr Halliday knew he had taken a load off my mind, because I was floundering in Electricity. My steel jacket had possibly saved me from failing Physics in the examination.

I passed Physics, Chemistry and Zoology and to my great surprise obtained a first-class in Botany.

So, the first year was behind me, and 1943 saw us at our new home at the Medical School up the hill next to the General Hospital, where we were to study Human Anatomy and Physiology.

On the day the term started, I walked into the Anatomy dissection room, dressed in my new white coat with a scalpel in my pocket. As the doors opened in the basement of the Medical School in Hospital Street, we could smell the powerful blast of the formalin from the dissection room.

We were rivetted by the rows and rows of corpses laid out on white slabs, lying like drained white and yellow Egyptian mummies motionless, legs outstretched, toes pointing to the ceiling and hands at the sides.

A few students ventured between the rows looking for the cadavers allocated to them for dissection. Many stood at the door taking in the bizarre scene, aghast at the thought of going into the room of dead bodies.

I well recall an image of the gas chamber atrocities that we were beginning to hear about from Nazi Germany, saying to myself that this picture of lifeless bodies was far too orderly.

I had been allocated a cadaver together with five other, older, students, friends from first year. Later I discovered that we all had something wrong physically, and I often wondered to what extent our physical and mental defects had brought us together to study medicine.

Hope Pletts, tall, lively and dark-haired had recently recovered from Pulmonary Tuberculosis. Leslie Weiner had one leg. I had a spinal disease. Jock Levy, a gifted musician, took one look at the corpses, and when he came to our cadaver went absolutely white with terror. Without saying a word, he walked out of our dissection room vowing never to come back. A week later, Nora Austoker, one of the women at our corpse went to see Jock, and she induced him to return.

The oldest student with us was a man of forty-nine, a doctor of theology from Stellenbosch University who had decided the study of medicine was God's wish. It was clear from the start that he could not cope with the work.

A few months later he left the course. We learnt he had opened a business making coffins for undertakers, no doubt inspired by the cadavers!

It was a very full and busy year. Anatomy and Physiology meant we were getting to grips with basic medicine, in the medical environment. One soon got used to the smell, the formalin, and the freedom of discussion around a cadaver that had lost its human identity and become merely an object.

Many of the world's problems were discussed over our corpse, especially the progress of World War II from which we were totally removed. South Africa was heavily involved. Many young men and women had interrupted their university courses to go "up North", and sometimes we heard of an injury or a death. The country's whites were sharply divided over the war issue, and at the Medical School there were deep divisions between certain nationalistic Afrikaans students and the rest of us.

In between the intricacies of studying the organs, the nerves and the blood vessels of the body, which my visual memory helped me recall, and the rushing to and from Medical School to business every few hours, I still managed to keep up activities like editing WU's Views, and participation in student politics. I had become treasurer of the Students Representative Council and was involved in student politics. I was no longer active in the Labour Party, but Tom Osborn, who was also my Physiology lecturer, kept me up to date about its activities.

Editing WU's Views took up much time. Many articles and editorial projects were discussed with Leslie and Johan over our inanimate corpse, which was becoming decidedly shabby from our assiduous dissection.

I had achieved further university notoriety. I had written an "open" letter to Arthur G Barlow, the owner and editor of a weekly newspaper in Johannesburg. He was constantly attacking university students as "yellow", alleging that they were hiding in the university funkhole despite the fact that General Smuts had excluded all medical students from voluntarily joining the forces.

My "open" letter to him was in response to his "open" letter on the front page of Arthur Barlow's Weekly, written in his own style, accusing the medical students of cowardice. He replied to my letter which was good "copy" for him, by reprinting my letter in yellow type on his front page, together with an open letter to serving soldiers at the Battle School at Zonderwater, the military training unit near Pretoria.

Barlow was a well-known MP, eccentric, outspoken, a thorn in the flesh of his political party and opponents. Neither of us knew that in the not too distant future we would clash again as political foes.

22

Second year was an important one for me. I met and formed friendships with several students, some of whom were younger than I was, but with whom I shared special interests. One was Harding le Riche, some clinical years ahead of me who, with Ray Bernstein a sociology student, were founders of the Fordsburg Clinic. This unit, of which Ray Bernstein became the first Director, operated in the run-down urban area of Fordsburg which included the Market and the police station where I went to bail my father out of gaol. I was extremely interested in doing socio-medical work although I was clinically experienced, and used my stethoscope for the first time at evening sessions at the Clinic. I then became its honorary secretary. The object of the Fordsburg Clinic was to find out why the area was running down, and what could be done in urban renewal terms to halt the slide.

Together with Harding I was one of the first students to spend a few weeks with Dr Sydney Kark and his wife Emily at the Polela Health Centre in the Natal midlands near Bulwer. It was in its infancy in the foothills of the Drakensberg escarpment and the "native" areas. There I studied the relationship between health, disease, nutrition, prevention and socio-economic circumstances.

Sydney Kark, who became world famous for his work, was pioneering the study in South Africa of medical and social problems. Like Harding, he eventually went overseas, because the Nationalists closed down health centres in order to consolidate the various "native" areas prior to implementing their Homeland apartheid plans. Countries like Canada and Israel gained experienced epidemiologists at South Africa's expense. Le Riche became Professor of Epidemiology at Toronto and Kark headed a unit in Israel.

For me, it was an opportunity early in my medical training to get to practical grips with medical sociology and to test my politics in the field, in relation to community health. Despite the pressures, I managed to devote some time to medico-social problems, which put into practical use the hours I had spent in countless political meetings and in the hustings.

Second year medicine was devoted entirely to Anatomy and Physiology. They are enormous subjects requiring a great deal of concentration and memorisation, and most nights I spent "swotting". Nevertheless, it was natural for me, despite the tough second year course, to continue involvement in extra-curricular matters. No matter how heavy the academic demands and the equally demanding business affairs, I continued to live at a furious pace.

I was still editing *WU's Views* in 1943 and one of the most serious problems was on our doorstep. The segregated non-European (black) hospital was in dire straits. NEH, as it was called, was next to the Medical School. It was a low building, with casualty in front and the wards behind. It catered for "Natives", coloureds and Indians, housed in overcrowded conditions.

To get early clinical experience I started attending casualty on Saturday nights helping the harassed and overworked staff. Casualty on a Saturday night was a carnage. Blood-soaked blacks were brought in hour after hour as a result of drunkenness, fights and assaults taking place in the segregated overcrowded "native locations" in the south-west of Johannesburg.

Anyone in casualty who was able to stitch battered heads or bodies helped, irrespective of their formal qualification, ability or experience. Medical students were specially welcome.

Often, our tutors in stitching were the untrained Zulu porters and casualty workers. The ability to bear pain and suffering by the injured blacks brought in for attention was salutary.

It was shattering to imagine how appalling the conditions in the Native locations must have been when one reviewed their ghastly injuries.

While white Johannesburg was enjoying itself on a Saturday night, many blacks were desperately resisting the mindless violence of the poverty-stricken in another world just a few miles away.

Medically sick cases were admitted as well, and it was here that I learnt my first lessons in clinical medicine. For me it was valuable, because I often had to miss lectures or clinical meetings because of business commitments, and the acute cases became priceless practical lessons for me. So I spent more and more time in the evenings both at NEH and the white hospital across the road.

There was no hospital in the Native locations, so all the sick and assault cases had to be brought across the city to NEH. The hospital's space and resources were so overstrained that patients not only lay on the beds, but on mattresses on the floors between the beds and even under them. Despite the outcry from students and newspapers about these terrible conditions the Provincial Health Authorities did little or nothing to build more hospitals or provide more staff. The City Council, which was responsible for the locations, also did nothing to improve these deplorable hospital conditions.

It was only when the war ended that the Provincial Authorities took over the military camp and hospital at Baragwanath adjacent to the locations for the blacks. Baragwanath is still there, probably the largest hospital in South Africa, consisting of the original rows of prefabricated wards which somehow have survived the rigours of time.

I decided to take action to expose the conditions at the NEH. I published a special issue of *WU's Views* with photographs showing the overcrowded conditions at the hospital calling for more money and improvements. This created a stir, and the local newspapers reprinted our story. Unfortunately, it was a nine-day wonder.

Nothing was done. It was ironic that thirty years later I was addressing a student conference on the socio-economic aspects of primary care, when I read them an extract from this issue of *WU's Views* without disclosing the date of publication in order to describe the hospital's conditions at the date of the conference. When I told the students the date of the special issue they could not believe that little or nothing had been done in thirty years. The situation in black hospitals had not changed.

It Takes 7 Minutes To Read This Page

LET US HOPE YOU ARE REALLY SHOCKED!

Appalling Conditions at Non-European Hospital

7,500,000 people in South Africa are facing extinction by disease. South Africa is heading for political, social and economic ruin unless the people and the Government of the Union realise their obligation to provide civilised health and medical services for the Non-European people.

The native masses are riddled with tuberculosis, a high percentage is syphilitic, and an astonishing number are rapidly succumbing to the ravages of malnutrition. Yet virtually nothing is being done to arrest the alarming progress of these scourges.

The conditions prevailing in one of the Union's largest and best-equipped Non - European Hospitals, located in the wealthy city of Johannesburg, is appalling. It is a hospital where 500 beds serve between 650-700 cases; where long queues of patient sufferers, wrapped in their coloured blankets, squat on the sidewalks, waiting hours for attention; where the wards are crowded to suffocation.

It is a hospital where the des-

one corner no larger than 15 ft. x 25 ft. nine cases were lying, four in beds, and the rest on the floors. In the women's ward, the situation was even worse. On one large mattress, four native women lay. Underneath most of the beds were patients. Some women had new born babies in their arms. In ward of 23 beds, 46 patients were present.

What of the children? These mites are kept in one ward. Fifteen of them have to sleep on the floors at night. During the day they have to play in the grounds of the Hospital, until they can go in at night. Between 30-40 per cent. of them are T.B. cases, with no means of isolation. Must this go on for very much longer? An official pointed to the bright-eyed feverish youngster suffering from broncho-pneumonia, sharing a cot with a wasted "skeleton," victim of malnutrition. What are their chances of survival?

The bed-population ratio in Johannesburg is one bed to 550

they are fighting, and they will continue to lose until the public helps them.

These conditions are prevailing in Johannesburg. The meagre statistics available prove that the same grim facts apply to the entire Union. In 1939, South Africa could boast of 280 hospitals for Europeans and 126 for natives, although there were 192,699 European patients compared with 354,535 natives. In parts of the native reserves there is one doctor in charge of 40,000 natives. Preventive medicine does not exist. Here are the breeding grounds of disease. From here death stalks the land.

● S.A. Lags Behind

In the development of public health services South Africa lags hopelessly behind the rest of the world. Yet the problems involved are not insoluble. They have been faced and overcome in Russia, in Sweden, in Denmark and in America. In Denmark, medical services have reached a high standard of efficiency. The

Central Government. Dr. G. D. Laing, Medical Officer of Health, recently stated that "the inadequacy of medical service for natives is a reflex of the general confusion due to divided control and divided responsibility."

It is obvious that there is no reason why the Union should not be able to reconstruct her medical services along progressive lines. War-time conditions do, unfortunately, necessitate short-staffing and financial stringency, but when the health, indeed, the survival of the native, and consequently the European population, is at stake, a bold policy of prevention as well as cure is essential, whatever the cost.

● More Money Needed

The crux of the matter is that a great deal more money is needed for native medical services. Present allocations should be doubled. Money is needed for new hospitals, sanitoria, health centres, for doctors, for nurses, for facilities to train

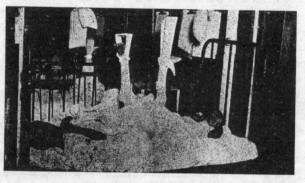

WOULD YOU ALLOW YOUR CHILD TO LIE IN HOSPITAL UNDER THESE CONDITIONS?

BROKEN LEGS, PAIN, INJURY, DISCOMFORT AND TWO IN A BED!

perately ill fill the beds and the floors between the beds and under the beds.

This appears to be the best Johannesburg can provide for the natives upon whom the economic structure of South Africa rests. If the future of South African civilisation depends upon the survival of the fittest, these people are certainly not being made fit to survive. The lack of adequate medical services for Non-Europeans in the Union has become a national scandal of the first magnitude. The native population is South Africa's reservoir of disease, and unless action of the most sweeping nature is taken immediately, the effects of the visionless, directionless State policy will be felt by all sections of the community for generations' to come.

● What We Saw

A visit to the Hospital a few days ago revealed that little change has taken place in the last eighteen months. The Hospital Board has done its very best to alleviate the position of the "T.B." cases which in the past were mingled with other patients. Hospitals have been built at Rietfontein and Waterval to accommodate T.B's and infectious diseases. But as quickly as they are removed they come in. In recent months in the male surgical ward which has 50 beds, as many as 140 cases have been housed, on mattresses, on the floors between and under the beds. When we arrived we found a little over a hundred cases. In

natives, excluding those who work on the mines. In the report of the last Hospital Commission which sat as long ago as 1927, it was stated that Johannesburg needed approximately one bed to 700 natives. The fact that there is an overflow of fifty per cent., even on the basis of one bed to 550 natives, illustrates the accuracy of this estimate.

Toiling under these fantastic mediaeval conditions, doing wonderful service, is a hopelessly small band of doctors and nurses. Each doctor has under his care approximately 70 cases. American experts estimate thirty is the maximum number of patients to which a resident medical officer can reasonably attend under ideal conditions. The doctors are doing sterling work, but it is utterly impossible for them to do justice to their patients or to themselves under the circumstances. The nursing staff would be adequate for five hundred patients. During March, 1943, there was a daily average of 686 cases.

● Beds on Floor

It is not easy to nurse a case lying under a bed; to look after sick children wandering about the grounds; to feed crying babies, two in a cot, with tireless cheerfulness, with kindness, with love. These women are doing magnificent work against heart-breaking odds.

The hospital staff is fighting a heroic battle against disease and death, but it is a losing battle

Danes have one doctor to 1,400 people, the Swedes one to 2,800. The South African ratio in the native reserves — approximately one doctor to 40,000 — constitutes a monument to criminal neglect.

In any attempt to improve medical services for the native, the factors precipitating the present chaotic state should be known. Obviously an absurdly inadequate sum of money is voted for the medical treatment of non-Europeans. This is in accord with the general policy of social and political victimisation of the African. The Transvaal Provincial Council subsidises European hospitals to the extent of 12/6 per patient per day; non-Europeans, 5/- per patient per day. The reasoning behind this allocation is obscure. Does a native who is suffering from the same disease as a European require less medical attention, less nursing, less medicine?

● Muddled Administration

On the administrative side, too, South Africa's hospital organisation is sadly deficient. Some cases fall under Central Government control, some under the provincial administrations, and yet others under the local authorities. If a man contracts scarlet fever he is provided for by the Municipality. Should he develop pneumonia as a complication, the Provincial Administration is responsible for his treatment. Finally, if he contracts tuberculosis (which is a reasonable possibility under present conditions) he falls under the control of the

nurses, for drugs, for dressings, for artificial limbs, with which natives are not provided. Money is needed for preventitive medicine on a large scale. The people should be taught what foods to eat, where pure water may be found. Swamps should be drained.

A comprehensive survey of Public Health throughout the Union should be undertaken immediately. There are few health statistics. There is no native census. Little is known about the cause of native mortality in the Union. Medical men have no facts on which to base their reconstruction.

● Statistics Needed

The infantile death rate in the native reserves is known to be a terrifying figure, but no official statistics or even estimates exist.

The answer for today is money — for tomorrow, a complete reorganisation of medical services in South Africa.

Organised medicine should be introduced under the control of a central, non-political body. Doctors should be free to work under reasonable conditions, removed from the field of monetary competition. In this way alone can preventitive medicine be raised to a high standard.

SOUTH AFRICA MUST REALISE THESE FACTS, TAKE ACTION, OR FACE THE CONSEQUENCES.

※ Printed by Prompt P. & P. Co., 94 Harrison Street, Jhb.

Ten years later, the "white" hospital had become "black" and NEH which had been closed, was re-opened as an additional "black" hospital because there is still an appalling shortage of facilities for staff and beds for patients.

In 1991 the crisis at Baragwanath still exists – the present-day doctors have come into open conflict with the authorities because of the chronic overcrowding, lack of staff, drugs, and poor facilities.

WU's Views, through its limited columns and circulation also gave me a chance to speak my mind as I saw the world of 1943 undergoing a giant catharsis in the struggle to rid itself of the fascism and the Nazis.

In a front page editorial headlined "This Year And All That", I optimistically wrote: "A new world will arise. The world that will give freedom and equality which is the right of man. The oppressed, the starving, the have-nots, the countless colonial underdogs, they will arise. Idle words will not convert those students who believe in a Fascist victory. Positive action will. We must go out and take part in the struggles to get better wages, better living conditions, with organised medicine and education for all."

There were students at the University and medical school who wanted a fascist victory. They were secretly organised and linked to the extreme right wing of the National Party. We knew who they were. Their organisation was called the Afrikaanse Studentebond (The Afrikaans Student Union) – the ASB. They profoundly influenced a large number of Nationalist-inclined Afrikaner students and attracted a number of English-speaking conservatives, not as members but as supporters.

At this time two significant issues arose that affected white-black relations at University. The first was that the National Union of South African Students (NUSAS), was unable to make up its mind about the admission to its ranks of Fort Hare, the only black university in South Africa. Innumerable meetings were held at the University, in which I took a prominent part, in support of opening up NUSAS to all colours, races and creeds.

Our efforts to admit blacks failed. I could not believe that white students at the most liberal university in South Africa opposed the admission of blacks. It was evidence of the growing desire of Afrikaners to separate the races.

The other incident occurred outside the post-mortem laboratory in the "white" General Hospital grounds opposite the Medical School.

I was due to attend the usual weekly post-mortem session. On arrival at the PM room all the students were standing outside the entrance somewhat confused. They were being urged by three Afrikaner ASB students not to enter the post-mortem laboratory because the post-mortem on a white man was being attended by the two black students in our class.

I was horrified. I immediately took part in an argument with the ASB activists, urging all the students to enter the post-mortem room together with our two black colleagues, which they did.

One of the ASB boycotters was Carel de Wet, a grandson of General de Wet who fought the British in the Boer War. He and I were destined to carry on our political confrontation in the future.

During the war period there was little in common between the Afrikaans-speaking and English-speaking students at the University and Medical School. We lived in separate worlds. It was all a result of the divided white society. As with Poppy, it went beyond the Boer War. English and Afrikaans students greeted each other and played sport together, but mostly that was the end of their association.

Despite the late nights doing extra-curricular work in Casualty or at the Fordsburg Clinic, swotting, or attending to business, I always rose early in the morning to study when my mind was fresh. Anatomy was not difficult for me because of my visual memory and drawing ability, but Physiology and Biochemistry I found a struggle. Student friends who knew my position often assisted, especially when I missed a lecture or a practical because of business commitments; they even made duplicate notes for me.

My family's problems faded somewhat into the background. I saw my father periodically. Leon was an officer in the Signals Corps "up North", and had a remarkable escape when Tobruk was overrun by the Germans in the Libyan desert. My father's main problem was still Max, who by now was at a cram school in Johannesburg, ostensibly under my father's care and helping at the Market. Max was enjoying the life style he had created, making his own decisions, and my father accepted the position. At least Max was at home. I kept myself at arm's length, because I had more pressing problems.

My business was very important in achieving my aims, which were crystallising. I realised that Kruger and Wilson (Pty) Ltd was going to run into a serious shortage of stock, because the remaining Ekco sets were rapidly being sold. No new stocks of radios were coming into South Africa because the world was making equipment to kill people instead. There was no South African radio manufacturing industry. Horace Dainty was now employed by the War Communications Department making basic communication receivers for the army. My urgent need was to import replacement stock. In the radio industry this was clearly impossible.

I had been racking my brains about our ability to keep things going because of the stock depletion, when a thought struck me while buying a book from the medical section of the Central News Agency, the only medical booksellers in the country. Why not import medical books? There were no import restrictions on text books. They were still being published overseas, and the CNA had no competitors. Here I was at the Medical School, in a favourable position to know what books were required. I decided to speak to Kruger as soon as possible.

"Mike, I have an idea. We can resolve our problem about stock by diversifying and importing medical books from England and America, which can be brought in permit-free. I would like to open a medical book section using half the shop space."

I showed him what would be needed. His face fell. Mike was not an innovator. The idea of pioneering something else created serious difficulties for him.

"Boris, I know nothing about selling books, let alone medical books."

"Don't worry Mike, most doctors or students who come in know what they want – all you have to do is take it off the shelf and get paid."

He was satisfied with my assurances. I promptly went off to the CNA to see what they had in stock, then checked on what books were needed for medical students, saw my shippers and the British Trade Commissioner and placed our first order.

Six months later the medical books arrived in good time for the 1944 term. We removed our radio stocks from the shelves on one side of the shop, and worked until the early hours of the morning pricing, labelling and putting books in their places. Kruger and Wilson (Pty) Ltd were now radio dealers and medical booksellers.

The most bemused person was our Asian next door neighbour, Mr Basmat of the Calcutta Fruit Market. He stood outside our shop looking perplexed at the books on the shelves and came in to ask us what it was all about.

Word soon got around about the books amongst doctors and students. Before long, we were very busy. The students were pleased that I had broken the CNA monopoly and lowered prices. The doctors in the army, back on leave, often visited the shop, walking out with a medical book and sometimes a radio. The venture paid dividends because it helped us to keep going until the end of the war, and above all it paid my medical school fees.

It was a great day for me when at the end of 1943 I passed Anatomy and Physiology. There was one more non-clinical hurdle to overcome – Pathology. I looked forward to the challenge because it was the key to future clinical work which I was already doing in Casualty at night and weekends.

To my regret I could not participate in the General Election that took place during 1943 when General Smuts was returned with an increased majority, through the aid of his military voters.

Right wing Nationalist opponents, egged on daily by Zeesen, were very active, prompted by the daily Nazi barrage over the air. Smuts in turn had to cope with continuing sabotage against internal military installations and amongst other tough measures he put leading Nationalist saboteurs in concentration camps.

Russia and the American entry into the war, had given us hope that in the end the Nazis could not win. Although I was not involved in the war, I could not ignore it. The awareness of violence, death and destruction, was very real when one learnt of friends or relations who were injured or killed.

The main war news came from the local radio broadcasts, and the newspapers. Cinema newsreels were irregular and of course delayed as they had to come by sea. I was fortunate that I was able to use good short-wave sets to listen to the crackling BBC wartime news services.

I passed Pathology in 1944 but of all things failed in an easy subject, Bacteriology. It was my own fault because I treated it too lightly. In retrospect, it is obvious I had to cut corners because of my nonstop life style between Medical school, the business, and extramural activities. Something had to suffer. My mental concentration must not have been good because

Bacteriology is probably one of the easiest subjects in the medical curriculum. I restored morale by collecting my second first-class pass when I wrote the supplementary Bacteriology examination six weeks later.

As I was now in the first clinical years, it was necessary for me to live close to the Hospital. Fortunately I found a flat across the road, so that I could work at night to make up for time spent away from the medical school during the day at business.

All I had to do was put on my white coat early in the morning, cross the road to Casualty and find out which patients had been admitted during the night. If a case sounded interesting, I'd get to the ward, inspect the patient, often doing a quick examination after reading the houseman's notes. In this way I gained much clinical knowledge. I would attend a lecture or ward round in the morning and at the tea break I would dash to the car, drive to the shop. There I would catch up with the morning's business activities and deal with problems which might have arisen.

The advent of the book division left no space for running the administration of the business, so we rented offices in a nearby building. From there I attended to the firm's correspondence, saw visitors, placed orders and dealt with the day-to-day management of the business.

I always tried to get back to the hospital for the main medical or surgical seminar of the day at eleven o'clock. By one o'clock I was back at my office, continuing the routine and having a quick lunch. Fortunately I had Molly Bell, a superb secretary, who carried a great deal of the administrative load.

The afternoons were spent in laboratory or clinical work, but additional subjects like Psychiatry and Public Health came later. The pressure of work became so great that I had to devise ways and means of fitting everything in. The hours of the day were not long enough for me. The fact that some clinical lectures were badly delivered was a help. I'd been told that the Psychiatry lectures were appalling, the lecturer simply reading from his notes which he handed out to everyone before speaking. I attended his first lecture, and stood in the doorway listening to him reading his notes. After five minutes I left the lecture theatre never to return. I saw no sense in wasting time when I could read the notes and swot in my own precious time.

I passed Psychiatry, meeting the lecturer for the first time at the oral *viva*, and he gave me a good pass.

Sometimes I was so tired that I could not remember simple things. Once, in the Public Health examination, the examiner asked me a simple question about a pig-borne disease affecting humans, a subject I knew well. My mind was blank. I could not recall its name. That lapse cost me the first-class he was hoping to give me, which he told me some months later.

Clinical work was demanding. At all costs one had to be there for the tutorials which took place during the day and could not be missed. Rare cases might never be seen again, signs and symptoms in acute cases could disappear within hours, or even minutes. I learnt more dealing with "cases" – sick people – than spending hours reading text books.

Students were allocated cases on intake days. Sick people had to be clerked with care and thoroughly examined. The "case" had to be presented to the registrar or houseman. When "God" – the chief or the consultant – came along, one had to be present to talk about the case and answer questions.

Because I was running up and down Hospital Hill all day, the only time I had for undisturbed practical clinical work was at night. So, at the end of a busy day, I would rush my evening meal and between seven and eight o'clock, be either at the "white" Casualty of the General or "Nigs" the black Casualty nearby.

All the Casualty officers knew me well. They taught me a lot in the years I was a clinical student, especially about acutely ill people. Students seeing the case at the following morning's ward round would no longer see the acute signs and symptoms I'd seen when the patient was first admitted hours earlier.

Attending Casualty in my day was not compulsory, so not many students bothered. Simply because I was there, I was allowed to do advanced surgical procedures under the eye of a casualty officer or a registrar. Often it would be the nurse in charge who would teach me all about the disease.

The big advantage of being in Casualty at night, which I soon realised, was that I could follow a case admitted to the wards and see how it was treated. If it was a surgical case, say, of appendicitis or acute gall bladder disease, I would help prepare the case in the ward for the theatre. In the early hours of the morning the surgeon or the registrar might invite me to scrub up in order to assist at the operation. This made up for missed lectures, tutorial time and reading. I relied more on what I saw and heard at the hospital to increase my medical knowledge than with my head buried in library books.

I enjoyed this because I was seeing hospital life and sick people in the "raw". Not only did it make an impact on me, but it taught me a great deal about the reactions of people under stress and in desperate situations. People often undergo a tremendous transformation when they are acutely ill. They have abnormal reactions when they believe that they are facing their last hours.

One or two incidents come to mind.

I was "hanging around" Casualty one night when the ambulance brought in a man whom they said was dead. I went to inspect the body in the ambulance before calling the doctor on duty, and asked the ambulance man how long he thought the patient had been dead.

"A few minutes," he said. As an afterthought he added "I think".

I took a quick look at the corpse's pupils, noted they were dilated, his lips were blue and he was not breathing.

"Rush him into Casualty," I instructed. In the cubicle I started resuscitating the corpse using a new method which in those days which could be carried out by one person. I had seen it demonstrated a few hours before at a lecture I attended given by Dr Beck, a visiting American cardiologist. In between mouth-breathing I yelled for the casualty officer to insert an intratracheal tube to help the patient breathe, because the dead body gave a shudder – and started breathing.

Froth was coming out of the mouth, but the pupils had become smaller, indicating that he was re-oxygenating. After the tube had been put in, the patient was rushed to the emergency ward for further treatment on the respirator.

I always followed up my casualty cases. A week later I went to see the "dead man" because I learnt he had made a good recovery. He was lying in bed, virtually covered to his chin by the blanket looking blankly at the ceiling.

"Hullo," I said, "I'm the student who rescued you from the dead, and brought back your breathing. I'm so glad to see you have recovered."

He stared at me blankly. Then his face distorted with rage, his mouth almost animal-like, baring his teeth in a snarl.

"You bastard, you bastard!" he yelled. " I wanted to die."

I recoiled with shock. He tried to struggle out of bed but could not. I fled.

I was not aware when he was admitted that he was paralysed below the hips, living alone, and had taken an overdose to end his life.

In another incident in my final year I had just walked into the professorial medical ward when a young patient screamed. I rushed to his bed because he was clutching his abdomen. I eased him back feeling his abdomen. It was rigid like a corrugated washing-board, with pain so severe he could not talk. Soon a senior doctor and nurse were at his bedside. "I think he has perforated a stomach ulcer," I said.

"Why do you think so?" asked the registrar. "You don't know why he was admitted and what his complaints and symptoms are?"

"Well . . ." I explained my reasoning, based on the shouting incident, with the patient holding his abdomen and the irregular feeling when I ran my hands over his abdominal wall. This is the classical description of a peptic ulcer perforating rarely witnessed by observers.

Within the hour the patient was transferred to the surgical ward and operated on. To my relief when the peritoneal cavity under the skin layers was exposed fresh blood appeared. My diagnosis was confirmed.

One night in casualty a small child was brought in looking very ill and almost comatose. The nurses were instructing the ambulance men to take the child to the Children's Hospital ten minutes away when "Shadow" (named after a comic strip character), the casualty doctor, intervened. He took the child in his arms, quickly examined it, noticing the child's neck was rigid and there was a skin rash. Asking me to hold the child, Shadow called for a large dose of penicillin in a syringe which he injected into the spinal canal. He instructed the ambulance men to rush the child to the Children's Hospital. He telephoned to tell them the child was coming and that it had cerebral meningitis, which is so severe that every minute counts. The child survived.

Acute medical situations like this, which I often witnessed, taught me how to make a quick diagnosis and take urgent action. Medical training is full of such happenings and one must be present to deal with these emergencies in the proper way.

Some students got through the medical course unaffected by these medical problems and the drama of the sick. Things often happened so quickly that there was literally no time to catch one's breath.

Late one afternoon I walked into our intake medical ward on the fifth floor of the Hospital, having just come from the business. I was checking on newly admitted cases. As I passed the first beds there were loud shouts from the patients.

"Stop him, stop him!."

A man in his dressing gown had rushed to a window and was opening it. I realised he was trying to leap out. I dashed over to him just as he opened the window. He had his hands on the sill, and was lifting his body ready to jump.

For a moment I thought I had caught him. I managed to grab his trousers with both hands. The next second I slipped on the highly polished floor, and I felt his ankles and pyjama trousers slip through my fingers as he slid to his death a hundred feet below.

I lay on the floor groaning and cursing the idiocy of the senseless polishing of hospital ward floors and the terrible error the intake doctors made of admitting a suicidal psychiatric case to a fifth floor hospital ward with unprotected windows.

The man who died was a school teacher who was severely depressed. Because of the shortage of beds in the psychiatry section he was admitted temporarily to our medical ward. He had been telling the other patients that he was going to commit suicide but for some unfathomable reason no one paid any attention.

I left the ward in a state of shock. I could have saved the unknown teacher had I not slipped on the shining floor.

When incidents like this happen, personally involving one, it has a traumatic effect. I realised more and more that studying medicine not only taught one about fellow humans and their problems but sometimes it left indelible scars.

As a child in the Market I had seen things happen to people which gave me the same sense of shock and despair as that day in the ward. The study of medicine is not only about patients and disease and curing them. It is about living people and their physical and mental problems and their reactions to their environment.

As I was older than the average student by six years or so, and carrying many other responsibilities, I tended to analyse what was happening all the time. Patients, to me, were not inanimate "cases". They were human-beings in need of assistance and help.

One got used to seeing dead people which started in second year in the dissection halls. We became blasé, not reacting to death. However to see someone die in a hospital when they are physically healthy and their death is due to human error in the hospital's administration is unforgivable.

I was reformist in my political beliefs. In turn I became a reformist in medicine. In my experience, the system, of which I was becoming critical, appeared to need many changes.

The white and black hospitals mirrored the life styles of the politically segregated ethnic groups in South Africa. Although South Africa has made many advances (1991) away from total segregation, the hospital system to this day reflects the dichotomous stratification between white affluence and black poverty.

Amongst the main causes of black poverty are racial segregation and wages below the poverty datum line. Family life is destroyed by the migratory labour system. Poor nutrition and wholly inadequate health services make things much worse.

Naturally my political outlook was influenced by daily experiences in Casualty, which was very important to me. I was constantly comparing the different environmental factors affecting whites and blacks as I saw them when they came in seeking medical help.

There were big differences. Whites hardly ever showed the serious effects of malnutrition, bad housing or poverty. Blacks invariably had evidence of these social deprivations, manifested often by diseases like scurvy, kwashiorkor and scabies which one did not expect to find in urbanised communities. On Saturday nights, both Casualties were full of drunks and assault cases, except that black casualty was totally chaotic. I cannot recall a case of a black neurotic, or drug overdose. If there was a black psychiatric case it was usually due to malnutrition. White Casualty always had its quota of peptic ulcers, coronary thromboses, overdoses and suicides.

Admission to the white hospital was by a means test on income; blacks paid a few shillings to be hospitalised for treatment. There were always long queues at black hospital Outpatients, but whites did not have to wait as long, because more money was spent on their facilities.

So, it was very easy not to notice the disparity in treatment if one did not have a social conscience. There were students who were very concerned about the different conditions at the hospitals. They not only raised their voices in protest but did what they could to alleviate conditions and establish voluntary health services where none existed.

During the last stages of the war, General Smuts received the Report of the National Health Services Commission which advocated a system of organised medicine similar to the British National Health Service. I was very interested in this report and and with other students strongly supported its acceptance. In the end the report was ditched, not only by Smuts but by successive governments. As a result there are hundreds of thousands people in South Africa, in the rural, urban and homeland areas without adequate health services.

Today there is still on the average one doctor for every 40 000 patients in the rural areas, whilst in the towns one doctor to 1 200 is more the norm. This is one of the iniquities of apartheid.

So it became increasingly clear as I went along the road to the final year, that I not only treated the medical course as a vocation qualifying me to practice, but I satisfied myself that I was equipping myself expertly to deal with socio-political and economic problems related to health and disease

108

should I return to political life. This in itself was worth all the effort, time and sacrifice in being trained as a doctor. I expected nevertheless that the time would arrive when conflicts would arise between business and medicine.

23

Early in 1945 it seemed likely that the war would be over in a matter of months. It became increasingly clear that we had to get in touch with EK Cole Ltd, the manufacturers of Ekco in England, about resuming radio shipments to South Africa.

The first importers to bring radio into South Africa would obviously do well.

Sparrows, our London shippers, advised us that it would be best if one of us could be in England as soon as the war ended. Ekco too said that they would welcome one of us as soon as we could get there. The medical book business was flourishing and it would be valuable to make contact with publishers, and widen the market.

I was in the fourth year of medicine, studying Pharmacology and most important of all the first courses of clinical medical and surgical training. To interrupt my medicine could be foolish.

At the business we were in a no-win situation. If Mike went overseas, I would have to look after the shop and the administration, and attend medical school. With all my experience I did not see how it was possible. If I went, which at the time was unthinkable, I would have to give up the medical course for a while, and I was totally opposed to this option.

In 1945, war or no war, the only way one travelled overseas was by ship. Regular passenger sailings had been suspended. The only ships that reached or left South Africa were troopships in convoy. No one knew exactly when the war would end and normal sailings to Britain be resumed. There were as yet no air services to South Africa.

By April we decided reluctantly that I should go to England and America. I was hoping that when I got back in three or four months the Medical School would allow me to continue and be understanding enough to let me sit the supplementary examinations in the new year. The Dean, Professor Watt, refused to commit himself.

I had several meetings with Laurie Harrison, the British Trade Commissioner, who by now was very enthusiastic that I should make the trip, in the interests of British exports. He thought he could get me away on a troopship in early May. There was no doubt then that the world's worst war would end in a matter of weeks. Berlin was destroyed. Hitler was dead. No official peace had been signed nor had the Germans surrendered.

Harrison told me to get a passport and have one bag packed, ready to leave at a moment's notice. I was not to tell anyone I was going overseas. He regretted he could not give me any more information.

Could I see my father and tell him I was going overseas? Yes, I could.

I went to see Father and told him in confidence what I was going to do, and that in all probability I would go to America if I got the chance, because I wanted to get a good American domestic appliance franchise for South Africa.

My father was getting older. He was a more relaxed person.

"Boris – you're going to America?"

"I'm hoping to, Dad."

There was a silence. He was drinking his favourite Russian tea in a glass.

"Do you think you can try and find my brother who lived in New York? I last saw him about thirty years ago, when I left for Australia. He was married and had two or three children."

I was astonished.

"Dad, you never told the family that you had a brother in New York – what is his name, where did he live?"

Father answered me slowly and carefully – his voice still had a faint American inflection.

"His name?" He hesitated. "His name is Meyer Tobin. He is two years younger than me, about my size and build. He used to repair sewing machines for the textile trade – the rag trade in New York. He lived in Brooklyn, but I can't remember the address."

Once more I was astonished.

"Dad – why is his name Tobin and yours Wilson? "

He described conditions under which Russian immigrants arrived in New York at the beginning of the century. In the chaos frustrated immigration officials, who could not decipher the Russian passports or speak the language, simply gave people names. Father was named Samuel Wilson. He did not say what his Russian name was and why his brother's name was Tobin. I was curious.

But I was asking too many questions. He shook his head and did not answer. It was left at that.

He made me wait while he wrote a note in Russian to his brother, should I be lucky enough to find him in New York. There were tears in his eyes when we said goodbye. A few days later I got an urgent call from Harrison who told me to get to Cape Town by train immediately and see the British Consul who would give me a ticket to travel on the troopship *Andes,* which would be taking about two thousand troops from the Far East back to England. As the *Andes* was one of the fastest ships in the world it should take about two weeks.

Only dormitory accommodation was available for about two hundred civilians, who were going back to England. He wished me luck and success because he wanted to see exports flowing again from Britain to South Africa.

When I told Leslie Weiner and other very close friends at the Medical School they were stupefied. Did I really want to take the risk of going overseas when the war was not yet over? There were still German submarines in the Atlantic! Why didn't I wait until things settled down?

I said goodbye to Mike, locked my flat and took the train to Cape Town.

I had never been on a voyage out of South Africa nor been on an ocean-going ship before. In Cape Town the British Consul was ready for me. He told me to go to the *Andes* which was already berthed in the harbour.

Greatly excited, I saw this sleek grey vessel of over forty thousand tons dwarfing the hundreds of people on the quayside. I walked up the narrow steps, not believing that I was actually leaving South Africa and going to see the England which I had dreamt about for years.

The ship was crowded with thousands of troops returning home from their service in the Far East. The war was still on. We were cheered to the hilt as we glided on a sunny afternoon out of Table Bay. The glorious sight of Table Mountain with its flat top receded into the distance and late afternoon mists. I was excited about the great adventure ahead of me.

The dormitory which was my home for the voyage was on one of the lower decks, and segregated from the troops. It was an open hold with several hundred hammocks strung up in rows. There were no cupboards. My clothes were kept in my travelling bag. We queued for everything – meals were served to us as if we were troops. We were not allowed to visit their quarters but at night it was not possible to keep some of the soldiers away from the few women on board, and vice versa.

Despite overcrowding and blackouts at night it was a memorable trip. Four days out, everything was called to a halt. The captain announced that the war in the West had ended in an Allied victory – the Nazis had finally surrendered.

The ship was a cacophony of cheering, shouting and celebration. There were tears and hugs. Civilians and soldiers let themselves go. A very moving service of thanksgiving was held in the open air under a blue cloudless sky, conducted by the Captain and several chaplains who were with us. As we were still close to the African coast, seagulls wheeled around us.

We were warned that blackout regulations would continue. There were still German U-boats around which could attack us, because they may not have had the news or refused to accept that Germany had surrendered.

The *Andes* had just been commissioned when the war broke out and had never been in civilian service. It was immediately converted into a troopship. It was able to travel alone, not in convoy; its speed could outdistance submarines as it zigzagged its way across the oceans.

On the tenth day we awoke to find our ship steaming slowly towards a peak on the horizon. To our surprise it was Gibraltar. We could see the shapes of several large ships anchored near the land. They were waiting to form a convoy to England. They had come from the Far East as well and were all troop carriers with returning war veterans. No chances were being taken on the last stage of the journey as there were submarines lurking in the waters of the Bay of Biscay and the English Channel.

As we came closer ships horns blared, minute figures waved at us from crowded decks. It was emotional moment for many of us and the soldiers on board. Small boats scurried around us with supplies. Later that day we sailed away, in what seemed an endless line of giants of the oceans – this time under the protection of warships.

Three days later, I awoke to the sound of a weather forecast given in impeccable English. It was the first time I had heard the BBC Home Service. I rushed to the porthole, and saw the brilliant green shores of England on a lovely summer day. I dressed in a great hurry; we crowded the rails as we steamed slowly past the patchwork quilt of hedgerows and green fields of the English countryside.

My first glimpse of England, from a distance, was everything I expected.

It was impossible to sleep that night. We were not told which port in England was our destination. The next morning when I woke the ship was stationary. We were outside the port of Liverpool.

The *Andes* had been edged into what seemed a partially reconstructed dock. The sight that greeted my eyes was of near total destruction. Around us there was hardly a building standing. I tried to take everything in, but we had to go through customs and immigration formalities before we could leave the ship.

In the excitement of the arrival I had no idea of what to expect. The day was grey, dull and cold. As we disembarked we were hurriedly put into buses and driven off to Aintree to the middle of the race course and told to wait there. Adding to the mystery were railway tracks on the race course.

Some while later a train drew up to take us to London. We clambered aboard. There was no chance to see more of Liverpool. What I saw of the docks and the city in the distance clearly showed the tremendous effects of wartime bombs. My memory of that day is mixed and unclear, but I do recall my emotional reaction to the damage inflicted by Nazi bombs. The first sight of the war's destruction was devastating.

Sparrows told me that when I got to London I should take the train to Bishop's Stortford in Hertfordshire where they had accommodation for me, because their original building in St Mary Axe in the City had received a direct hit and they had been evacuated to the country.

I learnt from several Londoners in my compartment that we would be arriving at St Pancras station about eight o'clock that evening. In order to get to the train to Bishops Stortford, I was told to take the Underground to Liverpool Street station and from there a train to Bishop's Stortford.

Nothing could be seen as we approached London into St Pancras because of the partial blackout. Grabbing my bag I walked along the platform looking for the Underground which I had been told to find. However I could not see it. In desperation I saw a soldier and asked him where it was. In a Yankee drawl he said that he did not know either – he was a stranger. So the first person I met in London was an American GI. It was a good start to my first day.

Eventually I found the Underground, and was soon on my way below the streets of London to Liverpool Street Station, where I bought a ticket for the waiting blacked-out train to Bishop's Stortford.

By this time I was exhausted. There were still two hours of travel ahead. I was not accustomed to the darkness because of the partial blackout.

Although it was two weeks after VE Day the British were not taking chances. It was a shock to my system on my first English day to be whisked from beautiful countryside to the loneliness of the blackout. I was cold and sat huddled for warmth in my coat. I had reached the stage of deflation, trying to rest as the train sped into the night. At last we arrived at what I presumed was Bishop's Stortford; there was nothing but blackness though I could hear voices outside the train.

The train was too long for the platform. As I clambered out and slowly walked alongside my eyes adjusted to the darkness. There were some shaded lights ahead of me and I made my way to them. The missing platform suddenly appeared. I struggled on to it with my bag, and wondered what I would do next, when a voice seemingly out of the dark called out:

"Mr Wilson, is that you?" I was flabbergasted that there was someone to meet me. I had been given an address and no meeting arrangements had been made, because it was difficult to communicate. I had carried out instructions given to me before I left South Africa and was wholly ignorant of what I would find at the other end.

"Yes," I called out into the blackness, "I'm Boris Wilson."

At that point a hand stretched out warmly clasping mine.

"Welcome to England. I'm Stanley Crabbe of Sparrows."

I could hardly speak. I was overwhelmed by the fact that there was someone to meet me well after midnight, in the dark, in an unknown place. I might as well have been on a desert island.

Stanley Crabbe, tall, dressed in an army coat, took my bag and I followed in the dark to his car, a pre-war Talbot, and we made our way to his house in Bishop's Stortford where he and the Sparrow business were situated.

In the light of the entrance hall I saw for the first time the well-built figure of a man with an angular face, a little moustache and a warm smile.

I was soon put at ease, shown a room and was expecting to fall into bed as I was dog-tired when Stanley said:

"You must be starved – did you have a meal today since you left Liverpool?"

I was embarrassed but admitted that I had not eaten and could do with something.

He took me by the arm.

"Come on," he said. "My wife has made you some bacon and eggs."

As I ate my way through a most delicious meal, two eggs and two rashers of bacon, we talked, getting to know each other. Then I fell into bed exhausted.

The next day I learnt that I had eaten Stanley Crabbe's entire monthly ration of bacon and eggs, which bothered my conscience for a long time after I left England.

I had arrived at a unique moment in England. Barely ten days had elapsed since the war had ended. Here I was in Britain, amongst strangers, ready to meet business associates and re-establish shipments of radios to South Africa, if and when I could get them. I had no idea what I would be seeing in England. In fact, looking back now, it amazes me that the British Trade Commissioner had the foresight to send me over when he did.

Talking to people every day in England was like speaking to people who were emerging from a dream or a nightmare. At first they could not comprehend that I was in England to carry out a peacetime function unrelated to the war – to buy British radio sets and ship them to South Africa.

Sparrows, through Stanley Crabbe, did not waste any time. The following day I met the company chairman at the nearby village of Much Hadham, and was delighted by what lay behind the beautiful old facade of the unspoilt village houses – quiet green gardens with the summer flowers and blossoms on the apple trees. Everyone was eager for news from me about South Africa which had not seen the ravages of war. That afternoon I was taken across country roads and lanes to visit EK Cole Ltd, where, to my surprise, flags were fluttering in the breeze in my honour. I was the first overseas business man to visit them since the war ended.

Eric Cole, the chairman, and I took to each other immediately. He was a very quiet unassuming man with a somewhat nervous laugh, giving the impression that he enjoyed his own jokes. Over the years we became very close friends. That day he took me around his factory and very apologetically told me that they had not yet started export designs, and felt it was better to begin production again with the designs they had when the war began five years earlier. During the war they had been major electronic manufacturers.

I paid several visits to them from London, where I had found a room in Knightsbridge at 7 Lowndes Street for three pounds a week which included breakfast. At the beginning I left myself very little time to look around London because I realised that unless I got to know what was going on at the Ekco factory my visit could be a failure since no export radio sets would be produced. So for the first few weeks, I went down to Southend twice a week, getting to know all the senior personnel and familiarising myself with factory production for 1945. It seemed that we would get nothing for about a year and the decision makers, the engineers and designers, were reluctant to use pre-war designs as had been earlier considered. I had to find another solution for supplies otherwise failure stared me in the face.

A few weeks after I arrived and had made several visits to the factory, I asked Eric Cole to accompany me on a walk through the main radio plant where I had noticed that radio sets were already being made for the home market and realised that if I could get some they were suitable for sale in South Africa. As we walked past the stacked sets I pointed to them.

"Eric, those sets for your home market would suit me for a start. I know they are not for export, they don't have all the wavelengths for short-wave, but I could put Ekco back on the South African market if you could let me have some."

He gave one of his nervous laughs.

"I don't know what home sales will have to say about this but we can ask them if you can have some. How many could you take?"

"Five hundred, providing they can be shipped to reach me before the end of the year. We could be the first on the market with a British set and it would be Ekco."

Eric Cole had a struggle with his staff about releasing the 500 sets for South Africa. They first refused to sell any for export. In the end it was agreed and I had achieved the main purpose of my visit. It had taken about six weeks. During this time I commuted on the drab, unkempt train from Fenchurch Street station having little time to explore partially blacked-out London streets congested in the West End with thousands of soldiers, sailors, airmen and American GIs milling about with few civilians.

The most striking memory I have of London was the terrible devastation from bombing and fires. St Paul's Cathedral stood alone in acres and acres of open space, broken walls and half-destroyed buildings. Flowers and grass grew where buildings once stood. In the East End near the River Thames and its docklands there was little to see because virtually all the houses and dock equipment were destroyed by Nazi bombs. Many City church towers stood like lonely skeletons, with naves bombed. I walked for miles until looking at the aftermath of the destruction. Often it brought tears to my eyes. By contrast it astonished me to walk into a local pub at night and see the returned soldiers, sailors and airmen celebrating the end of the war despite the formidable task that lay ahead in reconstructing Britain.

I was very lucky. Eric Cole lent me a car and as a visitor I was given a petrol ration which allowed me to visit Southend and further afield.

One of my first journeys was to Cambridge to savour what I had given up by not applying a second time for the Elsie Ballot scholarship. I had always dreamt about Cambridge and the first sight of the old colleges, the quiet gardens, the peace of the river Cam and the environment of the old university town made me sad for what I had missed.

Many of my London evenings were spent at the theatre, concerts at the Albert Hall, the Royal Ballet at Sadlers Wells, at the Angel in Islington. The excitement of buying a cheap seat for two shillings, and sitting high up in the "gods" looking down on the players or dancers was a unique experience.

I met many business people, friends of Eric Cole and Sparrows, and got to know some of the famous hotels and restaurants of London – the Savoy, Dorchester, Cafe Royal, Mirabelle and Etoile. On my own I visited many less famous restaurants where a good three course meal, by law, cost the huge sum of five shillings.

I discovered for myself all the tourist meccas ranging from Buckingham Palace to the Tower of London. The most memorable experiences were unexpected, such as the welcome the City of London gave to General

Eisenhower when it conferred the Freedom of the City on him. Tens of thousands of people – soldiers and civilians – crowded the streets and alleys in front of the Mansion House. I managed to get a position on a building opposite the main ceremonial platform and was able to hear and see General Eisenhower speaking. He was greeted with tremendous warmth and adulation by the large London crowd who were there to acclaim his military leadership in the victory over Nazi Germany.

Before I left South Africa I promised the National Union of South African Students that I would try and re-establish contact for them with the British Union of Students, whose first post-war conference was to be held in July at Leicester University. I drove there, introduced myself and the students were thrilled to have a voice from South Africa at this congress.

I was asked to address them and did so trying to explain the role South Africa played during the war, and its current political status. It became evident that there was, amongst the ex-service students, a strong movement against the Conservative government despite the great lead given by Churchill during the war. At Leicester I first heard talk of the welfare state and strong support for the Labour Party. The feeling was overwhelming that the Conservatives could not run the new society of post-war Britain.

I was not surprised on election day in July, at various constituencies, that voters were hoping to bring in a new era of social economic and political change in the country. The results of the first general election after the war started coming out during the night. I spent hours outside newspaper offices in Fleet Street cheering as results were posted showing huge Labour Party gains. The next day Londoners were delirious about the Labour victory over Winston Churchill's Conservatives. Clement Attlee formed the new Labour administration that was to take Britain headfirst into its post-war reconstruction after suffering so heavily in the cause of the world's democratic freedom.

24

I was reluctant to leave London. The days were passing too quickly. I had made many friends, experiencing the tremendous impact of the re-emerging cultural life of post-war London. There was a vitality as one toured the streets. The soft light and beauty of the English countryside during the long late summer evenings captivated me. It was hard to believe at times that this was the Britain that had not yet begun to recover from the terrible trauma of World War II.

I had achieved my objectives and had to be realistic. I had made up my mind that if I could get a seat on an aeroplane to America I would go there to see if I could find a domestic appliance franchise for South Africa despite the fact that America was still at war with Japan.

I had a stroke of luck. With the help of the US Department of Trade, I was told to stand by for a week and be ready to leave at short notice; they would try to book me on a special flight to New York. There were no commercial services to the USA. No one could tell me what sort of aircraft was available or from which airport I would leave, if in fact I would get away at all.

A few days later, on a cold, grey drizzly English day, I reported with a few other people to a RAF airport west of London. We were taken aboard a small twin-engined Dakota aircraft obviously used for military personnel and made a bumpy journey to an airport near Limerick in Ireland. We then went by coach through what appeared to be deserted villages and towns to the seaside port of the River Shannon. We had no information on what type of aircraft we were flying to the USA and were mystified because there was no evidence of a large airport in the area.

The mystery was soon solved. When we reached the estuary of the Shannon we saw our aeroplane for the journey across the Atlantic. It was a large four-engined Boeing Stratocruiser – a seaplane lying like a silver-blue whale on the calm water.

I had never seen such a large aircraft before and was excited by the prospect of flying in it. There were thirty passengers for the journey which surprised me. It was only when we boarded that I realised why so few were flying. The Stratocruiser was divided into two parts, the front had tables and chairs and the back of the aircraft had beds. We took off smoothly from the estuary and before long I was relaxing over a drink with other passengers.

The British Trade Office must have sponsored my visit to the USA because a number of the passengers were important political and military figures. The Stratocruiser, I learned, was used by the British and US governments during the war for crossings by senior military and political people of importance. It was luxuriously furnished providing every comfort for discussions and relaxation. I have never seen another commercial aircraft like it anywhere in all my years of international travel. After a good meal and a relaxed night's sleep in a bed, we landed at Gandar, Newfoundland where we stopped for fuel.

One more stop was made at Shediac in New Brunswick in Canada, where we took on two elderly ladies. An hour or so after we left Shediac, the purser came to me.

"Sir, two of our passengers who joined us at our last stop asked whether you would join them for a cup of tea. They would like to meet you."

"Are you sure it's me they want to speak to?"

"Yes, sir."

I followed him and was introduced to the two charming New England women, sisters, both grey-haired and elderly.

"Mr Wilson, we are delighted that you are visiting America. We have never met anyone from South Africa before. Do tell us about your country?"

Over cups of tea we chatted away. They asked many questions about South Africa. I did my best to give them a long-distance view of the country, its peoples and how beautiful it was. I was surprised by the interest they displayed.

As I got up to leave them, one of the sisters said:

"Before you go, do tell us – is South Africa anywhere near Casablanca?"

Later in New York I realised how little Americans knew about South Africa and when they did know something they expected me to be black, not white.

25

It is not easy to describe my arrival in New York for the first time in July 1945. Driving from La Guardia airport, one sees the great cluster of towering buildings in the distant haze coming closer and closer. Suddenly when the Hudson River is crossed one is overwhelmed by the buildings and deafening noise. The impact is electric.

In the middle of summer the heat is oppressive, the traffic noise cacophonic with non-stop hooting from large Buicks and Cadillacs mixed with swarms of Yellow Cabs. Looking up the narrow streets there is the endless perspective of the tall buildings trying to escape into the blue sky.

My hotel overlooked Central Park and it was about six o'clock in the late afternoon when I checked in. My business discussions were to begin the next day and I decided that the sooner I tried to find my father's brother the better, as I could get involved in business discussions that could take me out of New York.

Where to start?

In the hotel room I picked up the huge telephone directory and started paging through the list of Tobins with the initial "M" hoping there might be a Meyer Tobin. My search was fruitless. There must have been about twenty pages of Tobins but despite going through the list several times I could find no Meyer Tobin listed in Brooklyn.

I was just about to telephone enquiries when I noticed another large telephone book. It was boldly headed Brooklyn. I was unaware that there were separate telephone directories. Once more I began the exercise, paging through hundreds of Brooklyn Tobins – Irish Tobins, Jewish Tobins and unidentified Tobins.

Under the "M" Tobins I could not believe my eyes. There was only one first name listed – it was a Meyer Tobin, at an address in Brooklyn. Was this my father's brother, an individualist amongst the hundreds of "M" Tobins in the directory?

I dialed the number and waited. A man answered the call in a slow measured way, in a voice sounding exactly like my father's. I was so taken aback at the familiarity of the voice on the telephone that, for a moment, I was silent.

He spoke again. "Who do you want ?"

There was no doubt that this man was my father's brother. It was uncanny. Gathering my thoughts I answered.

"My name is Boris Wilson and I come from South Africa. Are you Meyer Tobin?"

"Yes."

"Do you have an older brother whom you have not seen for about thirty years? If so I am his eldest son. Before I left South Africa several months ago, my father, who is called Samuel Wilson told me about his younger brother who lived in Brooklyn in New York."

There was no response from the voice at the other end. I continued to speak.

"Father asked me to find out whether his brother was still in Brooklyn and to make contact with him. I have just arrived today from England."

There was still no response. All I could hear was breathing which had become faster. Then the silence was broken.

"Did you say your name was Boris?"

It was uncanny how similar the man's voice was to my father's – only the Brooklyn accent was more marked.

"Yes."

"I had a brother – his name was not Samuel Wilson. My name is Meyer Tobin – my brother left America over thirty years ago – I have never spoken to him since that day."

He said it in such a way that I felt I wanted to ask him why he and my father had not communicated with each other for so long.

Once more a silence.

"Where are you now?"

"I am at the St Moritz Hotel opposite Central Park."

"Can you come and see me tonight?"

"Yes, I can."

Meyer Tobin then gave me precise instructions how to reach him, which went something like this:

"Take the Sixth Avenue Express to Coney Island, change to the "A" train, then at 70th Street take the Culver Line."

It was about seven o'clock in the evening when I left the hotel and walked for the first time in the streets of New York. The St Moritz Hotel was on the corner of Sixth Avenue and 59th Street, and I went down Sixth Avenue looking for a sign such as London has indicating the Underground system. I could hear rumbling under the pavement as I imagined trains rushing by.

Periodically, steam rose up through pavement grates which was strange. The speeding cars, the yellow cabs and their klaxons, drug stores, flashing

119

neon lights, lightly clad New Yorkers in the early evening heat gave no indication that America was still at war with Japan.

It was a shock to enter the hot, dirty-drab subway station, full of New York commuters. But carrying out Meyer Tobin's instructions I affected all the train changes and about ninety minutes later left the elevated section of the subway system.

It was nearly 8.30 and dark, but I found the Tobin house and knocked at the door. It was opened after a moment or two. In the light of the room I saw a short man with thinning hair, squarish face and a firm expression.

The man was, without any question, related to my father. I knew I had found my Uncle Meyer Tobin of Brooklyn.

I forget what he said, but I went into the house and we sat down in the small simply-furnished lounge. The conversation began slowly. He asked me to talk first and tell him all I knew and how I had come to look for him in New York. He said little but kept looking very intently at me.

It was not easy to start but I gave him a quick resumé of our South African family's history, how I came to be in New York and amongst other things was looking for Meyer Tobin of Brooklyn.

At close quarters his resemblance to my father was confirmed. They not only looked alike, but spoke alike with the exception of the pronounced Brooklyn accent and Meyer looked liked a tired old man.

He neither confirmed or denied his relationship with my father, which was interesting. I had the feeling he was still weighing me up and unwilling to commit himself. His wife and two daughters were away, and he had a son, the eldest, who was a lawyer. His name was Boris. That was a coincidence and I hoped to learn more about him later.

We spoke for several hours over cups of Russian tea, and he conceded that he and my father were brothers. However, he was very cautious in divulging information or disclosing his feelings. When I rose to leave it was late. He refused to let me go and said I should stay the night.

Six weeks rushed by during which time I met my aunt, Lottie and Ruth the two daughters, and Boris the lawyer. In between attending to my business and visiting Boston, Cleveland and Chicago, I learnt a great deal about my new-found relations and my father's early days in New York, but few details about the family's early life in Russia. The Tobins appeared to be as reticent as my father in talking about their Russian background.

In Boston, I saw the eminent orthopaedic surgeon Smith-Petersen about my back troubles. He told me not to worry as I had sacroiliac bone disease which would not spread further up the spine. Regrettably his prognosis proved wrong. It did travel, in time, up the spine.

One evening about midnight I was returning to New York from Boston on the train when I realised on approaching Grand Central Station that the one place I should go to as soon as we arrived was Times Square. On the train an announcement had been made that the war with Japan had ended. I imagined that many New Yorkers would be celebrating the final end of World War II in Times Square.

I was right.

I took the shuttle to Times Square. From there it became a struggle to get into Times Square because of the crush of people trying to do the same thing. It was like daylight when I eventually got into the square, pushed by the force of the crowds behind me.

The noise of the cheering, singing, crying, shouting million or so New Yorkers who packed Times Square that night defied description. I just became part of it. Every neon sign was flashing, so that I was able to take pictures with my Brownie Box camera by simply pressing the shutter at will. Most of the time the crush of the crowd was so strong that I was unable to move, but kept changing direction because of the pressures from all sides.

Soldiers, sailors and airman were hoisted on to cars, cheered, kissed and thrown into the air. I saw women weeping alone when I managed to push myself to the periphery of the mass. Blacks were embracing whites, voices singing were drowned at times by sirens and the celebrations of final victory went on all night.

It was six in the morning before I managed to get myself out of Times Square, tired, exhilarated but thrilled that I had witnessed the uncontrolled joy of Americans saying goodbye to World War II.

My visit to the USA turned out trumps. I acquired a valuable domestic appliance franchise for South Africa. I said goodbye to my relatives who had been very kind. One of my cousins told me that my father and his brother Meyer had a serious family disagreement which led to their estrangement. Father left New York for Denver and eventually left the United States without saying where he was going.

I struggled to get a ship back to South Africa and eventually did so via England, where I spent a few more weeks and eventually arrived in Cape Town late in October 1945.

After I had settled my business affairs the first priority was to get back to Medical School to see if the Dean, Professor Watts, would let me write the examinations in February as I did not want to lose a year. He refused, probably quite rightly and I had to accept the fact that I would repeat Fourth Year in 1946.

As soon as I could, I went to see my father in Sydenham and told him in detail how I had found his brother Meyer Tobin and his family. He asked me many questions and at times seemed overcome with emotion. He told me he would write a letter to Meyer, which he did. I learned from Max that he telephoned Meyer in New York a few days later.

Despite further questions from me, my father was reluctant to throw any light on why his brother's surname was Tobin and his Wilson.

Mike Kruger was very pleased with the results of the trip and a few days before Christmas our first shipment of Ekco Radio arrived in South Africa. It was the first consignment of radios to reach the country after the war.

26

In South Africa it was seven months since the war had ended. Thousands of servicemen and women were coming back into civilian life while General Smuts was active on the international stage helping to found the United Nations.

Although the country had not directly suffered from the physical effects of the war, social conditions and rehabilitation were the important issues needing the government's urgent attention. One sensed amongst returning South African ex-servicemen that a major political change was imminent similar to the switch from the Conservatives in Britain to Labour because of the overwhelming need for policies of social and economic reform.

It had become increasingly clear that Smuts's United Party and its wartime coalition partner, the Labour Party, were too involved in the aftermath of the successful ending of the war to get their political priorities right. General Smuts in particular paid little attention to urgent internal matters while enjoying international acclaim. Important matters like the National Health Services Commission Report were still pigeon-holed. Housing of the returning soldiers, the prospect looming of serious "native problems", getting people back into jobs, training youngsters who had gone straight from school into the army and were now adults with few other skills, all had to be addressed by the government.

Failure to implement promises helped to fuel a serious undercurrent of protest against Smuts and the United Party. The Labour Party was too small to do anything of consequence and had little public support. Amongst the blacks there was evidence of serious disquiet in their leadership.

I had no time to participate in politics to the extent I would have liked, because I had a lot to do at the business and the Medical School.

Since fourth year medicine involved clinical training in the wards, it meant my nights were almost wholly dedicated to clinical work at the hospital. In a way, it suited me because I did most of my ward work at night as before with the advantage of seeing the acute cases. I knew the hospital better than most of my fellow students. During the day everything was organised, with many diversions. Often at night, when I was the only student "hanging about" I could follow an admission case from Casualty, to the ward, on to theatre for surgery or to the mortuary.

Casualty provided the main interest and excitement. Serious accident cases, alcoholics, drug addicts, attempted suicides, acute heart attacks, unusual diseases, resuscitation attempts were only part of the kaleidoscope and diversity of night time hospital admissions. Although I was forced by circumstance to do things this way I reaped great benefits in my training. During 1946 I became more competent in diagnosing and understanding causes of disease. The many late hours that I spent in Casualty and subsequently in the wards until early hours of the morning made up for the lectures and demonstrations that I often had to miss during the day because of business commitments.

Of course I had to find time to read and study. This I would try and fit in during the day in the quiet of the Medical School library, but this was less frequent than I would have liked.

Sometime in June 1946 my brother Leon, who had been "up North" in the Sixth Armoured Brigade returned to South Africa. He was offered his pre-war job back by his old firm at the same salary of five pounds per month which he received when he joined the army in 1941. Not much of a reward for a Captain in the Signals Corps. Mike and I decided it would be much better if he joined us as our first branch manager opening the Cape Town office of our company.

The business was rapidly expanding. We were regularly receiving radio and domestic appliance stocks which sold very quickly. The medical book section performed equally well.

I passed fourth year at the end of 1946, and in fifth year during 1947 an unexpected and serious problem arose. It was becoming very evident that Mike Kruger was growing more and more depressed at work. He used to sit at his desk hunched in his seat and deep in thought for hours, his left hand supporting his chin and staring into space. All my enquiries were rebuffed.

Important daily tasks at the shop were not receiving attention. When I was at the administrative offices during the day I would have to spend a lot of time trying to get him to deal with various urgent matters. We could not avoid altercations which became increasingly unpleasant. I was doing more and more, when in the year before finals I should have been doing less in the shop.

It was clear we were heading for a personal and business crisis. The final examinations were due in October 1948 and I was expecting that Mike would carry at least his share of the responsibility which was the intention when I took him into the business.

A new development added to my worries. The Medical and Dental Council announced that, from the end of 1948, all medical graduates would have to undergo a year's full-time compulsory housemanship. It was a severe shock. This would compound the already serious problems with Mike Kruger. It was not possible for me to do a full-time house-manship if I was completely involved in the business. The way things were going with my partner made the future now very uncertain.

I spent sleepless nights wracking my brains for a solution to all the problems. I was becoming depressed. One thing was sure: it was unlikely that Mike and I could continue much longer. Before everything collapsed I decided to take action. Mike Kruger had to go if we could not resolve our problems; the sooner the better so I could reorganise. I would employ a manager for the shop and control everything from my nearby offices. Although I had not worked everything out I decided that, whatever the consequences, this is what I would do.

As for the compulsory housemanship, I would deal with that when Mike had left the company.

I spoke to him one evening at the shop in an attempt to get at the root of his dissatisfaction – perhaps it was possible even at this stage for us to resolve our differences.

"Mike, you've been very depressed and uncooperative lately. I've tried to find out why, but you aren't very helpful. What has gone wrong?"

"Nothing."

"How can you say that?"

He was silent, refusing to look at me and to answer questions.

"Mike, there is something important but you won't tell me. If you won't we cannot go on like this. Finals are coming up next year. In our joint interests we had better resolve our problems now."

Then the thing I wanted to avoid happened. The discussion deteriorated into a hurtful personal argument. He suddenly broke it off.

"I am going to see my lawyer about it all."

Once he took this line I felt that we had come to the end of the road. He had to go. One way or the other I would buy him out. Unfortunately, during the years of our association we both used the same lawyer, never expecting this would happen. I had to get a new lawyer to look after my interests.

We held a meeting with both lawyers present. Mike's lawyer tried some bullying, trying to force an unacceptable solution on me. I agreed to pay Mike Kruger the enormous sum of twelve thousand pounds for his half-share of the business, over a period of three years. Guarantees were demanded from me, but I refused point-blank. In the end the deal was struck. Mike Kruger had done very well. His total investment had been five hundred pounds, paid for out of his profits from the business. After four years he was being paid a large sum of money for his half-share. I reckoned it was well worth it. As the business was expanding I was confident that the money would be found to pay him when due.

As soon as the partnership broke up I appointed a manager for the shop. Naturally, it meant much more of my time at the business, but as year-end holidays were approaching, this was less serious than it might have been. Of course I had to face up to the fact that some managers might not be satisfactory, and during 1948 I had to make several changes.

I was so involved in dealing with the daily routine of the medical curriculum that I felt I was on a merry-go-round. Early in the morning I would rush across Klein Street in a white coat with my stethoscope trailing, a quick visit to Casualty, then to a medical or surgical ward to inspect whatever of the night's intake that I might have missed, although I might have been at the hospital a few short hours previously. At nine o'clock there would be a formal ward round. Often I had seen all the cases and knew all about them, to the envy of some of my friends.

Then I would race by car to the business where I dealt with shop matters, administration problems, correspondence and telephone calls to Cape Town or the new Durban branch – or I might have a business conference – then off to the Medical School again . . .

I made sure that I attended the medical seminar in the Hospital Lecture Theatre every day at eleven in the morning. After this I would lunch with my friends in the students' refectory before again returning to the business.

The afternoons offered some variation. Such free time as I had was spent at the business. As likely as not, I ended the normal working day at the office.

After a short rest and dinner which I often prepared, I would start the evening's work at the hospital, mostly centred around Casualty. The interesting cases, surgical or medical, would determine where I would spend most of the night.

It was midnight or considerably later before I would give up and go back to the flat, dog-tired. If I was involved in surgery, I would follow the cases not only to the wards but to the theatre if an urgent operation was to be performed. I would ask if I could "scrub up" and assist the surgeon. In this way I gathered much of my surgical knowledge at firsthand. Often the sun would be rising when I reached home.

I enjoyed it all. It meant however that the pressure was tremendous. While I was interested in the momentous political events of post-war South Africa I was on the sidelines, only able to take a passing glance at what was happening. Politics was on the back burner for me.

In 1946 the Labour Party adopted a more liberal "Native Policy" resulting in a party crisis. Walter Madeley, its leader, resigned. Smuts appointed Judge Fagan to head a commission into Native Affairs which was due to report back in 1948. The blacks were making it difficult for Smuts. There was pressure from the African National Congress, boycotts by urban Africans in response to high bus fares and a large strike by black mineworkers There were strong moves by the Africans to get rid of the Pass Laws. The Native Representative Council asked Smuts, through their white Native Representatives in Parliament, for a new constitutional deal and Smuts said he would consider it.

Enmeshed as I was in medicine and the business, all these political events were peripheral as far as I was concerned. On top of all the problems I could see no solution to the compulsory housemanship at the end of 1948 when I was due to qualify.

I decided the best way to deal with the latter question was to ask the Dean of the Medical School whether anything could be done so that I could, if necessary, avoid the housemanship after qualification. Before visiting him, I read the relevant sections in the university calendar *vis-à-vis* requirements for the MB.BCh. degree, to see if I could get an inspired solution to my difficulties with the forthcoming compulsory housemanship.

To my surprise I learnt that the writing of final examinations was dependent on the number of clinical terms spent at the Medical School and not the calendar years as everyone assumed. Was there a case to put to the Dean that I could write in the middle of 1948 instead of October? If I could do so and pass the finals, I could avoid the compulsory housemanship. Reminding myself that I had interrupted the course in May 1945 to go overseas with about six weeks to go to term-end, could I convince the Dean that I had in fact completed my full clinical terms by mid-1948?

It was a challenge that had to be accepted and fought out.

I saw the heavily-built, moustached Dean, the Professor of Pharmacology James Watts.

"Sit down, Boris Wilson, what is it this time?"

Professor Watts knew me well. It was he who compelled me to repeat fourth year on my return from America.

"Professor Watts, I want to write my final examination in June and not December next year."

He interrupted me.

"You can't do that – your clinical year ends in the second half of the year."

"Professor, it should do so but in fact it ends earlier. You recall you made me repeat fourth year, but I had already nearly completed the first clinical term of that year when I went overseas. I've looked up the regulations. If you total the clinical terms I've been at Medical School I will have satisfied the requirements by the end of June."

"Rubbish."

He grabbed the calendar from me and read the relevant section.

"This has never happened before and I don't think I can allow you to write earlier than the year end."

We exchanged rapid and, at times, heated arguments. "Professor, I have the right to sit for the examination, and I intend to do so."

He glowered at me, and rose from his chair towering over me.

"Get out of my office," he shouted at me. "Get out, I don't care what you do."

I stood and slowly retreated backwards to the door.

"Professor, I'm going to write the examinations in June."

I left him shouting at me through the half-open door. I was in the clouds. I had overcome my most important hurdle. It was September 1947, and with less than nine months left, I was going to have a terrible battle to prepare for the Finals. However, I could do so without anguish regarding compulsory housemanship. I think Professor Watts secretly hoped I would make it. He subsequently took an interest in what I was doing and became a firm friend in later years.

Fortunately, there was a special group of ex-service students who had interrupted their medical course to fight the Nazis "up North". They were receiving special tutorials in certain subjects and were writing in June. I asked if I could join their group, to which they agreed, and preparation for my finals became a lot easier.

The pressure of running the business with little time before the examinations was enormous. I was working round the clock. To complicate things there were continuing difficulties with managers in the business. Post-war trade was expanding, because returning soldiers were setting up homes and I was selling all the radio sets I could import.

Personal problems did not escape me at this time.

I had met a young university student, who was also in her final year in Native Law and Administration. She was visiting a friend in the Pathology Laboratory when I first saw her a year earlier. We were in love, but there were family pressures on her to break the relationship with me.

A month before the finals, I could see that she was suffering from serious emotional stress. She was indecisive about our future, and ten days before I was due to start writing the examinations, Pauline terminated her association with me.

It was a terrible blow. The whole rhythm of my preparation for the examinations was interrupted. I lay awake, unable to sleep, making up my mind whether to accept her decision or not. In the early hours of the morning I came to the conclusion that she was as unhappy as I was. She was attached to her parents and respected their views. I was a Jew and an atheist; she came from 1820 settler stock in Natal with a long Anglican history.

That morning I would have to know whether she would marry me or not and I was determined to get a decision. I could not go on to write Finals which began the following week, engulfed in emotional trauma. If Pauline changed her mind and was prepared to get married we would do so in a civil ceremony before the week was out. Otherwise there was no option but to shut her out of my mind, if that was possible. I did not want crippling distractions while I was writing examinations which lasted about six weeks, with *vivas*, practicals and written papers almost every day.

Just after six in the morning I left my flat and drove out to the lodging house where Pauline lived. I knocked at the door of her room. Without speaking too loudly I told her I was outside.

I went in. She was lying in bed half-awake. I put my case to her and said that either we get married because we are the ones who count or we forget about our relationship.

I had done the right thing. She agreed to marry me. She told me afterwards that she had expected me to ask her months before, but as I did not do so the family pressures mounted and she decided to follow their advice.

We decided that we would marry by civil ceremony on the following Saturday, 1 May 1948, and telephoned her family who were in Pietermaritzburg. We did so at eight o'clock that morning. They were shocked by the news, but could do nothing about it and promised to come up for the ceremony.

We were duly married in the company of Pauline's family who came to Johannesburg the day before. We managed to organise a small celebration at a nearby hotel, and our "honeymoon" was spent that weekend at my flat.

On Tuesday 4 May, I started Finals with my long surgical case.

The strain of the six weeks was tremendous – but at least I was emotionally secure. The long case in Surgery nearly turned into a disaster for me. I could not remember some simple anatomy which did not surprise me. I had been through punishing times and expected setbacks. On the other hand there were breaks in my favour. I was shown X-rays in one oral examination which I correctly diagnosed. The next day the same ones were presented to me by another examiner. Luck was with me.

In the short surgical cases I was asked to examine a black man sitting hunched on a bed in an upright and uncomfortable position. I ran a hand down his spine and immediately concluded that he was an advanced case of Ankylosing Spondilitis, the spinal disease which afflicted me. I was right.

At times the Medicine *vivas* were difficult. I was unable to diagnose the cardiac case shown me. A few years afterwards I was told that as I was pacing a courtyard anxiously waiting to be called for the *viva* the Professor of Medicine told the other examiners that unless I had made a mess of the written papers and orals, he was going to pass me in Medicine. He gave as his reason that when he used to leave his office late at night or in the early hours of the morning, I might be seen with a patient going to the wards or walking alone in deserted hospital corridors. He said that I was often the only student he saw walking the hospital wards at night.

In the midst of all the Finals, General Smuts went to the country in its first post-war election, having concluded a pact with the Labour Party who were given six safe seats. On 26 May Smuts received the shock of his life. Like the British electorate three years earlier, the country turned him down and voted in Dr Malan's National Party with a slender majority of four seats. It shocked everyone who had given Smuts unstinted support throughout the war, and was a source of jubilation to the Nationalists, many of whom had opposed the war. It was the beginning of the apartheid era that was to socially and politically traumatise South Africa for decades to come.

The election was not an important event in my life at that stage despite its historical significance. I was nearing the end of my long drawn-out Finals. I was the only student in South Africa who had been in England when Churchill was rejected three years back, but my sights were directed completely away from political matters. One of the vivid reminders was hearing Dr Malan, the National Party leader, speaking on the radio in a very sombre voice before the voting took place, telling the voters to *"Dink, Dink, Dink voordat jy jou kruisie maak."* – Think, Think, Think before you make your cross.

The Finals were over at long last. I was in a state of utter exhaustion. The results were due the following day. It was a Saturday morning and Pauline and I went to Medical School.

We had been waiting for about an hour watching the notice boards. Suddenly there was shouting and jostling. The results were out.

I managed to struggle through the crowd to the lists. I saw at the end of the list: Wilson, B: Medicine, Pass. Surgery, Pass. Obstetrics and Gynae-cology, Pass.

I was through. I had succeeded. I grabbed Pauline and we hugged and shouted, congratulating all my ex-service friends who had also passed. No one had failed. It was great moment.

The jubilation and noise was almost like Times Square – a "VJ" night in miniature. The big battle was over. I was a qualified medical doctor at long last. Six and a half busy years had passed since I started to study medicine.

Here I was – Dr Boris Wilson MB.BCh., plus Pauline and the expanding Kruger and Wilson (Pty) Ltd.

My father was pleased in his undemonstrative way to hear the news. My one regret was that Poppy was no longer alive to celebrate with us, since she encouraged and helped me come to the decision to do medicine.

27

After the weekend and glowing with success I came down to earth. The future had to be reviewed and important decisions taken.

Was I going to sell the business and go into full-time medicine? Was there a way of maintaining the business and making medicine my career? When I started medical training I did so because I was deeply interested in the social and political aspects of health and disease. It was always my intention to return to politics and apply my medical knowledge in a constructive manner.

Things had changed since I commenced the course. The war had ended. Nazism was dead. South Africa had an unknown Nationalist Government. The United Party-Labour Party coalition was collapsing. The black people of South Africa were stirring and raising their voices for a better share of South Africa's post-war economic and political life.

Where did I fit in?

In terms of my original objectives I had not foreseen that when I qualified, I would be the sole owner of the business. I had always imagined that my business partner would have been there.

The practice of medicine and the return to politics would have been easier to pursue. Like most people, I did not expect Smuts to be defeated, although I should have been warned because of what I saw in Britain. I had been closeted in the Medical School with business and politics taking a back seat.

So, decisions had to be made.

Writing in June to avoid compulsory housemanship had been, in retrospect, a wise move.

One thing I knew was that, whatever else I did, I was yearning to get back to politics. It was an important time to do so, because the country was being lead into the political unknown by the Nationalists. No doubt there were going to be volatile and stirring times ahead for white and black South Africans. A strong white opposition was needed to deal with the sectarian threats of Afrikaner Nationalism.

Becoming a doctor satisfied my ego, but I had to ask myself again why I had done it. It would be entirely wasted if I did not make use of my clinical knowledge, because there was no denying that I had become intensely interested in general medicine apart from the wider horizons and political implications I had in mind.

Business responsibilities were now much greater. I hoped I would have more time to devote to it, whatever decision I made. The pressures of the Medical School were gone. There was a reluctance on my part to dispose of the business in any event apart from the fact that it was not easy to get rid of financial commitments at a stroke. Although I reminded myself I never wanted to be in business, I had to admit that the money I was making could help me in a political and medical career.

Compromise solutions stared me in the face. Would I take them? I wanted to get more clinical experience without doing the housemanship. There were several ways – locums for colleagues and casualty work at night and weekends. The latter offered me the princely sum of fifty pounds a month. I could not live on that sort of money and I was earning very much more in the business. I decided on the medical locums.

I would also take an active part in medical politics. I would maintain the business and streamline its organisation. As soon as possible I would try and sell the medical bookshop because I felt it unethical to maintain it as a qualified doctor. There was a new medical bookshop competitor, who was agreeable to buying me out. I did a deal selling them the total stock of books. At the time this happened my friends in the Labour Party urged me to come back to active politics and I was considering what I would do about this request.

My relationship with my father was much better. There was more understanding on both sides. I saw him frequently. He was still at the Market, helped by Ida. Business conditions had apparently improved and his financial problems were over. He still wrote letters to the newspapers, using Max to do the physical writing. He still had serious problems with Max, who was running true to form.

A year before the war ended Max disappeared. No one could find him. Eventually after six months he was found under the alias of Thomas Maxwell Wilson in the army at Potchefstroom military camp. He had bluffed his way into the army. Although he was only fifteen, he looked much older. My father had him removed and he was brought home, and sent to a private day school in Johannesburg. That did not last long. Once again he vanished. Father was very upset because despite all the troubles he was having with Max, he was no longer rejecting him but tried to look after him as best he could. I suspect this happened because I had made clear that because of my studies I could not be involved.

Max was not heard of until the end of the war. I was overseas when he was found. This time it was the Navy, and he was under the false name of Desmond J Leaney. Father gave up. Max was sixteen, removed from both Navy and school and found a job.

My business associates overseas were delighted to hear that now that I had qualified, I would be taking a firm grip on the business.

Some of them were sceptical about my future in the company, and were holding up new contracts. I was able to reassure them I was not giving up.

The business was improving all the time and I was thinking of further expansion.

I started medical locums at night and was appalled at the long hours general practitioners worked and how badly they were paid. I recall receiving all the fees from a doctor for whom I did calls while she was away, and it worked out at an average of about thirty shillings a visit to private patients at their homes in wealthy Johannesburg, which included the use of my car. I had already joined the Medical Association and was determined, at an appropriate time, to discuss with them not only the question of GP fees but their disinterested attitude towards the National Health Services Commission Report which both Smuts and the Nationalists had ditched.

28

My first political move was to get back to the Labour Party. I was immediately co-opted to the NEC and made assistant general secretary, an honorary post. It suited me because having been out of political life for so many years I was back at the top in the thick of Labour politics.

The party was in severe financial difficulty losing support at all levels. The larger trade unions no longer supported it. Most of them had been won over by the Nationalists. Trade unions were also barred by law from participating in political parties. As a result the Labour Party had become almost irrelevant. Smuts and then the Nationalists made sure that unions could not officially become multiracial. The large Mine Workers Union was now a white militant anti-black union.

All the trade unions now supporting the LP were small. Solly Sachs, an ex-Communist, was the general secretary of the Garment Workers Union and wielded an undue influence in the party. Ben Weinbren of the Laundry Workers was equally important. In 1946, a year after the war ended, there was still a split in the party over its more "liberal" approach to "Native Affairs", but still supporting residential separation. This pseudo-liberal drift helped to push many of its white trade unionists into the waiting arms of the Nationalists.

The small number of constituency members of the LP were completely overshadowed by the unions controlled by Sachs and Weinbren, who manipulated the card vote at annual congresses, so that the party's policies and the character of the National Executive was dictated by them.

One benefit of my NEC position was my friendship with the leader of the party, John Christie, a charming old Scotsman who replaced Walter Madeley when the latter resigned over the party's more progressive policy towards Indians.

John Christie tried his best to keep the right and left wings of the party in some kind of cohesion. However, on visits to his flat he told me all was not well in the LP because of the militant left wingers. He was getting older, enjoyed political life and his role in Parliament, and was all for peace. He was a wealthy man, a pharmacist who still had his shop in Mayfair, Johannesburg.

The LP General Secretary was Jessie MacPherson a large woman, a town councillor, who worked very closely with Weinbren and Sachs.

The LP was represented in the Johannesburg council, amongst whom there were a few bright stars, such as Colin Legum who subsequently left South Africa and joined *The Observer* in London, and Dave Epstein a lawyer who was also in the Transvaal Provincial Council.

The right wing of the party was distinguished by my friends Dr Tom Osborn and Margaret Mackenzie. In a sense I had aligned myself with the right wing of the Labour Party.

The Labour Party's survival depended on coalition with the United Party. At the last minute it succeeded in coming to agreement with Smuts for the 1948 election giving it six MPs. Leading parliamentarians were Tom Osborn and Alex Hepple, Tom having been elected when Madeley died. In the Senate, John Duthie was our sole representative.

The United Party under General Smuts after the disastrous defeat in the 1948 election was in a slough of despondency. Smuts had been the victim of a number of factors which lost him the election.

Failure to carry out reforms during the war, his paternalistic attitude to "Natives", the total rejection by conservative whites of Jan Hofmeyr's liberalism, accentuated the drift to the right into the arms of the unified Nationalists. Added to this was the fear of a deluge of English-speaking immigrants after the war.

The white Trade Unionists now in Nationalist ranks demanded intensification of the colour bar in industry, and loud was the rallying cry of Nationalists that had won them many elections, the *swart gevaar* – the black danger. All this brought Dr Malan to victory. The new 1942 constitution of the National Party, largely ignored by the English-speaking whites, set out the pattern of segregation – the future apartheid system.

The Labour Party was also in for shocks. The United Party refused to continue its electoral pact in the Provincial elections in 1949. Negotiations reached a crisis point and we had angry meetings with them. The UP said they wanted "friendly tussles" with us. On 17 August I issued a statement on behalf of the party criticising the UP of "flippancy" and accusing the UP of learning nothing from their general election defeat and wanting to leave the Nationalists in power. The LP at that time had twelve seats in the Provincial Council and one member on its Executive.

I accused the UP of ineffectual leadership and lack of policy. The "friendly tussles" left us with a reduced number of Labour MPCs in the Transvaal Provincial Council and no Executive seat. The result showed how weak the LP was as an independent party. Internal feuding between right and left increased and morale was low.

It took some time for me to realise that I was in a dying political movement. Tom Osborn and Margaret MacKenzie still thought there was a future for the Labour Party if the policies could be "modernised" and we could somehow bring right and left together. We tried to point out that the enemy we were facing was not the United Party but the Nationalists. They had won over most of the labour movement but "white" unions were prepared to sacrifice political freedom for the security of "white" jobs

All this perturbed me. I wrote several newspaper articles analysing the situation, with solutions. The impact was minimal. Trade Unionists were not interested in my views. As constituency members most of us came from "wealthy" northern suburb areas – in reality we were armchair socialists, anachronistic and dilettante, tolerated by our trade union colleagues because our money was needed. We were relics of the 1930 protest period.

Apart from money, we spent most of the time in the LP talking, with very little activism.

Tom Osborn was due to speak at a public meeting in East London on 24 September. The day before, in Port Elizabeth, he took ill. He had a valvular problem with his heart and sudden failure had occurred. He was hospitalised. I was urgently asked to speak in his place at the East London City hall.

To a small audience of the faithful, I called for "leadership in South Africa. We must uphold democracy imperilled by the present government. The United Party opposition is weak. South Africa needs a strong third party to hold the balance of power to protect the constitution."

I reminded the audience that the week before in the Johannesburg City Hall "an organised mob stormed a Trade Union meeting and the police, who were informed of the attempt to break up the meeting, were not present. When they did arrive they stood by and did nothing. This is mob violence. Are we going to stand idly by and let this go on? If we do, we are sounding the death knell of democracy in South Africa."

Brave words at the time, but in my heart I knew the socialists to whom I spoke had been politically outmanoeuvred and the LP would not be able to stop the Nationalist regime.

The Nationalists did not waste time. They were on the march, bent on carrying out the provisions of their 1942 Constitution, and were preparing the ground for full-scale apartheid.

The United Party plan to bring in immigrants from overseas was ditched pending a Bill to change the immigration laws. The Nationalists increased their small parliamentary majority from four to ten by incorporating South West Africa into Parliament giving them an additional six seats – all Nationalist MPs.

To get support from ex-servicemen Dr Malan announced he would implement some of Smuts's post-war promises while making plans to stop racial integration. The token Indian franchise was abolished by the Asiatic Laws Amendment Act.

The first moves to dismantle the previous government's infrastructure for the blacks, coloureds and Indians were under way. The legal black organisations at the time like the African National Congress, aware of the threat to their freedom by the Nationalists, met at Bloemfontein with a rallying call warning the country of the dangers ahead.

The New Year started with the most serious riots that South Africa had ever seen. Zulus in Durban went amok and attacked Indians. One hundred and forty were killed and over a thousand were injured. The Minister of Justice "Blackie" Swart said that Communism was a danger to South Africa. The Secretary of Native Affairs Eiselen started moves to take over Mission schools, which had provided education in the rural areas to blacks.

In general, those of us who for years had studied the political scene in the country were now apprehensive about the socio-political plans of Dr Malan's government.

In the midst of all this apprehension, Tom Osborn lay dying in Cape Town. Despite his weakened condition he made a few appearances in Parliament, speaking brilliantly for the Labour opposition.

One Tuesday in mid-July, I learnt from Margaret Mackenzie that he could not last long. I flew to Cape Town late that afternoon, saw him propped up in bed, pale, breathless and hardly able to speak. He was aware he was dying. I left him with a smile on his face and a handshake. He died two days later.

The sad part about his death was that if he could have survived for two years he could have had a valve replacement for his heart which would have saved his life. When Tom died new valves in the heart were uncharted territory.

In an appreciation I wrote about Tom Osborn, I praised his love of humanity and his belief in the unity of the human race. He had great visions for the future, which he often discussed with me. He knew that great social and political struggles had to take place before this unity was achieved. He was that rare sort of man who would not give up the struggle even if it shortened his lifespan.

The week after Tom died I was telephoned by a member of the Labour Party in Benoni, and asked if I would like to stand as the party's candidate at the by-election. I went to Benoni to speak to the local members of the party. After protracted talks I agreed to stand as Tom's successor. The seat was not opposed by the United Party because it came under the electoral pact that existed in the 1948 election.

Benoni is a mining town about twenty miles to the east of Johannesburg, and typical of the characterless towns that straggle along the so-called "Golden Reef". Mines were still producing gold there. This was Walter Madeley's old seat and in the early days Madeley was elected with the support of the white miners who were still imbued with the traditional spirit of British trade unionism.

By 1950 Benoni had changed. There was an influx of professionals and industrialists who outnumbered the original mining voters. I did not know if there would be a nomination contest, but I was advised by the people who supported me to visit the local members of the candidates' committee who would be important to me in a nomination contest.

I followed their advice. The first person I saw was a local solicitor, Leo Lovell. I was told that if I could get his support I would be assured of the nomination.

I was ushered into Lovell's office. He was a tall, well-built fair-haired man with the overworked, lined face of a busy lawyer. We had a very low key discussion. He wanted to know what my ideas were for Benoni and the Labour Party and my views on the current political situation. I had never met him before. As far as I knew he had never attended a national congress of the Labour Party.

The interview ended on a noncommittal basis.

Two weeks later the nomination meeting was called in Benoni. To my surprise I was the only candidate. I had expected an opponent. A small hall at Benoni Town Hall was packed. I addressed the delegates and they questioned me about my parliamentary plans. I made a short statement of my intentions. Then I left them while they debated the candidature. After a while I was called in and told that subject to the approval of the National Executive, they had chosen me as the parliamentary candidate.

I was reluctant to make the news public until the NEC approved of my success. I was very happy to follow in Tom's footsteps.

The following evening I was telephoned at about ten o'clock by a member of the Benoni branch to tell me that an urgent meeting of the branch had been held earlier that evening to re-discuss my nomination. To my astonishment reasons were found to rescind it, and Leo Lovell was nominated in my place for the seat.

At first I thought the message was a hoax or a sick joke, but it was true. I was shocked, and disappointed. It appears that after Lovell interviewed me, he decided to put his name forward for Parliament. For his own reasons he did not stand at the first nomination meeting, but arranged for the second meeting to rescind the decision on technical grounds, and had himself appointed as candidate.

I was still hopeful that the National Executive, who had to approve of the nomination, would investigate the circumstances and rule in my favour, or call for a fresh nomination meeting.

I was appalled at Lovell's behaviour. He had every opportunity to face me in a nomination contest which I would have welcomed.

Despite urgent requests by some members of the Benoni branch to re-open the nomination contest, the National Executive refused. To my surprise the decision went in favour of Lovell. I was hurt by the NEC's duplicity and the way it had manipulated the nomination in Lovell's favour. I knew that left wing members of the NEC did not support me and were suspicious of my political intentions. They knew I did not approve of the unacceptable influence of the few small unions who wielded the card vote, and I am sure this cost me the nomination. At the same time my faith in the democratic behaviour of the NEC was shaken.

I accepted the decision and did not pursue it further. I was learning fast about the subterfuge and double-talk that goes on in politics. Noble ideals aside, the Labour Party, as I learnt in later political life, was no different to all political parties with whom I came into contact. Politics is a tough environment for the young idealist.

One of my other activities was on the council of the Johannesburg Chamber of Commerce. I would often raise race relations or socio-economic matters. Now and then the press would report my views. At times this would upset the "old boy" network of the establishment. Several times I was accused of introducing party politics into the Chamber of Commerce. I tried my hardest to explain to tunnel-visioned, self-centred businessmen that there was a wide difference between party politics and the body politic of which they were part and parcel in their daily lives, and in which they had a most important role to play. My pleas fell on deaf ears. The Nationalists were in power, and businessmen through their own organisations were ready to be as subservient as possible, as long as they followed the narrow road of profits. They did not want to upset Nationalist Cabinet ministers or the senior bureaucrats.

In 1949, after import control was introduced into South Africa, they were petrified to raise their voices in case it damaged their prospects for import permits.

I was becoming tougher in my reaction to the local leaders of the Chamber of Commerce and I was not put off by their negative responses. Whenever it was opportune, I dealt with the growing number of intrusions by the government into the infrastructure of commerce. I tried to highlight the serious consequences, for workers and employers alike, when they came into conflict with apartheid. I was learning quickly how to use alternative platforms to attack nationalism.

It was becoming evident that although I was still wedded to "socialist" principles, business experience was modifying my political views in relation to national politics. I realised LP discussions were always theoretical. South Africa was not socialist and we had minimal influence.

By contrast, commerce reflected the viewpoint of the employers, and as a result I was able to widen my knowledge of the labour problem in South Africa, through the Chamber's Non-European Affairs Committee which dealt with white-black relations in commerce. It was here that I learnt how the average white South African businessman viewed the major racial and socio-economic problems of the day. My opinions often clashed with theirs because I did not exclude the effects of Nationalist policies on labour relations. Most businessmen, I discovered, lived in a dreamworld. They did not recognise the effects of apartheid legislation. At every opportunity I spoke about increasing governmental control over the social, economic and political future of white and black.

Their negative responses, the insular and narrow attitudes of the average South African in business, whose major interest was to defend his position of white affluence, was an eye-opener.

There were the exceptions on the Non-European Affairs Committee. A few members were as concerned as I was but our joint influence was minimal. There were no black, coloured or Indian members in the Chamber of Commerce. It was a white establishment with no contact with black

136

organisations, like the major white political parties.

Outside the Chamber, Johannesburg was facing a growing housing crisis. Rural blacks were flocking to the towns to seek work and were squatting in shanty towns in the south-west of Johannesburg.

The Chamber kept as far away as possible from getting directly involved in seeking financial solutions to solve the housing problems of blacks, despite the fact that its members were all very large employers of black labour.

Problems of transport arose for the black commuters who lived up to twenty miles away. Bus and train services were inadequate. Few owned cars. The blacks of Alexandra township, another large collection of sprawling shanties on the north-eastern edge of Johannesburg, marched in protest every day to their work in the city because they could not afford a few extra pence increase on bus fares. The bus boycott was one of the early demonstrations of emergent urban black power, regrettably unrecognised by most of white South Africa.

Organised commerce made suitable noises of sympathy but solutions were left to powerless local authorities who represented whites, and were not interested in blacks who did not pay rates or taxes.

29

For the first two years after qualification I kept up regular medical work, mostly on a locum basis. I also tried to make use of my medical knowledge to help the Labour Party formulate a new policy regarding the socio-medical problems of the country. It was clear that politics was the dominant factor in my life.

Although the Benoni experience was a setback, I was not seriously contemplating public life as a career. Instead, I had the reformist urge – I wanted my voice heard to improve the standing of the Labour Party in national politics.

The organisation was poor and the LP's political influence now virtually restricted to the Witwatersrand with little or nothing in the large coastal towns amongst the trade unions, liberals and "socialists". Our weekly newspaper *Forward* was read by the dedicated few.

All political eyes were on the Nationalists. True to our direst predictions, the apartheid steamroller was unleashed on the country through a series of Acts of Parliament.

The notorious Population Registration Act arrived in 1950, which made certain there were statutory definitions for the separation of the races. The Immorality Act was amended with severe penalties.

The Group Areas Act saw the beginnings of forced removals of Indians from their homes and businesses in white areas where they had lived and traded for years. The Suppression of Communism Act was introduced. On that day the SA Communist Party dissolved itself and went underground. The provisions of the Act were so wide that persons or organisations could be declared Communist if the authorities so decided. Newspapers could be banned if there was a "red" linkage. Restriction of movement and "naming" of people became an everyday occurrence. The government acted against anyone whose history showed ultra-left wing connections whether there was proof or not. Sam Kahn, the Communist MP, was banned from Parliament.

Multiracial trade-unions were frowned on, restricted from associating directly with political parties. Threats were made against the overseas press. Soviet journals were banned. Dr Malan, the Prime Minister, ignored the ruling of the International Court that South West Africa was mandated territory. Indians were threatened with repatriation to India.

There was nothing to stop the apartheid express. The United Party was in disarray, with no strategy to oppose the Nats. Mostly they supported what the government was doing by seeking faint-hearted compromises.

The response from the average white South African was one of ambivalence. It seemed as if people were at long last able to watch the government enacting all the laws that their fears and prejudices had desired for many years. Nationalist supporters applauded; English-speakers, other than liberals and left wingers, were silent. The only Parliamentary opposition came from the small Labour Party team. This in any event had little effect inside or outside Parliament.

Sporadic black unrest began on the Witwatersrand. The police attacked the African National Congress and Indian Congress at a protest demonstration on Labour Day – 1 May. Seventeen were killed and many injured.

I was frustrated and perturbed by the turn of events after two years of Nationalist rule. We had seen it all before in the 1930s when the Nazis could not be stopped.

Were the Nationalists taking South Africa along the same Fascist political road? To show it meant business the government appointed Dr Hendrik Verwoerd, controversial editor of its newspaper *Die Transvaler* as the new Minister of Native Affairs. The prospects for thousands of rural and urban blacks looked ominous.

In September 1950 the country was stunned by General Smuts's death. Shock and deep sorrow swept through English-speaking South Africa and the *"bloedsap boers"*. There was disappointment that Smuts had failed to rescue the country, not so much from apartheid but from the Nationalist politicians. Not many English-speakers read or spoke Afrikaans, so could not read the Afrikaans newspapers or comprehend proceedings in Parliament. They were content to leave politics to the "boers". As the days passed after Smuts's death people could not believe that "Oom Jannie" or the "Oubaas", as he was called, who had spent his life at South Africa's political helm, was no longer with them. They were suddenly confronted by his successor – JGN Strauss, his former secretary, colourless, with no personal following, instead of the liberal Jan Hofmeyr whose death earlier had also been a great shock.

Growing frustration amongst ex-servicemen at the failure of the existing political parties to stop the Nationalist legislative machine led to the formation of the War Veteran's Action Group, the "Torch Commando" in 1951. Its torchlight protests captured public imagination when Dr Malan and his partners, the Afrikaner Party, tried to remove the coloured voters from the Common Roll, to be replaced by four white MPs, two Provincial Councillors and one white Senator.

The problem facing the government was that "entrenched clauses" of the 1909 Act of Union did not allow voters to be disenfranchised, unless the government had a two-thirds majority of both Houses – the Senate and House of Assembly – sitting together. The Torch Commando took public protests to the streets – the only political group to do so. Many of us could not understand why it would not admit coloured and black ex-servicemen, who had fought side-by-side with whites in North Africa, to its ranks.

In 1951 there were many contradictions apparent in the actions and policies of whites who called themselves "liberals" – this was one outstanding example.

Nothing the "liberal" opposition in the country did could stop the Nationalists dismantling the remnants of the consultative bodies. The Native Representative Council established by Smuts was abolished because it made it clear to the government that it would not co-operate in implementing apartheid.

The BBC news service which had been re-broadcast daily to South Africa was discontinued, coming as a shock to English-speaking South Africans, whose links with Britain were to be severed as far as possible. A broadcast news monopoly was given to the South African Broadcasting Corporation, which rapidly became the government's propaganda mouth-piece. Passports were declared a "privilege", not a "right". Some passports were confiscated; other applications were peremptorily refused on political or "security" grounds.

The British Medical Association cancelled plans for its delegation to the SA Medical Association's annual congress because the government refused permission to BMA members and spouses who were not "white".

The government was frustrated by opposition to the removal of coloured voters from the Common Roll and set up the infamous High Court of Parliament which came to an ignominious end in the Cape Supreme Court and later at the Appeal Court.

Political turbulence was the order of the day. Somehow the government always got the upperhand. As the days went by in 1951 the United Party in Parliament became more and more ineffective, constantly failing to oppose the Nationalists or to find legal formulas to stop the erosion of the rights of blacks, Indians and coloureds.

I attended a public meeting of the United Party in the Johannesburg City Hall addressed by the UP leader Strauss. He kept saying the situation in South Africa must change, and we must get rid of the Nats. The meeting nearly ended in turmoil because most of the audience was yelling at him: "How? Tell us how?"

The situation in the Labour Party was equally bad. It was clinging desperately to political coat-tails of the UP. Only the parliamentary pact kept our MPs in the House. The large trade unions had deserted us and delivered us into the hands of Solly Sachs, Ben Weinbren and a few others from the small unions who wielded influence through the card vote. This completely outnumbered the diminished votes from the constituencies. Those of us who were not trade unionists had little say on policy formation nor could we be elected to the National Executive.

I had come to a watershed. The Labour Party's objectives were laudable and reflected much of my personal idealism – but it was dying on its feet. Nothing I could do would save it from eventually collapsing. Whether I liked it or not, I had to review my association with it.

I decided to take advice from John Christie, the leader, a politician of the old school. In his gentle way, he was firm and knowledgeable. We had candid and frequent discussions about the shattering changes brought about by the Nationalists and the weakness and futility of the LP. I told him of my lack of faith in the ability of the party to survive; one day the UP would refuse to support us, as they too were weakening.

However, the UP and the LP were not the only opposition parties in trouble. The fledgling Torch Commando's lights were burning out. In its place a Liberal Association was formed, with many ex-service members who wanted more than torchlight parades. There were others who thought there was still hope that the United Party could be revitalised by infiltrating its ranks and so changing its leadership and policy.

Julius Lewin and his wife, Eleanor Hawarden took a pragmatic view on the political situation. They believed that however weak the United Party was in Parliament, it was the only vehicle for change in the country. I was still attending their house meetings and had become a close friend. Often, on walks around the Zoo Lake near their home in Parktown North, Julius and I would discuss the political situation. As an academic and writer, his views were greatly respected in liberal circles. Discussions with him played a great part in getting a perspective on what was happening to South Africa under Nationalist rule.

In October, I'd just returned from a visit to England when I found an urgent message from John Christie. He would not talk to me on the telephone but asked me to see him at his flat.

Christie, a large man, somewhat overweight, wore spectacles and and always had a gentle smile. He welcomed me in his soft rolling Glaswegian accent.

"Please sit down, Boris."

"Well, John, you 've been very secretive this time – what is it?"

"I'll tell you. During your absence, a municipal seat become vacant – it's Ward 26 in Hillbrow. The NEC took a unanimous decision to ask you to be the party's candidate. I hope you'll agree to stand."

My immediate reaction was total rejection. I had not forgotten the shabby treatment from the NEC over the Benoni election when Tom Osborn died. It still rankled. Now they were asking me to help them out of a spot.

Christie saw that I was not co-operative.

"Boris, I know it's short notice, but there is no one else in the party able to stand. I know that party members will help you to set yourself up and do their best with the canvass. Before you give me your answer I must tell you we have no money to spend on the election."

I was flabbergasted. This was a real imposition – I was expected to pay for it as well. To start with, I had never thought of becoming a city councillor. The Labour Party was represented in the Council by people who had been there for years whom I knew well. Some were on the NEC. They had achieved little, unable to unseat the Independent Ratepayers who ran the Council – in reality the United Party. The Council as a whole was in deep water with the public and newspapers because of its failure to deal with the housing problems of the black people in the south-western areas and other peripheral "black spots". Enormous slums were building up in Moroka and Shantytown. I knew what it was all about because I was one of the council's strongest critics through the Chamber of Commerce.

Christie was quite keen on me fighting the election.

"You know, Boris, you've never fought an election. Don't you think you should give it a go to get some experience? We are not expecting you to win, but if you put up a good show it will strengthen our hand when we next have to negotiate with the UP. You must also get your name before the public – there is no better way than fighting an election."

We talked for a while. Should I seriously consider what he was asking me to do, just for the experience of an election fight?

"John, has anything been done to prepare for this election? Are voters cards written up? Is there an election office?"

John smiled wryly.

"Boris, nothing has been done – you'll have to start from scratch."

I decided I needed some time to think it over. I rose to go.

"I'll think it over and let you know on Monday."

"Boris, don't go. I need a decision now. I would like you to stand. The United Party candidate is already in the field. His name is Alec Gorshel. Nomination day is Monday."

It was Friday evening.

"It's an impossible situation. I don't know whether I want to go to the City Council; I have lots of commitments; I . . ."

He interrupted me.

"Boris, do stand, you won't regret it, believe me. It's good advice." I stood looking at him, thinking hard.

"Right, John, I'll stand. I must be mad. I'll do my best."

Christie was delighted that I'd decided to fight. I sat down and we discussed a plan of action – the sum total was that there was very little time and I could expect little help from the party.

Although it was after ten pm when I left I thought I would drive around the heart of Hillbrow, which in effect was Ward 26. I knew the area like the back of my hand. I was born there. I had lived in Pretoria Street. I knew the small cafes and Bohemian hide-outs and all the narrow congested side-streets overshadowed by the high-rise blocks of flats.

It was in one of these side-streets, just off Pretoria Street, that I saw an empty shop. I stopped the car and looked into the dark interior. There was a "To Let" sign on the door. If I could get it as my committee room it would be ideal – it was right in the centre of Hillbrow.

I stood on the pavement thinking about all the other things I had to do. I needed helpers, canvassers, posters and leaflets. Voters cards had to be written up. The election was in just under three weeks. Would I be able to do it?

Pauline took the shock announcement calmly. The next day I saw the agents, who were happy to let the shop to me. I was able, during the course of the day, to get a voters roll and checked to see how many voters I knew that might be enlisted to help. There were few likely prospects. I then telephoned several members of the NEC – and as I expected they were full of excuses, promising however, that they would assist me on election day.

I was on my own – I should have known when I said "yes" to Christie.

Just before the deadline I presented myself at the Nomination Court at the City Hall on Monday. Alec Gorshel and the United Party officials nearly had apoplexy when they discovered they had opposition. As Gorshel expected to be elected unopposed, he had done no canvassing whatsoever, although he had been in the field weeks before.

My entry gave me much-needed press publicity, attracting a few young people who offered to canvass and run the election room. It was like old times again – the business took second place.

I badly needed an issue on which to fight this election. It was pointless relying on the political programme of the Labour Party. No one was interested. Hillbrow was full of towering buildings, small flats and families looking for open space for their children or for the elderly. Most people there were itinerants and single office workers or retired. I learnt from early canvass returns that over sixty per cent of voters on the roll were no longer in Hillbrow.

I needed a local issue of importance to offset Gorshel's daily slander about me and the Labour Party. Within a few days I found one. There were no open spaces, no parks, no creches in Hillbrow. In the mad post-war scramble to build high-rise flats the people of Hillbrow were left without open spaces for recreation.

I got hold of Cliff Kallenbach, an architect friend of mine. We spent a few hours looking for a site for a park in Hillbrow. We found one. It meant expropriating a few ramshackle houses overlooked by developers near where I was born; it gave us a complete block on which we could get the Council to construct a park with other amenities. I drew up a plan showing a park on the site, with swimming pool, a creche and children's playground and printed a leaflet headed: "I will fight for these parks".

Choose the BEST MAN for Hillbrow!

VOTE DR. B. WILSON IN

Dr. B. Wilson understands Health & Housing Problems

HE WILL FIGHT FOR:

- TWO PARKS in Hillbrow;
- Day Nursery Schools and Creches.
- House and Homes at Low Rentals;
- Reduction in tram and bus fares;
- More money for slum elimination.

Transport: For Transport Telephone 44-0283 or call at THE COMMITTEE ROOMS, 106b Quartz Street, (between Pretoria and Kotze Streets).

FOUR YEAR OLD U.P. PROMISES HAVE GIVEN YOU

NO PARKS IN HILLBROW.

NO NURSERY SCHOOLS OR CHILDREN'S CRECHES;

LUXURY FLATS AT HIGH RENTALS;

TWO INCREASES IN TRAM AND BUS FARES; TRANSPORT AT A LOSS;

NATIVES LIVING IN SLUMS.

AND

Why did the United Party let in Dr. Ross (Nat. Leader) and 4 Nationalist Councillors into the City Council unopposed?

THE U.P. MANIFESTO IS AGAIN FULL OF PROMISES THE U.P. CANNOT FULFIL.

VOTE FOR DR. B. WILSON

OFFICIAL LABOUR CANDIDATE.

CORONA LODGE, 8, O'REILLY RD., WED., OCT. 31, 7 a.m.—8 p.m.

Published by the Candidate, Dr. Borés Wilson, Quartz Street, Hillbrow, and printed by Prompt Printing Co. (Pty.), Ltd., 11 Harris Street, Westgate, Johannesburg.

I challenged the UP to establish the park with its amenities and if elected, I would battle to get it for Hillbrow. For good measure I criticised tramfare increases and slums in Johannesburg.

My old *WU's Views* newspaper printer soon had my leaflet ready and my canvassers distributed it throughout Hillbrow. It created a great deal of interest. So much so that we discovered the UP had planted a "spy" in my committee room, whom we soon expelled.

Canvassing in Hillbrow had problems. The elderly could not be disturbed late at night – I would often conduct a conversation through a bathroom window. Many calls ended with a voter's promise or a brush-off because it was very much United Party territory.

There was no doubt that I had woken up the by-election. My canvass cards, however, came in with lots of "No" responses and many doubtfuls. I realised if I was to make an impact I would have to use other methods to get known to the voters and increase my support otherwise I would be ignominuously defeated, which would be bad. I knew I could not win but the last thing I wanted was to lose my deposit in the first election I had ever fought.

30

The obvious answer was to speak directly to the voters. There was no time to call meetings. In any event, very few would attend. The streets of Hillbrow are narrow, the buildings high. I asked my company's radio mechanics to provide me with a portable battery-powered amplifier with loudspeakers. I was driven around the ward and at a suitable spot, I would address a few buildings with a brief message. People came out on their balconies listening to me. In this way I started stimulating interest in the election and my canvass returns began to look a bit better. I used a different car every night because it was against the local by-laws to hold meetings in public places without permission.

As I was speaking one night, one of my helpers came running to tell me the police were looking for me. I stopped immediately. For the next ten days it was a game of hide and seek between me and the police – I can safely say I won that contest.

I think Gorshel put the police on to me. I learnt that he was upset at what I was doing through our "spy" in his committee room, to keep track of how he was getting on.

Gorshel and the UP in the end decided they would use the old smear tactic saying I was a communist. It was against the law to do so because of the Suppression of Communism Act.

If I could prove that they were behind it I could get an injunction, restrain them and claim damages for libel. I instructed my lawyer to issue a writ against Gorshel and his election agent, Gerald Alexander, a young advocate whom I knew. I received an urgent message from Gerald, asking me meet him in a local cafe. He gave me his assurance that smears would stop. I withdrew the injunction on his promise.

By time election day arrived I had no idea how I was going to do. My canvass returns showed a few hundred "yes" votes but there were too many doubtful voters for my liking. This was a bad sign when fighting the UP. It simply meant that UP voters were not disclosing their intentions to an opposition canvasser.

I was happy about my campaign. It had got through. *The Rand Daily Mail* and *The Star* gave me excellent coverage on the park issue – diverting attention away from Labour Party squabbles.

People were genuinely interested. Gorshel was caught because he could not oppose the need for the park, which he tried to belittle.

On election day voting was slow. As expected, this was the first time I saw any members of the NEC, who came, I suspect, to get their pictures into the newspapers.

There was a heavy downpour in the afternoon. After it stopped voters streamed in, a UP phenomenon I was to recognise in the future, time and time again.

At the voting count that night, to everyone's surprise, it became clear that despite the slow voting during the day I was getting more votes than both the newspapers and the forecasters had expected. Out of a total of nearly 2 000 I was beaten by only 250.

This was an exciting result. I had never fought an election before. It was not the Labour Party who did the work, in fact they gave me no help. I had confounded the political commentators.

Although I was satisfied with my campaign, it reaffirmed that the Labour Party had no hope of winning seats on its own. For me it proved that I could creditably fight an election on my own and enjoy the experience.

Of course the Labour Party was pleased with the result and endeavoured to capitalise on it, trying to convince the UP that the LP had sufficient political muscle to contest a seat. This was nonsense. My election had not been fought on UP vs LP policies. It was a personal fight on local issues.

Shortly after the election John Christie told me he was going overseas for a few weeks. He had learnt that his only brother was still living in Glasgow and was ailing. He decided that he would visit England and Scotland to see the remaining members of his family.

During Christie's absence I saw the Lewins a lot. The election I had fought made me think about my political future and my role in the Labour Party. The conclusion I came to was that the Labour Party was going to disappear from mainstream politics in South Africa. Eleanor Hawarden (Lewin – she was a staunch feminist) was highly critical of the United Party. Nevertheless she had firm opinions as to what I should do. As we sat in their lounge, with its book-lined walls, she told me that the only possible hope for South Africa was still a reformed United Party. She had already joined the UP in Parktown and was taking an interest in municipal politics. Julius Lewin was of a similar opinion. Much could be done in the field of race relations and the United Party's policy on Native Affairs had to be liberalised. Jan Hofmeyr was no longer there to do it. It was left to liberals to join the UP and change it – despite the UP's defects.

Eleanor's last words to me that evening were:

"Boris, you must leave the Labour Party. You are wasting your time there. Join the UP. Your energy and drive will add strength to the reform movement in the party."

"I'm not sure you're right," I replied. "After all, there is the insurmountable problem of the inflexible platteland attitudes. They will not give up support of the colour bar. I am sceptical. Despite liberals like you in the UP, I doubt whether meaningful reform can be brought about."

Her parting shot was: "What will you do if you leave the Labour Party?"

She was right, of course. There was little alternative if I wanted to be active in politics. I could join the Liberal Association. There were good political brains there; but it had never been in the political hustings – its role was extra-parliamentary. The Torch Commando was fragmenting – in any event it was not a political party. It had claimed a membership once of 250 000, but no one knew its real strength. As for the Labour Party, it had no appeal for returned war veterans, or to young whites who were not interested in socialism, let alone understood what it meant.

My talk with the Lewins prompted me to talk to John Christie when he returned from his visit overseas. I knew he would respect my confidence and be impartial enough when discussing the future of the Labour Party and my position in it.

Before speaking to Christie I tried to review the status of the political opposition to the Nationalists in the early 1950s. The most dramatic impact had been made by the Torch Commando. Its meetings all over the country electrified white opposition, who saw it as a saviour emerging from the long shadow left by Smuts.

But it was a temporary phenomenon of post-war anger. It faded before it could mature into a political party. The men and women who led it did not have the experience to turn it into a political party.

There was little else to stop the Nationalists. South Africa was no longer the preserve of the traditional British Trade Union movement and its old stalwarts who were responsible for the industrial legislation in this country. Of importance was the fact that white workers were replaced by cheaper black and coloured labour which flocked to the towns in the post-war industrial boom.

Militant white workers responded by openly supporting the NP because it promised "protection" of white jobs – job reservation – and maintenance of the colour bar.

Little was left for the Labour Party, except to oppose the NP in Parliament and expose the weaknesses of the UP when it tried to compromise in the implementation of apartheid legislation. South African whites, irrespective of their political affiliations did not want to give up their affluent life styles.

Labour's socialist policies did not interest them. Blacks could not involve themselves in white politics; most whites kept as far away from black politics as they could. The UP and its supporters openly approved of the Nationalist plans to maintain the integrity of the colour bar in industry. The UP opposed any form of integration. It believed in residential separation and advocated "white supremacy with justice" – a policy little different to that of the Nationalists.

Future indicators were there. The UP had been Labour's lifeline. The first break came as early as 1948. The UP had refused renewal of its provincial electoral pact with the LP. It had no option because it was losing seats and could no longer afford to give them away to the LP. It was clear that the next election could mean the end of the LP; without a deal with the UP it was finished.

On a personal level, my friends in the LP were dwindling. Tom Osborn was dead. The NEC meetings were dominated by Sachs and Weinbren – their pockets full of card votes. No doubt they both did great work for their unions; but their interest in the armchair socialists and liberals from the wealthy suburbs was nil.

I had to face up to the fact that my own attitude to socialist politics was changing. I was more interested in the hard realities of the race relations problem in South Africa. I had to concede, too, that my involvement in business was affecting my views, with the result that there was a widening gap between me and the minor union chiefs of the LP. My liberal principles were not changing. They were being enhanced. I saw clearly what the Nationalists were doing. I believed that everyone in South Africa, irrespective of ethnic origins and differences, was entitled to a share of the economic and social benefits of their own labour and productivity. I did not believe that a one-man-one-vote political system was possible within the foreseeable future – some qualified voting formula would have to first evolve.

In an unpublished article, written in 1951, I described what I believed were the essentials of a just and fair society in South Africa, involving the setting up of a new liberal movement.

We needed to maintain the rule of law and democratic rights of all races in South Africa; these were fast disappearing. All voting rights should be maintained with the extension of the franchise to all who qualified for it. A welfare state should be established.

I wanted the highest standard of living for everyone. I urged acceptance of the Fagan Report which called for the removal of the colour bar. All repressive Nationalist legislation should be repealed. South Africa should remain a Commonwealth member and develop and foster good relations with the rest of Africa.

I set this out trying to clarify where I stood. I obviously had to move on from the Labour Party. But to where? There was little choice if I wanted to remain in constitutional parliamentary politics and all it entailed in South Africa. I was not looking for a political career but more for policy achievement in which I believed. I was not prepared to remain in the LP subject to the dictates and political control of a few trade unionists who did not share my views. My background – the hours I spent with my father, his monologues, political poetry, the tough life at the Market, the struggles to qualify in medicine, the pragmatism in running my own business all said one thing – move on, leave the Labour Party.

John Christie was back from his overseas trip and the annual LP Congress was to be held at the end of the year. I decided it was best to talk to Christie again about my dilemma.

We met at his flat. He did not look well and complained of exhaustion. Before we got down to my problem, I asked him how he got on with his family in Glasgow and his brother whom he'd not seen for forty years.

"Boris, I took the night train to Glasgow. I booked into a hotel the next morning. Glasgow had changed a lot and I wandered around. I looked up my brother's telephone number and was ready to telephone him when something stopped me."

He was fidgeting uncomfortably and moving papers on his desk. He adjusted his glasses and avoided looking at me.

"I could not dial the number. I sat in the hotel room thinking that I had not seen him for forty years and we must have grown apart tremendously. I didn't want any emotional scenes. If I left Glasgow on the next train he would never know I had been there. It wouldn't make any difference to him."

There was a pause.

"Boris, that's what I did. I took the next train back to London."

Although I had been on a similar mission for my father in New York, I was astonished at what he told me, but I could understand his reaction. It seemed as if he had purged himself of some longing that he'd had for years, and just going to Glasgow was enough. He was unable to to take the final step.

We then got on to my problem. I had previously spoken to him about my future in the Labour Party so it was easy to reopen the subject.

In the strictest confidence he told me that he was sceptical about the Labour Party's ability to survive. It was in such a poor state that he doubted that, even if it improved basic policy, it would increase its appeal for the white electorate.

It had come to the end of its political existence; it had not kept pace with post-war political changes in South Africa. Smuts tried to give a better deal to the blacks, while the Nationalists were trying to reverse historical processes with separate development – they were severing the tenuous links that blacks, coloureds and Indians had with the white political infrastructure. Their attempt to undermine the constitution in this respect had disturbed opposition voters. The failure of the United Party to act as a responsible opposition did not help the Labour Party one iota – they were considered a UP appendage.

I told Christie that I was seriously considering leaving the LP at the end of the year. He was not surprised. I was not clear about my future plans, but there were two possibilities. One was to remain politically unattached, to assess the political situation; the other was to join the United Party and to link up with their liberals who were trying to reform the party from within. Despite the UP's deficiencies, it was the only Opposition party which English-speaking white South Africans supported – the party of Botha and Smuts, the "bloed-sappe", whom they believed would one day return to power.

Christie was outspoken in his reply to me.

"I shouldn't be speaking to you like this, Boris. If I was your age with your energy and outlook, I would take the bit between my teeth and resign from the party. You have the future to look to – I've had my political career, even as leader. The moment I go there will be conflict in the party and the NEC will split. My advice is to do what you think is right. I think you're on the right course."

The message was clear.

At the end of December the Labour Party could only muster forty delegates at the national congress. We sat at tables arranged in a "U" shape in the noisy Malvern Hall while the trams trundled by.

I had moved a resolution to abolish the Card Vote which, as I expected, was lost – all the Trade Unionists voted against it.

After the new NEC had been elected, I rose to make my resignation statement, which was listened to in silence.

The Sunday Times of 6 January 1952, under the headline "Resigns Because of the Card Vote" reported that "Dr B Wilson, for thirteen years a member of the SA Labour Party, startled the delegates to its annual conference in Johannesburg yesterday by resigning from the party in protest against the use of the Card Vote at the conference.

"The Labour Party must come to its senses," he declared. "The Card Vote is doing it harm and leading to frustration. I want to take a more active part in the struggle to defeat the Nationalists and I cannot do so under these conditions."

I recall that the conference appeared to be stunned after I had spoken. I heard angry and sarcastic calls and saw Solly Sachs getting to his feet. Before there were any personal attacks on me, I had gathered my papers and left.

I met John Christie again. He told me several of the NEC believed I had ulterior motives for resigning, others regretted my resignation. His own view was that I had done the right thing, and we agreed that we would continue to see each other from time to time. Later in 1952 I received an urgent call from his daughter Maude, who looked after him, to say that he was ill but refused to see a doctor. This was typical of John Christie, despite the fact that he was a pharmacist with many medical contacts. Maude suggested I should pay one of my customary visits and probe him about his health.

I really did not have to ask him questions. He looked very pale and had

149

lost weight. His clothes were sagging on him.His face was lined. When I asked him about his health he replied:

"Tired, Boris, tired – at the end of the day I feel washed out."

He did not object to me examining him. I found sufficient signs to alert me that he had symptoms of a well-developed disease. A blood sample I took established that his white cells were affected explaining why his spleen was enlarged.

I consulted a leading specialist, eventually getting Christie to see him. The diagnosis was confirmed. It was a battle to get consent to remove the spleen, but in the end it came out and gave him relief. I warned the family he did not have long to live. We had no cure for the disease in those days.

John Christie died a few months later. With his passing the country lost one of the stalwarts of the Labour movement who exemplified the best of the old British tradition and who had made a contribution of political significance to South Africa.

31

The break from the Labour Party gave me much needed time to develop some of the changes I had brought about in the business in 1951. I was regularly travelling overseas, the trips always benefiting the business. I began to expand it not only throughout South Africa but beyond its borders into Rhodesia, a promise I had made to myself when I was there in 1936.

As I owned the Ekco franchise for Rhodesia, I went back in 1951 and established Kruger and Wilson (Rhodesia) Ltd, with premises in the centre of Bulawayo. As a result I was driving to Rhodesia every two months, a very fast trip in my Jaguar over terrible strip roads from Beit Bridge on the Limpopo River to Bulawayo.

Southern Rhodesia was in the hands of Godfrey Huggins whose policy of paternalism kept relations between black and white on an even keel. Unfortunately, there was heavy black unemployment.

There had been an influx of Britons, who were mostly artisans seeking a new life but making little contribution to the development of industry or creation of jobs for blacks. As new immigrants they were not interested in the country's politics. They had escaped the post-war drudgery of Britain and were mainly interested in a life of sunshine, inexpensive black servants and swimming pools.

On the other hand, the locally-born whites I met were more concerned about the future of their country. There was a small core of young politicians in the Southern Rhodesian Parliament who gave me an insight into the country's problems which contrasted starkly with the turbulence south of

The official picture of the Mars Manufacturing Company, the first radio manufacturers in South Africa 1936. Botha Mabuza is left, sitting, in the second row; BW next, then Dr Sidley and Horace Dainty. Back row, left is Jack Sidley; Kronik, the cabinet maker is centre back.

Mr and Mrs Meyer Tobin, New York, 1945.

Reading my resignation to the annual conference of the Labour Party at the Malvern Hall in Johannesburg, January 1952.

Outside the polling station on election day in Hillbrow 1951, when I opposed Alec Gorshel of the United Party.

the Limpopo. Rhodesia had little strain between black and white. This influenced me in 1951 to establish a new business, Central African Radio and Electrical Ltd, unconnected with the South African company, in Bulawayo's industrial area.

As early as the 1950s, politics had taught me that South Africa was having serious financial, political and racial problems. I saw Rhodesia as a nearby independent base and haven. I expected problems of management and control, but was prepared to face these as they arose. I was motivated greatly by the utterances of leading Nationalist politicians like Eric Louw, who were frank about the Nationalist intentions to create a "boer" republic on racialist lines, based on the 1942 Republican Constitution of the National Party, which, if implemented, was ominous.

In South Africa I had just secured public company status for Kruger and Wilson (Pty) Ltd, without going to the Stock Exchange. I had no difficulty in disposing of the shares as we were highly thought of in the industry.

Eric Cole sent me a congratulatory cable and at the same time asked whether his company could purchase a thirty-five per cent interest in the South African business. I was flattered and accepted his offer. Ekco became my partner in South Africa.

As a result, we got new long-term agreements for distribution and manufacture and we had the right to make Ekco's products in Southern Africa. Until then I had had no experience in radio manufacture, but in 1949 the government was compelled to control imports by legislation. It was clear that I would have to manufacture Ekco locally if I was to hold on to our share of the market. I turned to Horace Dainty who had already opened his own radio factory at Pinetown near Durban. It was logical that I should entrust him to make my sets from the kits I imported from Ekco in Southend, and it was a great day when the first South African-made Ekco radio appeared in the dealers' shops all over the country.

Pauline and I had moved to our second house in Parktown. Adrian, our eldest son, was almost three. Nigel came in 1951 and Virginia in 1954. Life for me was very full supervising the South African and Rhodesian companies, keeping my hand in with a little medicine and an active interest in politics.

In April 1952 the Torch Commando managed to induce the opposition political parties to form a United Democratic Front. The Nationalists were gaining strength as reflected by their unexpected win in Wakkerstroom, a traditional UP platteland seat. The joint Defiance Campaign by Indians and Africans had begun. The only two Communist MPs, Sam Kahn and Fred Carneson, were expelled from Parliament. Solly Sachs was struggling to keep multiracial trade unions alive and himself out of gaol. The Pan-African Congress members were tearing up their passes and despite the arrests of seven thousand blacks, the government panicked and announced the end of the Pass system, substituting reference books (which wasn't much of a change), and tightening Influx Control laws.

The racist pressures of the Nationalists were succeeding in hardening the negative attitudes of whites and blacks; race relations were deteriorating.

Smuts had managed to keep blacks relatively peaceful by having a dialogue with the Native Representative Council, but Dr Malan, the Prime Minister, went off in the opposite direction. There was to be no political, social or cultural contact with blacks. It was like being thrust back to the days when I was a child, when Natives were pushed off the pavements by angry whites. I used to see this often at the Market and where we lived in the middle class suburbs of Johannesburg. A "kaffir" had to travel upstairs in a "whites only" tram where a few seats were reserved for a "Native", only if his white "master" was sitting elsewhere in the tram.

In our homes, black men and women were employed as domestics to make beds, look after white children and do all the menial work. They brought early-morning tea or coffee to many whites in their bedrooms. Living conditions in the backyards of even the most luxurious of homes were often primitive; a room with an outside toilet; and no bath or shower.

There were no statutory service conditions covering the employment of black domestics. Long hours were worked from six o'clock in the morning until after the "madam" and the "master" (baas) had finished their evening meal. Black families were not allowed by law to live together in the towns. Once a year the "girl" or "boy" would go home to their "kaia" (home) and family hundreds of miles away in some unknown kraal, often the only time the domestic servant would see family in a year.

This was the migratory system of labour which existed long before Nationalists came to power and which they legally refined under apartheid statutes. In white Johannesburg there were no parks or recreation halls for Natives even on a segregated basis. On "off days", usually on Sundays or Thursdays, the local blacks would dress up and meet on the street corners, often visiting the local "shebeens" (illegal backyard drinking dens), where many would get drunk and stagger in the streets. The police arrested them in periodic raids.

It was a common daily sight to see the police stopping blacks, demanding their passes. If these were not available, or the "baas" had not provided a "special" pass giving "Jim" permission to visit friends, the Native could be arrested and walked, handcuffed to another luckless victim, through the streets of the suburb where he worked to the nearest police station. The sight of such a small group of handcuffed blacks escorted to a police station used to anger me as a child because I respected and liked many of the blacks we employed at home and the Market. I was always upset when I saw them in handcuffs. All this was intensified after the Nationalists came to power. This was the reality of the master-servant relationship in white South Africa. Later, the only places I could meet blacks on an equal basis was at university, where a few had been admitted, or at the Institute of Race Relations.

From my earliest recollection of the fat, bosomy black woman holding me in her arms to the bustling Market, I was conscious of the black man in South Africa as a downtrodden human being.

I was always emotionally affected by black poverty and wondered why white South African society treated people of colour as inferior beings.

32

In the aftermath of my resignation from the Labour Party I knew that I had to devote much of my energies to improving the appalling race relations in the country. As a liberal individual I felt I had a duty to bring about change in white attitudes to blacks. The problem that faced me was how to do it. One thing was clear: it had to be through political effort. I decided not to join the Liberal Association because it was a talking-shop; peripheral organisations like this did not help because many were infiltrated by the "hard" left.

One evening in 1952, shortly after I left the Labour Party, I received telephone call at my home.

"Dr Wilson, Mayers here. You don't know me but some friends and I would like to talk to you about your political future. Can we arrange a meeting soon?"

"Mr Mayers, what organisation do you represent?"

"The United Party in Parktown."

As I lived in Parktown, I saw no harm in meeting him. Some nights later I met Morry Mayers and Hugh Ismay.

Mayers was a tall well-built man, sparse hair, glasses and a lilt in his voice. A self-made businessman, he spent much time in politics, but he had no personal political aspirations whatsoever. He was the Treasurer of the UP's Parktown Constituency. Ismay left all the talking to Mayers.

They proposed that I should join the local United Party. Mayers said he had followed my career with interest. He knew of me when I was at University. Both considered I had done a good job in the Labour Party and felt that the UP would benefit if I joined. Mayers was a veteran of the Torch Commando, who firmly believed that the UP was the only political vehicle that could remove the Nationalists from office. Mayers supported his views by saying that Parktown was the most liberal UP constituency in the country. An Afrikaner self-styled "liberal", Blaar Coetzee, was their MPC and they were in the process of choosing their new MP whom they hoped would be John Cope, a journalist and former editor of the liberal journal *Forum*.

I reminded them that I had always been a trenchant critic of the UP. They knew this, they said, from my statements in the newspapers. I wanted to know from them how my membership of the United Party could help to reform it. I told them:

"I am very interested in race relations – I have a liberal attitude to blacks. The UP's Native Policy is behind the times even for a so-called middle of the road party. To me the party's policy of 'white supremacy with justice' is meaningless jargon."

"I agree with you," Mayers replied. "That's why we need you in the party. We need your help to fight within the party to liberalise its policies."

"We need all the support we can get. Parktown is respected in the party because we usually raise the largest amount of money during the year and we're not frightened to open our mouths. Will you join us?"

I told them I'd think it over. I did not tell them that the Lewins had already spoken to me about the UP. I now wondered whether they had set up this meeting. I had to admit that Mayers and Ismay impressed me – but I was bothered that joining the UP could undoubtedly be considered a retrogressive move by liberals outside that party. What were the alternatives? I needed a political home, I was not a wilderness man. Joining the UP would be starting at the bottom. That did not worry me. I was not after prestige, but wanted to help in the struggle to change the government before it was too late. I wanted better race relations – I could not deny the fact that party politics was the only way to achieve it.

For days I struggled with my conscience about the options – but there were none. In the end I rang Mayers and told him I would join the UP. He was delighted and invited me to Parktown's annual general meeting which was shortly to take place. I was immediately made a member of the Saxonwold Branch.

A few weeks later I arrived at the AGM which was held at the Oxford Hotel. The room was crowded. Before we entered the meeting Mayers and Ismay took me aside.

"Dr Wilson, we have been instructed by our branch to nominate you as Divisional Secretary tonight. Will you stand?"

I was flabbergasted.

"Isn't it unreasonable to propose someone who has just joined the party to such a job? Won't it look as if I have joined the UP in order to get a senior position? That's not why I'm here tonight."

Mayers laughed.

"Forget it. We've had a struggle to find someone to take on this job. Everyone will be pleased if you accept and are elected."

"OK," I conceded. "If that's the way you want it – I'll stand."

The election of office-bearers took place early in the evening. Mayers was again appointed Treasurer. My name was the only one put forward as Secretary. However, before the nomination was agreed there was a high-pitched voice of protest from the back of the hall. I turned to see who the interrupter was.

A young man, dressed in a khaki army raincoat, with a thin and angular face, wanted to know how long I had been in the UP. As far as he knew I had recently resigned from the Labour Party. Was there not another candidate for the position who had been longer in the party?

I was embarrassed.

I whispered to Mayers: "Who is this man? This is what I wanted to avoid. Shall I withdraw my name?"

"Not at all. It's Harry Schwarz, one of our City Councillors. We expected his objection – but he won't get support."

Mayers was right. I was elected without a vote. I hoped I had not made an enemy of Schwarz whom I did not know. No doubt time would tell.

Morry Mayers and I became close friends. He was a tireless worker. Through him I learnt the rough road of UP political life. As secretary I was on the Witwatersrand Divisional Council and in turn on the Transvaal Head Committee.

In a relatively short time I had a good insight into the UP's political machine and how it operated. Throughout all the levels there was a dominant "verkrampte" (conservative) group who controlled all the major committees who believed that the "Native Policy" of the party should not deviate from "white supremacy with justice". The more liberal elements were hamstrung by the conservatives because of the fear that if there was any departure from right wing policy, UP platteland supporters and seats would be lost to the Nationalists.

The UP urban leaders were right wing generals leading moderate centre supporters constantly looking over their shoulders to see that the platteland was not upset by the liberal urbanites. One could distinguish the "old guard" by their frequent references at party congresses and committees to "keep to the policies of Botha and Smuts". General Botha, a Boer War fighter, was the first Prime Minister of the Union of South Africa in 1910; and Smuts, a young member of his cabinet, always affirmed his political allegiance to Botha's policies. In practical terms this meant maintaining the "master and servant" relationship, keeping blacks separate and subservient.

To the right of the Smuts-Botha followers were the real "verkramptes" emanating from the Transvaal and Orange Free State platteland areas. They enunciated their political credo often as: "Kaffir in his place, Coolie in the sea". These UP verkramptes wielded great power, the leadership and centre-rump dead-scared to upset them. Their bigoted and prejudiced views received great respect at congresses and meetings because of the spectre of Nationalists on the right ready to wean both supporters and parliamentary seats from the United Party.

To the left of centre was the small group of liberals I was seeking to meet. John Cope in Parktown, Helen Suzman in Houghton, Ray Swart and Ronald Butcher in Natal and Colin Eglin and Zach de Beer in the Cape. They all lived in the wealthier suburbs of their cities, and they had been out-voted at recent conferences in their attempts to liberalise in South African terms the UP's "Native Policy".

In Johannesburg, as elsewhere in South Africa, although liberals were vociferous, in the final analysis they were unable to influence the party along a liberal road because the "old guard" were firmly in the saddle, and they were just a vocal minority.

However the disbandment of the Torch Commando led to an influx of new blood into the UP. In 1953 a small group of liberal-thinking parliamentarians was elected under the United Party banner.

Helen Suzman, Ray Swart, Zach de Beer and John Cope were part of this group. Through Parktown's liberal connections in the UP, I was able to meet others who wanted change. As the new secretary I began to receive invitations to address other constituencies on current affairs, which I accepted, using the opportunities to speak frankly without compromising my views. At one meeting in Bezuidenhout Valley the chairman took me aside after the meeting and asked me whether I would consider standing as their candidate for Parliament in the forthcoming 1953 General Election. The previous MP had joined the Nationalist Party. The division was demoralised and wanted a younger MP, since it was a safe UP seat.

Although, at this stage with the UP, I had not considered standing for any public office, I decided to let my name go forward. At the Divisional meeting I was the unanimous choice despite the fact that I made clear at the outset that, as new member of the UP, I was not after a quick ticket to Parliament.

The Bezuidenhout Valley representative went to the Witwatersrand Candidates Selection Committee for approval and I was not surprised to learn that they refused to consider me. No official reasons were given for the rejection. I learnt afterwards it was the "old guard" who would not endorse me. If I had come over from the Nationalist Party there is no doubt that I would have been acceptable, but the Labour Party and anything left of it was taboo. My socialist and liberal leanings were the kind of political transfusion the UP could do without!

I was told that I was "too ambitious". My view was that to survive in the political jungle ambition was only one of a number of personal attributes one needed apart from a skin of the thickest hide. As I was a frequent critic of the UP's failure to stand up to the Nationalists this was not forgotten by the loyal followers of "Botha and Smuts".

At the time that Mayers made contact with me I was engaged in public controversy with the Town Clerk of Johannesburg over the lack of proper housing for blacks in the south and west of the city. In an address to the Johannesburg Chamber of Commerce I said that the "scheme for these (1 000) homes was passed in principle last May and it was ditched until Bishop Reeves of Johannesburg challenged the City Council."

I called for the resignation of GB Gordon, the leader of the UP in the Council, who had failed in his job to "give way to others who are prepared to spend the money available for Native Housing and rid Johannesburg of its gravest housing and sociological problem, that of slums, overcrowding in all forms, ill health, crime and lawlessness". (Letter to *The Rand Daily Mail*, January 1952).

The deplorable state of housing for all non-whites in Johannesburg had led to very bad slum areas. The UP, who controlled the City's affairs, had failed year after year to spend the money to clear them up. It was attacked by all its political opponents, the English-language newspapers, the Bishop of Johannesburg, Father Trevor Huddleston CR, of Sophiatown and liberals like me. We all wanted immediate action – but despite continuous on-slaughts we could not budge the UP in the Council.

As a result the United Party alienated many of its own supporters in the safe parliamentary seats. It gave me a "kick" to use the Chamber of Commerce meetings as a platform to attack the UP and the City Council on the housing question. This always upset the businessmen who controlled the Chamber's affairs because, although I was entitled to speak on these matters, the only press reports these meetings got was when I took trouble to give newspapers a copy of my speech.

It was obvious to me when I joined the UP that I had inherited a number of enemies from the Chamber who were also UP conservatives. This did not deter me in continuing to use the Chamber of Commerce as a vehicle for reformist policies. Johannesburg's so-called business elite were astonishingly naive and politically uneducated.

In June 1953 I raised the question of the non-white Defiance Campaign, stressing how important it was for Commerce to understand why it was taking place. I pointed out that the Pietermaritzburg Chamber of Commerce called for a national convention to solve the country's mounting racial and political problems as a result of the implementation of apartheid. They reacted in stony silence at my statement that "it is our duty to come out of our shelter and hit this government as hard as we can because it is ruining South Africa."

The Star gave me good coverage – but many Chamber members were incensed. I had to discipline myself in my attacks on the United Party from the safety of the Chamber of Commerce. It was a very useful conduit for liberal criticism from me, which the conservative Chamber did not how to stop, especially during the period that I was politically homeless.

White politics was in a state of flux, black politics in a state of ferment, when I joined the UP. Liberals were seeking political platforms and the Liberal Association was calling for one-man-one-vote, a very courageous move in 1953. In contrast, United Party liberals like me did not yet accept this dictum – we considered South Africa was not ready to accept equality between black and white. If one wanted to be politically active such a platform was a ticket to disaster. Anyone with aspirations in parliamentary politics was misreading the signs at that time with such a policy – it would confine one to a political life in the wilderness.

Unfortunately the only option for many was the United Party with all its faults – it was the main opposition political force, and through it we hoped to get rid of the Nationalist government.

From the beginning there were tremendous setbacks. The performance of the UP in Parliament over the Public Safety Bill and the Criminal Laws Amendment Bill, which the Nationalists introduced because of "Native unrest", was so full of compromise that the UP nailed itself to the cross. Despite public outcry and pressure from urban constituents, the UP voted for these Bills which reduced civil and political rights, because of pressure from their right wing rural supporters.

The UP made sure that it would not be seen to be aligned to left wing political organisations like the Liberal Association, the Congress of Democrats or the war veterans' Springbok Legion. It was openly moving to the right because it had sights on the voters it lost to the Nationalists in the 1948 election. It needed them if it was to return to power. I was caught up in this action with no option but to accept the realities having joined the UP.

After the Government announced the General Election for April 1953 I was visited by young Harry Cooper, who was referred to me by a friend in the Anglo-American Corporation. Cooper owned a printing press in Johannesburg and was active on the liberal wing of the UP. He wanted my help for a project which he outlined that was important in the coming Provincial Council elections.

The Provinces controlled the schools. One of the divisive ways in which the Nationalists created schisms between Afrikaans and English-speaking children was by segregating the children into single medium schools. English-speakers had to be taught in English; Afrikaners through the medium of Afrikaans.

This was backed up by almost total control of all school boards and cultural organisations. This is how they inculcated their narrow concepts of Afrikaner nationalism amongst the youngest children, laying down the foundations of disunity in later years with unexpected economic and social problems for school-leavers.

In the Transvaal the Nationalists were the majority party. They enshrined the principle of single-medium instruction into the new Language Ordinance which set up separate English and Afrikaans schools. Prior to this there had been dual-medium schools teaching subjects in both languages. The children, by and large, were bilingual, played together and cemented bonds which it was hoped would lead to unity in the future. It was evident that white children were growing up in different worlds with disastrous social consequences. Worse still, if the home language was English and the parents had an Afrikaans name, the child could be forced to receive instruction in Afrikaans and vice versa. School principals were trapped into holding inquisitions to determine the home language.

Parents rights to choose the language of instruction were denied by the Ordinance. Evidence was already accumulating that children leaving single-medium schools were having difficulties getting jobs because they could only speak and write one language properly, or they were not bilingual.

Over lunch, Harry Cooper and I talked about the iniquities of this Ordinance and Nationalist policies in general and how best to tackle the matter in the election.

"How can we sell this to the UP so that it becomes an issue in the election?" I asked Harry. "On the face of it this is not a parliamentary matter; on the other hand, it is vital. The Nats are strengthening their hold on the kids, separating them at school, indoctrinating them, especially in the Afrikaans schools. The Nats don't just go for apartheid between black and white, but white and white as well. Can we get white voters to realise what is happening to their children when the Nats are trying to make segregation between white and black the main issue in the election? That's the question to be answered."

"Boris, I think that you and I should run this campaign because if the UP is connected in any way, it will be suspect. We must set up an independent organisation to propagandise these issues."

"A sort of education group?"

"Yes, that's it, you've hit the nail on the head. Let's call it Education Action Group"

"OK, that's the name. But where's the money coming from? Who will be on it – who will run it?"

We sat in the restaurant drinking innumerable cups of coffee and ended up at his printing works nearby. By late afternoon we had evolved our plan. The Education Action Group was born. Its sole purpose was to expose the serious effects of the Language Ordinance and how it was being manipulated by the Nationalists. We would invite some well-known English and Afrikaans educationalists to sit on the committee, two of them as joint presidents, I would act as chairman. Harry and I would do all the work, issue press statements, leaflets and advertise in the newspapers.

Harry disclosed that he had spoken to Harry Oppenheimer whose Trust Fund had donated £5 000 for the Education Action Group. Harry Cooper made one condition: he was not to be publicly associated with the EAG – I would have to launch it, and organise all its activities.

I had no trouble in getting a committee together. Two eminent educationalists, Professor Arthur Bleksley, a leading radio personality and Professor Eybers, an influential Afrikaner became the joint presidents. Two of my former headmasters were induced to complete the committee. Professional help was needed for the leaflets and advertising campaign. I asked Leslie Walker, who ran my company's advertising, to take this on.

"A great idea," said Leslie at our first meeting, "but I don't think an advertising campaign in the normal way will have any effect. We must do something totally different."

"What do you suggest?" I asked.

"I don't know yet, but I would think something on the lines of a strip cartoon – stories of separated children, parents talking about children, youngsters unable to get jobs, hatred amongst kids – I'll have to give it lots of thought."

"Could we use the adverts as leaflets as well?"

"Yes, that's the idea."

Leslie Walker came back to my office a few days later with a prepared series of strip cartoons he had visualised. They were outstanding. One of the captions read:

"Why should our children be made to hate?" says Mrs Smith to Mrs Kruger. Let us be one nation, not two!

VOTE AGAINST THE LANGUAGE ORDINANCE!"

The cartoon showed Mrs Smith talking to Mrs Kruger, each with a child. Other cartoons dealt with different aspects of the case against the Language Ordinance. Walker explained that to make the best case, we had to get real-life examples of children who had been forced to go the wrong language schools against their parents' wishes. These had to be publicised first as press reports, and then used in advertisements nearer the election.

Harry and I wasted no time in approving the scheme. We agreed not to tell the UP about it, because we knew the kind of delaying tactics we would meet. On 4 April I gave a statement to the English and Afrikaans newspapers about the Education Action Group, which launched it in the Transvaal. The concluding words were that "state intervention against parents' rights to provide for the future of their children is causing the breakdown of family life and our group will help every parent whose home life is so affected."

Published by Dr. E. Eybers, P.O. Box 7108, Johannesburg, for the Education Action Group, Electro House, Gold & Fox Streets, Johannesburg, and printed by Prompt Printing Co. (Pty.) Ltd. 11 Harris Street, Westgate, Johannesburg.

The effects of the first news releases were better than expected. The newspapers carried interviews with our joint presidents Bleksley and Eybers following up with their own reports. To our surprise, the UP asked for leaflets to distribute. Our most important success was with parents. They telephoned us at all hours and wrote to us. A Parent-School Committee in rural Groblersdal in Eastern Transvaal asked for help as the principals were separating the children against the parents' wishes.

In Johannesburg a Mr and Mrs de Wet told us of their battle with the education authorities over their six-year-old daughter Yvonne. They lived across the road from an English-medium school but because they had an Afrikaans name (their home language was English) they were forced to send Yvonne to an Afrikaans medium school three miles away. I fought with the authorities about their rights, won the case, and Yvonne was allowed to go to the school of her parents' choice across the road. It was a major victory for the Group. While I was negotiating the case we had maximum press coverage. The De Wets said we could use them in any way we liked in our advertisements, of which we distributed over 200 000 with great effect.

The Nationalists reaction was one of fury and they derided the actions of the EAG as a United Party trick. Despite them the campaign gathered its own momentum. Parents all over the Transvaal came forward with their own stories of "separation". We much enjoyed it when the Groblersdal headmasters, loyal Nationalists, complained angrily to *The Star* about us.

The campaign was a success. With very little money, only three active people and a front of leading educationists, we achieved our goal of making parents of both language groups seriously aware of the way their children were being manipulated and indoctrinated by the Nationalists *en route* to their republic.

It was not just an electoral issue, but a matter vital to parents. The United Party benefited from the campaign in the election, but they were beaten by the Nationalists who gained over twenty seats. The United Party lost six and the Labour Party remained with four.

For me it was an invigorating experience, but I was also learning a hard lesson. There was little one could do when the Nationalists fought elections on the *swart gevaar* (black peril) ticket. It was impossible to divert the attention of voters away from the colour issue. However important other matters were, the ones that decided how people voted all related to the main issue of the survival of the white man in his overwhelmingly black environment.

It taught me other things as well.

It gave me greater experience in handling the newspapers. It proved to me that one could involve the ordinary man to defend basic rights if the issues were properly exposed. It also drew me closer to the mainstream of South African politics.

One fortunate offshoot of my business commitments was that I had sufficient time to devote to the long political fight against the Nationalists that now confronted us after the 1953 election.

The UP was dispirited nationwide. The Torch Commando had faded away. The United Democratic Front had collapsed. The Nationalists, now more powerful than ever, had in their hands the Public Safety Act and the Criminal Laws Amendment Act which they readily used to halt the non-white Defiance Campaign, ban meetings and invoke emergency powers.

In addition Dr Verwoerd, using the new Bantu Authorities Act started his notorious "Black Spot" removal schemes extending his control over black activists and leaders in the Native reserves. Although we were often hundreds of miles away from the scene of the removals, liberal groups persisted in opposing Verwoerd, trying to inspire the UP into active opposition. The English newspapers constantly attacked him since he was the dominating political personality in the country as apartheid's front-runner. The Provinces soon lost control of Native education to him making him all-powerful.

Political activists in opposition to Verwoerd were learning what intimidation by the Nationalists meant. Left wingers like Solly Sachs found that life was a bed of nails. To avoid being detained, Sachs packed his bags and left for England on a one-way ticket. On the other hand, the Liberal Association decided the time had arrived to form the Liberal Party for all races irrespective of colour. This move drew a number of leading UP liberals. It was a blow to those of us who still thought we had a chance of reforming the UP. We held urgent meetings in Johannesburg to see if we could keep them in the UP, before the Liberal Party founders met in Cape Town.

By coincidence Pauline and I were on our way to London as Eric Cole's guest at the Coronation of Queen Elizabeth. I asked for an urgent meeting with the Liberals before boarding the Union Castle mail boat. I had a faint hope that I might be able to persuade them not to ditch the UP, which despite its weaknesses and internal conflicts, still had fifty-eight Opposition MPs in Parliament.

The Liberals saw me in a small office in the centre of Cape Town. In the crowded smoke-filled room I saw several of my friends, including some I never expected would leave the party.

I put my case as strongly as I could.

"Remain in the UP," I implored. "I know it has many weaknesses, difficulties between right and left. UP liberals will be more isolated if you leave. A one-man-one-vote Liberal Party with no colour bar is ideal – but SA is not ready for such a move – it will take years to come. Please think again."

I realised my pleas fell on deaf ears. In fact, I felt throughout the interview that I was wasting my time. But I had to do it.

The next morning, before we sailed for England, *The Cape Times* front page announced the formation of the Liberal Party of South Africa.

While I was overseas the role of some of the former leaders of the Torch Commando became clear. Several had joined the Liberal Party, others in Natal had formed the Federal Party to protect the country's constitution.

Overall there was a state of flux amongst white liberal activists who could be classified into two groups. Those outside the UP, the majority, had political connections with non-whites and expected changes to come in association with them. The other group, the minority, saw reform taking place through liberal changes in the whites-only opposition UP, being able to defeat the Nats, with Smuts-Hofmeyr policies implemented radically if the UP was returned to power.

Liberals outside the UP considered those inside toothless. We were tied to the party's Native Policy which had not been changed prior to the 1953 election and remained a chain around our necks. Political power in the UP was in the hands of the conservatives; this was confirmed when post mortems were held after the 1953 election defeat. The Witwatersrand General Council right wing leadership brushed aside our calls for reform of the Native Policy, which had lost the UP many of its leading liberals to the new parties. We were left behind hoping that our resolutions to the Transvaal and Union Congresses might bear fruit later.

I was determined to get support for reform through UP branches because this is where pressures had to start for new race relations policies. My own branch, Saxonwold, had a mix of liberals and conservatives. They agreed to my proposal that we form a small group to "investigate the UP's Native Policy". I was asked to draw up a statement for debate. In a matter of weeks I had a memorandum ready which I called: "A New Approach – Race Relations".

My main thesis was that the UP should re-examine its attitude to its Native Policy adopting a race relations policy instead.

"The non-Europeans," I recommended, "are being more and more integrated into the life of the country and it would be suicidal to try and halt their progress. We cannot reverse their role in our industrial, commercial and domestic economy. Race relations itself must be improved in South Africa."

Some of the practical improvements I proposed included: "Children should be taught the fundamentals of race relations in schools they should learn at least one Native language, ie Zulu, Tswana, Sotho – there are many . . . our aim should be to uplift non-Europeans . . . the colour bar should be reduced not extended . . . trade unions should be allowed for non-whites . . . their earnings should be increased . . . Native Reserves should be developed in terms of the Native Land and Trust Act of 1936."

I went on to say we should consult with non-Europeans – we should believe in the gradual extension of political rights in accordance with the principles of Christian Trusteeship.

I realised at the time that my proposals were a compromise to satisfy the opposing right and left wing elements in the UP. "Christian Trusteeship" was a meaningless phrase; it meant, in effect, the continued white man's domination of blacks under the cover of Christian principles which appeared in our "Native Policy", an inheritance from the Smuts era which the right wing could accept.

My proposals were not revolutionary, but compared to existing policy they were a great advance. I had a struggle to get the branch to accept them, because the conservative members were suspicious. I then sent the proposals to many of Witwatersrand branches for discussion. There was a poor response. This did not worry me. I was happy that I'd been given the chance to circulate my proposals.

There was one important indirect consequence. One morning my secretary told me that two members of the Saxonwold Branch were at my office reception at about 8 am asking to see me.

Jean Suttner and Gertrude Gottlieb, two of my UP liberal friends, walked into my office. As I ushered them in, Gertrude went to the door, locked it and put the key in her handbag.

"What's that for?" I asked with some surprise.

"We want to talk to you – you can have the key back if you say 'yes' to our request."

I laughed. "What request?"

"Boris, we are here to ask you to stand as the UP's candidate in the municipal by-election in Saxonwold. Major Opperman, the UP secretary, has agreed that we can ask you to be the party's candidate. We want a liberal, not a party hack foisted on us. You are the only one who can save the seat for the UP against the Liberal Party."

"But Gertrude, I don't want to go to the City Council and I'm not prepared to fight the Liberals. I support their general principles and in particular their stand on the Western Areas Removal Scheme. As you know, I do not support the line which the UP has taken in the City Council on the Western Areas Scheme."

The Western Areas Scheme was a burning issue on the Witwatersrand. Dr Verwoerd, under authority of the Native Resettlement Act, had commenced his first major removal of thousands of people from Sophiatown, an old-established slum area. Blacks and coloureds had lived there for over fifty years, owning their freehold properties. Sophiatown was adjacent to white suburbs, mainly of Afrikaners, who pressurised Verwoerd to clear Sophiatown and move the blacks to newly-proclaimed Meadowlands township, in the black areas next to Orlando and Moroka, with the coloureds transferred to another area. Freehold rights were taken away in favour of of thirty-year leases. Father Huddleston, whose parish and priory of Christ the King was in Sophiatown, lead his famous campaign against the scheme. Liberals, churchmen and the English newspapers backed him, as I did. The United Party, however, who wanted to outdo the Nationalists, to secure the Afrikaner vote throughout the country, openly supported Verwoerd's policy. As liberals, we had failed to get the UP to drop its open support for this aspect of Nationalist apartheid ideology.

On the face of it, the proposal that I should stand as the by-election candidate in these circumstances was absurd. I was strongly against what the UP was doing and publicly said so. It seemed to me that at the time the two ladies came to me they knew my liberal reputation might get the liberal UP voters to support me against the Liberal Party, although the UP in the City Council officially endorsed Dr Verwoerd's Western Area removals.

I was having nothing to do with their carefully contrived scheme, and I told them so.

"Look, I've publicly opposed Verwoerd and what he's doing. I've criticised the UP City Council through the Chamber of Commerce. I've written letters to the newspapers. No, I could never stand."

Gertrude tried to be firm.

"Well, we're not leaving until you've changed your mind."

She held up her bag with the key of the office. All I could do was ring for tea. I reaffirmed my stand against fighting the election.

"I've no desire to go to the City Council. You'd better try elsewhere. I want to be free to oppose the UP's policy without being tied to its Caucus. I also won't fight the Liberal Party."

The Liberal Party was making its first entry into elections. Their candidate was architect Leslie Cooper. He was already in the field, condemning the UP and the Western Areas scheme. The Johannesburg newspapers were giving him excellent coverage.

It was already mid-morning . I had done no work, my secretary gave up putting calls through to me and I was fed up with the two women.

"Girls, you've already had two hours here – I think we should call it a day."

Gertrude, however, was not interested in being deflected.

"No, we're not leaving. You've got to see reason. We're liberals like you. We want you to stand to show that the UP has got liberals who can speak their mind. You are the only one who can hold the seat. We also want to see you in public life. You have to leave the fringe and get into the fight in the Council."

How was I going to get out of this impasse?

The idea that I might perhaps do something about the Western Areas Scheme by fighting the election was beginning to appeal. I would not alter my views opposing it, but would have to find a way of doing so, taking the UP in the municipal ward with me, then dealing with the UP in the Council and Verwoerd. Was there a challenge I should accept, complicated though it was?

In the end I decided I would take it, although I was very unhappy that my opponents were the Liberal Party. I had, however, a first loyalty to my liberal colleagues in Parktown.

At eleven o'clock I gave in and said I would stand.

"I am warning you, though, I intend to fight the election my way and will not be bound by the UP policy in the Council. If you accept that, I'll sign the nomination papers."

Jean and Gertrude were happy that they had persuaded me to stand. Gertrude, who was the leader in this political ambush, rang Major Opperman immediately to give him the news.

After they left, I was horrified at what I'd done. The die was cast. I could not withdraw with honour. The next day I met with my proposers at the nomination court. There were only two candidates – the Liberal Party's Cooper and me.

The English and Afrikaans newspapers had a field day speculating why I, a known liberal opponent of the UP establishment, was standing against the Liberal Party. I was unaware that the UP could not get a candidate for the by-election. Since my fight for the Labour Party against the UP, I had kept myself unencumbered so I could speak my mind about Native Housing and Verwoerd's Western Western Areas Scheme. Now I was going into the lion's den.

Fighting an election under the banner of the UP was much easier than under the Labour Party. This time the UP's organisers broke the back of the canvass. They had strict instructions that if voters raised the Western Areas Scheme, controversy should be avoided. The voters would be referred to me.

I saw them all myself when I visited every one of the 4 000 on the Voters Roll. I ignored the Liberals who saw me as a sitting duck. They attacked me mercilessly about the UP's support for Verwoerd.

I knew by then that loyal UP voters always ignored opposition parties, although as the canvass progressed there were too many doubtful voters appearing in our returns. Did it mean the Liberal propaganda against the UP and me was working? There were no Nats in the ward to worry about. My problem was how to fix the Liberals and the UP establishment and at the same time launch a major attack on Dr Verwoerd. I worked out a strategy. I decided I would have one public meeting two nights before the election day which would leave my opponents no time to reply or contact voters.

At every opportunity I got newspaper exposure. Once I was on the front page of *The Rand Daily Mail*, addressing the Saxonwold bus queues in town. The speech lasted a few minutes – it was the picture on the front page that counted.

I was ready with my *coup de grâce* to be delivered at a public meeting at St Columba's Church Hall. Every seat was occupied, the press well represented. My Liberal opponents were there in force, including their candidate Leslie Cooper.

I did not attack the Liberal Party in my speech. I attacked Dr Verwoerd and his Nationalist Party's policy of forced "Native removals". I then made the announcement which I hoped would dispose of the Liberal Party and make clear to the Nationalists where I and the UP stood. I told the meeting that my personal view, which was well-known, was that I opposed the Western Areas Removal Scheme, and that the United Party would support me "ultimately" in opposing the removals despite our differences. This was my policy in the Council.

The meeting exploded. The cheers were resounding, with Gertrude Gottlieb and Jean Suttner on their feet. The Liberals were taken by surprise and I had no difficulty in dealing with their questions.

I had thrown down the gauntlet compromising the UP establishment and gave notice to the UP in the Council and to Verwoerd where I stood. Tactically it was too late for the UP to act against me. They were as bad as the Nationalists on the Western Areas Scheme. I was certain there would be no public disclaimer by the UP forty-eight hours before the election.

The next morning *The Rand Daily Mail* not only carried a full report of the meeting, with a large photograph on the front page, but also predicted that as a result of my intervention the UP would be forced into opposing the Western Areas Scheme. *The Star* carried a similar report. Its newspaper editorial, as did *The Rand Daily Mail*'s, called on the voters of Saxonwold to support me. I did not rely on the newspapers. That evening I distributed to every voter in the ward a leaflet telling them exactly where I stood on the Western Areas Scheme. When the results were announced I had won the election by a large majority.

The results were: Dr Boris Wilson (UP)   1 955
Leslie Cooper (Lib)   809
Majority   1 146

POLITICS

If the impression can be created that South Africa is weak and divided internally, that South Africa can consequently be attacked and its government overthrown with comparatively little trouble or danger, in the interests of another one, then South Africa faces the bigger danger that we shall be involved in a struggle not only against boycotts, but in an armed struggle. That is where the danger lies. But once the world realises that South Africans will stand together to the bitter end to defend their rights as stated by this government, namely, the continued existence of the whites and the granting of their rights to the non-whites, in each case according to the method most fitting, they will think twice. If our assailants realise they will have to deal with a united South Africa, a united South Africa will resist any attempt to deprive it of this right by way of boycotts or armed force, it will not be easy to launch either of these two forms of attack.

Dr The Hon Verwoerd, MP,
Prime Minister
Republic of South Africa
House of Assembly Debate
Columns 4913/4914
24 April 1964

33

The next hurdle had to be faced in the City Council.

The United Party's City Councillors decided they would fix me. A week before, they had organised a special meeting of the City Council for the day following the by-election, on the Western Areas Removal Scheme. This was the welcome I was to receive. I was not told what the Caucus had decided to do.

The campaign had exhausted me. My telephone did not stop ringing, with both congratulations and abuse. Nevertheless, although I was so tired I could hardly stand up, I was welcomed by the Town Clerk at the City Hall, and clothed in my councillor's gown. Two former councillors, who had broken with the UP over the Western Areas, came to me as I was taking my seat in the Council Chamber to congratulate me on my stand. The rest of the UP councillors ignored me. Interest in the debate was high; the public galleries were packed with spectators and press.

The Council Chamber was typically Victorian, with councillors sitting in a half-circle facing the robed Mayor, the Town Clerk and his officials. The UP occupied most of the seating with a small Nationalist group to my right.

As I was going to take my seat I was handed a copy of *The Star*, which carried Dr Verwoerd's formal announcement that he was going ahead with the first removals from Sophiatown.

The debate began. During the early stages the Nationalists, lead by PZJ van Vuuren, attacked the UP, saying it was under the influence of liberals and me in particular. I could see the UP squirming. Due to the speed of events I'd given no thought to a maiden speech. However as the debate progressed I had no option but to stand up and clarify my position. I knew why I had come to the Council. I was going to make it crystal clear to Nationalists where I stood and where the UP should be going as far as the Western Areas were concerned.

I eventually caught the Mayor's eye and commenced my maiden speech. It was 1 November 1953.

Unknown to me the Council had for the first and only time decided to record all speeches on *Hansard* lines because of the importance of the debate, and no doubt the controversy that would arise over my election statements.

"Mr Mayor, two years ago when the Western Areas Scheme was first mooted, I took up an attitude against the scheme which I have consistently carried out and kept to. Accusations have been made by the Leader of the Opposition [Nationalists] here – he calls me a liberal, or as we think progressive, as to what we represent.

"In moving the motion for debate the Nationalist opposition already attacked me . . .

"Mr Mayor, I have been outside this Council Chamber and have come in at a stage when the whole City of Johannesburg and possibly the whole of South Africa is watching the outcome of this debate with the greatest possible interest . . . because of the very important implications of the Western Areas Scheme . . .

"It is not only the two per cent who own the freehold right who concern us, it is all people all over the country who own freehold who are our concern in this Chamber tonight."

There was total silence. I had their full attention. I could feel this strongly as I went on: (I again quote from the unique Council *Hansard*):

"I want to say this: I am proud that on the day I entered this Chamber the Leader of the Opposition should rise and be worried about the fact that one more liberal has entered the Council . . ."

Councillor van Vuuren (Leader of the Opposition): "It doesn't worry me that much."

I reacted immediately to his interjection.

"It did seem to worry Councillor van Vuuren this afternoon. Perhaps he has got over his troubles by now . . . I think what is worrying my friend is that he sees that change is coming and is being reflected not through me, but even in this chamber . . .

"Mr Mayor, the UP has gone through a most worrying time. No one would say – even those of us who want to hide the situation – that we have not got differences of opinion . . . I do not believe as a newcomer that we could make such a momentous decision tonight that would alter the Western Areas Scheme. But what I do say is this that the amendment put forward by Mr Gordon [the UP leader] affirming UP policy with regard to freehold and other factors is of the most vital importance. There is one person who is going to be responsible for the *ultimate rejection* of the Western Areas and all such schemes and it is Dr Verwoerd and the Nationalist Party."

I was able to make these remarks, especially about the *ultimate rejection* because it became clear as the debate progressed that I had won a signal victory in the UP. During the debate to save face the UP leaders hurriedly modified their stand and put in an amendment to the Nationalist motion on the removal scheme. They had found my remarks in the debate compromising and their amendment showed that they were prepared to go along the road that lead ultimately to total opposition to the scheme.

I was thus able to back what they had done by saying that "the policy of not giving in one inch to the Nationalist Party is unifying opposition to this scheme and what it represents. If Councillor van Vuuren is particularly worried by the fact that our democratic United Party permitted me to say that we will ultimately reject this scheme it is because I have been given full backing to say that as long as the Nationalist Party continues in endeavouring to dispossess people in this country of their rights and if it persists, the inevitable consequence of that will be the *ultimate rejection* by the UP . . ."

When I finished speaking, I sat down to applause from some of the Councillors and most of the spectators in the public gallery.

Councillor van Vuuren was immediately on his feet.

"Mr Mayor, it comes from the bottom of my heart that the honour is bestowed on me to congratulate the new member on the speech he has delivered here, his maiden speech . . . I think the speech he has delivered here will be a speech that will be referred to for many, many years to come in the future, and I can tell him this, that in his short and concise speech where he has expressed his heart, he has really given the Nationalist Party encouragement that will be used in the future to every advantage."

My recollection of the rest of the debate is hazy. Exhaustion had finally overtaken me a second time. The election effort, the tension of having to go to the Council almost immediately, making my maiden speech was almost too much for me.

One thing stood out. I had not only made more enemies in the National Party – I had made many more in the United Party. They would not forgive me for forcing them into a corner and compromise over the Western Areas.

It only dawned on me later that I had launched myself on a public career in a very exciting way. This was in stark contrast to the way I had started my medical training; then I had time to organise my business affairs. Once more I was rushing backwards and forwards – this time to the City Council. There were innumerable committee and party caucus meetings. My Ward 26 had issues constantly needing attention. I had to get used to dealing with pavements, street lighting, sewerage, bus stops and all the pedestrian paraphernalia in the life of a city councillor.

As a small boy I knew the outside of the City Hall with its long row of steps leading to the Mayor's parlour, and his old Rolls Royce with the TJ1 numberplate parked outside. I knew it best of all when Father used to take me to hear Bill Dunbar standing on his pedestal preaching his socialism. I knew something about the interior of the rates office because I was often sent to pay Father's overdue light or water account when they had been cut off. I knew the City Hall as the terminus for the Yeoville and Observatory trams when I was on my way in the early mornings to the Market.

It was a typical domed Victorian-type municipal building in the centre of Johannesburg. It housed the Council Chamber, a large public hall and all the municipal offices. To the west of the building was the old Market Square where Father first sold fruit from a barrow when he arrived as an enforced immigrant to South Africa. Market Square now houses a modern Library building.

Beyond this is the diminishing old Indian business quarter of Diagonal Street, with its dozens of colourful fruit shops and bazaars. *The Star* offices are still nearby. To the east of the City Hall, across the road is the historic old Post Office. Next to it was the famous Standard Theatre, which was demolished years ago. Surrounding the City Hall, interspersed with the new "skyscrapers" which make Johannesburg as faceless as any large international city, were many lovely old Victorian and Edwardian buildings dating from the "gold rush" of the late 19th century. Johannesburg's centre developed on gridiron pattern of streets between the dusty yellow mine-dumps and black headgears miles to the south, east and west. To the north was, and is, congested Hillbrow and Hospital flatland with the leafy suburbs and houses of the upper-middle class beyond.

The United Party controlled the City of Johannesburg through the Ratepayers Association, with forty-two members as against about ten Nationalists and a few independents. Most of the the work was done in committee and it took me some time to find out how local government worked. I soon learnt that most decisions were taken in our Caucus, or even by an inner leader's group, a sort of cabinet, so that some decisions were presented to Caucus as *fait accompli.*

There were very few "rebels" in the UP Caucus. Most councillors were only too happy to attend council or committee meetings, look after their own constituency needs and avoid controversy as far as possible. They were friendly with the minority Nationalist opposition, who had the ear of government, and in particular Dr Verwoerd. Our own Caucus meetings were rubber-stamp gatherings.

I soon learnt that to get anything done for one's ward it was best to go direct to the appropriate council officials, who were usually helpful. They would draft the necessary resolution to council, but often this had to be presented to Caucus before going to the committee concerned.

Council meetings were dull affairs in which we raced through the enormous monthly agenda all voting according to Caucus decisions. There was one bright spot. Under a standing order, a councillor could ask permission to address the Council on a special subject. I realised this was the best way to raise matters of "public importance" unknown to the Caucus, over which they had no control once the Mayor had given permission to speak. I decided I would use this facility whenever I could.

All councillors had to be on one of the standing committees. I opted to be on three: Non-European Affairs (black, coloured and Indian Affairs), General Purposes and Health. As the new boy the Caucus put me on Health since I was the only medical doctor in the Council. They kept me off Non-European Affairs because of my attitude to the Western Areas.

Dr Verwoerd had told them in no uncertain terms that he expected the Council to co-operate with him on the clearance of Sophiatown and resettlement at Meadowlands. UP liberals outside the Council were trying to pressurise their councillors not to co-operate as a result of the publicity given to this matter in my election campaign which had become a national issue. To satisfy the pressurising they withheld support, using freehold rights as the excuse – this was the way they compromised after my election statement that they would ultimately agree. The UP was having a rough time, being assailed on all sides. English newspapers who normally supported them were critical of their role on the Western Areas – the UP liberals were not leaving them alone and Dr Verwoerd kept his sword over their heads through his Resettlement Board and the letter of compliance the UP had sent him before I came to the Council.

There were only two or three liberally-inclined councillors in our Caucus. The Nats singled me out from the first day and used me as a stick with which to beat the conservative UP. The UP did not like the accusation of being under the control of Boris Wilson, the red bogeyman and the liberalist – this was the last thing needed in their political lives. I had few friends in the Caucus and was watched like a hawk.

One of the few Caucus critics was Harry Schwarz, the ex-soldier who opposed my appointment as Parktown secretary. As a councillor he often attacked the leadership. He was a lawyer with a sarcastic and biting tongue – they did not like him despite the fact that he was conservative politician. Although we differed politically I liked his aggressive and outspoken attitude.

The intellectual calibre of the Johannesburg's UP City Councillors was not very high. I did not regard myself as someone superior, but they really were a "collection of butchers, bakers and candlestick makers" trying to cope with serious urban problems, sociological, economic and financial for which they had little aptitude. They relied on advice of officials, many of whom were intellectually better equipped. Most councillors were interested in their own ward problems and getting results. They all had one characteristic fear in common – they did not want to upset the National Party in the Council, which as far as I was concerned was why I came to the Council.

Before I arrived in the Council, Richard Harvey a former Chairman of the Chamber of Commerce and Jack Lewsen a well-known barrister, resigned from the United Party, staying on as Independents. They were protesting at the UP's procrastination in Native Housing over which I had been fighting on the sidelines. They joined forces with Jack Cutten, a town planner, to expose the UP debacle.

In October 1953, when the new Council Committees were elected, I managed to get myself on Non-European Affairs as well as Health and General Purposes. In addition I became the Council's representative on the Council of my University, an appointment which delighted me. No one else in the UP wanted to take this job because it was "boring". This confirmed my impression about the average UP Councillor's interests and ability. I became more and more deeply involved in problems concerning the Non-European Affairs and Health Committees, especially becoming knowledgeable on the environmental problems of the black townships of the south-west. In those days it was easy to wander around the townships to see how the people coped in their appalling shacks, with primitive water and sewerage, poor hygiene and bad transport in the overcrowded townships. I took every opportunity to talk to residents and get first hand knowledge of living conditions, mostly without officials present.

My political and medical studies, knowledge of sociology and economics, experience with blacks at the hospitals and business were put to good use as a councillor. As a result, when issues were discussed in the Council, Caucus or committees I was able to make positive contributions speaking from direct knowledge. Councillors did not understand "investigative local

175

government" – getting at the root causes of local problems. They did not venture far from the club-like atmosphere of the City Hall.

Mostly, their sights were set on how soon their turn would come to be the mayor or the chairman of a committee. I soon-got the message that I would not be appointed to a committee chairmanship let alone a position of influence in the Caucus because of my liberal leanings. This never worried me, although it was clear that if one could get control of the Caucus the fight against the Nationalists could be intensified.

Too often I was the lone voice of dissent in Caucus. If it was on an issue of fundamental importance, I did not hesitate to get the help of the UP outside the confines of the City Council.

It was useless trying to take on the UP's political machine in the Council on my own. It was quite different from the small Labour Party. Pragmatism was the only sensible course. I was concerned to improve certain areas of the Council's domain and expose what had been concealed. It was more rewarding than trying to take on the Council or the UP Caucus single-handed to gain a political point.

I used the "public importance" standing rules to raise issues whenever there was something that needed attention. I had, therefore, to investigate the problem and present it properly. Council meetings were well covered by the newspapers, so I alerted those journalists who gave me good coverage, which annoyed many of my colleagues. My friendship with Ernest Shirley of *The Star*, who covered the municipal "beat", was a rewarding and valuable relationship during my years on the Council. My researches would often start with Council officials, who were always ready to co-operate if it was a matter that needed ventilation. In this way I became friendly with some of the senior men.

Dr Ivor Holmes, the City Treasurer, a tall angular and ascetic man, was one whose friendship and advice were of the greatest help and importance to me.

Ernie Shirley knew fully what the UP was doing in the Council, since he had covered its activities for years. It was through him that I learnt how the UP was controlled by a small clique headed by GB Gordon. Associated with him were two men who had political ambitions and who were waiting to snatch the leadership when Gordon retired.

One was a smiling Pickwickian councillor, Hymie Miller, a former mayor and everybody's friend; and Charles Patmore who became the mayor shortly after I arrived. Miller was a lawyer who, despite his public affability, was a shrewd political operator. He was elected leader when Gordon died. A former chairman of the Non-European Affairs Committee, (NEAC) he was very pleased to give it up because of the UP's failure to resolve the housing crisis in the townships. Major Opperman, the UP's local secretary took it over. I was certain that Miller surrendered the chairmanship because he did not want to clash with Dr Verwoerd. He wanted to maintain his image as a "neutral" politician.

Before I arrived on the Council, it was only the efforts of Harvey, Lewsen and Jack Cutten, who formed the Citizen's Housing Committee in

1950, that eventually got the Council on its way to build some Native houses. By the time I arrived the situation was bad again.

Local authorities were responsible for Native Housing, but blacks were too poor to pay economic rentals. The Council was scared of the political implications of increasing Johannesburg's rates; this would mean asking their white voters to pay for Native Housing. Dr Verwoerd adamantly refused to finance the City's housing needs because of his apartheid priorities. According to Verwoerd, blacks could not become permanent urban dwellers. They were temporary migrants to the towns and had to return to their homes in the rural areas when their jobs were finished, or they retired, or were unable to get work. The Urban Areas Act then compelled them to leave the area within 72 hours.

The Urban Areas Act was strictly applied. Blacks had just three days to find a job in Johannesburg – the notorious section 10 – failing which they had to go back to the reserves.

I only realised, when I became a councillor, that the UP was playing a double game; trying to placate Johannesburg's white ratepayers while implementing Verwoerd's apartheid laws.

The UP had appointed a Director of Housing, AJ Archibald. All he could manage out of a target of 10 000 houses a year was 2 000 because inadequate funds were available. Thousands of blacks lived illegally in the townships, in abject poverty. Critics outside the Council, such as the Citizens Housing Committee, Father Huddleston, the Chambers of Commerce and Industry tried to get the Council to clear slums and build houses. Verwoerd was not interested in either of these objectives. All he wanted was to remove Natives out of urban areas and keep the towns white. The UP had neither the will nor the motivation to initiate slum clearance or urban renewal.

Our UP Caucus meetings made clear why nothing was done. Leaders like Miller suffered from the same political disease as the UP's national leadership – a thinly-disguised Nationalism. In 1954 the UP adopted what they considered was a forward-looking "Native Policy"; it left the door wide open to "white supremacy" and residential segregation.

Many of the senior UP councillors had parliamentary ambitions and did not want their reputations destroyed, especially when their wards were full of "poor white" Nationalist voters.

The UP's leaders made it clear that they did not want the Council to do anything that would alienate platteland voters by being seen to act as "kaffer boeties" (kaffer lovers – perhaps the most damningly insulting of all political epithets).

This was a current UP nightmare. All UP public representatives had to become adept at speaking with two voices – one for the towns and one for the platteland. This political duplicity eventually killed the United Party; it has disappeared from the political scene in South Africa. But then it was all there was!

All this had a powerful influence on how I played my cards in the Council. I decided to concentrate on getting practical results, since the

Council bristled with long-standing unresolved problems. At local government level one could find solutions to most problems if one wanted to. Local authorities were responsible for the welfare of blacks. In Johannesburg, unfortunately, the United Party did not have the guts to stand up to Verwoerd and his apartheid legislation.

When I entered the Council he had the UP under his thumb. They had agreed to act as his agents to carry out removals; and they were unable to build houses because Verwoerd insisted that any houses built should be for blacks who were to be removed from the newly-declared "white" areas.

The United Party members were always going to Pretoria to see Dr Verwoerd or his officials about matters connected with Native Affairs. As I had only recently become a member of the NEAC, I was not invited to these meetings and was never part of the deputations. I was already known as one of Verwoerd's UP critics. The UP always had excellent reasons why houses could not be built for blacks. The Council was brewing its own "native beer" so that beerhall profits could be used to finance Native housing or amenities. Profits from municipal beerhalls were often the only way that local authorities could finance housing for blacks, but these were meagre.

One of the benefits of my election to the Council was that I was the recipient of invitations to speak to meetings of the UP on the Witwatersrand, during which I met more of the liberals in the party. Although many were vociferous and active, there was no organised liberal group. Most of the liberals lived in the wealthy northern suburbs of Johannesburg and did what they could to change the UP's right wing policies, but without much success.

All the local committees on the Witwatersrand were controlled by the conservatives and nominations to the important national committees were filled by these members.

At the general election Helen Suzman, Zach de Beer, John Cope, Harry Oppenheimer, Jan Steytler, Ray Swart and the other liberals were the progressive conduit which became important to the few liberals on the City Council. The MPs were trying to influence the party in Parliament to adopt an enlightened approach to the problems being experienced by the UP in Johannesburg. MPs had political problems in the parliamentary caucus similar to those we had in the Council, so that active liberals were always fighting on two fronts, one within the party and one against Nationalists.

My initial impression when I joined the UP in 1952 was that the conservatives did not want liberals in the UP. In my case they were not happy with the left wing "recruit" from the LP. What staggered me was that I discovered that there were UP "liberals" who were also not happy about left wing recruits from the Labour Party. Like the conservatives, they did not like socialist backgrounds. This no doubt had its origin in the wealthy life style of the liberals of northern-suburban Johannesburg who were somewhat ignorant of what socialism in the South African context meant. They were also full of the political prejudice which seemed almost universal in South African politics in the 1950s, whether liberal or conservative. They all

178

believed that if right wing Afrikaner Nationalists were induced to join the UP it would be a considerable coup for the UP.

Co-operation between me and the UP hierarchy on the Witwatersrand was like walking on a perpetual bed of hot coals. They spent most of their time trying to keep me off important committees. Mostly I ignored what they were doing and concentrated on the practicalities of what I could achieve.

From the start of my public career the National Party singled me out as one of the UP's leading "liberalists". They used this term instead of straightforward "liberal" as a political smear to imply that I was an extreme left wing radical. It was a response to my maiden speech in the Council, to rebuke the UP for their association with me. The Nat leader, Van Vuuren, took every opportunity to remind the UP what a formidable and dangerous "liberalist" they were harbouring in their midst, wooing the UP's conservatives.

The UP had political problems on its left, and its right. Dissident right wing MPs, which included Bailey Bekker, Blaar Coetzee, Frank Waring and Arthur Barlow (MP for Hospital) defected from the UP. They first formed an Independent Party, renaming it the Conservative Party, when the UP failed to support the government over the removal of the coloured voters from the Common Roll.

I knew Coetzee well, since he was Parktown's MPC when I was its secretary. He was young brash, aggressive, a rousing debater originally considered a great "catch" when he joined "liberal" Parktown, bragging of his liberalism to reassure the branch's financial backers. I recall him congratulating me on my liberalism at a meeting one evening, views which said he shared. This was noted in the minutes as I was still secretary. Personally, I did not believe him for a moment.

After Coetzee left the UP I became one of his political targets in Parliament. *The Rand Daily Mail* reported on 24 April that Coetzee asked Harry Lawrence, a UP front-bencher, whether "three of its City Councillors, Dr Wilson, Mr Harvey and Mr Lewsen held meetings in co-operation with natives to protest against the Western Areas Removal Scheme."

Coetzee told Parliament that "liberals controlled the UP as agitators by stirring up feeling against the Resettlement Bill,"which would cause bloodshed.

Barlow added that "two UP councillors held a meeting with Dr AB Xuma," (a founder and former chairman of the African National Congress), "and at another meeting UP City Councillor Dr Boris Wilson appeared with Natives on the same platform."

Arthur Barlow's statement was pure fabrication made under cover of parliamentary privilege. I had not appeared at any time on a platform with blacks or with the ANC – no one had ever invited me to do so. In 1954 the UP did not encourage its public representatives to appear on platforms with "Natives". We had to accept that there was a large gulf between us and blacks and it was party policy that we could only appear on political platforms with whites. Nationalists and their allies regularly made these allegations about the UP's liberals. Although the UP stood for consultation with blacks, it was frowned on when it took place because they were scared that Nationalists would make political capital out of it – which they did.

These accusations were used to give voters – the mythical average white South African – the impression that "liberalists", leftists and Communists were the only ones prepared to act in concert with political blacks on the same platforms. These accusations made by Nationalists against some UP representatives made the UP cower in collective fear. I was certain that this was only the beginning of "liberalist" attacks on me by my Nationalist opponents.

At UP congresses, conservative elements from both the urban and platteland areas would openly attack liberals in its ranks while the leadership of the party usually remained silent; this suggested that they tacitly approved of these actions. I expected attacks from Nationalists, but the vehemence of the UP's right wing was surprising. There was total cleavage between right and left in the UP and when the Nats attacked my liberal activities they were reinforcing the UP's conservatives.

As the "new boy" in the Council, this double attempt to tarnish my political image as an agitator in the struggle between whites and blacks, kept me always on the alert.

The UP was trying to steer a middle course in politics. It believed that line would attract the platteland Afrikaans voters it had lost in previous elections and since Smuts's dramatic takeover at the commencement of World War II. So the UP's policies and political statements were often biased in favour of rural voting opinion. In addition, liberal MPs and MPCs were confined to the urban areas like Johannesburg's northern suburbs. In our constituencies we sounded like liberals while our counterparts in the rural and semi-urban areas sounded like Nationalists. We were hardly ever sent to speak to voters in the rural areas. The UP acted out a political Jekyll and Hyde role – living in two worlds.

The Nationalists welcomed my advent to the City Council because I was outspoken and they hoped I could be used as a battering ram against the uncomfortable UP majority. The UP had to stomach this because the bulk of its funds came from the wealthy northern suburbs of Johannesburg and the Oppenheimers.

This was the background to the political scene when I entered the City Council in 1953.

In the early days I was not restricted when visiting the black townships. I spent a lot of time there with my 16 mm Bolex camera seeing how people lived, recording the poverty and the appalling slum conditions, getting as much insight as I could into the problems of being black in Verwoerd's apartheid society.

The townships consisted of the old areas of Moroka, Jabavu, Orlando and White City, the latter adjacent to the worst slum I had ever seen – Shantytown. Tin shanties, corrugated iron shacks and packing cases formed the bulk of the so-called dwellings into which over 80 000 blacks were crammed. No proper roads existed, only dirt tracks and narrow paths between the houses, no sanitation, no running water no communal services. Crime, disease, drunkenness were rampant. The Council had lost control of the slums, which had spread enormously since the war due to the influx of blacks into Johannesburg seeking work. It was also faced with Dr Verwoerd's unrealistic demands to rehouse blacks that he wanted removed from white Johannesburg.

Sprawling around Shantytown were some of the new houses being built on "site and service" stands for Natives moved there as a result of Verwoerd's demands that illegal city dwellers had first priority over slum-dwellers for new housing. These stands, on which the council would eventually build houses, had an outside pit privy and tap and were strictly controlled as to their usage by Dr Verwoerd's officials.

Verwoerd's instructions were that blacks could not be rehoused without first putting them on a site and service stand. The house was then built while they lived in a temporary shack on site.

The amenities in the black townships were bad. There was one garage in the centre with a few shops. Roads were untarred, pavements did not exist. There was no street lighting; few houses had electricity. In Eastern Native Township, schools were few and far between with no proper sports fields – just rough open ground as playgrounds for black children.

The City Council had established a number of health clinics, five in all, spread out in the townships and run by a few dedicated doctors and nurses. Through my contacts with these doctors I was able to confirm the extent of deprivation, poverty and ill-health. Tuberculosis was rife, malnutrition endemic, with all the concomitant diseases of overcrowded homes, low income levels and unemployment. Houses were basic. Walls, roofs with no ceilings, and mostly unmade floors. Water taps were outside as were the toilets. Heating and cooking was done with coal and wood fires often inside the homes, sometimes ending in disaster with carbon monoxide poisoning. Most times the townships were covered in a pall of smog which concealed them from the white man's sensitive gaze.

There was only one hospital for the townships – Baragwanath – the converted military camp. It was outside the townships. Today it is still the only hospital for Soweto's 2 – 3 million blacks.

Several of the clinic doctors in the Council's employ were at Medical School with me. They told me I was the first councillor ever to visit them to find out what was happening in the townships. Their conditions of work were bad, pay was low, most of the clinics had minimal facilities and the Council was totally disinterested in what went on. Some of the doctors wanted to leave the Council's employ and I promised that I would do everything I could to deal with their frustrations and the poor state of the townships.

I reminded myself that when I started medicine I had done so because of my interest in its social dimension. Here I was, confronted through politics, with my first challenge – medical and social problems that needed urgent attention. It was my first chance to put into practice all I had learned and to use political powers to do it.

Apart from what was on my plate at the Council, the ordinary work in my ward took up time, especially keeping in touch with constituents. In June 1954, the United Party was once again confronted, at short notice, with an election problem. The candidate for the Provincial Council in the Hospital constituency, a barrister called Lammie Snyman, (who later became a judge) withdrew at the last minute, just before nomination day. The UP, as usual, urgently needed a last-minute substitute. I was asked by the candidates' committee whether I would stand. The idea intrigued me, because Arthur Barlow was still the MP.

He had left the UP and there was no doubt that at the next general election the UP's MPC would be the obvious choice for MP. I was fascinated at the prospect of being able to harass Barlow, who did not like my liberal politics.

No doubt Barlow recalled my attempts to challenge him when he edited and owned *Arthur Barlows Weekly* and I was editor of *WU's Views* – the university newspaper.

The Hospital constituency was in disarray. The UP had neglected the infrastructure, as I discovered when I was invited to meet the local executive. They were a suspicious, conservative lot. Most of them did not want me and they made it very obvious. They had little alternative because no one else wanted the job at short notice and time was against them. It was made clear to me that I could expect little co-operation from the local organisation, which consisted of little more than a few individuals and depleted branches.

I was not unused to dissent; my limited political experience had been a good, hard dose of reality. So I decided to become the MPC and reorganise the constituency. The situation could not have been worse. I had to deal with an arrogant and defiant Barlow and an uncooperative United Party. Fortunately I was elected unopposed.

I was then able to apply myself to finding new people, restructuring the branches and creating a new divisional organisation.

There were many problems. The Hospital constituency was one of the most densely populated flatland areas in South Africa, with over 50 per cent of its voters constantly on the move. The only stable electors were the geriatrics: elderly ladies, widows, spinsters, who hardly ever attended a political meeting. For the rest, many were itinerant young people who lived in the cheap flats and lodgings; they could not be relied on to do any political work. As I expected, it was a very conservative area and my liberalism would be a hard sell there.

There were serious educational and hospital problems in the constituency. As I delved into Hospital, I found it a bottomless pit of unresolved issues. The sensible thing was to deal with the day-to-day matters, reconstruct the organisation and establish myself as the head of the UP in Hospital so I could challenge Barlow.

Fortunately, the Provincial Council met only three times a year, for short periods, was based in Pretoria, and dealt with education, local government and hospitals – all of which interested me. Several of my

The walkabout in Shantytown, Soweto; in the middle of the slums, surrounded by children.

Shantytown walkabout: BW, Sir Ernest Oppenheimer, leaders of the Native Advisory Boards (Mr Vundla is in the dark coat, centre), the Mayor of Johannesburg.

Announcing the £3 000 000 housing loan to the special meeting of the Johannesburg City Council, August 1956.

Sir Ernest Oppenheimer and BW congratulate each other after the special meeting, August 1956.

colleagues on the City Council were in the dual position of being MPCs as well. As far as I was concerned I was able to use the Provincial Council to strengthen my position on the City Council when dealing with issues that were common to both bodies. There were many advantages in being both councillor and MPC.

34

More of my time was now spent in politics. My business was still expanding. There were daily appearances at the office and rushed trips around the country. I still visited overseas suppliers annually. My Rhodesian company was over its initial problems and was flourishing. The only thing that suffered was my clinical medical practice. It was only possible to keep it up on an *ad hoc* basis but I was reluctant to stop altogether. I rationalised that I was active in the medical field through politics and fulfilling a useful function this way. In 1953 I was co-founder of the National General Practitioners Group with Dr Colin Cairncross, an older colleague, and I even indulged in an attempt to organise nurses into a trade union.

The main medical and social problem at this time was the terrible state of the City Council's health services in the black townships. I was determined to expose these and get something done about them. One of my ex-colleagues from student days, a polyclinic doctor employed by the Council, disclosed the horrific details of the Council's health services. Everything he told me was confirmed by medical records and corroborated by other doctors during my private tours of inspection. Although I was a member of the Health Committee, I decided I would carry out the investigations on my own because I intended to challenge the Health Committee's bona fides; they were responsible for what I was seeing. At no time had the Health Committee indicated to me or anyone else that they were sitting on a time bomb. In fact they were totally unaware of the seriousness of the township's health services.

The doctors and nurses to whom I spoke were devoted, but desperate men and women. For years the Council had paid little or no attention to the numerous reports and cries for help that came from the polyclinic doctors. Clearly, heroic action was required.

For me there was only one course – to attack the Council at its next monthly meeting, exposing it to the press and public to force it to remedy years of neglect in the townships.

One Friday morning in July, I gave notice to the Town Clerk that I wanted the half hour to speak on a matter of public importance concerning health services. There was no problem because I was the only one who ever used this facility. I went straight into describing the serious health conditions in the south-western Native townships to a full meeting of the Council.

"Mr Mayor, on Friday morning I went on a tour of the non-European so-called polyclinics established by the Council in the Native townships of Kliptown, Moroka, Jabavu, Orlando and Shantytown. They are travesties of what polyclinics are in properly run medical services."

I went on to discuss what I had found. I pointed out that doctors and nurses were grossly overworked, underpaid and housed in small, badly-lit, poorly-equipped buildings. I asked why Councillors had not bothered to visit these polyclinics.

I told the Council that there were 323 420 known residents in these townships, excluding illegal dwellers, with over 154 000 living in Johannesburg itself. The Council's health services had dealt with over 800 000 patients in 1953. Nearly 500 000 of these had been seen by the doctors in the clinics and over 300 000 in their slum homes.

"I want to shock the Council and the people of Johannesburg today and I am going to do so. To start with, I want to show you a photograph of pregnant mothers who have been standing in the sun for five hours waiting for an antenatal clinic to commence. The queue is over 120 yards long and is there every Monday morning. The women start coming at 8 am in the morning and can only see medical staff at 2 pm in the afternoon. It is bad for a pregnant mother to stand for hours on end."

The Councillors in the Chamber never said a word. The photographs which I handed out were first shown to the Mayor by the commissionaire and then passed on to the Councillors. It was the first of a series of photographs I was going to show them which I had taken myself, and which would condemn the Council's Health Committee for its failure to see that the blacks in the townships were provided with proper basic health services.

I did not tell the councillors how I got the photographs. I realised when I saw the pregnant mothers in the queue and other incidents, that I needed pictures urgently. As I did not want to implicate my medical colleagues, I borrowed a sophisticated camera from one of the retailers supplied by my company. A few days before addressing the Council I had gone to the townships and taken the pictures.

To make certain that I would get proper publicity I took Ernest Shirley of *The Star* into my confidence and gave him a copy of my speech with the photographs. While I was speaking to the Council he was in the Press Gallery. Meanwhile *The Star* was already out on the streets with a front page story and the photographs I had taken.

As I went on unfolding the tragic story of the health services, I handed round more pictures, including photographs of where the pregnant women were examined – a tin shanty with inadequate ventilation, badly fitted out and "the last place where a pregnant mother irrespective of her status should be examined."

By now the Councillors were giving me their undivided attention.

"At our major clinic, Orlando, I discovered what is the most shocking occurrence of all. Outside the Clinic, there was a Native mother, Rhoda

Majola, sitting on the lawn in the cold biting wind, huddling in a blanket. This woman had been taken to Baragwanath Hospital the night before, given birth to her child at 7.30 am and that morning was sent back to Orlando Clinic in the bus two or three hours later. From eleven to twelve noon she sat in the open, on the lawn, exposed to severe winter conditions with her three-and-a-half-hour-old baby waiting for a bed in the fifteen-bed maternity hospital at Orlando.

"Here, Mr Mayor, is the picture of the mother with her three-and-half-hour-old baby. As a medical practitioner words fail me. I can think of no greater disgrace."

I not only blamed the Council and the Health Committee but also indicted the Nationalist government because of its indifference to health matters affecting Natives and the bureaucratic red tape that hampered the Council's officials when dealing with provincial and central government.

Amongst other things, I told the Council how "doctors each saw about eighty to one hundred patients daily, giving each patient about one-and-a-quarter minutes of clinical time. Often patients are treated by doctors who never see them, because they have to rely on what the black domiciliary nurses tell them.

"It is not surprising that some of the nurses crack up – roads are bad and they have to walk for miles – there is no transport for them. The ambulance service is appalling."

I ended my half hour by calling for the establishment of ten new clinics properly staffed and funded, a proper hospital in the townships and a large maternity hospital.

I was not interrupted once by my UP colleagues or the Nationalists. Shortly after I sat down, Ernie Shirley sent me a note congratulating me, with a copy of *The Star* and its front-page story and photograph of the pregnant mothers in the sun. On page three Rhoda Majola was shown sitting on the grass outside the clinic, nursing her newborn baby.

The Health Committee and some of the officials were stunned by the disclosures. Some UP councillors said I should have spoken to Caucus before I publicised my investigations. I had rejected this because I knew that the Caucus would prevaricate and eventually kill the issue.

Native health services was the tip of the iceberg. What did emerge was that the Council was struggling with provincial authorities for money to improve health services and clinics. This had been going on for years. No one had the guts to bring it into the open until I spoke. The Council was stung into action. The Health Committee drew up plans for new clinics.

Although it took nine months to get the provincial bureaucracy to approve, new clinics were built early the following year, resulting in overall improved health services for Soweto's blacks.

I realised that the Council was merely a talking shop for a few of the UP's leaders. The rest of the councillors were silent puppets; they were intimidated not only by Nationalists, but by the UP's leaders, who did not want Johannesburg's UP-controlled city authority, the only one in the country, to do anything that would bring the UP into open conflict with the Nationalist government – especially on "Native Policy".

There was little difference between the UP and the Nationalists. Above all, liberals like me had to be kept silent.

I was not having this, and decided that I would use every opportunity to find ways of forcing the UP to improve in a real way the lives, the environment and the services that had to be provided for blacks in their segregated townships.

Dr Verwoerd was constantly threatening the UP – and they cowered every time he issued an edict. The Council's officials were hamstrung. They took their instructions from decisions made by our Caucus. Apartheid-delegated legislation constantly going through Parliament tightened the noose around the necks of local authorities, who could not move without government approval.

My attitude was different. The UP was expected to oppose Nat legislation, when it was found unworkable, disruptive or against our policies. Where necessary, we had to oppose implementation irrespective of political consequences, especially where it was not in the public interest. This was heresy to the average UP councillor. I was regarded as a rebel who had to be restrained and kept off all the important committees.

However, they could not stop me speaking. Under standing orders I had the right of free speech. The UP were a lazy lot – indifferent, uneducated and mostly unaware of what was going on around them. I was left the open field of investigative local politics.

In addition I was not frightened by Verwoerd or his threats. The UP without Smuts and Hofmeyr was, as I discovered, a demoralised party. The right wingers who ran it were were unable or unwilling to upset Nationalists because they hoped one day they would manage somehow to lure enough of them to vote them back into power. To do so one had to act like a Nationalist. That was not for me.

The conservatives in the UP, because of their ambivalence and failure to understand the real character of Afrikaner nationalism were unable to cope with the Nationalist steamroller. On the other hand, the Nationalists knew that the UP right wing could be kept in a state of political fear by telling them all the time that they were in danger of being controlled by the "reds" – the liberals in their ranks.

I found local politics absorbing because there were practical problems that could be solved. I was really too busy to take part in the events that were altering the face of national politics. The government was constantly putting through apartheid bills in Parliament affecting the rights of blacks, Indians and coloureds. From time to time, under pressure from UP supporters in the urban areas, public protest meetings were held which received good reports in the English press – and that was all.

There was an endless cry from the UP –"we must get the Nats out". The UP wanted to be back in power even though it differed little from the Nationalists. It also believed in "white supremacy".

186

When apartheid legislation reached local authority level for implementation, such as the removal of illegal blacks from white areas, work permits for blacks, problems relating to black trading, transport, health, the UP-controlled City Council of Johannesburg fell into its own political grave.

Under pressure from its Caucus right wing it would approve of government regulation over which the few liberals in the Caucus would struggle. When these Caucus decisions were made public in open Council, we were able to alert and activate liberal-minded voters from the northern suburbs of Johannesburg. In many cases these decisions were withdrawn. On the other hand, the Nationalists in the Council would attack the UP for not carrying out legislation and rush to Dr Verwoerd for punitive action against the obstructive UP Council.

Despite this political minefield I used the Provincial Council meetings in the Old Raadzaal building in Pretoria to attack the Nationalist government on two fronts. As it controlled all the local authorities through the Local Government Ordinances, I became extremely interested in the relationship between town councils, the Provinces and Central government. The provincial authorities were empowered to look after local government, hospitals and certain local health matters, education, roads and works.

Meetings of the Provincial Council were on parliamentary lines, in a similar setting in the Old Raadzaal debating chamber. It had a Chairman instead of a Speaker. Other than that, it was like Parliament. It published a *Hansard* of its proceedings. When Parliament was not sitting in Cape Town, the main party battles took place in the four Provincial Councils of South Africa.

As several UP and Nationalist City Councillors were MPCs, our political feuds were continued with greater ferocity and freedom in the Provincial Council where we had "privilege" as opposed to City Council debates where it did not exist.

As an MPC back-bencher I cemented my friendship with Harry Cooper of the Education Action Group. His liberal views coincided with mine. Like me, he was concerned about the failure of the UP to stand up to the Nationalists. We had lots of time to talk about this on the back-benches because debates could be dull affairs, livening up only when political issues were introduced.

It was on those back-benches that I began to wonder why I had joined the United Party. I could see from my association with the UP, through my offices as a City Councillor and a MPC, that my original idea of reforming the UP was turning out to be unattainable. All the UP MPCs in the Provincial Council came from urban areas, and some whose constituencies included rural voters spoke at times exactly like the Nationalists.

The UP had no newspaper of its own to support it, whereas the Nationalists had powerful Afrikaans voices such as *Die Transvaler* and *Die Burger*. The image of the UP in the platteland was controlled by the Nationalist media with disastrous political results. To counter this, one of the "plots" Harry Cooper and I hatched on the backbenches related to the founding of an Afrikaans newspaper for the UP called *Die Stem* (The Voice). It was Cooper's idea and he obtained money from Harry Oppenheimer to publish it. I provided some ideas for content and layout. When it was established we often had the early editions to enliven back-bench boredom.

Unfortunately *Die Stem* did not last. The Nats exposed it as a UP-funded newspaper, and it failed in its objective to gain the UP platteland support, and eventually died.

I participated as much as possible in the debates, prepared my speeches and questions carefully, and concentrated on matters I knew best – hospitals, education and local government. The latter became important because the Nationalists, frustrated by the UP majority Council in Johannesburg, decided to set up a Commission of Enquiry into Local Government with the intention of getting rid of Town Clerks and Council Committees, replacing them with Principal Officers and Management Committees.

I was the only member of the UP team who researched this issue in preparation for the commission's report. I became the leading spokesman against these Nationalist proposals. I wrote extensively in *The Star, Rand Daily Mail, The Sunday Times* and *Forum* exposing the changes as further steps of growing authoritarianism in South Africa. I was satisfied that the public did not understand the enormous changes Nationalists were contemplating in order to gain control of all levels of government.

As was to be expected, I was often the target of political abuse by Nationalist MPCs in the Raadzaal, who continued their attempts to portray me as the UP's liberal "bogeyman". I was never left alone. Piet van Vuuren, the Nat leader in the City Council was a front-bencher MPC and he took every opportunity to vilify me.

It was becoming clear that the Nationalists were going to concentrate on me as long as I was a public representative of the United Party.

I was flattered that the Nationalists singled me out for their special attention. It made my conservative colleagues unhappy when I was frequently involved in verbal exchanges in both chambers. I was a very vocal public representative in and out of the council chambers and especially at public meetings.

I was not compliant and silent, as the UP City and Provincial councillors would have preferred me to be. I felt it a dereliction of my duty as a public representative not to oppose or to be seen opposing the Nationalists. I was also aware that one had to keep in the public eye and the only way to do this was to be reported in the press. Journalists began to expect me to react to events. Often, when the UP preferred not to comment, I would speak up. Most of the councillors were not trained to research and investigate problems, so I had a distinct advantage. My experience as editor of *WU's Views* and the articles I had written for newspapers and journals were now standing me in good stead.

35

The latter half of 1954 was politically notable. Dr Malan resigned as prime minister. The "lion of the north" Johannes Strijdom took his place. In the same mould as Malan, he was a staunch conservative and Calvinist pledged to defend white control of South Africa.

In November 1954 there was a new City Council with several new councillors. I had already decided to try and gain control of the UP as an attempt to initiate reform, if I could get sufficient support from "progressive" councillors on a best-man-for-the-job ticket. Harvey and Lewsen were old hands at fighting the establishment before I came along. We were now joined by Kathleen Mitchell and Jean Sinclair, whom I knew to be outspoken. With the addition of some middle-of-the-road councillors it seemed as if there was chance to change the leadership in the Council.

I had drawn up a number of alternative "tickets" which I had discussed with some UP Caucus members. It did not take long for the newspapers to find out and speculate about attempts to unseat the establishment. If progressive-minded councillors could be appointed to chair the various committees it would be the most important step in gaining control of the UP Caucus and improving the quality of the administration in the Council.

Apart from press speculation before the committee elections *The Star* carried a report that the "liberals" were putting up a mayoral candidate. The last thing we were interested in was this ceremonial position. *The Rand Daily Mail* reported on our ticket – I had not given them the story, but I knew before I canvassed some councillors that there would be no such thing as confidentiality.

At the Caucus called to elect the new committees, councillors without any council experience were elected to head various committees, clearly showing that the inner caucus of the UP was very much alive and kicking. Hymie Miller was elected leader. My attempts at reform had failed badly. I had to come to terms with the fact that it was going to be difficult to get rid of conservative control in the UP. Many of these councillors had vested interests in their jobs as committee chairmen. This was obvious from the way they clung to certain of the chairmanships – such as the Licensing and Tenders Committees – for years on end.

After the Caucus meeting it was traditional to lunch with the outgoing Mayor in his parlour. I was wandering around the room with a drink in my hand, when I saw Charles Patmore, the Mayor, animatedly reading a document on his desk to several of my colleagues. I approached the group and was close enough to realise Patmore was reading from one of the "ticket" lists I had with me at the Caucus meeting, together with some notes made at the meeting about the appointment of inexperienced councillors to senior positions on committees. I was absolutely shaken. The papers had accidentally fallen out of my pocket in the Mayor's parlour.

I had to make a quick decision as to whether I would demand those notes and lists back or say nothing. Should I pretend ignorance of the papers?

I decided to claim them and interrupted the Mayor.

"Charles – how did you get those papers? They're mine."

I felt acutely embarrassed as he replied:

"They were found on the floor a few minutes ago and handed to me." He smiled as he returned them to me.

Under the headline "Exclusion of the Progressives Criticised" *The Rand Daily Mail* reported that "election of City Council Chairmen was a deliberate and successful attempt to exclude so-called progressives from holding important positions. A conservative ticket won the day."

My first attempt to oust the UP conservatives had ended in dismal failure.

There was a further shock at the Council meeting that afternoon. Harvey and Lewsen both resigned from the Council. They had kept this secret, but I felt they could have told me since they were aware of my plans. It was in keeping with their arms-length attitude towards me. I had the feeling that my presence in the Council as a "liberal" was not welcomed by them.

During the year I had noticed that they did not consult me or keep me in the picture, when we could have acted together. They could well have been protective of their established positions as "liberals". This was not the the last time I was to experience unexplained political jealousies. Reasons for their resignation emerged when they joined the Liberal Party.

At the civic reception after the Mayoral lunch and before the Council meeting, the leader of the National Party went against tradition by making a party political speech. The UP ignored it.

This was poor strategy, so I took independent action.

The following day *The Star* report of the new Council meeting dealt with one issue: Van Vuuren's political speech and my attack on him in the Council. It read:

"Before the Council adjourned, Dr Boris Wilson MPC moved the adjournment of the Council on a matter of public importance. He protested against the speech which Mr PZJ van Vuuren MPC, leader of the opposition in the Council, had made at the civic reception.

"Dr Wilson said that Mr Van Vuuren had been purely party political instead of paying his respects to the new Mayor."

To many it may not have been an important enough issue for a public protest. I was, however, protesting about the UP's lack of political integrity. Their failure to deal with the Nationalists had become pathological and chronic. As the Nationalists did not respect the governing UP in the Council, it was essential for some of us to let them know we would not be intimidated into silence.

36

Later that month the UP held their national congress. Pressure had been mounting for months for the UP to review its Native Policy, from which I had seen the UP retreating since the 1953 election.

There was great dissatisfaction in our Johannesburg liberal circles with this policy, which we felt was out of touch with the changing urban scene. The review was urgent – the double-talk had to end. We had numerous discussions at local branches and meetings prior to the National Congress at Bloemfontein in 1954.

I was clear about the changes I wanted. I had, since 1953, attempted to foster interest in a new race relations concept in the Saxonwold branch. I objected to the term "Native" and all it stood for in the white South African environment of colour and race prejudice. Like others I proposed the term "African" instead. This horrified UP leaders, who immediately thought it had something to do with the African National Congress; white Nationalists would think the UP was speaking for the ANC. The fears and prejudices of the 1950s made life very difficult for political reformists who wanted to break away from the shibboleths of the time.

This was very evident at the 1954 UP Congress which made some improvement to the UP's Native policy. It accepted that there was a permanent black population in the urban areas and that South Africa had to take into account economic changes that were bringing blacks into the post-war economy. It stated the UP wanted to improve the interests of "Europeans [whites] and Natives in the social, economic and political life of the country".

But, as usual there were qualifications. Liberal views at the congress were not strong enough to get support for a more open and honest approach. During the year in Parliament the new "progressive" group of MPs had made their mark, and their influence at congress heartened the liberals who were there.

For a time it seemed as if the UP was at last facing reality in regard to its policy for black people.

The Strijdom Government was testing the UP, promising more "baasskap", tough white control, to protect the white man by announcing that the first removals from the Western Areas would start on 12 February 1955. During 1954, whenever I could, I opposed Dr Verwoerd's Resettlement plans from my political bases in Johannesburg and Pretoria. In January, before the removals started *The Rand Daily Mail*, under a headline "Suspension of Western Areas Plans Requested", reported my plea to the government to suspend its removal plans.

"Instead of removal," I said, "the government should seek Native co-operation in clearing up the slums and their related evils."

I urged the Mayor to take a committee of leading citizens to the Prime Minister to intercede. "The removal scheme today is a matter of world interest because of its injustice and disregard of human rights."

It was strange. The UP never tried to stop my public opposition to the Western Areas Scheme. I was virtually the only UP councillor who raised his voice in protest against this plan. As I predicted during my election to the Council, the UP no longer supported the removal scheme. Amongst other things they realised it did not pay to alienate rich "liberals" in Johannesburg who were the main contributors to the UP's diminishing finances.

My opposition to the Western Areas was only a prelude to my future battles with Dr Verwoerd, whom I had not yet met.

When Dr Verwoerd introduced his notorious "Sky Locations" Bill in Parliament, he described the situation in my municipal ward, Killarney, as typical of an urban area that had to be cleaned up. The blocks of flats were serviced by black men and women who lived in segregated quarters on the tops of the apartment blocks, in bleak congested conditions. These were Verwoerd's "Sky Locations". The workers were mostly male Zulu adults recruited from the rural areas, living in Johannesburg on a permit system, working long hours, for low pay, with no recreational or other facilities in the white areas. On days off and at weekends they had no places to go to, and congregated in the streets of Killarney. Dr Verwoerd regarded Killarney as a "black spot" in a white area brought about by the UP.

I cannot understand why Dr Verwoerd got involved with me, unless he was out to teach me a lesson as to who was "baas". I was a relatively minor UP politician whose only distinction at the time was that I was not afraid to publicly condemn Verwoerd and his policies. When he chose to cite figures of whites allowing blacks to live in flats on rooftops, he could have chosen many other areas in South Africa because this was the normal situation all over the country. He probably wanted to discredit me as a liberal who approved of blacks living in white areas.

I was surprised one morning to read, in *The Rand Daily Mail*, Verwoerd's parliamentary statement dealing with Killarney's Sky Locations. I jumped at the chance to respond. I called together six supporters in the ward, spoke briefly to them about Verwoerd's attack on me, and then issued a press release from a "meeting held in Killarney last night."

It was obvious that the Sky Locations Bill was another form of urban removal; the burden of this removal would fall to the local authority. The latter would get no government help to pay for rehousing the rooftop workers, who would be sent to live in Soweto over twenty miles away and forced to commute daily to their jobs.

Verwoerd rejected other solutions, where blacks could have better recreational amenities and housing in the urban areas instead of on rooftops. This would cost more in terms of local rates and rents, but the so-called "liberals" of Killarney were unhappy that their black cleaning "boys" would no longer be instantly available. They were scared to protest openly against Verwoerd, leaving it to me to act for them.

Under a large headline "MPC challenges Verwoerd's Sky Location Figures" and "Minister Talking Through His Hat," *The Rand Daily Mail* reported my counter attack when I spoke to another hastily convened meeting, this time of the Hospital-Argyll Branch.

JOHANNESBURG IS LETTING VERWOERD GET AWAY WITH IT

—WILSON

"Control of City's Affairs Snatched by Government"

with the removal of civil liberties in the way that the Nationalist Government has done without general disapproval,' and resulting constitutional defence of those rights."

If the ratepayers and voters of Johannesburg continued to shrug their shoulders in reply and did not realise that there was no difference between the civil liberty of Native and White man, they would deserve what was happening and was still to happen.

Discussing the coming election,

APATHY MAY COST S.A. HER LAST LIBERTIES

–DR. BORIS WILSON

M.P.C. CHALLENGES VERWOERD'S "SKY LOCATION" FIGURES

Minister "Talking Through His Hat"

THE Minister of Native Affairs was accused last night by Dr. Boris Wilson, M.P.C., of "talking through his hat" on the "Locations in the Sky" Bill.

I WILL NOT BE STOPPED, SAYS VERWOERD

Warns Johannesburg City Council again

A RENEWED warning to the Johannesburg City Council to "put things right" in its handling of Native Affairs was given at yesterday's session of the Transvaal Nationalist congress by the Minister of Native Affairs, Dr. H. F. Verwoerd.

"I want to say very clearly that I found it necessary to give certain warnings and to carry out certain negotiations in the public

DR. BORIS WILSON

ing facilities in and around the big towns, lack of transport, absolutely no recreational facilities for Natives in the urban areas, and a lack of hostels for single men and women.

In Hands of Public

"There is only one way to deal with Dr. Verwoerd, and the solution lies in the hands of the public at the present moment. If the owners of flats, estate agents and flat dwellers are worried, let them get in touch with their present public representatives and let them smother Parliament with telegrams of protest.

...REPLY BY WILSON,

It was attended by six co-operative old ladies of the Hospital constituency. I could rely on them in an emergency and it added some interest to their quiet flatland lives.

"I am horrified," I said, "at the inaccurate statements made by the Minister in the House of Assembly. He has taken Killarney as an example of what he calls a great evil. This is astounding. It is probably the most select flatland suburb in South Africa."

After demolishing the accuracy of his statistics, which fortunately for me were wrong (I had them checked by the Non-European Affairs Department of the City Council), I ended my attack on Verwoerd by saying that "the sacrificial animals are the European areas of Hospital and Killarney – to satisfy government propaganda directed at the platteland. There is a problem in the urban areas, but it is a problem caused by inadequate Native housing facilities in and around the towns, lack of transport, absolutely no recreational facilities for Natives in the urban areas and lack of hostels for single men and women.

"There is only one way to deal with Dr Verwoerd. The solution lies in the hands of the public at the moment. Let them smother parliament with telegrams of protest."

This attack on Verwoerd heralded the beginning of a series of newspaper clashes between him and me on the subject of the Sky Locations. It was major apartheid legislation with serious effects. Verwoerd was determined to force local authorities to carry out his edicts under the Act. Despite the fact that the United Party controlled Johannesburg's affairs and proclaimed their opposition to apartheid, they said they were forced by Verwoerd to implement Sky Locations.

I refused to co-operate, making my position clear to Verwoerd, the UP and the public. I did not have the political clout in the Council to influence the UP, but I did not hesitate to deplore their weak response to Verwoerd as a political bully. The UP hid its fears behind an innocuous exchange of correspondence with Verwoerd through the Town Clerk which got the Council nowhere.

Verwoerd insisted they remove blacks from rooftops. They meekly accepted that the law had to be obeyed. My view was that the Council had independent rights granted to it under the Local Government Ordinance, and could legally refuse to act as the government's delegate in this politically sordid situation.

To a great extent my fight was a lone one. The UP refrained from associating themselves publicly with what I was saying, which left me free to continue my attacks on Verwoerd and his policies without hindrance from the ineffectual UP. The public did not at first realise the consequences of the Sky Locations Act. When it became evident that they were going to lose their black servants, panic erupted. I was bombarded with letters and telephone calls by my constituents, including the landlords of buildings who feared a chaotic situation if the black workers could no longer live on the rooftops.

I took advantage of the situation to challenge Arthur Barlow, the renegade Hospital MP, to resign his seat and fight a by-election on the issue of the Sky Locations Act which he supported in Parliament. Of course he ignored my challenge.

It was a golden opportunity to have a "go" at Barlow as well, as we had no parliamentary representative in Hospital since his defection. I was expected to monitor his parliamentary performance.

Naturally, it suited me. I had to keep myself prominently before the public as successor to Barlow in the next election, since I was the sitting MPC.

Barlow attacked me from time to time, usually protected by parliamentary privilege. He lied in Parliament when he alleged I associated with the African National Congress. I felt duty-bound to harass him in return.

Overcrowding was the main problem of the Hospital constituency, due to the unregulated development of high rise buildings. It was the largest flatland area in South Africa. Together with adjacent Hillbrow it crowded more people into a square mile than New York.

One of the casualties of the overcrowding was the neighbourhood Twist Street School in the centre of Hospital. It was surrounded by towering blocks of flats, narrow streets, main roads, and noisy traffic going up busy Twist Street on the east side. To the west the lumbering green diesel-polluting Putco buses from the black township of Alexandra traversed Edith Cavell Street.

The children of the school did not stand a chance. They were deprived of good teaching because of the noise. It was so bad during the day that teachers had difficulty in being heard. At breaks no suitable area was available for sport. Children had to play in a small confined space. Some had been run over by cars and parents had been trying for years to get the education authorities to improve the situation with no success.

As the MPC I was determined to find a solution. I had to find some land on the borders of Hospital or Hillbrow to build a new school. After spending weeks looking at maps and exploring the constituency, I found a few derelict houses below the Fort, the large old prison, on the Hospital borders. "Roseneath", to my surprise, was owned by the Johannesburg Council. I decided to ask them to transfer Roseneath to the Province for a new "Twist Street School". I discovered that Alec Gorshel, the councillor whom I opposed in Hillbrow when I was in the Labour Party, had already asked the Council for Roseneath to be the site of a new opera house. My request infuriated him.

Gorshel was appalled when I joined the UP, even more so when I became a UP councillor. He made his antipathy quite obvious in the UP Caucus. I realised that I was facing a political storm by proposing Roseneath as a site for the new school. I was not deterred. The children's needs came before a low-priority opera house. Gorshel had already applied to the council for the rezoning of the site and a subcommittee was already at work.

I discussed the matter with the headmaster of the school, Mr Viljoen, met the parents' committee, addressed several meetings and as a result a

195

deputation of the Parent-Teachers Association put their case to the General Purposes Committee of the Council.

Gorshel was in a rage, loudly declaiming that I would not succeed in my plan. I ignored him. Instead I saw the Administrator of the Transvaal, Dr William Nicol, who showed great interest in the proposal.

To make sure that the Administrator and his advisers would accept my invitation to inspect the Twist Street School and the proposed new site, I raised the matter in the Budget Debate in the Provincial Council. To make it more interesting for the education authorities, I found more land adjacent to Roseneath suitable for extending their educational complex in the area.

The Administrator's visit was a success. Despite protracted delays and opposition by Gorshel I was able to get a promise in the Provincial Council that the site would be expropriated for the new Twist Street School. In December Roseneath was sold to the Province, and the new school built within a year. The Parent-Teachers wanted to name the school after me, but the Nats could not stomach that idea of perpetuating my name. It stayed Roseneath. As far as I was concerned, I was happy that the children of the congested Twist Street school had a safe new home.

37

Business in 1955 was going through a recession. Problems of finding adequate turnover to meet overheads were arising. Fortunately I managed to diversify by securing the English Electric domestic appliance franchise for the company. This meant a great deal of reorganisation and additional staff to handle the appliances on a countrywide basis.

Unfortunately it coincided with tremendous pressure on my political time since I was heavily involved in City and Provincial activities while keeping an eye on national events.

Under Prime Minister Strijdom the National Party was still determined to remove the coloured voters from the Common Roll. Dr Malan had been thwarted with his "High Court of Parliament" because the Appeal Courts declared it illegal. The NP abandoned their bizarre plans. They found another solution. They packed the Senate instead, increasing its size by appointing more Nationalist Senators, so that when the Separate Representation of Coloured Voters Bill came to Parliament it would be passed with a two-thirds majority.

By May 1955 there was political uproar in the country, mostly by English-speaking South Africans, over the NP plans to remove the coloureds from the roll by this cynical constitutional trick. The Bill was to come before Parliament on 23 May. This time the UP organised a nation-wide series of public protest meetings.

As a member of the Organising Committee of the General Council in Johannesburg, I became heavily involved with the setting up of these public meetings.

English-language newspapers were building up hysteria in South Africa. Car convoys were driving to Johannesburg to join the protest. The newly-formed Anti-Republican League also launched its campaign.

The rhetoric was powerful. "The time for mere talk and use of kid gloves is over. This power-drunk Government will stop at nothing."

The UP's Union secretary HL Horak tried to inspire voters country-wide – he told them that the next week would see prominent United Party speakers calling on thousands of South Africans to make a last ditch stand against the government.

Tracy Bielski MPC, the leader of the UP in the Provincial Council, predicted in *The Rand Daily Mail*: "South Africa was about to retreat into the dark ages."

Even the Conservative Party, to which Arthur Barlow now belonged, opposed the Nats' attack on the Senate and the Constitution. The press called for the disbanded Torch Commando to be revived. Nationalists retorted that the UP was to blame for the new Bill because it had not co-operated with the government.

The NP maintained that it was within the law to enlarge the Senate. Eric Louw, then Minister of Finance told the UP leader Strauss not to "squeal" when government took action hurting the UP in a vital spot – its represen-tation in the Senate. He cited how the British government appointed additional peers in the House of Lords to ensure the passage of legislation. The purpose in packing the Senate was to ensure the survival of "white civilisation" in South Africa.

In the midst of all this crisis manouvring, I received an urgent telephone call from Jean Sinclair and Ruth Foley, two leading UP liberals who wanted to see me. It was a Saturday and they both arrived in tennis dress at my home in Valley Road in Parktown.

We talked in my study.

Jean Sinclair was agitated, her face more intense than usual. She was a poor public speaker, but articulate enough in private.

"Boris, Ruth and I and some other UP women are very upset. We want the women of the UP to show their opposition to the Senate Bill and we would like to organise a separate women's march next week to end at the City Hall just before the protest meeting commences. We spoke to Harry Rissik [the local UP chairman] and he refused to let us do it. We believe the UP women should stand up and be counted. We want you to help us. What can we do? How can we get Rissik to agree?"

"I'm flattered you've come to me, but you know what Rissik's attitude is to me. If it was in my power, I'd not only tell you to go ahead but I'd help you to organise the march. I'm not the chairman of the council, just a member of the organising committee."

Ruth Foley intervened: "Someone has to support our idea. Boris, you're not frightened of Rissik – you must help. Haven't you any ideas as to how we can march?"

We talked for half an hour. All I could promise at the time was that I would put my thinking cap on and telephone them the following day, hoping that I would find a way that the UP women could have their march to protest against the Senate Bill.

I had little time for Harry Rissik and his conservative friends on the General Council. They had a stranglehold on the UP on the Witwatersrand. It was mostly their double-talk that had dumped the UP in its present political mess. They mistakenly believed the hoary United Party myth that if you wanted to beat the Nats, the way was to speak and act like a Nationalist!

Harry Rissik's coterie retained control year after year because they had the support of the majority of the conservatives on the Witwatersrand. When Jean Sinclair asked for permission to hold a protest march the answer was a flat "no".

Rissik and company did not like the UP to protest on the streets.

That evening an idea emerged. The obvious solution was for Ruth and Jean to form an organisation outside the UP, but to use the women of the UP for the march.

I sat down at my typewriter. As I typed I created a women's organisation. What do you call an organisation of women to defend the constitution? "The Women's Defence of the Constitution League".

I went on to draft a short declaration of aims of the League.

"The time has come for the Government to listen to the voice of the women of this country. We are the ones who have borne the children of today who are the South Africans of tomorrow who will have to bear the brunt of the sins of their fathers. We cannot stand by doing nothing. The Government has stated it will listen to no protests. As mothers and grandmothers, as wives, career-women and professional women, as young women looking forward to a peaceful South Africa we are uniting to take common action.

"As women we intend to bring this government to its senses. We therefore call on all women, English- or Afrikaans-speaking to join us in this march. Let all women who value liberty heed this call to action."

The next thing was to arrange first-class press publicity. Before I put the idea to Jean and Ruth I telephoned Jack Watson, the political reporter on *The Rand Daily Mail*.

"Jack, what political story have you got for Monday morning's *Mail?*"

"Nothing, Boris. I'm scratching around. Have you got any ideas?"

"Yes, Jack. I can't tell you now, but if it comes off I'll telephone or see you in good time tomorrow evening."

Jean and Ruth came to see me on Sunday afternoon. I sketched out my idea of the Women's Defence of the Constitution League, reading them the proposed declaration and aims that I had composed for them. They were thrilled with the idea. We got down to details. They undertook to raise the women for the march. I would handle the publicity and have the posters for their march printed. I promised to deliver the posters personally at Joubert Park, which was in my constituency and where they would assemble.

I rang Jack Watson and he came to see me after they left. He was impressed with the plan and the formation of the "Women's Defence of the Constitution League", undertaking to get the story a front page position, which is what happened. The march was planned for Wednesday, 25 May, at around three o'clock. There was a magnificent response to Jean and Ruth's call to the women of the United Party.

Several thousand women were brought together on the pavement in King George Street on the west side of Joubert Park. I handed over the posters and in a short while the march set off. White women were protesting in the streets of Johannesburg, followed by hundreds of black people. The procession wound its way to the City Hall where thousands had gathered for the open-air UP meeting.

Having tasted success, Jean and Ruth made sure that "The Women's Defence of the Constitution League" continued its protests. It even marched on the Union Buildings a few weeks later to face the government in Pretoria. Eventually, under the leadership of Jean Sinclair and others it converted itself into the famous Black Sash of South Africa.

The Black Sash has grown from strength to strength, outliving the United Party. Throughout the lifetime of apartheid it has epitomised the spirit of white liberal opposition to this draconian system of the Nationalist Party.

The silent women with black sashes standing at busy highways all over South Africa have been a

THE VOICE OF CONSCIENCE
– Robin in the *Natal Mercury*

thorn in the side of apartheid's architects from the day the "Women's Defence of the Constitution League" started marching. As the Black Sash it widened its activities, opening aid centres in the main cities to help blacks caught in apartheid's sordid infrastructure of influx control, group areas, population registration the iniquitous pass laws.

An official history of the Black Sash has been written by Mirabel Rogers. On page 14 she writes:

"On May 19 six Johannesburg women met to take tea. These women were not only good friends with a liking for each other and a trust founded in common ideals, but they shared a mutual temper in the steel of their

199

principles. The thought uppermost in the minds of them all that day had pushed out other thoughts of social consequences. And it was not long before Ruth Foley voiced that thought.

"We can't sit still and do nothing – I don't know what we can do, but we must do it. We must act. There must be thousands like us and we must get together."

"In such manner, in those simple half reluctant words, The Women's Defence of the Constitution was born."

For the record, Mirabel Roger's version of the birth of the League is incorrect. It wasn't born as she describes it. The women who met were all in the UP. Their meetings took place before and after Jean and Ruth had seen me twice over the weekend.

Ruth Foley is reputed to have said: "I don't know what we can do." This sums up their position before they saw me, and the reason why they called on me very urgently that weekend.

I am glad I set them on their way, because for nearly thirty-six years they have shown grit, determination and leadership serving South Africa's struggle for democracy with dignity and civility, fielding with success the Nationalist Party's constant attempts to destroy them.

On the day the "Women's Defence of the Constitution League" marched, I watched them from the steps of the Mayor's parlour as they approached the biggest political meeting South Africa had ever seen. They received a tumultuous welcome, putting to shame the political sheep in the UP's Johannesburg hierarchy.

Meanwhile, a thousand miles away in Parliament, the Minister of Justice, CR Swart, threatened that he would not hesitate to take action "to maintain law and order in the country," if anyone acted on the "inflammatory speeches and proposals" made during the campaign against the Senate Bill. He accused the UP of incitement.

For once it was not silenced and continued to protest at nationwide public meetings, albeit confined to the cities where the UP had voters.

Unexpected support came from thirteen professors and lecturers at the University of Pretoria, a spiritual and intellectual home of apartheid. They protested against the government's attempt to alter South Africa's constitution for apartheid's sake.

Prime Minister Strijdom objected, condemning these Afrikaner academics for giving the UP support which, he said, showed their real sympathies. This was not the case. Strijdom was trying to besmirch an early rebellion amongst Afrikaner intellectuals against the rigid party line. Their warnings shook the NP. We did not know then, but it was a historic declaration – the forerunner of many Afrikaner academic protests to be made in public.

Later that week Strijdom told a meeting in the City Hall that the Separate Representation of Coloured Voters Bill would bring about peace and stability to the political situation. *The Rand Daily Mail* reported that the City Hall was packed with Nationalist banners proclaiming: "The Nationalist Party is the Guarantee of White Supremacy in South Africa."

Two days later I attacked Strijdom and called on him to answer questions from me, at a speech I made at a public meeting in my constituency. My call to him received wide press coverage, but that was all. He ignored me.

A succession of controversial apartheid laws found their way onto the statute books in Parliament and in three of the four Provinces controlled by the NP; Natal remained under the UP and was less affected.

In 1955, between September and November, I was fully occupied studying the important report which had been released by the Nationalist-controlled Executive on the future of Local Government in the Transvaal. In essence, if recommendations were implemented, increased autocratic control of all local authorities by the state would ensue. The UP, under pressure from me, agreed to discuss the report at the monthly City Council meeting. When we came to the matter, Nationalists refused to debate it on the grounds that their leader, Van Vuuren, was a Commission member.

"Dr B Wilson, MPC," reported *The Rand Daily Mail*, "asked the Council to oppose the Commission's recommendations, and said that all city councils should call for an enquiry instead into the local government department of the Transvaal Provincial Administration. The whole report is unsound from the viewpoint of political science, and it does not line up with political theory."

For a change I was supported by the UP establishment. They did not want further state interference either.

For the next few weeks I kept this issue alive in the press and the Council. My view was that "the people of the Transvaal must open their eyes to what is happening to their town councils. It looks as if the Nationalist Party would start to write off Transvaal town councils in 1956 and pave the way to Mr Strijdom's republic."

I was aware that the proposed abolition of Town Clerks, replaced by Principal Officers appointed by the Province, would simply make local government subject to total state control. This might be fine in a democratic society, but in 1955 democracy in South Africa looked to be in grave danger. The average white person seemed unconcerned about what Nationalists were doing to political rights. However, some of us were very conscious of our responsibilities, trying to enlighten people. I wrote numerous articles for newspapers who had been alerted to Nationalist intentions and did not like what they perceived.

One of the articles appeared on the leader page of *The Sunday Times*, the largest weekly English-language newspaper headlined: "An Ominous Cloud Hangs Over Local Self-Government." This was followed by others in the liberal monthly journal *Forum* and *The Star*.

I was blunt about what the Nationalists were doing to local government:

"When Hitler was at the height of his career, one of his last acts was to destroy local government as it existed in Germany, substituting local *gauleiters* to do his work and so retain final and complete control of the German nation.

"Is South Africa facing a similar situation today? "

My conclusion was that "there are 108 cities, towns and village committees in the Transvaal. There will be 108 Principal Officers with local executives acting through the Provincial Administrator, his Executive and the so-called Advisory Board for the Advancement of Local Government. And the Nationalist party will be in power and there will be a Republic."

38

On 13 October 1955 my father died in Margate where he had lived in retirement. He was reputedly 83 years old. We knew the end was near and the family was at Margate. We sat with him in the front room of his house, and with the noise of the sea in the distance I held his hand as his life slipped away.

To the end, he was still writing poetry, one of the last of which was read at his cremation in Johannesburg. Before he died he said that he wanted no religious ceremony, which we respected. His doctor, who had become his friend, read an oration which included one of the last poems he had written:

> Today, a day of sunshine, I advanced on the old rocks
> Armed with a rod and line
> Attacked the fishes with hooks,
> Climbed from rock to rock,
> Step by step and jump by jump
> Reaching a cosy cave . . .
> But the turbulent waves
> Rushed into my caves . . .
> With a silver brush
> In a lightening rush
> Brushed me deep down
> With my rod and line . . .
> I stood up again
> With might of a younger man . . .
> Held fast my rod and line,
> It was not in vain,
> I hooked a silver bream.

39

Later in October 1955 the City Council elected new committees. I was in a much stronger position publicly, and my conservative UP colleagues had difficulties in keeping me off the committees of my choice. I found myself not only on the Health and Non-European Affairs Committees, but I had inexplicably been appointed vice-chairman of the latter, with Major Opperman, the UP's organising secretary still its chairman – one of the "perks" of his job.

Being a councillor helped pay his party salary. He was no liberal and did not know much about "non-European Affairs". I suspect he was there to keep me in my place and make use when necessary of my knowledge of race relations. I liked Opperman because, as far as he could, he was open with me and there was a good rapport between us.

He was a friendly person and tried to keep the peace between the UP's fractious right and left factions.

Hymie Miller was still the Leader in the Council. It was well-known that he would liked to have been the chairman of the Non-European Affairs Committee. At least Opperman would keep the seat warm for him. I think the establishment's attitude to me was that as long as I was his deputy I could not harm their control.

The City Council was in continuous bad odour with Dr Verwoerd because it was ambivalent in its co-operation with his Sky Locations and Resettlement plans. This was due to the conflicts in the UP, and as far as I was concerned I did my best to thwart Verwoerd and keep the UP acting as an opposition and not a collection of *ja-broers*, yes men, for the government.

By making the UP's local secretary, Opperman, chairman of the NEAC the party could bear the odium if he failed in the job. I was there as the compromise to satisfy liberal pressures from supporters.

40

After two years in the Council I still found the United Party's Caucus interesting. It met regularly once a month to discuss and approve of everything that was going on in the Council, but there would be special meetings for specific issues. The Caucus was a law unto itself when it came to municipal policy. This led to many arguments because of our differing views and interpretations of policy.

There were two types of councillors. One group believed that party politics did not enter civic affairs and municipal matters should be restricted to rates, street lights, pavements and other uncontentious subjects. These councillors said little in Caucus and were equally silent in Council meetings. The other group, led by Miller and Patmore were politically orientated since they were MPCs as well.

When Harvey and Lewsen resigned from the UP, I was joined by Jean Sinclair and Kathleen Mitchell, which made the three of us the total liberal strength of the UP in the 42-member Council.

The corpulent, smiling, Miller always gave the impression that he was a middle-of-the-road politician. His political progress in public life relied on this image. Like most of the councillors, his knowledge of political philosophy was restricted to the slogans and jargon that were standard fodder in the council debates and UP public statements. In fairness, I must add that this simply reflected the general political level of the population as a whole. I have always regarded South African whites as amongst the world's most politically illiterate. The inevitable result was seen in UP confrontations with Dr Verwoerd, the most formidable and dynamic leader the Nationalists ever had.

He was intellectually streets ahead of the average UP and NP politician. He was implacable and knew exactly what relationship he wanted between whites and blacks. It was clear that Verwoerd only had to threaten the UP councillors and they wilted and fled, panic-stricken. If it was not so serious it would have been hilarious. Stalling decisions were taken in the UP Caucus; letters written; Council officials sent to intercede with Verwoerd's subordinates; deputations sent to Pretoria. Urgent consultations with parliamentary leader Strauss and later with De Villiers Graaff, constantly looked for compromises.

The arguments and rows that ensued in the Caucus were often bitter. Most of the goings-on in the Caucus were often leaked to the press, especially Nationalist newspapers, who revelled in the disclosures. Most of us knew who gave Caucus secrets to the journalists, and the NP, but the UP leadership wanted no expulsions.

It was rare for the UP to stand up to Nationalists in open Council – they were poor debaters, hating political confrontations with the sneering Piet van Vuuren, who tied them up in knots.

Above all, the UP believed it was bound to carry out the government's instructions never wanting to test them in the courts. They feared the government might take over the City Council if they did not comply with Verwoerd's edicts.

In the Caucus I constantly fought the party to stand up to Verwoerd and his Council Nationalists. This was not a popular role. Sometimes I would lobby support from so-called moderates. It never got far – my approaches were leaked to the UP leaders, who were archetypal fence-sitters.

I began to notice in Caucus that Harry Schwarz, who originally opposed my entry into the UP, was also outspoken despite his conservative outlook. He often criticised the UP's leadership to the extent that sometimes we found ourselves fighting the same battle, though for different reasons. Not only was he an able speaker but his prowess as an outstanding young lawyer was invaluable to the UP in its unequal and intricate struggle with

Verwoerd. Trenchant and logical, he was head and shoulders above the rest of the Caucus.

I came to admire his stand, although we did not speak to each other. I felt he still disapproved of my rapid rise in the UP.

One thing I loathed was the arrogance of some of the committee chairmen in Caucus. Many of them held on to their jobs for years. One wondered why they did.

After one particularly acrimonious meeting of the Caucus, when Schwarz and I both attacked the establishment, I happened to walk out of the Council with him. Halfway down the City Hall steps, I spoke to Harry, a slight well-dressed figure of a man.

"Hold on a moment. You know, I don't understand what you've got against me. You didn't welcome me in the UP for reasons of your own. I find that we often differ in our basic political attitudes to council problems. Yet on many issues we have found ourselves on the same side in Caucus. You can't stand some of our colleagues and neither can I. Why do you dislike me?"

I cannot recall the details of his reply, but we stood on the steps talking for nearly half an hour about our differing roles in the Caucus and the problems of the UP as we saw it.

We took a big decision that afternoon on the steps of the City Hall. We came to the conclusion that we were not so different after all. We faced the same problems in the Caucus, and had the same critical views of the leadership.

That half-hour on the steps established a friendship that lasted for years.

41

One of the dark corridors that opened up to me was the workings of the Non-European Affairs Committee. As vice-chairman I had the status that allowed me to get information from officials, and I took every advantage of this facility. From the manager, Bill Carr and Mr Archibald, the Director of Housing, I received on 7 November a report of the serious state of the housing of blacks in Soweto. It was the Council's biggest problem. Not only was the Council unable to cope with the building of houses for "Natives" but it was impossible to get money from Dr Verwoerd's department who refused to budge from the unacceptable conditions that Natives were first to be removed from the rooftops and sent to the site-and-service plots, to live temporarily in shacks until permanent housing could be built. Ultimately when money became available, a house could be built for them by the Council.

Dr Verwoerd was not interested in the truly homeless, the clearance of slum areas or urban renewal. Removal of blacks from white areas was the first of apartheid's priorities.

As a NEAC member I moved freely around Soweto, often without officials, to see the bad slum conditions for myself.

To add to the miserable black housing picture, I found Indian and coloured housing just as bad. Indians lived in run-down Vrededorp houses beyond Fordsburg near the Market – the coloureds wherever they could find a roof in Johannesburg.

I became, daily, more determined to do something about the appalling housing situation that confronted Johannesburg and which appeared to be the concern only of a few committed liberals and churchmen.

Although the number of Indians and coloureds was relatively small, their housing needs had also been neglected for years. Verwoerd, whose power as Minister of Native Affairs appeared to be absolute, was forcing the Council to rehouse the Indians twenty miles out of Johannesburg at Lenasia, their "group area". Roads and amenities did not exist. Coloureds lived in slums on the periphery of the city centre in Ferreira's Town, one of the original mining camps next to the palatial Anglo-American Corporation head offices. The coloureds were worse off than the Indians; their lack of housing was coupled with social problems and miserable earnings.

I came to a decision. I was going to concentrate on problems of non-whites; the Natives, the Indians and coloureds almost to the exclusion of everything else. Apart from the fact that their medico-sociological state needed investigation, the UP did not care about these terrible conditions as long as they were able to placate Verwoerd and the City's ratepayers. The UP's concern was with white privilege. Blacks only came into the picture when their living conditions affected whites. The UP always reflected the general attitude of whites in the 1950s.

Whites gave little thought to the dreadful way in which their servants lived segregated in the backyards of their own homes.

I began to draw a lot of political flak during Council debates. I was always raising matters in Council about the poor conditions under which non-whites lived, constantly attacking Dr Verwoerd his policies and those of his Nationalist government.

42

I found that the UP had been negligent and guilty of dragging its feet in other areas as well. In January 1955, as the result of newspaper reports of dreadful conditions in private nursing homes in Johannesburg, the Health Committee went on a tour of inspection.

Unannounced, we arrived at some of these private hospitals and confirmed what some overseas nurses had told the press about the unhygienic conditions. We found cockroaches in the operating theatres, the wards and the kitchens; dirt all over the place and in general unacceptably low standards. While this was happening, the Nationalist-controlled Provincial Council advised us that it was suspending the Public Hospital Services Ordinance. This was my opportunity as MPC to raise the nursing home issue in the Provincial Council since it was the responsible authority. Before doing so I went to see Dr Wassenaar, the MEC in charge of hospitals on the EXCO. He told me he was thinking of holding an enquiry into the nursing homes.

I drew his attention to the fact that overseas nurses were being threatened with deportation because they exposed the bad conditions. To make sure that the issue was aired, two medical colleagues and I initiated a Provincial Council debate. This had the desired effect of frightening nursing home owners. A clean-up took place. Many nursing homes were put under closure notices if premises were not immediately renovated and hygiene standards improved.

The debate on the ordinance took place late in February. *The Pretoria News* headline: "MPC Says Nursing Homes Shook Him" aptly summed up my feelings when I spoke in the Provincial Council.

"The appalling state in which food is kept in private nursing homes, cockroaches, filth and theatre floors covered with dirt made it mandatory to pass the Ordinance – not suspend it."

Some other things came to light as a result of our action. The provincial authorities were hiring beds in nursing homes, but did not inspect them and knew nothing until we exposed the matter. We also highlighted the failure of the City's Health Committee and officials to properly understand and cope with health matters.

It proved that councillors or officials without special knowledge or training could not work efficiently in the public's interest.

As I was the only medical doctor, at this time, on the City Council, my colleagues had a hard time convincing me about some of their actions. When they would not take what I felt was sound advice, I would use the privilege of the Provincial Council chamber to make them come to their senses. In the City Council I repeatedly used the standing orders on Matters of Public Importance as a platform for exposing and attacking malpractices.

For example, on 30 January I discussed the need for community centres. Between 1950 and 1956 Johannesburg had an average of 400 cases of juvenile delinquency a year, 2 000 cases of truancy, snowballing alcoholism and thousands of lonely and at times desperate citizens with nothing to do in their leisure hours. Two people a day committed suicide.

These were statistics for whites; figures for blacks were unavailable.

The Finance Committee had a "power of veto" which it used to frustrate the Social Affairs Department. Since 1949, fourteen Johannesburg suburbs wanted to establish community centres – all had been vetoed. This was the

UP establishment at work which was not acceptable to me, and I tried hard to educate them.

"A community centre was not necessarily a place for poor people or those in need of care. It was a place in any area for the enjoyment of leisure time."

I called for a twenty-year programme and a rate increase to cover £2 000 000 needed for a crash programme. Council officials backed my proposals, and the local newspapers added their weight.

"The Lonely Heart," was the headline to *The Star* editorial. "Dr Wilson has recognised the problem and this is a step forward."

The recognition of the problem was what mattered first in this UP-controlled council. Most times it was beyond them. They were obsessed with rate-pegging and favourable budgets. They talked of "charity" and left it to the service organisations like Rotary and others to relieve them of the burden of social responsibility. Individual councillors would plead for money for their wards – and if it was street lights, pavements or roads they would get it. Expenditure on social needs had a low priority. I tried to remedy this. The social problems of communities came first – roads, pavements and street lights followed. City Council meetings became my crusading platform for social change. I made full use of them.

As a result I was called upon to speak extensively at UP branches on the Witwatersrand and Pretoria. I was able, on these occasions, to attack the Nationalists, their supporters and some of the bizarre theories they propounded and which were believed by many whites.

For example, Professor Strauss of the University of the Free State was reported as saying that "the Afrikaner and Nationalists believe that the Prime Minister is sovereign in the sense he receives his authority from God. He merely uses Parliament within the framework of the Constitution to endorse his legislation."

Professor Strauss went on to say the "allegation of the 'liberals' that parliament would have to account to the coloureds for depriving them of their vote was misplaced, because it made the authoritative power subject to the demand of the will of the people". He was backed by Prime Minister Strijdom, Dr Verwoerd and Minister of Justice "Blackie" Swart. Later when Verwoerd became Prime Minister he claimed his power was derived from God.

I was asked to comment on these statements and pointed out in the newspapers that these views were serious evidence of the perverted mentality of the Nationalists, who were prepared to use the Christian religion to uphold their apartheid beliefs, which were condemned by true Christians. Furthermore, I warned that all the Nats were doing was to discredit South Africa internationally, with these unChristian beliefs. To them, all power was derived from God, both "good" and "bad". In the platteland the religious voters lauded these views. To the farming community in South Africa, God and government are intertwined.

The UP did not criticise these utterances. As usual they did not want to upset potential platteland voters. The average white South African swallowed these ideas with little or no comment – in the 1950s no one wanted to disturb the high standard of living and peace of the whites. People like me who spoke out were considered political mavericks and prophets of doom.

I was constantly alert to every political move the Nationalists made and used every available opportunity to remind people of the real issues confronting them, such as the local government changes which were now occupying the headlines as a result of my efforts months before.

The Rand Daily Mail headed a speech of mine "Gauleiters and Juntas May Run SA Towns". This was my response to the legislation which the Nationalists were now pushing through the Provincial Council, as a result of their Commission of Enquiry into Local Government. Two days later I was again in the headlines: "Apathy May Cost SA her Last Liberties". Speaking in Pretoria I forecast that "apathy, indifference and inertia were a fifth column threatening the remaining liberties of the South African people. In Germany it was the division in the democratic ranks that let the Nazis in".

In 1956 some of us were still reminding people of the Nazis' enslavement of the Germans, drawing comparisons with Nationalists, many of whom supported the Nazis during the war. They objected to the Fascist label. I had no hesitation, however, in using this term. There was mounting evidence that they were destroying the democratic process by the infiltration of school boards, trade unions, and cultural organisations through their secret and feared Broederbond, all a carbon copy of Nazi technique. The United Party and most of its supporters gave lip-service to anti-Nationalist protests and only acted when they were pressurised and left the few on the liberal wing to continue verbal protests. Indifference and apathy by the UP created severe problems on the Witwatersrand. Dispirited UP supporters gave it the cold financial shoulder and constituency organisers and other staff were being retrenched.

Late in April Major Opperman telephoned me and gave me news which dramatically changed my political life in the Council.

"Boris, I have to resign from the City Council – now! Things are so bad at the party office, that I have to concentrate on the party's affairs and finances on the Witwatersrand."

"But Oppie, why resign from the council? You're chairman of Non-European Affairs and I can always stand in as vice-chair."

"No, it's not on. Harry Rissik wants me to be here full-time. You must take over the chairmanship. I know most of the Caucus will oppose this, but I have told the powers that be, that as vice-chairman you have done an excellent job and must take over on 1 May when I resign."

I was astonished. The chairmanship of the most important committee was in my lap, to be confirmed by our mainly conservative Caucus. With unbelievable haste it was done that day through a newspaper release. The statement said that Opperman was recalled to prepare for the forthcoming 1958 general election – partly true. The real reason was the UP's dire financial straits.

There was speculation in the press about what I was going to do about the serious unsolved problems of Johannesburg's non-white inhabitants. I said nothing but made some important decisions.

The first was to find a solution to the appalling housing conditions in the townships of the south-west, the second to initiate social improvements and thirdly, to put an end as far as possible to the role into which the Council had deteriorated as Hendrik Verwoerd's "whipping boy ".

I didn't waste time. I telephoned the Director of Housing, Mr Archibald, and asked him to see me at my home in Parktown. In the warmth of a balmy autumn afternoon we sat in the garden talking.

"Archie, I don't know how long I will be chairman of the committee, because I don't trust the UP establishment. The next election for committee chairman will be in October. Before that I want to solve Soweto's housing problem. I want to build houses on a large scale. I've read the report you sent me last year. How can we put the Housing Division on the road?"

Archibald, a slender man with a sense of urgency, reputedly a member of Moral Rearmament, gave me the answer without hesitation.

"We can build all the houses needed. I've started training black bricklayers, and we could train more. The Council has no black plumbers or electricians. The only way to get them is to train them ourselves. We're already making our own breeze blocks. The biggest need is for money – that's your job. If you can get it nothing will hold us back. I can build all the houses needed.

He then told me that the week before, Sir Ernest Oppenheimer the chairman of the Anglo-American Corporation had been to see him at Soweto. He had asked whether Archibald could build 42 houses for the black employees at Brenthurst, his large Parktown home. They could no longer live there – the Sky Locations prohibited it. Sir Ernest was prepared to pay for the houses if the Council would agree to build them. While he was at Soweto, Archibald showed him the slum areas.

After a very satisfactory discussion with Archibald, I spent the rest of the weekend thinking over ways and means of tackling the huge problem of getting money to clear the slums of Soweto.

On Monday morning, I walked into the office of the City Treasurer, Dr Ivor Holmes, with whom I had become friendly, and who made a great impression on me. I got to the point.

"I have decided my main priority as NEA chairman is the housing problem in the townships. I want to get rid of the Moroka and Shantytown slums. How much do I need, and where would the money come from?"

Ivor Holmes leaned over a pile of ledgers and quickly did some calculations.

"Boris, you'll need at least £3 000 000 to build about fifteen thousand houses. I don't see you getting it from the government. Verwoerd is determined that any houses built by the Council must be for Sky Location removals – you won't change his mind on that."

I was not discouraged. We agreed that in the first instance an official approach be made to Verwoerd's Native Affairs Department for the money.

This was expected to fail – both Archibald and Holmes were in no doubt about this.

I would then have to find other ways of getting the money.

"I have an idea, Ivor. At the weekend I had a wide-ranging talk with Archibald about the housing problem, and my desire to clear the slums. He told me about Sir Ernest's visit during the week and his wanting to help. My plan is that, having made certain we can't get the money from Verwoerd, I should see Oppenheimer and ask him to lend the Council the money. It is Johannesburg's Festival year, and who knows, we might succeed with Oppenheimer? What do you think?"

Ivor Holmes was delighted at the idea, and promised me a memorandum for study. He'd lived long enough with it and knew the answers – he also wanted the slums to go for Treasury reasons.

I instructed the NEA officials to make an urgent application to Verwoerd's department in Pretoria, and within two weeks I was assured that no money was available. There was no objection to non-government funds, but if we got them, we would need Verwoerd to approve before we could use the money. This was the law.

While this was going on I wasted no time making an appointment to see Sir Ernest Oppenheimer at 44 Main Street – the Anglo-American head office.

I had never met him. We sat alone in his office. Here was a man whose name was virtually synonymous with the gold and diamond wealth of South Africa, and who was known as a generous benefactor.

I put my case to him, and asked him whether he could help Johannesburg to get rid of the slums in this Festival Year. I traced the City Council's poor record in housing over the years in slum clearance. I told him I this was my absolute priority as long as I was the NEA chairman. To do the job properly, at least £3 000 000 was needed as a long-term loan or a donation. I assured him that we could start building houses without delay.

When he had read the memorandum I could see from his attitude that he was extremely interested in my proposal.

As we talked about the specific proposals in the memorandum, I sensed that Sir Ernest and I had reached some accord. We were on the same mental wavelength.

Sir Ernest asked me:

"Do you think you can do it, if the money is found? I cannot guarantee to make it available but of course I will happily look into it."

I was unequivocal in reply.

"All I can say, Sir Ernest, is that in my opinion there are only two people who can break the housing backlog and clear the township slums, and both are sitting in this room – you and me."

He smiled, and thought for a moment.

"All right, Dr Wilson, leave it with me. I expect I won't be in touch with you for some weeks, but you will hear from me."

We shook hands. I was sure that something would come of our meeting. In 1956, £3 000 000 was an astronomical amount of money. If we got it, either as a donation or a loan, it would be the turning point in the sad history of the UP's housing debacle. Only Carr, the NEAD manager, Archibald and Holmes knew about this meeting which was otherwise confidential. I was not telling the Caucus. If I did so, I knew what would happen. Miller, Patmore and others would want innumerable committee meetings and reports, leaking news to the press. Miller, I was sure, would find a way to exploit the loan for personal glory. Overall, I was certain negotiations would get bogged down by Council routine. Furthermore, I was not going to have Sir Ernest embarrassed by low-level UP antics.

So I told no one, and put my mind to all the other problems of the Non-European Affairs Committee, of which I now knew a great deal. Bill Carr, the NEAD manager and I had several meetings to sort out priorities. I knew from experience on the committee that he was a difficult man, competent, not lacking in guts to stand up to his chairman or committee if he disagreed. Senior staff often resented interference from councillors who were there for a relatively short time. Carr assumed, quite rightly, that a new chairman did not know much about the work of his department. I hoped that he would treat me differently.

He knew me by reputation and as vice-chairman and I realised that I might have a rough passage with him, because he was used to telling the NEA committee what was best. This of course did not suit me. I was more than prepared to deal with "Native" and race relations problems, but not interested in perpetuating the conditions which had brought about frustration, fear, delay and failure, leaving the great problems of the blacks, coloureds and Indians unresolved.

It took hours of discussion with Carr to get an overview of NEAD's problem areas. The list was formidable, endless. The most important were: the failure of Native Advisory Boards to co-operate with the Council, the disclosure that transport to and from Soweto was on the verge of breakdown and almost no money for school buildings.

Amenities hardly existed; there was no electricity except in one township; and little running water in the houses. It was difficult to control illegal dwellers – the list seemed to go on forever.

Despite all this, he was defensive of his department's reputation. I did not blame his caution in the face of the prying eyes of his new chairman.

I decided to exert my authority when necessary.

I was not interested in what had happened before my term. I knew the terrible weakness of the Caucus system that elected ill-equipped councillors to important committees; and from what Carr told me it was even worse than I envisaged. There was a formidable job ahead of me, with no certainty of how long I might be in the chairman's seat.

Carr explained to me that almost everything that was done by the NEAD was subject to the scrutiny of Dr Verwoerd or his department. Apart from constant delays, letters, visits to Pretoria and the chaos that went with it, there was a real fear in his mind, and that of the UP, that Verwoerd would take over the Council's Native Affairs Department. Carr's morale was at a low ebb. He had been in in the frontline and the hot seat of "Native Affairs" for a long time. His initial cold response to me was pathognomonic of the state into which a senior official could get, when dealing with a domineering personality like Dr Verwoerd.

Amongst the many pressing problems was transport to and from Soweto. Verwoerd had been forcing more and more blacks out there through his removal schemes. The homeless seeking work were also illegally drifting in from rural areas, clandestinely living there. The railways could not cope. Workers overfilled trains risking their lives hanging on to doors of fast-moving carriages.

Service was erratic and blacks were often late for work.

The only way to deal with this was to get at the facts. To do so I instructed Carr to arrange that we should meet with the senior South African Railways staff at Soweto at 3.30 am on 8 May, which turned out to be a bitterly cold winter's morning, to witness what was happening at Nancefield and several township railway stations.

The Star's front page story later that day best described what we saw, under the headline: "Native Station Scenes Shock City Councillors" – "Workers in Hundreds Jam Platforms From 4 am." It continued: "They saw thousands of native men and women – the non-European labour force of the city – arriving rain-soaked at stations like Nancefield, Pimville and Dube, there to stand for half an hour or more in puddles of muddy water before they could get into muddy coaches. A hard-boiled police officer commented: 'My God, this is terrible'."

It was terrible. There was virtually no control at the stations. Passengers exposed themselves to serious danger by jumping on to trains in motion, travelling on the buffers and on running boards. It was an incredible sight. Masses of people surged forward as trains arrived, pushing and shoving for a place.

Trains often moved off while people were still desperately trying to enter carriages. Doors remained open, leaving hundreds hanging on for dear life. It reminded me of the black man I attended to in Casualty several years back who had been brought in with both legs severed while trying to board a moving train.

The Star went on: "There was only one ticket office open for business. Natives jammed the stairway of the overhead bridges so that we had to force our way to the top. Natives stared at us with sullen eyes."

The councillors, the railway officials and police were silent.

The Star interviewed several commuters on their background and experiences.

"Lazarus Powane who works for an engineering firm in the city has to be on duty at 7 am. To make sure he is, he rises at about 4 am and catches a bus to Nancefield Station. This costs him two shillings and six pence a week. His train ticket costs 4/4d a week. He earns £2/9/4 a week, and although he finishes at 4.40 pm daily, he only manages to get home by 7 to 7.30 pm each night."

As *The Star* remarked, there were thousands more like him. The newspaper publicity was as vital as the inspection. The whole question of

213

public transport, its costs and the tremendous burdens on the Soweto blacks became issues of public debate. The impression was also gaining ground that the UP was at last doing something tangible.

Five weeks later my committee had a meeting with the railway officials, Verwoerd's staff and others to take practical steps and improve the services. The Railways, despite being a government department, criticised the fact that Verwoerd's laws insisted on blacks being housed in Soweto and not in Johannesburg, which created much of the current problems, making forward-planning difficult.

The response of the blacks and coloureds was heartening. For the first time non-white residents of Soweto responded to me, as NEA chairman, by writing letters.

Mr ME Mcwana of 388 Dube Village wrote me a four-page letter which opened: "We were thrilled when we read in *The Star* that you were one of those who went out on a tour of inspection in the Western Native Townships to study the conditions under which we travel every day. Now you know the true facts . . ." The letter went on to give details of train delays and why blacks arrived late at work so often.

As important were his remarks about serious crime in the townships. He asked for more co-operation with the township boards: "There is not a week that passes without someone being shot or stabbed to death by *tsotsis* [young black gangsters] who take advantage of the dark streets."

"Sir," he ended, "we beg of you to do your utmost in easing up all these painful conditions we live under."

The Moroka (Emergency Camp) Advisory Board wrote to me through the Revd Ray Phillips who devoted his life to the people of the townships: "At a meeting of the Moroka (Emergency Camp) Advisory Board held last evening I was asked to write to you and express genuine gratitude of Board members for the trouble you took in visiting Nancefield Station in the early hours of the morning. I was informed that the whole township has been influenced favourably by your action and that of other councillors and officials."

At the stations when we did our inspections members of the Advisory Boards were unofficially present on the way to work. Carr told me that councillors never met them, but he and his officials did so from time to time, when he reported to the NEA Committee.

I told him this was not good enough and I wanted regular meetings between the Boards and councillors. Carr was pleased and said it would be a great step forward in relations with the people of Soweto.

The first-ever meeting between Joint Advisory Boards and the Non-European Affairs Committee held at the NEAD offices was fully attended. In many respects it was an emotional start of face-to-face talks. Every black man present reiterated that this was a step forward in the Council's relations with the black people. In turn, from the chair I told them not to be inhibited by what they had to say. We wanted them to know that they would get the NEAD's co-operation through Mr Carr and in order to make progress we had to know from them as frankly as possible

Part of the Shantytown slums to be cleared by the Housing Division and rebuilt with the £3 000 000 loan.

AJ Archibald's achievement: the £160 three-bedroomed dwelling in Soweto.

Rhoda Majola and her newly-born baby three-and-a-half hours old, waiting for a bed outside the Moroka clinic.

Ante-natal clinic at Moroka – pregnant women who have been standing in the sun for over five hours to see the doctor. (Photograph by BW)

about their problems so that we could do whatever was necessary to assist them.

It did not take long to learn of their frustrations. One elderly man made his points very emphatically. He appealed to the white councillors to bear in mind that "because I am black, it does not mean that I should not educate my children or own my house or not have proper transport. When I buy clothes in the shop, I buy the same kind of shirt as you do, or the same suit."

Carr was stimulated by this first meeting with the Advisory Boards. For me these meetings were vital because blacks in the 1950s had no direct say in running their affairs. Unless we spoke directly to their leaders through the Advisory Boards, a meaningful relationship between the City Council and black leaders was a sham. We needed undiluted, direct, information from the people who lived and struggled in Soweto and not the watered-down views of officialdom which had previously been the case.

During the course of these meetings I was struck by the sincerity of the black leaders. One man, Vundla by name, educated and well-dressed, impressed me because of the rational way in which he was able to present his arguments. After one meeting, he came up to me and asked me whether I would like to visit him at his home in Soweto and meet his wife and family. I gladly accepted. To my knowledge this was the first time any councillor, let alone the chairman of NEAD, had been invited to the home of a Black Advisory Board leader in Soweto.

I made my way unaccompanied through the rutted streets of the sprawling townships, and found his house in Dube, one of the better areas, with single houses built individually to higher standards. His wife was a pleasant lady who said little. In their simple lounge/kitchen/diningroom, we sat at a large dining table drinking tea. Vundla spent most of the time answering my questions about life in the townships. He told me he was a member of Moral Rearmament. He was cautious in his answers to me which I felt was natural because relations between whites and blacks on official levels was a new departure for us both.

At the next monthly Council meeting, while I was addressing the Council, I heard an interjection from Piet van Vuuren the Nationalist leader: "*Vundla, jy is 'n Vundla*" (Vundla, you are a Vundla).

The interjection did not register at the time, but later when it was repeated I realised what it was all about. I was either being shadowed or informed on by persons unknown in my movements as chairman of the NEAD and no doubt Verwoerd and his Nationalist lackeys on the Council knew all about it.

Since 1948 the Nationalist government was reputed to have built a large network of paid informers, who had infiltrated churches schools, sports and cultural organisations in the black townships. This was known to most Africans who lived there. I was a marked man, once I had become the NEAD chairman.

Neither Verwoerd or the Nationalists ever expected the UP to put the "liberal Boris Wilson" in the "hot" seat. I was not surprised that my movements were being monitored – if the Nats were running true to form this is what I had to expect.

In calling me "Vundla", apart from being a clumsy smear attempt, Piet van Vuuren was warning me to watch my step. It was a signal that they knew what I was doing and that I was being watched. I decided to be careful but it would not deter me from what I had to do as the chairman of the NEAD nor would it intimidate me.

In the Provincial Council Van Vuuren repeated his Vundla jibes. He sat on his front bench, and in his sneering way, at a suitable point in a debate, he would interject "Vundla, Vundla".

I ignored him.

Shortly after I became chairman I listed my priorities in a speech to the City Council:

"Acceleration of house building to double, equal to about 5 000 houses a year; the slums of Moroka and Shantytown to go. Medical services must be expanded. Street and home lighting introduced. Recreational facilities fostered and developed. The underlying sociological causes of crime to be identified. The restoration of family life an urgent need. Commerce and Industry should pay higher wages. Married couples should be encouraged to live in the city where accommodation was available. The Council should establish a public relations department of the NEAD to keep Africans informed. The press should be careful of its reporting – inaccuracy was kindling racial passions."

My answer to the Nationalist jeers and attempts to hinder me, was to make them understand publicly what I would be trying to do, and to alert the UP that they should give me the support that was necessary.

My final statement told the Council that "all this costs money and with it a change of attitude towards the African. I can only say to the people of Johannesburg, you cannot have your cake and eat it. You must realise that the position of the African people is no longer that of an uneducated mass. The comforts you want for yourselves are desired today by the non-European. If you herd him by the thousands in the beerhalls and hope he will be satisfied with his mug of beer, then you must think again."

I hoped that the UP and the Nationalists were absolutely clear where I stood, as long as I remained chairman of the NEAD.

43

Problems and difficulties were the order of the day. It was a bitterly cold June, winter had come early. Thousands of people in the townships had no heating and lived in slum conditions; in crates that originally contained Austin cars imported from England; in hovels built from any kind of metal scrap; in tents; and the only heat they had was when they huddled around their open fires in the unmade dirt passages that separated their homes. Many were unemployed, relying on friends and family to keep them fed and housed.

The Star reported the hardship on 13 June.

I called an emergency meeting of the NEAD and we launched the Non-European Winter Clothing Appeal and Financial Fund to help the needy. Public response was overwhelming. We recruited extra staff to deal with mountains of blankets and clothes that were donated. Distribution centres were set up in the townships. It was a small help for poverty-stricken blacks in the middle of winter.

I was also watching the confidential negotiations between the City Treasurer and Anglo-American representatives about the £3 000 000 loan. Ivor Holmes kept me in touch and nothing had been leaked in the usual way to the newspapers.

Since I was convinced that we would get the money, on 6 July I wrote to Archibald, the Housing Director, requesting him to prepare draft plans for clearance of the 12-year-old slum camps of Moroka, Shantytown and Pimville. By 30 July I was studying Archibald's report. Because of apartheid laws he had to take into account the ethnic origins of the slum-dwellers. Verwoerd had already laid down ground rules that there was to be no mixing of the black tribes in the townships. Archibald had to do a quick survey of the ethnic breakdowns. Fifty-three per cent were Zulu, forty per cent Sotho and seven per cent were mixed. Families had then to be divided into those who could pay economic rentals and those who had to be subsidised.

There were 15 000 families, amounting to 80 000 people and these were the people I wanted to rehouse, in addition to the normal housing programme of 2 500 houses. Our figures showed that the loan would cover 5 000 extra houses a year for three years.

Archibald's plan had to ensure that before families could be rehoused they had to move to the site-and-service plots insisted on by Verwoerd, which would require negotiation with him for his agreement. The scheme would cost £2 286 500 and with provision for services, schools and administration this would bring it to £3 000 000.

The astonishing fact was that we could build a three-bedroom house with minimum facilities for £160 to £180, using our own trained black labour.

As we waited for the final decision on the loan, I was getting to know more about the problems that the NEAD was having with Verwoerd. The City Council had meekly accepted Verwoerd's Sky Location conditions in November 1955 and they were committed to carrying them out. I was not told of the serious problems with the delegated powers that the Council had taken on. In terms of Verwoerd's regulations the Council had agreed that it would build a large hostel complex at Dube to accommodate the thousands of single migrant workers who worked as cleaners in the city's flats, hotels and office buildings and who lived on their roof tops – the Sky Locations.

The Act allowed no more than five, but numbers required by buildings were far in excess of this figure.

According to the Council's officials the 1955 agreement with the government gave the Council the right to vary the removals to the townships if they found industry or commerce was being disrupted.

I was determined not to implement the Sky Locations Act because it was entrenching apartheid. Unlike the UP in the Council, I was not prepared to do Verwoerd's work for him.

The Council believed they could not refuse to do so and that is why they agreed to carry out the removals in November 1955. Archibald was busy on the large Dube Hostel complex when I took over; and hotel, flat and other employers of "excess" labour had already been told to house their labour at Dube.

The first time I learnt that something was wrong was at a UP Caucus meeting. Councillor Miller pointed out that, in terms of the agreement with Verwoerd, inadequate notice was given to employers. They were up in arms because a serious position had developed regarding lawfully resident Natives. Miller told the Caucus that he had received many telephonic complaints. I was astonished that he had not come first to me as chairman. It was then that I realised that Miller was out to embarrass me by going to the Caucus. They were looking for excuses to blame me for things that were going wrong as a result of their agreement with Verwoerd.

There was no love lost between Miller and me. I knew that he now regretted that he was not able to become the NEAD Chairman when Opperman went.

After a noisy and bitter Caucus meeting I was instructed to suspend the removal notices for a month so that my officials could meet Verwoerd's to sort matters out. It was evident that if Verwoerd's instructions were carried out there would be chaos amongst the non-licensed hotels and luxury flat-dwellers in Johannesburg.

I dutifully made a public announcement temporarily suspending the removals on the grounds that the new Dube hostels were not ready. This lead to deputations from hotels and many requests for exemptions from elderly flat-dwellers who wanted to retain their servants on the premises. Many of my medical colleagues wrote to me after they received notices from NEAD officials about the removals because they needed their servants on call.

Letters started appearing in the newspapers condemning the Sky Locations Act. The public became aware that the hostels which were being built were unsuitable. To overcome public dissent I invited employers to visit Dube and to inspect the buildings. This did not help matters because I had to admit that the type of accommodation was not good enough. I was saddled with an impossible situation. All the Sky Locations arrangements had been made before I took over control. It was becoming clear to me that my opposition to implementing Verwoerd's apartheid legislation was correct.

A *Rand Daily Mail* editorial headed "Slow March to Dube" just about summed it up. "Apartheid always puts the cart before the horse. The government promulgates the regulations first and worries about the accommodation later."

The Dube complex, expected to be ready by the end of June, was nowhere near completion. Senior officials dealing with it were on holiday. I had no option but to postpone removals yet again. Every day the newspapers carried stories on the Sky Locations and the Dube hostel problem. Explanations had to be given to Verwoerd for the new delay. Staff discussions were going on with his officials.

Verwoerd, however, did not wait. On 4 August he issued a press statement saying that he would shortly give new directives to the Johannesburg City Council on Sky Location removals. He referred to our decision to delay the removal of legitimate residents from the buildings until such time as the "illegals" had been rehoused.

Verwoerd said he did not agree with my interpretation of the Sky Locations legislation, and criticised the Council's decision to delay removals.

"Unfortunately," said Verwoerd, "Dr Wilson, the NEAD Chairman, said that his [Dr Wilson's] proposals and the City Council's resolution concurred with my policy and wishes. Dr Wilson added that I would have applied the law similarly. Unless I react to this immediately it will be said later when I have to judge the achievements of the Johannesburg City Council that I tacitly approved of its actions. This I do not do, and Dr Wilson is obviously the last person I would elect as my mouthpiece to interpret my policy."

Dr Verwoerd accused the Council of wanting to use the Sky Locations Act for its own reasons and so did not carry out his directives.

I did not bother to reply to Verwoerd. It was what I expected. The only thing I could agree with was that we were poles apart. I waited for his new directives.

Verwoerd did not know about my plan to raise the £3 000 000 from Sir Ernest Oppenheimer and Ivor Holmes finally brought the news that negotiations had been successful. We were getting the money to clear the slums. It would be in the form of a thirty-year loan on the same terms that the government offered for loans to the Council, at four and five-eighths per cent per annum.

Sir Ernest had been shrewd and had gone to his mining finance house colleagues and drawn them into a consortium.

The news could not have come at a better time. We had to have government approval to use the money, and this meant that I would have to see Dr Verwoerd about it. Perhaps, on the strength of this, he would soften his attitude on the Sky Locations, since we would be rehousing slum-dwellers and taking a great financial load off the government's shoulders.

The loan negotiations were miraculously still confidential. Holmes and I met the mining chiefs with Sir Ernest on 8 August to finalise the deal. I explained to them that I would lead a deputation to Verwoerd for approval as soon as possible. I also hoped that as a result of my meeting with Dr Verwoerd that there would be a better understanding between us and that we could iron out some of our differences with the government.

Throughout the negotiations I had kept Paddy Cartwright, the editor of *The Rand Daily Mail* fully informed, because I wanted to get maximum publicity for the loan and the slum clearance. This would help to restore the image of the UP and maximise the importance of the loan to the people of Soweto.

A week before we saw Dr Verwoerd, Holmes and I saw the Treasury and the Transvaal Administrator to tell them our plans. However, before seeing Dr Verwoerd we had to let Caucus know about our coup, which I did at a special meeting. Several members were fed-up that I had kept the negotiations secret from the Caucus, which decided that the delegation to Verwoerd would include its senior party members – Miller, Patmore and others.

Once the Caucus was told, I knew that there was the risk that someone would let the press know about the loan – the days of confidentiality were over. We had to see Dr Verwoerd, meet the mining finance houses, settle the arrangements for the special Council meeting called to announce and ratify the loan, inform the Native Advisory Boards and above all to tell the slum-dwellers that at long last the Council was going to build houses.

On the day we were to meet the financiers about the £3m loan, we saw Dr Verwoerd in the boardroom of his office at the Union Buildings in Pretoria. At long last I was to meet the most formidable Nationalist politician in South Africa. He was a large man with well-brushed silver hair, bluish eyes and had a fixed smile. He held himself well, and spoke clearly in a high-pitched voice. I felt, because of our frequent newspaper confrontations, that Verwoerd was no stranger to me, although this was our first face to face meeting. I told Dr Verwoerd why we had come and asked him to approve the £3 000 000 loan which, I emphasised, would clear South Africa's worst slums.

It was hard to believe what followed. He refused to sanction the loan. He was truculent and said that the mining finance houses were trying to dictate to him how he should run his site-and-service scheme for the Sky Locations removals. He accused them of trying to "steal" his sites. (We needed 6 000 sites for the slum-dwellers annually).

I immediately challenged these extraordinary allegations. The meeting had started on a bad note. It was clear that he had decided to tell us how we were to spend the loan money – if he gave his approval. He told us that the site-and-service scheme came first because the number one priority was removal of the Natives from the rooftops. They had first claim on any houses the Council might build with the loan money. This was preposterous. I pointed out that we were not only going to clear the slums, but we were going to include other natives who were on our housing list who had waited for years.

Verwoerd was adamant, implacable. Everything I told him went in one ear and out of the other. It was a stalemate. Unless we housed Sky Locations dwellers there was no approval from him.

220

"Dr Verwoerd, this is a remarkable offer from the mining finance houses and Sir Ernest Oppenheimer," I told him, "and it will solve our most serious slum problem, which is severely criticised overseas harming South Africa." I tried all the arguments to influence him. There was dismay at the confused discussion that took place around the table. It seemed as if the meeting would break up when Verwoerd made a new offer.

"I might consider allowing you to use a 1 000 sites a year."

I rejected this. He had a hurried discussion with his Secretary for Native Affairs, Dr Eiselen, then he said he would consider 1 800 to 2 000 sites yearly, providing the rest of the houses were used for the Sky Location blacks.

It was like an auction, absolutely unbelievable. Here was the Minister of Native Affairs bargaining with a City Councillor over the number of sites we could use to clear slums that affected the lives of 85 000 people, simply because he refused to depart from his doctrine of apartheid. He was totally inflexible. Verwoerd was obviously carrying out a preconceived plan of action.

My colleagues were speechless. My immediate reaction was that we could be tough too, because if he did not come to agreement the private sector loan might not be available.

"Dr Verwoerd," I interjected at a point in the horse-trading, "I don't understand why you are bargaining. This loan was obtained for slum clearance, and I doubt whether the lenders will consider it if its main purpose is to move Natives already housed, when there are thousands living in appalling slum conditions."

Eventually Dr Verwoerd evolved what he called a "final offer".

"I will confirm the loan, if the Council makes available 6 000 sites on which they will build houses for Johannesburg's illegal dwellers. It is only on these terms and against my will that I will approve the loan."

I had to admit that Verwoerd was in the driving seat as the Minister of Native Affairs. It was a case of take it or leave it. Time was running out. I told him that we would urgently report back to the Council. My problem was that we had to back in Johannesburg by 5 pm to meet the financiers and then see Ernest Oppenheimer for drinks to report on the day's events. The meeting did not end without further controversy. Just before we left, Dr Verwoerd threw his final spanner into the works.

"Well, we have settled the question of the Sky Locations, the illegal dwellers and the slum clearance . . ."

I interrupted him.

"Dr Verwoerd, we have not yet discussed the Sky Locations matter, and if we can meet again in the next few days I will do my best to find a settlement."

Verwoerd said he could not see us for a fortnight. As we left Dr Eiselen, the Secretary for Native Affairs, came up to me.

"Dr Wilson, I'm glad we met you. It has a been a good frank discussion today. I want to say that if you can arrange the loan on the terms agreed by Minister Verwoerd – it will help everybody."

"I'll do my best to help *everybody*, Dr Eiselen." I replied.

On the way to Johannesburg Ivor Holmes and I talked about Verwoerd's offer, and came to the conclusion that the Council was in a cleft stick. Verwoerd had powers to hold up everything. Despite my refusal to implement his apartheid schemes we had to consider the 85 000 slum-dwellers and what it meant to them. I also had to accept that the UP Council could override my views, which was very likely once they knew the details of the scheme I had in mind.

They did not not approve of my constant opposition to Verwoerd and the Nationalists anyway. We decided to advise the mining finance houses to accept the terms – there was a long road ahead for manouevre. If it took us another two years to rehouse the slum-dwellers, well then, so be it.

Back in Johannesburg we met the chairmen of the seven mining finance houses, and told them of our meeting with Dr Verwoerd. I do not think that some of them were too worried about his offer, because the general attitude of the gold-mining fraternity was not in conflict with government policy. They left it to us to find the best formula as long as we built houses. The bulk of the funds would be used for slum clearance. Dr Holmes assured the meeting that if there was a shortfall, the Council would most likely find the money to complete the rehousing of the slum-dwellers.

We then went to see Sir Ernest at Brenthurst, his home in Parktown. He was relaxed in an armchair surrounded by lovely Impressionist paintings. One, a lovely Renoir, caught my eye. Holmes and I explained the day's happenings, and what went on at our meeting with Verwoerd.

When I had finished describing how Verwoerd reached his final offer, Sir Ernest put his hands out and said:

"Verwoerd is *meshuga*." This was a colourful Jewish expression meaning off his head or mad in the descriptive sense. When Holmes understood what it meant he heartily agreed. We came to the conclusion we had done the best we could with the Minister. I was apprehensive about Verwoerd's statement that we had settled the Sky Locations matter, because I foresaw further disagreements, verbal battles and attempts by Verwoerd to use the £3 000 000 loan as a bargaining point. I decided to hold my fire until he made his intentions clear.

I arranged to meet the Native Advisory Boards before the special Council meeting on 14 August to ratify the loan. They were extremely happy at what we had achieved.

I told them that we proposed to visit the townships the following day, when I and other councillors would do a "walkabout" with Sir Ernest, Lady Oppenheimer and their mining colleagues.

The special Council meeting was at 5 pm. I had given *The Rand Daily Mail* editor full details of the gathering, with copies of my speech, but about an hour before the meeting began I learnt that *The Star* had broken the story in late afternoon editions. It had been leaked to them by someone in Caucus, or at Anglo-American.

This was not unexpected, because councillors like Miller and Patmore would want to get on the bandwagon. Unfortunately, *The Star* story was incorrect, reporting the initiative for the loan from Oppenheimer and the mines, without mentioning my role in it.

Instead, only Miller received mention in connection with the delegation to Verwoerd. It was clear who had leaked the story.

I telephoned Paddy Cartwright of *The Rand Daily Mail*, who assured me that he would set the record straight.

"Don't worry, Boris, I've got permission to take photographs at the Council meeting – our story will be taken up by the news agencies."

The Star told me that their story came from an unnamed councillor.

The Council meeting started at 5.30 pm. It was packed with visitors with only one resolution on the order paper – the £3 000 000 loan, which I officially announced after I rose to speak. I told the story of the negotiations, paying tribute to Sir Ernest for his help when I originally approached him.

I also paid tribute to the mining finance houses, Ivor Holmes and Housing Director Archibald.

"To say thank you to Sir Ernest Oppenheimer is of little value in terms of what he achieved for us. I believe that he knows the humanitarian motives that inspired him to assist us will reap just dividends, when he sees the new townships that will commence to arise early in 1957, giving new hope to thousands of African people."

Afterwards, we had a cocktail party and a national broadcast.

The following morning *The Rand Daily Mail* appeared with the front page almost wholly taken up by the news of the loan.

"The scheme was explained to the Johannesburg City Council last night by Dr Boris Wilson, chairman of the Non-European Affairs Committee who first suggested it to Sir Ernest Oppenheimer." I was photographed addressing the council, the only time a photograph had been allowed of the Council in action. There was another picture of Sir Ernest and me shaking hands captioned "Sir Ernest and Dr Wilson were originators of the idea."

The next morning we met at the City Hall, and I travelled with the Oppenheimers, followed by a large procession of cars to Moroka, Shantytown and Pimville.

The news had got around the townships. People lined the route and cheered. We walked around for several hours, accompanied by members of the Advisory Boards. We saw the worst slums, spoke to many black men and women and received first hand accounts of life in the townships. The newspapers were full of pictures of our visit. I doubt if there had ever been such a warm reception given by blacks to whites, who not only came to see how they lived, but who recognised them as ordinary human beings needing help.

My telephone rang constantly for days afterwards and I received dozens of letters of praise and congratulation, not only from my white friends but from blacks. The Moroka (Emergency Camp) Advisory Board wrote that the "people of Moroka see their hopes of nine long years for homes coming true." Telegrams expressing goodwill arrived. The Institute of Race Relations praised my efforts. It was good to know that people were encouraged

223

by what had been done, but the task was not finished because we had not yet settled with Verwoerd and houses had to be built.

One letter from a stockbroker was down to earth.

"I happily and most sincerely congratulate you a thousand times for your magnificent coup, which tremendously heartened me. It is the first political ray of sunshine in eight years. I sincerely believed that you had every chance of destroying yourself politically by accepting the chair of Non-European Affairs. I am very happy that I was hopelessly wrong in my fears."

The newspaper editorials were brimming with hope. They foresaw the end of the worst period in the UP's control of the Council over the last ten years because of their failure to deal with the housing problem in the townships. The press had thoroughly and repeatedly castigated the UP for its failures over the last ten years. I hoped it would teach the arch-conservatives in the UP a lesson and let me get on with the job of building houses and restoring faith in white liberalism.

The Golden City Post, a newspaper for blacks, wrote that "we wish every influential South African in the country would make a personal tour of the rotten slums which are a disgrace to South Africa."

On 17 August I wrote to Sir Ernest thanking him for all he had done, and on the 20th he sent me a personal letter: "I appreciate your kind remarks in regard to the £3 000 000 loan towards native housing. Full credit for the scheme, of course, must go to you, who initiated the proposal, and its success is in no small measure due to your untiring efforts in its cause. I am happy that I have been associated with the project and that all the mining houses co-operated so readily."

A generous letter but understating the role he played. I am certain that no South African other than Sir Ernest Oppenheimer could have raised such a large sum of money so quickly at the time.

As I told Oppenheimer when we first met, only two people could succeed in clearing those slums – he was one, I was the other.

In those days the United Party failed to find a solution to the housing problem. All they did was to whimper in the face of Verwoerd's threats, and carry out his removal instructions.

Oppenheimer's role came at a crucial time.

Later that year Jack Cutten, an independent City councillor and town planner, writing in *The Forum* described the history of the struggle by civic minded and liberal people to try and get the UP council to deal with the slums in the last ten years. Paying tribute to the loan success, he said it "was left to Dr Boris Wilson to climb the summit." He was correct in that much work had been done by the Citizen's Housing Committee, Father Huddleston, Richard Harvey and Jack Lewsen, but they all failed to find a formula. It is obvious that if I had not joined the United Party I would never found the formula. Out of a political evil came good for the poverty-stricken blacks of Johannesburg.

Despite public acclaim from whites and blacks, a few days later Verwoerd issued a careful public statement on the loan which caused

OFFICE BOX 4902
EPHONE 34-1547
GRAPHIC ADDRESS:
"SPECTRUM"

44, MAIN STREET,

JOHANNESBURG.

EO/AMM/   20th August, 1956.

My dear Wilson

Thank you for your letter of the 17th August, 1956.

I appreciate very much your kind remarks in regard to the £3 million loan towards Native Housing. Full credit for the scheme must, of course, go to you who initiated the proposal, and its success is in no small measure due to your untiring efforts in its cause. I am happy that I have been associated with the project, and that all the Mining Houses co-operated so readily.

*With best wishes
Yours sincerely
E. Oppenheimer*

Dr. Boris Wilson, M.P.C.,
P.O. Box 11252
JOHANNESBURG.

225

problems. He insisted that he and I had settled the Sky Locations issue. Unless his wishes were carried out, loan approval would be withheld.

In the Caucus, councillors avoided dealing with this and instead voiced their complaints that the negotiations on the loan had been kept confidential from them until the last minute. Miller, Patmore and others were sullen because of the acclaim that was showered on Sir Ernest and me. Miller was most affected. He loved the limelight. It was incredible to hear members of the Caucus complaining that they should have been told about the negotiations from their inception. This was the level to which the issue was reduced. I was not having any part of this nonsense and made clear that I was not interested in Miller, Patmore or the UP establishment. I was satisfied that most of them were councillors only for the status and benefits it gave them.

If they had wanted to find a way of clearing the slums they could have done so years before I came along.

Instead they fell into a political stupor in the face of Verwoerd's threats and lost sight of the real target. That is why they compromised themselves in November 1955 when they agreed to take delegated powers and carry out Verwoerd's Sky Locations removals.

When they found it to be an impossible task, they had to find other excuses for not implementing the removals.

Unfortunately for me, everything happened at once – the £3 000 000 loan, the failure to have the accommodation ready at Dube for the single men removed from the rooftops, and mounting hostility in the Caucus towards me.

Verwoerd used the loan as a lever against the Council and me. Unless I carried out his wishes he would hold up loan permission.

In retrospect I often wondered why there had been no opposition by the UP establishment to my appointment as chairman of NEAD. Could it be that they calculated that I would bear the brunt of the problems they were experiencing with Dr Verwoerd and when all broke down, I could be blamed? It would be an easy way to discredit me and dispose of me in the Council.

I did not realise, when I became chairman, how serious the Sky Location problem had become. Opperman, the former chairman, never disclosed it, because the senior staff had a habit of confining most of the day-to-day happenings to discussions with the chairman. The committee only got to know about problems when a report had to be made. So, when Miller openly attacked me in the Caucus because some flat owners had complained to him about the disruption to their lives, I was taken unawares.

The Council had sent out notices in terms of the Sky Locations Act to flat owners that all natives in excess of the five permitted, had to reside in Dube irrespective of whether they had a lawful right to be on the premises or not. Flat owners said they could not service their tenants homes any longer; private hotels, the indigent and the sick complained. The press reported that a number of "Zulu boys" had packed their bags and gone home to Zululand rather than be sent to the Dube single men's hostels.

Here was I, one of Verwoerd's implacable opponents, now trapped into implementing his apartheid Sky Locations policy. It was ironic. I had forecast that the Sky Locations would bring chaos. It had come. Verwoerd disputed my view that the loan and the Sky Locations were separate matters. He now told the Council that they would only get loan approval if they implemented his apartheid legislation. It was political blackmail.

I was in a Catch 22 situation. I was attacked on all sides. Verwoerd was lambasting me in public, the UP was blaming me for not agreeing to Verwoerd's terms, and the building of the sorely needed houses was held up. I was standing firm, refusing to let Verwoerd use our loan money for Sky Locations. The dispute went on for six weeks. Eventually, I compromised in that I was prepared to move illegal dwellers because it was the law, but I was not prepared to use the loan money to house them. If Verwoerd wanted them moved he had to provide the money to house them.

The more Verwoerd attacked, the more the UP Caucus cringed and ran for cover. There was a newspaper story almost every day about the Sky Locations, the loan and the Council. The Council halted the movement of blacks, which we believed we could do. Verwoerd objected. Eventually I telephoned Dr Eiselen to make an appointment for a deputation to see Verwoerd to try and settle our differences. I wanted an end to this conflict and to get on with the job of house-building.

Neither Verwoerd or Eiselen could see us. Instead an official's meeting was arranged. This was a good idea, because if the officials could agree, it would save a confrontation and possible breakdown between Verwoerd and me. The Council's officials knew how far they could go and in any event they supported my stand.

Carr, the manager told Verwoerd's officials that "at no time had the Council departed from what it was delegated to do. The Council felt it had the right to shift the emphasis from the removal of the lawful natives to the unlawful. The Minister's original directive said the Council should proceed with caution and that is what the Council was doing."

The Council's legal adviser told Verwoerd's officials that the Minister had placed Johannesburg in a difficult position in that the Council would have to decide whether it wished to carry on, "or hand back the delegated powers". This upset them and our official's were called back to an urgent meeting in Pretoria, where they were given a veiled threat against "other schemes of the council" if the present dispute should result in further estrangement between the Minister and the Council.

At the next NEAD meeting the Nationalists attended in force. They insisted on discussing the £3 000 000 loan and the Sky Locations Act. Piet van Vuuren threatened that the "whole three million pound loan could go down the drain as well as any further loans."

My reaction from the chair was to tell the Nationalists that we would not be intimidated. We would wait for the results of the officials' meetings. It was obvious that the Nationalist councillors were in collusion with Verwoerd – their truculence, their obvious attempt to put a squeeze on the United Party and their timing was enough evidence for this assumption.

While waiting for the news from Pretoria we had frequent Caucus meetings. The UP establishment did not like me standing up to Verwoerd. They wanted to give in and call it a day. I stood firm, backed by the Council's own officials who were giving me legal and practical policy advice.

Early in September, after a meeting with the Town Clerk and Bill Carr, we decided that the Town Clerk should make one final attempt to get Verwoerd to accept our proposals and approve a scheme for reduction of licensed natives in the European (white) areas on a voluntary basis. There was a swift reply from Pretoria. The Minister was not prepared to accept it, and threatened the Council that unless it carried out the removal of legally accommodated Natives on a quota basis, the £3 000 000 loan and other building schemes were in jeopardy.

Verwoerd had already attacked the council publicly and Miller as leader put up a half-hearted defence.

My interpretation was that Hendrik Verwoerd was going to stand firm because the Sky Locations was one of the bastions of his apartheid policy. He could not deviate one iota. His repeated threats were not based on reason – they were politically motivated – the threats of a political bully. The Town Clerk and the Legal Adviser both confirmed that the Council had every right to take the stand we had adopted.

If they had told me that we were in the wrong I would have reviewed our strategy and considered my position. One thing I was not going to do was to give in to Verwoerd's vindictiveness. My difficulties were compounded because I had an unwilling caucus in the struggle with the Nationalists.

Verwoerd's next tactic was a public attack from the platform of the Transvaal Nationalist Party Congress.

Under the headline "I Will Not Be Stopped" *The Rand Daily Mail* reported Verwoerd's onslaught on its front page together with his warning to the Council to put things right in its handling of Native Affairs.

"I want to say very clearly that I found it necessary to give certain warnings and to carry out certain negotiations in the public interest. No irresponsible reproaches, no loud talk, no attempts by the UP to sow suspicions against us will stop me.

"We know what is going on in Johannesburg. The Council will have to put things right, United Party or not, or we will put them right."

These were the bluntest threats to the council's sovereignty and to the governing United Party who were being reluctantly dragged into the arena against Verwoerd.

Then a terrible catastrophe occurred. There was a serious "faction fight" at the new Dube single men's hostel, and forty blacks were killed and scores injured.

The UP caucus was called urgently and it was decided that Miller would issue a statement blaming apartheid's ethnic grouping and calling for an immediate Commission of Enquiry.

Verwoerd's reaction was to attack the Council yet again.

Once more the front pages of *The Rand Daily Mail* were dominated by his arrogance and threats:

"It appeared that anyone, a Miller or a Boris Wilson, was considered worthy of the front page in the English Press if they were prepared to attack him or his department. My warning is intended to upset the UP regime. The more they are upset the more the ratepayers may hope for more control in Native Affairs."

My response was on the front page next to his statement.

"At a time when 40 people have been killed and scores injured, Dr Verwoerd indulges in polemics and political bullying such as have not been witnessed publicly in South Africa before in order to excuse his failures and the shortcomings of his policy. Neither I, the ratepayers of Johannesburg or the United Party will be intimidated by a Minister of Native Affairs whose dictatorial methods we thought had died with Hitler and Mussolini. The blame lies not at the United Party's doorstep but at the foot of the Minister's unscientific and tragically repressive apartheid schemes."

I challenged Verwoerd.

"What proof is there that ethnic grouping is not the root of the riots? Is not the Minister's policy of large hostels of 5 000 single men a contributory cause? Is it now not evident that the haste in which he compelled the City Council to move thousands of raw natives to Dube Hostel under the Sky Locations Act a further major cause?

"Does he not think that *tsotsism* (juvenile gangsterism) has resulted from the slums and the breakdown of native family life due to the failure of the government to raise minimum wages so that natives could afford to educate their children and live in better circumstances?".

Verwoerd was trying to make political capital out of a very serious riot. Even Miller, in his reply, had to admit this fact.

Meanwhile Archibald and the housing division were going ahead to accelerate plans to build more houses. One way or another, I knew that Verwoerd would have to allow house-building for slum-dwellers even if it meant we could not use all the loan money.

By now the Johannesburg public and the politically conscious elsewhere were aware of my struggle with Verwoerd. I received many messages of encouragement from all over the country which contrasted with the UP's sullen attitude towards me.

On the 18 October I decided to issue an official statement to *The Rand Daily Mail*: "City Can Go Ahead With £3 000 000 Plan for Houses – Wilson" ran the headline. I reviewed the course of events in the dispute and pointed out that the "Minister had originally welcomed the loan. The Minister was now trying to make the loan conditional upon the implementation of the Sky Locations Act. This attempt at this late stage to impose new conditions and to act like a political bully should be resisted." I emphasised that the implementation of the Sky Locations Act would be better done if the Minister would leave us alone to get on with the job instead of imposing new quotas and interfering all the time.

"It is impossible to co-operate with the Minister if he does not stick to decisions already made. The City Council would be well advised to return the delegated powers (*vis-à-vis* Sky Locations) and let him try to implement his impossible legislation."

I had crossed the Rubicon as far as Dr Hendrik Verwoerd was concerned. I had also thrown down the gauntlet to the United Party who were not giving me the support I needed and wanted once again to send a deputation to Verwoerd. The whole dispute cried for action from the unwilling council.

I tried to nail the Caucus once and for all on 7 November. I moved a comprehensive resolution calling on the Council to rescind its decision to send a deputation, confirming that it rejected allegations that it broke agreements and that Verwoerd's view that the Sky Locations and the £3 000 000 loan were linked was unacceptable. In terms of the Council's discretion, it handed back the delegated Sky Location's powers and expected Verwoerd to honour his verbal approval of the housing loan, failing which the Prime Minister should intervene to protect the rights of the City of Johannesburg.

Not unexpectedly, there was a great struggle in the Caucus where debate was bitter and long. They refused to take a decision and opted for sending the deputation. Tension in the caucus was heightened by the fact that the annual struggle was taking place for the leadership, mayoralty and committee positions.

As usual, the newspapers had details within hours of what went on in the Caucus and rumours were rife about a split. The Verwoerd dispute was linked to councillors who were struggling for UP leadership, reputedly Miller, Patmore and me.

The Star reported that a subordinate contest was going on for the chairmanship of the Non-European Affairs Committee. This was now considered the most important Council committee, and should be in the hands of the Leader of the United Party, either Miller or Wilson. This was an indication to me that this inspired piece of reporting emanated from Miller. It was evident he had his eyes on the Non-European Affairs Committee. The Council election results were not surprising. Patmore became the leader, Miller chairman of Non-European Affairs and I was demoted to vice-chairman of the General Purposes Committee.

The United Party establishment had won in the end. It was not Verwoerd who defeated me, but my own political party. I was upset, especially since I was looking forward to the day when the slums would be eradicated. Instead my future was decided by the uncaring political councillors whom I despised, who were prepared to negotiate with Verwoerd at any price for the sake of peace and petty positions of power.

Public reaction was overwhelming in the newspapers. Many letters condemned the United Party. *The Rand Daily Mail* on 13 October published a leading editorial:

231

LET'S SACK THE CHAIRMAN

The United Party in the City Council works in a mysterious way its wonders to perform. On Thursday it met in a secret conclave to choose the chairmen of the various Council committees. The one chairman who, in a comparatively short term of office seemed to have earned the distinction was Dr Boris Wilson MPC, who has been in charge of Non-European Affairs since May. The Caucus sacked him and decided to appoint Mr Hyman Miller in his place.

Dr Wilson had played a large part in securing a £3 000 000 loan from the principal mining groups on the Rand. This probably represents the biggest single advance towards a solution of the housing problem made in this past ten years. In fact, it would not be exaggerating to say that it is the only advance since the council appointed Mr Archibald to speed its building programme. Here were the sinews of war which Mr Archibald has needed ever since he took up his job. Dr Wilson seems to have been the *deus ex machina*. Some Councils would have awarded him a medal or an illuminated address for this service. Our council gave him the sack.

There may be excellent reasons why this decision was taken. Perhaps the United Party has discovered that Dr Wilson has become too close a friend of Dr Verwoerd's. For all we know Dr Verwoerd may have offered him a job finding the finance for the Government's housing plans. Heaven knows they are going to need it. But, if this is so, the bewildered ratepayers who have watched five chairmen of this committee come and go (especially go) in the past two years are entitled to an explanation.

It really looks as if the essential qualification of the chairman of our Non-European Affairs Committee is that he should not build too many houses. Three million pounds worth of houses is obviously making the pace too hot. Sack the chairman and let's get back to normal.

The UP establishment had done what Verwoerd wanted them to do. They had got rid of me as their solution to the dispute, and I was certain they would try this tactic again. Miller's first pronouncement after he took over again was a cynical ploy – "We shall tackle this issue [Sky Locations] honestly and with realism".

A reply was awaited from Verwoerd about the Council's deputation.

The Star reporter wrote that he had reason to believe that the Council will honour the agreement they had reached with Verwoerd the year before.

So, the Council was turning tail and bowing before the might of Dr Verwoerd as they had done over me. Disappointed as I was, I realised that I was almost alone in opposition in the ranks of the UP to what they were now going to do. They were not going to oppose apartheid, they were going to carry it out and do the Nationalist's work for them. This is why the United Party could never defeat the Nationalists.

Apart from what I could say in Caucus, I still had the right to speak in the open Council meetings. I decided to follow the course I adopted when I opposed the Western Areas scheme – to speak out in open Council.

On 29 November I told the Council that "I am strongly opposed to the Johannesburg City Council accepting the delegated powers to implement proclamations in accordance with the Group Areas Act. Local authorities should keep their hands clean and have nothing to do with his [Verwoerd's] legislation. The Council had a sorry experience when it accepted delegated powers to carry out the provisions of the Sky Locations Act . . . There was no law that compelled local authorities to accept delegated powers from the government."

I was on safe ground. The week before I had told the Union Congress of the United Party in Bloemfontein the same thing, and no one, including Miller and Patmore who were present, challenged my words. It was clear to the delegates who came from all over South Africa where I stood and that I was not prepared to be Verwoerd's political lackey.

My personal relations with the UP caucus were at their lowest ebb. I had no more time for their duplicity and weaknesses *vis-à-vis* the Nationalists. The time had come for me to get out of the Council.

I had done my job. The slums would be cleared. The UP could not turn back on this one. The newspapers, the mining barons and the liberal elements of the UP would see that the reluctant City Councillors would rebuild the black townships.

44

A general election was due in August 1958. I decided to concentrate on getting the parliamentary nomination for the Hospital constituency. If I was successful it was a safe UP seat. I knew that if Arthur Barlow stood I would beat him. I believed I had a duty in Parliament to challenge Verwoerd and the Nationalists on the grand designs of apartheid.

Sadly, Sir Ernest Oppenheimer died in 1957 after a short illness. Some months later the City Council announced it was erecting a memorial to him in Soweto. Miller and the officials did not consult me as to the form it would take, or when the ceremony to honour him would take place.

One evening at about 7 pm my home telephone rang. It was Lady Ina Oppenheimer, his widow.

"Dr Wilson, I would be very pleased if you would let me take you tomorrow morning to the memorial ceremony for Ernest at the townships. Can I pick you up at eleven o'clock?"

I was stuck for words. I had not been invited by Miller or the Town Clerk. I explained this to Lady Oppenheimer as tactfully as I could. She was

233

obviously embarrassed and upset when I told her why I could not accept her kind invitation. She tried to persuade me to come.

"I will be there in spirit," I said.

I have often wondered whether she in fact did know that I had not been invited and had decided to take me along to put the Council to shame. It was deplorable, but this is the level at which UP councillors operated. I was not surprised. I knew the moral calibre of the UP men of the City Council.

I later visited Sir Ernest's monument on my own, paying my respects to him, on the small hill where a slender obelisk had been erected. In the distance in the hazy smog of a spring morning I could see the matchbox landscape of houses. I knew that Sir Ernest and I had set the black builders to work rehousing their people, which is really what counted!

I reflected on my father's own struggles in the Market with the Market Master and his inspectors which I witnessed as a child. Father was never intimidated by authority, especially if he believed he was in the right. I suppose I had inherited some of his stubbornness in this respect. In my struggles against the Nationalists and the apartheid regime, I now found that I was battling on two fronts because the small men of the United Party in Johannesburg had given in to the Nationalists. The loss of status did not worry me. In fact it encouraged me to intensify my personal opposition to Afrikaner nationalism and to help blacks who had few or no rights whatsoever. The £3 000 000 loan, the picture of houses being built, improving the quality of life, was the real reward.

At the height of the Sky Locations crisis, nominations were called for the Parliamentary seat of Hospital. So to add to my problems, I had to busy myself in the evenings visiting UP supporters and branches who held valuable votes to support my candidature. There was opposition to me from several people in the constituency and determined attempts were made by a group who would not have me at any price because of my liberal views. Despite this, in a secret ballot during October, I secured the nomination by 15 votes to 2.

In general, my relationship with the voters in Hospital Hill was good. Since Arthur Barlow's defection, I was regarded as the senior UP representative, and I restored the morale of the organisation which was very low. However, I was constantly harassed by the "anti-Wilson" faction led by a stern middle-aged woman, a Mrs English, who from the moment I arrived in Hospital conducted a non-stop vendetta against me. Apart from her wholly right wing sympathies, she was openly racialistic and prejudiced and had no difficulty in recruiting a few supporters, especially a young man, Ernest Rex, who was to cause me a lot of trouble.

Rex was invariably rude to me at branch meetings. He was a short man, in his mid-twenties, had a very ruddy complexion, close-cropped hair and his small cynical mouth fitted in with his anti-Wilson behaviour. On one occasion he threatened me with violence. The divisional committee tried to censure him but Mrs English always came to his defence. I concluded that he was able to act like this because he must have had backing from outside the division, probably from senior conservative members of the party on the

General Council, who wanted to make my life intolerable and were trying to stop my nomination even although I had secured it legitimately.

I decided to be as cool as possible, but would watch Rex and stand no nonsense. He formed a Youth Branch in the constituency whose sole purpose was to try and block my nomination. I was told this by a sympathetic supporter who attended their meetings.

However much they tried to provoke me I was not drawn. I simply countered by seeing that, of eight branches in the constituency, at least six supported me. It meant that I had to have constant contact with them. Through some of the dear old ladies of Hospital Hill, who had lived there for years, I had a constant flow of information about the activities of Mrs English and Rex in their anti-Wilson crusade.

I was a busy man, shunting from business, to the City Council, the Provincial Council and keeping an eye on the internal feuding in the constituency. No longer an office bearer in the Council, I was able to write for newspapers and speak at public meetings.

In March 1957 there was an extraordinary event in the Provincial Council. The Leader of the Nationalist Party, Dr Wassenaar, resigned from his governing party on the important grounds that the Nationalists were denying English-speaking South Africans proper rights on School Boards. The composition of the School Boards was very important. Ever since the Nationalists had come to power their chief method of controlling educational policy at individual schools was to obtain control of the boards.

They did everything in their power to influence decisions once they had control with propaganda onslaughts on parents, pupils and staff. This is the technique used over and over again since 1948; control of cultural societies, school boards and trade unions.

White children had to be Afrikanerised – the parents somehow had to be forced to change their views. This would have devastating effects on the social, educational and economic life of the people of South Africa in the years to come.

In 1953, when Cooper and I set up the Education Action Group, we attacked the Nationalists on these very points. We believed the inspiration behind the Nationalist strategy was the secret Broederbond organisation.

Wassenaar, in his historic denunciation of the Nationalists in the Old Raadzaal in Pretoria, our provincial Council home, accused the government of creating a one-party state which he said would lead to eventual dictatorship. His defection was a watershed.

He was the first of the Nationalists to expose what they were doing, backing his expose not only in strong language but by resigning from the NP.

Although he was the senior Provincial Councillor, the Nationalist hierarchy was able to minimise the consequences of his defection.

The Rand Daily Mail asked me to analyse the political motives behind Wassenaar's actions.

"Is There a Crack in the Nationalist Machine?" ran the headline of my leader page article.

235

"These accusations were remarkable [I wrote] because from the mouth of a leading Nationalist they underwrite the accusations the United Party has made of the Nationalist Party since its coming to power."

During the debate that followed, the new leader of the National Party, JH Odendaal MEC, predicted that South Africa would have a Republic outside the Commonwealth in the foreseeable future.

Wassenaar, a lonely bespectacled figure, conservatively dressed, grey-haired, now occupied a cross-bench. Without reacting, he was attacked by the portly Odendaal, who came from the platteland in the North, in "an onslaught which was like a sudden Transvaal storm of great violence." Odendaal accused Wassenaar of being a second Lord Milner wanting to anglicise little Afrikaners. He was followed by every member of the Nationalist Party like a pack of South African wild dogs pursuing their unfortunate prey in the veld, from which there was no escape. It was Wassenaar's political demise.

Of course, I tried to make political capital out of this astonishing event.

"Sitting on the United Party back-benches during the session and reviewing what has happened, I believe most certainly there is a crack in the Nationalist armour. Nationalists deny this. They say Wassenaar is finished politically."

In the end they were right.

This small incident, which assumed great political meaning, was at the time really insignificant. The Nationalist political machine and its Broederbond masters were far too powerful for anyone to start a revolution amongst Afrikaners. They were very much in control. Questions I put in the House to the Administrator and the new Nationalist Leader about the basis on which school and hospital board nominations were made in the Transvaal threw no light on their secret election procedures.

As a result of the additional time I now had because I was no longer a a mere committee chairman in the City Council, I was in a far better position to deal with Verwoerd. I had more time to concentrate on his tactics, especially his attempts to force the council to carry out his policies. The senior officials in the Council were always ready to provide me with the facts. Miller, the NEAD chairman, pretended he was opposing the Nationalists. I delighted in upsetting him and his colleagues in open Council whenever I attacked Verwoerd. I wasted no time on side issues or irrelevancies. For months on end I kept up a political barrage on what Verwoerd and the government were doing to civil liberties and the rights of local authorities.

On 24 April *The Rand Daily Mail* headline "Johannesburg is Letting Verwoerd Get Away With It – Wilson" and "Control of City's Affairs Snatched by Government" set the tone and summarised most of my attacks.

"The people of Johannesburg no longer have the power to run their own city in a democratic way. As ratepayers and municipal voters the people were supposed to control Johannesburg's affairs, but their powers were snatched from them by government decree and statute. The government, aware of the political apathy of many of the people of Johannesburg and the

Witwatersrand, was proceeding quite calmly to enact new powers to further tie up Johannesburg and politically paralyse the Witwatersrand."

My final message in the newspaper was frank.

"The Nationalist government has cracked its whip, and the people of Johannesburg have bared their backs. Few realise how serious things are. There are twelve months to go before the General Election. If the Nationalists are returned it will set a seal on this country which may be irreversible."

This was a prophetic statement, but it fell on the deaf ears of the UP and most of the rich whites of northern Johannesburg. The UP was plagued with two enemies – the National Party and its own lethargic supporters. Anything I said publicly was regarded by most of them as stirring up trouble for no good purpose.

I warned in a speech at a public meeting:

"Many of the people of Johannesburg still believed that the rights that had been taken away from their Native servants had nothing to do with Europeans [whites]. But they should be made to realise that their own rights had gone too. They did not realise that Dr Verwoerd, Minister of Native Affairs, was making the city waste thousands of pounds annually on his decrees and threats. Thousands of people are being shifted from point to point without recourse to normal processes of justice. The Native Laws Amendment Bill before Parliament showed that the Nationalists were now taking the final plunge in the process of tying up Johannesburg, lock, stock and barrel.

"I doubt if in any other country in the world it would be possible for a government to get away with the removal of civil liberties in the way the Government has done without the general disapproval and resulting constitutional defence of those rights. If the ratepayers and the voters continued to shrug their shoulders in reply and did not realise that there was no difference between the civil liberty of the native and the white man they deserve what was happening and was still to happen.

"The Prime Minister has been quite outspoken about the future of the Broederbond Republic. The Union Jack has been hauled down; the universities were fast losing their academic freedom; the nursing profession was being involved in a crisis in the interests of apartheid and the doors of the churches could only be opened by orders of the Nationalist Government."

The newspapers liked my speeches, but I was depressed at the lack of response from my colleagues and the opposition voters. It was only twelve years after the ending of the worst war the world had ever seen to destroy Fascism. But here in South Africa in 1957, Fascism was developing at a pace which put it on a par with events in Spain, Portugal and the South American republics.

Miller and his friends in the Council had given in to Verwoerd to the extent that they were implementing the Sky Locations Act under the eyes of a "Watchdog Committee" of Verwoerd's which had Nationalists sitting on it. The only ray of light was that Archibald was going ahead, training black construction workers, building houses; slum-dwellers were getting new houses every day, albeit side by side with blacks who had been removed from the rooftops – the Sky Locations. The houses were only costing £160 each – this was an incredible achievement.

Late in June, I told the Council at another open meeting as reported in *The Star*: "Government interference, provincial autocracy and public apathy are spreading like a neurosis among Johannesburg Municipal officials and a sense of doom among city councillors. A darkening curtain of frustration sits like a huge frontal headache on the brow of the City Council. A mass of paperwork, legislation and dictatorial commands of the Minister of Native Affairs have merely made our municipal Non-European Affairs Department an appendage of Dr Verwoerd's ministry."

In many ways I was now glad that I was no longer in charge of the Non-European Affairs Department. I was free to attack Dr Verwoerd and the Nationalist government at will.

The newspapers were turning more and more to me for forthright comment and I was prepared to give it to them.

In July the Final Report of the Commission of Enquiry into Local Government was published. I was asked for an assessment of its findings and how it would affect the future of local authorities.

It amounted to the "back-door way to Nationalist control because of the powers given to the Principal Officer which each Council had to appoint". Despite my warnings councillors and municipal voters were lethargic on this issue. Lethargy was a disease endemic to the UP – and and many of its supporters.

In 1956 the United Party realised that JGN Strauss, its national Leader, had to go. Sir De Villiers Graaff took over in November at the Bloemfontein Congress.

Strauss had been replaced because he lacked charisma and political judgement. This was evident in the platteland. Graaff represented a middle-of-the-road breed of UP parliamentarian who might attract back those voters who had deserted the UP since Smuts's death. Graaff was no "liberal", but he created around him a "shadow cabinet" of advisers both from the right and the left of the party which was to his credit.

I had never met Graaff. Through the Witwatersrand General Council I knew all the Johannesburg members of Parliament, especially John Cope and Helen Suzman. They were part of the "liberal" nucleus from the north who associated themselves with Dr Zach de Beer and other MPs from the Cape. They had little to do with public representatives like me despite my "liberal" activities on the Council. We seemed to work in our own spheres of influence. No attempts were made to co-ordinate the liberal forces in Johannesburg. We often met at UP branch meetings but never as a liberal group. This was a grave weakness in that the control of the UP on the Witwatersrand remained in the hands of the "old guard" like Harry Rissik and Henry Tucker.

At the time I began to reflect on what had happened to all my ideas of "reform within the United Party". It was proving to be a myth. All I had achieved was being a "one man band", a liberal by UP standards, and as such by the English press. To the Afrikaans press I was a dangerous UP "liberalist" no longer a "pink" but a dangerous "red".

I was now so involved in my own struggle with Nationalists that there was really no time to organise the liberals in the UP.

The first priority was to stiffen the party's attitude to the Nationalists. The 1958 election was on the horizon. From my 1956 congress discussions with other liberals and my observations of the views of right wing delegates, it was obvious the United Party was not going to win the 1958 election.

During 1957 I decided on a lone offensive. After much thought I drew up an election plan which I believed was the kind of fight the UP should make if it was to put up a good showing in the election. Not only was I interested in the organisational problems, but I gave thought to the specific election issues. At the time the UP's attitude was one of apprehension and confusion. It was floundering.

The Nationalists were making tremendous advances. The UP leadership was no match for them, with no ideas on how to fight the Nats powerful *swart gevaar* tactics – the old proven formula of the "black danger" – their successful appeal over the years guaranteed to whip up the fears and emotions of South African whites from across the spectrum.

Amongst the new friends I had made in the UP was a young Afrikaner lawyer, Peter de Kock, who came from the Cape. He was now working in Harry Oppenheimer's office as his personal assistant. Peter and I found we had a lot in common. A few years before, as a student at Stellenbosch University, the home of the National Party intellectuals, he had been a leading Nationalist. His views changed when he objected to their interference with the constitution and he joined the UP, fighting an election against the Nationalists in the Cape and losing it. He and I had similar political ideas.

I had been considering what tactics the UP should use in the 1958 election. I was anxious to test plans I had drawn up which were not based on the race question, because the UP did not stand a chance against the Nationalists in an election on this issue. Its own Native Policy was a watered down version of apartheid. It had to find other election issues – the obvious ones related to the constitution, security and economic matters.

One weekend I sat down with a sketch pad and roughed out my ideas, based on a series of posters. The main motif was a Key – the "Key to Security and Prosperity". I selected about twenty of the posters and wrote a summary of what they represented as a basis for the 1958 election campaign.

On Monday morning I asked Leslie Walker, the managing director of the agency who did my company's national advertising, into my office and explained my ideas to him. I told him to reproduce, from my sketches, improved full-size posters as soon as possible. Leslie Walker, a witty Englishman with a handlebar moustache, a very politically-conscious man, was enthusiastic. A few days later he turned up with about twenty posters based on the ideas from my sketch pad drafts. He had done a marvellous job, just as he had for the Education Action Group.

We arranged them on the walls of my office, spending several hours evaluating them and making changes. The posters set out in a simple, bold way the line the UP should pursue on the questions of security, prosperity and the economy.

I telephoned Peter de Kock.

"Can you come down and see me – soon. I've got some interesting political material which I can't bring to you – it's at my office. I'd like you to give me your opinion before I show it to anyone else in the party."

I wanted his reaction before the election committee saw it. Peter arrived later that day. He was tall, carrying himself well but looking far older than his years because of his prematurely grey hair. He walked around the office inspecting the posters:

"Explain it – where do I start – what's it all about?"

He listened carefully while I unfolded the ideas which I intended to put to the Union Division of Information.

"Boris, I wouldn't do that – yet. You might be wasting your time. I know the type of people who would have to judge your plan. They could easily miss the point because they have their heads and shoulders deep in the political mud of the tired old issues. You know them as well I do. I think your ideas are a tremendous breakaway from the stereotyped campaign the UP is considering. I like the bread and butter basis of your scheme. The 'Key' theme is not new – but its new for a South African election between the UP and the Nats – and what we desperately need is something new."

"What do you suggest I do?"

"Look, Boris," said Peter pointing to all the posters, "there is only one man who can influence the UP about all this. One of my functions in Harry's office is to keep him abreast of political happenings in the country. His opinion is greatly valued by the UP bigwigs. Don't forget he is the biggest contributor to their election funds. I'll talk to him tomorrow and perhaps bring him here to look at all this, and see what he thinks. If he is enthusiastic, then we can decide who we should see in the UP."

The next day Peter telephoned to say that Harry Oppenheimer would come at about 1.30 pm to my office to look at the posters and discuss the plan. I did not know Harry well, because the negotiations about the £3 000 000 loan were done with Sir Ernest, so I was pleased to meet him when he came with Peter.

He strongly resembled Sir Ernest, and with his head at a slight angle walked around asking questions about the Key Plan. He said little, thanked me and asked Peter to keep in touch with me.

A few days passed – it was Peter on the telephone.

"Boris, the UP are interested and want to see the scheme as soon as possible."

The Union Division of Information committee met me at their offices. The chairman, Marais Steyn, a UP front-bencher and Jack Higgerty the Chief Whip, were there.

I did not have to press them too hard. I don't think they had too many ideas, and they were only too pleased to adopt the plan for the 1958 election.

240

GENERAL ELECTION

APRIL
16th
1958

Dr. Boris Wilson
M.P.C.

**OFFICIAL UNITED PARTY
CANDIDATE**

Hospital

Dr. B. Wilson	X

I was asked to join the division and supervise the implementation of the "Key" plan.

I was made a member of the Information Division, and insisted that Leslie Walker be co-opted to do the practical work. Marais Steyn was De Villiers Graaff's right hand man, a front-bench MP, a captivating speaker with a powerful platform presence. He said he needed my help to reorganise the unit. It was transferred to Johannesburg from Cape Town and after investigation I produced an acceptable reconstruction proposal.

It envisaged direct liaison for the first time with the General Councils, Divisional Committees and election candidates. There would be one representative on the Union Committee for each province and improved local and national press liaison. As soon as the marginal seats were known, a local information machine would be set up. All the Key Plan brochures we had drawn up were accepted without demur – "Key to Racial Security" and a constitutional leaflet.

Through my association with the Information Division, I began to meet leading UP politicians from all over South Africa. I was aware from many of my meetings with them (most of whom were of the *bloed Sap* type, true-blue old South African Party conservatives) that they were suspicious of my liberal views. This did not worry me because it gave me an opportunity to try to understand their politics – in any event Marais Steyn backed what I was doing. My contacts with the editors of the main English-language newspapers all over South Africa increased. As soon as De Villiers Graaff started his pre-election campaign I was invited to join a small confidential group of "speech advisers" and "ghost writers" to Graaff when he came to speak in the north.

Marais Steyn was the leading figure in this team.

We usually met at the Information headquarters in Hillbrow, Johannesburg. We would spend hours in a smoke-filled room constructing Graaff's speeches. In fact we would often get the speech or the section affecting the local area done in advance.

Graaff would read it over and give us his reaction. He was always clear about what he wanted to say – we never succeeded in bullying him into accepting anything he did not like. Despite my own criticisms of Graaff and his lukewarm middle-of-the-road policies, I admired him as I got to know him better.

Marais Steyn, with his fine sense of rhetoric, would often get worked up, as if he himself was going to deliver the speech and we would have to cool his enthusiastic outbursts.

There was always a last-minute rush to type the speech. On many occasions I would drive Graaff in my Jaguar to a City Hall meeting where crowds were waiting to give him a triumphal entry.

Graaff was well-built, sallow, moustached with dark curly hair. The Nationalists attributed this to "coloured" blood, which angered him. At his meetings he spoke slowly and carefully, fluently switching from English to Afrikaans at will, which was the custom in South Africa. Apart from the fact that I was ideologically a reluctant supporter of Graaff's, I did my best to inject into his speeches some liberal views. But I had to be careful. Graaff was no fool. Like most South African politicians his speeches were far too long and often drifted away from the points being made. South African political audiences expected these marathons and seemed to like them.

Graaff's press publicity was good. It had to be. The government-controlled South African Broadcasting Corporation gave little time to Opposition politicians. The Afrikaans press completely supported the National Party. In Johannesburg, I handled Graaff's press releases, usually with advance copies, and if there was time, with good photographs. I would frequently brief editors or political reporters beforehand, handing out his speeches at meetings. At weekends I would be at the *Sunday Times* or *Sunday Express* making sure we got good weekend coverage. Editors like Joel Mervis of the *Sunday Times* would take me into the printing rooms to look at page setting or to see the early editions as they rolled off fast machines.

All this brought me back to the exciting days when I edited *WU's Views* at the University. Some of these editors became close friends and were very supportive during my political career.

I often asked myself why I allowed myself to play a role of the middle-of-the-road politician when in fact I regarded myself as a liberal rebel. There was little alternative in the 1950s in white politics. Political association between blacks and whites was at a very low ebb and confined mostly to the radical left wing groups. There was little political option. I had to be a pragmatist.

Besides, I wanted to get to Parliament where I felt I could do constructive things and be heard throughout the country.

The United Party was run by an upper class urban group of professional and business men in collaboration with well-to-do farmers in the platteland. Because of the wide divergences in outlook, even as a generally conservative group, the control of the party was in the hands of a select few who surrounded Graaff. He appointed a "Leaders Committee", which was always looking for compromises in its approach to the country's political problems. Above all they did not want to alienate Nationalists more than necessary because their objective was to wean them over to the UP. Their eyes were always on the platteland, which was almost totally in the hands of the Nationalist machine. As opposed to me they believed the key to their victory was in getting conservative plattelanders into the UP. In turn the party's officials were mostly die-hard conservatives. Smuts, with few exceptions, was responsible for these policies, to the extent that most supporters referred to the UP's policy as that of Botha (the original South African Party Leader) and Smuts. This political label identified the UP. The officials ensured that the party's affairs were boringly run to this fixed formula. They lacked imagination, using conservative political techniques. This was evident at every level in the party.

When I arrived on the scene the UP's morale was low. They had lost the 1953 election, and were politically worse off. Verwoerd was a new phenomenon on the political stage – a tiger they could not tame. The Nationalist

243

strategists kicked the political football – the UP ran haphazardly after it. Prime Minister Strijdom carried on the policy of Daniel Malan – to make the white man secure and to keep him in control. The UP's answer that they could make it safer their way never worked with the Afrikaner Nationalist. It was a failure and this is what faced me as I became more and more involved in the United Party's inner political life.

The UP could not stop the spate of Bills rushed through Strijdom's Nationalist Parliament. Despite Graaff's charisma, the lack of an aggressive political plan did not help the new optimism engendered by his accession.

Winning the coming 1958 election seemed remote. My Key Plan was not to be overrated in this political scenario. It concentrated on two points: the way the constitution was being raped by the Nationalists and a solution by facing the economic realities if apartheid was implemented. Its success depended on how effectively the UP created a new party infrastructure. Because I was also involved in the implementation, much rested on my shoulders. The fact that Harry Oppenheimer supported my ideas, the second Oppenheimer to do so, was the main reason why the UP hierarchy tolerated me at the highest level. In the political climate of 1957, both Oppenheimer and I were part of the UP's liberal wing – examples of "liberalism" of the northern suburbs of Johannesburg.

His political power was enhanced by his financial support of the UP. Unfortunately when Sir Ernest died, Harry left politics to become chairman of the giant Anglo-American Corporation which was a great political loss to the white opposition.

In a sense, I was more fortunate than he was – he had to give up active politics to run his business. I was still able to run mine, minuscule compared to Anglo-American. I had got used to arms-length control. There were many management problems from time to time, but I was determined that whatever happened I was not going to let my business stop my political ambitions. I was doing the sort of work in politics that I enjoyed.

What did suffer was my medical career. Although I practised my knowledge of medicine when I was consulted, to keep it alive, it was really on the back-burner.

In the belief that 1958 would see me as the Member of Parliament for Hospital, I reorganised the business, brought my brother Len from Cape Town to Johannesburg, and installed him as deputy managing director. I would supervise Cape Town as I expected to be at Parliament for at least five months in the year. Business visits around the country were combined with political activity. I had branches in Durban, East London and Port Elizabeth as well as Cape Town, and when visiting these cities I would often contact the local UP for discussions or a public meeting.

The "Key" symbol was now visible in many constituencies throughout the country. The nationwide information and publicity machine was now beginning to operate more efficiently. Speaker's notes for meetings were issued. An election newsletter was produced and the important Constitutional leaflet distributed – in form and typestyle quite new to United Party handouts. Our relations with the press improved, especially the English-language papers.

Graaff's meetings were drawing bigger and more enthusiastic audiences. In October 1957 we started a national advertising campaign. The experience that Les Walker and I had gained during the Education Action Group campaign stood us in good stead.

We called for a De Villiers Graaff government. Our leaflets and advertisements appealed not only to the ordinary voter. We called on the women of South Africa to play their part in putting an end to the Nationalist government.

As Marais Steyn was busy with organisational matters as well as publicity, it was agreed that I would be responsible for the organisation of the Information Division. Everything we produced had to be translated into Afrikaans and fortunately Peter de Kock was at hand. He not only helped translate but was available for advice and had the ear of Harry Oppenheimer. There was now a general air of confidence in the UP which had previously been absent.

Despite this there were difficulties. They arose mainly with the General Councils who were not used to being told or guided from the top about political propaganda. In Johannesburg, the local publicity committee totally ignored the advice and assistance we offered and made no use, in the October local Municipal elections, of material we offered. They discarded the Key symbol, rejected our leaflets and support and handled the newspapers with indifference. We encountered this situation with monotonous regularity all over the country. The average UP worker in the constituencies often expressed the view that he knew better about local publicity needs than us or the professionals. Neither Marais Steyn nor I wanted the parliamentary candidates to be caught up in this situation, and it created a lot of extra work for our already extended publicity machine.

In the midst of all this countrywide activity, I became embroiled in the most serious political dispute of my career – the question of my Hospital parliamentary nomination.

45

Since my nomination by the Hospital Division in 1956, the opposition to me, headed by Mrs English and Ernest Rex, did not cease. They were determined to upset it, despite the fact that it was reaffirmed in 1957. It still had to be endorsed by the Candidates Committee – that was considered a formality. No one was expected to oppose me. Word kept coming to me from time to time about the activities of Mrs English and Rex, but I ignored them and left it to my supporters in the Division. Rex continued to be rude and often very aggressive. To my surprise, he was appointed full-time assistant to Major Opperman, the UP's General Secretary at the Witwatersrand office.

Rex did not waste any time. On 5 December, four days after he was appointed, he asked one of the delegates in Hospital to sign a nomination form for Alec Gorshel, who was asked to stand against me when the Candidates Committee met. Mrs Vermaak, the delegate, protested that she did not know Gorshel. Nevertheless, she signed the form, saying that she would not vote for Gorshel as she was supporting my candidature when it was ratified by the Candidates Committee. I asked her why she signed the form. Rex had spun her a story and it did not seem to her that it would affect my position. Simple as she was, she thought she was doing the right thing.

So Gorshel, my old adversary from the Labour Party days, had been induced to oppose me. He always said he would do so, whatever I did in the UP after I joined it. In fact, he often clashed with me in the UP Caucus in Council. I never took him seriously. He was a maverick politician, professing great interest in the Arts, a persuasive speaker, satirical and physically a red-faced, untidy personality, with a straggly, matted, greying head of hair.

I realised from what I knew about Gorshel that he would try every political trick to stop my nomination and so put an end to my parliamentary aspirations.

Later that day Ernest Rex canvassed others in Hospital for more signatures for Gorshel's candidature. I learnt from them what was going on. At the time I did not know that the lithe, smooth-featured, sharp-eyed, thin-mouthed Rex would dog every stage of the nomination contest. He spoke in a typical high-pitched guttural "platteland" accent; and, much worse, he spouted the usual platitudes about "white leadership with justice" – the political fodder that made conservative UP followers happy.

Gorshel had every right to stand against me, even though the constituency did not propose him. The Candidates Committee was composed of fifteen members of Hospital and fifteen members from the Witwatersrand. I was confident that Hospital supported me, but I was unsure about all the Candidates Committee members.

Some were right wing establishment personalities and openly opposed to me. Mrs English and Rex were able to get this joint meeting because they convinced the officials that a serious dispute existed. They hoped that, with support of the outside delegates, they would stop me becoming Hospital's MP.

Naturally, I was upset by this development. I monitored their moves with the help of my friends. Gorshel had already canvassed some of the Candidates Committee before the meeting. In the end I decided to address the Committee although they all knew me well enough.

The usual resuscitation of "dead" branches had taken place and Rex arrived at the meeting with "delegates" from the dormant branch to vote, which included himself.

Jan Steytler, leader of the break-away Progressives, arrives at Johannesburg Station, August 1959 for the first steering committee. (L to R) John Cope, Colin Eglin, BW, Jan Steytler and Zach de Beer.

The Progressive Party's MPs on the steps of Parliament, January 1960. (L to R) Walter Stanford, Jan Steytler, BW, Townley Williams, Clive van Ryneveld, Ray Swart, Harry Lawrence, Zach de Beer, John Cope, Helen Suzman, Colin Eglin and Ronald Butcher.

March of the Women's Defence of the Constitution League, 25 May 1954.

BW and brother Len in the United Radio and TV factory.

Gorshel addressed the meeting, denying that I had anything to do with the £3 000 000 Loan and that the rebuilding of the new school for Twist Street was not due to my efforts. My speech to the joint meeting was brief, and I was not surprised when I was confirmed as the parliamentary candidate for Hospital by the narrow margin of 15 votes to 13. Gorshel got 9 votes from the Candidates Committee and four from Hospital. The verdict was clear.

I expected the UP to announce my candidature in the newspapers as the official representative together with other nominees from other constituencies. Once more, to my surprise, my name was omitted from the official candidate list. *The Star* reported that a decision had not yet been taken in Hospital!

I spoke to Opperman at the party office and he informed me that Gorshel was appealing to the Witwatersrand General Council on the grounds of voting irregularities in the nomination contest.

I was astonished that Gorshel's group was still going on with this vendetta. Supported by conservatives on the Witwatersrand, they had decided to fight me all the way. The battle was on. I was determined to stop Gorshel once and for all.

Only one person could help me. It was Harry Schwarz, who was now accepted as one of South Africa's most brilliant advocates at the Johannesburg Bar. I had no doubt that a long and protracted struggle was ahead of me. I was deeply disappointed that the party hierarchy, for whom I was devoting all my time at national level, did not step in and squash this charade. All it was doing was wasting valuable work-time for the coming election.

I told Harry the whole story, giving him a copy of Gorshel's speech to the joint meeting.

Gorshel's case rested on the fact that the dormant Union Grounds Branch in Hospital, which supported him, had not been allowed to vote. My immediate question to Harry was how did Gorshel know of this branch's existence? He was not a member of the Hospital division.

The only one who could have told him of its prior existence was someone at the party office. The obvious culprit was Ernest Rex who had access to party records. Gorshel also complained that he was refused the right at a divisional meeting to put forward his candidature, and address branch meetings.

In his appeal document Gorshel wrote: "I must emphasise that this appeal is lodged not to further any personal ambition that I may have to become a Member of Parliament for Hospital, but because I regard it as a matter of vital importance that the good name of the party should not be brought into disrepute through deliberate flouting or evasion of the nomination regulations by individuals and divisional or branch committees."

Harry and I burnt the midnight oil going through Gorshel's appeal.

A week later, I lodged my reply, mainly Harry's work. I was satisfied Gorshel would now need a competent lawyer to deal with it. Harry was an expert on the party's constitution. Apart from his own interest in the success of my candidature – he was going to stand in my place as member for the Provincial Council – he was as determined as I was that Gorshel should be defeated.

Gorshel was no friend of Harry's, for very good political reasons.

There was clear evidence of active participation by Ernest Rex, who was a paid party official. This was forbidden by the constitution. Gorshel's allegation that there was deliberate flouting or evasion of the nomination regulations had no substance.

On Harry's advice I lodged a cross-appeal.

Letters passed to and fro. I was meeting with Harry almost every day, which played havoc with my timetable. There were innumerable discussions with the chairman and committee members of Hospital who, by now, were incensed with Gorshel.

The UP establishment on the Witwatersrand stayed absolutely quiet on the sidelines. The whole story was leaked to the English and Afrikaans newspapers and they had a field day.

The Afrikaans press widened the reasons for the struggle, by declaring that Gorshel represented the voice of the conservatives who wanted to keep "the dangerous liberalist Boris Wilson out of Parliament".

The UP hierarchy were still silent. Other nominations throughout the Transvaal were announced daily – with no Hospital result.

It was now February, with the election in April. I pressed on with my election plans while battling out the nomination struggle. On 17 February I met Senator Henry Tucker, one of Graaff's senior advisers on the Leader's Committee, Major Opperman and Gorshel at the party offices in Johannesburg. We agreed that my cross-appeal be heard at a later date, if it was necessary after a decision was made on Gorshel's appeal. I insisted that if this came about it should be heard by the Union Candidates Committee (Graaff and the four provincial leaders were on it) because this was the only way to end Gorshel's filibuster. This was finally agreed.

The Witwatersrand General Council Executive would hear the appeal. Gorshel's case was pure obstruction. I could not see how he could overturn my nomination. I was upset and concerned, although, in a perverse way, it did me good because by keeping the matter in the public eye, it made the position of the Appeals Committee a public one, and they had to act speedily and with objectivity.

The Nationalists made much of it whenever I spoke in the City or Provincial Council.

In the Budget Debate in the Province, Odendaal, who was the Executive Member in charge of Finance intervened in the debate. I quote from *Hansard:*

Dr Wilson: "I want to make a couple of recommendations to the Hon Member for Kempton Park before he leaves here [he was the Nationalist candidate for a safe Parliamentary seat] because I don't want to have this fight with him in another place, Mr Chairman . . ."

Mr Odendaal (MEC): "You're not there yet."

Dr Wilson: "The position is this, he will be responsible – I'll be there, I'll be there sooner than he will."

Mr Odendaal: " You still have to become the candidate."

Dr Wilson: "I am the candidate, don't worry about that."

Mr Odendaal: "Don't count your chickens before they are hatched."

Despite my confident manner I was not only fed up with the nomination fight, but I was depressed at the thought of going through the whole appeal procedure.

However, a few days later Gorshel's appeal was heard, and it was rejected. It was ruled that it was not necessary to hear my cross-appeal. On this occasion the UP did not waste time, and announced that I was the parliamentary candidate. My relief was short-lived. Gorshel, taking advantage of the regulations filed another appeal, to higher authorities. It went to a senior executive committee on which Marais Steyn and a prominent lawyer Andrew Brown, sat as members.

Suddenly it all ended. Gorshel withdrew his appeal, which dealt with the fact that I had already opened my committee room in the constituency declaring myself the approved UP candidate as announced by the party to the press.

The Hospital Division was delighted. At last we could get on with the election fight. But it was not the end of Gorshel. He decided to oppose Harry Schwarz for the Provincial nomination.

It was now an incredible situation. Gorshel was not wanted by the Hospital Division. This was made clear over the farcical role he played in the parliamentary nomination contest. He was thick-skinned, wanting to be my Provincial Councillor. The relationship between MP and MPC is a close one. Gorshel was a die-hard conservative – I was liberal. Harry Schwarz was already my favoured successor. Everyone knew Gorshel did not stand a chance. Schwarz, a dynamic character, had made a big impression and there was no way Gorshel could impede his selection. The work he did for me in the parliamentary nomination fight was not wasted when dealing with Gorshel, who, I believe was doing this because he thought he had another vehicle with which to harass me. In the end Gorshel failed again – Schwarz was nominated my MPC.

The conservative wing of the UP had been defeated in my nomination struggle. They had tried every device to stop me going to Parliament, to the extent of putting Ernest Rex in the party office. He and shadowy conservatives backed Mrs English and Gorshel. Many misleading statements were made by the party office to newspapers. When the dispute was over I wrote to the editor of *The Star*, Horace Flather, putting the record straight about some of the lies and innuendoes that had appeared in the press. At the time I could not deal with them because I did not want to prejudice the appeals procedure.

Hospital was a safe UP seat. It was the "Manhattan" of South Africa, possibly the whole of Africa. The streets were narrow, congested, with a jungle of high-rise tower blocks. The old General Hospital was in the middle, and the boundaries stretched to the railway line in the south which marked the border of the city centre. Its northern boundary was Hillbrow, where I was born – as congested as Hospital. I knew it well, especially since my Labour Party battle with the ubiquitous Gorshel. Bedsitters and small flats were found in almost every building, cosmopolitan restaurants and cafés abounded. The people who lived there gave it a "Chelsea" atmosphere. It was alive at night when the rest of Johannesburg was fast asleep.

But the people who lived there were urban nomads. So the biggest problem was trying to find thousands of missing voters, which gave us grey hairs. My voluntary helpers spent hours tracing them, because although we knew the Nationalists would not oppose me, we expected they might assist a third-party candidate to do so.

On nomination day, at the last minute, the leader of the South African Bond, Charles Retief, appeared at the Nomination Court with the requisite number of voters supporting him as my opponent in the election. So I had an election fight on my hands. Once again I would be opposing a candidate from a new party, as I did when I fought the Liberal Party for my first entry into politics. I would have preferred a Nationalist – at least I could have had a good go at Verwoerd. Nevertheless fighting the Bond would be positive work, not wasting time with Gorshel.

I was busy on three fronts, fighting my election, organising the UP's national propaganda machine – and when I could do so – my business.

The "Key" was now the party's emblem, the Constitutional leaflet a success. The local Witwatersrand Committee made our lives a misery – they had their own ideas. John Cope, Parktown's MP and I had a meeting with them and worked out an "understanding".

Sir De Villiers Graaff came to Johannesburg to address large public meetings and much of the organisation fell on my shoulders. As far as the public and the daily press were concerned, these meetings were successful. The feeling was that UP support was growing, but of course, it was not Johannesburg and its environs who would decide the election, but the far-flung platteland. There were no pre-election polls in the 1950s to determine voting trends, and it was really a hit-and-miss affair.

I knew that our meetings were crowded with the party faithful who came from all over the Reef and as far afield as Pretoria. Few Nationalists attended the meetings. Those that did, came not to hear the UP point of view but to heckle and ask awkward questions, which Graaff was adept at answering. The Nats always asked the same type of "Yes/No" questions.

"Would you like your sister to marry a black man? Say Yes or No."

The UP produced a lot of its own political jargon. Policies were unclear and relied greatly on phrases like "the United Party is the party of Botha and Smuts," or "white supremacy with justice".

UP supporters were inundated with this kind of meaningless rubbish. The leadership of the UP did not want to deal with the country's problems in a radical and pragmatic way, but hoped it could entice Nationalists to a new loyalty by mouthing cliches.

It did not work, and I made certain that none of our literature was written in this style. Our presentation was so different and interesting that the leadership missed the fact that we were using more direct language. They were pleased that there was someone with ideas and able to get the propaganda out. Nevertheless, everything had to be vetted by die-hard establishment watchdogs, before being issued. There were always crises because they wanted changes.

The selection of speakers for public meetings in the Transvaal showed clearly the party's approach to the Nationalists in the platteland. There were 78 pre-election meetings, and liberals like Helen Suzman, John Cope and I were used very sparingly or not at all – they did not want to be tainted with "liberalists" in the rural areas. We were kept to the urban and semi-urban seats. The only platteland seats were small English-language enclaves like White River, where we would not upset the UP conservative Afrikaans-speaking voter. Liberals were not to have platteland exposure. We did not exist.

The Afrikaans press followed us like hawks; they wrote good copy, which in turn helped us to make our reputations. The press was polarised - Afrikaans meant Nationalist, English the United Party. There were no Afrikaans newspapers on our side. The South African Broadcasting Corporation, supposedly independent, took a very pro-Nationalist line in its comment and reporting. Graaff got little coverage.

Graaff was linked to Oppenheimer and there were often vitriolic cartoons in the Nationalist newspapers reviling the Oppenheimers. On the other hand, the Prime Minister was fully reported whenever he spoke. His presence was charismatic and severe; he was the real *volksleier* (people's leader) and spoke only in Afrikaans. His Cabinet were on the radio every day – there was no television.

Walker and I came to the conclusion that the dice were loaded against the United Party. The election was a fascinating study of the politics of frustration, as far as liberals like me were concerned. I no longer had illusions about about reforming the party. I had come to the conclusion that my main job was to get to Parliament and see what I could do to influence the wider electorate in concert with the few liberals I expected to find there.

My early canvass returns showed overwhelming support for me, but I had to take the South African Bond seriously. I knew that their leader would get Nationalist backing, and I was expecting my campaign to be demanding.

I did not have long to wait.

On nomination day, when I first met Retief, he stated for press consumption that there would be no "personality clashes". During the course of the previous three weeks, however, reports from people who came to my rooms indicated that Bond canvassers were making personal attacks on me, saying I was a Communist. In addition, they said that I had changed my name from Hymie Wulfson to Boris Wilson. Anti-semitism had emerged for the first time.

The Bond canvassers who made these remarks were identified by my informants; one of them was Retief's right-hand man, a Mr Van Wyk. To make certain these allegations were not hearsay, I sent a colleague to the

Bond Committee room, ostensibly to check the voter's roll. She met Van Wyk, who repeated some of the allegations. I discussed the matter with Harry Schwarz and the party office; the consensus was that I should pay a visit to Retief and ask him to deal with the matter.

On the evening of 31 March, accompanied by an official from the party office, I visited my opponent's committee room. Retief, a well-groomed man with receding hair and a small moustache, greeted me effusively and offered me coffee. I told him my complaint, reminding him of his promise to keep the fight clean. I asked him to deal with it as I was not anxious to take action for defamation.

At this point Retief lost his temper.

"Get out," he shouted, "go to court if you like."

He was furious. I stood my ground.

"Mr Retief, calm down, let us talk in an adult way. I can shout as well as you can."

Glaring at me, mumbling under his breath he calmed down.

His election office was a small shop opposite the General Hospital. Several people were working there when we arrived. When Retief lost his temper, they all stopped to listen.

He turned to them.

"Is there anyone on my staff who is responsible for such statements? You will be fired immediately if that is the case."

Before anyone could reply, I said: "Do you have a Mr Van Wyk on your staff?"

"Yes."

At this point he called his workers over and asked them to listen to the conversation.

"I am Van Wyk," said a tall, thin man.

"Did you tell Miss Roets, who called to check a vote, that if she voted UP she would let a Communist into Hospital?"

"I don't know Miss Roets, she is just a bloody liar." He was very angry.

It was obvious we would get no further, and I considered we had made our point. Retief and Van Wyk became amiable and asked me why I would not debate the election on a public platform. I explained it was not UP policy to share the same platform with election opponents. We then left.

Two days before the election I received a writ from Van Wyk claiming the sum of £500 for defamation. He alleged that I made defamatory remarks against him in the offices of the South African Bond. They had expected me to sue and pre-empted any action by me. I entered an appearance to defend the action and four months later, when Van Wyk showed no signs of proceeding, my attorneys applied for absolution from the instance with costs, which the court granted.

This was the continuation of many of the attempts by the Nationalists in the City and Provincial Councils to harass me, which I expected would follow me to Parliament.

The point about this incident was that it was an offence to call a person a communist since the Communist Party was outlawed in South Africa. One can sue for defamation and claim damages. No doubt my allegation in his presence that he called me a communist was the basis for his claim for defamation. It was a turn around – like a black comedy.

No one could forecast the Union election results. The most we in the Information Division were expecting was that we might win back some of the marginal seats. We did not expect to win platteland seats. We relied a great deal on the last-minute "bombshell" we had sent out. The leaflet had mainly been drawn up by the UP's Research Section; Walker and I had little to do with it. In fact, although we expected to be consulted about it, this was not the case. The UP's conservatives kept it a close secret. We were asked simply to produce and distribute it on time.

The "bombshell" was an attack on my favourite political enemy, Dr Hendrik Verwoerd. The leaflet looked like a typical National Party release in blue and white, and on the front page there was a straightforward presentation with a picture of Verwoerd – his Past, Present and his Future. The design was intended to lead the Nationalist reader beyond the first page.

It began by saying there were strong indications that if the National Party won the election, Strijdom would resign and Verwoerd would be Prime Minister. It proceeded to examine Verwoerd's strength and stated that he was the most powerful Cabinet Minister in South Africa. It claimed that seventy per cent of the NP caucus were behind Verwoerd. He was not a real South African. He was a foreigner, born in Holland and ruled with an iron hand. Headstrong, he was a known Nazi sympathiser.

During World War II, when Verwoerd edited *Die Transvaler*, the National Party's newspaper, he was charged in the Supreme Court, as a Nazi supporter. Politically he favoured an authoritarian control of South Africa, which it was claimed he would bring about if he became Prime Minister. The prospect facing South Africa because of Verwoerd's strong apartheid views was that agriculture, mining and industry would lose eighty per cent of their workforce and economic ruin would follow.

Verwoerd intended to establish independent Bantustans, which, the UP's leaflet said, would form links with Communists and Russia.

The "bombshell" spelt out in millions of pounds the extra cost of a Verwoerdian Republic, which included money for black universities while white universities would be financial losers. It was hoped when Nationalist supporters read this literary time-bomb, they would switch their allegiance to the United Party.

Swart Gevaar politics was always a vote winner in South Africa for the Nationalists. It played on the crude fears, sub-thalamic prejudices and reactions of their supporters, and most of the English-speaking whites. The UP was trying to use the same tactics. It presented a spectre of blacks infiltrating white areas, sharing the same toilets, travelling in white transport, black men living with white women. It was enough to make white voters cringe. With this stale ingenuity, the UP hoped it could outbid the National Party in horror tactics and win the election.

There was not a word about the promised land of the Key campaign. While I was working on the Key programme the inner sanctum of the UP was busy ditching it. Its secret weapon was a recycled *swart gevaar*. This cynical action by the UP's hierarchy was a real jolt to my political ideas of reform even before I reached Parliament.

The leaflet pointedly asked the voter: Where is Dr Verwoerd going?

The UP answered: He is going to move all the blacks out of the white areas. Yet during his term as Minister of Native Affairs blacks increased from 1,2 million to 1,7 million in the large cities; 59 more black locations have been established in the towns and only thirteen in the rural areas. Under "this man who supports total apartheid white South Africa has become blacker."

"Dr Verwoerd is the most dangerous man in South Africa. Here is our new Prime Minister if the Nationalists win the election on April 16. Vote for the United Party and get rid of Dr Verwoerd."

I was appalled by the leaflet, its presentation and its content. It was a mishmash of truth, fabrication and fantasy, a compound of all the fears and prejudices that could be imagined, all blended into a political cocktail designed to strike fear into the hearts and minds of white South Africans, using their black compatriots as the targets of hate.

If it was not the eve of the election, I would have rebelled openly against the UP establishment. There was nothing I could do to stop this disastrous political diatribe from seeing the light of day – but something nearly happened to kill it just as it was going out to the voters.

A final proof-reading was done by Dr Louis Steenkamp, a Graaff senior adviser, a very conservative pillar of the establishment. He found a spelling error in one word, which might have caused a sentence to be misinterpreted. He was adamant that the leaflet could not go out with this mistake. More than 100 000 copies had already been printed. His request was ridiculous; of course, I hoped he would veto the entire leaflet. He contacted Graaff and Marais Steyn and they gave in to him. The ludicrous instruction was telexed to us – correct mistake and reprint!

The printers worked all night. The leaflet went out only to selected marginal and platteland constituencies, two days before voting. The liberal suburbs of Johannesburg, Cape Town and Durban never saw it.

This was the end of the black comedy. The United Party leadership were committing the same errors as their predecessors in elections. Their target, Verwoerd, was good but instead of leaving it to a garbled and unfocused "bombshell" at the last-minute, they should have attacked him months before the election.

They may have succeeded in opening the eyes of Nationalist voters who did not really understand what Verwoerd was doing. All that the UP leaders achieved, wasting thousands of pounds and our time in an ill-conceived crackpot campaign was confusion.

From my own experience in fighting Dr Verwoerd, I knew that he was a formidable opponent. I approved of a sustained attack on him – but not in the way the UP did it. He was the most powerful man in the National Party who understood the psychology of the whites, especially the Afrikaner. He had convinced all Nationalists his plans meant future white security.

The United Party misread the signs. Instead of a real alternative it simply tried to "out-Nat the Nats" and fell into a near fatal trap of its own making. Verwoerd had already shown the country that he could implement apartheid. The fact that the Constitution had been raped in the process was irrelevant. No cost was too high to protect white supremacy. The real truth in the 1950s was that the Afrikaner Nationalist *was* prepared to pay any price, even if it meant sacrificing political democracy in the process.

For me election day was free of untoward incidents. Retief, my opponent, sat expressionless in his marquee. His efforts to entice voters to his table before voting were unsuccessful. When at midnight the result was declared, I was the victor by a majority of over 5 000 votes. Retief saved his deposit; the Nationalist vote was sufficient for this but not much else.

I was going to Parliament. Exhausted, surrounded by jubilant supporters, my friends and my wife, I was now the Member of Parliament for Hospital. Although I had always been confident of victory, the result was very satisfying. But there remained a sense of foreboding about my future in Parliament.

The United Party as a whole was not successful. As the results came through in the early hours of the morning, it was clear that the Nationalists were well on the way to winning their third election in a row. Their majorities increased. Record polls were achieved in many of the constituencies lost by the UP. Many marginal seats won by the Nationalists were now beyond the reach of the UP.

It was a sad day for the United Party. Morale at headquarters was low. Verwoerd and the Nationalists had once again outwitted the United Party.

The South African Labour Party, with whom the UP had no electoral pact was wiped out. Their leader, Alex Hepple, lost his deposit as did two members of the Liberal Party in the Cape. South African political opinion, in 1958, was firmly trapped in the tunnel vision of apartheid. Liberalism in any form was unwelcome. The increased platteland majorities confirmed this the next day.

More shocks followed. Marais Steyn was defeated at Vereeniging. Sir de Villiers Graaff lost his seat of Hottentots Holland – the defeat of the UP's leader was a devastating blow. The Nats were jubilant.

Obviously the UP had to get Graaff and Steyn back into Parliament. There was speculation as to which newly elected MPs would give up their seats for the UP leaders. Yeoville's new MP Leo Kowarsky surrendered his seat to Steyn; Pilkington-Jordan, a UP front-bencher, went to the Senate so Graaff could return to Parliament.

Post-mortems held by the UP threw did not reveal the idiocy, or convince members of the stupidity, of trying to beat the Nationalists at their own game. Party leaders tried to compare the defeat of Smuts in 1948 with that of Graaff ten years later. It was a pointless exercise. Graaff was not a General Smuts, who had been a political philosopher of deep insight and wide horizons. Graaff's ideas were dictated by the narrow, simplistic backwaters of the platteland. His cardinal error was that he encouraged the duplicity of the UP; one message for the towns and another for the rural areas.

He and his advisers failed to understand the dynamics of South Africa's changing industrial economy in which the white man had to make provision for the integration of blacks into industry and commerce.

The United Party failed to grasp the fact that in the long term security would ultimately depend on a new approach in which, whether whites liked it or not, they would have to share power in the end with blacks.

46

In 1958 white South Africa was still mesmerised by Dr Hendrik Verwoerd's visions of apartheid which heralded the promised land. Verwoerd the architect and innovator appeared at the right time for whites. He knew he was on a good political wicket because the theory of racial separation enjoyed the support of many English-speakers, as well as Afrikaners. People felt secure with the "whites only" notices in the post offices, the buses, trains, parks and taxis. Resettlement plans were reasonable, logical.

Bantustans were no longer paper dreams. The Master and Servant relationship was the correct social and economic order. If a "Native" or a "kaffir" was pushed off a pavement it was because the white man was a superior being. The white man was "baas".

Elections to political bodies of town, province or central government was only for the white man. Blacks were the wards of the white people. When laws were made involving the blacks it was not necessary to consult with them because they were ignorant and helpless children. The Nationalists had entrenched this notion as soon as they assumed power and they had already been ten years in office. They said that blacks could have their own system of political power in the Bantustans. The white man ruled the blacks from the cradle to the grave, as was only proper. Little was known about black reaction to white elections and whites cared little about black opinion.

Symptomatic of the times was that the small number of white liberals, who maintained contact with blacks through organisations like the Institute of Race Relations or the liberal universities, found that very few blacks were interested in white politics. The black attitude was that as white elections did not concern them, why should their opinion count?

The massive number of restrictions barring interracial contact made it difficult for whites to visit black areas or maintain contact with blacks except in strictly defined relationships.

In this respect I had early warnings that I was being watched by the security police both at university and on the City Council.

Parliament was due to meet in August, which was fortunate because I had time after the elections to rearrange my business and family affairs to prepare for the move to Cape Town.

One morning in July, Molly Bell came into my office. In a whisper, she told me that there were two detectives waiting for me in the anteroom.

"What do they want, Molly?

"Doc, I don't know they wouldn't tell me."

"Well, I'll have to see them. Send them in."

She ushered in two men, one in a grey suit, the other in sports jacket and slacks. They introduced themselves as detectives from the Witwatersrand region. I invited them to sit down.

"Well, what can I do for you?" I asked.

"Dr Wilson," said grey suit, "we wish to speak to you about your recent visit to the Pietersburg location where you addressed a gathering of Natives belonging to the African National Congress – this meeting was held on . . . [unfortunately I cannot recall the date because the papers relating to this incident were stolen] . . . You are aware that it is illegal for a white person to address meetings in Native locations without permission from the authorities."

For a moment I was astonished by the allegation which sent shivers down my spine. What the hell were they after? However, I decided not to react but keep calm. There were two of them. I was alone, and I did not even have a tape recorder on. I had never been in Pietersburg location in my life. I did not even know where it was. I decided to keep quiet until I had more information.

"You say I addressed a meeting of Natives in Pietersburg in the Northern Transvaal, which was held by the ANC? Are you sure it was me?"

"Yes we are sure, we have your address here. It is . . ." He gave me an address in Helen Suzman's constituency totally unknown to me.

Bells started ringing. I recalled that before the election, my predecessor in Hospital, Arthur Barlow, alleged that I addressed meetings of the ANC in locations. At that time all I could do was write a disclaimer to *The Cape Times* denying the allegations made by Barlow under privilege in Parliament, saying I was not averse to speaking at such meetings if I received an invitation.

While the two detectives and I sat sparring with each other, I began to sweat, my pulse was racing, heart thumping, waiting for the next move. I blinked first.

"You say I addressed this meeting without a permit in Pietersburg location. Who gave you this information?"

"I am sorry, Dr Wilson, we are not permitted to tell you, but we have reliable information otherwise we would not be here."

This was clearly an attempt to get me into trouble before I got to Parliament. Barlow and his Nationalist friends could have been behind it. I knew there was something odd because the address they gave was not mine – I had to have some proof that I was not in Pietersburg that night.

"Have you any evidence, like a photograph, showing me at the meeting?"

"No, sir."

Throughout the interrogation the second detective remained silent, staring coldly at me. Suddenly I had a brainwave.

"What did you say was the date of the alleged meeting?"

For the third time it was given to me. In the opposite corner of my office was my personal safe which housed my passport. While I was being questioned, my memory was dredging up the fact that at the time of the alleged meeting I was not in South Africa.

I got up without a word, took out my keys, unlocked the safe and found my passport. They watched every move. Under their silent gaze, I paged through the passport. The two date stamps were quite clear – one when I left South Africa and one on my return. In between these two dates, when I was supposed to have committed an "offence" in South Africa, I had been in England.

I returned to my desk.

"First of all, I wish to reject the allegation on three grounds. Since 1954 I have lived in Parktown and I have never lived at the address in Houghton. Secondly, I have never visited Pietersburg location, not on the night in question, nor any other night, nor have I addressed any meetings of the African National Congress, or meetings of natives at any location. Thirdly, please examine my passport. You will see that I was not in South Africa at the time you say I addressed a meeting at Pietersburg."

I handed the passport to the two detectives, who scrutinised it, the silent one making notes. They gave it back to me.

"Is there anything else you wish to ask me?"

"No, sir."

"I have another appointment. Please excuse me. Thank you for your visit. I will be writing to the Commissioner of Police."

They left. I was as exhausted as if I'd run a gruelling road race which I'd narrowly won. All sorts of things were going through my mind. Was I being framed before I got to Parliament? Was there any connection between the allegations made during my election and the South African Bond? Was this part of a wider plan which the Nationalists had hatched to intimidate me and which would continue when I got to Parliament?

Molly came in and I dictated a letter to the Commissioner of Police, asking him for an explanation of the visit by the detectives and setting out for the record my rebuttal of the allegations.

A week later I received an apology from the Police Commissioner. There was no explanation. Naturally I still asked myself who was trying to frame me even before I went to Parliament?

In the past I had been able to ignore or reply to the direct attacks made on me by political opponents in the National Party. I knew from where they came. This episode however was different. The police were obviously briefed by a higher authority. It was sheer luck that my memory for dates and places outwitted them. My alibi was watertight. If there had been no alibi, I might have been brought before the courts with unforeseen results.

This was a serious warning which I could not ignore, particularly on the eve of my parliamentary career.

As the MP for Hospital, a thousand miles away from Cape Town, I had to establish a separate home for my family during the session. Pauline and I debated the prospects of moving from our comfortable Parktown home for a half year. We did not want to disturb our children's security and education by frequent moves to the Cape. In any event the first session would be short, giving us a chance to see how things worked out. Cape Town is the legislative capital of South Africa from January to June. For the rest of the year, Pretoria is the executive seat of government.

As we made our way to Cape Town through the endless open landscape of the dry and cold scrublands of the Karoo, the excitement of getting to Parliament a few days before the official opening grew. I parked my car in the private road in front of Parliament. A uniformed policeman approached me. I addressed him in Afrikaans. *"Ek is 'n nuwe volksraadslid."* A new MP.

He promptly saluted me and directed me to the Sergeant-at-Arms. I walked past the Senate steps with its colonnade of slender Greek columns and found my way to his office in the 1910 old Cape Parliament building next door, which was to be my new political home. What was in store for me in the corridors of power?

I then made my way to the Clerk of the House, who was friendly and explained all the procedures to me, including what he thought were pitfalls for new MPs. I then went to see Jack Higgerty, the UP's Chief Whip, a heavy, taciturn man, who found it difficult to smile. One of the points I raised with him was with whom I was to share my back-bench. Some new MPs were known to me, and I was not anxious, for the foreseeable future, to spend day in and day out with an MP like Hymie Miller or some other conservative whose politics and personality would be unsympathetic. Experience in the Transvaal Provincial Council had warned me.

I asked Higgerty to seat me, if possible, with Colin Eglin whom I had not met but who was known to me as a Cape liberal and whose speeches in the Cape Provincial Council had sometimes been favourably reported in Johannesburg newspapers. I had also heard him speak at UP Congresses. He was a politician of promise several years younger than me.

I spent the first few days exploring Parliament and the Senate. Both are beautiful old buildings, modelled in the British parliamentary and Victorian tradition of spatial grandeur. The old South African prints and historical paintings on the walls gave me a quiet feeling of triumph as I savoured my new surroundings. Parliament's lobby was empty as I looked at paintings of the former Prime Ministers, Chief Justices and Governors-General. There they were – Louis Botha, Smuts and Hertzog and the Kings and Queens symbolic of Britain's interest in South Africa.

I walked alone into the silent House of Assembly with its dark green benches on which many of my famous predecessors had lounged. I inspected the beautifully-carved stinkwood Speaker's Chair, which had been brought from the old Cape Volksraad. In 1958 the main dining room of Parliament was dominated by two large paintings of previous Cabinets. The Private Member's diningroom, a small intimate place, is next door. Along the same corridor is a bar and further eastwards I found the spacious library next to the Senate, now (1991) the Coloured House of Representatives.

The United Party Caucus room was on the ground floor of Parliament. At the first meeting Sir De Villiers Graaff welcomed us and various committees and portfolios were allocated. The Whips had put me on Posts and Telegraphs, a minor portfolio, without asking my preference. The only interesting aspect was that Broadcasting came into this portfolio.

As I was one of the few doctors in the House I was put on the Health committee. I learnt that if the new MP is a good establishment supporter, he is looked after by the Whips. For example, he is allocated a good time for his maiden speech, which is an enormous hurdle.

The "new boy" in Parliament is understandably very timid. My experience in Johannesburg and Pretoria stood me in good stead and gave me confidence. One of the problems of Parliament was the paucity of office space. If one was lucky enough to be appointed a secretary of a specific portfolio group, it helped in the scramble for office space. It also was the route to a "shadow" portfolio. In government, I discovered, this was the recruiting ground for cabinet ministers. The competitive spirit in Parliament permeated everything. MPs jostled for the best times to speak because this ensured the best publicity. The struggle for the attention of the newspapers and radio never stopped.

The knowledge I had gained in the Provincial Council about procedure and Standing Orders was useful, because it was the same as Parliament – and rules of procedure can often make or break debates. The Provincial Council had taught me about the clever use of questions on the Order Paper, exposing government failure, trying to embarrass a Minister or uncover a "scandal".

One of my first tasks was getting to know the Press Corps. I knew from both the Council and the Province that without their co-operation there might be little success in Parliament.

I took the plunge and placed two questions on the Order Paper, for the opening of Parliament. One was for my *bête noir*, Dr Verwoerd, the Minister of Native Affairs who was responsible for the special investigation his officials were making into Johannesburg's Native Affairs Department. The other was to the Minister of Justice.

At the commencement of every session, Private Members motions are placed on the Order Paper with the consent of Caucus. Mine were accepted with alacrity because few had been put forward. Most Private Members motions never reach debate, but it gives the new MP the opportunity to make some of his interests known.

Select Committees are elected to deal with matters such as Public Accounts, Pensions and Native Affairs, but as I knew I would not get on Native Affairs I did not bother to apply for a place.

We were warned by the Whips about debating procedure in the House. An MP had to continue a speech in the language in which it was started. The MP could not switch from English to Afrikaans or vice versa.

I was to find that the Nationalists rarely spoke in English because of their patriotic urge to Afrikanerise South Africa. We had the same system in the Provincial Council. It was a crazy debating method. Speakers often conducted acrimonious debates across the floor of the House, Nationalists in Afrikaans, United Party speakers in English.

Most of the UP spoke English; some could not speak a word of Afrikaans. How they understood the debates was a mystery to me. Cabinet Ministers rarely spoke in English. Graaff, I was told, varied speeches. If he started the "No Confidence" debate in English, he would reply in Afrikaans. What the visitors in the public galleries who were unilingual made of this was also beyond comprehension. Parliament must have been a cacophonic bore to the spectators.

I found that I was better than some of my compatriots because of the Afrikaans I had learnt and spoken at the Market in my dealings with farmers. I was going to have to concentrate hard when Bills of a technical nature were being discussed in Afrikaans.

47

The opening day of the first session of the Twelfth Parliament since the formation of the Union of South Africa arrived. From early on MPs and their wives filled the lobby. Pauline was ushered to the wive's gallery – I and the other "new boys" were hustled into the House by the Whips, six at a time; we stood before the Speaker who administered the Oath to us. Then we proceeded to our seats where I found I was sharing the bench with Colin Eglin, a very sombre and serious young man.

The opening of Parliament followed the form of the "mother" of Parliaments – Great Britain. The first few hours were concerned with the Speech from the Throne, read by the Governor-General, followed by Private Motions and Notices of Bills. It was a good opportunity to take it all in. The constant mumble of noise from the floor of the House and the Speaker's attempts at keeping order was something I would have to get used to. The Press Gallery and the *Hansard* reporters sat above the Speaker's Throne. To the right and left of the Speaker were the senior government officials ready to provide information to Cabinet Ministers during the course of debate.

In front of my back-bench was the very reduced United Party team – the front-benches occupied by Graaff and former Cabinet Ministers in

Smuts's government – Harry Lawrence and Sydney Waterson, with Marais Steyn and the arch-conservative from Natal, Douglas Mitchell.

To the UP's left was the small team of Native Representatives led by Margaret Ballinger, the remarkably erudite liberal, and her two colleagues Lee Warden and Walter Stanford. The Native Representatives were elected in 1936 to represent blacks in the Native Reserves, some of whom had previously been able to vote for white members of Parliament. However, in 1936 General Hertzog's Parliament took away their votes and substituted three white MPs as their parliamentary representatives.

Next to them was Dave Bloomberg and his three MPs who represented Coloured voters. Across the aisle, on the cross-benches and around us were the government MPs, most of them from rural constituencies; many were farmers.

The "Lion of the North", the Prime Minister, was supported on his front-benches by the burly, silver-haired, smiling figure of Hendrik Verwoerd; the tall ostrich-like "Blackie" Swart, Minister of Justice with his deep voice; and the rotund figure of Paul Sauer whose father had been a famous figure in the old Cape Parliament. Eric Louw, Minister of Foreign Affairs, small and perky, was easily singled out in conversation with the chubby Interior Minister, Dr Ebenezer Donges.

On the Nationalist back-benches sat some of my old political foes from the City and Provincial Councils – Fritz Steyn, PZJ van Vuuren and others who would no doubt continue to attack me.

As I looked around the House on that first day I must have felt like most new MPs. Exhilarated, "here I am, I've made it" to the top political forum in South African public life, the House of Assembly. I was 39, and it seemed a long way from the cold noisy days of the Market where I was first intrigued by the behaviour of my fellow human beings. I was reminded of a poem my father had written to me when I was eight years old:

> You will keep right to the truth . . .
> You will stand up for human-hood.
> From sunrise to sunset,
> That shall become your human fate.

Was this the place where I would "stand up for the truth?" I hoped so, in the hurly-burly and political excitement of the struggle between United Party opposition and Nationalist government.

My thoughts were interrupted by the Clerk of the House who read the Proclamation of the Opening of Parliament and announced that the Governor-General would open Parliament at midday in the Senate.

We then elected Nationalist MP Johannes Conradie as Speaker, a post he had held since 1951. Despite the effusive eulogies on his re-appointment from all sides of the House, he was unpopular. We then made our way to the Senate for the Speech from the Throne.

The Speech from the Throne, purports to set out the Government's programme but is really a vapid version for the voters and the press – the political shocks follow during the session. We already knew that voting age was to be reduced to eighteen and separate universities for Natives were to be established. And then there was all the other apartheid legislation buzzing around in the fertile brain of Dr Verwoerd.

The real business of Parliament would begin on Monday, when Graaff would introduce the UP's Motion of No Confidence. This would be my first direct experience in sizing up the quality of the UP's top MPs and the strength of the Nationalist front-bench.

So, we were on our way. As the No Confidence debate proceeded I realised that, with exceptions, it was a rehash of the continuing serial of the Afrikaner's struggle, his determined rejection of British imperialism, his fixation about the security of the white man, the need for separate development. I was sure this would be repeated *ad nauseam* during the short session ahead.

In between these speeches there was a serious attempt by a few speakers on the Opposition benches to introduce reality into the proceedings, which the Nationalists studiously ignored.

The main message from the government, through the speeches of the Prime Minister and Dr Verwoerd, was that the establishment of a South African Republic was a top priority.

The No Confidence debate is a high level introduction to Parliament and its leading party speakers. I was specially interested in seeing and listening to MPs who were well-known personalities through the newspapers and the radio.

The Prime Minister impressed me as a forthright political opponent, committed to Afrikaner nationalist ideals. Dr Verwoerd towered above his colleagues as a speaker, but he had the fatal weakness of being too long-winded with his arguments. He believed everyone needed a lecture. I had had a sample of this when I met him in Pretoria.

I was disappointed in the No Confidence debate. The race relations issue was so polarised that much of the discussion could be summarised in *swart gevaar* terms; the comments were of the "do you want your sister to marry a black man" variety. After the first day, apart from the few MPs who had special subjects, both sides of the House were locked in tiresome and repetitive badinage, scoring petty party political points. Not even Graaff was innocent of irrelevancies and obscure references which weakened the good points in his two speeches. The power of the party bosses reflected itself in the stereotypical sloganeering on both sides of the House.

The UP was tied to its 1954 Native Policy and Graaff said he was seeking a common agreement with the government. This was cloud-cuckoo political nonsense, because we were supposed to be totally opposed to apartheid. Back-benchers had no voice at that stage and I had a long way to go before I could speak up as a liberal.

Bills were introduced, select committees started functioning, time was spent enjoying the pleasures of the "club" – the diningroom, the lobby talk and the library. There were lunches with constituency supporters; I learnt the technique of writing letters or reading papers while supposedly listening to a debate.

The first few weeks passed rapidly. Some new MPs had broken the ice by making their maiden speeches, one of whom was Colin Eglin. A few were allowed to do so in the No Confidence Debate – this was a signal from the Whips to the House that they were likely UP establishment favourites. Most early business was concerned with minor legislation and private motions. One afternoon I was listening to speeches on the need for a national education policy, when I noticed De Kock, a deputy-whip, sitting next to me.

"Boris, when are you going to make your maiden speech?"

"Soon, soon. Perhaps next week, if there is a chance."

"What about later today – this is a good time to come in, man!"

I thought he was mad. I had no speech prepared.

"Ag man, Boris, you don't need to prepare. You've been in the Province and you know a lot about education. Come on."

I gave in. He told me I would be the last speaker of the day before the Minister of Education wound up the debate.

I left the House and went to the Library, and considered what my maiden speech to Parliament would be.

De Kock sent me a note to say that the Speaker would "see" me after a Nationalist back-bencher, Hilgard Muller, a former mayor of Pretoria, had made his maiden speech.

"Don't forget to congratulate Muller on his speech," the note warned, "and good luck!"

When Muller got up to speak, I was tense and hardly heard what he was saying. When he sat down to *"hoor hoors"* and "hear hears", I looked at the Speaker and stood up.

"The Honorable Member for Hospital."

The Speaker's voice was clipped and precise. I congratulated my "brother-in-arms" Muller on his maiden speech and commenced mine.

I tried to widen the horizons of the debate by talking of the changing world and technological development, the future role of uranium and atomic weapons. I posed the question of whether "we are heading for a brave new world or total destruction."

In a future world war "an intercontinental ballistic missile could blot Cape Town out and no one would know from whence it came." South Africa should train more scientists and technologists with a humanistic outlook to work for peace in the world. I asked for money for technological training and a ten year development plan.

The House was silent, as is the custom for maiden speeches, and all I could recall is my dry mouth, the Speaker's attention, and the sea of faces around me. I spoke without notes and sat down to muted approval, as the heavily built Minister of Education, Arts and Science stood to wind up the debate.

"I want to congratulate the Hon Member, who has just sat down, most heartily on his maiden speech. He has made a real contribution to this debate and if he continues in this way he will develop into a very useful member of this House."

The initiation was over. I could now speak my mind and take a more active part in debates. Parliament was now beginning for me.

How did the press see the "new boys"?

"New MPs Rush to Make Their Maiden Speeches." *Cape Times*. Not true as far as I was concerned; the Whips were forcing us to speak.

"New Members from the Rand – Dr Boris Wilson [two others quoted] made the best impression. Dr Wilson opened the international door and let in a little wind of chill reality to the cosy remoteness of the House by reminding it that a ballistic missile could destroy Cape Town."

. *The Sunday Express*, under a headline "Select Half Dozen" included Colin and me as maiden-speech makers lingering in the memory longer than most. We were big-city products marking the new age in South Africa's affairs. Dr Boris Wilson "was a political sensationalist – I do not mean this unkindly – for we all love sensation. He showed this in his first entry into the debate by dropping considerations of the Atomic Age into an otherwise cosy little exchange on local education."

The press had not ignored me; neither had my constituents and friends for whom the press, I think, had magnified the quality of my speech. Letters and telegrams filled my postbox.

It was now a nice feeling to know that, within the limits of the Whips restraints, I could attack the Nationalists, interject and in turn be attacked. I was ready for it all.

I decided to be careful and speak only on issues that interested me or were important in the subjects that I knew best. At all times I would try to be as objective as possible. I did not want to join those MPs who spoke indiscriminately on a multitude of subjects. To make the best impact on Parliament and the voters, one had to be expert on a few subjects, researching them properly. I already saw that some of the new MPs without special interests were somewhat lost.

Parliament in the late 1950s was composed of a large number of farmers. The agricultural debates were well attended, and the government took note of grievances because it needed votes in the loaded platteland constituencies. Most of the MPs used their speaking time in expressing the needs of their constituents. Pleas could be made directly to the Minister concerned, instead of wasting Parliament's time, but these private approaches would not be reported and read in a local newspaper by the MP's constituents.

It was a case of "we ask the Minister " and "we thank the Minister."

This first session was called mainly to provide funds until Parliament reconvened in 1959. The Budget debate took precedence so no fireworks were expected until then.

Debates could, however, suddenly explode into clashes across the aisle, especially when it involved a volatile MP like Eric Louw, a Minister with a venomous tongue.

In the evenings, a mellow Harry Lawrence one of the UP's leading front-benchers was certain to enliven debates and we looked forward to his presence. His irrepressible wit and interjections could reduce the Speaker to a furious pulp, turn a lethargic debate into a sudden uproar, with Harry Lawrence perhaps ordered out of the House.

It is not generally realised how important the role of the party Whips is. They are there to protect members at all times, especially to ask for points of order or withdrawal of unparliamentary language. No one can be called a "liar" or said "not to be telling the truth" or "deliberately telling an untruth". Whips are there to ask the Speaker to insist that unparliamentary allegations are withdrawn. If an MP fails to withdraw a remark he can be ordered out of the House, and exchanges between the Speaker and MPs can be gripping.

I witnessed many such events, in addition to the times when I was myself required to withdraw allegations I had made. I suspected that the UP Whips did not always give me the same measure of protection when smears or unjust attacks were made on me. Was this a deliberate tactic of the UP conservatives to embarrass me? I have no way of knowing.

The Afrikaans newspapers impressed on their readers that the UP was being lead by *linksgesindes* – left wingers – and *liberaliste* out of all proportion to speeches I had made. I was singled out as an important acquisition to the UP's liberal wing in the House.

I was sure that the UP leadership was not happy about these constant reminders in the Nationalist press about their newest liberal. I did little to encourage this and kept to my intention to play on muted political strings until I had the measure of the Nationalists and my own conservative front-bench.

Obviously both the National Party in the House and their press were doing their best to create political instability in the UP – not a difficult job. The UP leadership hated any suggestion of a liberal brush.

Journalists supporting the government were very effective in labelling and segregating MPs into groups. Over the years it had built up the concept of a separate liberal parliamentary group in the United Party. By the time I arrived in Parliament, I was the liberal group's important acquisition.

In truth there was no such thing as a liberal group in the UP – there were liberals by South African standards varying anywhere from the political centre in concept to the fringes of Marxism. In the 1950s if anyone in the media, a political reporter, or an MP, Nationalist or United Party, who was not a liberal was asked to describe a liberal in South African politics, the answer would be couched in a range of platitudes from the centre to the extreme left. For the Nationalists a liberal became a "liberalist" – a term of direst abuse. For the conservative UP MP or supporter, a liberal really had no place in the party of Smuts and Botha.

The so-called UP liberal group, when I arrived in Parliament, consisted of John Cope, former journalist and colleague of JH Hofmeyr; Helen Suzman; Dr Zach de Beer; Ray Swart; Townley Williams; Ronald Butcher; and Dr Jan Steytler. In July 1958 Colin Eglin, Clive van Ryneveld and I were added to the list. On opposition benches were the outspoken Native Representatives – Margaret Ballinger, Walter Stanford and Lee Warden.

In the Nationalist newspapers I was the *éminence grise* of the new arrivals, mostly I imagine because of the fight I waged in Johannesburg against Dr Verwoerd.

If the truth be known, I had great difficulty in finding out what the UP's parliamentary Cape liberals thought about the UP's problems. They were not very communicative. As Cape members, De Beer and Eglin were close to Graaff and sincerely believed they could influence his political stance. De Beer was an outstanding young debater, with a fine flow of language in English and Afrikaans, and he was used with effect by the Whips in major debates.

The Budget debate gave a good insight into the calibre of many of my colleagues and the Nationalist MPs, several of whom were good speakers. The problem was that much of the content of their speeches was marred by poor argument and cluttered with political jargon.

The first time I heard Margaret Ballinger in the House I realised why she was regarded as someone of formidable stature, knowledgeable and erudite, who always raised the general level of discussion. The amendment she moved in the No Confidence debate called upon "the authorities in the interests of internal peace . . . to abandon the practice of arbitrary government now in operation among Africans". It was pivotal.

The restoration of civil liberties, the extension of political liberties and rights to Africans and setting the country on the road to true democracy was urgent. These were forthright demands, expressed clearly and not in the cliches and slogans which were used by UP and Nationalist policy-makers and MPs to disguise their real intentions.

Her amendment was in stark contrast to the United Party's, which requested a "common approach to certain aspects of non-European policy on which there is general agreement between the major parties."

As debate followed debate where there was discussion on the "Native question", there was reluctance by the United Party to face reality on this most important matter.

The reality was escalation of the conflict between black and white, fuelled by the apartheid policies of the Nationalists. Time and again the only MPs who sincerely tried to address the race relations problem were the liberals. When the Prime Minister and Verwoerd replied to Graaff they were easily able to ridicule the obscurities and contradictions in UP policies.

The exchanges between MPs across the aisle were often vitriolic and reflected the enormous gap between government and opposition. This was even more pronounced between liberals and NP right wingers. Carel de Wet, who had led the student demonstration against black medical students attending post-mortems on white cadavers came to the House in 1953, and was expected to go far up the NP ladder.

I watched him, an overweight, heavily-built, inscrutable man, arrogantly defending the ideological legislation passed by the Nationalists during the last ten years:

"The white man must remain the master of the white areas of South Africa today and in the future. When I refer to *baasskap* [white man's authority] I do not merely mean the master of the black man. I mean the master of the white man as well . . . There is only one way of remaining master, only one way of maintaining white supremacy: by ensuring that only the white man will vote for a white member of Parliament. That is the only way we can remain master . . . At the moment the aim of the Honorable Members opposite [the UP] that the non-whites should sit in this House as well, that they should vote with us on the Common Electoral Roll is realised, the white man will no longer be master of South Africa."

De Wet was speaking with the voice of the deeply committed Afrikaner nationalist. These sentiments were echoed by every Nat MP when dealing with blacks and whites; in such precise terms there was no ambiguity. White meant being "baas". When Graaff said he wanted to find common ground with the Nationalists on Native Policy I do not know where he thought the common ground lay. De Wet's speech set out the parameters. Either Graaff and the UP accepted them or there was no coming together. It reflected the social and political outlook of the Nationalists in the 1950s environment.

The Nationalists came to power unexpectedly in 1948, and this gave them the opportunity, for the first time since Union, to gain absolute cultural and political control of South Africa. They were able to pursue unhindered their survivalist policy of separation – apartheid – while the UP wandered without direction in the political wilderness.

The politician who reached the pinnacle in setting out the Nationalist policy, the arch-exponent of apartheid, was Dr Hendrik Verwoerd. In Parliament I was able to confirm that I had been more than justified in opposing his policies, which I now heard at firsthand.

In 1942 the Nationalist Party announced their Republican aims. In a few words, Carel de Wet had summarised this policy; it was all about white survival through "white baasskap". In the House the endless puerile, repetitive and boring but dedicated debates filled the pages of *Hansard* as a testimonial. All we could do on the opposition benches was listen, interject, object and vote against apartheid Bills.

From my early days in Parliament, I was constantly reminding myself why I was there – to remove the Nationalists from power and end the iniquitous apartheid system.

It was easy to succumb to the lazy clublike life of Parliament, the exclusive parliamentary diningroom, the freedom to move in relaxed surroundings, the constant attention from the staff and the unmistakable feeling of achievement that the MP suffix meant to one's position in the political life of the country.

There were also the constant flow of diplomatic invitations to cocktails and dinner. For some, free trips overseas to the USA and the UK. Inside South Africa, we had travel concessions and free wine from the KWV (the wine co-operative). It was tempting to fall into line with the older MPs and coast along, enjoying the life, making sure that one was in Parliament long enough to get the ultimate, a pension for life at the end of one's parliamentary career.

It was not for me. I was in a hurry. I wanted to get things changed. Unfortunately as a back-bencher, I had to stay in line, obey the Whips, stay with the system and all the rules and traditions of the all-powerful party Caucus.

The United Party was composed mainly of members from the urban and peri-urban areas. Since coming to power the Nationalists had, in three elections, made tremendous electoral inroads into safe UP seats, helped by the fact that Smuts had committed a grave error in not having a delimitation before the 1948 election.

The Nats were shrewd. They loaded seats like mine where votes did not count, unloaded the rural areas and created more seats in the platteland. They were assured by their leaders that the white survivalist creed was there for all time.

They increased their political targets by planned invasions to control cultural, educational and trade union organisations into which they planted party hacks. They co-operated with the secret society, the Broederbond (Band of Brothers), established in 1921, to which all their leaders belonged – Strijdom, Verwoerd, Donges, Louw and Swart.

English-speaking South Africans were content to let Afrikaner nationalists dominate the country's political life, leaving the English free to be seduced by the social and economic advantages of apartheid. Although Afrikaans was taught in all schools, English speakers were mostly not bilingual, never read the struggling Afrikaans newspapers or listened to the Afrikaans "B" radio service. They were more interested in the banks, the mining investment houses, the July Handicap, the weekend and holiday trips to Natal, the Cape and periodic overseas visits – England was still referred to as "home" by many.

Despite all the political objectives of the United Party, its congresses and public protests, it believed that the road to power lay in acting like camouflaged Nationalists in the hope that dissatisfied members of the NP would join its ranks and in time it would win enough votes to become once again the government of "Botha and Smuts".

The realities were the other way around. Leading members of the UP – Bailey Bekker, Blaar Coetzee, Frank Waring and a steady constant stream of lesser lights left the UP to join the Nats, either directly or through short-lived new movements and splinter parties. Some of them like Blaar Coetzee became Cabinet Ministers or occupied high offices in the Nationalist Party.

So, it did not take me long to realise that my original aims to reform the UP with the help of other liberals was "pie in the sky". More than ever I realised that liberalism, as seen by many indoctrinated affluent whites, had become a sinister relative of the radical left or the Communists. From my back-bench in the House the view that the white electorate was one of the most politically illiterate anywhere was confirmed. Most South African whites believed the Nationalist theory that to share power with blacks would be disastrous. It was a sombre, chilling, realism which held little hope.

The UP's dilemma was profound. On the one hand it wanted to regain the (white) seat of power, for which it needed the votes of right wing Nationalists in the platteland, the mines and from the thousands of young Afrikaners in the segregated "white" universities. Above all, it needed support from the Calvinist-orientated Dutch Reformed Church, which gave apartheid its theological justification. On the other hand, it relied on the strong English-language newspapers and wealthy South Africans like the Oppenheimers, who kept the United Party alive because it was the only political party which represented the English-speaking community. There were no other political alternatives.

This was the UP's problem and why it was unable to take a stand against apartheid. It was always faced too, by the dangers of a split in its ranks which could break it. The hard right in the UP was led by people like Douglas Mitchell, from Natal, and Harry Rissik and Henry Tucker in the Transvaal. On the other hand, liberal MPs – Cope, Suzman, De Beer, Eglin, Steytler, Swart, Butcher, Van Ryneveld and myself – took every opportunity to oppose apartheid.

As the session progressed I swallowed my disappointment and frustration. I was constantly flying to Johannesburg to my business, my constituents, my wife and growing family, who periodically joined me in Cape Town.

Our children were now at school and, as we had agreed, they remained in Johannesburg for schooling and security. The South African parliamentary system demands sacrifices. Six months of the year are spent in Cape Town. Then for everyone, MPs and officials alike, executive government transfers back to Pretoria sometime in midyear to continue its administration.

While I was in Cape Town I had my own problems running my business. Although I had from medical school days run it at arm's length, it was a great responsibility. Apart from this, I had to maintain good contact with my constituency. Fortunately Harry Schwarz, my MPC, was a loyal and energetic friend who watched over our constituents' activities and needs like a hawk.

My first session in Parliament took place through the depths of the Cape winter, when it rained a lot. Night sittings had commenced. One became exhausted sitting in the House all day followed by a dinner break and at least another two hours in the House.

At the end of a long day I would return to my lonely apartment for sleep. The next day the routine would commence with a morning sitting, caucus or meetings. Every day in Parliament our desks and pigeon holes were full of reports, Bills, Acts, proceedings of the day, notices and other official memoranda. I was conscious all the time of the subtle methods the government used to increase and retain control by regulation. At the end of many Bills there were regulations which greatly increased the powers of Ministers without having to consult Parliament. In many cases this was against the Rule of Law and government was being carried out by decree and delegation.

Often, MPs did not read Bills that did not interest them. However the message was clear – the government increasingly used delegated powers to run state departments – a dangerous form of autocracy. Hence it was very necessary to scrutinise every Bill placed on our desks, whether it was of direct interest or not. Opposition meant politically watching the Nationalists.

The first of several all-night sittings was the Electoral Laws Amendment Bill. We had already spent four acrimonious days on it, and tackled every clause in this long Bill in the Committee stage. The government decided the debate had gone on long enough; our main objection was the granting of votes to eighteen-year-olds. The UP believed this was a government ploy to get the votes of a decade of Afrikaner schoolchildren who had been well indoctrinated by the single-medium language system.

An all-night sitting can become a tiring talking shop, irrelevant and unnecessary unless there is a crisis. The biggest problem is to keep it going. As the night lengthens, arguments become obtuse, speakers filibuster and the Speaker spends his time stopping repetition. Exhaustion ends the debate. On our benches it was Harry Lawrence once again who provided the light relief, like the following exchange with the Speaker in the early hours of the morning.

Mr Lawrence: On a point of order, I want to ask – it is no longer necessary because I see the Minister is entering . . .

The Speaker: Order! If the Hon Member does not have a point of order he should not rise on a point of order.

Mr Lawrence: It was merely a temporary point of order. (Laughter).

In the national newspapers, I was beginning to get good reporting, the Afrikaans journals giving me increasing coverage and paying the occasional backhanded, barbed compliment. *Die Burger* reported that "Dr Boris Wilson, a young doctor now a businessman, is one of the few MPs who is always correctly dressed. He speaks well and clearly and has attracted attention in the Transvaal where he is a leader of the liberals. He can be very useful to the UP in certain debates, but it looks as if he has views which can create problems for his party."

Not only had the "NP press boys" in the Gallery correctly assessed my views, but they were happy to sow discord in the UP.

By coincidence, my Private Member's Motion calling for the appointment of a Commission of Enquiry to investigate growing interference of central government in the affairs of local authorities attracted some press attention.

I was pleased about this despite the fact that my motion would never be debated in Parliament because of my lowly back-bench status. It so happened that Cape Town was at loggerheads with the government over municipal non-European voting rights and job reservation, Durban over the financing of Group Areas, Pietermaritzburg over bus apartheid and Johannesburg over public gatherings in the city. The newspapers gave my motion as much publicity as if it had been debated. Parliament, as I learnt from my Council and Province days, is the same kind of battle to interest the newspapers not only from the floor of the House, but by other means such as questions, motions, interviews, interjections and walking out of the House – at the right time!

Fighting the nationalist ideology in South Africa has its risks – even when one is a Member of Parliament. I was harassed in the past – usually in the City Council, the Province or when the detectives visited me at my office. However, a new phenomenon now appeared. Pauline telephoned me one day in distress. She said that someone was telephoning at various times during the night, not speaking, but breathing heavily into the mouthpiece. Then the receiver was put down. She first noticed it when a Parliamentary speech of mine was reported in the newspapers attacking the Nats.

The unknown caller would telephone several times early in the morning from about 5 am, or in the evening anytime after 8 pm and then at intervals throughout the night. She was upset, unnerved and apprehensive apart from the fact that her sleep was disturbed. If it stopped for a few days and then recommenced around 5 am she knew she would read a speech I had made the night before in Parliament, reported in the early editions of *The Rand Daily Mail* and *Die Transvaler*, the Nationalist Party mouthpiece.

This was a new situation for us. I could not advise her to unhook the telephone, nor would we be intimidated into having an ex-directory number. I discussed it with my colleagues and they told me I was not alone in getting these calls. This negated my initial view that there was a maverick at work. It was obviously designed by Nationalist Party sympathisers on night duty to intimidate outspoken anti-Nationalists in Parliament like me.

One morning when I was at home, I was woken by the telephone around 5 am. All I could hear was the sound of heavy breathing.

"Hullo, hullo, speak up – what do you want?" I said.

There was still just the heavy breathing. I tried another tack.

"Look, my friend, I know you don't like my speeches in Parliament, but why take it out on my wife. Why don't you meet me for a cup of coffee and let us talk over our political differences. What about it, man?"

Silence, only the continued heavy breathing. Then the caller spoke in a very guttural but typical Afrikaans accent:

"You bleddy fool," and put the telephone down.

He was probably right – I was a "bleddy fool" trying to reason with an unknown political foe who was using unorthodox and frightening ways to intimidate my family and me.

48

Not unexpectedly, I was studiously ignored in Parliament by Dr Verwoerd. This did not worry me. There was time for the right opportunities. Dr Verwoerd was in the limelight because he was the leading apartheid protagonist and innovator. I had no doubt that when his vote as Minister of Native Affairs was taken, there would be ample opportunity to take up the fight.

Parliament was in a state of uncertainty. For some while Prime Minister Strijdom had been unwell. He had not been seen in the House for a month, and was now in hospital for treatment.

On Sunday, 24 August, he died, leaving the National Party with the important task of choosing the sixth Prime Minister for South Africa since Union in 1910.

According to *The Sunday Times* each former Prime Minister represented a particular phase of history: Botha and Smuts the concept of English-Afrikaner unity; General Hertzog, the painful and erratic unfolding of the "twin stream" policy; Dr Malan the triumph of Afrikaner nationalism. Finally Strijdom – the stream gathering pace for its unknown destination. Strijdom's death focused attention on that political destination.

Who was to lead the Afrikaner to the promised land?

The weekend newspapers had heavily speculated on who would be Strijdom's successor. "Blackie" Swart, Minister of Justice and acting-Prime Minister, was widely tipped to become *hoofleier* (chief leader) of the National Party and so the next prime minister.

Other newspapers speculated on a range of candidates, who were all eliminated in their columns. The final decision was to be taken by the NP caucus of more than 170 MPs and the enlarged group of Senators. It was "hardly likely", wrote *The Sunday Times*, "that a contrary choice would be made which would be embarrassing to the cabinet."

Two other possible candidates figured in the media. Dr Eben Donges, the Cape Leader who had piloted the "Teenager Bill" through Parliament, was considered the choice of the Cape MPs. If Swart did not get it Donges would get the votes of the hard-line MPs from the Transvaal, if only to keep out the other possibility, Dr Verwoerd, who was only eighth in seniority in the cabinet. Overall, the press reported that Verwoerd was not popular with the Nationalist MPs. A sudden "Verwoerd for Prime Minister" campaign was turning into an anticlimax, concluded *The Sunday Times*, whose views were echoed by the English dailies.

Monday morning in the House was tense. The corridors and the Lobby were full of rumours about the succession. It was difficult to concentrate on anything else. I spent most of my time talking to the press. It was clear from "leaks" from the NP caucus that intense lobbying was going on behind the scenes.

I was told that BJ Vorster and Carel de Wet were prime movers in the attempt to have Verwoerd elected with the support of the bulk of the

Transvaal and Free State MPs. The cabinet's choice by ten votes to three was Swart, so the dice were heavily loaded against Dr Verwoerd.

On Monday afternoon, when the House met, Swart as acting-Prime Minister, moved an unopposed motion of condolence. Speeches were made about Strijdom and the House adjourned for a week of mourning, the funeral, and to give the National Party in Parliament time to elect its new leader and Prime Minister.

The Cabinet was requested by the Governor-General to remain in office. It was expected that by the time the House met again there would be a new Prime Minister and Cabinet. The country was given little time to speculate. The Nationalist Caucus was due to meet the following day at 10.30 am for its fateful decision.

I went early to Parliament to hear the result. The Lobby was full of opposition MPs, the press and diplomats. TV cameramen were on the Senate steps outside in the beautiful sunshine of the Cape winter's day. The sky was blue without a cloud. Hundreds of people stood waiting on the pavements to see the new Leader of the Nationalist Party and Prime Minister.

The Cape Times reported that the NP Caucus rooms were boarded up. Whips voices calling Senators and MPs to vote could be heard. At about 11.30 am, Whips came out with the ballot boxes for the count. Fifteen minutes later they returned. I heard someone in the Lobby say *"Verwoerd tagtig,"* (Verwoerd eighty). If so, Swart had been eliminated and Verwoerd had won. Some Opposition MPs had opened a "book" in the Lobby on Strijdom's successor.

I found it difficult to concentrate on what was being said because of the mêlée in the Lobby. It was an historic election – the first time a Prime Minister was being chosen within the precincts of Parliament. If it was Verwoerd, then it was more than historic. He was formidable, an intellectual and master of the of the future ideological strategy of the National Party.

He knew what he wanted and where he would take South Africa. Swart did not rate against him. He was unprepossessing, a party hack; Donges was more educated and stable, was well-informed, commanding respect in Parliament. Nevertheless,the Nationalists were committed to elect a leader who would take them further along the apartheid road that had been traversed by Malan and Strijdom, the road of white supremacy, irrespective of political opposition and cost.

Only one man could meet these criteria – Dr Hendrik Verwoerd. Would the National Party Caucus elect him?

Suddenly the noise in the Lobby was overwhelmed by the distant singing of *Die Stem van Suid Afrika* our national anthem, followed by cheers and clapping. All eyes, from journalists in the gallery surrounding the Lobby to MPs, were fixed on the Caucus room. The new Leader and Prime Minister, Dr Hendrik Verwoerd, came into the lobby with his party colleagues.

It was a memorable moment for me. Here was the man whom I had fought tooth and nail in the City Council over his inflexibility, his ruthlessness and his aim to establish total apartheid in South Africa with the promise of the Afrikaner Republic. Here was the smiling victor, who would lead South Africa into the promised land.

It was an emotional experience as he walked past me followed by the National Party Caucus to the Senate steps outside. It struck me that Verwoerd was honouring Strijdom in choosing to speak from those steps, because it was Strijdom who had enlarged the Senate.

We realised afterwards that it was the "enlarged" Senators who had voted Verwoerd into office. The Nationalists had also honoured Strijdom because they knew Verwoerd was uncompromising and imbued with the spirit of white survival.

On that beautiful day, against the beautiful background of Table Mountain and Signal Hill, Hendrik Verwoerd promised the "volk" (the Afrikaner people) fulfillment of their political and social aspirations, the security of the white Afrikaner dream, apartheid.

Verwoerd did get eighty votes in the first ballot, which disposed of Swart. In the second ballot he beat Donges by 98 votes to 75. Thus 23 Nationalist MPs set the seal on a turbulent future for South Africa.

Dr Verwoerd had only been a member of the House of Assembly for four months. Before that he was Leader in the enlarged Senate. It was as a Senator that he was first made Minister of Native Affairs and confirmed that the Senators had voted him into office.

Despite all the forebodings before his election, the result was a shock to the English press with whom he was no favourite. *The Cape Times* considered that he has "wielded much power without responsibility to an electorate, and his qualities must be mainly inferred from his administration of the Department of Native Affairs".

As one of the few UP politicians outside Parliament who had fought Verwoerd, I knew it was not only the quality of his administration that counted, but the quality of his intellect. I had no doubt that he would be a strong-willed Prime Minister. Naturally, my earliest thoughts on his election made me wonder whether the relative calm I was experiencing from the Nationalists in the House would continue. I realised that in Parliament I was small fry.

Verwoerd had ignored me. He had been forced to deal with me in the past when I was Chairman of the Non-European Affairs Department, whether he liked it or not. I had asked him a few questions in the House, and his replies were perfunctory and dismissive. Nevertheless the old conflicts were always in my mind. We had not reached the Native Affairs Vote so I had no chance to take up the many issues that I knew were plaguing the City of Johannesburg and its "non-European problem".

I expected that government MPs like Vorster and De Wet would take up the cudgels on his behalf – the signs were there. I had made no contentious statements or drawn fire from the Nationalists; it was early days and I was watching both fronts – the United Party and the Nationalists. I was also still learning about Parliament and trying to get the "feel" as an opposition legislator. For support I haunted the pages once again of JS Mill.

Here I was in Parliament, in opposition, the pinnacle for many politicians seeking a public role. I wanted to make a real contribution to democracy. The difficulties were immense. I was apprehensive of Verwoerd and all he would do to South Africa. At the same time I was in an opposition party which was in a chaotic state.

Dr Donges, when winding up the Electoral Laws Amendment debate said: "The United Party is a pathological case. We have heard a lot about their dual personality and how in certain parts of the country they have certain policies, and in other parts of the country other policies."

Simply put – and how true it was.

Of course the unexpected could happen. Verwoerd might help the UP to emerge as a proper opposition. No doubt, as he went along he would spell out and implement his aims – and the UP could show him whether it meant to oppose him or not with positive policies.

The day after Verwoerd was elected he told South Africa and the United Party where he intended to take the country:

"All [his] energies would be used to establish a Republic in such a way and a time that will be lasting . . . the policy of separate development is designed for happiness, security and stability . . . despite the differences between South Africa and the black states the government will try to find a means of co-operation . . . The right of people who have other convictions to be maintained, the state after all is responsible for good government in the interests of all."

This declaration was viewed with scepticism by many of his white and most of his black opponents. His record on civil rights did not inspire confidence.

The Cape Times was scathing. It wanted to know how it was possible for him to absorb the traditional conventions and tolerance which make a parliamentarian, when he had written that "our system of parliamentary government was British-Jewish Liberalism". Through his newspaper he had endorsed a draft constitution for a "volks" republic which made English the second language. He described this document as "very precisely interpreting the ideology of the National Party."

"As Minister of Native Affairs he had been autocratic, contemptuous of public opinion and criticism. He is a declared racialist and a champion of baasskap. He is an advocate of what he calls strong leadership, which almost always means thrusting on the public radical policies devised by a small group of men arrogantly convinced of the rightness of their views. Only in the last twenty-four hours has he referred to democracy and this is in his own election by a majority of 23 votes in a caucus swollen to preposterous size by nominated Senators. After all, he is dedicated to a fantastic and fanatical conception of apartheid, to a lunatic attempt to unscramble the South African racial omelette at any cost in human privation and dignity. If Dr Verwoerd the Prime Minister is going to be a projection of Dr Verwoerd the Minister of Native Affairs, this country is faced with disaster. At no time less than now could this country afford a government based on regimentation, fanaticism and authoritarianism."

This editorial was published on the morning of the day that Verwoerd was to meet the House as Prime Minister for the first time. There was no doubt in the minds of the perceptive English-language press and most political commentators that Verwoerd's appearance on the scene as the Prime Minister and the reality of what his accession meant was of major historical importance.

I had no illusions about his views and objectives. On these I had spoken out frequently, with little or no support from the UP. In fact the UP got rid of me as soon as they could when I stood in Verwoerd's way as Chairman of the NEAD. Would the UP in Parliament now repeat this to placate Verwoerd? Would the UP support his call for national unity by muting its own opposition to apartheid?

One message that Nationalist leaders always repeat is the religious basis of the rule of government – all important decisions emanate from the Will of God. Verwoerd, in his broadcast to the nation, was no exception:

"It must be stated at the outset that we as believing rulers of a religious country, will seek our strength and guidance in the future as in the past from He who controls the destinies of nations. The grief which plunged the whole country in mourning was His will. But the life of the nation goes on. In accordance with His will, it was determined who should assume the leadership of this government in the new period in the life of this people of South Africa."

Verwoerd and his followers arrogantly believed that he was chosen by God to lead South Africa. His message to all its people was that Separate Development would continue. His accession to leadership did not overtly affect them.

They had no say in the voting that brought Verwoerd to power. Their only knowledge of him was as a ruthless Minister of Native Affairs who enforced segregation and forced removals. They were not impressed by his promise that bringing in "separation, whether it be residential, territorial or social does not envisage oppression . . . that the policy of separate development is designed for happiness, security and stability."

Did Verwoerd really think that some of us in the House were naive, like the Nationalist MPs who surrounded him?

During the dramatic days in Parliament when he took power little appeared in the newspapers reflecting the views of the non-whites despite its importance to them. Verwoerd provided the first indication of what his government would be like before the House sat on 3 September. There was no change in Cabinet appointments – he would be both Prime Minister and Minister of Native Affairs. He thus made clear from the outset who would be "baas" of the blacks.

We all wondered whether as Prime Minister he would be isolated from the everyday political shadow boxing in the House and whether its character would change. As he retained his position as Minister of Native Affairs he would still be vulnerable as far as I was concerned. Much could be done by questioning and challenging him in the House on his policies and, equally important, his actions. Overall, we knew he would dominate political events.

49

It was clear that certain Nat MPs were increasing their attacks on me, obviously trying to "smear" me as the UP's most dangerous "liberalist". I ignored them, constructing my early speeches so that I did not "rock the boat" as Nationalist newspapers were predicting. My outspokenness occurred in the Caucus – it was there where it mattered most. One had to be doubly careful since "leaks" occurred literally within minutes of our Caucus ending.

We knew the names of Caucus "moles" but the UP Whips were powerless to stop them. Liberals in the Caucus never acted as a group and initially never met to plan strategy – the media had it wrong. Most Nationalist pressmen were too involved in their own party affairs to get facts right – they simply played political games to sow discord.

Even journalists supporting the United Party glossed over the UP's internal problems in spite of the leaking of Caucus secrets upon which much of their political comment was based. They knew of the sharp differences in policy discussions but did not try to cause any rifts, leaving that to their Nationalist colleagues.

The ending of the session was near, when a most unexpected event occurred in Caucus. A Leader's Propaganda Committee was set up to review the party's propaganda objectives in relation to its Native Policy. When the names were announced, I was included. I could not believe this – I was never consulted by Graaff about the appointment. However, there it was!

It was a high-powered committee, with Marais Steyn as chairman; Jack Higgerty, the Chief Whip; Frans Cronje the establishment's favoured new MP; JL Horak, party secretary; Vause Raw and Douglas Mitchell the arch-conservatives from Natal. From the centre was former Witwatersrand chairman Andrew Brown with Hamilton Russell from the Cape. The accepted liberals were John Cope, Zach de Beer and me. I presumed that my inclusion was due to my work in the Division of Information, my association with Graaff as a speechwriter and that my liberal views on the party's Native Policy were known. As Cope, De Beer and I were a minority, we could never dictate the Committee's line, but Graaff was in the clear because he had constructed a committee representative of all views in the party which in those days of UP infighting was very much to his credit.

This surprise appointment to the Leader's Committee on the issue of the day – Native Policy – had the dramatic effect of erasing the pessimism and gloom that engulfed my first two months in Parliament. I was catapulted on to it, I assumed, so that liberal views could be taken into account. Had some pragmatism permeated into the minds of Graaff and his close advisers that they should remove inconsistencies in the Native Policy before the party collapsed? I suddenly saw it as my last chance to deal with the whole race relations issue. I was going to take it. Was my hope that it was possible to help bring about internal reform in the UP going to become a reality? Were liberal views going to receive consideration?

I would soon know. We were told to work during the parliamentary recess and complete our job before the new session in January. A set of draft proposals was placed before us at the first meeting sending a few shudders down my spine. It was headed:

"Suggestions of an answer by the United Party to the National Party's exploitation of the Native Policy."

Summarised, this draft concluded that the Nationalists had created a fear-ridden society in South Africa, by "ruthless reckless propaganda"; their policy of segregation will "succeed in maintaining the white man's baasskap." By contrast it said the UP's 1954 policy remained a practical and sensible approach, to white supremacy with justice, pretending to debunk apartheid with all its economic fallacies and impossibilities. To support its case it juggled with population figures, predicting that by the year 2000 the people of South Africa would reach 30 million. It proposed a white majority solution, with a national home for Natives in the reserves which "will be a reality and not a mere chimera as the pipe dreams of Dr Verwoerd."

In my notes on this paragraph I had written on my copy: "surely this is apartheid?" Which is precisely what it was. The UP's leaders were displaying their usual preference for the apartheid solution, seeking a new presentation to satisfy its critics. We were back to square one – the constant attempt to clothe the UP in the apartheid regalia of the Nationalist Party. John, Zach and I realised there was a tremendous task ahead of us to swing the committee towards a liberal policy since it was inherently conservative.

It was early days, but at least we were on the committee.

In the House, the government lagged behind in its programme. Numerous Bills still had to come with debates on Ministers' Votes. I found a controversial issue on the the the Post and Telegraphs Committee despite my lack of interest in it. It related to the SA Broadcasting Corporation, which came into the Vote. I drew the attention of the House to the English radio programme which I said was dull, unimaginative and stereotyped. I also attacked the commercial channel, Springbok Radio, with its violent serials. In one of them, seven men were murdered, one stabbed, one hanged and one had his throat cut! I also complained that there were no broadcasting services for Natives.

Instead of broadcasting to the rest of Africa to counteract "Red propaganda", I recommended that the SABC spend its money on radio programmes for South African blacks instead. Nationalist speakers countered that there was no obligation on the Minister to do anything – the SABC was independent, and it was not Parliament's concern. The Nationalists had the same attitude to local government, although it was Parliament's responsibility. When it suited them, they refused to discuss such matters. This did not deter me.

In 1958 South Africa was one of the few countries in the world without a television service. I asked Dr Albert Hertzog, the grey-haired, bearded, dapper Minister of Posts and Telegraphs why this was so?

"Because," he said, "there is a difference of opinion as to what the cultural value or otherwise of television is."

This was an evasion of the truth. The Nationalists at this stage in their career, were scared of TV. It was a medium they did not know enough about and they worried whether they could control it – or whether it would control them. I decided I would watch SABC matters in future.

I was on tenterhooks about Verwoerd's Native Affairs Vote. As a new MP I hoped I would get into the debate – I was sure he would soon appoint a new Minister to succeed him. Before that I wanted to confront him about his dictatorial methods now that I was free of the shackles of the Johannesburg City Council Caucus.

Minister's Votes are taken in a Committee of the House. MPs are allowed ten minutes to make their points. Technically, there is no limit to the number of times one can speak. The Minister periodically replies until he finally ends the debate, knowing that the Committee of the House will approve his Vote because of the Nationalist majority.

All my previous battles with Verwoerd were through the Town Clerk and newspapers, virtually at second hand, with the exception of the visit we paid to Pretoria to get his consent for the £3,000,000 loan.

I was looking forward to seeing him in action as Minister of Native Affairs so that I could initiate a more intimate struggle with him in the House. He was a good orator, taking his time. He was known to speak for several hours on Native Affairs and apartheid, and his plans to change the face of South Africa.

During his Vote he clarified repeatedly how apartheid would take root and be developed.

"The ideal of total apartheid," he told us, "gives one something to aim at . . . We have said clearly, Dr Malan said so, Advocate Strijdom said so, I have said it repeatedly and I say it again – that the policy of apartheid moves in the direction of ever-increasing separation. The ideal must be total separation in every sphere, but everyone realises today that it is impracticable. Everyone realises that such a thing cannot be attained within the space of a few years . . ."

From such general statements he would go on to deal with the specific issues relating to the use of labour, job reservation, and influx control. He could speak for over two hours answering the many criticisms that came from us without giving way one iota on his apartheid plans. He was a mine of information on his department which did not produce annual reports in time.

The last report saw the light of day in 1954. He said he had given Parliament full enough detail every year, keeping it constantly informed, which was good enough reason to reject our complaints about his failure to issue the annual reports.

Verwoerd's "performances" in the House were masterly. He handled the "big guns" of our front-bench with aplomb, always polite and with a smile, in his slightly singsong voice which became plaintive when he was hurt.

We had several experts in Native Affairs, but when replying it was Verwoerd giving them a classroom lesson. Patience was one of his virtues, and he explained the minutest detail of his plans; or he would correct someone about a place-name in a reserve or urban township of which he had a profound knowledge. He blamed the UP for all the economic integration that had taken place in South Africa over the years, which he was now untangling.

I found the discussion on his Vote fascinating. Everyone from Graaff down who had an interest in Native Affairs wanted to speak. I was lucky enough to be seen by the Speaker early on in the Vote. In the ten minutes allocated to me I decided to tackle Verwoerd on the way he had forced Johannesburg to submit to the "watchdog" committee, and challenged his right under the South Africa Act to compel Johannesburg to implement his policy of apartheid.

There was, as I expected, no reaction from Verwoerd. He was still keeping to his policy of ignoring me.

I took the opportunity, too, to deal with Johannesburg's black housing programme which had been held up by his department. Normal housing activities of the Council six months after the disputed £3 000 000 loan had been settled, were still in a limbo.

"What is going on?" I asked. "What methods of threat and intimidation are being used by the government against the city council of Johannesburg? I think this is the place where the Minister of Native Affairs must come clean about the manner in which he is dealing with the largest local authority in South Africa. Is the Minister and the Hon Member for Westdene [chairman of Verwoerd's Johannesburg 'watchdog' committee] denying local authorities the right to think independently about apartheid legislation and about the policies of the government . . . never mind the legislation, have they no right to criticise the policies of the government? Some of us who were in local government know that the only way you can protect the rights of local authorities is to stand up and criticise the policies of this government. It will be a sorry day for this country when apartheid and the resultant legislation will smack down on the freedom of thought, speech and criticism in South Africa. But what is the Minister doing?"

To my surprise, Verwoerd was making notes. I pressed on.

"The Minister is using his 'watchdog' committee, ostensibly like the spider and the fly. He is drawing the Council in as Hitler did with the Prime Ministers of Czechoslovakia and Austria – he says come and see me and I will help you. And what happened when they came? He used a political sledgehammer to knock them out."

I wondered whether I had provoked Verwoerd enough to reply to me. Just before the lunch break, Dr Naas Coertze (Standerton) came into the debate. He was a reputed "hatchet man" for the NP in debates. As I came to recognise later, he invariably followed me in reply.

He went straight into a personal attack on me, saying there was no obligation on my part to advertise my ignorance in the House as I had done on the eighteen-year-old franchise Bill. I should not think I was still a member of the City Council or the Provincial Council!

Coertze was a legal academic and he proceeded to give the House and me a lecture on the South Africa Act:

"I do not want to give him a lecture on constitutional law, but he has asked for it."

Then came the stock-in-trade of the NP back-bench attack.

"He was making propaganda for himself . . . I assure him he need not keep an eye on the Press Gallery. Those gentlemen will faithfully report every statement he makes besmirching South Africa, and those statements will appear in the foreign Press. But it did not escape our notice."

I interjected: "I think this is scandalous."

He was not dismayed – his last words were:

"I accuse the Hon Member for Hospital of having an ulterior motive and this was his motive. He was very eager to make all sorts of disparaging statements about the Union, and having made them he was eager they should appear in the foreign press. That is why he kept one eye on the Press Gallery. He is very anxious that international pressure should be exercised on the Union to make all sorts of concessions to the Liberalistic group in South Africa. We on this side regard this as political blackmail which will not succeed." His time was up and the House adjourned for lunch.

This was the first intimation of a personal political attack provoked by my questions to Verwoerd. There had been no sign that Nationalist MPs were paying me much attention. It was more than coincidence that my intervention in Verwoerd's Vote made them show their teeth in what I was to recognise as a mixture of smears, sneers and ridicule. I was to learn that they would go to any lengths to "smear" a "liberalist" – their technique was a potent part of the armament used to deal with articulate parliamentarians who espoused liberalism.

In this respect my reputation had preceded me. An attempt was made by Coertze and several Nat MPs, like John Vorster, to belittle me and "put me in my place". Coertze had devoted the whole of his speech to me in a very snide, sarcastic way, which was characteristic of him. He was tallish, thin, moustached and spoke very good Afrikaans. I thought his speech full of veiled threats – interesting, in a cynical way.

Hymie Miller, my erstwhile City Council colleague who succeeded me as chairman of NEAD, was the next speaker after Coertze. It was customary for a UP speaker following an attack like Coertze's to defend a colleague and to reject the allegations and threats. I presumed Miller would follow the convention and put the record straight as to what went on in the Council when he took over from me. Not a bit of it.

Full of smiles, Miller dealt with Coertze by saying he "hoped the previous speaker will forgive me if I do not refer to what he said". Miller was distancing himself from me. If there was one man in the House who was able to defend me, it was Miller – yet he chose not to. Miller had a rough time from the NP. The Speaker had to warn him several times not to read his vague and pointless speech.

Mentz, Johannesburg's "watchdog", then spoke, also making short shrift of Miller. He also attacked me, but paid me a compliment which made up for Miller's failure to defend me:

Mentz: "I want to say to the Hon Member [Dr Wilson] that I like a man who can stand up and fight, not a man like the last speaker [Miller] who, although he probably agreed to drag me across the floor of the House, collapsed like a pack of cards and leaves it to the Hon Member for Hospital to continue the fight. But I want to say to the Hon Member for Hospital he must not think he is still in the Johannesburg City Council. He will find that this bombastic attitude of his will get him nowhere. If he brought the City Council to its knees, I just want to tell him he will not succeed in doing so here."

Mentz, who was a polite little man, thought he had done a good job by exposing Miller's tactics to the House and at the same time putting me in my place. He did me a favour by lambasting Miller. He was concerned that information I had at my disposal about his *"sub judice"* discussions with Johannesburg and questioned me as to the source of my "leaks". Naturally, I refused disclosure. Eventually he admitted I was correct, reading from the minutes of the "watchdog committee" and the City Council.

I hoped that this was the extent of the Nat attack. Not so. Later that afternoon Verwoerd replied to the debate. In the middle of his speech he said that he wanted to discuss the behaviour of the City Council of Johannesburg when Miller and I were members.

He immediately accused me of launching the attack in the debate, especially that I alleged that the government could not indicate constitutionally its powers preventing Johannesburg from pursuing its own native policy.

Minister of Native Affairs: "He [Dr Wilson] alleges that we cannot indicate any section in the Union's Constitution which prevents the City council from laying down its own basic Native policy. I think I am correct in saying this is what he maintained."

Dr Wilson: "I asked where the South Africa Act provided that local authorities must implement the policies of the government of the day. I said they had to obey the laws of the land."

Minister of Native Affairs: "That is exactly what I maintained. That is the bone of contention."

Dr Verwoerd went on to explain in great detail the official view, quoting relevant sections of the South Africa Act:

"It is provided in clearest terms that the administration of all Native Affairs in South Africa is vested in the Central Government. This is in accordance with the spirit of the discussions at the National Convention . . . that the country should have one national policy in respect of one great issue . . . we cannot have a variety of Native policies."

Verwoerd then went on to give a history of the UP in the City Council before my election.

Dr Verwoerd: "I now turn to the latest developments which the Hon Member has referred because he has levelled the charge at me, that we are bringing compulsion to bear on the City Council. What are the latest developments?"

Then followed a detailed history of the role the government played in giving help to local authorities, who assisted with the government's removal plans, which I was unwilling to do, recounting the £3 000 000 loan through Sir Ernest Oppenheimer raised by me.

"I discovered," he said, "that the Johannesburg City Council under the leadership of these present two members of the House were violating what had been a clear 'gentleman's agreement', an agreement that had been put into writing and accepted."

I interjected: "I never violated any agreement." Miller was silent.

Verwoerd continued: ". . . if the Hon Members had still been on the City Council the fact that the government had UP councillors who were willing to sign an agreement and co-operate with them would never have come about. People who cannot keep their word when they have entered into an agreement with the State are not people with whom we can operate." (Interjections)

Dr Verwoerd ended with the following words:

"Now I say this: what great temerity is it not to make an attack on this government as though we are the cause of of these difficulties while it is obviously their fault and more specifically not the present responsible councillors, but their predecessors! With that I have come to the end of what I have to say about the Hon Member and I hope he is as ashamed of himself as he should be."

Of course I was not ashamed; at last Dr Verwoerd, the grand architect of the removal schemes, had finally acknowledged my presence in Parliament. I had never co-operated with him and his apartheid plans despite the fact that they had statutory backing, nor was I the compliant UP City Councillor willing to implement his detested removal plans, in the hope that the carrot he dangled before the councillors would produce financial assistance to house the homeless and the slum-dwellers.

He did not tell the House that I only went to Sir Ernest because, when I became NEAD chairman, I found that all attempts by the Council to obtain funds from his department for housing were refused. Which left the homeless and slum-dwellers out in the cold because Verwoerd's first priorities were the needs of apartheid. At least he had made clear to Parliament on our first encounter that I was not one of the UP compromisers nor the object of his political bullying. He also exposed the fact that the UP, by carrying out the removals of thousands of blacks, was actually acting as his agents in implementing apartheid, which they said they opposed.

The following day *Die Transvaler*, the Nationalist daily which Verwoerd formerly edited, had a large cartoon on its leader page. It depicted Miller and me with large dunce caps on, holding our caned backsides, jumping about in pain. The caption read:

"Verwoerd deals out the punishment."

The Native Affairs Vote was the first indication that Verwoerd and the Nats took my presence on the back-benches of the UP seriously. I was certain I could expect no mercy in the future. They would do all they could to curb my zealousness, using whatever tactics and language suited them.

I knew that I would probably have to fight alone because it was already evident that few on the UP benches would want to defend me in debates including, regrettably, the Whips. Verwoerd alleged that I had ulterior motives, to weaken my position on the UP benches. I could not rebut his statements in the Vote because I was not allocated time to reply. I could understand the tenor of Verwoerd's and Mentz's criticisms, but Coertze's vitriolic words indicated that I was a marked man. The UP front-bench recognised the scenario – but, as always, they believed in silence.

Before the Native Affairs Vote terminated, there was a remarkable contretemps between Dr Verwoerd and the slightly-built Native Representative, Lee Warden. A member of Mrs Ballinger's team and a trade unionist, he asked Dr Verwoerd why the government refused to answer his questions on the Order Paper referring to "Africans".

Until Verwoerd was appointed Prime Minister, the word "African" was used by all the Native Representatives with regularity and some questions on the Order Paper received answers. It was even proved later that several members of the National Party had used the term to describe the many black tribes of South Africa.

But Lee Warden decided to thrash this out, if he could, to show how inconsistent and stupid the Nationalists were because they would not officially refer to "natives" as "Africans".

According to the government, the term "African" was unknown to them. Lee Warden succeeded in making the Nationalists look foolish. He told the House, when Verwoerd was present, that "we heard the Hon Minister declare in this House, for all the world to know, that he did not know what an African was, and furthermore his department kept no records on Africans . . . I think it is just arrogance on the part of the Hon Minister to refuse to answer questions on Africans . . ."

It was more than arrogance; it was a bizarre situation where the Minister concerned with the welfare of the overwhelming majority of the blacks refused to acknowledge their African heritage.

Later, in his reply, Dr Verwoerd let the cat out of the bag.

"The term African quite clearly has a wider meaning than merely the Bantu of South Africa. The word African is used by certain people for propaganda purposes. They want to impress on the world that Africa is not the home of the white man or of other peoples. They want the world to believe that Africa belongs to the black people alone, and that is why they are trying to make the world accustomed to the use of this word.

"There is a third reason why they want to use the word. They want to hurt Afrikaners. They know the English word African can only be translated by something like Afrikane, only the 'r' of Afrikaner falls away. It is quite clear we are faced with a propagandistic concept."

He lashed out at some of the English-language newspapers for using African instead of Native or Bantu: "This is part of a propaganda trick and I have no intention of being deceived by a trick of the members opposite."

This quite ignored the fact that the United Party front-benchers, for once, had come to the aid of Lee Warden, by launching a full-scale attack on

Dr Verwoerd on this issue. Philip Moore, an ex-teacher, an expert on English, told the House African used as a noun means "a native of Africa and one ethnologically of the African race . . . when the English-language press uses the word African they are doing so in conformity with the usage throughout the world, not only in South Africa."

In the year 1958 Verwoerd was not only trying to change the character and physical status of blacks and whites in South Africa. He was determined that there should be no semantic confusion between the white Afrikaner volk and the overwhelming number of African people whom he intended to move about on the chessboard of his future vision of South Africa.

This also told us how the Nationalists under a powerful leader like Verwoerd would resist any attempt to divert them from establishing their apartheid state, even if it meant decreeing that an African was not an African in the white state of South Africa. A few minutes later the Native Affairs Vote was passed.

The days to come under Dr Hendrik Frensch Verwoerd were ominous for South Africa. There was a clearer indication of what was in Verwoerd's mind later in the Appropriation debate. Verwoerd made the shock announcement that he was going to abolish the Native Representatives in Parliament once Natives had taken control of Reserves as envisaged by the Bantu Authorities Act. On the republican issue, he refused to tell us whether South Africa would be in or out of the Commonwealth. But we had to be a republic in order to achieve "white" national unity.

Answering Graaff, Verwoerd said South Africa could not get enough white immigrants because of the role of liberalism in many parts of the world. Immigrants had to be allies of white people, if they were to help solve the non-European problem. Coloureds, and not Natives, should take part in the industrial development of the Cape.

Verwoerd's strong personality, once he became Prime Minister, dominated Parliament in a few weeks. His greatest problem was that he spoke far too long and gave too many detailed explanations. Nothing was too much trouble if he had to make a point, especially when he dealt with the UP's Native Policy. From the Nationalist point of view he exposed it as a muddled, dangerous, road to integration. He focused attention on the UP's attempts to out-Nat the Nats, which was my own point of view as a liberal.

Before we could fully adjust to Verwoerd's accession, Parliament was prorogued to January 1959 – my first session had ended.

50

I was ready to get back to Johannesburg to be with my family, attend to business and report back to my constituents.

The Leader's Propaganda Committee met several times, and I was not surprised to see that John Cope, Zach De Beer and I were a minority group. It was obvious that the majority of the members were looking for ways and means of presenting the UP's current policy on Native Affairs clothed in more acceptable robes. This did not interest us. We wanted real change

During the recess, Harry Lawrence told our Transvaal Congress "not to be a pale shadow of the National Party". His call was ignored – congress endorsed the party's Native Policy. Lawrence, as far as I knew, was a conservative. I began to speculate whether I had misjudged him. Was he more liberal than I thought?

I had several public speaking engagements, taking the opportunity, whenever possible, to deal with race relations. I was trying to convince people that the UP could change – that there were real alternatives to Verwoerdian baasskap. I often spoke in general terms because, for many organisations, politics are taboo – such as the Brakpan Rotary Club. *The Rand Daily Mail* was impressed with my speech and wrote an editorial headed "Sound Steps".

"Dr Boris Wilson's proposal for improving race relations and easing tensions between whites and non-whites in South Africa may not be applicable in all its eleven points, but it does suggest an approach to the problem that is sensible and practical. It breaks with the all too prevalent habit of thinking that the only choice in this country is between two opposites – on the one side, the restrictive policies of the Nationalists designed to preserve White *baasskap*; on the other, the egalitarianism of the Liberals.

"It indicates that between these two attitudes is a wide range of possible measures and courses that would do much to improve conditions and improve resentment."

During the recess the United Party public representatives contented themselves with report-back meetings. Generally they kept discussions on UP policies to the closed confines of branch and divisional meetings or to Congresses, which lead to serious infighting and differences on Native Policy. It was clear that we were a divided party, which we could not hide from the press who knew what went on in our inner sanctums.

My own constituency did not provide me with great intellectual challenge. It was composed of white collar workers, retired or young flat-dwellers, middle class settled people and thousands of itinerants, typical inhabitants of the congested tower-blocks. It also included University students who lived on the campus. I formed a student branch outside the campus, because political parties were not allowed at the University. As a political workshop this branch was no great success. The reasons became clear. Students and lecturers actively interested in politics avoided the "political dinosaur", the United Party. I was extremely disappointed, but it made the point of what academics thought of the UP's political policies.

To overcome this I spoke on public platforms wherever I could to offset my Hospital constituency's shallow intellectual base. I received increasing invitations to address northern suburbs liberals. I made sure that my speeches got press coverage by giving journalists extracts beforehand. Newspapers, during the recess, were short of political copy. It was essential for a politician to speak to a wider audience and this was how it was done.

At last the deliberations of the Propaganda Committee produced an interim report which I could not accept. It was full of political cliches, some of which came from the 1954 Native policy like:

"Maintaining western civilisation and the leadership of the white race" – "the party stands for a positive approach to strengthening the position of the European." It recommended ways of increasing the white population by the end of the century to parity with blacks. Coloureds should be reinstated as appendages of the white man in relation to Natives. In fact it was no more than a total restatement of the main points of the existing Native Policy, which was not acceptable to Cope, De Beer and me.

We decided to submit a minority report to Graaff.

I am not certain whether the work of the committee was leaked to the press, but a week before Parliament re-assembled in January 1959, *The Rand Daily Mail*, edited by Laurence Gandar, ran a story that the "liberals" wanted to settle the Native Policy once and for all.

Aubrey Sussens, a leading political reporter, predicted "a colour row likely in the UP. A number of United Party MPs are going to parliament this session determined to settle once and for all the question of the party's colour policy. Although all members of the Party accept the broad principles there is a noticeable difference in the way it is interpreted – and put over in public – by members of the two main schools of thought. The so-called liberal group which draws most of its support from the Witwatersrand and the Cape believe the opposition should take a firmer stand against the government and interpret the Party's colour policy in a much more progressive manner.

"The conservatives [UP] complain that they suffered during the general election when platteland audiences asked them to explain statements made in the cities by members of the liberal group."

Sussens's report was traumatic for the UP. It was obviously timed for maximum effect, but as far as I was concerned, the only independent action I knew about "of a concerted effort by a liberal group" was what we might do on the Propaganda Committee.

No UP liberals, to my knowledge, met independently. We did not proclaim we were liberals – it was the press and the conservatives who were trying to split the United Party, who used these tactics.

288

51

Unfortunately, I felt extremely ill when I reached Cape Town for the new session. The night before Parliament opened, Zach de Beer diagnosed infective hepatitis. I went to bed, missed the No Confidence Debate and realised that I would be unfit for at least three weeks. I flew back to Johannesburg, to the comfort of my home. In the early stages I was too ill to worry about politics.

In the No Confidence Debate Verwoerd reaffirmed that he was going ahead with the Republic, the Native Representatives would be removed and many apartheid Bills were coming during the session. Lying in bed, convalescing, reading newspapers and *Hansard* reports convinced me that problems in the UP were compounded by the obscure nature of its language and propaganda material. Liberals and conservatives interpreted policy differently. By contrast, in the No Confidence Debate, Graaff was forthright and to the point, which was a welcome change.

"During its period in office it [government] has shown a greed for despotic power which has resulted in the erosion of the foundations of democracy and liberty as we know them in South Africa, a process which somehow has lost us the goodwill of the rest of the world. No Minister in the history of South Africa has ever increased his own powers or taken more powers for his own department than the Hon Prime Minister when he was Minister of Native Affairs. He has extended the powers of summary arrest and removal, he has removed the right to interdicts. Through the Bantu Education Act he is virtually in charge of all Bantu Education.

"The Bill to extend University Education will place all higher education for Natives under the complete and exclusive control of the Minister and his department. We know the Church clause did. We have seen that during this gentleman's period in the office of Minister of Native Affairs that department has virtually become an *imperium in imperio* and more, and Parliament and the Supreme Court are being excluded not only from the administration of the reserves but from increasing fields of native life outside the reserves. At this time when the need for contact between the Native and the European is perhaps greater than ever, powers exist under the Act of 1957 to prohibit the establishment of any interracial organisation."

Graaff went on to say that the Nationalist government was not governing according to Western standards and quoted the retired Chief Justice who said that "the course which the Union is following cannot be reconciled with the principles of Western civilisation."

Graaff deplored both the plight of Indians under the Group Areas Act and the removal of the Native Representatives from Parliament.

"We on this side of the House," he affirmed, "stand by the 1936 settlement . . . the responsible class of Native should have a greater say in the election of Senators, in the electoral colleges."

In bed, reading these words, I concluded that Graaff had clearly put his finger on the main points of what apartheid was doing to South Africa. Zach de Beer told me that he and Eglin were trying to influence Graaff to make a stronger stand against Verwoerd. I wondered if they were succeeding, because the *swart gevaar* tactics of the Nationalists could only be countered and exposed if the UP leaders spoke out without compromise.

Somehow they had to wean themselves from the political verbiage of the Native Policy, originally adopted to satisfy the retarded, prejudiced and emotive thinking of the platteland voters who, like Nationalists, were reluctant to surrender their visions of the white republic.

Dr Verwoerd, in his reply to Graaff, told the House that Owen Vine, writing in *The Rand Daily Mail* stated: "To put it crisply the party's [UP] colour policy is out of date . . . White leadership with justice will no longer do." Verwoerd was unaware that he was quoting the words of an important liberal journalist of the day, Laurence Gandar, *The Rand Daily Mail's* editor writing under a pseudonym.

Verwoerd used further quotes from the article: "It used to be said that the UP would be better off if it shed its liberals. That was a point a year ago; now the need of the party is to shed its conservatives."

Dr Verwoerd, with apposite reasoning, but with different objectives, was telling the country what we were trying to tell the United Party. I wondered whether it would make sense to the UP establishment. Verwoerd wanted the UP conservatives to come over to the Nationalists. This was their real home. Then we could get on with the job of handling the country's difficulties with pragmatism, realism and the liberalisation of a restructured UP. I did not expect that Verwoerd's call would affect the UP at this stage, despite the fact that since 1948 it had been going downhill in Parliament and the constituencies. Its main support was from urban voters. Verwoerd's use of Gandar's words showed that he fully understood what was going on in the UP.

He was attempting to break the UP with logic – but he would not succeed because the UP clung ferociously to their conservatives because they feared that they would be engulfed by the urban liberals.

One could not argue with Verwoerd's tactics; they suited me, anyway! It could not have come at a better time in view of what we were trying to do on the the Leader's Propaganda Committee.

If Graaff was going to grasp the nettle, he would have to analyse where the UP was heading under its conservative mentors and whether it was the road to extinction or success for the United Party.

Verwoerd was beckoning. It was a call to the white faithful. Would Graaff let the party split, or would he listen to what we had to say on the Propaganda Committee?

The first week of March saw me recovered and back in Parliament. The UP were putting up a good fight against the Extension of University Education Bill, opposing the First Reading "because it provides for serious interference in academic freedom and university autonomy".

Opposing the First Reading of the Bantu Self Government Bill, the combined opposition showed the government that for once it was united against this most important piece of legislation.

It was a watershed – intended to give apartheid its teeth. Graaff said South Africa was entering upon a pattern of legislation which in some degree placed us at "the crossroads in which an ineluctable choice has to be made, and the choice seems to be the choice between the continued existence of this Union of South Africa or its partition into a number of separate states, economic deterioration and perhaps ruin for all the peoples who inhabit South Africa."

I realised, as I sat in the House listening to the exchanges between the front-benchers on both sides of the aisle, that this legislation would segregate whites and blacks as never before. Worse still, it meant the end of the 1936 Settlement upon which much of South Africa's Native policy and the rights of blacks were entrenched. No wonder Verwoerd was adamant that the Native Representatives had to go.

Graaff made a very good point: "You are going to have two forces pulling in different directions. One the force of economic integration, the other the force of political separation".

Marais Steyn reminded Verwoerd that whatever happened, the "white state", despite the legislation, would have a majority of non-whites and Natives . . . and they will never be able to enjoy permanent rights as permanent inhabitants of South Africa".

History was in the making when Verwoerd stood up in the tense House. He wasted no time in attacking the UP, who, he said stood for a multiracial South Africa governing in partnership, while the "whole National Party, the whole of the government party with all the power of its supporters, support the policy that the white man wants to retain his domination over his part of the country, and is prepared to pay a certain price for it, namely by giving Bantu full rights to develop in their own areas."

Margaret Ballinger, the leader of the Native Representatives, backing the UP's case, moved an amendment which stated that the "African" people would be deprived of all say in the government of their own country and were not being consulted by a Parliament who is shaping their future. The Bill would reduce Africans to a subject race and endanger good relations inside and outside the country.

"It was the shortest route to disaster in the country," she said.

Other than newspaper comment, I had the impression that the silent white majority accepted that the Verwoerd plan was on the right lines. Laurence Gandar, writing in his newspaper two weeks after the Bill was introduced, said there was the "prospect of stirring and perhaps momentous debates ahead . . . This measure goes to the heart of the South African political struggle, and it does so at a time when interesting new trends of thought are becoming apparent in this country . . . the Bantustan proposal is undoubtedly making an appeal to many opposition supporters whose faith in any form of multiracialism or racial partnership has been thoroughly shaken by recent events in Central Africa. The Bantustan idea is politically potent . . ."

Gandar, farseeing in his evaluation of the Nationalist proposals, believed the "forthcoming debates will draw from both sides of the House

291

clearer definitions of outlook than we had before."

The Bill had to be debated through the rest of its stages in Parliament. We knew from the very nature of the government replies in the First Reading, that whatever we said in the House would make no difference. The Nationalist apartheid steamroller was on its way and could not be stopped.

52

I was in Johannesburg for the short Easter recess when I was telephoned by "Bunny" Neame, a journalist friend of mine, the political correspondent of *The Rand Daily Mail*.

"Boris, I've just learnt that our newspaper group are going to close *Forum*. This month is the last issue. Its a real tragedy. We're all upset about it. You know *Forum*. It's the only truly liberal journal left in South Africa – there's nothing else. Some of us were discussing the news and we wondered whether you would consider rescuing it by buying it and keeping it going. We are desperate that something should be done quickly. We think the company will sell it to you."

It was a shock to learn that *Forum* would close. I did some rapid thinking, discussing it at length with Neame, whose idea it was. He was a regular contributor, as were most of South Africa's known liberals since Jan Hofmeyr's day, when he formed a Trust to keep it published. Other contributors were John Cope, one of its early editors, Julius Lewin, Margaret Ballinger and many more. I first wrote for it on the dangers to local government when I was in the City and Provincial Councils. Originally it was weekly, then a fortnightly. Now, with a few thousand circulating to the faithful, it was a monthly edited by Joel Mervis, *The Sunday Times* editor.

I agreed with Neame that if *Forum* closed it would be difficult to start another journal in its place. It was symptomatic of the Verwoerdian era. The decision of South African Associated Newspapers to close *Forum* was not because they did not want to bear the minor financial loss, but because it was a small venture and not worth their while.

I promised Neame I would look into the matter urgently. The closure of *Forum* bothered me so much that I telephoned Henry Kuiper, the managing director of SAAN, whom I vaguely knew from my political activity in Johannesburg, and arranged to see him.

I was not clear about what I would say to him, but I thought the best thing was to meet, find out the situation and take it from there.

I saw Kuiper the next day in his office in Main Street. He confirmed that SAAN had definitely decided to close *Forum* after the next issue. I tried to make him reconsider, explaining *Forum*'s importance and that it was unique in contemporary South African journalism, especially in the present political climate. Kuiper was adamant – the SAAN was closing *Forum*.

"Will you sell it to me?"

"Do you really want to buy it?"

"Well, I haven't really thought this out, but in view of the fact that you are closing it, I would like a day or to to think about it and see if I can plan to keep it going."

"Boris, I can't alter the Board decision, but I can give you until Thursday to let me know if you are interested. If you want to make an offer contact me on Thursday and we can talk it over".

I then asked him how much he would take for the title and records. He thought for a moment:

"I think in the region of a thousand pounds."

"No, Henry, that's too much. You are closing it anyway. I would have thought about five hundred. Would you print it if I bought it?"

"No, Boris, there is no chance of that. It's not our policy to print for others. In any event the print order would be too small."

I left him, my head full of ideas, wondering whether I was unbalanced in even thinking about buying *Forum* and running it. Not only was I an MP, but I had a large business commitment with no time to spare. All I knew was that *Forum* had a small circulation, very little advertising, and that it was incurring losses.

If SAAN, the second largest newspaper group, could not make it pay, how could I do so, with minimal resources at my command? Then there was the all-important question: Who would edit *Forum* for me, full-time or part-time? Where would I find an editor?

All these salient points flashed through my mind. Above all, could we South African liberals afford to lose the *Forum*, the only mouthpiece we had, however small it was?

Obviously, if I did want to take it over I would have to act quickly, because the next issue had to be prepared. I would need temporary help until a permanent editor could be found.

Despite the difficulties, the idea of rescuing *Forum* and owning a liberal journal fascinated me. The first thing to do was to speak to John Cope, fortunately also in Johannesburg for the recess. Cope had been the second editor of *Forum* in its early days. He was appalled to hear the news.

"Boris, buy it. Buy it, man! Until you find an editor I'll do the next two issues."

It was a marvellous offer. Then I had a brain wave. I spoke to my friend Morry Mayers who had brought me into the UP. Although a wealthy man, he ran a small business from an office in the centre of Johannesburg. Without demur, he agreed to manage *Forum* although his knowledge of newspapers was nil, let alone journals like *Forum*.

I reminded myself that I did have sufficient experience to look after *Forum* – I had edited and produced *WU's Views*, and had published newsletters for the UP's information division.

I telephoned Prompt Printing, my old *WU's Views* printers. They agreed to print *Forum* on a monthly basis, as it was similar to several small magazines they were already printing.

By Thursday morning I had estimates of printing and distribution costs involved; I had consulted CNA, the current distributors, who also agreed to continue selling *Forum* in their shops throughout the country.

Full of enthusiasm, I saw Henry Kuiper that afternoon.

"What have you decided, Henry? To sell or fold up *Forum?*"

"Boris, we'll sell to you. Five hundred pounds – but we cannot help you one bit. Our staff are not available for assistance. We'll let you have all the financial information you need to run it, but bear in mind we are not print jobbers and our costs will not help you. We'll give you the current subscriber list."

He went on to discuss further details.

"Well . . . ?" he asked me.

"I'll buy it, Henry."

I wrote out a cheque for five hundred pounds. We shook hands.

I walked out of the newspaper offices feeling that I had done the right thing. I was going to try and develop *Forum*. It had to continue its historical role in fostering liberal thought in SA.

First things, however, came first.

Forum had to be owned by a private company. It would not be good policy for me to known as the owner. If it was to keep its independence and liberalism, it should not belong to a politician. It should reflect the reality of all shades of opinion in South Africa, and maintain its traditional role.

I named the company Independent Journals and Newspapers (Pty) Ltd. Mayers and I were the directors. John Cope was as good as his word – he took editorial control. I spoke to the few advertisers it had to reassure them that *Forum* was alive and well. Additional advertising was sorely needed. I took this job on to see what I could do.

Forum's front cover and layout were dull. I drew up some cover ideas, and Cope, Mayers and I chose one, agreeing on a new layout.

We had three weeks to get the next issue out. John and I spent a hectic time in Parliament working on the content. Unfortunately, it coincided with a heavy Order Paper which commenced with the Second Reading of the Extension of University Education Bill which the UP strenuously opposed. The Bill would destroy academic freedom, separate students ethnically and enforce a colour bar.

Helen Suzman accused the government of having "spies" at universities. Professor "Sakkies" Fourie charged that universities would become "slaves" of the government. Verwoerd entered the debate. He told the House that all non-white students enrolling at universities in future would have to study at segregated institutions. It was a non-stop four day debate, with everyone taking part. After an all-night sitting the Second Reading was passed.

The NP did not like our tactics and did not take long to show their teeth. The Committee Stage was guillotined. After four clauses had been debated, the discussion was cut short and we spent two days voting against thirty-eight clauses which Parliament had never discussed. It was a sham. Verwoerd was showing his scorn for Parliamentary democracy. He was using it and the opposition to steamroller his apartheid legislation. Whether we liked it or not, the Official Opposition was manipulated to give the impression that the Verwoerdian Parliament was a democratic institution. I was appalled by what I was witnessing. It was authoritarianism at work in the South African Parliament.

My original fears about Verwoerd and what he would do to democracy in South Africa were justified. I knew that this would not be the first time I would see Bills rushed through the House in order to get apartheid laws on the statute books. There was little I could do as an individual. The Official Opposition under Sir de Villiers Graaff was a puppet of Dr Hendrik Verwoerd.

Normally an opposition expects to be outvoted, with the government having the final word. But, and this was what I had witnessed, the Nationalists were simply using us as a rubber stamp for apartheid legislation, as they had done in Johannesburg's City Council. Verwoerd had not changed and the UP was forced to give him the appearance of legality.

To many the UP appeared "united" in its opposition to the Nats. Most of its confidential Caucus discussions were leaked to newspapers. The "moles" made certain the outside political world was informed. Unfortunately, many of these "revelations" were gross distortions. The UP Caucus was split into a majority of right wingers and a small number of liberals or progressives. Afrikaans newspapers used this evidence of the rift in the UP and that Graaff was led by "liberalists" in Caucus.

For example, when we had to decide on the University Bills, Caucus unanimously agreed the line we should take, because there were few problems relating to Native Policy. We showed "unity" in the House. However, sharp divisions of opinion flared up when Group Areas, Separate Amenities or powersharing with Natives were discussed.

The political views of the conservatives in our Caucus differed little from the racial separation theories of the Nationalists. Our approach was indirect approval in sustaining our type of segregation. The Nationalists went straight for the target – segregate. The UP's conservative Caucus vacillated, compromised, looking for grey areas in political solutions. The reason was simple. Most of them had the same prejudices and fears as the Nats.

All feared the consequences of white backlash in their constituencies. The worst offenders were English-speaking leaders from Natal like Douglas Mitchell and Vause Raw. This did not surprise me. The press revelled in the fact that the MPs they designated "liberals" were the cause of Caucus strife when the UP was faced with contentious apartheid Bills.

This was often true. Our views were known from congress and party meetings. Not only did we oppose the Nationalists in the true sense, but we had to oppose our right wing colleagues as well. Consequently we were watchful in Caucus about the official line the UP was taking when the Government produced apartheid Bills tightening the net around the blacks.

OCTOBER, 1960

THE CASE AGAINST A NATIONALIST REPUBLIC

The **forum**

The Verdict Must Be . . .

NO

Contents

ONE SHILLING AND SIXPENCE

Volume 9, No. 7

The MPs who leaked Caucus deliberations and confrontations were known to the UP leadership, but they were not disciplined because our numbers were already reduced by election defeats. The UP could not afford to expel conservatives from its parliamentary group.

The story, repeated in the columns of newspapers, propagated the myth that the liberals were a co-ordinated Caucus group. But this was never the case. I do not recall a meeting of liberals ever being called to discuss Caucus problems where we might take separate action. We acted on an *ad hoc* basis or as individuals. Mostly there was no need for meetings – we knew where we stood.

Our thinking was empirical – we had no conflicts as to our attitude to the Nationalist's apartheid ideology. Often we did not know what was on the Caucus agenda. In Caucus Graaff was was fair – he always heard all shades of opinion; too often the device of "leave it to the Leader" was taken. This was dangerous because all he would do was take the advice of his Leader's Committee, which consisted of the chairmen of the provinces; with the exception of Jan Steytler in the Cape, they were leading conservatives. Despite this, we did our best, when we spoke in the House, to place the most liberal interpretation on UP policies because of their "grey area" vagueness.

As opposition MPs we were aware of the importance of our role in the Verwoerdian era. We often repeated publicly and in the House, that not only did we represent our white voters, but we spoke for the voteless – the Natives, Indians and coloureds.

It was now urgent to repeat this, because we knew of Verwoerd's plans to remove the Native Representatives from Parliament. Individually and collectively, we liberals and progressives wanted the United Party to shed itself of its hidebound colour prejudices and face up to the facts of economic and political integration; not overnight, but in an evolutionary way, in a society dominated by a large black population and a small white minority in control.

We did not hide our views, but naturally in a debate we did not try and embarrass the UP when we could not support the official policy. Thus many ways were found for interpretation, which of course were pounced on by the press, especially Nationalist newspapers. Their headlines often read:

"Liberalists Control United Party policy." We were usually linked with extreme left wing movements, like the African National Congress or the Communist Party. Many allegations began in the House.

From my back-bench, I often pondered about the low level of the political debate, which consisted chiefly of slogans, prejudice and insults. Certain Nat MPs were masters of this type of innuendo. I wondered what on earth I was doing, sitting for hours in this unreal environment listening to this political garbage. Did the Nationalists ever know the real meaning of liberal thought and philosophy? How could farmers and party organisers, very much in the majority, understand what some of us were talking about.

Not many had been to university or studied political philosophy. One had to hand it to Dr Verwoerd. His political views, of the extreme right wing, were streets ahead of the average rank-and-file Nationalist MP. The ebb and flow of the dialogue across the aisle in the House, the jargon, political abuse and slogans making up the exchanges, made one despair that real solutions for the great racial problems that divided black and white in South Africa would ever be understood and solved.

Next to *swart gevaar*, the black peril, was the Nationalist fear of Communist infiltration. Liberalism was regarded as the evil conduit pipe along the road to Communist dictatorship. Hence it had to be fought tooth and nail. Those of us who were labelled "liberalists" always received special attention. The technique was to belittle what had been said. I was, for example, "ignorant, bombastic, did not read the Bills".

Later it became more serious impugning my political affiliations. On the UP back-bench, I was the "liberalistic" target. I tried to ignore NP attacks, by raising serious matters and not being drawn into inconsequential political disputes. I was regularly reminded that I was no longer in the City Council, where I was a "big boy".

As a new MP, I received a great deal of attention from the parliamentary press corps, not only in their reports but in the special parliamentary columns. For example, in the Third Reading of the University Extension Bill, I ended my speech quoting the respected Dr Xuma, one of the Founders of the African National Congress in 1912.

"The educated African is our hope, our bridge. He is an asset that responsible and thinking white South Africa cannot either afford to ignore or alienate without disastrous results in the long run.

"He also should be brought into close contact and co-operation with the thinking community. It is he and he alone who can best interpret the European to the African and the African to the European."

MC Botha, a Nationalist MP, who later became Minister of Native Affairs under Verwoerd followed me, opening with these words:

"We have listened here to a whole series of nonsensical allegations by the Hon Member for Hospital [Dr Wilson] and I really do not feel like replying to all he has said because I think the sooner the contents disappear from our memories the better for him and all of us." He ended by saying I wanted to make "all Natives imitation little Wilsons".

These remarks were typical of the kind of response my speeches in the House often evoked from Nationalists. It became impossible to have real dialogue on serious issues with them.

Shortly afterwards the Deputy Minister of Education, Arts and Science, John Vorster, who later became Prime Minister, tackled me.

Unfortunately for him I was not paying him attention when he addressed the House. I was busy opening a large envelope which a messenger had brought me and for which I had waited all day. It was the first issue of the new *Forum* sent to me by express post.

As I paged through this historic new issue with its modern red and white cover, I vaguely heard John Vorster mentioning inferior "university education for the non-whites", about which I and other speakers had been critical earlier in the day. I still paid no attention to him, admiring the first rate job done by John Cope.

Then, in the distance I heard Vorster, who was a competent and at times satirical speaker, address me:

"I should like to put this question to the Hon Member for Hospital. He will not find his answer in the book he is reading at the moment."

I looked up to see him, in his characteristic pose, one foot on a bench, staring at me, waiting to get my attention.

Hansard records the following:

Dr Wilson: "Remain calm. We know that you are only a Deputy Minister". I then continued reading *Forum*. For a moment there was silence. Then Vorster spoke, in his gruff Afrikaner accent:

The Deputy Minister of Education Arts and Science: "It is perfectly true I am only a Deputy Minister, but I did not go and take a medical course during the war because I was afraid to discharge other obligations in the war."

I slowly looked up at him.

Dr Wilson: "At least I never learnt your prejudices. I have never blown up a bridge; I have never been put behind iron bars; I have never had that privilege."

Mr Speaker: "Order, Order."

John Vorster stood and glared at me, as I looked down again and continued to read *Forum*.

During World War II, Vorster was one of the banned Ossewa Brandwag (Oxwagon Sentinels), who blew up electrical pylons and engaged in other illegal activities. He was arrested and General Smuts put him and other saboteurs in prison for the war's duration.

When Vorster became Prime Minister, this spicy interlude was often quoted by newspaper biographers. Later in this debate he demanded my attention again. I was getting used to the fact that I was constantly being referred to, whether I spoke or not, by leading Nationalists. They were always trying to ridicule, denigrate or disturb my equilibrium in Parliament; to give the impression that as a liberal back-bencher I was an important UP leader. Dr Verwoerd followed a few days later. In discussion on his Vote, he attacked Graaff for allowing the liberals in the party to "exert great influence on him" and urged Graaff to "stand firm".

Verwoerd went on to say that the "public and the voters of South Africa . . . have taken note of the statements made on occasion by many of the United Party representatives in this House – such as the Hon Member for Parktown [Mr Cope], and they have taken note of the statements made by the Hon Member for Hospital [Dr Wilson] and other members who speak as liberals. The entire nation has taken note of the statements made by the liberalistic group. We have no illusions as to the nature of the struggle taking place in the United Party . . ."

By attacking us the NP was constantly trying to split the UP. It used every opportunity to point out to the UP conservatives that they were harbouring dangerous "liberalists" in their midst. It was the cause of great concern at the top. The leadership was trapped – our constituencies provided most of the money for the party. We were tolerated; this was reflected in the personal relations in the Caucus. As if by edict, right and left were separated – we knew that if there were contentious matters for discussion real feelings would come to the fore. There was no mingling, no *bonhomie* between us, even socially.

I decided to take note of the NP attacks made on me. Their regularity, recorded in *Hansard* told me that I was one of the prime "liberalistic" targets for the Nationalist bully-boys.

Fortunately the boredom, the stupor and the low level of debate in the House was relieved by the fact that the special Propaganda Committee was at work, and meetings were held regularly. We were trying to establish the basis for a comprehensive overview of the Native Policy and whether we could could get some kind of consensus. Newspapers and NP were aware of this committee. Although we were not in the public eye I was certain Nationalists and our conservatives did not want to see a liberal race relations policy emerging from our deliberations.

This view was reinforced from the nature of the debate between Graaff and Verwoerd on the PM's Vote. *The Cape Times* commented that as the debate was on race relations it ended in a stalemate. Verwoerd and Graaff traded questions on coloureds, Indians and blacks, and Verwoerd praised Graaff when he said, as far as the UP was concerned, coloureds would be represented only by whites if the UP came to power.

"The United Party leadership and the UP conservatives have triumphed over the liberals in the party," said Verwoerd.

The venomous nature of his attacks on liberals, the fact that many of our conservative MPs shared the views of Nationalists when it came to Native Policy, meant that debates between UP and NP were politically sterile most of the time.

Most of the United Party MPs came from urban English-speaking constituencies, the wealthier parts of South Africa, with a minority from semi-urban Afrikaans areas. The UP was supposed to be a party of moderates, whatever that meant in the South African context.

In reality UP conservatives supported apartheid. The difference was in technique. The UP would implement apartheid as "white supremacy with justice". As liberals, we could express our views in Caucus, and these were leaked to the newspapers, who splashed the story, especially the Nationalist press who lampooned the United Party unmercifully.

Cape newspapers were reporting that there was intense political interest in our parliamentary Caucus deliberations over the forthcoming Bantu Self Government Bill. A bold headline in *The Cape Times* contrasted the UP with the NP caucus unity, pointing out that "things are not so simple on the United Party side, (they never are) because this party always likes to have a twofold approach to everything. It will tie itself into political knots at the drop of a hat." It went to ask what the UP would put forward as its own alternative to the Bantustan plan and the government apartheid ideology, since it was groping around clutching its 1954 Native Policy booklet "costing sixpence".

It was the last opportunity for the UP to clarify party policy before the end of the session.

The Cape Times further reported that a large section of the party Caucus wanted Graaff to offer a definite clear-cut alternative, accepting that South Africa was a multiracial country, with increased political rights for non-Europeans. Others wanted a restatement of the UP's 1954 Native Policy and no more. The article concluded by dividing the Caucus into two factions and suggested that the balance lay in the hands of the "progressives".

The truth was that there was a wide-ranging debate in Caucus on the Bantustan Bill. Some of us wanted Graaff to go further than just rejecting the Nationalist proposals. We urged the inclusion of improved political rights for non-whites. The all-powerful Caucus chairman ruled that we were bound by existing party policy in open debate in the House. This was the general pattern in Caucus. From time to time we thought we were converting some of the so-called middle-of-the-roaders in the Caucus, but when it came to the vote, they either abstained or were not present.

So we struggled on, as individuals, trying to get the UP to take a pragmatic line – to really oppose the Nationalists, but were defeated all the time by the nationalist-thinking MPs in our Caucus. In contrast, when a Vote came up where party principle was not at stake, I was given a free hand.

One such an occasion was during the Vote of Eric Louw, Minister of External Affairs. As a result of my frequent visits overseas I came across misleading pamphlets and news handouts from the Information Department which did not correctly reflect conditions in South Africa.

Eric Louw was a sharp-featured, sallow little man, who spoke in a clipped voice and who overreacted sharply to personal criticism. He was an avowed anti-Semite and a racialist. As far as I was concerned the only positive thing about him was that he made good caricature material in the newspapers.

From my back-bench I called on him to explain glaring inaccuracies in a pamphlet distributed overseas called "The South African Indian", which opened with the following statement:

"In four years short of a century, the Indians in South Africa have advanced from the depth of want, illiteracy, physical and spiritual degradation to heights of plenty, liberty and opportunity. Everywhere today are to be found prosperous Indian merchants, industrialists, agriculturists, including wealthy sugar farmers, builders, brokers, doctors and lawyers. All the amenities of civilised life are open to them."

Louw interrupted me: "Don't leave it at that. Tell me what is your objection."

I replied: "My objection is that the statement 'all the amenities of civilisation are open to them' is absolutely untrue, and the Minister knows it and so does the Government".

Although Louw was getting angry with me, I went on, detailing other untruths. At one stage the Nationalist Chief Whip interjected: "You are stabbing your country in the back."

By now Louw was fuming. I then drew his attention to another leaflet headed "The Black Man's Progress in South Africa". It stated that "thousands of Bantu are enjoying the amenities of modern townships. In various cities large blocks of bachelor apartments for migratory workers have also been erected." Where were they? I asked. The leaflet went on to describe how teachers, technicians, doctors, secretaries and lawyers were being trained.

"In all honesty, Mr Chairman, I would like to know where we are training secretaries, lawyers and technicians in this country."

Vorster, then Deputy Minister of Bantu Administration and Development followed me and accused me of being one of those members who "will leave no stone unturned to stir up the outside world against South Africa," apart from the fact that he spent the whole of his speech vilifying me from my City Council days.

"I am pleased that Johannesburg is rid of him". A Nat MP interjected: "And now we are saddled with him."

Eric Louw was running up and down from his front-bench to the officials in their bay asking for help. There was more to come. Several Nat MPs then attacked me. Finally Louw replied.

He said I ought to be ashamed, and I would probably send my *Hansard* overseas with the message: "Here is stuff you can use against South Africa". Interjecting I told him: "I think it is a most disgraceful thing thing to say."

Louw continued that what House had heard was "repetitive, exaggerated, unjust and verbal nonsense . . . what we have heard from the Hon Member is the sort of thing we have been getting at United Nations from the Indian and Soviet and other delegations. He is playing about with one's opponents and is supporting them in their opposition to South Africa and the white people of South Africa."

He may have thought that he had dealt me a mortal blow. But I was on my feet again.

I quote *Hansard* (5626 May 12 1959).

Dr Wilson: "I hope this house will never have occasion again to listen to such a speech by the Hon Minister of External Affairs. He could not sink any lower in the manner of his reply. He has deliberately distorted what I have said." (Interjections).

The Chairman: "Order. The Hon Member must withdraw that."

Dr Wilson: "I will withdraw that . . . and I will say . . . many in this publication which I again reaffirm tell a distorted picture with regard to South Africa's position and which have been, I repeat again, deliberately designed in order to give false information to the outside world."

An Hon Member: "And it is not the only one."

Dr Wilson: "Yes, I have more to show the Hon Minister. The answer to me is not vilify me and not to make the most appalling suggestions, which I fling back in the Minister's teeth, that I will send my *Hansard* over in order to collaborate with our so-called enemies. Who created the enemies of this country? It is the Minister and his party who have created these enemies of South Africa. We did not. While the United Party was in power we had friends overseas. (Interjections). I do not want the Minister of Justice to intervene. I do not need his interventions."

The full pack of Nationalist MPs were now barracking and harassing me. Ignoring the noise, I ended my speech.

"Consequently, the money (£500,000) on this vote is wasted. The money spent in the last ten years has brought us nothing. One man comes from a newspaper in America and gets on television [there] and wipes out everything the Minister and the Information Service has done. So until such time as the Minister is prepared to clean up his own house, there is no point whatsoever in coming to this House and asking for more money . . ."

The Deputy Minister of Bantu Administration was on his feet once again, coming to the aid of Eric Louw, who returned finally to the debate with another attack on me, quoting extensively from United Nations deliberations. "I suppose the Hon Member even calls himself a patriotic South African!"

It was a turbulent time in the House and the newspapers made headlines of it. I did not realise at the time the extent of the hornet's nest I had disturbed, but the role of the Information Service had to be exposed. It was apartheid's lie to the outside world and if it continued I knew that in the future it would cost South Africa dearly in terms of international friendship.

I was aware that most MPs never read Information leaflets even though they received them from time to time in their cluttered parliamentary mailboxes. When they went to South Africa House in London they never looked at them. All the leaflets from which I quoted I had obtained from South Africa House. From my experience as City Council Chairman of Non-European Affairs I knew the position of the blacks and Indians intimately. These leaflets bore no relationship to the realities of their lives in their segregated ghettos. Louw and the Nationalists knew I was right, but they resented my exposures, or as Louw admitted I was attacking the position of the white man and apartheid – the heart of their political ideology, for which, in the late 1950s, they wanted a worldwide cover-up.

The Justice Vote followed. It was a full-scale attack by the NP on the UP because of the issues we had raised on conditions in the police force. The Nationalists hated anyone exposing police misdemeanours because they had turned the police force into guardians of the white people, keeping blacks under control.

John Cope complained about the activities of the Special Branch, citing their attendance at meetings of the Institute of Race Relations and as "spies" at English-speaking universities. He accused the government of using the police to intimidate public opposition.

Hans Abraham, a swarthy, corpulent Nat MP from the platteland tackled Cope: "He [Cope] asks why only certain universities are selected for the attention of the Special Branch. The answer is obvious. If those universities were not contaminated by liberalism of which the Hon Member is a high priest, it would not have been necessary for the Special Branch to concentrate their attention on them."

I immediately interjected: "Are you using the Special Branch for political purposes?" (*Hansard* 5698 May 12).

Abraham replied: "The Hon Member for Hospital should be the last person to talk, and those students, Mr Goldstone and Mr Wentzel who came from the Rand, from Wits, in connection with the tape recording of the blonde spy to who reference was made, is sufficient proof of the part the Hon Member played in their activities. For that reason I say the Hon Member is the last person to talk."

Two things emerged. Cope had elicited the fact that the government was using spies on the campuses and that without any evidence I was accused of being behind student opposition in the universities. As it was late at night, the debate was suspended before I could deny Hans Abraham's lies.

The next afternoon a crowded House continued with the adjourned Justice Vote. Hans Abraham was on his feet, reminding Cope that "many of the Hon Member's intimate friends are receiving the friendly attention of the Special Branch."

Mr Abraham: " . . . One of the bodies which is active in this country and which therefore receives the attention of the Special Branch is the ANC. The United Party has continually taken the ANC under its wing in this House. I still recall the days when the Hon Member for Hospital [Dr Wilson] held meetings in the Native locations in the Johannesburg area together with a Native named."

I could not believe my ears. I jumped up.

Dr Wilson: "That is a lie."

Mr Von Moltke: "Is the Hon Member not obliged to withdraw that?"

The Chairman: "Order! The Hon Member must withdraw that."

I stood at my bench, hesitating. My inclination was not to do so, but I knew Abraham. He probably had more to say, and I could speak later in the Vote.

Dr Wilson: "I withdraw it."

Mr Abraham: "One can see that until recently the Hon Member still enjoyed the protection of the City Council of Johannesburg where there are no proper rules of order and where one is at liberty to tell another person that he is lying . . . I repeat that together with a certain Vundla and other members of the African National Congress . . ."

I was on my feet in a flash.

Dr Wilson: "That is a downright lie. The Hon Member accuses me of having attended meetings together with members of the African National Congress . . ."

I remained on my feet, angry, amidst general uproar. I saw the tall, bespectacled Justice Minister, "Blackie" Swart, at his front-bench addressing the Chairman in his deep voice:

"On a point of order, Mr Chairman, may I have your ruling. If an Hon Member continually ignores your ruling and repeats the same word which you ordered him to withdraw, I suggest you take steps against him."

The Chairman: "The Hon Member for Hospital must withdraw those words."

I had to think quickly again. If I stood firm and did not withdraw, I would be sent out of the House. This was pointless because I was certain the Nats were trying to "frame" me. If so, my place was in the House watching events from my back-bench. I had made my objections. Withdrawal did not mean the allegations were true.

Dr Wilson: "I withdraw them and say that what the Hon Member has just said is absolutely untrue."

The Chairman called on me to "withdraw" and obey his injunction.

I was saved from further action because at this point the UP front-benchers woke up. The Deputy Whip attacked Hans Abraham; then followed Douglas Mitchell and Henry Tucker, who told the Chairman that it was the duty of the member for Groblersdal (Abraham) to accept my word. The argument then hinged on the fact that Abraham's allegation referred to something that occurred outside the House. But the Chairman was not going to change his mind. He said I could deal with the allegations later in the debate.

Hans Abraham continued, saying that the NP leader Johannesburg, Piet van Vuuren had "occasion over and over again to pull up the Hon Member for Hospital because he was associating so closely with the African National Congress and their activities in Johannesburg and in the Johannesburg locations, and now the Hon Member wants to come along together with the Hon Member for Parktown [Cope] and launch an attack on the Special Branch of the South African Police."

The ten minute time limit rule stopped Hans Abraham from continuing his litany of fabrications. I was on my feet, and amidst Nationalist catcalls, told the House that what the MP for Groblersdal had said was a "tissue of untruths. It is a deliberate attempt to frame members on this side."

I challenged him to produce any evidence whatsoever that I had any connection with the ANC. I invited him to repeat the statements outside the House and I would know what to do with him.

"He has not got the guts or the courage to do so."

I reminded the House that, as Chairman of the Johannesburg Non-European Affairs Department, it had been my duty to visit the townships. If Hans Abraham was relying on the evidence of the then Leader of the National Party in Johannesburg (who was now in Parliament), "I say that he is relying on the most unreliable evidence quoted in this House." I then dealt with problems in the Police Force – my original intention. As I sat down, Abraham was on his feet again, making accusations, trying to draw me into the debate, to link me with reputed subversive ANC activities.

My decision to stay and defend myself was right. It was clear that the Nationalists had made their first major onslaught on me in Parliament. It was a warning. When would the next move be made?

Did I know a man called Vundla, Abraham wanted to know. Harry Lawrence, Smuts's former Minister of Justice, intervened, asking what this had to do with the Vote under discussion. Ignoring Lawrence, Abraham retorted it was necessary to have a Special Branch to watch the ANC. By this time, all the front-benchers and our Whips were using points of order to stop Abraham, who was now saying that "members on the other side . . . are clearly connected with the activities of the ANC in South Africa."

The right wing establishment members on the front-bench of the United Party were horrified at the allegation, but Hans Abraham fought his way through their objections. Then he returned to me saying, *inter alia*, that the Hon Member for Hospital was formerly "Benjamin" without giving any reason. It was obvious that the Nationalists had been investigating my background, not very efficiently, but they were now using the discovered "facts" to suit their own ends in Parliament.

I reminded myself of the two Special Branch detectives who had come to my office with the phony story that I had been to Pietersburg location and addressed meetings. Was this all part of an unfolding plan? The Justice Vote appeared to be the launching pad for their attack on me. I decided to await events and keep my eyes open for further innuendoes and personal sniping.

I did not have to wait long. Most Nationalist speakers who followed Hans Abraham made some snide references to me. Coetzee, the Nat MP for Langlaagte (Johannesburg), opened his speech: "The Hon Member for Hospital [Dr Wilson], was very upset when the Hon Member for Groblersdal [Mr Abraham], referred to some of his activities. If my information is correct, the Hon Member for Hospital [Dr Wilson], was Chairman of the Native Affairs Committee of Johannesburg, but the remarkable thing is this – and this is my information – that the Hon Member touted for that position for one reason only, namely, to have access to the locations in order to carry on with his activities there. That is my information. It subsequently became known what his activities were and the City Council simply got rid of him as Chairman . . ."

Unfortunately, I was at tea when Coetzee spoke, otherwise I would been on my feet again. Hymie Miller was in the House while I was out. I was not surprised to learn that he made no attempt to refute the allegations, which he knew were blatant lies.

If I expected the Nationalists to leave me alone that afternoon it was forlorn. They used all their political hatchet-men. Hans Abraham was only the first. JF Schoonbee (Pretoria West) soon followed. I quote from *Hansard:*

"Now I want to deal with the Hon Member for Hospital [Dr Wilson]. In my opinion he behaved himself yesterday and this afternoon like an undisciplined schoolboy, practically like the notorious ducktails that wander around the streets. I want to ask him whether he was not kicked out of the Labour Party, because he went about trying to form branches of the Labour Party amongst the Natives . . ."

Our Whips were protesting that these remarks had nothing to do with the Vote. Schoonbee was allowed to continue his bizarre allegations. It was now evident that the Nats were using the Justice Vote to implicate me in subversion and denigrate my bona fides.

Undeterred, Schoonbee, speaking from the cross-benches then revealed what the Nationalists were trying to plant on me with the connivance of the Minister of Justice.

Mr Schoonbee: The Hon the Minister has a list now of the names of people who have gone from this country to pay a visit behind the Iron Curtain. I want to ask the Hon Minister whether the name of one Benjamin Woolfson does not appear on the list. If so I should like to know . . .

The Minister of Justice: "Did he by any chance change his name later on?"

Mr Schoonbee: "He did change his name; that is no longer his name. That was his name at the time . . ."

The importance of this by-play between Schoonbee and the Minister of Justice did not escape me. I doubt if many of the UP realised what was going on, but the Nationalists were obviously enjoying themselves and had prearranged this smearing attack on me with the co-operation of the Minister of Justice. The Nationalists were intent on establishing that I had changed my name from Benjamin Woolfson to Boris Wilson, and linked me with someone of that name who appeared on a list that the Minister of Justice had of people who had illegally been behind the Iron Curtain – in other words, they were by implication, Communists.

I said nothing in the House. It was not the time to react. I knew the Nationalist mentality. They believed what they said in Parliament would be reported as the truth.

I was certain that this was the tip of a "Red iceberg" in the House and that I would be hearing more of this. One by one, members of the Nationalist Justice group were taking part in the charade.

A short while later, John Cope, intent on exposing the Special Branch, was listening to the Minister of Justice replying to him, when I heard a Nat MP call out to the Minister, "What about Benjamin Woolfson?"

Unbelievably, the Minister interrupted his reply to Cope to deal with the interjection:

Minister of Justice: "Unfortunately he has changed his name, and I do not know what name he has at the moment, and therefore I cannot reply . . ."

At which point he continued with his reply to Cope.

I was now more than intrigued by what was happening, but concerned that the UP Whips were ignoring the nature of the innuendoes and concentrating on points of order. I expected they would have told me to get back into the debate and deal with the implied smears. I decided to take independent action.

During dinner I briefed one of my back-bench colleagues, Percy Plewman, a former Auditor-General, who had listened to the debate. Later, he told the House that he "would like to refer to the very unwarranted and shameful attack which the Hon Member for Pretoria District [Mr Schoonbee] had made on the Member for Hospital [Dr Wilson]. It was quite an unjustified attack which cannot be established, and it carried insinuations against an Hon Member of this House which should never have been made in this House."

The message was clear to the Nationalists – their attack on me had been noted. Would they heed my message to them?

The Nationalists had long memories. During February, I asked the Minister of Justice questions about informers at universities. The Minister refused to reply, saying he would not satisfy my curiosity as to whether the police were using informers to report on the activities at certain universities. Cope had raised the question of the "spies" in the Justice Vote and the Nats were now using this as the vehicle to harm me politically.

The Cape Town newspapers were full of reports the next day. *The Cape Times* headline read: "Pile Into Them – Swart – And The Dirty Day Begins". The *Cape Argus* headlined: "The Push and Tackle Justice Vote". There were columns of verbatim reports of the Justice Vote, but in "Notes in the House" written by "Adderley" (*The Cape Times* parliamentary correspondent Antony Delius) the scenes in Parliament were graphically described.

"Pile into them, fellows," said Mr Swart, Leader of the House and Minister of Justice, "and the day became one of the nastiest seen in parliament for a long time."

Delius went on: "Slightly built Dr Boris Wilson, who had made some particularly wounding remarks about government policy, was the particular target of the Nationalist hatchet-men. Corpulent Mr Abraham of Groblersdal was practically pounding his chest with challenge even before the the wild accusations began to fleck his lips against Dr Wilson. Dr Wilson had addressed the African National Congress on behalf of the United Party, he roared."

" 'That's a downright lie,' said Dr Wilson with equal gusto.

"Mr Abraham stood there ducking and weaving like like an eager heavyweight sent to his corner. Yells and counter shouts, interjections and imprecations flew as Dr Wilson was ordered to withdraw the word 'lie'. Reluctantly the member for Hospital substituted the words 'tissue of untruths'."

Delius went on to describe the rest of the Justice Vote and an interjection by Harry Lawrence which I did not hear: "Just a campaign of vituperation – a disgraceful attempt to cloud the issue of mishandling of Justice by the Minister."

After Schoonbee called me a "ducktail", Lawrence called Schoonbee a thug. Delius noted that nobody was terribly surprised when Schoonbee said he was proud of the *herrenvolk* [superior race] idea, "because we have a *herrenvolk* idea we are a white nation."

I was so involved in the debate that many of the interjections were not heard by me, nor reported in *Hansard*. The press, above the Speaker's Throne had acute ears for verbal exchanges in the House. I was used to the Nationalists attacking me in the City and Provincial Council chambers. But this was a pre-planned attack involving the Minister of Justice. This was serious. I did not like it and decided to be doubly alert.

Who was behind it? I could not believe that Prime Minister Hendrik Verwoerd would approve of the bizarre events in the Justice Vote, yet his Minister of Justice was part of the scenario. Nat MPs like Piet van Vuuren had attacked me in the Transvaal with taunts of "Vundla" which I had ignored. I was sure that Van Vuuren had primed Abraham and Schoonbee. It was important for the Nationalists to succeed in their attempts to name me as a Communist follower, a man who had changed his name and who had been behind the Iron Curtain, because they knew the effect it would have on the United Party leadership in Parliament. In addition, they could have me removed from Parliament on this ground.

It was a strange kind of political life in the UP. Nothing was said to me about the concerted attacks made by the Nationalists despite press publicity all over the country. The UP leadership pretended it never occurred. It was not raised in Caucus.

The Nationalists in the lobby treated me as usual, with a smile and an occasional chat as if nothing had happened. The storm had abated. I seemed to be the only one waiting for the next moves on the parliamentary chessboard.

The attacks that were made on me by Abraham and Schoonbee were all made in Afrikaans. I replied in English. The Minister of Justice spoke in Afrikaans. Our Whips mostly spoke in English. Harry Lawrence, John Cope and Percy Plewman spoke English. Our Caucus meetings were all held in English. Nationalist Caucus meetings were held in Afrikaans. The Speaker read prayers one day in Afrikaans, the next day in English. The Order Papers were published in both languages, so were Bills and *Hansard*.

Unfortunately for all of us, because of the policy of equality of the official languages but separated single-medium language schools, it was not possible to find many politicians who were fluent in both languages.

I began to worry about this. If we could not fully speak each other's languages how on earth could we ever understand each other's arguments and problems?

The status of our all-white Parliament was another incongruous situation. It took decisions affecting blacks and coloureds, who had no direct representation in either House; it was at that time indirect, by a few white MPs and Senators. Indians had no representation direct or indirect. As far as blacks were concerned laws were debated as if blacks did not exist as human beings – just as part of the environment to be kept in their place. It was up to the Native Representatives, Margaret Ballinger, Walter Stanford and LB Lee-Warden to do their best to make the news known to hundreds of thousands of blacks in the rural areas who had no direct contact with the government. This was the same for the coloureds, although their numbers were smaller. Indians were out in the cold.

I used to sit on my back-bench wondering at the astonishing number of Bills put before Parliament affecting the lives of blacks, about which they knew nothing. To most MPs this was normal.

My experience at Johannesburg's Non-European Affairs Department taught me that the only way of co-operating with blacks was to consult directly with them as equals at all levels. The Council's relations with their Native Advisory Boards improved instantly once black leaders in the townships realised I would talk to them face to face. There was no such thing in the white Parliament, nor in central government. Smuts was the last Prime Minister who had consultations with the Native Representative Council which the Nationalists promptly abolished on coming to power in 1948.

The atmosphere in Parliament, especially after the attack on me in the Justice Vote, was brittle. There was no doubt that the advent of Hendrik Verwoerd, the protector of white civilisation and the separator of the races, had encouraged the Nationalists in Parliament to wage an all-out war against liberal MPs like me, linking us with subversive black left wing political groups.

At every opportunity, the United Party was accused of racial integration, although its Native policies in many respects were hardly different from the Nationalists' in terms of segregation.

The UP's 1954 Native Policy which the Propaganda Committee were reviewing spoke of consultation with Natives and offered them limited representation in the white Parliament and Senate through whites. It vaguely hinted at local and community level black control. The UP's Senate Plan on which we went to the country in 1958 spoke of "checks and balances". It was all tentative, and almost furtive, but such was white fear of eventual black domination that passions roused in Parliament often led to threats, intimidation and bitter hatred between Nats and the UP.

In the United Party we were not encouraged to meet Natives; it was virtually impossible to have a black man to lunch, or to listen in the public galleries. If one was seen with blacks, one could expect Special Branch activity. Even organisations like the South African Institute of Race Relations, of which I was a council member, had few blacks on it, whose status amongst their people was very low.

In the UP we had no committees or internal organisations monitoring black-white relations, so that our ideas in the party were all theoretical, dictated by the 1954 policy.

All in all, in the late 1950s, associating with "Natives" was a risky business. I am certain that the movements of the Native Representatives amongst their widely spread electorate were closely watched by government security. From my knowledge gained in the black townships of Johannesburg, I knew that the government was recruiting black informers to report not only on underground black organisations, but on whites who associated with blacks. There were a few other MPs in Parliament who were experts in black-white relations – they were constantly harassed in the House by the Nationalists and had similar experiences in their work in the constituencies – Ray Swart, Helen Suzman, John Cope and Douglas Smit. We were all called *kaffer boeties* by the Nationalists, and even by some of our colleagues, if we showed special interest in the welfare of blacks.

This was a cross we liberal MPs bore with fortitude in the 1950s. Life for opposition MPs who were seriously concerned about race relations was like riding in a small boat in turbulent seas. Many things we did were risky,

Dr HF Verwoerd, the Prime Minister (R), Eric Louw, Foreign Minister (Centre) and
SA ambassador to the Court of St James, Hilgard Muller (L), at Lancaster House,
London, after South Africa left the British Commonwealth.

Helen Suzman and BW at the election victory of 1974.

Progressive Party founder members at the 1975 Conference. (L to R) Zach de Beer,
BW, Colin Eglin, Sakkies Fourie, Ray Swart.

because we knew that we were constantly watched by the Security Police. We never knew when we were in the company of an informer or not. Often suspicions were confirmed because the Nationalists would give themselves away, as Van Vuuren did when he called me "Vundla" in open Council, indicating that the Nats knew when I had visited the Native leader's home.

The Nationalists in the House never varied their approach. They constantly linked efforts at open consultation, which I regarded as normal for members of Parliament, with organisations like the ANC, which they had driven underground, creating the impression that we were firmly part of subversion.

In my case they were going all out, lying and creating connections that never existed. Nationalist strategy was straightforward; attack everyone who publicly criticises or opposes apartheid, smear them, intimidate them and, if necessary, ban them. Since 1948 they had been ruthless. Leading churchmen suffered most of all. Fr Trevor Huddleston, who opposed the Western Areas Removal Scheme, and Bishop Reeves, were both forced to leave South Africa. Every thing they did was under the shadow of the Special Branch. They were openly vilified as "subversives".

The average white South African believed that there was a widespread plot by left wingers from Moscow to Peking, from the banned SA Communist Party to the African National Congress, and that anyone who dared speak against the implementation of apartheid was an ally of the "Red" onslaught on white South Africa.

Dr Verwoerd was a master at creating fear amongst the whites. He had a firm base for his political plans. Afrikaners had a long history in South Africa, as did English-speakers, of sustaining the master-servant relationship. Most whites wanted their protected and (comparatively) affluent white society to survive. As Verwoerd's plans for "control" and "separation" unfolded, the scared, indifferent white voter, UP or NP, gave support openly or clandestinely to "grand apartheid". All whites relied on this philosophy which provided cheap labour, the security of job reservation, separate white residential areas, segregated schools, trains, buses, universities, post offices and exclusively white seaside beaches.

This was a powerful political platform. The UP, most of whose supporters in the platteland and urban areas had the same fears and prejudices as the Nats, were no match for Nationalist propaganda. They could not find an alternative to apartheid.

The "Senate Plan" was one of the UP's abortive attempts to find a solution in terms of "white leadership with justice". It fell on stony ground. South Africans knew that, historically, whites were only safe because of apartheid. Blacks, coloureds and Indians were never to be involved in the white man's politics – they were never to be consulted. Non-whites had to bear the penalties of apartheid as the voteless, the carriers of passes and permits, acknowledging that whites were superior, masters.

This was the background to the introduction of the "Bantustan Bill" by the government, the most important legislation that would implement segregation on a scale never before dreamt of in South Africa.

For this debate the House was full, the public galleries crowded, when the Minister of Bantu Administration lifted his cumbersome frame, and with the vociferous support of his MPs, introduced the Second Reading of the Promotion of Bantu Self-Government Bill.

For two hours he explained the Nat view of black-white relations, while Dr Verwoerd sat smiling benignly on his front-bench.

Supported by occasional *"hoor hoors"* from his benches, he wound up his laborious arguments by saying that "everywhere the Bantu have acclaimed this as a new day and a new era has dawned for the Bantu of South Africa . . . It creates a future of hope, and expectation for all the population groups for South Africa, a future of peace and security not only for the white population of South Africa but also for the Bantu population groups. Now every group will know in what direction it is moving. It removes the mist of doubt and uncertainty which are the greatest cause of mistrust of the white man. Those mists and doubt and uncertainty have now disappeared. Everyone will know in which direction he is heading and it is that certainty which gives man his greatest satisfaction."

I sat on my back-bench marvelling at the euphoria of the Nationalist leaders who believed they had found the formula for black and white peace in Southern Africa, while the rest of the four hundred million of Africa's peoples were busy breaking, or had already broken, their colonial links with the whites who had dominated them for so many years.

De Wet Nel, the Minister, told the House the only opposition he had to his Bill he saw as he entered Parliament – he had to pass a silent group of Black Sash women holding posters which read: "No taxation without representation". His earlier contacts with Native Chiefs and black leaders revealed full support for him.

To our cheers, De Villiers Graaff rose to oppose the Bill, moving his amendment, which cut through the "misty" camouflages of De Wet Nel's oration. The first two clauses read:

"The House declines to pass the Second reading because, *inter alia*, it aims at the division of South Africa into black states, and a multiracial state, and, if implemented will involve great dangers for South Africa." This Bill "is repugnant to principles of natural justice in that it removes long-standing rights without giving anything of substance in return and leaves the Native population without any voice in Parliament which governs them . . . and will leave millions of Natives permanently settled outside the reserves without any means of political expression whatsoever."

Graaff's case demonstrated the illogicality of the Nationalist grand apartheid strategy, pointing out that they were not following the advice of their own Tomlinson Commission, which highlighted the demographic problems of scattered communities and consolidation of black areas. The weakness of his case was that he relied on the 1954 Native Policy "that seeks above all the maintenance and the continued existence of South Africa as a united land in which the people of all races can build together harmoniously and in peace . . . Hon Members opposite are prepared to fragment South Africa . . . we believe that in the Union the present leadership of the white

312

race must be maintained . . . the white race is the bearer of Western Civilisation."

One of the fallacious ideas of the UP leadership was that if they kept repeating "white leadership" and "western civilisation" for long enough, it would penetrate the Nationalist mind that the UP had an alternative policy to apartheid. But it did not wash with Afrikaner nationalists. They wanted proof that white security would not be endangered and no powersharing with Natives would take place.

Powersharing lead to integration; integration meant the end of white rule and security. To hear Graaff repeating phrases about "white leadership" and "western civilisation" in Parliament, simply underlined the fact that the Official Opposition did not understand the mentality of the average Nationalist voter. Douglas Smit, former Secretary of Native Affairs, followed Graaff and succinctly put it this way:

"People spoke of a native problem but in reality it was a European [white] problem. Hon Members are called upon by the government to deprive 9 500 000 of its underprivileged subjects . . . to whom we stand in the position of guardian of the meagre representation they have in Parliament – three in the House of Assembly out of 163 members, and four in the Senate of 90 members."

The most impressive speech was made by Margaret Ballinger, who was to lose her seat as the Leader of the Native Representatives. In her clear, incisive Scottish voice, she slated the Nationalists for their sophistry:

"This Bill is the culmination of a process of destruction which was initiated in this country by the present Prime Minister and has gathered momentum since his accession to power as Minister of Native Affairs – destruction of all that was built up over the last hundred years in the field of political organisation and development."

Her amendment opposed the Bill because "it seeks to lay the foundation of a political separation which will deprive the African population of all say in the government of the country to which it belongs and to which it forms an essential part . . . it is being introduced without consultation and against the wishes of the African population whose future it wishes to shape . . . it will reduce the African population to a complete subject race."

Amongst other points, she criticised the government for its failure to implement the 1936 Land Act, which promised to increase the amount of land available to Africans. Finally, she flailed Verwoerd on his ideas of democracy:

"The Prime Minister has no place in his philosophy for an Opposition at all. The place for an opposition in this philosophy is – out!"

It was a speech that history will applaud. The Nationalists tried to distract her. Verwoerd sat motionless in his front-bench studying her, as she told him:

"I am quite certain that the task imposed on us, unworthy as we are, is to prove to the world that the democratic principle can be made to work in a multiracial society, that people can be taught to live together respecting one another, people of different race and of different colour; that they can be taught and can learn to live together in peace and harmony in one country. That is my firm conviction, my profound belief. That is the foundation on which I have conducted my whole political life."

For three days the Bantustan debate dominated Parliament.

Eventually the Minister closed the Second Reading in a state of euphoria: "Mr Speaker, it is my deep and sacred conviction that we stand before a choice today, one of the greatest decisions South Africa has had to make, a decision for which South Africa has been criticised, threatened and belittled, but in the end has proved to be the only salvation for South Africa . . .

"We are being criticised in many circles – there is no doubt about that – but in the depths of my heart I am convinced that the day will arrive when the people of South Africa will look back with gratitude to 20 May 1959 as one of the great days when the right choice was made in the interests of South Africa."

As we waited for the fateful vote to be taken, I had enough time to think about De Wet Nel's last words. I was certain that one day South Africa would "look back", not with "gratitude" but with horror at the final decision taken on that day in May 1959 by Dr Verwoerd's Nationalist government to dismember South Africa and create years of discord and unhappiness for whites and blacks.

The Nationalists had applied a guillotine to this Bill, which we strenuously fought in April. Dr Verwoerd was not interested in allowing the Official Opposition more time than he thought was necessary to maintain a semblance of democratic debate. We had limited time in which to fight this and three other important Bills.

During the Committee Stage of the Bantustan Bill which followed, the important Clause 15 was debated which proposed that the Native Representatives should be abolished. That meant that Margaret Ballinger and her colleagues would leave Parliament for ever after Graaff had spoken. When the Minister of Bantu Administration rose to reply, Harry Lawrence immediately objected.

Mr Lawrence: "No, no, no! I object to the Minister talking again. Our time is limited." (Interjections).

The Chairman: "Will the Hon Member resume his seat?"

Mr Lawrence: "If you allow the Minister to talk . . ."

Mr Moore: "I appeal to the Hon Minister to speak after the guillotine."

Mr Lawrence: "I think it is most unfair. Why cannot the Minister talk later?"

The Chairman: "Will the Hon Member resume his seat?"

Mr Lawrence: "No sir, you can do what you like with me. I am making a protest. What do you wish me to do, sir?"

Harry Lawrence, amidst cheers from us, catcalls from the Nats and a puzzled De Wet Nel, stood in his seat, defying the Chairman.

The House was in uproar, its collective blood pressure rising.

The Chairman: "The Hon Member must withdraw from the House for the remainder of the day's sitting."

Harry Lawrence, straightening himself up, very loudly replied:
"Yes sir, I will leave the Chamber."

Gathering his papers, Lawrence walked down the aisle and left the House. Both sides were suffering from tension. The week had been emotional and heated. De Wet Nel did speak again, but before he ended, another UP MP was sent out of the House by the Speaker.

The guillotine was then applied. By 72 votes to 43 the Native Representatives, who had been in Parliament since 1936, were voted out for ever. Verwoerd had won a major victory.

The next day, the House went into Committee on the Interior Vote. Since 1956, the government had issued 27 Proclamations banning books, all of which I had carefully studied. There was no doubt that political censorship was their motive. Parliament was the place to get at the facts. The press and the public needed to know what was happening. I regarded it as part and parcel of South Africa's drift into authoritarianism under Verwoerd.

I accused the government of using "strangling political censorship over political works and opinions not in accordance with the Government's views. Why were *Passive Resistance in SA*, by Leo Kuper, *The Colour Problem* by A Richmond and *Gestation* by Edward Crankshaw banned? Novels by Erskine Caldwell, James Farrel, Elmer Rice, DH Lawrence, Albert Moravia and John dos Passos were banned. Many South African novels breaching the colour line were prohibited. Books on religious subjects including Bertrand Russell's *Why I am not a Christian* and books from Russia by Tolstoy, Gorky, Turgenev and Dostoevsky were banned. Since 1956, 2 678 books had been banned.

Where was it going to end? In charge of the Interior Vote was the newly-appointed Deputy Minister who was making copious notes. He was a former organiser of the Nationalist Party in the Cape, a very aggressive younger MP on the Nationalist cross-benches.

His name was PW Botha.

I told him that the government was carrying out "careful political censorship, interfering with the freedom of the conscience of the people, the freedom to read and learn, to study other political systems, colour questions and race relations . . . the government is invading the civil liberties of the people with deliberate intent . . . if you ban the reading material of the people and by negative means you indoctrinate them, you can extend any political power."

PW Botha replied to me immediately accusing me of making "irresponsible statements". He denied the Government wanted to interfere with religious freedom but said that "as far as Communistic works are concerned this Parliament put an Act on the Statute Book . . . The Government, representing the National Party stands for freedom of conscience and religious freedom."

He then made the astonishing statement that only certain soft cover books I had mentioned were banned, not the hardcover versions, because "we feel that the hardcover book which is sold at a high price is read in circles

315

and spheres where they cannot do any harm . . ."

It was a remarkable revelation, showing that the Nationalists were permitting whites to read certain books, but non-whites who could only afford the cheaper books, were prohibited from buying them. (A good example of the fatuous ideas of the government at that time).

Botha then came to the real nub of the Government's policy: "He [Dr Wilson] mentioned books which definitely advocate intermingling between whites and non-whites . . . does he want us to allow these books to enter South Africa which attack the historic and traditional policy that has been followed in South Africa?"

In reply, I told Botha that he had confirmed my allegations that there was political censorship of books in South Africa. From what he had revealed, there was no doubt that one of the greatest democratic freedoms in South Africa was rapidly being eroded.

It may be significant that I was the only MP to speak in this debate. PW Botha was carefully trying to make his mark as a responsible Deputy Minister. Despite the fact that he said I was "irresponsible", which was now the stock-in-trade NP response to me, he spent considerable time dealing with my arguments. The newspapers gave good coverage – but that was the end of the story. It faded into the depths of *Hansard* and history.

The 1959 session was nearing its end. Tempers were short. Minister's Votes still remained, with Bantu Administration expected to be acrimonious. Most important of all, however, were the problems that were being experienced in the United Party Caucus.

Bitter differences on policy were emerging between liberals and conservatives. The newspapers were intensifying their coverage of Caucus meetings. Leaks were rife. Rumour-mongering was mounting. One story consistently repeated that Natal MPs were behind an attempt to rid the UP of its liberal elements at the next Congress in August. This emerged from the party grapevine and the Afrikaans press. It became increasingly obvious, as the session progressed, that liberal MPs' relations with Douglas Mitchell and some of his MPs from Natal were on a knife-edge, but there was no hard evidence that a "putsch" was in the offing. The fact that three of us were forced to put in the minority report on the Propaganda Committee no doubt sent sharp signals to leading right wingers on the Committee who surrounded Graaff. We knew that pressure from them was mounting. He was walking a minefield. The Propaganda Committee was unexpectedly dissolved. The minority report that Cope, De Beer and I had drawn up may well have been the catalyst for a crisis in Caucus. We were forced into the open because of the attacks on us by MPs like Douglas Mitchell. There was a realisation in Caucus that, although we were not an organised group, our influence on Graaff for reform was important.

In this respect, Zach de Beer played a key role. He told me that his friendship with Graaff helped him to convert Graaff to progressive policies. Graaff was forced to "eggdance" far too often, caught in the middle between right and left, with the Nationalists casting an enormous shadow over him.

We hoped that our views on the Propaganda Committee would give Graaff the courage to introduce more realistic liberal changes to the crucial issues affecting white-black relations in South Africa.

The Congress in August at Bloemfontein would have before it issues relating to more land for Natives, political rights and the 1954 Native Policy, which were all expected to cause great friction.

Graaff's position had become unenviable. Overall, he never veered from set UP policy, but it was clear that it was the right wingers who were calling his shots. His arguments were too often couched in language that made us squirm, clichés like the well-worn "western civilisation", "white supremacy with justice", "the traditions of Smuts and Botha"; all to satisfy his conservative platteland and urban supporters.

The Nationalists persisted in charging that our Native Policy would lead to political integration. In the Justice Vote they had hoped to split the UP Caucus, egged on by their own newspapers with the English press revelling in the Caucus leaks.

In Parliament the UP tried to show it spoke with one voice. Differences between us in Caucus were not allowed to get to ignition point in the House. Graaff did not want to preside over a party that was breaking up. In his favour, he made attempts to placate right and left in the Caucus.

The basic problem was that the majority of Caucus was dissatisfied with the 1954 Native Policy. The conservatives said it went too far – Native political advancement should stop at local authorities. They did not want more money spent on acquiring land to fulfill the 1936 Land Act promises. They openly called for policies that would seduce NP voters back to the UP and so to regain power.

As liberals we condemned this strategy. We wanted the reverse: Native Representatives to be increased and Parliament to give better political rights to blacks. We insisted that 1936 Land Act promises to which the UP was committed should be fully implemented. We urged the UP to fight more openly and honestly for civil liberties which the government was eroding. We opposed the restrictive legislation that the Nationalists were putting on the Statutes, mostly under the guise of anti-communism, which not only went down well with Nationalist voters but most of the whites in South Africa.

Anything anti-communist was a vote winner; it was in the same league as *swart gevaar*, and Verwoerd knew how to make the best of these tactics. Under this Red umbrella the Nationalists were able to interfere with fundamental rights and freedoms, because in the late 1950s the overwhelming number of white voters believed Communism was the greatest enemy, and whatever the Nationalists did to eradicate it they applauded.

It was easy for Verwoerd to trade on their fears. His political career was based on exploiting white fears, and his authoritarian beliefs made it easy for him to convince Afrikaner voters that his draconian legislation was essential. So they gave the fullest support to apartheid legislation in order that blacks should be controlled by whites in perpetuity. White domination and white security was to be protected at all costs. Most whites in South Africa accepted the poverty level of the Natives as normal and consistent with their "primitive civilisation".

It was part of increasingly believed doctrine of the absolute rights of whites and found its confirmation in the growing affluence of white society.

As liberals we had two fronts – one in the Caucus against our own right wingers, and the other in open Parliament fighting against the Government's inroads into civil liberties. This constant Caucus infighting seeped through to the press, with the result that parliamentary reporters were predicting an early split in the UP Caucus.

The 1953 group of urban liberals like Helen Suzman, John Cope and Ray Swart were already in the forefront of the struggle to protect civil liberties and represent the rights of non-whites.

In 1959 in Parliament, apart from the Native Representatives (soon to go), there was only one liberally inclined Afrikaner MP from a rural area. This was Jan Steytler from the Eastern Cape, a staunch member of the UP who became the Cape leader of the party.

He was a well-built man, a farmer and a medical practitioner. Emotional, he was a speaker whose rhetoric could easily sway people, and he had the advantage that he had been nurtured in a family who were in the forefront of the Afrikaner's struggles.

53

What had happened to all the great plans for reforming the UP from the inside that I thought possible? What had I achieved in six years since I joined the UP? The slum clearance in the townships, cheap housing, new clinics and opposing Verwoerd's apartheid policies and forced removals. I had done so in the face of the reluctant UP in Johannesburg's Council. However, the reality of the UP in Parliament was a rude shock. It did not want apartheid changed. It wanted it retained, hoping to manage it in what it believed was a more humane way on the road back to power in South Africa. Unfortunately, it was no match for the NP tacticians who outmanoeuvred the UP at every turn.

Nationalists knew the UP would be glad to shed its liberal minority, and they continued to attack us in order to embarrass the Party. We were fortified by several giants of the English press, notably *The Rand Daily Mail*'s Laurence Gandar who, both in his editorials and under the pseudonym "Owen Vine" wrote trenchant articles urging Graaff to show real opposition to Verwoerd's apartheid.

Regrettably, Graaff was a prevaricator. Speaking to sophisticated urban UP supporters, he used the "liberal" language they liked to hear. In the platteland he was equally at home assuring voters that he was the guardian of their white security and privilege.

I realised, as the session drew to a close, that the Nationalists fully understood the dichotomous nature of Graaff's politics. He was a prisoner of his right wing majority. The more apartheid legislation was introduced, the more internal strains it created. The UP right wingers demanded conciliatory opposition as opposed to our demands for confrontation. As a result, the UP was moving more to the right and not the left.

The Prime Minister's Vote brought Verwoerd into the debate three times. He rebutted Graaff's arguments, accusing him of supporting discrimination in the 1954 Native Policy of the party. He told us that Natives, coloureds and Indians wanted equality, and not the qualified representation the UP offered them under its "white leadership" policy. He said that Graaff, together with his conservatives, had "for the moment evidently triumphed over the liberal section of the party."

Graaff was stunned. Verwoerd spoke as if he had been a constant eavesdropper on our Caucus meetings.

"Everyone sitting here on both sides of the House, knows how all the newspapers which support him in South Africa – I think I am correct in saying all the newspapers – have told him that he must once and for all submit a clear policy, and what is more a policy which is not in part a copy of the National Party's policy, but a policy which will not provide for any form of discrimination but will be a liberal policy accepting total integration in the economic and political spheres . . . The demand is consistently being made that he should once and for all gather together his courage and adopt a policy directly contrary to that of the National Party . . . not some sort integration mixture accompanied by segregation, but total integration."

I do not recall what some of my liberal colleagues thought of Verwoerd's analysis, but it was to the point. His final injunction to Graaff was a warning:

"Unless he changes his attitude he will now have these newspapers opposing him . . . The public and the voters of South Africa have taken note of everything these papers have published; they have also taken note of the statements made on occasion by many of the United Party representatives in this House –such as the Hon Member for Parktown [Mr Cope], and they have taken note of the statements made by the Hon Member for Hospital [Dr Wilson] and other members who speak as liberals. The entire nation has taken note of the attitude adopted by the whole liberalistic group, including the Hon Member for Zululand [Mr RAF Swart] . . . We have no illusions as to the nature of the struggle taking place within the United Party . . ."

It was a brilliant and timely attack by Verwoerd which must have sent shivers down the spines of Graaff and the UP right wingers. It showed that Hendrik Verwoerd not only dictated where South Africa was going, but he was almost the master of the fate of the Official Opposition in Parliament. He knew that by using the "liberalistic group" as the political stick with which to frighten and whip the UP, he would drive them more and more into internal conflict in the party.

I was no longer surprised that he had cited me as one of the liberal leaders in the Caucus, but I realised that he was using me as a weapon to force the UP conservatives to the edge of the precipice. The increasingly aggressive nature of the attacks on me during the session now seemed to make sense, and Verwoerd was confirming that he was part of this strategy. I was certain, from Verwoerd's remarks about me, that I would hear more before the 1959 session concluded.

Native Affairs was still going to dominate the rest of the session. The Vote of the Minister of Bantu Affairs was pending and Ray Swart, Helen Suzman and I had several important matters to raise in the House. Above all, we were concerned about the 1936 Land Act and the promises that had been made to provide more land for the Reserves, to which the United Party had subscribed. The Nationalists were using it to further apartheid and the Bantustans, causing conflict in our ranks. When the Minister of Bantu Affairs told us that he wanted to provide more land for Natives in the Eastern Cape, Miles Warren the UP parliamentarian for the area, objected because additional land would have to come from white farmers in his constituency.

Conservatives like Douglas Mitchell, Vause Raw and Sannie van Niekerk of Natal rushed to support him. Despite the rifts in Caucus, Warren was allowed to object in the House.

One of the leading Nationalists complained that he "did not know what the Hon Member [Miles Warren] wants. If I understand him correctly he wants the Minister not to give the Natives more land . . . It seems to me that together with certain of his colleagues he has gone on strike against the 1936 legislation."

Warren's speech could have been made by a Nationalist. It was typical of the real attitudes of the UP's conservatives from the white farming areas, and once again reflected in the House the nature of the struggles in the United Party Caucus.

In the Bantu Administration Vote, Ray Swart asked the Minister the reasons why ex-Chief Luthuli, the African National Congress leader, had been banned. Was it, he asked, because Luthuli had dared to criticise the government, or because he believed in a multiracial society in the future?

Swart was interrupted by the Nationalist's Chief Whip with the remark: "You are winning elections for the National Party." In a heated exchange, the Whip told Swart:" That is a criminal speech you have made." Blaar Coetzee followed, saying that " if the Minister has made a mistake he waited too long to ban Luthuli. He is one of the worst and communistic agitators in this country."

We could see from the virulence of the attack on Swart that this debate on Bantu Administration was going to be lead by the NP's toughest parliamentary shock troops. They regularly reduced, by snide remarks and taunts, any serious attempt by opposition MPs to elicit information, implying that we were in league with communists and agitators.

No one on the Opposition benches was safe from what one of the gallery correspondents called the Nationalist "bully boys".

Gray Hughes, a UP deputy Whip and member for the Transkeian Territories, asked the Minister to clarify what the government euphemistically called the "farm labour", scheme about which disturbing reports were beginning to appear in the newspapers.

There had been court cases in the Eastern Transvaal where some white farmers had been sent to prison for ill-treating their farm labourers. The farm labour scheme had been introduced by the Government, the Minister explained, to avoid sending Natives to prison for Influx Control and Pass Law offences. Instead they could do their sentences under supposedly controlled conditions on farms in the Bethal and Ermelo areas of the eastern Transvaal.

It was evident that the scheme had got out of hand. Natives were being coerced to the farms, either under threat by the police, or were not given the option of paying a fine. Men disappeared for months on end.

Conditions on the farms were bad. Workers were ill-treated by the farmers and their employees and Bantu Affairs had lost control of the scheme. The Minister tried to excuse what was occurring by saying that "every month Natives come to town to seek work, while it is difficult for them to earn a living elsewhere . . . If we allowed this we would once again be creating conditions of squatting, theft, murder and so on which we have experienced in the past . . . Natives in the towns complain their work is being taken away from them by people who are coming in from outside . . .

"We had two or three aims in mind in introducing this system. First to treat these people in such a way that they did not go to prison, that they would rather be guided to employment . . . secondly that squatting did not take place . . . thirdly to protect the urban Native who might lose his job. The average number of Natives who have been entering the towns is between 3 000 and 4 000 per month . . . it was far better that they spent the night in a cell and to be taken to employment on the following day . . . of 25 000 who came before the officials, 4 000 elected to go to the farms on the platteland . . . the farmers treated them very well . . . but I do admit there were a few cases where the farmers treated their Natives badly . . .

"I do want to say tonight of the 115 000 farmers in South Africa there are only four or six who can be quoted as examples of farmers who treat their Natives badly . . . on that basis a campaign of vilification has been launched . . . here I once again wish to mention the English press and also certain spiritual leaders and the Black Sash . . .all the Black Sash is doing is to besmirch South Africa . . . the United Party is giving support to the campaign of vilification of the farmers . . . I have decided to appoint an inter-departmental committee to enquire into the whole matter for the sake of the good name of the farmers . . ."

The repudiation by the Minister was clear evidence that the Nationalists were concerned about the newspaper disclosures which had appeared for some months about the behaviour of the farmers. The Black Sash, church leaders and the English press were upsetting the Nationalists because the government's main support in the platteland was from the farmers. We suspected that the Minister wanted to whitewash matters with his inter-

321

departmental committee. A lawyer, Joel Carlson, was repeatedly reported in the press as the expert in court proceedings over farm labour scandals.

Carlson telephoned, asking to see me. He told me of the seriousness of the allegations, which were widespread. In his possession were many affidavits from Native men who had been on the farms, some of which had already been used in court cases. I asked him if I could use them in Parliament. He said that that was why he called me. He had already spoken to Helen Suzman, and she intended to raise the whole issue in the House.

I said I would speak to Helen and co-operate with her.

The extra-Parliamentary attack on the farming community drew in platteland MPs from both sides of the House to reject the allegations. The UP put its MPs from platteland constituencies into the debate, emphasising that it was not attacking all farmers, wanting to keep its image clean.

The Nationalists were not to be outdone. They saw the debate as a golden opportunity to hammer the UP on its attitude to the ANC, Luthuli's banning, the 1936 Land Act and its ambivalent attitude to apartheid, with the object of diverting attention from the farming community. It developed into a major debate on the policies of the UP not the NP, whose Chief Whip, JE Potgieter, summarised his party's attitude:

" . . . It is quite clear to me that the liberal wing has triumphed today . . . There is not a party which has acted in more politically criminal way than that party [the UP] has acted today . . . Slowly but surely the United Party is deteriorating into being the political front for the leftists in South Africa. That is why they put the crown on the head of Luthuli. There is a conflict in that party. The left wing was in full action, and what is their aim? It is to incite hatred against the farmer, and to incite the Bantu against the white man."

As the UP appeared to be sinking deeper into the political mire, its conservative members entered into the debate to convince the NP and the white electorate, that the Party opposed Luthuli's views, the views of the Liberal Party, and plans of the Nationalists vis-à-vis the Bantustans. It had been pushed into a corner by the NP who savoured the UP's embarrassments it tried to distance itself from Luthuli and the Liberals.

The NP gave the UP little respite on this Vote. At every opportunity we were accused of being fellow-travellers with Luthuli and vilifiers of the farmers of South Africa. All the ingredients were there for a major attack by the UP on Verwoerd's policy of shunting Natives back to the rural areas by whatever means possible, to give cheap labour to farmers which was the basis of the scandal. The UP was outwitted. It found itself in the dock – the NP had neatly turned the tables – and lost the initiative.

What did emerge, which was not denied by the UP, was the charge made by MJ van den Berg, a NP front-bencher, that "Miles Warren did not want the Minister to implement the obligations resting on the Government as the result of the 1936 legislation . . . They [the UP] want to go to the country and say that this Government wants to buy up all the land and give it to the Bantu . . . In regard to the implementation of the 1936 legislation

Hon Members opposite are divided into at least three groups. There is only one factor that binds them together – that is the Luthuli factor."

The only way the UP could reply was to call on its right wingers like Vause Raw to proclaim: "The United Party is opposed totally and unequivocally to the views of equality advocated by Chief Luthuli. The United Party is equally opposed to the views put forward by members of the Liberal Party who sit in this House [the Native Representatives]. The United Party is totally opposed to the Bantustans."

It gave the UP conservatives the chance, in the face of the Nationalist attack, to distance themselves from UP liberals, who had hardly entered the debate, to express their anti-liberal views.

By the evening of 16 June, the scene had been set for further confrontation – the UP right wing, who had so far dominated the proceedings in reacting to the NP accusations, had revealed that some of them were prepared to ditch the 1936 Land Act commitments, which was what we had long suspected. This was a serious departure from party policy and could cause major difficulties for the parliamentary team. Graaff had not intervened in the debate to put the record straight, nor did he repudiate Miles Warren's remarks; nor, for that matter, some of the statements of other right wingers.

My confidence in the ability of Graaff to stand up to the right wing pressures on the 1936 Land Act was diminishing fast, and I regarded remarks by people around Graaff, who said the UP would carry out the Land Act provisions, as specious. The Nationalists had widened the cleavage in the UP since Ray Swart put his questions about Luthuli, adding fuel to the fires already fanned by the media.

On 17 June Helen Suzman criticised the farm labour scandal in relation to its causes: Pass Laws and Influx Control which brought Natives to the courts. She told the House:

"He [the Minister] does not know how the scheme is implemented or about the abuses and he should have appointed an impartial judicial commission. I want to make clear that in criticising the operation of this scheme I am not attacking the farmers as such or the labour tenant scheme . . . I will tell the Minister what I am attacking. I am attacking the system which lends itself to great abuse. I am attacking the farmers who committed the abuses.

"I am attacking the way the system has been implemented and the lack of supervision by the department."

Mentz, the Deputy Minister of Bantu Administration, replied to Helen. Mentz's main complaint was that Helen Suzman had no right to attack the farmers. Helen, on her feet a second time, continued to question Mentz, while the temperature in the House rose. Mentz accused Helen of being the "mouthpiece of the Black Sash in this House". Unmoved, she persisted in trying to establish how the farm labour scheme worked.

The root cause was the notorious Section 10 of the Urban Areas Act. Under this Act, any Native who was not born in an urban area or had lived there for at least ten years, could be arrested. Instead of sentencing him to prison, the farm labour plan was adopted with disastrous results, and farmers took advantage of it.

Mentz reiterated: "She is the mouthpiece of the Black Sash in the House," accusing the UP because "the mouthpiece of the Black Sash is the megaphone of the United Party . . . This campaign against the farmers is one of the biggest scandals that we have ever had in South Africa, and I deprecate it that a political party like the United Party, who after all have farmers who support them, associates itself so actively with this campaign."

Helen catalogued factual information about the abuses and where the scheme went wrong. She gave details of the sleeping quarters, reference books confiscated, how people were locked up at night as if in prison, bad rations and attacked the failure of government inspectors to do their jobs properly.

The fury of the debate continued with Mentz protesting again that a few cases of farmers being brought to the courts was insufficient reason for condemning the scheme.

When Mentz sat down I immediately challenged him. He had read selectively and only partially from the affidavits made in the court cases and omitted to tell the House that several of the presiding judges had criticised the officials, commenting that "irregularities have taken place in the operation of the scheme."

I read out the affidavits that Joel Carlson had given me, saying that "this Committee has not heard what has gone on with regard to forced labour . . . the affidavits show that in every single case these Africans who were apprehended were given no opportunity whatsoever to appeal to their families and they were not told there were alternatives . . ."

I wanted to know from Mentz: "Who gave the instructions to officials that they should tell individuals that there was one or two years at Baviaanspoort [a large and notorious prison] and not the £1 or £2 fine as the alternative?"

I supported this with quotations from the court affidavits confirming the fact that many Natives had been arrested, not by uniformed police, but by the plainclothes "Ghost Squad" in Johannesburg. These Ghost Squads consisted of teams of white and black police who suddenly appeared at the "Second Class" [black] bus stops in the Johannesburg suburbs, demanding passes from waiting Natives. If passes were not immediately produced, arrests were made, with appearances in court the following day. Sentencing was perfunctory and inevitable: immediate transfer to forced farm labour camps miles away.

Apart from some questions from the Minister and his Deputy, I was able to get on with the reading of some of the affidavits by Natives who had undergone the forced labour. I quoted the case of Daniel Mahloane from the court records:

"Do you know why you went to the farm, how you came to go to the farm? – The police forced us.

"Why? – He told us we had to go to the farm to get work, and if we did not we would be sent to Baviaanspoort."

324

My time expired before I could finish quoting from the affidavits so I was determined to speak again. The main complaint of the Nationalist Chief Whip, amidst increasing interjections from both sides, was that Helen and I were put up by the UP to attack farmers, and we were challenged to go to the platteland and make our speeches there.

The debate was becoming noisier, the atmosphere more tense and questions and challenges were come from all sides. Helen was told to take up farming for six months and that "the difficulties which farmers experience today have their origin in people like the Hon Members for Houghton and Hospital, people who know absolutely nothing about the Native." The UP was ridiculed for putting up two urban MPs to discuss farming problems. The NP was wide of the mark. If Helen and I had not been interested, I am certain the UP's farmer-MPs would have remained silent.

I managed to catch the Chairman's eye after the Chief Whip, and as soon as possible continued reading from the affidavits which I wanted recorded in *Hansard*, one of which was typical:

"The European foreman sometimes carried a *sjambok* [a large leather whip]. When the boys in the fields rested after they they had been continuously digging potatoes and bending over for a long time they would be beaten and told to work. The only rest we were allowed was at lunchtime."

"The Hon Minister knows about this affidavit . . . Is it true he is paying costs . . . and not fighting cases?" I asked.

I also quoted a trial judge's remarks: "It appeared to be common cause that when a Native was sent to a farm he was not given the opportunity to communicate with his family or his employer or even to fetch his clothes."

This was all damning evidence, but all the Minister did was to deny the allegations and stand by what he had said about our motives for raising the farm labour scandals.

Helen and I had made out a substantial case against the farm labour scandal. It was quite apparent from the NP's replies in the House that the Minister had been caught out, with the Nats desperately trying to diminish our charges, without success.

The plain facts were that Natives had been hijacked to farms by the police under instruction from the Minister of Bantu Administration's officials. One thing I could not pass was the Minister's criticism of the role of the English press:

Dr Wilson: "An attack has been made here on the English-language press. I want the Hon Minister to repeat or withdraw, but I think in all honesty he should withdraw this allegation."

The Minister of Bantu Administration: "I repeat everything."

Dr Wilson: "Well, it is a shameful thing that he should have attacked the press, which only came into the picture because of the court cases . . .until writs of habeas corpus were before the court."

The Minister: "They blamed the whole farming community."

Dr Wilson: "They never did anything of the sort, and I challenge the Minister to produce a press-cutting or a press report in which it is stated. In fact what the press did do was ask for a judicial commission of inquiry. And I am going to say this, if the Hon Minister does not appoint a judicial commission of inquiry he is a coward." [Interjections].

The jovial Minister of Bantu Administration, De Wet Nel, was surprised, and his expression seemed to ask: Do you really mean it?

The Chairman intervened immediately: "Order! Order! Will the Hon Member withdraw the word coward at once."

Dr Wilson: "I withdraw, Mr Chairman, and I will say he knows the only honorable thing is to appoint a judicial commission of inquiry."

This set off a tremendous uproar on both the NP and UP benches.

The Chairman was now having an altercation with one of the NP back-benchers, Kotze, who yelled at me: "You are a ducktail."

The Chairman: "Order! Order! Will the Hon Member withdraw?"

Mr Kotze: "I withdraw, Mr Chairman."

The uproar continued. It was very difficult to make out what MPs were shouting to each other. However, when the afternoon newspapers appeared, we realised that the Nationalists had created another diversion by attacking the Jews. Many interjections are not recorded by *Hansard*, and at the time we did not hear them.

I was followed by Herman Martins, a small, rotund, goatee-bearded farmer from Wakkerstroom in the Transvaal, reputedly an NP hatchet-man in the House. His opening statement astonished me.

Mr Martins: " . . . The Hon Member who has referred to the Minister's so-called cowardice should remember that we know of a certain Benjamin Woolfsohn who was an agent of Barlows and who was so scared to join the army that he became Boris Wilson." [Interjections].

Dr Wilson: "That is absolute nonsense."

I was thinking rapidly as Martins continued with the refrain that we were attacking farmers but he had introduced the first notes of racialism into the debate.

Mr Martins: " . . . But what does the Hon Member for Hospital do? He read out a number of sworn statements . . . He remained silent because he knew that the Jewish Board of Deputies had sent a message to their Rabbi the day before yesterday to the following effect: Don't get involved in this farm labour question; don't organise those people no longer to employ farm labour."

Dr Wilson: "Is that so?"

I could think of nothing else to say. It was absolute rubbish, but it was obvious he was now trying to make out that it was Jewish farmers who were solely responsible for the scandals.

Martins continued: "He remains silent because he knows that those six or seven farmers who are alleged to be guilty are not Afrikaans-speaking people."

Dr Wilson: " Are you anti-Semitic?"

Martins ignored this, but continued his attack. What was he really up to? Martins had let the cat out of the bag about my name.

I could not leave the House, to consider the importance of Martins's allegation, because the debate was at its height. Martins was venomous, drawing many MPs into the debate. It was incredible how the Nationalists had injected a "Red" scare into the farm labour scandals, linking us to Luthuli and the African National Congress. The Opposition was trapped once more into squandering most of its time discussing Luthuli instead of hammering the Nationalists about their farm labour scheme. Every NP speaker continued the refrain that Helen and I were put up by the UP to attack the farming community. The UP's right wing response only clouded the issue – they did not know what to do next.

The Nationalists repeatedly flung Luthuli, the African National Congress, the Black Sash and the Liberal Party at us. The UP's right wingers dutifully rushed in:

Vause Raw: " . . . this side of the House have made it absolutely clear that we do not have anything in common, that we are totally and unequivocally and implacably opposed to the policy advocated either by the African National Congress or by the Liberal Party . . . nobody on this side has supported the policy advocated either by Luthuli or by the Black Sash . . ."

The Minister of Bantu Administration finally wound up the debate, near the end of an exhausting day. His was a short speech, mostly devoted to Helen Suzman and Boris Wilson.

"I just want to point out once again that the whole morning has been taken by just two members of the United Party. The one was the Hon Member for Houghton, the other the Hon Member for Hospital. They have, in effect, dominated the the debate from beginning to end. They were the two main speakers and their attack dealt with the labour in the employ of our farmers. They have now come as the high priests who are to teach the farmers how they are to treat their labour. Where are the farmers of the United Party? . . . This will stand on record in future as one of the distasteful methods used by the United Party, that is to say, to allow its liberal wing to vilify the most noble section of our population . . . I repeat the United Party have made only two contributions. They have honoured Luthuli and they have vilified the farmers of South Africa."

The press, however, did not see it that way. For three days and over the weekend all newspapers, English and Afrikaans, headlined the debate with full pages. We learnt from their detailed reports that there had been an organised anti-Semitic outburst by the Nationalists in an unprecedented racial attack because Helen and I were Jewish. It was pure coincidence that we had investigated the farm labour scandals and obtained affidavits to expose it.

We were the only members of the UP Caucus who took the trouble.

The UP farmers in the House would never have done so because they did not want to be seen criticising their farming colleagues. The UP had to

327

support us, but were also completely caught up in the major counter-attack launched under the Nationalist smokescreen. The NP had been cornered too, so they took out their long intimidatory political knives and slashed in all directions, in the hope they would destroy their liberal opponents and expose the United Party's pretense. They might have succeeded but for the journalists in the Press Gallery who wrote graphic accounts of the day's events in the House.

Front-page banner headlines in *The Cape Times* the next day read:

"Anti-Semitic Outburst By Nat MPs" – "Two United Party MPs who launched a vigorous and well-documented attack on the farm labour scandal in the Assembly yesterday, were made the target of the most violent anti-Semitic outburst heard on the Nationalist benches since the war days. They were Mrs Helen Suzman and Dr Boris Wilson. They were told by Nationalist members, that being Jews, they should be the last people to criticise farmers for ill-treating their workers because of the number of Jewish farmers who had appeared in court in ill-treatment cases. JF Schoonbee (NP) in a highly emotional speech said: 'I just want to say that if I were today of Jewish descent I would be the last person to raise the matter in this House.' There were exclamations of the 'countrymen of Suzman and Wilson' when Schoonbee mentioned the names of four allegedly Jewish farmers."

The *Cape Argus* gallery correspondent wrote: "For passions rose to such an extent that everything normally murmured confidentially in voters' drawing-rooms was roared across the Chamber."

He added: "By the end of it all Mr Schoonbee was roaring in reply to Mrs Suzman's persistence: 'Go and preach in the synagogue'."

The Sunday Express headed its parliamentary report: "Nats Use Hate to Boost Morale".

"There is one new feature about the increasingly hostile and truculent attitude now being shown by the Nationalist members of Parliament towards the English-speaking Jewish and non-white citizens – they have never been so outspoken and unashamed before. It is an attempt to fuse the two great hatreds of the Nationalist Afrikaner into one grand sweeping passion . . . It was started by the Prime Minister himself.

"One wonders why the Nationalists are becoming so careless about concealing their real sources of inspiration any longer. But why should one conceal such minor peccadilloes when Dr Verwoerd is getting away with bannings, Bantustans and guillotines and all the rest of it?"

Stanley Uys, political commentator of the largest newspaper in the country, *The Sunday Times*, pulled no punches.

"Since January when Dr Verwoerd had his new vision of Bantustan, life has hardly been worth living for some Nationalist MPs. As propagandists of the new vision they had to revise their political vocabulary. Such fruity terms as *kafirs, coolies* and *Hotnots* [Hottentots, in this context a pejorative name for the coloured people], were replaced by more respectful ones like the 'Bantu must be given their freedom' and 'Bantu culture is a rich culture'. This week finally the muzzles were off and with whoops of delight that section of the Nationalist MPs who can best be described as the 'bully boys' went into action again. Who better to instruct us in the realities than the profound student of the Native mind, than Mr DJ Potgieter (Chief NP Whip).

" 'Did the opposition know,' asked Mr Potgieter, 'that the Native on the platteland is still virtually a barbarian?' "

Stanley Uys pointed out that the one redeeming feature of the debate was that, as in previous debates this session, "the more sensitive Nationalists sat silent or else beat it out of the Chamber leaving the field to the Schoonbees, the Martins, the Potgieters, the Fronemans and the Blaar Coetzees."

Uys ended: "Dr Wilson's hair-raising quotations from affidavits filed in forced labour cases were heard in silence by the assembly – there was no answer to these facts. The farm labour scandal is South Africa's current disgrace . . . Through the efforts of Ray Swart (on Luthuli), Mrs Suzman and Dr Wilson, the UP won a moral victory – and in the long run the moral victories are translated into political victories."

The farm labour scandal debate was a watershed in Parliament. The Nationalists grasped the nettle, and launched full-scale attacks on the two wings of the United Party, hoping to break both. It brought into the open the brutal and ugly innards of Nationalist ideology and tactics when its very existence was threatened by exposure in Parliament from sworn liberal enemies.

It also showed that beneath the fine words of the UP's "white leadership with justice", there was its craven capitulation to Nationalist political dominance. When it came to the line, they retreated into their conservative trenches, denying any political affinities with Native leaders and movements, the real victims of apartheid.

This debate signified a turning point in my attitude to Parliament and the UP. It was impossible to reform the United Party. I was faced with the prospect of fighting on two fronts in Parliament – against both the UP and the NP. I had to accept that there was no proper home for liberals in the United Party; it would not hesitate to rid itself of the liberal members if this could be done.

The sad truth is that in 1959, although some of us called ourselves "liberals", the real liberals were certainly not in the United Party. Most of us were products of the affluent armchair urban intelligentsia who wanted reform, but saw it as a possible evolution within current political structures. Margaret Ballinger and the Liberal Party were far ahead of us. They were already asking for one man one vote – we still did not accept that this was wise. We did not believe that the blacks of South Africa, who for centuries had been kept in political and economic bondage to whites, were ready to share power on that basis.

The tension of the farm labour debate did not end for me when we proposed a reduction of the Minister's salary as a protest. I only half-listened to the final assaults by the NP on us, and turned over in my mind the innuendoes and allegations made by Abraham and Martins about my

329

background, my supposed political attachments to the ANC and the lies that I had changed my name and been behind the Iron Curtain. Clearly, the Nats had planned to destroy my parliamentary career, implying that I had been elected under false pretenses and had committed offences against the laws of the country. The staggering consequences dawned on me. Tired and exhausted, I went to the library and looked up all the *Hansards* of the debates in which I had been attacked, from the time I entered Parliament. There was no doubt about what they were doing. I had to take urgent action to defend myself.

I went to speak to Sir De Villiers Graaff that evening for his advice on how to deal with the NP's allegations and tactics. After studying the evidence, as a lawyer and an experienced MP, he agreed the charges were so serious that I had to repudiate them in Parliament without delay. It was 7 pm. He immediately telephoned Senator Pilkington-Jordan, one of the senior legal UP experts on parliamentary procedure. An appointment was arranged that evening at his home in Rondebosch. I arrived just after 8 pm with all the *Hansards*. We sat until midnight going through all the allegations about me in the House. Pilkington-Jordan concluded I had a prima-facie case against Herman Martins because he had defamed and libelled me. We drew up a statement, which I was to present to the Speaker the next morning, together with my birth certificate.

On Wednesday at 9 am Pilkington-Jordan and I saw the Speaker in his rooms. He listened carefully to what we had to say, read the statement and examined the *Hansard* quotations. He immediately confirmed that a serious breach of parliamentary discipline had occurred, and that under Standing Orders I would be allowed to read my statement to the House before the first Order of the day. There could be no discussion by any member of the House. If Martins did not apologise properly in the House later in the day in the Appropriation Vote, he would appear before a Select Committee and risk expulsion from Parliament.

It was 24 June 1959, a week before Parliament prorogued. The House was full. Dr Verwoerd and all the Cabinet Ministers were in their seats. The Whips on both sides knew what was going to happen and Herman Martins was told to be present in the House.

The Speaker read the Prayer, and then immediately called on me to speak, to the surprise of the Press Gallery and most MPs.

In tense silence, I stood up.

Dr Wilson: "Mr Speaker, I rise to seek your indulgence and that of the House to make a personal statement regarding the most serious reflection upon my character and reputation as a member of this House.

"On 17 June, in the course of debate in Committee of Supply on the Vote of the Hon the Minister of Bantu Administration and Development, the Hon Member for Wakkerstroom, Mr HE Martins said:

'The Hon Member (he was referring to me) who has referred to the Minister's so-called cowardice should remember that we know of a certain Benjamin Woolfsohn who was an agent of Barlows and was so scared to join the army that he became Boris Wilson.'

"Mr Speaker, I ignore, as I believe you would wish me to do, the imputation of cowardice contained in the reference to my not having undertaken service during the last war. Such service was not or could not be undertaken by many persons for a large variety of reasons.

"The gravity of the charge that my true name is Benjamin Woolfsohn and that I am masquerading in this House under the name of Boris Wilson needs little emphasis, even if it stood alone in the context of the Hon Member's remarks. The words, 'The Hon Member . . .must know that we know of a certain Benjamin Woolfsohn who is an agent of Barlows,' carry an innuendo of some grave impropriety which unfortunately was left entirely undefined by the Hon Member."

As I spoke I could see Dr Verwoerd and "Blackie" Swart, the Minister of Justice, looking at me intently. There was absolute silence.

The correspondents in the Press Gallery were writing furiously, as I was not able to warn them or issue my statement beforehand.

"But, Mr Speaker, the name of Benjamin Woolfsohn has figured on another occasion in the debate in Committee of Supply on the Vote of the Hon Minister of Justice. I now quote from the current issue of *Hansard* (No 15 of the weekly edition) at Col 5744 as follows:

'*Mr Schoonbee*: The Hon the Minister has a list just now of the names of people who have gone from this country to pay a visit behind the Iron Curtain. I want to ask the Hon Minister whether the name of one Benjamin Woolfsohn does not appear on that list. If so I should like to know . . .

The Minister of Justice: Did he by any chance change his name later on?

Mr Schoonbee: He did change his name; that is no longer his name. That was his name at the time'."

I was told by colleagues that Schoonbee and Martins, were now looking very uncomfortable.

"Mr Speaker," I continued, "the lists to which the Hon Member for Pretoria District [Mr Schoonbee] referred, were mentioned by the Hon Minister of Justice the same day, *vide Hansard* No 15 Col 5711 where he is reported as follows:

'*The Minister of Justice*: In the course of our enquiries into communistic activities we found that at the University of Witwatersrand there was an active branch of the Communist Party amongst the students. That was forbidden under the Act. There are many members of the lecturing staff of the Johannesburg University at this moment who are named Communists. I have here a list of at least 15 students and ex-students of the University of the Witwatersrand. I mention this in order to show that at the University there was an active Communist movement which influenced students; many of these students went overseas to countries behind the Iron Curtain; others were members of the Communist Party.'

"The implication of what was said on 13 May 1959 by the Hon Member for Pretoria District is that Benjamin Woolfsohn is a Communist or a suspected Communist and what was said on June 17 1959 by the Hon Member for Wakkerstroom in express terms is that I am in truth Benjamin Woolfsohn and am, therefore a Communist or a suspected Communist.

"In fact, I have never borne the name Benjamin Woolfsohn nor have I ever been employed as an agent of Barlows. I entered this House under the name with which I was born, and my birth certificate, which confirms that at birth my name was registered as Boris Wilson has been handed to you, Mr Speaker, in your chambers.

"Mr Speaker, to your care is entrusted the guardianship and reputation of every member of this House and I leave mine in your hands."

For a moment I stood and looked at the full benches of the Nationalist Party government and sat down to total silence in the House.

The first reaction came from Hamilton-Russell on the the UP front-bench when he called out:

"Are there no apologies?"

The House came to life. I recall murmured approval around me from the UP. The Nationalists were talking animatedly amongst themselves as the rest of the day's business commenced.

I was fortunate that I had been able to make my statement under Standing Orders without interruption, because I am certain if I had tried to make it in a debate there would have been uproar.

I felt a deep sense of relief. I had stopped the Nationalist "bully boys" who had thought they had cornered me and in all probability would have called for a Select Committee to investigate their allegations against me.

About five minutes after I had spoken, I left my seat to go to the Lobby because I received a message that some journalists from the Press Gallery wanted to interview me. As I left the House to enter the Lobby, Herman Martins blocked my way.

"Ag, man, Boris," he said in his gruff platteland accent, "why didn't you tell me what you were doing? I really didn't mean it."

I gave him a withering look, and strode past him to the waiting journalists.

The newspapers all over South Africa gave front-page coverage to my statement under headlines: "Boris Wilson Is My Name" and "Serious Reflection on MP". *The Sunday Times* ran a story that "Herman Martins will apologise to Dr Boris Wilson, the MP for Hospital, during the Appropriation Bill in the House of Assembly the following day, Monday. He will also deny he is anti-Semitic."

The more I thought of what the Nats had tried to do, the more I felt I should have demanded in my statement a Select Committee to investigate the actions of the Minister of Justice and Schoonbee, who were part of the "plot" to libel and defame me. Pilkington-Jordan reminded me that the Nats were the government and ran the proceedings of the House. It was obvious that the Minister of Justice and Schoonbee were involved, but Martins made the vital allegation. He was the one who should apologise, and this should warn the NP, including Dr Verwoerd, that I was aware of what they were doing, that I was no political pushover and that I would fight back.

I was told by the UP Whips that Herman Martins would formally apologise to me in the House during the Appropriation Vote.

Knowing the Nationalist Party, I was fully expecting some weaseling. I was not disappointed. Martins complained to the House that "after he [Dr Wilson] had made the necessary arrangements with you, Mr Speaker . . . I think it would have been fair and reasonable . . . to have notified me that he was going to make this statement, so that I could have prepared my reply . . ."

This was not true. It was not my function to warn him. It was the NP Whips' job to instruct him what to do. In any event, neither he or his co-conspirators informed me of their intent to mislead Parliament about me, when they made their allegations.

Martins went on: "If I cast any aspersions on the Hon Member personally, in that portion of my speech where I said we knew of a Benjamin Woolfsohn who had changed his name, I am prepared to offer him my full apologies, because in the political sphere and in my daily life, I at all times try to be nothing but honest reasonable and sincere in my dealings with all persons, no matter how much I may differ from them, and no matter what I may think of their courage.

"I am therefore prepared to offer him my apologies, but in addition I want to ask him a question. He has linked this statement with two things. He has referred to his baptismal certificate [sic] and he has linked that to his courage and the lack of courage which resulted in many people not serving during the war.

"Why did he himself not take steps to correct this prevailing belief regarding his Woolfsohn extraction? This belief has its origin in the fact that for many years the Woolfsohn family operated on the Newtown Market, Johannesburg, as market agents. This accusation was levelled at the Hon Member in the Johannesburg City Council and in the Provincial Council of the Transvaal.

"A year ago, the impression was created in this House that the Hon Member was possibly a Woolfsohn who had changed his name to Wilson. Now I think the Hon Member owed it to himself to put it right at the first opportunity and to ensure that he put an end to these beliefs and to these statements which have been made . . .

"I want to tell the House as far as the one section of my speech is concerned in which I spoke about Woolfsohn who had become Wilson I accept the Hon Member's word and I apologise . . ."

What Martins told the House was untrue. The NP never accused me in the Council or Province that my real name was "Woolfsohn" or that I had changed my name. He was doing his best to wriggle out of the mess he had created for himself and the NP by accusing me of being responsible for the misconception. What was evident was that neither Martins or the NP realised from my statement that I had been aware for months what they were up to.

My intention was to end their attempts to frame and harass me. It was patent that Piet van Vuuren, the former NP Council leader hopelessly misinformed the vicious but amateur plotters of the NP Caucus.

To what extent they had been aided by the Security Police was a mystery, because the latter visited me at my office after I was elected to Parliament. They too had their "facts" wrong, but they could have been directed from Dr Verwoerd's department, since it began when I entered the City Council.

Martins went through the whole spectrum of Nationalist "bogeys" – all the supposed leftist connections of the UP – having nothing to do either with his apology to me or the farm labour scandal. It was typical and revealed the low level of their political trickery. Regrettably, parliamentary debating standards were, and still often are, at unbelievable levels of moronic absurdity; we had to endure this from time to time.

Martins's speech was no exception. I said nothing, listening with cynicism as he tried to lay the blame on me while virtually admitting that the NP had been plotting about me from City Council days. He finally droned round to the farm labour scandal, and accused the English press of spreading "vilification, untruths and division and fear in South Africa". I was accused of quoting speeches out of context "to sow hatred between the Jewish community and the Afrikaners".

Then came the usual smearing refrain, that I "spoke on liberalistic lines" during the debate. He added gratuitously: "I differ from him but I respect him. It is his right to act in this way."

Harry Lawrence from his front-bench interjected:

"You have a strange way of showing it."

Martins then proceeded to deal with all the aspects of Jewish involvement in the scandals, including the Jewish newspaper *Zionist Record* and the English newspapers allegations of anti-Semitism. He objected to the stand they took because "the National Party reproved the Hon Members [Suzman and Wilson] because they have helped to spread this impression that the farmers of South Africa are enforcing a system of slavery. In carrying on this campaign of vilification are these two members acting here as the mouthpiece of the Jews of South Africa?"

Helen retorted, "Nonsense". A minute later she told Martins: "You are now making the position worse than it was before", when he tried to prove the press was alleging that 100 000 farmers were treating their Natives badly. Then he dragged in the UP's right wingers Raw and Warren because they had criticised the press who said the UP was divided on this issue. Finally, Stanley Uys of *The Sunday Times* became the target. Under the head line "No More the Velvet Glove", he had written:

"To show they were not one-sided in their racialism, Mr Schoonbee and Mr Martins fired an anti-Semitic blast such as South Africa has not heard since the days when Mr Eric Louw was the country's leading anti-Semite . . ."

This provoked Blaar Coetzee to interject: " . . .and for the rest he [Uys] lies."

The pinnacle of absurdity was reached when Martins announced: " . . .the National Party has changed its constitution and has made provision that a member of the Jewish community can also become a member of the

National Party . . .The National Party is not a racial party. This party is not a racialist which sows hatred . . . ."

Mercifully the debate at this point was adjourned for dinner, but Martins was not finished. When we returned he continued attacking everyone in sight, including one of our right wing members, Mrs Sannie van Niekerk, a portly woman from a Natal constituency. Earlier she had put questions about Bantustans coming to her constituency.

Mr Martins: " . . .But before asking those questions in this House she had gone to Pongola (in her constituency) and told those voters: 'Come here so that I can comfort you and press you to my political bosom because,' she said, this Prime Minister, Dr Hendrik Verwoerd . . ."

Harry Lawrence: (the master of front-bench interjection after a good dinner and wine): "You really are an awful swine."

Mr Speaker: "Order! The Hon Member must withdraw that and apologise."

Mr Lawrence: "He must not refer to a lady member in that way . . ."

Mr Speaker: "Order! I again ask the Hon Member to apologise."

Mr Lawrence: "I won't."

Mr Speaker: "I again ask the Hon Member to apologise."

Mr Lawrence: "I shall not apologise to the Hon Member. I withdraw."

At this point, Harry Lawrence was on his feet, gathering his papers ready to leave. MPs were hurling insults at each other, enjoying the postprandial interlude; but not the Speaker.

Mr Speaker: "No, the Hon Member must apologise."

Harry Lawrence, pausing in the melodrama, turned to the Speaker. His sharp brain had sensed something from the Speaker's persistent demands.

Mr Lawrence: "To whom must I apologise, to you or to him?"

Mr Speaker: (very diplomatically) "To the House."

Mr Lawrence: (Putting down his papers). "I apologise to the House."

Martins continued his bizarre political diatribe, hitting out in all directions at Luthuli, the ANC, the Black Sash, Helen and me.

By any standards, it was an astonishing day in Parliament, worth recounting because it illustrates the Nationalist technique of utilising innuendo, half-truths and racialism to convert serious attempts to debate matters of great public concern, into political farce.

I had at last cornered the Nationalists where they had to be cornered – in the presence of Dr Verwoerd in Parliament. Their vendetta was exposed, written into the Parliamentary record, plus tremendous publicity throughout South Africa. I had a personal interest – would they continue to harass me in the future? Time would tell.

If any debate in Parliament confirmed that there was an unbridgeable gap between the conservatives and liberals in the UP, it was the farm labour scandal. The Nationalists had forced our right wingers in the House to denounce, with tortuous arguments, left wing organisations and individuals who were compromising the UP's conservatism. Any taunts from the NP that the UP was aligned to liberals or "leftists" terrified our right wing MPs – they were always on their feet denying these allegations.

An example was the late entry into the Bantu Administration Vote by Vause Raw of Natal, three times confirming the UP's attitude to Luthuli's banning, that of the Liberal Party and the serious matter of the land provisions of the 1936 Land Act. He denied the NP's accusations that the UP were hand in glove with banned organisations and individuals, at the same time spelling out in no uncertain terms the wide differences between UP conservatives and liberals like Ray Swart, Helen Suzman and me. Very noticeable was the reluctance of our Whips to protect its liberal MPs from the constant National Party battering.

Our response in the House was not to be drawn into internecine warfare with the conservatives, but rather to concentrate on the government's actions and legislation and do what the UP should be doing – opposing the National Party. We could easily have protested about the negative role of the UP conservatives, but were waiting for the forthcoming National Congress of the UP in Bloemfontein in August to do what we could to alter the UP's policies and its weakness and vacillation in the face of the NP's attacks.

The English-language newspapers like *The Rand Daily Mail, The Cape Times*, the Port Elizabeth *Evening Post*, edited by John Sutherland, and the *Daily Dispatch* of East London, all urged the UP to shake off its stubborn reactionary right wing compromisers who for years had forced it to speak with two voices. They urged Graaff to end this infighting at the coming Bloemfontein Congress, having a good idea of caucus differences and having already published names of MPs who were leading conservatives, and those reputed to be "liberals or progressives" in Parliament.

The UP Whips were conservative and protected the establishment at all times. They were ready to attack the Nationalists when the leaders of the UP were the targets, but when "liberals" were in trouble with the NP they hardly ever intervened to protect us. In the farm labour scandal, with the exception of an objection by one Whip, they were largely silent. When Martins made his half-baked apology they did not react. Consequently I was more than pleased when Harry Lawrence, in his last speech of the session, attacked Martins.

"I feel it is my duty," he told the House, "to express my surprise that when the Hon Member for Wakkerstroom [Mr Martins] apologised to the Hon Member for Hospital for having been under a misapprehension, he should have found it necessary to qualify the apology by various questions and rather tortuous arguments . . . Sir, the position is this, and I think it should go on record that we can have an end to this unsavoury incident. Those allegations were made against the Hon Member in the City Council and the Provincial Council. He denied that at once and they were accepted by the person concerned. He made the position absolutely clear in this House. He never changed his name. He was born under the name that appears on his birth certificate. That is perfectly clear, and I would have thought as a matter of chivalry and as a matter of practice in this House that explanation would end the matter."

As General Smuts's former Minister of Justice, Harry Lawrence commanded respect in the House. He was fearless, with a deep sense of personal justice and not frightened to protect the rights of anyone in Parliament. I always regarded him as part of the UP establishment but this intervention in the Appropriation debate, quite unsolicited, raised questions in my mind about his political stance in relation to the conservative elements in the party. For some while he had given me the impression that he was dissatisfied with the ambiguous role that leading conservative elements were playing in relation to Nationalist pressure and in particular to the nature of the UP's Native policy. It appeared he was leaning more and more towards the "liberals" of the UP.

Liaison between the Cape MPs and those of us from the north was not a close one. The main co-operation was in the joint report that De Beer, Cope and I sent to Graaff's Propaganda Committee.

Lawrence did not figure in our talks on our differences with the leadership and the right wing. In reality it was the media who were stoking things up, latching on to statements by conservatives who, more than once in the dying days of the session, made no bones about where they stood in relationship to the government's banning of Luthuli, the UP's attitude to the Liberal Party and liberals in general including implementation of the 1936 Land Act. It was significant that Vause Raw spoke three times in the Bantu Affairs Vote.

Mostly we held fire. As liberals we had not made joint decisions on strategy in Parliament as to where we or the UP stood on vital matters. Our technique was to tackle specific issues, as Ray Swart did with regard to Luthuli banning, or Helen Suzman and me on Influx Control, making clear our total opposition to apartheid.

Open confrontation in Parliament was not our strategy. We would only play into Nationalist hands.

As the session reached its last weeks, the Nationalists had a one-man revolt in their Caucus. "Japie" Basson, an MP from South-West Africa, a former United Party organiser, considered a NP intellectual, staged single-handed his rebellion against the removal of the Native Representatives from Parliament. It was the first sign of uneasiness in the Nationalist monolith under Verwoerd. It led to NP crisis meetings in Caucus and Basson was expelled. The NP tried to minimise the incident, but were powerless to stop Basson's trenchant remarks when the Appropriation Bill came up in the House.

"Mr Speaker, I have come to the conclusion that the National Party and this government have no love for South Africa; their only love is the National Party . . .Can any Hon Member opposite get up and say in all honesty that the coloured people were removed from the Common Roll in order to protect the white man in South Africa? . . . The Hon Prime Minister has told us that it was necessary to abolish the Natives Represen-tatives if we want to save white South Africa. Is there one single member in this House who believes that the Bantustans and those local authorities which the Natives are going to have will in any way contribute to the safety of the white man? These Native Representatives are being removed as the Prime Minister himself has said because they oppose his apartheid policy."

As the diminutive Basson lashed the NP, his former colleagues interrupted and abused him in anger when he said: "The National Party had been
built on racial prejudice. When they did not attack the Jewish community
they attacked the coloured people; when they did not attack the coloureds
they attacked the Natives; when they did not attack the Natives they
attacked the English-speaking section of South Africa. In that way the whole
National Party has been built up on prejudice and hatred for other sections
of the population . . ."

This was an unusual public purgation by an Afrikaner nationalist,
indicating deep-seated emotional problems arising from Hendrik Verwoerd's tight grip on the Nationalists. We were not surprised by this
catharsis, since earlier, in the Bantu Administration Vote, Basson had
mercilessly attacked the NP indicating he was not resigning from Parliament. His defence of democratic government was a welcome change. In the
past he had not protested about the erosion of democratic rights as a result
of apartheid laws passed by Parliament affecting both blacks and whites.

Nevertheless, it was important when he said as an ex-Nationalist:
" . . .there is not the slightest doubt that we have gone a long way in
restricting personal freedom in this country".

Basson's break with the Nationalists was the first sign of strain in the
NP since Verwoerd took over, indicating hidden problems in their ranks.
The UP conservatives were waiting with open arms to have him back in the
fold. He had no hope of remaining an independent or forming a new party.

54

It was a dramatic ending to my second parliamentary session, a session full
of political turbulence, uncertainty and infighting in the ranks of the United
Party with evidence that the Nationalists could not suppress, in its large
Caucus, the first strains of rebellion against the hard-line policies of Hendrik
Verwoerd.

The South African Parliament, I discovered, loses all its political and
moral inhibitions at the end of the session. MPs who have sat through the
cold wet Cape winter, hundreds of miles away from their families and
constituencies become short-tempered, tired and want to get home. Party
jealousies, personal attacks, innuendoes and even threats and abuse can be
unleashed and the Speaker has a tough job keeping the proceedings more or
less decent. In this atmosphere the "political dogs of war" on all sides of the
House had field days trying to destroy the liberal elements of the UP.

We were grateful that the media was there to record the ugly face of
Verwoerd's nationalism, which had given the impetus his party needed to
implement apartheid. He had pushed through as much legislation as

Parliament could absorb. This had the effect of exposing the deep divisions between right and left in the UP.

The hypersensitive right wingers of the UP were infuriated by the NP's taunts that Graaff was lead by the nose by UP liberals. This accounted for Vause Raw's repeated declamations disowning the liberal wing. In the corridors of the House and press enclaves, there were persistent rumours that Douglas Mitchell, Vause Raw and the conservatives were going to the UP's National Congress in September in Bloemfontein with the objective of organising a "putsch" to get rid of the liberals. We did not know how true these rumours were, but could not ignore them, because it was clear from the atmosphere in Caucus that matters were coming to a head.

Despite this, and contrary to the political commentators' predictions, we liberals did nothing strategically to prepare a counterattack. Our problem was that we were an uncoordinated group – liberal MPs who came from urban or peri-urban areas, light years away, politically, from the average UP or NP parliamentarian from the platteland. We spoke a different political language. We saw the South African racial dilemma without the restraints of the fears, emotions and prejudices that so dominated the UP and NP right wing circles.

Because we endeavoured to expose the real problems that faced multi-racial South Africa, laying bare the ruthlessness and cruelties of apartheid, we were not only attacked by conservatives everywhere, but told that we were undermining the white minority in South Africa.

The media, however, had sold the idea to South Africa that liberals in the United Party were a unified bloc.

Nothing was further from the truth. The Cape liberals like Colin Eglin and Zach De Beer were as remote from us as were MPs like Ray Swart and Ronald Butcher in Natal. The same power struggles went on internally in the party. Graaff was aware, but did nothing to bring people together. How long he could continue with this unsatisfactory state of affairs was unknown. He was polite and pleasant to everyone, but kept his political options open by consulting with both factions, as he did in the appointment of the ill-fated Native Policy and Propaganda Committee whose reports never saw the light of day.

55

I was glad to leave Cape Town for the rarefied air of Johannesburg with its crisp winter mornings. There was much to do in the business, and *Forum* needed attention. It was now being edited by Neville Caley, the retired editor of *The Sunday Times*. I was very fortunate that he took it over, because he was one of the most experienced senior journalists in South

Africa and it relieved me of tremendous responsibilities. *Forum* was struggling both for circulation and advertisements. The liberal readership it had once enjoyed was greatly reduced, which reflected the waning liberal political influence.

Advertisements were hard to come by despite my efforts, but I was prepared to subsidise the paper, determined to keep it alive. It was run on a shoestring with Morry Mayer's help.

It was usual for an MP to hold his report-back meeting in the constituency soon after Parliament ended. This I did, sharing the platform with Harry Schwarz, before a muted gathering of Hospital UP die-hards. They listened attentively with little reaction, which was to be expected, given the character of my voters in the congested flatland, the General Hospital, the Old Fort Prison and the preponderance of retired people.

Resolutions for the national congress were top priority. In my absence Hospital had sent a resolution on the party's non-European policy to Congress which asked for "the preservation of the European community and its civilisation in South Africa and the necessity to give human rights . . . and satisfactory political representation to the non-European people." I was critical because it was too vague and not explicit enough, but it had gone forward while I was in Cape Town.

More important was the fact that the press were daily reporting on the widening split between the UP conservatives and liberals, publishing lists of MPs and senior party supporters who would be involved if a break came.

I cannot recall that Helen Suzman, John Cope and I had any serious discussions about particular joint action we might take at Congress. Nothing was heard from our liberal colleagues in the other Provinces. I learnt more from my contacts in the press, such as Stanley Uys, who had his ears tuned to UP undercover activity.

A message, loud and clear, came from the UP Youth Congress which took place before the main Congress. It was, according to Uys, "under the control of the right wing MPs and voiced its opposition to any liberal thoughts the UP might have."

The UP went to great lengths to avoid liberal involvement. For instance, the UP would not allow MPs or officials to participate in innocuous "Brains Trust" discussions which the Black Sash were holding all over the country; nor did it want to be seen on the same platform as the anti-Nat Black Sash.

At long last, on 11 August 1959, in a tense political atmosphere, we arrived at Bloemfontein for the UP's National Congress. The media had built up a crisis situation for the 750 delegates.

The City Hall was packed for Graaff's opening speech. He attacked Verwoerd's Bantustans, believing that the UP could get back to power on this issue, because it was "a desperate expedient which will lead inevitably to the dismemberment of our fatherland."

Earlier that day we had heard on the grapevine that Douglas Mitchell had raised the 1936 Land Act issue, indicating that he intended to speak against it at Congress, about which Graaff was not happy. We were most concerned, as there was no resolution on the Land Act from Mitchell in the confidential agenda.

The confidential agenda contained what UP officialdom regarded as contentious resolutions, to be discussed behind closed doors, on Native Policy, race relations and constitutional issues.

It was a charade, because, although journalists were excluded from the secret sessions, copies of it were in their hands within minutes. It was riddled with controversial motions fully reflecting the divergent views of the United Party.

The section on non-European affairs had calls from Hospital and Pinelands (Cape) for "proper consultation with responsible leaders amongst the non-European people affecting our mutual interests. North-east Rand (Transvaal) demanded "adequate representation in Parliament of the various non-European communities, the right to acquire freehold".

Parktown (John Cope) and Wynberg (Cape) wanted the UP to make provision for all races to be represented in Parliament "by their own people".

The usual calls for the "maintenance of white leadership and Western Civilisation" appeared. Platteland constituencies were forthright in opposition to the common roll. The longest resolution was from Vause Raw's constituency of Durban Point starting with a demand for a "positive white population policy, the party stands for white leadership and political control, rejection of a common roll and that any public statement in conflict with this policy be dealt with as an act hostile to the interests of the party and that no person uses the United Party to propagate personal views in conflict with the basic direction (above)".

Roodepoort called for Party policy to remain conservative, and Worcester in the Cape was concerned "in view of the liberalistic principles attributed to our party, we ask Congress to reaffirm our policy on matters of race relations."

Germiston backed this up with "the UP must be conservative in its approach to South Africa's problems and avoid at all times the liberal view so prevalent in the Party's debates in Parliament".

The hard right of the platteland supported discipline against "any party member who makes statements not in conformity with party policy and congress disassociates itself from the principles of the Liberal Party and demands that the spokesmen of the UP refrain from expressing support of such principles."

The confidential agenda was a messenger of hostile intent riddled with implied threats to UP liberals. It looked as if the UP's right wingers intended that congress should show Verwoerd's government that the UP totally opposed the one-man-one-vote system, and conservatives called the political tune in the party.

If Congress was to debate these motions as set out in the agenda it would lead to repetition, chaos and possibly an explosive situation. Hoping to overcome this, Graaff was invited as Leader to discuss his parliamentary proposals in the Bantustan debate that Natives to be represented on a separate roll, a franchise for the responsible class of Native, Europeans to

341

represent Natives and not more than eight Native Representatives in Parliament.

The debate began amicably, but did not remain so for long. Speakers started coming to the rostrum solely to attack the liberals in the party, without paying much attention to the content of Graaff's proposals. This raised the temperature in the hall. By the time Louis Steenkamp, one of Graaff's moderate right wingers had finished, Colin Eglin stepped in hoping to restore some order to the debate. He failed to stop the anti-liberal attack which approached hysteria. Speakers like Leo Kowarsky and Leo Boyd, leading extra-parliamentary liberals, condemned Steenkamp's proposals and rejected the accusation that that those of us who wanted a common roll were *kafferboeties*.

Graaff sat expressionless, silently listening to the furore. At one point late in the afternoon he intervened calling for calm and all shades of opinion to be heard. The Congress was dominated by platteland delegates. It was clear from the abuse they hurled at us from the platform and the vitriolic nature of the attacks that there was a serious organised attempt to make the position of UP liberals untenable.

I made notes as opposing speakers followed one another, some in English, others in Afrikaans, with frequent interjections from the floor. It was impossible to keep a record of what speakers were saying, other than fragments of importance. Late in the afternoon I could contain myself no longer. I went to the platform and spoke on the political intimidation that was taking place, attacking Steenkamp's resolution which would destroy the 1954 Native Policy of shared responsibility. Steenkamp's views had lost the UP five previous elections – it would be a day of "no hope for the UP" if his resolution was accepted. Zach de Beer followed with similar warnings.

The marathon debate raged late into the night. Every liberal or progressive delegate had been in the debate – it was a make or break situation for us.

By ten that evening we had been locked in the Congress Hall for nearly nine hours, and mostly in a state of exhaustion. We had listened to seventy speakers when Graaff rose to reply to the debate, trying to pour his often-used balm on the political wounds of the day. "Every single member of the UP can come to Congress and deliver himself of criticisms of me," he proclaimed.

He unhesitatingly supported the Separate Roll which he said the people of South Africa understood. He was satisfied that the (white) electorate would not tolerate non-Europeans in Parliament, and appealed for Congress to unite on the issue, to reject Kowarsky and Boyd's resolution for twenty non-whites in Parliament.

The policy statement of the future should be tied to Steenkamp's resolution. He made no mention of the day's disastrous events. The open cleavage between right and left, as far as Graaff was concerned, had not happened. Most of us were worn out and remained silent. We realised that the UP leaders had not retreated. Graaff's final remarks clearly indicated that

de Villiers Graaff, leader of the United
~~rty~~ty.

Harry Schwarz, leader of the Reform
Group, now South African ambassador
to Washington.

My family in Johannesburg, 1962. Virginia in front, Adrian, Pauline and Nigel.

Raymond Louw, Oliver Tambo (ANC President), and BW in London, May 1991.

Steenkamp's resolution was in reality the views of the UP's Head Committee. Its express intention was to tell South Africa that the UP would not allow the Separate Roll to submerge white South Africa, that the UP's head Committee did not envisage a change in UP policy and it was sending signals that "the Common Roll" would never come. As a late night sop, Graaff said that Steenkamp's resolution would not bind the party for the future.

So ended a day of political drama, not unexpected, but the intensity of the attempt to sledgehammer the liberals into submission once and for all was shattering. For many of us, a great rethink was needed. The United Party was ruptured, but Graaff was not openly strong enough to restrain his right wingers who were now thirsting for the kill. Surprisingly, Mitchell's promised Land Act resolution had not surfaced. The question we liberals were asking each other was: Would it still come?

The next day we discovered that many liberal delegates had left Congress, disgusted with the turn of events. The morning's business was uneventful, so much so, that after lunch I asked John Cope whether there was any point in staying on. I went to the opposite side of the hall to Eglin and De Beer to find out their views. They also thought nothing would happen.

They were going home at the end of the day. Cope and I decided it was all over, and we left Congress just after 4 pm for Johannesburg, arriving home about eleven that night.

About 1 am, I was woken by the telephone. Instinctively I thought it was the telephone intruder, and was going, in my sleepy state, to pull it off the hook and leave it at that. However I answered it.

"Boris, sorry to wake you, its Terry Spencer, *Rand Daily Mail*. There's been a break at Bloemfontein. We've been given a statement by some United Party MPs and others who have decided to leave the UP because of the Mitchell Land resolution which Congress accepted late in the afternoon. Can I read it to you? And will you tell me whether you agree and will join the break?"

"Terry, I'm half asleep," I muttered. "Did you say Mitchell introduced a land resolution? It must have been late; I left Congress after 4 pm."

I listened as Terry Spencer told me all he knew. Mitchell introduced the Land Act resolution, which we had expected, at a late hour because it was known that many liberals had left Congress.

It was eventually accepted by Congress after an acrimonious discussion resulting in Steytler, Helen, Zach, Colin and a few others meeting at the Maitland Hotel, from where they issued their statement of intent to resign from the United Party.

Spencer's shock news, by then, had my complete attention. I asked him to repeat everything.

"Boris, do you associate yourself with what they've done?"

"Of course."

"Can I quote you?"

"Go ahead. But Terry, do not call us liberals at this stage, call us progressives. We don't want to be confused with the Liberal Party. Get hold of John Cope, he must be home now, because he left Bloemfontein about the time I did."

So the expected schism had become a fact. The conservatives had succeeded in forcing the liberals out of the United Party. For a moment I was sorry I had not stayed on at Bloemfontein. On the other hand, my views were known, and although I had no details about plans for the future, I was certain that Cope and the others, as soon as they knew, would also associate themselves with the break. I decided not to contact Zach or Colin, but dozed fitfully.

Early next morning I was woken by telephone calls from constituency members and friends wanting to know what it was all about. I could only tell them what Spencer had told me – I had not yet heard from any of the breakaway MPs. I contacted Cope and we decided to say nothing more until we had met as a group to decide on the future.

All the newspapers carried details of the fateful last few hours of Congress when Mitchell introduced his resolution. It expressed total opposition to the acquisition of more land for the government's Bantustan policy, from which it would form independent sovereign states. Graaff said he would oppose the resolution but, if passed, would not regard it as a vote of no confidence in his leadership – a clear message to Congress to pass it. The vote was taken. Congress supported Mitchell to the dismay not only of the liberals, but moderates like Sydney Waterson, a senior front-bencher who signed the Land Act in 1936 with Smuts and Hertzog.

Jan Steytler, Helen Suzman, Zach de Beer, Colin Eglin, Ray Swart and others had met at the Maitland Hotel. After long debate they saw that their only course was to issue the statement of intent.

It read: "The United Party Congress today took the decision to oppose further purchases of land for Native settlement by the present Government. This is a clear breach of the promise given by the United Party government in 1936, and as such a backward step from the 1954 statement of policy. None of us can accept this decision. It is indicative of the general unwillingness of the Congress to face up to what we believe to be the increasingly urgent problems of our multiracial country. For this reason we doubt whether we can any longer serve any honest and useful purpose as members of the party and we therefore have to consider our position and discuss it with Sir De Villiers Graaff. We have had no opportunity of consulting with other party members who may share our views."

The statement was clear enough. There was no doubt that Mitchell's Land Act resolution was the straw that broke the camel's back. As far as I was concerned, the message from *The Rand Daily Mail* was only one reason to end my connection with the United Party. My reformist-from-within mission had failed. The political role I was playing was a sham. If I was going to stand up and be counted as a liberal, it had to be outside the moribund United Party.

The newspapers telephoned all day wanting more news of our plans. However, if ever there was lack of liaison it was the day after the announcement of the break. It was impossible to locate Zach de Beer and

Colin Eglin. Their Cape Town offices did not know where they were. Steytler was on his way back to Queenstown, his constituency. Ray Swart, Townley Williams and Leo Boyd were on the road to Durban.

Eventually, Zach and Colin were inexplicably located in Johannesburg, not in Cape Town. I could not believe this at first, but it was true. They should have been in the Cape to explain to their regional and divisional supporters why they had broken with the UP and rallied support for their actions. Even more important was that Graaff, as UP leader was in Cape Town and the field was left clear for him to influence local party leaders to his side, especially MPs like Waterson and Hamilton-Russell who were on the brink of joining us.

The *Cape Argus* and *The Cape Times* were left high and dry, with the two most important MPs, De Beer and Eglin, a thousand miles away. I was appalled when I learnt that they had gone to Johannesburg, ostensibly to see Harry Oppenheimer and local newspaper editors, without bothering to contact Cope or me. Since we were not with them when they made the landmark decision, a first priority should have been a discussion with us and urgent talks on future strategy. Harry Oppenheimer and our local newspaper editors could have been dealt with by us.

De Beer and Eglin had their priorities totally wrong. As a result of this initial tactical error, valuable support was lost in the Cape.

I suspected that they had intended to break away all along, but for reasons best known to themselves, we were never told of their plans.

Was it because they wanted to obtain control of a new party if it was formed? If so, they lost the initiative in their own Cape constituencies. By the time they got back three days later Waterson, Hamilton-Russell and other important MPs were backing Sir De Villiers Graaff.

Graaff had grabbed the initiative. It was a bad start for the new group. Political inexperience in the crisis did not augur well for future personal relationships if a new party was formed. Instinctively, I was wary of the kind of leadership to expect from De Beer and Eglin.

John, Helen and I quickly convened meetings of our UP Divisions, explaining the reasons for the break. Harry Schwarz and his wife Annette were very upset at my proposed move. The Hospital Division gave me an almost unanimous vote of confidence, pleading with me not to resign. I told them I was seeing Graaff in Cape Town after the weekend and would do my best to straighten things out, reporting back within days. I was not confident that I could avoid resignation. The Division passed a resolution that there was no reason for a person of progressive thought to resign from the UP, and condemned Mitchell's Land resolution passed by Congress.

At the weekend I flew to Cape Town with Colin on the same flight. It was the first time I'd seen him since the break. At Cape Town airport we were met by several hundred supporters who gave us a rapturous welcome when we entered the arrivals hall.

Those of us who joined the break had temporary headquarters in Cape Town at the old Grand Hotel where I met Jan Steytler and other breakaway

MPs. This was our first coming together after United Party congress in Bloemfontein.

Steytler's hotel room was our "office". We had a full discussion about Bloemfontein, the interviews with Graaff which some already had; and future strategy. Steytler, Suzman and Cope had resigned from the UP. I was due to see Graaff next. Our main task, however, was to convince Waterson, Hamilton-Russell and Clive van Ryneveld that they should stay with us.

Clive had got himself into an emotional mess, retracting his resignation. We all got to work on him in the hotel, and after some time he realised his future was with the unknown and us.

By the time I went to Graaff's office I was sure I would get the same reception he had given to Helen and John. To my surprise, I spent an hour with him. He was sympathetic and argued the land question with me, stressing he did not want me to leave the UP.

He praised my party work. He could not have been more friendly. I was firm and told him that unless there was a complete change in the running of the party's affairs in relation to Native Policy and a reversal of the Mitchell Land resolution, I was resigning.

This is how we parted.

I reported to Steytler and the others. When everyone had seen Graaff, we sat down to plan strategy. Steytler had agreed that we would not issue a statement until Graaff had done so, which appeared on 19 August. The *Cape Argus* gave it the front-page lead.

Graaff accepted resignations from the six of us he'd seen, and three in Natal, Swart, Townley-Williams and Butcher who had not consulted him. South Africa knew that nine of us had left the United Party. Of immediate concern to all of us was our constituencies and our personal futures.

Before we issued our reply, which I drew up for Steytler at his request and sent to all newspapers, we decided that it was essential that Steytler should consult with a Native leader on the land question. We managed to get a telephone call to Professor ZK Matthews of Fort Hare University, the current president of the African National Congress. Steytler asked him the questions and Cope, on an extension, recorded it for posterity.

As I have Cope's notes, I can quote from the conversation.

Dr Steytler: "Professor Matthews, the United Party has passed a motion at its Union Congress to the effect that further purchases of land for Native occupation under the 1936 Act should be suspended while the Nationalist Party is in power and wishes to use this land to add to its Bantustans. It is argued by those who support this motion that the situation has been altered by the Bantustan policy – what is your view of the situation?"

Prof Matthews: "Does anybody seriously believe that the proposed Bantustans can ever materialise? Does your Party [UP] not say that the economy of South Africa is indivisible, and that territorial apartheid is impossible from the economic point of view?"

Dr Steytler: "May I then ask you another question? Do the Bantu people attach any special importance to the 1936 undertaking to purchase 7,5 million morgen of land?"

Prof Matthews: "I assure you my people attach the greatest importance to this undertaking."

Dr Steytler: "Do they regard the 1936 undertaking as a pledge to the Bantu people?"

Prof Matthews: "You must please understand, Dr Steytler, that this question of land is a burning issue amongst my people. It is not just an ordinary question, but a very important matter. My people feel they have insufficient land. They have been promised more land by the white people and they would regard any departure from this promise as a breach of the white man's word."

Dr Steytler: "But if it is to be argued that the additional land to be bought is to be added to the Bantustans?"

Prof Matthews: "My people would not be impressed by such an argument. The crux of the matter is the need for more land, not Bantustans. In any case, they know in their hearts that Bantustans are impossible. They would regard such a proposition as a breach of the white man's word."

When Steytler put down the telephone, and John Cope read out his shorthand notes, we knew that what we'd done was more than right.

Prof Matthews's firm replies elevated our morale. It was now full speed ahead. We had clear proof from a Native leader that promises given by the United Party had been abrogated. We could now reply to Graaff, so the statement I drew up for Steytler was amended and approved by all present. On 20 August it appeared in all the country's newspapers:

"The crisp point at issue is whether or not the United Party in a Congress decision went back on a solemn undertaking in the 1936 Settlement to buy further land for the Native areas of South Africa. We believe that it did . . . What concerns us and what should have concerned Congress is the question of how the Native people will react to this decision . . .

"We believe the time has come when white people should stop taking important decisions affecting non-white people without proper regard as to how the latter think and feel. Since Bloemfontein Congress we have in fact consulted a number of responsible Natives and we have found they deplore in the strongest terms this decision taken at Congress. They most certainly regard it as a breach of faith on the part of the white man. It is our view that South Africa cannot afford political tricks of this kind which destroy the trust and respect of Native people in the guardianship of the white man."

The statement then dealt with the other issues:

"For a long time now we have been made to feel more unwelcome in the Party . . . we found at Bloemfontein a spirit of hostility towards us that amounted to political intimidation. This bore every sign of having been organised in advance, and it soon became evident that a concerted attempt was being made to drive us out of the party . . .

"The action of issuing a statement after the Congress was taken quite spontaneously . . . surely none of this looks like a prearranged plot? . . . The impression we have is of a party reluctant to move with the times . . . we shall try to develop United Party principles in a dynamic and realistic way offering to South Africa and its different race groups real hopes of security, mutual trust and the boundless progress which is our natural heritage."

The media were screaming for more. This was the largest split the United Party had suffered. Their right wingers and the Nationalists were equally jubilant that we were at last out of the United Party. While they celebrated, we got down to work, because before we parted company to explain to our local UP divisions what had transpired in Cape Town, we had to decide on our immediate strategy and political future.

At this stage we had no organisation whatsoever. All we knew was that Jan Steytler was acting as our leader and spokesman.

We decided that we would form a Progressive Group to be attended by the breakaway MPs, Provincial Councillors and party members from all over South Africa. The inaugural meeting would be in Johannesburg, which I had to organise. Before that we had to see our local UP Divisions, because, apart from explanations, we hoped to induce as many of our voters and UP office-bearers to join us if we decided to form a new party.

I returned to Johannesburg on Tuesday. That evening I attended the special meeting of the Hospital Division which was held at Harry Schwarz's house. It was a traumatic meeting. It was public news that I had told Graaff I was leaving the UP. Harry Schwarz emotionally appealed to me to remain; some of the women members wept, creating a tense atmosphere.

The only reply I had was: "Harry, you and others will join me in the Progressive Party in the future."

"Never," he said.

The rest of the week was non-stop organisational activity. The Cranbrooke Hotel was booked for our meeting, with accommodation for delegates. The newspapers were kept informed of all our arrangements. A few days before our inaugural meeting, Jan Steytler came by train from Queenstown. I arranged a photograph of Cope, De Beer and me meeting him at the Johannesburg Station, which appeared prominently in most newspapers.

On 24 August we held our historic first meeting of the Progressive Group at the Cranbrooke Hotel, following an agenda which I compiled. Preliminary meetings were held at Helen Suzman's home and at my house.

The main items were a statement about the split, discussion on the political objectives to be attained, advisability of forming a new party, its name and the establishment of offices in key centres, and the details of organisation and finance.

As the Steering Committee, we decided to have two more meetings, one in Durban and the other in Cape Town, after which we would be in a position to make arrangements for the launch of the Progressive Party.

We all fell into temporary jobs. Helen set up subcommittees on various aspects of future policy. I concentrated on organisation and publicity. Mayers handled all financial matters. We found money urgently, and established our first headquarters in Johannesburg. There was non-stop consultation between all of us.

The most important job at this point was our relations with the media. The break was still news in the daily papers. Announcements were being made of UP office-bearers from all over the country joining our group. It was essential that the press be fed with news items and I took this job on, since there was no one else who would do it.

The one difference of opinion we had at that stage was whether we should put up candidates in the forthcoming Provincial elections.

Leo Boyd and Lester Hall, two of Natal's MPCs, were determined to fight as Progressives. After protracted discussion they agreed to stand as independents. Elsewhere, we left the Provincial elections alone. I felt it wrong to fight elections before we had formed a party, a view shared by others. Zach and Colin did not want to oppose the UP because we could be accused of letting in the Nationalists. Some breakaway MPs felt morally guilty and did not want to harm the anti-Nationalist front, such as it was.

So we did not directly contest seats in the Cape and Transvaal. All that concerned me was to get the Progressive Party under way. In this respect it was a matter of importance to get the support of Harry Lawrence, who was overseas. He was opposed to Graaff's action in the Bantustan Debate. Zach and Colin believed he would join us when he knew the facts. If he supported us, then we would have a senior United Party politician and front-bencher with us since we had lost the backing of Waterson and Hamilton-Russell.

Johannesburg was confirmed as the group's head office. Several committees were formed to run Finance, Organisation and Public Relations. As chairman of the latter, my suggestion that I edit and produce fifty thousand copies of a newsletter carrying our two statements and the facts behind the Progressive break, was accepted. We continued, in the initial stages, as we had started when we broke with the UP. Helen, Zach and others on policy initiatives; myself with a small team on organisation and publicity.

In between all this the UP was calling on us daily to resign our seats since we had signed pledges to do so. We refused. We said the UP had reneged on the agreement they made in 1936 to implement the Land Act. Their threats left us cold.

Public interest was high. Letters of support were coming in, our public representatives were busy setting up their local organisations. All of us felt as if a load had been lifted from our shoulders. My greatest relief was that, at one stroke, I had got rid of Mrs English, Ernest Rex and the few who tried to make my life a misery in Hospital.

Most of my Hospital committee joined us, but Harry Schwarz remained with the UP since he was now the Provincial Councillor and I was sorry that our relationship was strained. This was sad, but I hoped the day would come when we would come together again. He was to become UP Provincial Council leader and ironically the spearhead of the next breakaway from the UP several years later before joining the Progressive Party.

Organisationally, I knew what to do and did not waste time consulting with others. I drew up memoranda on the infrastructure of the new party and on 28 August, two weeks after our break, it was in the hands of all our key personnel. Its acceptance allowed us to work almost from the beginning as a new political party.

I was in daily contact with Steytler at Queenstown drawing up all his major press statements which he amended and approved during the first weeks of the breakaway until our inaugural congress.

These were issued to all the national newspapers from my own office at Kruger and Wilson (Pty) Ltd. Molly Bell, my secretary, told me she did not know whether she worked for the new party-to-be or the company. It was an exciting time and I used my business facilities to the full to help us on the way.

In a "Plan of Action", I advised the group not to waste its time attacking Mitchell and the UP but to get on with the job of organising our party.

In Johannesburg we had the support of Laurence Gandar of *The Rand Daily Mail* which was of great significance because *The Star* was committed to the United Party. Leading newspapers elsewhere like John Sutherland's *Evening Post* and *The Natal Witness* backed us. The success of our first group meeting made us feel that we were, in a real sense, writing history. We were purged of the UP right wing. We were politically alive and independent. We had fixed the date of the inaugural congress of the Progressive Party in Johannesburg.

We were lucky that amongst the people who joined us from the UP was Max Borkum, the chairman of the their organising committee in Johannesburg. He was a wealthy stockbroker and friend of Helen Suzman. He played an important role in establishing the party in the early stages. Several of us kept in touch with Harry Oppenheimer, who had made public his support for the Progressives, and Zach de Beer and Borkum were the connecting link between Oppenheimer and the early funding of our proposed party.

I sent out organisational circulars to all our supporters, advising them that a Union Organisation and Public Relations Committee and a Finance Committee had been formed, and that our headquarters were in Johannesburg at GB Centre.

"The purpose of this first circular is to report progress and to provide for regional and local organisations; a proposed basis for the establishment of suitable methods of organisation, carrying our of public relations work and the development of a suitable financial structure for the proposed new party. In addition the circular contains the latest information with regard to the establishment of various offices and personnel who are carrying on the preliminary work with regard to the establishment of the new party."

While I was busy at national level dealing with the establishment of the party, I had to deal with the sniping from the Hospital UP. My own Hospital supporters rallied to my defence by writing letters to the newspapers, most of which were seen or initiated by me.

On 21 September we met in Durban for our second Steering Committee meeting. It was at this meeting that the first rift appeared between Zach de Beer and me about the way the Progressive Party should be organised. I cannot recall the details of our differences, but I know that we were so emotionally charged that on our way the following day to Port Elizabeth to attend a meeting we did not even speak to each other on the aeroplane.

It became worse because we had to share a hotel bedroom. In the morning, when Zach was in the bath, I had it out with him. I was opposed to his ideas on how the party was to be organised. I was frank with him. In my eyes he was inexperienced, and I did not approve of his leadership ambitions. Furthermore, he and Colin had already made cardinal tactical errors at the outset, confirming to a large degree their political immaturity.

They had allowed Graaff to regain the initiative and outwit them. I saw nothing in De Beer at that stage, which would lead me to accept him as leader should he be nominated. Zach was a doctor, like me, whose heart was in politics. He had been elected to Parliament at the age of 24, was married to the daughter of JGN Strauss, who had been the leader of the UP at the time. There was no doubt that, in Parliament, he was an outstanding member of the opposition.

Fortunately we ironed out our differences and had a successful meeting with the local Progressives in Port Elizabeth, helping them to establish themselves.

The 16th of September 1959 was a great day. We received news that Harry Lawrence had resigned from the United Party. He was deferring his decision whether he would join us, until he returned to South Africa, but we knew he would do so. By now the list of MPs who had resigned from the United Party was had grown to twelve. We had been joined by five MPCs, two in the Transvaal, two in Natal and one in the Cape, as well as four aspirant candidates for the Provincial elections, plus hundreds of leading UP office-bearers and supporters.

During the latter part of September, amongst all the activity, I was busy preparing the first issue of *Progressive News*. I sent a copy of the first draft to Colin Eglin for his approval, and a letter came back saying that "frankly I don't like the editorial. I believe that it will give support to the accusation that we merely used the Land Resolution as an excuse to leave the UP and that we had planned in advance to form a new party. Suggest that you delete in any case the phrase 'non-racial in character'. While I hope that our party will acquire a multiracial character as it develops, I think it most unwise to use the phrase you have at this stage while we are in the process of planning the party."

My editorial read as follows: "South Africa has entered a new political era. The Progressive Group has been born out of a political crisis. It is determined to create for South Africa a new political party that will be non-racial in character, realistic with regard to race relations and able to give hope to all the various races who together constitute our Country . . ."

Eglin, cautious as ever, put his foot into it. I never expected anyone to object to a straightforward message that spelt out our task. His reasoning was fallacious, but by now I was inured to contrary responses because everyone was somewhat "hyped up" and although I thought Colin would regret it one day, I left it out of the Cape edition of *Progressive News*, for the sake of peace.

By the time the October meeting of the Inaugural Committee in Cape Town arrived, we were almost ready to form our party. We felt like old hands. We approved of the party's constitution. De Beer reported on his talks with the Stellenbosch "intellectuals" and Donald Molteno was appointed to convene the Constitution Commission, regarded as a top priority.

Our Congress to form the party would be held on 13 November in Johannesburg, in committee, and would only deal with a number of essential items necessary for our formation. We had appointed our first General Secretary, Don Horak, and we were on our way.

The day before Congress, our Parktown house was like a hotel. Jan Steytler, Clive van Ryneveld and Leo Boyd were house guests. Clive, a former South African cricket captain, even found time to teach my young sons, Adrian and Nigel, the rudiments of cricket. It was all part of the remarkable canvas over those few days, when we held a new-style inauguration of the Progressive Party. The Cranbrooke Hotel was decorated in the party colours of red and blue, filled with delegates and a special observer Charles Whitehouse, political secretary of the American Embassy. I saw that we had good facilities to allow the press to give us full reports.

At least thrice a day, at set times, journalists were given statements of Congress decisions. Overnight, after the Progressive Party was formed I produced a special edition of *Progressive News* as a memento of this historic occasion.

My main contribution to Congress was the short motion I moved proposing the formation of the Progressive Party and seconded by Leo Boyd. It was carried unanimously "amid scenes of great enthusiasm, by the fully attended congress of 200 delegates and 150 observers from all parts of the Union." (*Progressive News*).

Steytler's opening speech set the tone: ". . . colour and colour alone should not be the yard stick by which people are judged. All South Africans should be given the opportunity to render a contribution to the political and economic life of the country."

Steytler was elected Leader amidst cheers, and Harry Lawrence became the party's first Chairman. We were over the first hurdle. By the end of the second day we knew that we had introduced three-party politics back into South Africa.

We stood for the abolition of pass laws and influx control, for free trade unions for all, the ending of the migratory labour system and the colour bar in industry. At long last we had a multiracial political party, unrestricted by the double-talk of the United Party; we were free to speak without frustration. As yet we had no black or coloured members, despite the fact that in those days there was no bar to membership.

Blacks were in ferment. They were engaged in an anti-pass revolt and had no time for white political parties or politicians no matter how liberal our ideas were.

The government's determination to go ahead with the Bantustans was a burning issue amongst blacks, and, as they did not have representation in

352

HE
PROGRESSIVE NEWS

A Newsletter of the
Progressive Party

OVEMBER, 1959   SPECIAL INAUGURAL CONGRESS EDITION   NUMBER 2.

Progressive Party Formed

The most significant politi-
l event in the past decade,
as how Mr. Harry Lawrence
.P., described the formation,
the new Progressive Party
South Africa.

A resolution adopting the
w Party's constitution was
rried unanimously, amid
enes of great enthusiasm, at
fully-attended congress of
'0 delegates and 150 obser-
rs from all parts of the
nion.

Gathered in the conference-
ll, as one delegate put it,
as "the biggest concentra-
on of the best political
ains in the country" and
e standard of speeches was
precedentedly high. Public
terest in the Congress and
e formation of the Party
s shown by the great pro-
inence given to the proceed-
gs throughout the South
rican press.

JAN STEYTLER LEADER

Harry Lawrence Chairman

Dr. Jan Steytler, farmer,
medical practitioner, ex-service-
man and son of a Boer hero,
was unanimously elected leader
of the Progressive Party at a
moving scene during the Progressive Congress on Friday.

Congress rose spontaneously
and acclaimed him. In reply, Jan
Steytler regretted that Harry
Lawrence had found it impossible to assume the leadership.
Mr. Lawrence would, however,
be a tower of strength as chairman, Parliamentary leader and
personal adviser.

Dr. Jan said he was determined
there would be a full spirit of democracy in the leadership. He would
never hesitate to give a firm lead,
but whenever humanly possible he
would consult those responsible
officers of the Party placed around
him.

DR. JAN STEYTLER, M.P.

●

NATIONAL EXECUTIVE
Dr. J. van A. Steytler (Leader of
the Party), M.P.
The Hon. H. G. Lawrence, M.P.
(Chairman of the Party).
Mr. R. Butcher, M.P.
Mr. J. P. Cope, M.P.
Dr. Z. J. de Beer, M.P.
Mr. C. Eglin, M.P.
Mr. C. van Ryneveld, M.P.
Mrs. Helen Suzman, M.P.
Mr. R. A. F. Swart, M.P.
Mr. T. O. Williams, M.P.
Dr. Boris Wilson, M.P.
Mrs. Jacqueline Beck
Mr. I. J. Bleiman
Mr. M. M. Borkum
Mr. L. Boyd
Mr. F. de Kock
Mr. A. Einstein
Dr. B. Friedman
Mr. I. Gordon-Forbes
Mr. I. Hall
Dr. Ellen Hellmann
Mr. M. Hofmeyr
Mr. L. Kowarsky
Mr. H. Marcus
Mr. M. H. Mayers
Mrs. Kathleen Mitchell
Mr. D. B. Molteno
Mr. B. Muir
Mr. R. S. Parrott
Prof. Hansi Pollak

Principles of the Progressive Party of South Africa

(1) The maintenance and extension
of the values of Western Civilisation, the protection of fundamental human rights and the
safeguard of the dignity and
worth of the human person irrespective of race, colour or creed.
(2) The assurance that no citizen of
the Union of South Africa shall
be debarred on grounds of race,
religion, language or sex from
making the contribution to our
national life of which he or she
may be capable.
(3) The recognition that in the
Union of South Africa there is
one nation which embraces
various groups differing in race,
religion, language and traditions; that each such group is
entitled to the protection of
these things and to its due share
in the government of the nation;
and that understanding, tolerance and goodwill between the
different groups must be
fostered.
(4) The maintenance inviolate of the
Rule of Law.
(5) The promotion of social progress
and the improvement of living
standards through the energetic
development of a modern economy based on free enterprise,
whereby the natural resources
of men and materials can be
fully utilised.
(6) The promotion of friendly relations with other sections, more
particularly the members of the
Commonwealth and those who
share with us the heritage of
Western Civilisation.

The Republic

The Progressive Party is resolute-
ly opposed to the Nationalist
Party's proposed republic, because
we believe it will endanger our internal peace and will lead to our
leaving the Commonwealth.
When proper constitutional reform has ensured democracy, and
if membership of the Commonwealth
is secured, the choice of governmental form — if it is still an issue
— should be left to the choice of
the electorate. No change should
however be made without the support of a substantial majority.

MAIN POINTS OF POLICY

Constitution

The Progressive Party stands for
NSTITUTIONAL REFORM in
uth Africa.

The new Constitution must be a
id one: that is, unalterable ex-
pt by a large majority of the
ctorate.

MUST:

Give political rights to those
who deserve them on a basis of
civilisation, regardless of race.

Protect the white and all racial
groups against oppression.

Increase the powers of the provinces, and make it possible for
new provinces to be created and
for neighbouring territories to
join the Union.

Franchise

The Progressive Party believes
at it is unjust and extremely
ngerous to deny any say in
vernment to civilised persons on
ounds of skin colour alone. There-
'e we stand for a system whereby
tably qualified people can obtain
l voting rights, while special
angements are made for the re-
esentation of less highly qualified
'rsons.

SOCIAL, RESIDENTIAL ASPECTS

The Party recognises the social
conventions which exist in South
Africa. It will not force residential
or social integration upon anyone,
and it will continue to provide separate amenities as desired by the
different races. But it will not deprive individuals of freedom of association.

The Party will repeal the Group
Areas Act, simultaneously making
provision for those who so wish to
live among their own people, but
opening the industrial and commercial areas to all races.

Economic and Labour Policy

The Party stands for the energetic development of a modern economy based on free enterprise. Its
policy will be directed to the conquest of poverty by increasing the
National Income, maintaining a high
and stable level of employment and
improving the living standards of
all sections of the population.

This envisages the removal of certain restrictions e.g. those on mobi-
lity of labour, and job reservations,
that prevent the fullest utilisation
of our human and material resources, the expansion of home and export markets, development of a
stabilised labour system, the restoration of freedom to the trade unions
and the extension to certain African
employees of full trade union rights.

Education Policy

The Party will extend the provisions for compulsory schooling as
facilities become available; while
ensuring that there is no basic difference in the type of education for
the various racial groups it will provide separate schools for the children of each group.

The Party recognises the right of
parents to determine the medium of
instruction of their children, the
right of universities to academic
autonomy and of teachers and university staff to freedom of conscience.

It will repeal the Bantu Education and the "University Apartheid"
Act.

Parliament, there seemed no point in their joining or supporting whites, who did not carry passes, did not have influx control and were not poverty-stricken.

Charles Whitehouse wrote to me after Congress thanking me for inviting him, and in my reply I told him that I was too involved in seeing it ran smoothly and looking after the journalists, to participate in policy debates. Zach de Beer wrote me a note saying how he was "impressed with the public relations side of Congress."

From my point of view, we had achieved a successful launch, despite the daily pounding we received from the United Party's newspapers. It seemed a far cry from the Bloemfontein break. We would no longer share the same benches as Mitchell, Vause Raw and the right wingers of the crippled United Party. We were our own political masters, and it was up to us to convince the country that the road we had chosen would lead to a new deal for all the people of South Africa. I had no illusions about the fight ahead, but at that stage we were hopeful of the future.

The tension and pressures were over. Since the break, all of us had been subject to every kind of mental trauma, ranging from personal insults from UP stalwarts, calls to resign and all the indignities that our former colleagues could heap on us. This was all coupled with the need to organise ourselves and our constituencies into the basics of a new parliamentary party. It was natural that in the process we would step on each other's toes and we did, frequently. On the other hand, the break threw up colleagues who were seeking personal power in the new situation, which was again natural, since politics is not just a game, but for some a fierce, individual and competitive struggle for power.

Prior to the Congress, while we were all busy organising, it was clear that difficulties were arising amongst a few of the leading personalities, as had happened in the case of Zach and me. On 22 October I wrote to Colin Eglin: "Over the last few weeks it has been clear to me that the various members of the Steering Committee in different parts of South Africa are not willing to work together as a team; there is far too much personal undercurrent; a number of people are wanting to build personal empires. Furthermore, it is impossible to get answers to letters; if circulars are sent out, people don't acknowledge or react to them."

At the same time I wrote a letter to Margaret Roberts (formerly of the Labour Party) who had joined us, mentioning that I was "unhappy about the personal manoeuvres that are going on behind the scenes." I was particularly referring to Zach. It seemed to me that he wanted the organisation and constitution shaped so that the leadership could ultimately fall his way. "There is no reason for me to interfere with his aspirations, except that it appears the Constitution of the Party and the way it will be run may be streamlined to suit his particular tastes. He put up a proposition that he should be appointed organising secretary and party manager and that he should do all the donkey work for the Leader."

My feeling was that we had been through all this in the UP. I wanted to see the end of this personal struggle for control. I was hoping that the breakaway had put paid to personal aggrandisement.

I suppose, in the flush of success in coming together as Progressives, one hoped that a new era had begun in personal relationships.

We were called prima donnas by the media. There was no doubt that in a smaller party the impact which individuals made was more marked. There was a failure in the early stages of people in various parts of the country to work together or leave power in the hands of the most competent. When I was in the small Labour Party there were many personal clashes, and I was used to it.

On the other hand, I was no longer interested in power polarisations in our new party. In December 1959 I flew to London, and was invited to speak to the Commonwealth Parliamentary Association at the House of Commons. I spoke about the background and formation of the Progressives to a crowded meeting and John Dugdale, a former Labour Party Minister, mentioned the fact in the House of Commons, calling us "brave people". At the meeting itself I was criticised by Sir Hugh Fraser, the blind MP who was a keen supporter of the Nationalists.

Helen Suzman was in London as well. She said in a press interview: ". . . people generally regard the Progressive Party as a gleam of light in the darkness of South Africa. There is a marked bias in Britain towards liberalising policies in Africa."

This was my experience as well. At a private dinner at the House of Lords, where I was the guest of honour at an exclusive small dining club, I was told to "let my hair down" as everything said at the meeting was confidential.

Away from South Africa I was able to reflect on a very full and eventful year. Things were not only happening to me in politics but the country as a whole. My relationship to the business was still at arm's length, but I was in touch with it daily.

The Hospital constituency was not a "progressive" one by any means. The people who joined the PP were loyal hard workers and we struggled to develop a strong political base because we had a constantly changing conservative electorate. Our liberal views were too far advanced for voters who for years had been fed non-controversial theories.

Cope and Suzman whose constituencies were wealthier and more stable, had better grassroots Progressive support; most of their voters could afford to be liberally minded in politics from their comfortable affluence.

In reviewing 1959, it was evident that under Dr Verwoerd the Nationalists had become obsessed with the implementation of apartheid. Amendments to existing Acts had gone through Parliament, shaping the country's destiny at a headlong pace. Apart from our break with the UP, most white voters were content to let Verwoerd and his Nationalists get on with the job.

The blacks, however, would not shut up. All over the country there was evidence of mounting opposition to the Pass Laws. Hardly a day passed without newspapers reporting incidents involving black protests ending in skirmishes with police. A general air of black dissatisfaction prevailed in large urban areas like Johannesburg, the eastern and western Cape Province.

The government's moves to establish black homelands was gaining momentum, and Verwoerd was hell-bent on achieving his targets. It seemed as if 1960 was going to lead to some kind of racial confrontation. The omens were bad.

I reminded myself that Verwoerd, at the end of the 1959 session, promised the country an independent Republic if the Commonwealth rejected South Africa's proposed membership. The Nationalists, he said, had taken "a clear step forward in this historic session in relation to apartheid". Verwoerd said he had overwhelming support for his moves and it was only a handful of liberals who objected.

56

It was in this unsettled environment that the Progressive Party commenced the 1960 session of Parliament, sitting to the left of the United Party in the House. Jan Steytler and Harry Lawrence were our front-benchers, Colin Eglin became the Chief Whip. I remained a back-bencher. There was no caucus room in the main part of Parliament available for us and we had to "make do" with an old storage room (for *Hansard*) in the basement of the building, which we also used as a general office.

Our Caucus meetings had a totally different atmosphere from the start. They were without rancour as far as policy and strategy were concerned. There was an intellectual kinship which we had not experienced in the UP, because we now created political policies in which we believed and which we all supported. Professor "Sakkies" Fourie left us shortly after our Congress because he felt that our opposition to a Republic under Verwoerd was wrong. In December we were joined by Walter Stanford, a Native Representative, who saw a future for the Progressive Party.

It was an historic moment in the 1960 No Confidence Debate when Jan Steytler stood up to make his first speech as Leader of the Progressive Party in Parliament. He stated, in dramatic and sometimes emotional terms, where the Progressive Party stood, and the role we intended to play in fighting apartheid, by making it clear also that we stood by the 1936 Land Act and that we were opposed to Verwoerd's Bantustan concepts.

Dr Verwoerd rose after Steytler and warned the House that if the Progressives policy ever came to fruition, South Africa was doomed as a white man's country.

"At least I want to admit this: he and his party have the courage to say: This is the road we choose – down the precipice". He later elaborated by saying we wanted to hand over to the blacks. He forecast (quite correctly) that the United Party would lose more of its liberal followers in the years to come to the PP and the more conservative to the Nationalist Party.

Verwoerd announced that South Africa would hold a referendum on a Republic, indicating that it would be decided by white voters to "at last see the end of the disputes in regard to our constitutional future between the two language groups so that we can become one united nation".

On 25 January, Graaff moved that the No Confidence Debate be adjourned so that a matter of public importance be discussed. The day before, the Cato Manor black slum near Durban, had erupted into a riot and nine policemen were killed. This urgent debate in Parliament brought back the reality of apartheid, and the cynical role the government was playing.

This was the second time in a year that a riot had occurred. The government blamed all sorts of people, including the English press, and refused to appoint the judicial commission which we requested. Once again, all that the debate did was to evoke party political jibes and empty rhetoric.

It was this sort of debate in Parliament that made me realise that my long-standing belief that it was the place where open and honest discussions could take place, was not so.

Parliament under the Nationalists was merely a conduit through which their apartheid legislation would pass. We could object, call for commissions, give constructive advice, criticise – but all we got in response was ridicule and a level of discussion that was sterile and pointless.

Serious and bloody outbreaks between blacks and the police, inter-racial conflicts and other incidents were blamed on the multiracial views of the opposition. The lead was given by Verwoerd and the Nationalist MPs followed obediently.

Cato Manor was a slum which housed thousands of black workers in appalling conditions near Durban. It emerged that on a peaceful Sunday the police, in typical fashion, were raiding the homes of black people and arresting them for minor technical offences such as Pass laws, illegal residence and Influx Control infringements. Whatever the causes, some residents of Cato Manor objected. In a flash there was a riot. Nine policemen were killed.

Years of government neglect had exploded at the cost of nine unlucky policemen. The government did not concern itself with underlying causes. Poverty, overcrowding, bad housing, unemployment and police harassment were ignored. The unnecessary implementation of the worst apartheid laws were their prime objectives. The real issues, the degrading state in which the blacks lived, due to a host of sociological and economic causes, were overlooked.

Ronald Butcher, the local MP, pleaded for a judicial commission of enquiry, without success. The Minister of Justice replied that he considered the "debate ill-timed . . . I am sick and tired of Cato."

He blamed incitement at public meetings at Cato Manor. Mrs Ballinger, ending the debate said: "When the African people behave as they do in this way, they behave like slum populations the world over, and the reason they behave like slum populations is because they are left to rot in slums."

This was an early demonstration in 1960 of the failure of Parliament to get to grips with significant social upheavals caused by apartheid. The

Nationalists simply ignored unrest and dissatisfaction amongst blacks and blamed black and white political "agitators" for the killings. (With hindsight, it is remarkable how enduring these Nationalist rationalisations have been. Much the same sort of thing is still being said and believed).

Our independence in Parliament as the Progressive Party demonstrated early on the basic differences of our attitude towards apartheid from that of the United Party. We were determined to expose the UP's double standards.

An early opportunity came when the government introduced an amendment to the Separate Amenities Act relating to beach apartheid. In the UP we would have had to accept the amendment, which the UP did. With a free conscience we voted against it.

Unfortunately, we needed fifteen votes to secure a Division but we made our point. We had a similar opportunity in the Appropriation Bill that followed. We moved that "the House declines to pass the Second Reading of the Part Appropriation Bill unless the government abandons race policies which are in conflict with economic facts and devotes itself to raising opportunity earning power and prosperity of all sections of the people of our multiracial state."

We were not the only ones who made political history. The following day Harold Macmillan made his famous "Winds of Change" speech at a joint meeting of the House and the Senate.

The parliamentary dining room had been cleared, leaving only the enormous old paintings on the walls. Harold MacMillan and Dr Verwoerd sat alone on the platform. Members of both Houses filled the room. Macmillan, in quiet measured tones, developed his theme of the changing Africa and the emancipation from colonial rule.

He explained that "the most striking of all the impressions I have formed since I left London is the strength of this African National consciousness . . . The wind of change is blowing through this continent . . . And whether we like it or not this growth of national consciousness is a political fact. We must all accept it as a fact and our national policies must take account of it . . . This means I would judge that we come to terms with it."

To the obvious consternation of Verwoerd who was listening intently and to the many Nationalists present Macmillan set out some guidelines: "Our judgement of right or wrong and of justice is rooted in the same soil as yours – Christianity and in the rule of law as the basis of a free society . . . and that must in our view include the opportunity of an increasing share in political power and responsibility; a society finally in which individual merit and individual merit alone is the criterion for man's advancement whether political or economic."

He reminded us that the official policy of Britain was non-racial and near the end of his speech said: "..but I hope you won't mind me saying frankly that there are some aspects of your policies which make it impossible for us to do this without being false to our own deep convictions about the political destinies of free men to which in our own territories we are trying to give effect."

Macmillan had delivered an open challenge to Dr Verwoerd and the Nationalists: after twelve years of increasingly repressive rule, which ignored the rights of blacks in Southern Africa, there was little time left to make changes which would not only meet the needs of the African national consciousness but that of the the civilised nations of the West.

How would Verwoerd take Macmillan's warnings?

Most Nationalists present, I am sure, expected Dr Verwoerd to give an immediate reply – and he did. Instead of a "Thank you," speech, Verwoerd reminded Macmillan that whites were not expendable and that only the Afrikaners could solve their own problems and did not need the assistance of the outside world.

As I left the old parliamentary dining room I felt both a sense of elation and deflation. Macmillan had done his job to point out to Verwoerd that he could not go it alone because both the outside world and the forces of black nationalism would rise up against Afrikaner volk hegemony. Dr Hendrik Verwoerd brushed it all aside. The Afrikaner course had been charted – South Africa would go it alone.

Die Transvaler published an editorial after this speech which said that what Macmillan had said about South Africa "went to the very roots of the existence of the whites here." Sitting at the back of the room and watching the scene I wondered to what extent Macmillan's warnings would effect the Nationalists in their approach to South Africa's problems.

A month later I was speaking in the House on a Nationalist Information Services motion and I reminded MPs that "Macmillan had jolted South Africa out of a dream". *The Rand Daily Mail* approved of what I said, because under large headlines it quoted me as "thanking the British Prime Minister for doing more than any other man during the past 12 years to jolt the people of South Africa out of this dream world of apartheid."

Macmillan's words were timely, with reverberations throughout the whole of Southern Africa. Nationalists faced increasing black hostility to apartheid legislation. They condemned Macmillan's interference in South Africa's internal affairs, and ignored his warning. They demanded "strict action against foreigners permanently or temporarily resident in the Union who, while availing themselves of the country's hospitality, are guilty of malevolent and undermining activities against the interests of South Africa."

Lord Poole, a former chairman of the Conservative Party told South African newspapers in Johannesburg that what Macmillan said to the people of South Africa "is without doubt fully representative of what is in the minds of the majority of people in England, regardless of their political party."

Nationalist Party politicians reacted through their newspapers, demanding that the sooner the country became a Republic the better – away from the influence of Britain.

The whites began organising either to support or oppose the Republican referendum, while the blacks, who had nothing to do with the referendum, were concerned with matters nearer their doorsteps – apartheid.

We were opposed to Verwoerd's Republic, and we started protesting early. Leo Boyd, in Natal on the day that Macmillan spoke in Cape Town, told a Pietermaritzburg audience of 1 200 that "people should clearly see now the path they must take in the future. The only path which offers any hope to multiracial South Africa is the path towards racial co-operation, and sooner or later we must take that path."

The Progressives saw the Macmillan speech as underlining the fight for multiracialism in South Africa – the NP and the UP saw Macmillan's message as an opportunity to say to outsiders: Keep your nose out of South Africa's affairs.

The obvious interpretation is that Macmillan was fully aware of what Dr Verwoerd's Nationalists were doing to South Africa and timed his speech to raise a voice of protest from the outside world. The speech heartened us. We felt it was historically important and would help us to achieve our political goals.

57

The pressures on our small team of eleven MPs were great. Most of us had to shadow more than one portfolio. At the same time there were a few of us who were very involved in party affairs. My job was to look after the Progressive Party's organisation and public relations division. I soon found it impossible to manage everything.

I persuaded the party to appoint a director of public relations to assist me. Miles Malleson, a young, successful advertising executive took over the post. I had already completed all the initial planning from the date of the founding of the party. My first confidential circular was sent out on 12 February 1960 and party structure was organised on this basis.

However, there was an additional burden. In addition to the massive work entailed in building up the party, we had to run the referendum campaign to oppose the establishment of a Republic.

Miles Malleson made it clear to me that we could not run this ourselves and that we should get an overseas expert to do so. He had in mind Al Toombs, who had worked in West African political elections. Harry Oppenheimer helped, through his London office, to investigate Al Toombs, who eventually came to South Africa to survey the scene and advise us. We engaged him and most of the referendum work opposing the establishment of the Republic was carried out by Miles and Al Toombs.

The thought that South Africa could become a Republic under Verwoerd and the Nationalists was depressing. The fact that South Africa was a member of the Commonwealth and that we had the links with British democracy had always been of comfort.

To abandon this for unrestrained Verwoerdian republicanism was horrifying. I had studied Nationalist policies and I had in my possession a copy, in English, of the National Party plans for a Republic drawn up in 1942 when Dr Malan was their leader.

In essence, South Africa would become an Afrikaner-controlled Republic, dominated by the Broederbond, with the possibility of English-speaking citizens relegated to second place, with the fullest implementation of apartheid and increasing inequalities for the blacks, which were already barely tolerable. Macmillan's hope, and ours, of a non-racial society was pure fiction. The country would be ruled by an oligarchical military clique backed by a Calvinistic church. South Africa would be a white laager of immense proportions in black Africa – kept together by machine-guns

The 1960 Parliament continued with one Bill after the other making inroads into every aspect of South African life to make apartheid a reality. We were constantly reminded of what an Afrikaner Republic would mean. Verwoerd was in a hurry; his great plans for separating the races had to be carried out as quickly as possible. It was clear to me that his target was to implement the 1942 concept of the Republic.

He was determined to achieve his republic, no matter what it cost. When it came, it would mean radical constitutional change in the country. Verwoerd announced in the House that a simple majority of even one vote either way would decide the issue.

It was a devastatingly simple solution.

In Parliament there was now a new kind of politics. We faced implacable Afrikaner nationalism. I, and many others, considered that it would be impossible to exist in Verwoerd's republic. The monarchy did not mean much to us, but the link we had with the British Crown represented a democratic lifeline which Dr Verwoerd was going to destroy.

Personally, I had no wish to live in a society dominated by the harsh reality of Verwoerd's apartheid. I saw no hope of peace in race relations, for which I had been struggling for so long.

I had spent a lot of my life trying to find a formula that would help put my country on the road to peaceful multiracialism. The gulf between the Nationalists' apartheid beliefs and our liberal voices seemed unbridgeable. The Nats only wanted the survival of the white Afrikaner Volk – nothing else mattered to them. It was clear that 1960 would be a watershed year in my political life.

Outside Parliament, almost every day, there were signs of mounting hostility by blacks to Verwoerd's repression. It was true that some legislation had been on the statute books long before the NP came to power, but previous governments had not enforced many of the laws in the same draconian way as Verwoerd. He amended and updated, and these were the Bills that came to the House with regularity.

The strengthening of apartheid was a warning of grave times ahead, which the Nationalists took in their stride and viewed with equanimity.

The Republic referendum, therefore, required maximum opposition from us. Organising a "NO" vote was no easy task. Blacks did not take part nor were they asked to. It was a white man's matter which did not interest them. They had no votes and no legal status, and by no stretch of imagination could we see a situation in which Dr Verwoerd would try and get black views on a republic. The main concerns of blacks were their own immediate survival – poverty, passes, restrictions on movement, arrests, deprived social conditions, appalling educational facilities and humiliation by the whites.

Verwoerd constantly assured whites that democratic institutions would be preserved. I never believed him. The Nationalist idea of democracy was simply defined: "The white man is Baas".

One saw it every day in the House. Bills gave Ministers discretion to act as they thought fit or by regulation. Whilst Progressives objected, the white people of South Africa, in the main, approved, and believed the Nationalists were on the right road. Blacks responded dramatically. There was open activity against the government's apartheid laws. The interesting thing was that on the surface the government was impervious to the countrywide disturbances which were being dealt with by the police. Blacks, and some whites, were detained almost daily and hundreds were already inside gaols with no access to their families or the law.

In the face of all this, our fledgling political party was succeeding in Parliament by dissecting every Bill that came along, dealing with matters of national interest protesting about the repressive way the government was implementing apartheid.

We asked questions, to expose covert attempts by the government to hide from public scrutiny the real nature of their rule, and in general focused on the hollowness of the United Party's so-called anti-Nationalist stance.

Underlying everything, in February and March, was the continuing effect of Harold Macmillan's speech. Two days after he delivered it, Jan Steytler moved a Private Member's motion rejecting partition of the Union of South Africa, calling for reform of the constitution based on the multiracial character of the state.

It called for guarantees on fundamental rights and liberties of people of all races and ensuring political rights for all citizens irrespective of colour.

Steytler and De Beer made excellent speeches. The surprise was the interest the Nationalists took in the debate. As usual, they proposed an amendment, reaffirming segregation of races and white survival. The UP took the opportunity to move an amendment proposing the social and residential separation of races. These amendments demonstrated the great divide between the Progressives, the NP and UP. We were clearly telling Parliament and the country that no policy would succeed in the future which did not fully recognise the social and political needs of all the races of South Africa on a basis which initially would still require voting qualifications and minority protection.

In 1960 this is as far as we would go, but it was light years ahead, in its goals, of any of the other white political parties with the exception of the Liberal Party's one-man-one-vote.

During February I had spoken on a number of Bills and it was noticeable that the NP no longer harassed me as they had in 1959 when they were forced to apologise in the House. It was evident that I had silenced them. My speeches were treated more on their merits, with less abuse and fewer smears. I was able to pay more attention to debates. However, what depressed me was the great gap between our thinking and the Nationalists.

I began to believe that we would never find common ground in order to solve race relations problems. The Nationalists were entrenched and, under Verwoerd, proceeding arrogantly to create the "grand apartheid" South African state. The Nationalists could be in power for many years to come.

In the debate on the Factories Act Amendment Bill I tried to raise the importance of the long-term effects of apartheid on the actual day-to-day working on the factory floor.

In the Third Reading, Harry Lawrence, following me, said I had made a "most lucid speech . . . given the House some of the effects on industry and on industrialists."

A leading NP member, GLH van Niekerk, criticised and dissected my speech. It is worth quoting from *Hansard* because it demonstrated the implacable prejudice and fears that dominated the average Afrikaner's attitude to colour in South Africa.

Mr van Niekerk: ". . . Laws are passed to ensure that order is maintained and by virtue of that fact alone this amending Bill is justified. The Hon Member [Dr Wilson] talked about the effects this measure would have on race relations. I maintain it will have the most wholesome effect; it seems to me that those two members have never yet been in a factory. They have not as yet seen whites and non-whites leave at the same door . . . I have seen people at clothing factories, white and black enter at the same doors and rushing out from the same doors. I have heard the insults they hurl at each other."

Dr Wilson: "Haven't you got non-whites in your home?"

Mr van Niekerk: "I have, but I'm not like Solly Sachs who said: 'Because my Native girl looks after my child she has the right to bath in my bath'. The Hon Member for Hospital may be of the same opinion but I am not. In my home the relationship is that of master and servant and that is also the relationship which is maintained in the factories. There is no social equality. The white man is superior. That is why I am sure that this legislation will be welcomed by all who wish to maintain white leadership . . . No mention is made of the additional benefits the workers will derive from this Bill . . . furthermore there is the extension of apartheid facilities, separate entrances, separate first-aid rooms, clocking devices, pay offices and eating utensils . . . I do not know whether the Hon Member for Hospital uses the same eating utensils as his non-white domestic servants. We do not do it. It is not our tradition and it is not the tradition of any true South African, whether he is Afrikaans-speaking or English-speaking."

Harry Lawrence, replying, went straight to the point: "What you are making in the second half of the twentieth century is a nightmare of South Africa."

Van Niekerk's statement was not an isolated viewpoint. He had summarised in a few sentences the attitudes of the average white person in South Africa towards the blacks. I am certain that not many parliamentarians paid much attention to this speech, nor did the newspapers. It was, however, the brutal truth about white attitudes to blacks, and why the Nationalists had no problems in coming to terms with the legislation they were pushing through the South African Parliament. They knew that in making these declarations they were *de facto* speaking for the overwhelming majority of white people.

I was not surprised to find myself questioning how long I would be able to continue to participate in the daily parliamentary charade of rhetoric aimed at halting the march of apartheid. We were up against a wall of granite – be it Hendrik Verwoerd or a back-bench Nat MP. I never realised how strongly the Nationalists would characterise left-of-centre Progressive views as inconsistent with those of the average white South African voter.

Outside Parliament, at many public meetings in order to get our message across, we explained why we had broken away, why it was necessary to make radical changes to the laws of the land so that in our lifetime we could avoid serious confrontation with blacks before we achieved a multiracial society.

But outside Parliament we came up against another wall of granite. The average white voter was not ready to support our views. They said we were 20 years ahead of our time. Nationalists smeared us as Marxists or followers of Lenin. I began to understand that speaking to them in Parliament was a sheer waste of time. Our views that blacks were entitled to the same civilised treatment as whites was unacceptable to the majority of MPs.

Apartheid legislation was making itself felt throughout South Africa. The rigidity of the application of the laws stiffened non-white resistance; there had, of course, been no consultation with them at any time. Their response was to rebel; they refused to carry passes. Police were attacked. Civil disturbance began in the rural and urban areas.

Parliament seemed unaffected by the awful results of apartheid in the black areas. White people in their segregated residential areas, distanced themselves from the social disruption they did not see or hear.

The political atmosphere was depressing. There was an undefined apprehension amongst the people who lived in the northern suburbs of Johannesburg who were mainly the professional and wealthier business class. They were opposed to what Verwoerd was doing, but they did not want their comfortable life style disturbed. Many tried to turn a blind eye to the forced removals, the arrests and detentions, the frequent clashes with the police and the restraints that were increasingly placed on them as employers of black labour. It was the same kind of endless depression that people felt during the war years.

Will it ever be different? Will it ever end?

58

As the Progressive Party grew, new internal conflicts emerged. I was trying to co-ordinate the activities of the public relations section, but it was becoming more and more evident that the Cape members were often taking unilateral action without consulting me when it involved matters of national importance. Things were going wrong. Statements on the referendum circulating throughout the country often ended up emasculated due to the differing views of our Cape Town office. Eglin and De Beer openly indicated that they did not like the centre of control in Johannesburg.

Leo Boyd, from Natal, and I became increasingly fed up with this situation. Early in March I wrote to him:

"With regard to the mess-up in Cape Town about the Reject the Republic appeal, I am deeply disturbed about the continuous bungling on major matters. This is not the first time this has happened; it's about the third or fourth time. And the net result is that we do not get the press that we should get."

All this was a big disappointment to me. I was reading more into these incidents than they deserved, but there was no question that Eglin, De Beer and I differed very greatly on running the Progressive Party's affairs when Parliament was not sitting. Steytler spent most of his time at his home in Queenstown instead of Cape Town or Johannesburg. The irony was that control passed into Eglin and De Beer's hands; they now had the *de facto* control of the party and its Cape Town-based research department. These developments did not please me.

It was not a happy period. The early feelings of euphoria when we formed the party had long gone. We were all up against the realities of building a new party in the midst of the most serious political developments and social havoc in the country. The way ahead was not going to be easy.

I was certain that in the not-too-distant future there would be a power struggle for leadership – De Beer showed all the signs of a frustrated leader. It was obvious that he wanted it. After all, it had been he and Eglin who had set the ball rolling for the break; he was an Afrikaner like Steytler, but much more sophisticated and astute. He was an outstanding orator in Parliament but he needed much more political experience in dealing with people.

Steytler was a likeable and genuine personality. He was easy to get on with; I soon formed a close friendship with him. I was able to speak freely to him, and on several occasions I spoke to him about the general futility of the debates in the House and that I was most unhappy about spending my days in this environment. I was also thwarted by personal confrontations and lack of co-operation from the PP's organisation. Apart from anything else, we were a small team. Our time was fully taken up studying Bills, making speeches, asking questions. I was not interested in playing political games in the in the party. In the House I had the additional task of cultivating the parliamentary correspondents. The PP needed the best publicity it could get, and the journalists welcomed speech handouts and tip-offs about parliamentary events.

Apart from the referendum, the important priority was to establish the Progressives by putting our policies across to the English-speaking electorate who had been dominated by the Smuts-Botha tradition of the United Party and whose ideas on race relations and the colour question had made few advances since Union in 1910. Most of them did not understand why we had broken away. Many condemned us as left wingers, communists and fellow-travellers and were relieved that we were no longer in the United Party. We also had to face the fact that we had little hope of getting Afrikaner support. The UP's liberal wing had been painted for years by both UP and NP as political untouchables and "Reds".

There was a small movement at Stellenbosch University where some of the Afrikaner intellectuals were beginning to speak out. We also knew that if there was an election all of us could lose our seats. Therefore we had to do as much as we could to enlighten voters of at least the English-speaking constituencies that it was vital to keep us in Parliament.

Hence the media – the press was very important to us. We were the only politicians in Parliament who were constantly evaluating what the Nationalists were doing, scrutinising every word of the Bill, attacking and harassing Dr Verwoerd on every move he made in and out of the House. We put the United Party to shame as they continued to use double-standards in dealing with Nationalist apartheid plans.

Dr Verwoerd dominated all the proceedings in Parliament. He was a powerful personality, an independent thinker, patient and we could always expect speeches that lasted two hours and more.

They were political lectures, most of the time. We listened with concentration, because this was the master of apartheid speaking. Verwoerd would painstakingly spell out to Parliament almost every stage of his plans and was ready to defend them from opposition attacks. He overshadowed the government benches; they voted as a bloc. There was no dissent. Every time an innocuous-sounding Bill came along we had to study it carefully to see where the apartheid catch was.

Mostly, we were on the lookout for the delegated powers which were given to Ministers and which were the hallmark of the Verwoerd era in Parliament.

More important than what was happening in Parliament was the daily news of increasing rebellion amongst blacks. The breakaway Pan African Congress was telling them not to carry passes, organising protests to take place during late March throughout the country. In the large urban areas like Johannesburg, police raids by the "Ghost Squads" were frequent.

If a black servant did not turn up for work, the white employer would telephone the police station to find out whether the servant was there because of a pass offence. If he was, the next move was to go to the Native Commissioner's Court, where daily hundreds of blacks were summarily sentenced to prison or farm labour. Cope elicited from the Minister of Bantu Administration that in Johannesburg alone 55 475 cases were heard by the

Native Commissioner's Court in 1959, of which 48 126 were charged under the laws governing Influx Control.

The extent of the police action on the streets could be judged by these statistics. Projected countrywide, they showed the great injustice done to blacks by the architects of apartheid. No wonder black resentment was rising. It was no surprise that they were fighting back.

It is fair to comment that 1960 Parliamentary debates were dominated by what was taking place in the black areas. When the PP raised these issues, we were called agitators or ANC and PAC supporters. We were accused of fuelling black resentment.

Private Motions by MPs on the Order Paper were often hotly debated, with several there as political kites to herald impending government action or new legislation.

Dr Carel de Wet, now one of Verwoerd's closest supporters, introduced a motion in the House deploring anti-South African propaganda, which he blamed on liberals. His motion called for action to restrict activities of foreign correspondents, many of them "stringers" for overseas newspapers, whom he said were "guilty of malevolent and undermining activities against the interests of South Africa".

In this debate, after the Minister of External Affairs, Mr Eric Louw, had spoken in support of De Wet's motion, I moved an amendment to the effect that "South Africa's prestige overseas would not be restored until it reverses its apartheid policy, and withdraws its threats of imposing political censorship."

I accused De Wet of planting his motion to pave the way for political censorship. As usual Eric Louw erupted and strenuously denied the accusation.

The following week, by contrast, there was a motion from Margaret Ballinger, the liberal leader of the Native Representatives.

Her motion read: "The Pass system now applied to our African population constitutes an unjustifiable invasion of personal liberty and should be replaced by a system in keeping with modern democratic practice".

The UP amendment to Mrs Ballinger's motion asked for modifications in the Pass laws and that they should be applied with "greater fairness and justice." We fully supported Margaret Ballinger. If we had still been in the UP, we would have had to toe the line and vote against her motion, which was contrary to what we believed. How could one apply the stringent Pass Laws with greater fairness and justice? The only solution was to scrap them.

From the PP benches I wondered how I had ever joined the United Party believing that it could be reformed from within. Parliament had changed my views, especially the experiences in the UP's Caucus and the futility of the debates in the House. Going to Parliament for the UP ultimately brought me into the Progressive Party.

Equally important, as members of a small party we did not spend valuable time on arguments amongst ourselves on party policy or legislation.

It was mostly clear-cut. In this sense, a great political burden had been lifted. In the UP one was constantly fighting on two fronts – against the Nationalists or embroiled in a never-ending fracas with our right wingers. In the PP we saw the country's problems in a holistic way. Even votes on Committee of Supply would not be supported by us until the government "abandons its disruptive apartheid policy, adopts an economic labour policy dedicated to the conquest of poverty . . ."

The Nationalists often lost their sense of perspective in their desire to implement apartheid and widen the black-white gap. Question time in the House often revealed their stupidities.

On 8 March the Minister of Bantu Administration told Mrs Ballinger that white school inspectors were banned from shaking hands with black teachers and chiefs while on official duties. He said that "instructions should be given that European officials of [my] department were not to greet Bantu persons in the European manner by shaking hands."

If this situation was farcical, it was nevertheless symptomatic of the astonishing influence of Dr Verwoerd on the National Party and the tremendous fear engendered in most Afrikaners that if you shook hands with a black man, he would next ask to visit your home and maybe fall in love with your daughter. It sounds surrealistic, but this was the attitude of many MPs in Parliament and what Afrikaner voters believed. The Afrikaner was insecure under Verwoerd. He strengthened the master-servant relationship in the country, and this explains why our liberal ideas were fought tooth and nail.

59

Of course, there were debates in the House unrelated to racial problems. As I was involved in the radio industry, the PP left me to deal with all broadcasting matters. In Committee of Supply, I raised two matters which the government did not like. The first was the appointment of the new chairman of the South African Broadcasting Corporation. Under normal circumstances, this would not be raised in Parliament because the SABC was independent, reporting annually to the Minister of Posts and Telegraphs. My reasons for speaking were important. The NP did not like what I had to say.

Ever since the Nationalists came to power they had increased their influence on the media, especially broadcasting, to further their apartheid aims. They packed the SABC board with NP supporters and the Nationalist propaganda that flowed from the SABC was at times nauseating. Several of my friends who worked for the SABC told me how deep was the Nationalist infiltration and influence.

The *coup de grâce* was the proposed appointment of the head of the Broederbond, Dr Piet Meyer, whose personal history was known to me, as the new chairman of the SABC.

Apart from the Broederbond connection, Meyer had been a member of the Ossewa Brandwag, the illegal organisation banned by Smuts, for sabotaging South Africa's war effort. Meyer had published a book called *Trek Verder*, in which he postulated that the "Afrikaner was placed by God to make a stand against Russian and Chinese Communism, Indian Imperialism, European Liberalism and American Capitalist sentimentalism", whatever the latter was. The book was full of prejudice, mumbo-jumbo and political jargon. I could not see how such a bigoted and confused person could head the SABC.

In my speech I asked the Minister of Posts and Telegraphs, Dr Albert Hertzog, whether, amongst other things, Dr Meyer was the right and proper person for the job which needed a man of stature, impartial and objective. While I was speaking I noticed that Dr Meyer was listening in the public gallery. This did not deter me from voicing strong opposition to his appointment. I was sure the Nationalists would unleash a tirade, which they did, in the form of a personal attack on me. I was told that I should be ashamed of myself for daring to attack Dr Meyer, whose appointment was a foregone conclusion. Under his rule the SABC became the full propaganda arm of the government, which is still the position today, whatever new arguments are produced to conceal this.

I had also been tipped off by friends in the SABC that the government was going to introduce Very High Frequency (VHF) broadcasts in the near future. I saw this as another formidable way for the Nationalists under Dr Meyer to to control the dissemination of news and propaganda on a racial and tribal basis. Because of the technical constraints, these broadcasts could only be received in line-of-sight, distances of twenty to thirty miles.

I asked Dr Hertzog how true this "rumour" was. I also asked about the introduction of television. Hertzog did not reply, but Verwoerd emphatically rejected the idea that TV would be introduced into South Africa. He was opposed to it. The Nationalists were almost neurotic at the thought that they would never control what was shown on TV. However, the subject of VHF was always avoided by Hertzog.

I was convinced it was coming and would be used to indoctrinate and control the various black ethnic populations.

Verwoerd, in the Prime Minister's Vote, devoted most of his speech to the role of the white man: "The white man is the leader and the creator," giving us the full blast of his Verwoerdian philosophy.

Once more he took the opportunity of attacking Macmillan's "Winds of Change" speech:

". . . If the white official, the white entrepreneur, the white scientist and the white adviser are taken away from these states, what remains? Can the blacks govern such a state themselves and can they maintain their economy?

"They cannot . . . I am not discussing a political struggle. I am making a plea for the right of whites . . . Do not let anybody suffer from the psychosis that the white man in Africa can just be swept aside in order to satisfy world opinion."

Dr Verwoerd mesmerised his Nationalists. He chose the right time and the right place to put Macmillan's views in perspective. He had the advantage that whatever he said could no longer be rebutted by Macmillan. All this was against the background of rising unrest in South Africa, and luckily for Verwoerd, unrest elsewhere in Africa.

The political aces were all in his hands. He emphasised to his South African followers that they should not be influenced by visiting politicians, whoever they were. He criticised the "over-hasty handing over of independence" and foresaw the establishment of black dictatorships, despite the fact that he was establishing a white dictatorship. All the ills of Africa, for Verwoerd, were linked to the West's failure to deal with Communism.

Dr Verwoerd gave South Africa, through Parliament, his solution.

"We say there should be no mingling anywhere – no intermingling in the political sphere nor the swallowing up of the white man by the black masses in any other sphere of life. Wherever suitable a white state should be established . . . from which will emanate the influence which will lead to the gradual development of the neighbouring state which will be black."

Whether one liked Verwoerd or not, it was fascinating to hear him expound his theories in the House. He ended this speech by saying that the "supremacy of the white man in the Union is not only in the white man's interest but also in Britain's interest." (This was for the benefit of the British government and Macmillan)

Without doubt this was one of Verwoerd's most important statements of policy. It reflected the great strength of the man as Nationalist leader; whether one liked it or not, he was apartheid's philosopher, commanding the attention not only of all South Africans, but of the world outside.

I had my turn again when Carel de Wet's motion was continued the following week. I did not hold back. I told the House that the attitude of people overseas was largely due to the accurate reporting of the events in South Africa's Parliament. I conceded that there were cases of inaccurate reporting, which however were outweighed by the fact that "adverse propaganda will not cease and be successfully countered, nor South Africa's prestige restored in the eyes of the world, until the government reverses its apartheid policy, gives an unequivocal assurance that deportation threats against foreign correspondents will be withdrawn and renounces any intention of imposing political censorship in the Union."

60

Monday 21 March 1960 brought us back to reality in Parliament. We were listening once again to Dr De Wet who this time was criticising De Villiers Graaff on his reaction to Macmillan, whose "Winds of Change" continued to reverberate throughout almost every debate. Before concluding De Wet said:

"Just a final word before I sit down. Serious riots have taken place at Vanderbijl Park [De Wet's constituency]. My information is that one black man has been shot dead. They have marched on the police station and the white people in the town are very alarmed and I want to make an appeal to the government today. The one thing I am concerned about is that when there are riots whether on the part of whites or on the part of blacks, if it is necessary to shoot, only one person is shot dead."

Mercifully the time limit cut De Wet short.

Like others on the opposition benches, we were horrified by what we had heard. For a moment the House was stunned. Steytler was on his feet as the next speaker. I looked over at Verwoerd, who had lost his cherubic calm.

I could not believe my ears, as De Wet was a medical colleague. Although I had little time for his views, it was unbelievable that a medical man should call for more people to be shot. He and I had both taken the Hippocratic oath in order to protect life, and here before Parliament and South Africa he was asking for more killing of blacks.

The shooting he referred to was to change the course of South African history because he was giving us the first news of the Sharpeville massacre.

Steytler, also a medical doctor, lashed into De Wet before he went on to his main speech, expressing his horror at De Wet's callousness. He called on Verwoerd to explain De Wet's remarks.

The House was tense. We awaited more news. We knew that the PAC were demonstrating about passes, but never expected violence to erupt. It was ironic that Sharpeville occurred on the day we were still discussing Macmillan's speech.

Speaker after speaker on the Opposition benches went for De Wet and his "only one black shot" remark. As each spoke, Dr Verwoerd grew more and more uncomfortable. It was obvious that he would have to intervene about De Wet's remarks.

In the Committee of Supply later, Carel de Wet was once more on his feet. He tried to explain to us that that when whites needed protection they should get it and the blacks were marching through a white area. His explanation was unacceptable. He had clearly deplored the fact that only one black man had been shot. It was difficult for the House to concentrate on Macmillan's speech. MPs were leaving the chamber to look at the telexes to get the latest news on Sharpeville. Later that afternoon, Verwoerd, who had been absent from the House returned, and made a statement.

The House was full. Our worst fears about the events at Sharpeville were confirmed. The Pan Africanists had carried out their plans to burn or destroy their passes and had gathered in many places throughout South Africa. Sharpeville was a key black township in De Wet's constituency.

Dr Verwoerd reminded us that the PAC said it would demonstrate on the 21 March. In fact their protests had started the night before. Blacks had stayed away from work. Verwoerd said they approached police stations to "create trouble". About 5 000 eventually congregated at the Sharpeville police station. Telephone wires were cut. The crowd swelled to 20 000.

PAC leaders had been arrested. When Verwoerd spoke to us all he could say was that one man had been killed. Independent reports from outside the House confirmed that many more had lost their lives. The demonstrations were widespread throughout South Africa.

Dr Verwoerd then referred to De Wet's remarks and said that he interpreted them as not meaning that only one man was killed but that De Wet meant the government should not be frightened to take strong action when threatened. I personally think that Verwoerd knew how many had been killed, but in order to let De Wet and the government off the hook, he withheld the information until later, leaving us to believe that only one person had died.

The Opposition refused to accept Verwoerd's explanation. All that he did was once again to let De Wet address the House saying that he accepted the Prime Minister's interpretation as "precisely what he intended to say" and that "it is neither my intention or my desire to advocate that more violence should be used than is necessary to preserve law and order."

Throughout this charade I reminded myself of the time De Wet, at Medical School, tried to stop white students from entering the post-mortem room because two of our black students were going to watch a post-mortem on a white cadaver. Verwoerd should, as Prime Minister, have called on De Wet to withdraw his scandalous views in the House.

Soon the sad truth was out. Sixty-nine blacks had died at Sharpeville, shot in the back while running away from police armed with guns. They included women and children. This tragedy has cost South Africa dear in the eyes of the world. It acted as a catalyst for black unity and demands for change. It was the forerunner of the violence and unrest that was to continue in the years to come.

It was also the brutal symbol of apartheid that South Africa was to endure in the future.

As a member of the opposition, I felt totally frustrated and politically impotent. All we could do in Parliament was to talk incessantly, while throughout South Africa the struggle between black and white was intensifying.

We were brought back to the referendum by Verwoerd, who within a few days was lecturing at length to the House, denying that a republic would lead to a dictatorship. He spoke too about the Bantustans and once again about the white man's position in Africa.

I quote from *Hansard*:

The Prime Minister: "I do not think that Mr Macmillan impresses anyone of us as an authority on the right policy to follow in South Africa with reference to South Africa's colour issues . . . I said to him one should live in South Africa before one is able to form a proper opinion as to the solution of those problems. Not only has Mr Macmillan not lived with our problems, but in the nature of things he was only able to pay an extremely superficial visit to South Africa. He did have discussions with people here and he was able to pick up ideas from all sides but that does not enable him to decide whether the policy of the South African government is a good policy or a bad policy . . . I am not impressed therefore when he says that he regards the policy of the Union of South Africa in respect of the Native or non-white populations as the wrong policy . . ."

He had made the South African government's position clear in relation to Macmillan and emphasised that no outsider would deflect him or the Nationalists from their task of implementing apartheid to protect whites. Verwoerd was a clever parliamentary tactician. In this discussion he trapped the UP into facing up to the fact that if they followed through on their own 1954 Native Policy they would in effect be closer to the Progressives. In that eventuality a black majority would take control.

The UP did not like this. Dr Verwoerd, however, had hijacked the debate. We were compelled to stay in the House while the republic and Macmillan were taking priority over the violence outside.

Harry Lawrence brought the debate back to reality that evening.

Mr Lawrence: "While we are speaking here in this House tonight there is firing going on within five miles of this House of Parliament. The latest information I have is that the police at Langa, traditionally a peaceful Native residential area falling within the jurisdiction of the Cape Town City Council, have opened fire. Information is that they have done so with Sten guns and there are several dead. Huts are set on fire; cars on fire and no communication is available with the police station at the moment . . . Earlier today, in the course of his preliminary statement, the Prime Minister told the House about these most disturbing events near Vanderbijl Park . . . But quite obviously at this stage four hours ago when the Leader of the Opposition raised this matter with the Prime Minister it was clear to every member of this House that a most serious situation has arisen in this country today."

Harry Lawrence, as a former Minister, then criticised "the deplorable remarks of the Hon Member for Vanderbijl Park [De Wet]." He told De Wet that "if ever there was an incitement to persons who might be placed in a position of difficulty, that was incitement. If ever there was an inflammatory statement in the House at a time when it was for members of the legislature to be calm and give a lead to those who maintaining law and order it was the statement by that Hon Member. He is a member supporting the Prime Minister. He made this shocking statement; this deplorable statement; this most reprehensible and unsavoury remark."

The House was, by this time, very anxious. All day the news had been bad. We learnt in the dinner recess the truth of shootings, deaths and unrest in many places in South Africa.

In 1960, although there were sporadic incidents from time to time, this was the first occasion when it seemed as if blacks throughout the country were taking matters into their hands irrespective of the consequences – they were determined to fight apartheid with their bare hands. The country was unused to this situation. In Parliament we had been warning the Nationalists that an eruption would come and 21 March was the day. It was a watershed in our lives.

Harry Lawrence ended his speech on a prophetic note: ". . . the Prime Minister must not quibble if there are complaints both inside and outside South Africa, that it has become necessary in order to maintain law and order, to shoot. This complex of the pistol, this trigger consciousness of many persons in this country has developed in the last few years . . ."

This complex of the pistol! How true. The hidden clique of the militarists backed Nationalist governments in their role as the "protectors" of white supremacy in South Africa.

All the predictions of violence as the weapon of apartheid were beginning to surface. The whites, in the final analysis would turn more and more to guns for protection. Sitting on the back-bench, one had much time to grieve about the events of the day.

61

It was not difficult to become depressed about South Africa in 1960. The media kept us fully informed. Press restrictions had not yet reached an impossible stage. In Natal, Chief Luthuli, the ANC leader, burnt his own pass and called on other blacks to do so while he was in Pretoria giving evidence at the mammoth trial of 156 persons already in its fifth year. Luthuli called for a national day of morning on 28 March, thus joining with the PAC.

Robert Sobukwe, the charismatic and intelligent leader of the PAC, instructed his anti-pass carrying supporters to burn them.

This started the unrest in the black areas.

Luthuli called for non-violence. We learnt that the blacks who gathered at Sharpeville were not armed. Dr Verwoerd told the House that the police were forced to fire, because of some violence and the crowd could not be controlled. When shots were fired, the blacks panicked and had run away; that is how nearly all were shot in the back. The news about the extent of the killings at Sharpeville came out piecemeal. We knew that riots and pass-burning were taking place all over South Africa. To verify what was happening, some of the Cape Town MPs tried to get into Langa, but the police refused to let them into the township.

Fortunately for us when we returned to the House the next day, it was the Prime Minister's Vote. The House was full as Verwoerd gave an extensive account of the the events of the last 24 hours.

As we suspected, there were incidents all over South Africa, with the main unrest in black townships at Sharpeville, Johannesburg and Cape Town. During the night Sobukwe had been arrested, together with others, and charged "under Act No 8 of 1953 for protesting against the laws of the country."

De Villiers Graaff, in the usual UP double-speak, talked of Native agitators and the need for consultation:

"I think it is necessary that as South Africans we should get together to consider the situation which is now developing in South Africa at present. What happened in Sharpeville and Langa yesterday are not isolated events . . . There was the disgraceful murder of a policeman at Cato Manor [near Durban] . . . trouble at Windhoek [SWA], Harding [Natal], Zeerust [Transvaal], and Paarl [Cape] . . . these events over the last few months warn us that what happened yesterday is not an isolated event, and it seems clear to me that certain Native leaders – call them agitators if you like – are systematically experimenting in organising the masses of Natives to resist and to protest against administrative measures which they tell the Natives are oppressive . . . we of the opposition want to reiterate today and emphasise that the necessary bridges between responsible Native opinion and Government seem to have been destroyed in a large measure."

This statement criticised the government for failure to consult blacks, and voiced the Nationalist jargon about "responsible Native leaders", while at the same time talking of Native agitators and murderers, smearing their chosen leaders – not elected leaders – like Sobukwe and Luthuli.

The problem that faced the UP was that it ignored the wishes of the blacks; it did not have links with their leaders nor did it practice the consultation it demanded in its Native policy.

On our side as Progressives we tried hard to meet with blacks. We had talks with many of the them, but they did not want to have anything, overtly, to do with white political parties. Black consciousness was in the process of development due to the repressive policies of white government in South Africa.

All that Graaff got for his criticisms was ridicule on the UP's policies when it was in power – the Nationalists went to town, using this debate as a mudslinging session.

Steytler, who followed Graaff, condemned the Nationalists for their inter-party politics while South Africa was burning.

"I do not think for one moment," he said, "that the objection to the Pass laws and Influx Control is the only cause of the trouble that we have in South Africa. I do not believe that the poverty, the hunger, the misery of the non-Europeans in South Africa can be excluded in diagnosing the basic causes of this trouble. I do not believe that any responsible man on the government side can ascribe these actions by the non-Europeans in South Africa to the work of agitators or the politicians or Mr Macmillan."

Before Verwoerd replied, we had the usual charges from the Nationalists that the troubles were all due to us – the liberals.

The Nationalists had a rigid formula. When they were confronted with
evidence of the political unrest in South Africa involving blacks, they refused
to admit their 1948 policies were the root cause. They immediately placed
the blame on the liberals whom they always linked to agitators.

They had a ready audience for this – South African whites, not the most
politically educated people in the world, swallowed these allegations hook
line and sinker. The liberal movement had always been the whipping boy for
the country's black-white problems. It was easy for the Nationalists to drag
this out as and when required, because the white voters never tired of
hearing it. Since Union the nature of South African white governments has
always been conservative.

I agreed with Margaret Ballinger, who told the House that commissions
were endless and useless. Unless governments acted on their findings, "you
might as well not have commissions of enquiry because they only lull the
community into a false sense of security . . . of course, I have not the
slightest doubt about the cause of things that are happening today. For
twenty years in this House we [the Native Representatives] have said what
would happen; but alas, there is no joy in being a Cassandra; there is no joy
in foretelling tragedy and having one's prophecy fulfilled."

Herman Martins, the NP member for Wakkerstroom who in 1959
apologised to me, inadvertently hit the nail on the head when he told the
House, after Margaret Ballinger had spoken, that "I [Martins] could
summarise the entire speech of the Hon Member for Cape Eastern [Mrs
Ballinger] in one sentence: We have these uprisings because there is not
complete equality, because the Natives do not enjoy equal rights in all
spheres in South Africa."

Dr Verwoerd said he did not want to make party politics at a time like
this, but pointed out that when the UP was in power there were riots and
uprisings in 1946 and 1947, before the Nationalists came to power.
Correctly, he pointed out that the Pass Laws and Influx Control had existed
ever since Union. "Troubles and unrest are worldwide; we should not lose
our perspective."

Sharpeville and Langa focused Parliament's attention on the racial
situation. Reports were sent all over the world. From the outside it looked
as if South Africa was blowing up.

In the House, Verwoerd reiterated that "those countries will never stop
criticising, whatever government might be in power, unless eventually we
accept the principle which would mean that this country would be given by
the white man to the black man of South Africa . . . we must follow the
difficult road and try to show how we must organise South Africa in such a
way that the continued existence of the white man and his rights will be
ensured and at the same time the Bantu, in whose rights we also believe, gets
his rights . . . and the coloured, in whose rights we also believe gets those
rights . . . Now I ask, if we look at how South Africa has developed, can we
simply give away the white man's rights; can we do what other countries ask

us to do and try and force us to do in various ways . . . are we to give up all that in order to adopt the policy they want to enforce upon us?"

We had asked him to lift the ban on Luthuli and talk to the ANC "to bring about peace". Verwoerd brushed this aside. "The ultimate aim of the ANC is the same as that of the PAC . . . The ultimate aim is the Bantu domination of the whole of South Africa . . . These persons are simply using the reference book system [passes] as a starting point but their ultimate aim is the same as that of the Progressive and Liberal Party. What they are trying to achieve is Bantu domination."

The Prime Minister's Vote lasted four days, leaving Parliament in ferment. The unrest in South Africa showed no sign of abating. The police, and in certain areas the military, were fully extended.

Unexpectedly, as a back-bencher, I had a chance to speak in the Prime Minister's Vote. I reminded Dr Verwoerd that we had confirmed reports that Nyanga, a black township next to Langa, was virtually in a state of siege. The streets were impassable, people were not going to work. Buses were not running, fires were indiscriminately started. I asked Verwoerd if he was going to declare a state of emergency or martial law.

We had pieced together this information from various local sources, confirming that the authorities could not handle the situation. This type of unrest was virtually new to the South African black townships. Although there had been incidents before, they had been easily brought under control.

"The important question," I asked of the House, "is what is the Prime Minister going to do now in order to resolve the state of tension in South Africa?

"Why does he not take extraordinary steps at this time of crisis to act like a statesman? Why does he not invite the accepted leaders of the African people to come forward and give their co-operation? The Hon Prime Minister has rejected our plea to him to release ex-chief Luthuli to assist him to restore order in South Africa. With whom will the Prime Minister consult? With whom amongst the urban Africans can he consult?

"What outlets are open to these urban Africans? Are there Trade Unions? Are there proper political opportunities for expression of their views? The Prime Minister must tell this House what is going to happen, because in this debate he has stated that the proper machinery for consultation does exist? What is precisely that machinery and why is it not being used? Can the Hon the Prime Minister give this House the names of six responsible Africans from all over South Africa whom he could call together and with whom he could even have a private meeting in order to find out their grievances?

"Can he tell us the name of one urban African Churchman? Can he tell us the name of one urban African businessman? The name of a single African lawyer? An urban African doctor? Does he know the name of an urban African woman to whom he could speak instead of Chief Luthuli?"

Jan Steytler wound up the Prime Minister's Vote by spelling out the PP's plans if it came to power. Passes would be abolished, the labour bureaux would stabilise labour unrest. Facilities would be created in the urban areas to prevent conditions from developing again that led to the present violence and unrest.

After the debate I was left with the undeniable fact that all we had achieved in the nine days of the violent unrest was more verbiage and propaganda in Parliament. There were no black voices in Parliament. How could we or they affect Verwoerd's apartheid policies when blacks were not sitting in the House, and the Nationalist Government refused to talk or negotiate with them?

On 26 March, in what seemed a move of desperation, the police announced that Reference Books (Passes) would not be demanded by the police with immediate effect. The chaos at police stations had brought this about. Police were needed to contain the unrest rather than waste time demanding passes in the streets.

I flew to Johannesburg that weekend. There was an air of depression amongst my friends and constituents who felt the end of the road had arrived. Everyone agreed that peace could come if Verwoerd would talk to blacks – but there was no hope he would. On Monday when Parliament reconvened the Government announced its plans. The Minister of Justice introduced the Unlawful Organisations Bill, which banned the ANC the PAC and other black organisations involved in the disturbances.

The relaxation of action on "passes" had been no more than a ploy. Consultation and talks with blacks were out. *Kragdadigheid* (toughness) was the Nationalist government's road ahead.

We were wasting our time in Parliament urging the Government to talk to the black people. Instead we now had another fight on our hands against the new Unlawful Organisations Bill, which no doubt was the beginning of more and more repressive legislation and police action.

Margaret Ballinger said we were forcing peaceful black organisations underground: "If this is all the government has to offer, they are sacrificing the whole of South Africa to their complete incapacity to understand how society works and their complete incapacity to govern this country."

For once, all the Opposition parties, the UP, the Native Representatives and the Progressives opposed the introduction of this Bill. The Government was undeterred. The Second Reading took place the next day, while the rioting and burnings continued in Langa, Nyanga and other black areas in South Africa. It was unbelievable The House then went on to discuss the Cape Town Foreshore Bill and the Soil Conservation Bill as if nothing else was happening!

In opposing the the Second Reading of the Unlawful Organisations Bill, we pointed out that it gave the government a blank cheque to ban political organisations.

Colin Eglin told the House: "This is not an emergency measure, this is to be a new pattern of legislation in South Africa."

The ANC and the PAC were in a dilemma. The ANC told its supporters to go back to work. The PAC said they should stay out until the Pass Laws were abolished by legislation. The unrest continued, unabated. The newspapers were full of reports of fires, looting and deaths. It seemed

378

as if the Nationalists were unable to control the disturbances, spending time bringing in Parliamentary Bills instead of talking to blacks about grievances and possible solutions.

Wednesday began dramatically. Before lunch there was the astonishing news that a column of about 30 000 blacks, lead by a young man, Philip Kgosana, a university student, was marching from Langa and Nyanga to Parliament, to stage a peaceful protest.

With some press colleagues and other MPs, including Nationalists, we stood outside Parliament in the company of soldiers watching the long column of black protesters coming down Roeland Street, past its gaol and heading for Parliament. I had seen something like this before in Johannesburg when the Alexandra township bus boycotters walked daily to work.

It was a shock to the white people of Cape Town, who were lining the streets, watching this group of black people peacefully protesting in the same way as whites had done over Nationalist legislation. Cape Town realised on that day that even voteless blacks, if organised properly, could protest no differently from whites.

I looked at some of the Nationalist MPs who were standing with us, in the beautiful summer sunshine of the Cape, with Table Mountain dwarfing the long row of marchers. The MPs were pale, their faces drained. This was a new phenomenon to them. Something was wrong when blacks could stage such a massive protest in Cape Town, the seat of Nationalist power. They were speechless.

We learnt afterwards that none of the blacks marching had passes. As the column neared us it was confronted by the police. We could see some discussion taking place between police officers and the march's leaders. To our surprise, the marching blacks split into two columns, and to the relief of the Nat MPs next to us, they turned round and marched back to their townships. Later we were told that the police had come to an agreement with Kgosana that he would not be arrested if the march to Parliament was stopped, and he and his supporters went back. Kgosana was promised that he would be able to lead a deputation to the Minister of Justice.

Kgosana accepted the word of the Police Commissioner. That is why the dramatic column turned around and faded in the distance. We had witnessed a piece of South African history in the making.

Philip Kgosana did not get his interview with the Minister of Justice. Instead he and others were arrested the next day. The police were forced, by the Government, to break their promises. It was an ominous end to peaceful black protest. Kgosana, in turn, while waiting trial, broke his word and fled the country.

That afternoon Verwoerd told Parliament in a special statement that everything was under control. He described the march as an "influx of a large number of Natives who mainly congregated near Caledon Square. I can tell the House those Natives are busy moving back to Langa and Nyanga in two columns."

He refused to admit that it was an organised black protest. He also said the situation of the last few days had to be tackled by force, because the tendency "to revolt spread to rural towns . . . but in view of the fact that there is a possibility that this may lead to more widespread violence, the government is prepared to extend the steps it has hitherto taken whenever it becomes necessary to do so."

What these steps were, other than police reaction, shootings and strong-arm tactics, was not made clear.

By now the world outside was taking an interest in what was going on inside South Africa. The Prime Minister told us that the Afro-Asian Group of the United Nations had asked the Security Council to take action against South Africa as a result of the riots in the country. Verwoerd's reply was to tell the UN not to interfere in the internal affairs of South Africa.

As soon as he finished addressing the House, the Minister of Justice rose to make an announcement. The Government, he said, had declared a State of Emergency. This was unbelievable. Verwoerd had just told us that everything was under control. We did not have the time to collect our wits.

Paul Sauer, leader of the House, moved the suspension of automatic adjournment of the House. We proceeded immediately to debate the Second Reading of the Unlawful Organisations Bill, followed by the rest of the stages so that it could become law without delay.

Dr Verwoerd and his Nationalists were taking action at last. They were going to use all the might of the police and army if necessary to put down the growing black revolt. This put an end to our hopes of peace by consultation around a table by all parties.

When Margaret Ballinger moved her amendment to the Unlawful Organisations Bill, she said it was the most tragic day of all her political experience. So was it for many of us on the Opposition benches. It brought home to us how powerless we were in dealing with Verwoerd's government. The role of the Opposition had become inconsequential. From now on the Government had all the power it needed, playing all the cards.

I wondered how ordinary Nationalist MPs reacted to what Verwoerd was now doing. Did they feel more secure? Margaret Ballinger had no doubts. She spoke for all the Opposition:

"I have a very strong feeling that a great many of the people sitting on the other side of the House are suffering from acute fears today and wondering where they are going. And they are not the only people . . . their fears are justified."

She got no response from the tense faces of the Nat MPs across the aisle.

The State of Emergency had never been experienced in South Africa before in peacetime. Obviously the unrest and the disturbances must have been greater than we knew. I detested the fact that we were forced in Parliament to vote on a Bill that gave the government of Verwoerd *carte blanche*, the right to act against blacks without further consultation with us.

To cap it all, Dr Verwoerd, the Minister of Justice and other senior Ministers were constantly out of the House, no doubt dealing with the extra-parliamentary crisis happening outside.

Our function was to go on talking. It was difficult to produce new points. Our own arguments became repetitive – it was a merry-go-round in a discussion that went nowhere. We simply had to await events. Instead of replying to our protests, we just got the usual litany of abuse from the Nationalist MPs.

Harry Lawrence injected a dose of reality into the debate once again: "I hope that this House and I hope the country realises the gravity of the situation. Do Hon Members know what this means? Do they know what the effect of this proclamation is? It means as far as the government is concerned Parliament can be ignored. For the purposes of the eighty magisterial districts of South Africa the government can govern by procla-mation."

Lawrence had been through this all before when he was Minister of Justice in Smuts's government during the War. He wanted to know from the Government how many people had been arrested by the Secret Police (Gestapo, he called them); why Luthuli had been arrested and assaulted with other Treason Trial accused so they could not even be present at their trial? Leading members of the Liberal Party had been arrested. The State of Emergency had been made retrospective by one day. It was clear the Government had acted during the night, and was now rubber-stamping its arrests, which were widespread throughout the whole country.

At midnight we were still debating the Second Reading of the Unlawful Organisations Bill. Discussion was heated, tempers frayed; allegations, threats and counter-threats flew backwards and forwards across the aisle of the Chamber. We struggled on during the night keeping the debate alive, and after the all-night sitting we voted at eight in the morning.

The Vote vindicated our action in leaving the United Party. The UP, after opposing the introduction of this Bill, voted for it in the Second Reading. It was a major political sell-out by the UP after all its pious condemnation.

That Vote established the small Progressive Party as South Africa's only real Opposition. At the same time it strengthened my growing belief that Parliament in its present form was a cynical charade. As long as there were no blacks, coloureds or Indians in one House, the future for South Africa would remain in white hands, using all the powers of Government through the iron fist until ultimate confrontation and explosion.

Later that day, at 2.20 pm, we were back at our benches to start the Committee Stage of the Bill. By Monday morning the Third Reading had been completed – it would soon be law.

Again I was left with the feeling of *déjà vu* – we were being used by the Nationalists to put the democratic seal, in the name of Parliament, on legislation we knew went against the Rule of Law, giving tremendous powers to the State with no recourse to the courts.

Question time in Parliament became very important during the first few weeks of the Emergency. It was the only way we could learn about happenings in major trouble spots – Langa, Nyanga and Soweto. Continued ministerial questioning gave information on the many people who were being detained every day. Many members of the Liberal Party had been arrested. Leading blacks, like Nelson Mandela of the ANC had gone into hiding. Robert Sobukwe was reported to be in prison on Robben Island.

Parliament went into recess for the Easter weekend, and we had a conference of the Progressive Party at the Cranbrooke Hotel in Johannesburg. Delegates came from all over South Africa.

As usual, I was in charge of press relations.

On Saturday afternoon I was telephoning Charles Blumberg, the political reporter of *The Sunday Times*, with some conference information when he stopped me with these words:

"Boris, reports are coming in that Dr Verwoerd has been shot at the Rand Easter Show. He's still alive and has been rushed to the Johannesburg General Hospital. I can't tell you any more. I'll ring later."

The news was shattering. I could hardly believe it. Obviously I had to tell the delegates through the public address system.

I spent much of that afternoon trying to get details of what had happened. It appeared that while Verwoerd was giving the opening address at the Rand Show arena, David Pratt, a wealthy white man, shot him in the throat. Chaos ensued, Pratt was arrested, Verwoerd was rushed to hospital.

This news was electrifying but it did not surprise me. I knew of David Pratt. He wrote to me when I was chairman of Non-European Affairs in the City Council and because of the anti-Verwoerdian sentiments in the letter I thought it wiser to keep its contents to myself to avoid problems in the future.

In this letter, he was highly critical of the havoc Verwoerd was creating between black and white in South Africa. The contents of this letter were never disclosed – it was a very incriminating document lost from my files when a theft occurred at my office. Pratt, considered insane, was put in a mental home and finally died by suicide.

On the Tuesday after the attack on Verwoerd, the House was in a sombre mood. Paul Sauer, the senior Minister, opened proceedings with an unopposed motion of sympathy on the shooting of Verwoerd.

The attempted assassination of the Prime Minister by a white man, not a black, confused South Africans. If it had been carried out by a black man, there is no doubt that there would have been an upsurge in violence and further reprisals by the police.

However the Minister of Defence, JJ Fouche, summed up the attitude of the Nationalists: "I believe that if we show the slightest degree of hesitation in our actions at this time it will have disastrous consequences for South Africa."

Parliament was now becoming a Jekyll-Hyde institution. It was able to turn immediately from the most serious event like the attempt on the life of its Prime Minister to the consideration of mundane matters. The House went on to discuss the amendments to the Broadcasting Bill as if nothing had happened. I had to speak several times in the Committee Stage, when I was strongly condemned by the NP for criticising the appointment of Dr Meyer as chairman of the SABC, but I did manage at last to get an admission from Dr Hertzog that VHF broadcasts would be introduced in South Africa, in particular for the black people.

My mind was mostly on what was happening outside the House. The events since Sharpeville had become menacing. There is no doubt that it represented a watershed in South Africa's political life. Nationalist apartheid legislation had bared its teeth, but the blacks were on the march against it. Outlawing the ANC and the PAC would be detrimental to our interests in the future. The blacks would assuredly go underground, and resort to violence as one of the means of retribution and to finally secure their place in the government of the country. They would never forget Sharpeville. Nor would the outside world. Oliver Tambo of the ANC had already been invited to address the UN on South Africa.

On the other hand the Nationalist government intensified internal control by calling out the army to surround known trouble spots. No time was wasted. The Pass Laws were reimposed. The Public Safety Act was used to the full. No one knew how many blacks or whites had been arrested. Hundreds of foreign correspondents converged on South Africa. Every day thousands of words were reported overseas on events here. We could not rely on the South African Broadcasting Corporation for unbiased news, because, as I had predicted, it was the Government's main propaganda tool and we were fed what the SABC wanted us to hear.

There is no doubt the English-speaking whites and some Afrikaners were in a state of profound shock, especially after Pratt's attempt on Verwoerd's life. The Stock Exchange had slumped. In Parliament it was the Progressive Party that opposed the NP at every turn. We received the plaudits of the leading English-language newspapers for the lead we gave in Parliament.

The Natal Witness, in an editorial on 11 April under the headline "Salute to the Progressives", wrote:

"South Africa owes a debt of gratitude for its Parliamentary conduct during the past ten days or so . . . In the first place they and they alone have kept Parliament in being as a functioning body . . . The United Party has totally abdicated the function of an Opposition, at any rate on all matters bearing on the Emergency . . . the Progressives have done well to repeatedly bring to light facts which in the interests of good government ought to be made known . . . have continually directed attention to necessity of finding a way to a better condition of affairs when the Emergency is over . . . In doing all these things the Progressives have established a fifth title to our praise and gratitude. It is that they have been an inspiring beacon of courage and devotion to duty at a time when such inspiration is sorely needed."

This editorial, written in Pietermaritzburg, a quiet enclave of English-speaking South Africans, who normally gave full support to the United Party, and who were always ready to compromise, was clear evidence of the effect our small party was having outside the confines of Parliament.

The government was obviously very worried despite the flow of *kragdadige* statements from Parliament. Paul Sauer unexpectedly broadcast an appeal by the Government promising that new methods would have to be found to restore peace and better race relations. It was, however, in such general terms that to those of us monitoring the overall scene and involved in the heart of the white political struggle this broadcast was simply the NP's attempts to calm the electorate, while the Government continued to use Verwoerd's mailed fist. He had survived but was out of the picture for a while, which made very little difference.

It was difficult to believe Sauer because the Government wasted no time in enforcing its repressive laws which were at the root of the trouble. My reaction to Sauer was one of resignation – I did not believe that the Nationalist Afrikaner would change to policies that would compel him to share power with black people. I had never altered my view, and could see no evidence that unrest plus an attempted assassination would alter the basic direction in which Nationalists were going. All we could do was act as the people's watchdog, and constitutionally oppose the government wherever possible.

Information was badly needed. The country was a hotbed of rumour. We needed facts. Arrests, assaults on detainees, censorship needed explanations. As an example, on 22 April our questions embraced: Indemnity to witnesses at Sharpeville and Langa; censorship of news dispatches; reference books; facilities granted to detainees and publication of their names; assaults on Treason Trial witnesses; detainees held in solitary confinement; members of legal profession detained; and, total number of whites, coloureds and Bantu detained.

In order to put these questions on the Order Paper we had to do a lot of extra-Parliamentary research. During all this critical time the government indicated that it was going ahead with the Referendum on the republic. In the House it used its guillotine powers to curtail our intensified protests.

The Government knew we could hold up the progress of Bills with insistence on proper discussion. Their only counter was the increasing use of the guillotine. All the Opposition parties protested – to no avail. To save time, the Government introduced further amendments to the "Guillotine Bill", reducing markedly the hours to be spent on all stages of two Bills – the Senate and the Referendum. We bitterly opposed this stratagem.

Professor "Sakkies" Fourie went to the nub of the matter: "The guillotine, which is increasingly being applied under the regime of the present government, is of course something undemocratic . . . This type of measure forms part of the inevitable pattern which will have to be followed on an ever increasing extent in this country. We have long since been on the road to dictatorship away from democracy . . . Hon Members opposite who so easily sacrifice rights should realise that this sort of thing also leads to the destruction of freedom of those who are in the process of curtailing that freedom. History teaches us that. All the dictatorships have had a similar fate. When I look at the measures which my own Afrikaner people have introduced I can only say I feel sorry for them as far as the future of South Africa is concerned and I pity South Africa . . .

"If you are unfaithful to the idea of freedom, you do not know what may happen. It will end in slavery".

These words in 1960 from a liberal Afrikaner academic in our ranks in opposition to Verwoerd's government were profound, prophetic and sad. They went unnoticed at the time by the people of South Africa but were ridiculed by Nationalists in Parliament. Thirty years later these words ring out with the peal of truth.

The sledgehammer tactics of the Nationalists showed to what extent their ruthlessness would go in order to implement apartheid and achieve their republic. All Opposition was cast aside. We were there to rubber-stamp apartheid laws. Although we were in the epicentre of this political earthquake, we could do little more than record our objections. One must bear in mind too, that very few blacks knew or understood what was going on in the white man's Parliament. Most were illiterate, there were few vernacular newspapers, no radio or TV. All they were left with was to retaliate with violence and unrest against the hated Pass laws and Influx Control. On our side we were trying constitutional means. In the 1960s both were doomed to failure.

Since Sharpeville, in answer to a question from us, the Minister of Justice told the House that over 18 000 blacks had been arrested and detained in police raids all over South Africa. This will give some indication of the size and extent of the unrest. In an answer to me as to when the arrested would be brought before the courts, the Minister said: "I should like to give a considered reply to that question." It was never referred to by him again.

This type of evasion under the umbrella of the Westminster democratic constitution made a mockery of the Opposition's role.

We were pawns of the Nationalists. The pressure was on. Morning sittings commenced and the Government wanted to end the session within a month. Celebrations on the Act of Union were being held, which was to the political advantage of the Government because of their republican plans. We felt we should be in session while the Emergency was on. Furthermore, several of us refused to join in the celebrations because of the state of Emergency.

Hamilton-Russell (UP, who later joined our Parliamentary team) and I, told the House before the Emergency that we would not attend the celebrations as long as apartheid existed. South Africa was no longer a unitary state. Verwoerd's Bantustans had begun the fragmentation of Union. We also objected to the celebrations because they would be for the NP's benefit. Blacks, coloureds and Indians, under Emergency conditions, had little to celebrate. I agreed with Margaret Ballinger, who said 31 May should really be a day of mourning in South Africa.

I was highly critical of participating in a Parliament where decisions on Government spending, on labour, agriculture, transport, health, Bantu and coloured affairs were taken without any consultation with non-whites. It is true that blacks and coloureds still had white MPs in the House, but they were forced to operate at arm's length. The Native Representatives, Margaret Ballinger, Lee Warden and Walter Stanford, were to disappear from Parliament at the end of the session. Blacks would then lose the slender link they had with white legislators and white politics.

Debates on black politics tended to become boring and futile at times, despite the flow of rhetoric. Black organisations paid little attention to the white Parliament – I felt that they had lost faith even with whites like us who were fighting for their rights and upliftment. My experience as a member of the Institute of Race Relations and on the City Council reinforced this viewpoint.

The other objection I had was that however much we tried to raise the level of debate on race relations, all we got in response were insults – we were "liberalists" and the "mouthpiece of the ANC".

The Minister of Bantu Administration, referring to the unrest and violence, blandly told us: "It is certain that whites are behind the whole affair."

The euphoria of the Cabinet under Verwoerd reached bizarre heights when De Wet Nel told the House: "Never before in the history of South Africa has there been such sound co-operation, such good relations between white and Bantu as there are today. Mr Chairman, I say that with utmost emphasis."

I felt as if I was listening to a madman. He was speaking six months after Sharpeville. The Emergency was still on; the government was still arresting people, and protests and unrest were the order of the day.

Our roles as MPs were becoming impossible. We were trying to democratically legislate through the narrow conduit of Verwoerd's apartheid ideology. We were caught in his political straitjacket.

This Bantu Affairs Vote nevertheless had historic connotations for us. Graaff, for the UP, moved an amendment reducing a provision of £750 000 to £250 000 in respect of the purchase of Native Trust land the Government wished to buy in terms of the 1936 Land Act.

This was a volte-face by Graaff who had supported us at the UP Congress against his right wing in 1959. We had a field day in the House. Almost every Progressive attacked the UP without interruption. The only speaker on the UP side was Graaff. When the amendment was put we voted with the Government for more land for the blacks. Graaff had become the prisoner of his conservative Caucus and the credibility of the UP was destroyed.

It was now common knowledge that the Government wanted the session to end in a few days. We were reluctant to agree. We did not want Parliament to prorogue while the Emergency was still on. While there was Parliament, we could probe, ask questions and keep the country informed about the Emergency as far as possible.

We still had the Justice Vote to debate. We succeeded in drawing out of the Minister that the Pass Laws were not by any means the main reasons why blacks were in a state of unrest. He contended that behind it all was a Communist plot – that is why so many had been detained – especially whites, some of whom had gone on hunger strike. Many women had been detained. In some cases husband and wife were arrested, leaving children to be cared for by neighbours, relations or strangers.

The Minister of Justice told us that he was doing no more than Harry Lawrence did in Smuts's government when Lawrence detained people for sabotage and subversion. Paying back old scores was a favourite way of condoning what the Nationalists were doing.

Margaret Ballinger wondered whether the "government was engaged in a policy of revenge . . . to go back into the past for justification for what we are doing today seems to me to be the most awful approach to the subject . . ."

In the discussion on the Emergency regulations one Nat MP told the House: " . . . with an opposition such as this I believe it is necessary for us in South Africa to have a Secret Service, which will also keep its eye on some members sitting in this House."

The Minister admitted that some of the detainess were important because the Treason Trial was still on.

We had to listen to Carel de Wet, arrogant as ever, say: "If I were a Communist and I had to listen to what Hon Members say here, I would never wish for a better ally than the Opposition."

Attacks were made on the "British Press": *The Rand Daily Mail* was described as an agitator.

It became impossible to argue coherently with Government MPs. The Chief Whip, JJ Potgieter declared that "the Minister of Justice is correct in saying these disturbances are inseparably linked with the pattern that we see throughout Africa. It is this spreading of ultra-liberalistic ideas, this pernicious mental poison of Communism which the Communistic agitators are injecting into the susceptible minds of the black man, and this intermingling, this multiracial society . . . that is why we must not have a multiracial society. We must have separate development."

Harry Lawrence commented on the Chief Whip's views: " . . . it certainly demands a particularly optimistic nature when one looks towards the future not to be alarmed by them. It would be a very black day for South Africa if one were to regard the speech made by the Chief Whip seriously . . ."

Lawrence was wrong. Unfortunately we had to take it all very seriously.

The NP believed that liberalism and communism were joint enemies and agitators of South Africa's unrest; their beliefs were being used to influence the people of South Africa in every possible way. Once more the Emergency Regulations debate was interrupted by a Standing Order Suspension calling for further "guillotines" on "urgent" Bills which the Government wanted to be on the statutes before the session ended.

We vociferously objected. Instead the Government solemnly gave, as one of its reasons, the forthcoming celebration of fifty years of the Union!

Our last attempt to attack the government on the Emergency was in the Appropriation Bill. Graaff called the situation grim. The debate was notable because of a speech by Walter Stanford, a Native Representative who was making his final speech to Parliament.

He spoke for me when he said: "I had come to this Hon House with the naive hope that by putting the human and economic facts of South Africa to

387

the House I could in some small measure help to bring this Government and the country to face the facts that are happening all around us outside . . . I have been bitterly disappointed. These six years here have been for us one desperate rearguard action after another, as one right or institution after another was removed from non-whites and particularly the Africans in the name of apartheid . . . Always it has been the erosion of liberty, and freedom of rights and always it was argued it was absolutely necessary for white preservation by denying to others in our country that which we demand for ourselves."

Addressing the Speaker in a silent House, Stanford ended his last speech as Native Representative with a stinging attack on the Nationalists:

"Rather have we seen, to our despair the storm troops of baasskap dictatorship thrown into these recent crucial debates. Sir, they now seem in control of the Nationalist Party. They are pressing for the continuance of the Emergency and the use of force. They, Sir, are pressing for Government by the Saracen tank."

Harry Lawrence's last words for the session also echoed in my ears: " . . . apart from one or two lucid intervals . . . these proceedings have had an air of complete unreality."

62

The session ended. I left Parliament emotionally drained and depressed. Lawrence was correct in describing the proceedings as having an air of complete unreality. It had taken three sessions of the South African Parliament to make me realise the political odds against our small Opposition – faced by Verwoerd's juggernaut. The prospects of staying on in such a Parliament began to prey on my mind. There was already one announcement of resignation from Parliament by a UP back-bencher, Andrew Brown, who saw no future for the UP as the Opposition in Parliament.

The life I had been leading, rushing between Johannesburg and Cape Town, to see the family, attend to the business, looking after constituency affairs was frenetic. In Parliament one was busy with Caucus meetings, preparation for debates, sometimes speaking, but overall there was the terrible waste of time having to listen to the low standard of debate, all of which led to terrible chronic boredom and the desire to renounce it all.

Great demands too, were made on my time as chairman of public relations. Both I and Miles Malleson ran into continuous problems in getting other regions to carry our requests. The Cape Progressives were not co-operating. It came to a head over the anti-republican campaign. Al

Toombs had been engaged to draw up a plan so that the Progressive Party could fight against the republic on a nationwide basis.

The campaign was to be directed from Johannesburg, but it became clear early on in the year that Zach de Beer and Colin Eglin had other ideas. They wanted the control.

Toombs's plan was already upset by Sharpeville, the unrest at Langa and the Emergency. For reasons I could not understand, our PP Executive decided to put De Beer in charge. Malleson was upset. He wrote to Steytler on 9 September: "Dr Wilson's undoubted talent and great experience in public relations were lost to the party."

Prior to this the Anti-republican Action Committee met after Parliament's ending, when Eglin secured modifications to Toombs's plan which Malleson described "as a grave error". Malleson found it impossible to work with De Beer a thousand miles away in Cape Town. He asked that De Beer and he get together for the rest of the campaign, or that I resume responsibility as public relations chairman, with a free hand to complete the job. By now I was in no mood to get involved in any kind of party struggle, least of all with De Beer and Eglin.

This sort of development in the PP was not what I had expected. During the year I had spoken to Steytler several times about these tactics, and told him that we were slipping into the old UP ways, characterised by political intrigue, self aggrandisement, and internal power-struggles. Had I not been one of the original founders of the PP, I might have ignored the uncooperative attitude of De Beer and Eglin, and their desire for control. I was also aware of their growing antipathy to Steytler.

It was easy to adopt a *laissez-faire* attitude, make a few speeches in Parliament, and avoid party responsibility. That was not my nature, nor was it the reason why I was in politics. I was quite prepared to sacrifice personal and business affairs in order to work for the Progressives – but in the Verwoerdian era obstructive tactics by party colleagues was totally unacceptable.

We had been through the most traumatic session that senior MP's could recall. Twelve years of Nationalist apartheid strategy and legislation had forced the blacks to fight back with the only weapons they knew, unfortunately violent, bringing out the worst reaction from whites such as Sharpeville. Despite the attempt to assassinate Dr Verwoerd and Paul Sauer's appeal, oppression was tightened through the Emergency. Negotiation with blacks was out.

Apartheid was going to be implemented, come hell or high water.

All the criticism and advice we gave in Parliament was ignored. Most of the time we had to listen to recurring replays of the "Boer War" to divert Parliament from the realities of 1960, brought on by the granite-like Dr Verwoerd.

Worst of all were the hours one spent in the most boring environment listening to MPs talking on subjects of no interest whatsoever, about which they knew nothing anyway, in language that made one wonder what one was doing in a Parliament of MPs, some of whom seemed, at least part of the time, to be politically and mentally disorientated.

The glamour of Parliament and the views one had of achieving changes in our society had evaporated, and one had to make a choice. Ignore it all, or reject it before it turns one into one of the old Parliamentary hacks who remain ineffective, spending their years in Cape Town during summer, in its club-like atmosphere, waiting for a pension and retirement.

This club-like atmosphere did not include social fraternisation of MPs from opposing political parties. This in the main was taboo. I had been through a baptism of fire in my first two sessions and the pros and cons of where I was going weighed heavily on my mind. In the end I decided to speak in confidence to Steytler about how unsettled and dispirited I had become. I had not lost my high ideals but I had no time to be a pawn in the personal ambitions of some of my colleagues, nor for the irrelevancies of the rhetoric of Parliament. We were a small group of MPs in a small party. I was used to working with small groups of politicians at top level and I was at the stage where I was no longer interested in people whom I considered inexperienced or politically selfish in their aims.

I also felt let down by the Progressives. I was battling to get *Forum* on its feet. When I took it over, I thought it would in a short while become the journal of the liberal and progressive movement in South Africa. I was prepared to lose money to achieve this end. After many appeals to the party to help, it was evident that they were not particularly interested in *Forum* as the only liberal journal still published in South Africa. Despite the fact that we supported the PP, made copies available at meetings, and had *Forum* improving under Caley's editorship, we got little or no help from the PP. I had purposely kept a low profile so that *Forum* would not be seen as Boris Wilson's political mouthpiece. Nor did I want political adversaries to know my connection. However, by the time Parliament prorogued *Forum* was losing circulation fast.

Also, I did not relish the prospect of the anti-republican campaign for the next six months. English-speaking South Africans did not seem to care whether we had a republic or not. It looked as if we were going to fight on two fronts. The idea of trying to organise the voting pattern in my Hospital constituency with the UP was not a beguiling prospect. It was regrettable that Harry Schwarz, now the UP leader in Hospital, adopted an indifferent and almost hostile attitude towards me since our break. This was a pity because formerly we had a close personal relationship. White politics is a great divider in South Africa.

It was hard for me to comprehend the change that occurred in my outlook. Here I was, a Member of Parliament, having reached the goal after years of effort and sacrifice, suddenly stopping in my tracks and reviewing once again where I was going and whether I would be able to "stand the strain", as my old headmaster at Yeoville School used to thunder from his assembly platform.

One of the motivating factors was my growing family. My three children were at an age where decisions had to be made about their education on a long-term basis. I was critical of my life style because it left me little time to be with them when I was most needed. Was my immersion in the maelstrom of South African politics worth it? I kept asking myself this question. I also kept asking myself whether I wanted to educate my children in a system that was controlled by the state, full of dogma narrow-mindedness and secular direction. I did not want them indoctrinated with the dead-end notions of apartheid. This was my state of mind at the end of the 1960 session of Parliament.

I left Steytler in no doubt that I was considering resigning from Parliament. He was very upset and pleaded with me to think it over, pointing out the problems it would create for the Progressives. I assured him I would not act hastily during the recess and would see him again before I took a final decision.

In Johannesburg the business kept me occupied. I was able to pay attention to my Rhodesian company, which was flourishing and was expecting the introduction of television, for which a campaign had to be organised. Neither I or my Rhodesian managing director knew anything about TV, hence we had a lot to do.

I made a major change in the running of the South African company. I appointed my brother Len to become the company's chief day-to-day executive. This left me free to attend to all my other activities unhindered.

THE FUTURE AND POLITICS

63

My political future and that of my family continued to occupy me. I could not escape from the underlying reasons for my unsettled state.

Countrywide unrest, apartheid, the Emergency, white liberal fears had generated feelings of insecurity. In my view, the whites would not desert the Afrikaner volk.

I had seen, over the years, how National Party dogmatists succeeded in convincing young white people. We could reach a stage where the liberal values I cherished would be under severe legal restraints. We were already the enemies of the volk; the agitators, the allies of the ANC. Dr Verwoerd, who had recovered from the attempted assassination, strongly backed action against left wing movements. He was tough and uncompromising. Over and over he declared that the whites were in South Africa by virtue of the Almighty and that God approved of the doctrine of apartheid. He said this in the name of Christianity, backing the bannings, detentions and arrests of thousands of blacks for statutory apartheid offences such as Pass Laws, curfews, and infringements of the Group Areas, Mixed Marriages and the Immorality Acts.

I could not avoid coming face to face with the reality of apartheid. The daily arrests in the streets of the affluent suburbs of Johannesburg, the small line of dejected handcuffed blacks who did not have their passes or had no right to be in the area being marched to the nearest police station was enough to make one sick; the white passers-by who gave scant attention and accepted this as part of life in South Africa.

We had become a brutalised society.

I had always been aware of the extreme poverty of black people and the results of social deprivation and lack of education since I was a child. The Market taught me a lot, making me very conscious and sympathetic to black problems. Later in the City Council I faced the same realities in what I saw in Soweto. The image of tens of thousands of blacks herded into their matchbox houses travelling like Orwellian hordes to and from white Johannesburg in overcrowded trains, standing patiently in hospital queues, never left me and always haunted me.

Johannesburg's whites rode in their large American cars and hardly ever walked in the streets. For the blacks it was different. They congregated in the streets or illegally occupied white parks because there was no where else to go in white suburbs.

Recreational facilities did not exist for blacks in white areas – most whites objected to any assembly of blacks there and in any event the Group

Areas Act forbade it. Suburban domestic workers were not allowed to to live with either wife or husband or family even in the backyards of houses where they were normally accommodated. Black family home life was a pathetic social structure, destroyed by the demands of apartheid. A black servant would come to his employer on his or her day out:

"Master or Missus, can I have a pass to go out today – I'm going to see my children in Soweto." The employer wrote out a simple pass.

"To whom it may concern, please pass Jim my cook, who is going to Soweto to see his family. He is in my employment."

Many thousands of black men and women came to Johannesburg illegally from the rural areas, or as far away as Rhodesia, Malawi and Mozambique to seek work. Sympathetic whites, or those wanting cheap labour, employed them, risking police raids and fines.

One incident, several years later, involving me, illustrates how easy it was to get embroiled in the problem of the illegal black work-seeker.

Simon Dube, a Rhodesian gardener, came pleading for daily work as he was starving. My wife gave him work as she was sorry for him. He turned out to be an excellent gardener, and a very pleasant personality. We learnt that he had no home to go to in the evenings and lived with friends. It became a daily hazard for him to come to our house because he had no legal documents. If the police challenged him he could be arrested because of his illegal status. Simon told me his story.

He came from Plumtree near Bulawayo. There was no work, so three years earlier he decided to make his way to Johannesburg because his family was starving. He walked for days to the South African border in Botswana. From there he illegally entered the country at night, hiding in the dense bushveld during the day. He walked at night for over two weeks, somehow feeding himself, being helped by other blacks and keeping out of the way of the police. Several times white "Boers" (farmers) chased him off their lands, but luckily he avoided police.

Arriving in Johannesburg, he went to stay with Rhodesian friends, some of whom were legally here. Simon earned a living working "tog", doing gardening on a daily basis when he could find it. It was a cat-and-mouse game avoiding the police, but he survived and was able to send a little money to his wife and three children in Rhodesia.

One day he was caught in the street, handcuffed, walked to the police station and sent to Fordsburg to the Native Commissioner's Court. He was fined, but because he could not pay went to gaol for a month and then deported to Rhodesia. He tried to get work in Bulawayo but it was hopeless. So back he came over the slow, laborious route to Johannesburg, this time via Beit Bridge in the northern Transvaal. He crossed the Limpopo River at night braving the crocodile and hippopotamus and eventually reached Johannesburg. Once again he started working illegally, living with friends sending money home. Then he was caught for the second time. On this occasion he was sentenced to three months in gaol without a fine and sent back to Rhodesia.

The work situation was even worse in Rhodesia, his family's plight had deteriorated. For the third time he made his way back to South Africa. This was when we met him.

Our black servants liked him, so we decided the best way he could keep out of trouble was to stay on our property, where we had a spare room at the bottom of the garden. He was warned not to leave our house at all. He was to be a virtual prisoner. He had to accept this because I knew he would be caught if he went on the streets as the arrests were now a daily routine.

One day he wandered down the street and was confronted by a black policeman – somehow he got away. I asked him how he did it. He shamefully confessed he had bought his freedom with a Rand note.

I promptly read him the riot act. He apologised.

He had one weakness. He smoked cheap cigarettes and he had to rely on our other servants to buy them for him. He saved money, sent food and clothes home. He was a good talker, spoke English well and had views of white-black relations.

One day he was missing. Our servants said he had no cigarettes and he decided to go to the local shop to buy some. A neighbour's servant told us he saw Simon being arrested in the street.

I immediately visited the nearest police station and was told that Simon was there and would be taken to the Native Commissioner's Court the next day.

I had not been back to Fordsburg since I had bailed my father out of his cell at the police station, next to the Native Commissioner's Court. It is a depressing building. Every day hundreds of blacks are brought before several tired and jaded magistrates and charged with statutory Pass Law offences under the Urban Areas Act, sentenced to fines, imprisonment, or farm labour as Helen Suzman and I knew when we raised the matter of farm prisons in Parliament.

Mostly, there are no lawyers to defend the black offenders. One by one, blacks are called out, often by numbers. They come up from the basement, are read a charge and in a few minutes are sentenced.

They then disappear into the basement. Sometimes a white employer makes a plea, pays a fine or gets an acquittal. In later years the Black Sash was very much in evidence helping blacks in trouble.

Over two hundred thousand people were sentenced in 1959 for not carrying the hated "dompas" (pass) or for being illegally in urban areas.

I arrived early at court and saw a young prosecutor. I told him I wanted to help Simon, and that we gave him work which did not surprise him. He told me to wait while he spoke to the magistrate.

A dejected Simon came up from the basement. The magistrate remanded the case. I then received a note that the magistrate would see me at the tea interval in his office. He was an elderly civil servant, who offered me a cup of tea. I told him how we had befriended Simon, how good a worker he was and that we had no option but to assist him in his present troubles. The magistrate reminded me that I had broken the law. But I was not the one before the court. He then told me that this was Simon's third offence which could no longer be condoned or tolerated.

"Dr Wilson," he said, "you are a man with a public record and you have done a lot for Soweto. You shouldn't be harbouring an illegal black from Rhodesia, should you?"

He proceeded to do his duty and lectured me. My concern was to get Simon off with a fine. I told him it was a waste of time and the state's money to send Simon to gaol again. I promised that if he would give Simon the option of a fine, I would pay and guarantee to send Simon back by train to Rhodesia within two weeks.

He listened carefully and said I should see him at 9.30 the following morning at his office.

Promptly on time I presented myself at the magistrate's office. He was seated at his desk. He called in the young prosecutor.

"Dr Wilson, this is a court in session."

Turning to the prosecutor he said: "Bring the accused Simon Dube to the court."

A few minutes later Simon was brought in. His face lit up when he saw me. The prosecutor read the charge.

The magistrate then proceeded to question Simon on his previous record, patiently writing it all down in longhand. He then asked me to confirm that I would pay a fine and be responsible for returning Simon to Rhodesia. I nodded assent. He then pronounced Simon guilty.

"Simon Dube, I sentence you to three months imprisonment and R100 fine for contravening Influx Control regulations, Section 10 of the Urban Areas Act, and illegally entering South Africa for the purposes of employment. The prison sentence is suspended for three years. I warn you the next time you will be very severely dealt with by the law. Do you understand me?"

Simon nodded. I paid the fine and thanked the magistrate. I realised that he had gone to the trouble of this "private" court, because in open court he would have had no option but to send Simon to prison for a long time. He was an understanding man.

I collected Simon, who was overwhelmed with gratitude for what I'd done. In turn, I lectured Simon and told him he was never to return to South Africa, whatever the circumstances. I telephoned my Bulawayo office, instructing them to give Simon the equivalent of R100 and if possible to find him a job. Unfortunately there was no work in my company, due to the bad state of the Rhodesian economy.

That is the story of Simon Dube. He was fortunate that I was able to help him in a small way. Hundreds of thousands who are arrested for being illegally in urban areas aren't so lucky. Instead they waste years of their lives away from their families, in South African gaols.

64

The Pass Laws, the Urban Areas Act with the notorious Section 10 which allowed a black exactly 72 hours to find a job before coming up against the law, the interminable raids, are a sordid reminder of the effects of apartheid. For blacks it is a destroyer of the social fabric of their lives.

It was this sort of thing that made one hate the kind of life we led in South Africa in the 1960s as privileged whites in an affluent society. For us it was not possible not to be emotionally, morally and politically involved in the lives of blacks. The lives of whites were inextricably linked with that of the blacks.

Verwoerd was trying the impossible, to unscramble the omelette. His grotesque plans, the uncaring brutality and the resultant social crisis played havoc with one's conscience.

But to be fair, the Pass Laws were not the invention of Verwoerd. They had dominated South Africa's control of its blacks since the earliest mining days. It was the Nationalists who refined their implementation.

I looked back to the days in Parliament when new amendments to these pernicious statutes became law. Delegated authority tightened control of black movement in the country, which not only affected the blacks, but also restricted the freedom of white employers dependent on black labour.

In the recess, as I thought about Parliament and my other commitments I realised that I would find it very hard to continue. I was drifting away from the family, my business, which was growing, needed my attention, I was not doing any medicine. Above all, I had become an unwilling tool of the apartheid machine in Parliament.

I came to the conclusion that I and the liberal presence in Parliament could do little more than ask questions and protest. There was no social intercourse; Government and Opposition MPs lived in separate compartments. The surrealism of the conduct of the debates, in which each side stuck to its own language, the Afrikaners to Afrikaans, the English-speakers to English was not normal. The Nationalists were mostly products of their own single-medium school system, and their desire to protect Afrikaans was part of their identity maintenance. Some could hardly speak English. Some of our opposition MPs could not understand a word of Afrikaans. Add to this the puerile level of debate and the constant failure to face up to the real problems of the country, my continued participation in Parliament was was an exercise in futility. What on earth was I doing in this strange legislative House of Assembly?

It was fascinating to see the Nationalists in action, especially Dr Verwoerd. But that was not my purpose in going to Parliament.

I had no desire to be reduced to the level of a Parliamentary hack, an occasional interjector or a primed asker of questions. That was no way to make a contribution.

I weighed up the years I had been in Opposition and concluded I was tired of the constant battle against the Nationalist tide. I had been actively opposing them since 1943.

The other disappointment was the less than satisfactory development of the Progressive Party. We were back to square one as far as non-cooperation was concerned. I wrote to Leo Boyd in March about "continued [party] bungling on major matters." Things had not improved. I could not ignore the fact that I was a key figure in the organisational and information infrastructure of the party. I felt very deeply the continued mismanagement by my political colleagues, which was associated with an emerging struggle for power in the party.

Steytler was a non-controversial politician, without the sophistication of MPs like De Beer and Eglin. For professional and personal reasons he had to spend a lot of time in Queenstown, and had to rely heavily on telex and telephone. Much of the key work, however, was done by others in Johannesburg, Cape Town and Durban. I regarded myself as politically more experienced than most of the leadership, and continual differences, especially on organisational strategy, not only depressed me but wasted my time. I wanted efficiency.

Finally, the anti-republican campaign was a mess.

The evidence was mounting that once more in my life I should make some important decisions.

On 20 July 1960, I wrote to Jan Steytler:

"I have now had sufficient time to go into this whole question. I have come to the conclusion I should resign from Parliament as the MP for Hospital as soon as possible. I would like to suggest that I resign my seat at a point convenient to you and the Progressive Party; and since it is my intention to take six months holiday overseas commencing some time in October or November this year, I suggest I could delay this until the end of the year if it is suitable to you."

Steytler was upset on receiving the letter, and came to see me in Johannesburg to try and dissuade me. In the end, I agreed to hold it over until the New Year, but I doubted that I would change my mind.

No one else knew about my decision and I went ahead to make my personal and business arrangements.

The anti-republican campaign was in full swing, with Dr Verwoerd back in office and vigorously propagating the Government's case.

On 3 August I addressed my own report-back meeting in Hospital, the day the five-month Emergency ended.

Voting on the referendum was due to take place on 5 October. Verwoerd was giving people the impression that he was "convinced that if South Africa decides to become a Republic within the Commonwealth and puts the request to other members of the Commonwealth, the influence of Britain, Australia and Canada would see to it that South Africa is retained within the Commonwealth."

What Verwoerd did not tell South Africa was that Hillary Marquand, a British MP, told the House of Commons on 4 July that "the South African

Government are on trial at the bar of humanity." I had been on a quick visit to the UK and my British political friends in the House of Commons told me that they were convinced that, if the Nationalists did not change their apartheid policy and South Africa chose the path of a republic, it would not be allowed to remain in the Commonwealth.

Meanwhile reports were coming in from the platteland that Nat MPs were telling their supporters that South Africa was to become a republic outside of the Commonwealth. Who was telling the truth?

The electorate was confused. At my report-back meeting I tackled lethargic English-speaking voters:

"I must sound a warning to certain English-speaking people in places like Johannesburg who spend their time in their clubs, on the golf courses, the stock exchange and in business circles . . . saying: Let the Nationalists have their republic. After all, once they get it, there is very little else they will want."

I was a lone voice in a very confused political wilderness. The recent Prime Minister's Conference was aware that the House of Commons had unanimously declared that "repression in South Africa is threatening the security and welfare of all races living in the Union of South Africa and the good relations between members of the Commonwealth."

This important declaration was not brought to the attention of South Africa by the NP.

At my small meeting in Hospital I warned the audience: "Apartheid has brought fear and frustration and disappointment to millions of non-white South Africans . . . Apartheid, with its racial discrimination, its laws that permeate every facet of our political, industrial and social life will be the cornerstone of the Verwoerdian Nationalist Republic."

English-speaking South Africans hardly ever read Afrikaans newspapers or listened to Afrikaans language radio stations, because they could speak Afrikaans. They were totally oblivious of how the Afrikaners saw the republican issue. The republic, to the Afrikaner, was to be the culmination of the long struggle against British imperialism and colonialism. It was winning back all they had lost in the Boer War, which they had never stopped fighting.

It was very easy, therefore, for Nationalist politicians to tell English-speaking voters one thing, and the Afrikaners another. Some of us, who were involved in the referendum, realised that Verwoerd would get his "Yes" result due to the laziness, gullibility and economic preoccupation (greed) of the English voter.

In September, Verwoerd sent a letter to every voter in the country. It was full of every cliche that his propagandists could muster and dealt with national unity, our children's future, blaming racial enmity amongst the whites on the monarchical system – to which he added, for good measure, the chaos in the Congo and the Communist threat. He threw the book of Nationalist horror, prejudice and fear at all white South Africans.

My enthusiasm for this campaign, of which the result was predictable, waned by the day. This was not helped by the fact that problems arose in

Hospital and elsewhere in the country.

In Hospital the co-operation between the UP and the Progressives was formal. Unfortunately, it was not helped by Harry Schwarz's attitude. Elsewhere, Miles Malleson was frustrated by De Beer who had taken over from me. He had not carried out his promise to come to Johannesburg.

Once more Malleson wrote to Steytler asking for my return.

I was glad that Steytler did not accede to that request.

On 6 October the republican issue was settled. Verwoerd had triumphed, but only by a narrow majority. There was great jubilation on the SABC and in the Afrikaans press. For me, it was a very sad day.

Verwoerd's majority was only 75 733 in a 90 per cent poll where 850 458 voted "YES" for the republic and 774 725 voted "NO". Nevertheless, it was questionable whether it gave him the right to go ahead with his radical plans for the republic and the balkanisation of South Africa.

Stanley Uys, writing in *Forum*, said: "The alacrity with which the Opposition circles have accepted the result of the referendum is evidence of the muddled thinking in South Africa about the republic . . . The majority is meagre enough . . . the inadequacy of the Opposition organisation . . . aided the republican cause. At least the majority is insufficient to justify such an important constitutional change as the establishment of the republic. The current theory in Opposition circles is that if the republican theory can be pushed aside the the ensuing conflict over the race policies will split the Nationalists and bring about a change of government."

Uys continued: "This is fantasy, because the republic and the race policy are inextricably related and Dr Verwoerd is going to keep it that way."

Neville Caley, in a masterly leader in *Forum*, was strongly critical of the English voter's "stupidly superior attitude to party politics . . . to leave politics to the Afrikaners. Above all the blacks have not been consulted".

Hillary Marquand warned in *Forum* that if South Africa became a republic the Commonwealth would not accept it if Verwoerd continued with apartheid as a policy.

Bernard Braine, a Conservative back-bencher, told *Forum* reader's before the referendum that "if the vote is in favour of a republic . . . he [Verwoerd] will plunge South Africa into perilous isolation."

There had been enough warnings before and after the referendum for the average South African to realise what Verwoerd was doing to the country. What astonished me in 1960 was the total amnesia displayed by English-speaking South Africans about Verwoerd's journalistic and political history. They were prepared to believe that the republic was the last claim that the Nationalists would make.

It reminded me of Hitler in the 1930s, who assured the world: "This is my last territorial claim."

The majority of English-speaking voters ignored the sinister influence and control of the secret Broederbond in South Africa. As they were excluded from its membership they knew little of what it did.

Almost all Verwoerd's Cabinet Ministers were members. "Broeders" were said to have infiltrated all public bodies, school committees, trade unions, churches, cultural and political circles where they directed decisions wherever the Afrikaner was active. When the Republican Constitution was published in 1942, Dr Malan, the former NP leader, demanded "a free independent Republican Christian National State based on the word of God, eschewing all foreign models . . . with the Christian National Education system . . . and the stringent emphasis upon the effective disciplining of the people."

Nationalists had no hesitation in keeping the idea of the republic alive before the volk. Dr Nico Diederichs, Minister of Finance, called for "a disciplined Christian National Republic, Afrikaans in core and content with strict state control over press, radio and mines."

Dr Verwoerd, when editor of *Die Transvaler*, the Nationalist's mouth-piece, wrote that the "Nationalist Republic would eliminate the evils of British-Jewish capitalist democracy."

"Blackie" Swart, former Minister of Justice who participated in the attempt in Parliament to frame me, and who became Governor-General, echoed these views: "We must eradicate British-Jewish democracy root and shoot and in its place we shall have the old republican system adapted to modern conditions."

In the 1940s, during World War II, when Smuts and the UP were in power and the Nationalists were the Opposition, their attitude to the British connection was made very clear.

In 1941, FC Erasmus, who later became Minister of Justice, had said: "The un-national press and the radio will find, under the republican order, that it is regarded as treason to undermine or attempt to overthrow the Republic. The press and radio will have to keep in step with the interests of the Republic or keep quiet."

The Minister of Defence, JJ Fouche, had been equally outspoken in 1942. "We nationalists are in agreement that we want to get rid of British liberalistic democracy in this country."

In 1944 Eric Louw was notorious for his rabid anti-Semitism. "As long as we remain within the British Commonwealth," he had said, "either as a dominion or as a sham republic, we shall be continually hindered by British liberalism in our attempts to solve the colour problem and the Jewish question."

These statements by National Party leaders went unheeded by the generation that voted twenty years later in the referendum. Whatever the English press and the Opposition parties recalled from history had little effect on the voters. The English and the Afrikaners were too busy fighting their little war of hate.

In 1942, when Dr Malan published the draft constitution of the Republic the document made clear that "the Afrikaans people acknowledge that their national destination is embodied in their Voortrekker past. The Republic is to rest on a Christian National foundation . . . Afrikaans will be the first official language . . . at the head of the state will be the State President . . . only responsible to God . . . altogether independent of any vote in Parliament."

The provisions of the 1942 Republican Constitution made a strong impression on me. I always believed that when Afrikanerdom established its republic it would be based on the the narrow Calvinistic precepts of this document, which is what happened.

In the post-Sharpeville days of 1960 and the turbulence created by Verwoerd in South Africa, the 1942 Republican Constitution was of major importance when I made my decision that my Parliamentary career was at an end, despite all my high ideals.

I could no longer support the political hypocrisy expected of white politicians. I did not accept that the Nationalist Afrikaner would ever change his survival credo for himself or the whites – but above all for white Afrikaners. I could not see how, in the end, a small number of white people at the bottom end of the continent of Africa, with its hundreds of millions of blacks would ever be able to repress the blacks of South Africa, in order to run a white-dominated political society, other than at the end of a machine-gun.

I also saw that despite the advent of the Progressive Party, we were not acceptable to the blacks, just as we were not acceptable to the conservative whites of South Africa. Furthermore, in the longer term the white-black connection would become the white-black divide. I had been through the whole gamut of bitterness of race prejudice and colour hatred in South Africa and no longer wanted to be part of it in the future, since I had seen through the ghastly political innards of the Nationalist Afrikaner in Parliament.

I was not prepared to let a Dr Verwoerd or a CR Swart or the secret police, the phone-tappers or the nightly telephone callers dictate to me and my family what we should be thinking and doing, or how we should run our lives. The world had seen all this in the 1930s when Hitler was enslaving millions.

In early November I took the family to England. I needed time to think and reorganise our lives. Many questions to be answered. It was helpful to view South Africa's grief from thousands of miles away.

Parliament was due to start in late January. As we were still in England, I decided I would fly back to South Africa in order to personally hand in my resignation to the Speaker of the House of Assembly.

On the aeroplane from Jan Smuts airport to Cape Town, were several members of Parliament flying to the official opening and the new session.

Walking up and down the aisle, as if he was taking the air, was Dr Albert Hertzog, the Minister of Posts and Telegraphs. He was in his shirt-sleeves, smiling at colleagues, with a word or two here and there.

He was an unusual character, with an angular, small face, goatee beard and round spectacles with eyes that peered intently.

I got up and stood near my seat to stretch my legs.

Albert Hertzog came up to me.

"How are you, Boris, did you have a good holiday?"

We exchanged pleasantries. We inevitably came to the new session of Parliament, and started talking of South African politics.

"Albert," I said, "I don't know how you can stand it."

"Stand what?" he asked.

"All the tension in the country that we had last year and are still having. How can you put up with it all the time?"

Albert Hertzog looked at me as if I was mad.

"Tension," he said. "What tension?"

He put his hands out wide, and smiled.

"There is no tension in the country – everything is beautiful."

65

Twenty-nine years later, on 2 February 1990, I was in Cape Town watching the ceremonial opening of Parliament on television, listening to the new State President, FW de Klerk. Near the end of his speech, he gave South Africa the dramatic news that the government was going to release Nelson Mandela from prison, unban the African National Congress, the outlawed South African Communist Party, the Pan-African Congress and release many political prisoners.

The Separate Amenities Act, one of the cornerstones of apartheid was to be repealed, curbs on the media scrapped and the conditions imposed on released detainess rescinded. There was the possibility, in the future, of re-incorporating the Bantu homelands into South Africa.

President De Klerk declared that South Africa was entering a "new era".

In a television interview after the announcement, Dr Gerrit Viljoen, his right hand Cabinet Minister and former President of the Broederbond, declared that the National Party had come to the end of apartheid's road, with no option but to make a radical change in political direction.

Later, President De Klerk told South Africa that for forty-two years the Afrikaners had struggled to reach their promised land, but had failed. Afrikaners had to face up to the fact that if they wanted to survive they had to compromise with the black people of South Africa and rebuild the South African nation without discrimination in which everyone irrespective of colour would have a vote and share alike in its future. De Klerk shattered the beliefs of many of his supporters and enemies by forecasting that the National Party might not be in power within ten years.

He expected that a black government could take over under a new negotiated constitution with a Bill of Rights that protected all minorities.

I found it hard to believe that after all the human suffering inflicted by the National Party over the last four decades, in particular in implementing Dr Verwoerd's apartheid plans, it was now doing a radical about-turn, hoping to consign the theory and practice of apartheid to the dust-bin of history for ever, embracing the liberal policies we progressives had proposed for over thirty years.

My first reaction was "I don't believe it – there must be a hidden agenda." If there was one, I had to find out what it was, before the deluge of words camouflaged it.

I reminded myself that, thirty years ago in Parliament, I had listened to the British Prime Minister, Harold Macmillan telling Dr Verwoerd and the country that the "winds of change" were blowing through Africa, and South Africa could not, in the end, escape from these political whirlwinds and tornadoes.

The announcement was a shock to me, because I believed I would not see the end of apartheid in my lifetime. Yet here in February 1990, the political leader of the Afrikaner volk, Frederick de Klerk, was telling everyone, black and white that the struggle for white supremacy was over, admitting it had failed.

On 11 February I was one of the many thousands who thronged the Grand Parade in Cape Town waiting to hear Nelson Mandela speak on the day he was freed from prison. My purpose was to experience what was undoubtedly an historic event, and get the "feel" and mood of the tens of thousands who waited for hours to catch a glimpse of Nelson Mandela, the black leader whom no one but his jailers, certain National Party cabinet ministers, his wife Winnie and Helen Suzman, had seen or heard for twenty-seven years.

On the crowded Grand Parade, there was a sense of excitement and euphoria, coupled with disbelief, that at long last millions of blacks, coloureds and Indians could look forward to a place in the sun in their own country, which had been denied to them by the ruling Nationalist government for forty-two years, but which had been there since the white man came to Southern Africa over three centuries ago.

Throughout the country, amongst the whites, there was an immediate rush of support for De Klerk from English-speaking South Africans. From his right wing enemies, the Conservative Party, the Herstigte Nasionale Party (HNP) and the Afrikaner Weerstands-Beweging (AWB), there were howls of rage that De Klerk had sold the birthright of the Afrikaner to the ANC and the Communists. They vowed to fight to the bitter end to save white South Africa from this terrible sell-out by the National Party.

There was muted reaction from leading liberals, who were cautious because many previous National Party "reforms" in the last few years were stillborn. Some of us who had been monitoring South Africa's progress over the forty-two years of National Party rule expected that the road De Klerk had embarked on would be a dangerous and rocky pathway to the "new South Africa."

66

A year later, on 1 February 1991, President De Klerk was still on the road to the new South Africa. He announced, at the opening of Parliament, that he was repealing, in this session of the Tri-Cameral Parliament, the last three major apartheid Acts which would spell the final passing into history and oblivion, the pillars of Dr Hendrik Verwoerd's vision.

The Land Act of 1936, the Group Areas Act and the Population Registration Act would all go before the session ended. By the time Parliament had prorogued in June 1991 the three Acts, the last remaining buttresses of apartheid, had been repealed from the statute books.

It was another momentous declaration from De Klerk and it was clear even to the political sceptics that despite the social and political trauma which followed his 1990 announcement, he was on an irreversible road to his new South Africa.

De Klerk had not been deterred by the appalling black-on-black violence in Natal and the Transvaal, nor the widespread unrest throughout the country. He had not deviated from his goal, although nearly 10 000 blacks had died since 1984 when the violence began, nor did he flinch from threats of the white ultraconservatives, who vowed that they would fight tooth and nail against the National Party's march to democracy.

I was present in February 1991 at the Joint Sitting of the three Houses when the debate on the State President's speech took place, and witnessed the extraordinary role adopted by both National Party ministers and MPs who followed each other in an almost evangelical "confession" of their own and their party's apartheid sins. They were determined to purge themselves before the coloureds and Indians in the multiracial Chamber. It was history, all right, but watched by only a small number of whites, coloureds and Indians in the public galleries.

Who would have thought it possible that one could sit in Parliament, in 1991, listening to the Afrikaner successors to Dr Hendrik Verwoerd, the upholder of the white volk, rid themselves of the final solution of apartheid which had brought South Africa very nearly to the brink of racial and economic catastrophe. It was hard to believe that De Klerk and his National Party MPs were going to the podium as the new disciples of democracy, rejecting with scorn the objections that came from the official opposition, the Conservative Party prophets of doom.

The coloured MPs spent their time trying to justify the role of the Labour Party in the House of Representatives since the inception of the Tri-Cameral system, pleading that they were an essential part of the future political infrastructure, even though few coloureds had voted for them. Some were brave enough to ask for "reparations for the land and homes" that had been taken from them by the demands of apartheid.

I was struck by the fact that, in this debate on the new South Africa which had at stake, amongst other things, the future political role of thirty million black South Africans, there was not one BLACK member of Parliament to participate; nor did I see more than one or two blacks, in the public galleries to witness this catharsis coming from the country's white Nationalist leaders.

The irrelevance of the Tri-Cameral Parliament was never more starkly evident than in this debate, which the blacks ignored, because it was a fraudulent edifice, in its final throes of collapse.

67

Much had changed in my life and in South Africa since the fateful day when I flew to Cape Town in 1961 to resign from Parliament, when Dr Albert Hertzog told me: ". . . there is no tension in the country . . . everything is beautiful".

In 1961 I was unsettled after six months in England and returned to South Africa to take charge of my business because of deteriorating economic conditions and management problems.

My two sons, temporarily attending a private school in England, pleaded to be allowed to remain there. After much thought and rationalisation my wife and I agreed to let them stay in England, knowing that they were happy at their school, they would be getting a liberal and progressive education and be out of the clutches of the national education system that the government was introducing into the South African schools with its indoctrination, apartheid and dogma.

Subsequently they passed "A" levels at Harrow, securing places on merit at Cambridge, to study the biological sciences and medicine. This gave me great satisfaction, as I was never able to take up the invitation to appear before the Elsie Ballot Scholarship Trustees for selection to Cambridge in the late 1930s. Eventually, Adrian and Nigel studied for their medical degree, and Virginia, our daughter surprisingly left the London School of Economics to take up medicine as well. In time, all three qualified as medical doctors.

I became deeply involved in my business, as the chairman and chief executive, constantly on the move, organising and planning, driving my car or flying to my branches in South Africa and to my Rhodesian company's offices in Bulawayo and Salisbury. Or on a business trip to London, to see my sons at Harrow and Virginia at Wycombe Abbey, and later at their universities and medical schools.

In South Africa I kept myself on the periphery of politics. I was often urged to take an active part in Progressive Party affairs when liberal and progressive views were unpopular. Much as I would have liked to be in the thick of things again, I declined, keeping to my business and family priorities, with half an eye on medicine, which I did not want to desert. Although I had left Parliament as a disappointed man, I could not get politics out of my system, and watched the important political happenings from the sidelines. However, every time Helen Suzman had to fight her seat at a general election, I was one of the helpers.

Nineteen sixty-one was the eventful year when South Africa left the Commonwealth, the Treason Trial ended with all the ANC accused acquitted, and the Nationalist government under Dr Verwoerd relentlessly pursued its apartheid objectives. Blacks unsuccessfully continued to harass the white government with strikes. Sabotage in 1962 was increasing, and conviction was a capital crime. Then, in 1963 the first of the "gaol without trial" Acts, the notorious 90-day detention law was passed, followed in 1965 by its draconian extension to 180 days to cope with mounting opposition, not only from blacks, but by militant white liberals opposed to apartheid.

This law meant the end of habeas corpus in South Africa, which was a serious diminution of civil rights.

One of the most significant events in opposition politics in South Africa from 1961 to 1974 was the extraordinary role played by Helen Suzman the sole Progressive Party member of Parliament after the original founder MPs were defeated in the 1961 general election.

As the lone Progressive Party spokesman left in Parliament she fought against both the Nationalist steamroller and the weak United Party who continued to find ways of compromising with the government as it piled on the agony of Verwoerd's race laws. Verwoerd wanted to see the end of the Progressive Party in Parliament; it could have been one reason why he called the 1961 general election. He could cope with the United Party, he knew how to put them to shame and create political situations in which the UP would, in the end, support his legislation. But he had problems with the lone Progressive survivor, Helen Suzman, who opposed his apartheid legislation at every opportunity, showing South Africa and the outside world that there was a flicker of progressive opposition left in Parliament. Helen hoped to keep this opposition alive until the Progressives were returned one day in the not too distant future.

Much has already been written about the unique role Helen played, objecting to every new apartheid law, asking hundreds of parliamentary questions with the able help of the PP's research team, finding time to visit political prisoners and detainees, and the way she fought for the rights of individual South Africans who fell foul of the many laws and regulations that were the innards of the apartheid monster.

This petite woman, whose shrill voice in Parliament often drove the Nationalist leaders to distraction, has received praise and honour from the civilised world for her courage in her lonely fight against the might of the National Party.

When I first joined the United Party in 1952, I had visions that I would make early contact with Helen and her friends because they were known as liberal reformists in the UP. I was disappointed however, to find that they appeared to keep me at arm's length. It eventually dawned on me that some of the so-called liberals of the United Party were suspicious of my credentials because I was a "socialist" Labour Party recruit – a socialist background was not the best introduction to the wealthy armchair liberals of Johannesburg's northern suburbs, whose epicentre was amongst the leading stockbrokers and financiers. Helen Suzman was no political leader and has never claimed to be one. She and the Progressive Party knew her best role was to fight for the underdog, the voteless, the banned and the detained, and for those who needed someone courageous in Parliament who would speak without fear against apartheid's damage to society.

Since the Native Representatives had been removed from Parliament, the United Party wanted its hands clean in the fight against the Nationalists. As a result, Helen's life throughout the thirteen years of her parliamentary battles, was so full and tiring that the political loneliness began to tell on her and sometime in 1969 she was ready to quit Parliament if a successor could be found. I was approached by some of her close friends to consider standing in Houghton in her place because she did not want to fight the next election. Fortunately, after a visit overseas her strength and motivation returned and she carried on alone until the Progressives had their breakthrough in 1974.

Over Helen Suzman's parliamentary career I have only one serious criticism where I believe she made a wrong decision – namely her opposition to sanctions against South Africa, which received worldwide prominence, in which she allied herself with Margaret Thatcher, the Conservative British Prime Minister, Mangosuthu Buthelezi, the Zulu homeland and Inkatha leader and subsequently with the Progressive Party MPs who were elected to Parliament after 1974. Like others, I thought that Margaret Thatcher was using Helen Suzman and Buthelezi as pawns in order to justify her own anti-sanctions policy for Britain, who has large investments in South Africa and could not afford, unlike the Americans, to let them be reduced or withdrawn because of the negative effect it would have on unemployment in Britain, and the need to maintain British exports to South Africa.

Helen turned a deaf ear to the advice given her by black trade unionists in South Africa, leading churchmen like Bishop Tutu, and other black leaders, that the black people of South Africa would gladly suffer sanctions if it meant that apartheid would die. This, after all, was what Helen's own lone struggle had been all about.

Helen actively campaigned in support of the no-sanctions policy against South Africa, particularly in Britain and the USA over a number of years, disappointing many South African liberals like me and thousands of black people who felt she was simply acting out the Nationalist government's wishes and helping to keep apartheid alive.

Helen Suzman, in her own right, is an economist who fully understood the consequences of a full-scale sanctions onslaught on South Africa, its effects on the economy of the country and on the mass of lowly-paid blacks; she had every right to adopt the no-sanctions policy she advocated, but it was wrong political strategy.

I believe too, that her close association with liberal businessmen and other financiers of wealthy Johannesburg, were important factors in her decision to oppose sanctions. She lost the moral support of many blacks over her anti-sanctions stance and one cannot believe that she is now not aware that probably the main reason that forced the Nationalists to abandon apartheid, after their forty-two year struggle, was the effectiveness of the financial sanctions imposed on South Africa in 1985 by the USA through the withdrawal of large loans to South Africa, amongst other economic pressures, coupled with the country-wide wave of black defiance that followed.

68

In 1964 I realised that there was going to be a political crisis in Rhodesia. Ian Smith's Rhodesian Front would not give way to the demands of the British government that they should come to a proper settlement with the black people of Rhodesia if they wanted the country to become independent. Political experience persuaded me that it would be better to sell my Rhodesian business before the situation erupted.

Friends in the Southern Rhodesian Parliament after the dissolution of Federation were certain that a break with Britain would come with disastrous consequences for the economy.

I initiated talks with my partners, Pye of Cambridge, (who had absorbed Ekco in Britain) to buy the Rhodesian company. Pye depended on me in Southern Africa because, after they took over Ekco in 1964, they approached me to take over management of their faltering business interests in South Africa, reorganise them and merge them with mine.

This relieved me of a tremendous burden and I was able to concentrate on my South African business affairs, spend more time on observing South African political events, writing for the newspapers, making speeches to nonpolitical organisations and doing some medical practice, which I had neglected.

I started doing clinical sessions as a casualty officer at the Johannesburg General Hospital in the evenings and at weekends. It was surprising how easily my medical knowledge surfaced after several years of non-use.

69

On the afternoon of 6 September 1966, South Africa was startled by a dramatic news report from Parliament in Cape Town.

The Speaker of the House of Assembly had just read the prayers, and MPs were settling in their seats, when a uniformed messenger came down the aisle and stopped in front of Dr Verwoerd, who was about to sit down. He bent over Dr Verwoerd, raised his right hand, in which was a sheath knife, and plunged it downwards into Dr Verwoerd's chest. The Prime Minister fell back and then slumped forward over his bench, bleeding copiously.

Dr Hendrik Frensch Verwoerd, almost 65, the architect of legalised apartheid, the Prime Minister who set South Africa on the road to separate development and the Afrikaner's hope of their promised white fatherland, had been assassinated by an unknown man later certified as a psychopath. No one has ever, since that momentous day, been able to disclose whether the assassin was a "loner" or part of a plan by enemies to remove Verwoerd.

On the floor of the chaotic House of Assembly, PW Botha, the future President of South Africa, stood screaming at Helen Suzman that she and the liberals were responsible for Verwoerd's death.

The Star, reporting Dr Verwoerd's assassination on its front-page later that day, carried another report beneath it, also in bold print. A 75-year-old Indian general dealer, his wife and thirty year old son (together with R10 000 worth of groceries and furniture) were evicted from their shop and living quarters that very day in the white suburb of Turffontein in Johannesburg, under the provisions of the notorious Group Areas Act, whereby a court order, obtained by the Minister of the Interior gave him power to invoke the provisions of this front-line weapon of apartheid.

Mr Hassan Kara, the bearded and bewildered old man, said: "I've held a general dealers license in Turffontein for 37 years."

Mounds of tinned foodstuffs and other groceries piled up alongside mattresses and wooden furniture on the pavement outside his shop and dwelling-place.

No one noticed Mr Hassan Kara's tragedy, as a victim of apartheid, on the day that Hendrik Verwoerd died. While most of the whites mourned Verwoerd's death, the tragic plight of millions of blacks, Asians and coloureds, whose lives had been dislocated by apartheid through the political philosophy of the late Prime Minister, went unnoticed. After all, Dr Verwoerd had proclaimed that he had been chosen to lead South Africa because it was the wish of the Almighty.

Balthazar John Vorster, former Minister of Justice, was elected by the National Party to succeed Verwoerd and to carry out his unfinished tasks, so that apartheid's monster could complete its agenda despite Verwoerd's death and Vorster's promise to humanise it.

Instead, by 1968, Race Classification was refined. It now depended on descent as well as appearance and acceptance. Terrorism was made a capital offence. The coloured parliamentary and provincial franchises were abolished, and inter-racial party politics were prohibited.

Although I was deeply involved in business affairs, I had to have some vehicle for political expression. I often used business organisations to which I belonged as a platform for my political ideas to see to what extent I could bring realism into the minds of organised industry in some of its relations with its workers.

On one occasion, when an industrial tribunal had been called to settle a new wage agreement for the radio and television industry, we found that our meeting was held up because no representatives of the Bantu Labour Department had arrived to represent the black workers in our industry.

My business colleagues were prepared to negotiate new terms without the blacks being represented. I strongly opposed this procedure, and said that I would step down as the chairman of the industry, (I had been elected in 1965) and act as the workers representative if the tribunal agreed. Surprisingly, they did, and my vice-chairman replaced me on the side of the employers. I argued the case for the black workers and secured better terms for them than they would have got if they had not been represented. This incident illustrates the gap in the minds of industrialists in a colour-conscious environment like South Africa where at that time black trade unions were not recognised by the government or the industries themselves.

In my own radio assembly plant, I visited the manufacturing lines daily, and made myself, as chief executive, available to any of the employees who wanted to speak to me. In this way I was able to learn at first hand about personal problems and could often help with housing difficulties, pass laws, compulsory removals and family matters. I got to know some of the workers well; they, in turn, kept me informed of what was going on in the black townships.

There was a production problem on our radio manufacturing line that would not resolve itself and which the factory manager could not explain. The daily rate of production in the mornings was always about thirty per cent lower than the rest of the day which increased our costs and lowered our production rate. Numerous studies did not help us.

Like a bolt from the blue the solution hit me. The black workers on our lines all came from the segregated townships of Soweto, and their day started between 4.00 and 5.00 am. They had a long walk to the train or bus, in which they usually had to stand, arrived at work somewhat exhausted, in time to commence the first few hours assembling small components on to the intricate radio chassis.

The first morning break was about 10 am, when they had tea and perhaps a piece of bread. It was evident that with no intake of food from the early hours of the morning, they were physiologically in no condition to maintain a high degree of expertise and efficiency because of a lack of essential calories with resultant energy depletion.

I decided to carry out an urgent "clinical trial" and arranged for milk, bread and jam to be given to all the black, coloured and Indian workers before they started work at 7.30 am. The results were remarkable. The morning production rose to the best levels of the day, and we were able to justify the extra cost of the food we gave them by the lowered cost of production and the increase in the number of radio chassis they assembled.

I wondered how many tens of thousands of workers in factories in South Africa were suffering from this problem which had at its roots the fact that blacks were forced by apartheid regulations to live miles out of white cities or towns, where they were burdened by transport problems; they earned low wages that kept them in circumstances of social deprivation and poverty. My training as a medical doctor and my early morning inspection of black township workers problems on the railways when I was chairman of Non-European Affairs stood me in good stead in resolving this difficulty on my own factory floor.

Some of my business colleagues, who secretly objected to my liberal views, relied on me nevertheless to negotiate with the government, as in 1967 when I secured the abolition of resale price maintenance. The radio industry itself was having a hard time and we looked forward to the advent of television, but the government was adamant that it would not introduce TV until it suited them.

By 1969, at the age of 52, I decided that I had enough of business. The political climate was more depressing than ever. Thousands of whites were leaving South Africa because of the inhuman effects of apartheid legislation. Many people feared the open hostility of blacks. Many of my friends were now living in Britain, Australia or Canada.

My business was doing well. Pye expressed an interest in buying a majority stake if I would remain on as chairman for a number of years, with my brother Len as managing director. I thought long and hard about this, and decided I would do it because it was a way for Pauline and me to spend more time with our children in England.

I had no other ties in South Africa and although my political interest never waned, I knew that I would never go back to Parliament, even if the opportunity arose, because I believed that the struggle in South Africa would not be settled in the white Parliament, but by extra-parliamentary negotiation between leaders of the black people and the whites outside its walls. If settlement was to come in Parliament this could only happen if the blacks, Indians and coloureds were properly represented by their own people.

The way was clear, therefore, to talk to Pye in England.

Having made my decision to negotiate with Pye I flew over to Britain with Len and we agreed on a deal with them in which they acquired our joint stakes.

There was a serious misunderstanding with Pye as to nature of the management contract they settled with me, and I had to resort to a legal tussle to secure my rights; it was settled amicably in the end, with a payment by Pye to me of damages and compensation. This left me free to leave Kruger and Wilson (Pty) Ltd, the company I founded, with no obligations whatsoever.

While I was negotiating my way out of the Pye impasse, my shippers asked me to advise them how to solve a serious problem they had with a well-known radio manufacturing competitor which owed them more than a million rands. It was in an insolvent state. They knew I would soon be a free man so they asked me to look at United Radio to see whether this troubled company could be rescued under new management. I refused at first to consider their request because I had already made up my mind to go overseas with Pauline for a while to spend more time with the children, relax and enjoy life in London away from the growing political turmoil in South Africa.

The shippers nagged me until I agreed to help them on the basis that I would commit myself for no more than three weeks doing a survey of United Radio's problems. I would then advise them what they should do to rescue it and save their investment – if this was possible.

I was to regret my weakness. In three weeks I had become so involved in the problems of United Radio and Television, that I had worked out a formula for rescuing it. I agreed to carry out the rehabilitation, providing I could purchase sixty per cent of the equity for a nominal sum, namely one rand, with the proviso that I would in time pay back their past advances to United Radio.

The shippers jumped at my suggestion. The owner of the business and his sons retained forty per cent. I thought I could rehabilitate United Radio in a year and do well in the process. In fact it took me more than five years, because television came to South Africa in 1976.

Within three months, to achieve my objectives, I put an ultimatum to my shippers that I had to own 100 per cent of the equity. They promptly transferred the rest of the shares in United to me, and I became the sole owner. Gone were my ideas of a relaxed life overseas. I was plunged, for the second time since Pye, into the role of a company doctor, to put right the years of mismanagement in United Radio, whose main business was making radio receivers for the black community.

In due course, when Pye made other plans for the control of Kruger and Wilson, my brother Len, my wonderful secretary Molly Bell and several members of staff, including black employees who had worked for me for years, joined me at United Radio.

70

In 1974 I was asked to stand for the Progressive Party in the general election in April. I declined the offer.

I was certain that I could not go back to the South African Parliament and waste my time there in a political dialogue with the deaf, when I believed that the white Parliament was not the place where matters would be settled between black and white. I saw no reason to change my mind about a

Parliament dominated by the Nationalists in which for the foreseeable future there would be no blacks, coloureds or Indians to represent themselves on an equal basis.

Because of the Progressive Party's many electoral setbacks, especially its defeat in 1961 and 1966, Jan Steytler, its leader, became despondent. Colin Eglin had been elected Chairman of the National Executive. In an interview with Dr Brian Hackland who was researching his D Phil thesis on the Progressive Party 1959-81, Eglin told him:

"Jan Steytler went into decline. I think he lost heart. He was still trapped in the leadership position." Steytler resigned in 1970 and Eglin took over as leader.

After Colin Eglin became chairman of the National Executive in 1966, he and Zach de Beer decided that as the Progressives did not have the resources of a national party they "were going to look for six seats, so we chose two-two-two for Natal, Cape and Transvaal . . . in areas . . . where we can get the quickest returns. We're going to go for business-oriented South Africans and we're going to go for young South Africans. Believing that our policy made more sense to these two groups more than anyone else . . . and so in the six seats we chose between 1966 and 1971 there was very sharp improvement."

Despite further setbacks, Eglin pursued a positive policy outside Parliament looking for a new power base amongst "modern city Afrikaners", speaking to frustrated Afrikaner academics in Pretoria and, in his own words, "stomping of the platteland".

He also tried to show that the party was sympathetic to blacks, visiting all the homeland leaders, including visits to the rest of Africa, accompanied on one occasion by Helen Suzman. Colin Eglin's leadership resulted in electoral success.

The 1974 election was the first breakthrough for the Progressives for thirteen years. *The Rand Daily Mail*, in a front-page editorial described it as a "spectacular vote for change".

Progressive Party candidates were returned in six constituencies, in a remarkable swing of 13 per cent.

"The United Party has been knocked for a six," said *The Rand Daily Mail*. Helen Suzman was back – but no longer alone in Parliament. Colin Eglin, the PP's leader, won his seat as, unexpectedly, did a new candidate, Dr van Zyl Slabbert, in the Cape.

I was encouraged by this result and began to give more of my time to the party's affairs in Johannesburg. In June I was elected vice-chairman of the Regional Council and chairman of the organisation committee. I had been approached by worried members of the Regional Council who hoped to make me the chairman the following year as they wanted a change of local leadership and felt the current chairman, Max Borkum, had gone stale, having been in office for many years.

At this time I was intrigued by infighting in the United Party. There was strong evidence that Harry Schwarz now an MP and his group of "young turks" were having problems with the "old guard" of the United Party. There was, however, a big difference between the underlying reasons for the "young turk" conflict – by no means could they be considered the same class of liberal – and the reasons of principle that motivated the Progressives 1959 break from the UP. Nevertheless, in my first public speech at a meeting in Vereeniging I appealed to the "young turks" to join the Progressive Party as individuals, not as a group, because they were wasting their time in the collapsing United Party.

Harry Schwarz and I, over the years, had drifted apart because of the Progressive split, but nevertheless I believed that my original prediction that he would be in the Progressive Party one day was on target.

71

Behind the public scene in the Progressive Party I soon found I was confronted with chronic infighting and animosities between local leaders. Nevertheless, in the Southern Transvaal Regional Council I was not frightened to speak my mind on matters that affected the party's image in the public eye.

One such issue was the praise heaped on the prime minister, John Vorster, by leading Progressives both in South Africa and while on visits overseas. I believed it was not the function of Progressive Party leaders to speak, particularly overseas, as if they were supporters of the Nationalists, and I was puzzled by this development when I returned to party work. My views were endorsed by other members of the Regional Council.

The minutes of the regional meeting in January record that "Dr George Cohen said he was disturbed by a report that had appeared in the press as a result of a statement by Mr Piet Vermeulen (Transvaal leader), in which he praised the PM by calling him a statesman, and said "all right-minded South Africans would stand behind Mr Vorster". Dr Cohen said that he felt it was not the duty of leading members of the Progressive Party to praise the prime minister in view of our attitude to apartheid."

The minutes further reported that "Dr Boris Wilson then spoke, stating that he considered that Dr Cohen had done a service by raising the matter. He too was disturbed by Mr Vermeulen's statements, as well as statements by Dr Alex Boraine MP, in London, also praising Mr Vorster . . . Dr Wilson said the government had got themselves into trouble and he felt it was not the function of leaders of the Progressive Party to praise Mr Vorster's actions, because in fact he had been driven into this position as a result of the policy of apartheid which we all opposed."

The Rand Daily Mail reported on 11 January 1975, under a headline "Boraine Hit For Defending PM", that Boraine had been accused of being an apologist for the prime minister John Vorster, by a member of the British Council of Churches in London.

It was obvious that my outspoken views were not appreciated by some leading members at our regional meetings. I concluded that some of the Progressives who were newcomers to the Regional Council during my long absence did not like the frankness and criticism I displayed even in the inner sanctums of the party's organisation. I, for my part, felt fully justified in objecting to our MPs when overseas praising the National Party prime minister. There was no logic in this behaviour and I strongly made my views known.

What was evident at this point was that I was becoming unpopular in certain circles of the Progressive Party hierarchy because of my criticisms. My comments had struck particularly sensitive nerves.

72

The 1975 session of Parliament opened dramatically in the No Confidence debate. Harry Schwarz threatened to "walk in the wilderness" rather than be the political executioner of one of his UP colleagues in the House of Assembly. The debate, which was was supposed to be devoted to an attack on the government by the United Party, erupted instead into an open split between the "young turks" and the "old guard" in Parliament. Dick Enthoven, a "young turk", had been expelled from the UP caucus over complicity with the *The Star*'s poll earlier in January which showed the United Party in a very poor light.

I did not think the issue was important enough for the drastic action taken by the UP, but it was typically an excuse for the right wing to get rid of the "young turks" in the same way as they put up Douglas Mitchell and Vause Raw in 1959 to create the situation that made us walk out of the party.

The next day Harry Schwarz refused to vote against the Prime Minister's motion to "encourage the promotion of sound race relations", defying the UP party whips. It was predicted that within a few days Harry Schwarz and the "young turks" would be out of the United Party.

The Rand Daily Mail told Harry and his friends to "cool it". They felt that the issue did not warrant breaking up the UP. I did not agree with this view, because I knew once the UP's "old guard" had made up their minds, they would pursue their aims to get rid of Schwarz's group as quickly as possible irrespective of the consequences.

Within a week the expected break in UP occurred. Schwarz, his "young turks" and most of the MPCs in the Transvaal Provincial Council, together with UP office-holders throughout the country, left the United Party and formed themselves into a new party – the Reform Party of South Africa.

Once again the UP was in crisis.

There was the same tired response from Sir De Villiers Graaff to the break. He said he expected the Reformists to resign their seats in Parliament and the Provincial Councils. The United Party had reached the stage where it was so chronically ill that it no longer had insight into its dying political condition, and why it would ultimately disappear from South African political life. The Reformists struggled hard to find some real issues as to why they had resigned, despite long explanations in the Transvaal Provincial Council by their MPCs. No one was seriously interested, because there were no important principles behind the new split.

As I expected, Schwarz was chosen as the leader of the Reformists. I was satisfied that Schwarz and his few MPs could not survive an election – they were really a fragment of the UP with no ideological basis or political principle.

In 1991, I was reading through Hackland's interviews with everyone involved in the formation of the Progressive Reform Party and came across the transcript of the interview he had with Sir de Villiers Graaff, the United Party Leader, in Cape Town on 5 August 1980.

It gives Graaff's opinions, at that time, of Schwarz and the "young turks" – views not previously published.

Graaff: " . . . and this lot [the young turks] got the ear of Joel Mervis, the editor of *The Sunday Times*, who put his boys on to try and denigrate the United Party as much as they could, and me in particular . . . "

Hackland: "Was the idea to force you left . . . ?"

Graaff: "Yes, well, young turk ideas, they were really half-baked, but what they thought was that if they could present a picture of patriotism, black support and sound finance they'd get support . . . and very soon we had a terrible feuding in the party . . ."

Graaff goes on to relate the all-important incident in the No Confidence debate which I mentioned earlier.

Graaff: "Well, they were becoming more impossible . . . In the No Confidence motion which I moved, Vorster waited until the last day to reply . . . moved an amendment to have the support of everybody thanking the government for all it had done to achieve detente, maintain law and order and security of the state and then, wickedly, stuck in 'and approved its policies on relations between the races' . . . I didn't get a copy of the motion until I stood up . . . Schwarz was sitting behind me (having gone out and returned) . . . just as I was finishing saying that it was impossible for us to support the Prime Minister's motion."

When Graaff sat down, "Schwarz simply leaned over and said, 'No, Div, I'm not doing that,' and walked out. So I said, 'Good God, what can I do with an idiot like this?' "

Graaff: "I sent for him on Monday morning and he was in a terrible state, because by that time I think he'd . . . He said 'Do you still want me in the party?' I said, 'No. You chaps have caused so much damn trouble since you've been here . . .'."

Later in the interview, Graaff told Hackland: "Well, there's not much more to tell except that he [Schwarz] rallied his crowd and they went with him . . . They formed the Reform Group which quite obviously could not exist unless they could do a deal with the Progressives, which they did in due course after a tremendous amount of squabbling . . . Well, it's still going on very happily. It's amusing sitting on the sidelines now and seeing the same people who caused me trouble now causing trouble in the Progressive Party. Well, they finished poor old Eglin off, and now they're [sitting] with Van Zyl Slabbert, but I wouldn't like to be in his boots."

Colin Eglin watched Schwarz and the Reformists with growing interest because he saw in them potential allies to strengthen the Progressives in Parliament if he could merge with them. The Reformists could be manna from the political heaven. Eglin did not at that time know of Graaff's experiences or opinions of the "young turks".

Some of the media were critical of Schwarz. The influential *Financial Mail* wrote on 14 February that: "Morally, (the Reformists) the defectors have no right to keep their seats . . . neither do they enjoy the moral and tactical advantage of having decamped on a crisp issue of principle." The *FM* went on to say: ". . . ideologically the right home for all those who have now had their fill of the UP's vacillating leadership, double talk and double standards and who feel instinctively that time is running out for South Africa . . . is the Progressive Party."

I decided it was time for me to act again. I wrote an article that appeared in *The Rand Daily Mail* on 1 March explaining why the Reform and Progressive breaks differed – why we progressives failed to reform the United Party. I emphasised that in 1959 we broke from the UP on several fundamental issues of principle while the Reformists did not appear to have a basic philosophy. Raymond Louw, the editor of *The Rand Daily Mail* (Gandar's successor) relied on me for political perspective – which is what I hoped I achieved in my article.

Reformist moves for a merger with the Progressives came quicker than expected.

Four days after my article appeared Harry Schwarz indicated in Cape Town that he would be willing to serve under Colin Eglin should Eglin be elected by a congress of "verligte parties". Harry was addressing the first meeting of the Reform Party in Cape Town. He did not waste time in making his views known that the Reformists urgently needed a home with the Progressives, but making it abundantly clear that he was not prepared to be gobbled up by the Progressive Party.

"We will only join a new political party if we can come to terms over policy," he boldly announced.

He disclosed that had already had talks with Eglin. On 13 March I wrote to Colin about the discussions he was having with the Reformists. I sent him a copy of my article of 1 March in the *RDM*, and asked him to be patient: "Given a little time they would join us, accept our policy and our terms because they had no other home to go to; but not at a price of any sacrifice of policy and without question a change of name".

To Helen Suzman I wrote a similar letter: "I heard that HFO [Harry Oppenheimer] wants a merger to be done quickly. If so, it is wrong. I've had a lot of experience with some of the Reformists. They're not liberals or Progs and they won't change overnight."

I knew Helen's views. She had no time for Harry Schwarz – she always referred to him sarcastically as "your friend" when she spoke to me about him.

On the same day I wrote to Harry Schwarz: "I hope you'll join the Progressives . . . I hope you will not insist on any policy changes or a change of the name of the party . . . I think you will be lauded by the country if you accepted the position and joined the Progressives without strings . . . what counts now is for you to strengthen the opposition to Nationalism . . . I hope you will accept from me a warm invitation, even if it is a repeat of the one I made to you in your house sixteen years ago to join the real opposition . . . which is now a reality."

I was overseas until the end of April. By the time I returned plans were well under way for a merger with the Reformists. Raymond Louw and I discussed the matter a few days before the PP National Executive met in Johannesburg to ratify the merger.

We decided I should write another article for *The Rand Daily Mail* on the alternative to the merger which simply called on the Reformists to join the Progressives as individuals to retain the Progressive Party image, name and status which had been built up by progressives over 16 years. The Reformists, we had been assured, accepted Progressive policy; therefore there was no need for a new party. At our Congress they could then be integrated into positions throughout the party which should satisfy their aspirations to be on its councils. A survey by *Rapport*, the Afrikaans national Sunday newspaper, gave the Reformists no more than 2,4 per cent voter support so, in effect, they did not mean much to the voters.

I once more appealed to Harry Schwarz as an act of statesmanship to support my proposals. Many old Progressives telephoned and wrote to me approving of my viewpoint, which was in direct conflict with the attitude of the executive of the Party who resented my intrusion into the controversy surrounding the arranged merger at this late stage, and needed ratification. My public views irritated the members of the National Executive who were gathered in Johannesburg.

On 7 July the Southern Transvaal Regional Council of the party held its annual meeting when new office-bearers were elected. It was no surprise to me when I realised during the meeting that I was opposed for nomination as the region's senior vice-chairman and its chairman of organisation. I knew there was trouble ahead. Originally I understood that I was to succeed Max Borkum as chairman. However some weeks before this meeting I was asked to meet at Helen Suzman's home with Max Borkum and Peter Soal, the local director of the party. I did not initiate the meeting but it was clear to me that Borkum wanted to hold on to his chairmanship. The meeting was a farce. I told Borkum that I would not stand in his way. He said that he would see that I was nominated at the AGM, but I should then withdraw in his favour, to which I agreed, as I had no real desire to be the chairman.

At the elections when Max Borkum was nominated as chairman my name was never put forward. To my surprise, Zach de Beer was proposed instead of me as senior vice-chairman. I withdrew immediately in his favour as I realised that opposition was organised against me. The Borkum establishment had made plans to oust me from senior positions in the party. I was nominated for chairman of organisation but beaten by Peter Nixon, Gordon Waddell's MPC, who had no experience whatsoever of organisation or publicity.

It was clear that the anti-Wilson faction was out in force.

I flew to Durban the next day and was disconcerted to read a prominent report in the early edition of *The Star* that "Progs Axe Anti-RP Rebel." It stated that the "man in the Progressive Party who publicly opposed the planned merger with the Reformists, Dr Boris Wilson, has been axed from all positions on the Party's Southern Transvaal executive."

It went on to say "that Dr Wilson, one of the party's original 12 MPs, came in for criticism because of his stand that there should not be a merger with the Reformists but that the Reformists should join the Progressives (as individuals)."

It was evident that this was "inspired" reporting, designed to discredit me politically. I had a good idea who planted this report and I was indeed very angry. I decided that I would set the record straight.

On 21 July, at the last meeting of the Southern Transvaal Regional Council of the Progressive Party, before it went out of existence, I read a statement indicating that certain persons were determined to keep me out of office at all costs. I also reminded the regional members that I had every right to criticise any leader of the party and voice my views in the inner sanctums of the party, but pointed out that internal criticism appeared not to be welcomed in the party. I noted that some members objected to the fact that, although I was one of the founders of the Party, I should not have written the *RDM* article opposing the merger with the Reformists.

For the record, I told the regional executive about the personal attack made on me at Zach de Beer's house-party the evening after the national executive meeting. Gordon Waddell angrily criticised me in the presence of other MPs – Van Zyl Slabbert, Alex Boraine, and Colin Eglin, for publishing my anti-merger article in *The Rand Daily Mail*. He said if it was in his power he would have had me "chopped". There was no reaction from any of the MPs present. I did not waste words with Waddell whom I suggested had lost "his cerebral connections to his vocal chords". It left me with a clear impression that he could have been one of the Progressives behind recent events both to discredit me publicly and to keep me out of office in the regional council.

I ended my statement: "The function of our party has been to fight for freedom and enlightenment, which I will continue to do, and not to fall into the trap of indulging in the muckrake of personal politics, and political jealousies which was the obvious aim of those who inspired the unfortunate report in *The Star.*"

The whole issue reminded me of the manner in which the United Party did not re-elect me to the chairmanship of the Non-European Affairs Committee in the City Council – the only difference was that this time it was the Progressive Party who decided that the best way to deal with Boris Wilson was to remove him. It was this series of events which made me abandon active party politics and continue my political interests as an observer and critic from outside the Progressive Party ranks.

The day before the special congress of the Progressive Party on 25 July to ratify the merger between the Progressives and the Reformists, Raymond Louw asked me, as one of the founders of the Progressive Party, to write an article for the record in *The Rand Daily Mail,* since the PP was going out of existence. I suggested that I would write the article as an interview with his chief political reporter, Bernardi Wessels. This resulted in the full-page "Milestones To A Merger", in which I went through historical events, of my first meeting in the UP with Harry Schwarz, the early days of the Progressive Party, our struggles, what we had achieved, and what I thought of the future of the merged party.

This interview in *The Rand Daily Mail* is a contemporary newspaper record of the rise and demise of the Progressive Party, at which the PP and Reformists merged to form the Progressive Reform Party.

The Progressive Party which we had founded in 1959 no longer existed – an era had passed.

73

Having reached another watershed in my relations with the Progressives, it is opportune to review what happened to the Party after Colin Eglin took over and masterminded the breakthrough in 1974.

As mentioned earlier, I had heard that Dr Brian Hackland had written a D Phil thesis at Oxford on the Progressive Party 1959-81. I was busy collating information on the period from 1974 to the present, so I contacted Hackland in London, and he very kindly lent me his thesis. I discovered that in the course of his research he had interviewed all the leading players in the progressive movement, except me. I then recalled that in 1980 he had asked for an interview, but for some reason we never met.

As I was busy with this chapter and had to hold over finalisation be-cause of the rapidly changing events in South Africa, I had time to read his thesis.

I found that I disagreed with certain of his conclusions about relations between Progressive Reform MPs, the subsequent Progressive Federal period and Harry Oppenheimer, who continued to support the progressive movement.

I differ from Dr Hackland's suggestions that there could have been some kind of "collusion" between Oppenheimer and his companies and the Progressive Party over the question of their overseas anti-sanctions stand, and the policies they advocated on their numerous visits. Aside from this, Hackland's thesis is a remarkable document, since much of it is based on interviews he had with leading Progressives, including Oppenheimer, between 1978 and 1980; and also the United Party Leader, Sir De Villiers Graaff and his colleague Douglas Mitchell, Natal leader of the UP.

Most interesting of all are the interviews with Oppenheimer, Helen Suzman, Zach de Beer, Van Zyl Slabbert, Harry Schwarz and Gordon Waddell. These conversations shed considerable light on what was happening in the progressive movement after the break in 1959, Helen Suzman's lonely fight in Parliament and Colin Eglin's rehabilitation of the Progressive Party.

It helped me to understand why, after 1974 in particular, the Progressive MPs were wandering around the capitals of the USA, UK and Europe: the House of Commons, Whitehall, Capitol Hill in Washington, Bonn, Paris, Amsterdam, year after year, which became their stamping grounds as they defended South Africa against the "total onslaught" of sanctions and other world pressures which were being intensified against the apartheid government of the National Party.

I could not easily fathom what motivated these Progressive MPs to make so many of these long trips overseas when perhaps they should have been pounding the hustings in South Africa during the Parliamentary recess as crisis succeeded crisis after the 1976 Soweto uprising.

I vividly recall an evening when Helen Suzman, Donald Woods and others debated the issue "for and against sanctions" at the Oxford Union in England. When the debate ended, Helen's daughter called out to me as we walked through the division doors: "Boris, you're going through the wrong door!" I looked up to see whether I was going through the "right" door for me, which was a vote FOR sanctions. Helen and her daughter went through the other – AGAINST sanctions.

I have been told that for some the question of sanctions is a highly emotional issue. That may explain why MPs like Helen Suzman, Alex Boraine, Harry Schwarz, Zach de Beer, Colin Eglin and others went on the anti-sanctions trail for so long.

Had the Party accepted any specific standpoint against sanctions which would justify their overseas activities? Not to my knowledge. This was never formally decided. Then why were they doing it? And were they doing so with the help of Oppenheimer the Anglo-American Corporation and other corporate donors to the Progressive Party?

These visits were extensive. Hackland records some of them. Helen Suzman went for a five-week tour in 1975 to the USA, lecturing and giving TV interviews opposing sanctions and disinvestment. Waddell went to Mocambique in a "dual capacity" as both a Progressive MP and a top Anglo executive. In September 1975 Boraine went to the USA to "refute a strong body of opinion in the US which was advocating total disengagement from South Africa."

Hackland points out that the "international isolation which followed led the Progressives to close ranks with the government even more in international relations." This might possibly account for the praise Vorster got from Boraine when he was in London about which I complained. Harry Schwarz declared the Party's support for the government's efforts to overcome this isolation. He was reported to have said: "We have the credibility, the credentials and the connections in western Europe and the US and I offer the government my services unconditionally in doing whatever I can to re-establish the kind of relationship we need abroad." (*The Rand Daily Mail*, 28 October 1977)

Two weeks later Schwarz went to Europe to "persuade business people with South African links to oppose economic sanctions and to invest further in South Africa." Two months earlier Helen Suzman had been on a similar mission to the USA.

Hackland says that the campaign by the Progressive MPs to encourage investment in South Africa occurred synchronously with a similar campaign launched by Aubrey Dickman, a senior economic consultant to Anglo, which appeared in the form of a major article in the Group's well-known journal *Optima* late in 1977. In May 1978 Harry Oppenheimer addressed the International Monetary Fund and urged foreign investment in South Africa.

No one can object to senior executives of South Africa's larger multinationals appealing for investment and capital – that is after all part of their job and what shareholders expect.

The conundrum is why the Progressive politicians seemed to be doing the government's job when the government was getting into deep international trouble because of its doctrine of apartheid.

I have no doubt that the Progressive MPs firmly believed that sanctions were wrong and that a healthy economy would make it easier to destroy apartheid, and that the lowest-paid workers would suffer most – the black worker – and that there would be increasing unemployment, which was bad enough long before sanctions.

However, the African National Congress and other organisations speaking for blacks repeatedly pointed out when criticising the anti-sanctioneers, that when the South African economy was healthy and burgeoning no attempts were made by the government to modify or abolish the stringencies of apartheid that kept blacks at low income levels and denied them the economic and financial privileges enjoyed by the higher-income whites.

I have learnt from members of the PRP caucus that the Progressives decided informally that as there was no other political party in opposition to the government who could speak against mounting sanctions, that it should be their duty when overseas, especially in the USA and UK, to speak up for South Africa. In the interests of unity and patriotism they felt that they should do so because they felt that it was better to keep black people in jobs; if there was a healthy economy, apartheid would eventually go. That, at least, was the theory.

This I regarded, then as now, as an illusion and a pipedream. Nothing would move the Nationalists away from apartheid except the strongest world sanctions. We all knew what the National Party's kragdadigheid and Dr Verwoerd's wall of granite meant.

Surely by now Helen Suzman, her Progressive Party colleagues, and Harry Schwarz in Washington, whose prime task is to hasten the end of sanctions, are aware that it was the financial sanctions and the package of economic pressures, that were the crucial reasons why the National Party was no longer able to continue the policy of apartheid, and FW de Klerk made his historic declaration in 1990 abandoning it forever.

Can they advance any other reasons why on 19 June 1991 the last of the Acts of Parliament, the Population Registration Act was finally and totally repealed by the Tri-Cameral Parliament, the apartheid edifice set up by the nationalists as the constitutional cornerstone of their policy; why the 180-day detention without trial provision was withdrawn and why after twenty-eight years South Africa had its rule of law and habeas corpus restored?

Dr Hackland also reminds us, in his thesis, of a very interesting statement Harry Oppenheimer made in 1961 when speaking in support of Helen Suzman at her final election rally: "I have decided to vote for the Progressive Party because I am really a conservative."

Was this declaration a slip of the tongue, or was it really intended to identify the true political views of one of South Africa's leading "liberal capitalists"? Does it help us to explain the important developments that affected the Progressive Party and the leading anti-apartheid English-language newspaper, *The Rand Daily Mail*, some years after Gordon Waddell arrived on the scene?

The position of Waddell is interesting. Because of his relationship with Oppenheimer, Waddell very quickly became an important player in the Progressive Party.

Waddell arrived in South Africa as a member of one of the British Lions rugby tours, met Harry Oppenheimer's daughter Mary, married her in a "wedding of the year" in 1965 and, not unexpectedly, became a director of the Anglo-American Corporation.

Waddell acquired South African citizenship, becoming involved in Progressive Party affairs mainly through his connections with Oppenheimer and his circle of Progressives.

Waddell told Hackland in October 1980 that he became involved with the Progressives because it was the only sensible policy. Helen Suzman particularly inspired him. His decision to stand for parliamentary election in 1974 was to increase Progressive seats in the House. If Helen Suzman was again to be the only MP, then the whole Progressive Party position would have been reviewed and many supporters might have abandoned the party.

Gordon Waddell appeared to take over Harry Oppenheimer's role as the direct contact with the leaders of the Progressive Party, especially on matters of the party's finances. To my surprise Waddell, who could neither speak or understand Afrikaans, was selected as the PRP's parliamentary candidate for Johannesburg North in the 1974 general election. No doubt Oppenheimer and the Progressives were happy that Waddell would make a positive contribution in Parliament for the Progressives, and was expected to be their spokesman on financial matters. At the same time, his rise in the party's hierarchy and his Oppenheimer connection was expected to encourage other financial leaders in South Africa to follow Oppenheimer's example and contribute to the PRP's election and party funds.

Waddell's connection with the Oppenheimers was not broken when his marriage to Oppenheimer's daughter was dissolved. What was even more interesting was that Waddell became very powerful in the Progressive Party's political affairs. The top leaders did not appear to act without his approval. In effect, for a while he became the *eminence grise* of the party.

Of importance was the influence he wielded as a director on the board of the South African Associated Newspapers (SAAN), who owned, amongst other morning newspapers *The Rand Daily Mail*.

The SAAN group, in which Anglo had a complex interest, was showing large losses in part attributed to the fact that the *RDM*, since Laurence Gandar's editorship, supported the Progressive Party, which became the policy of successive editors like Raymond Louw and Allister Sparks.

In 1984 there were strong rumours that *The Rand Daily Mail* would be closed because the losses were so large that they were affecting the stability of the SAAN Group.

Not only were there rumours that Anglo-American was going to close *The Rand Daily Mail*, but the government had clandestinely in 1977 used R30 000 000 of taxpayers' money when it started *The Citizen* newspaper to force closure of the *RDM*. This was part of the "Info Scandal", or Muldergate, which *The Rand Daily Mail* under Allister Sparks uncovered.

Three past editors of *The Rand Daily Mail*, Laurence Gandar, Raymond Louw and Allister Sparks warned Gordon Waddell that the policies adopted by SAAN would lead to the closure of the newspaper, and appealed to him to stop the rot.

At the first meeting he gave assurances that something would be done, but in fact – even after further meetings between Gandar, Louw and Waddell – nothing happened, and Waddell announced the closure of *The Rand Daily Mail*.

The excuse Anglo-American had given was that the newspaper was losing money and endangering the whole of the SAAN Group. No one, however, enquired about the efficiency and effectiveness of the advertising department, which is the mainstay of any newspaper.

SAAN's management had embarked on a disastrous sales policy a few years earlier, which involved *The Sunday Times* – the largest newspaper in South Africa – the smaller *Sunday Express*, and *The Rand Daily Mail*.

The space salesmen gravitated to the easy-to-sell *Sunday Times* and neglected the *RDM*. In addition, the losses of *The Rand Daily Mail* were compounded by the fact that management had created its own distribution scheme which increased the *RDM's* losses by 400 per cent (R3 000 000 to R12 000 000).

Those were some of the factors which ostensibly led to the closure of *The Rand Daily Mail*; but what is the saddest fact of all is that the management had intended closing the paper at least four years earlier.

In 1981 Raymond Louw, who was then general manager of SAAN, told me that Clive Kinsley, the managing director, informed him that if *The Rand Daily Mail* was closed, SAAN would become extremely profitable. Louw protested, but was ignored. Kinsley and his financial manager were completely wrong, because after *The Rand Daily Mail* closed, the company's overdraft shot up in a couple of months from R10 000 000 to R40 000 000. SAAN was forced to sell its assets to retain viability.

Raymond Louw explained that it was that remark by Kinsley in 1981 that aroused his suspicions about Kinsley's intentions, and which resulted in the visits and warnings given to Waddell by Gandar, Louw and Sparks.

I was in London when Raymond Louw, told me of the imminent closure of the newspaper. I was appalled because not only did I have a close association with the *RDM* in my political career, but, like many liberals, there was a bond of affection in the mutual struggle against Verwoerd and apartheid. *The Rand Daily Mail* always gave me unswerving support, and its loyalty to the Progressive movement was unquestioned.

Raymond Louw and I discussed what we might do at the last minute to stop the tragedy if that was possible. Louw decided to speak to IPI, who sent a cable to Harry Oppenheimer.

The International Press Institute represented over 2 000 editors and publishers all over the world. The Institute asked Oppenheimer to try to stop the closure.

"In view of the role you personally and Anglo-American have played in liberal affairs in South Africa in the last twenty-five years in opposing the Nationalist government's policies of oppression through its apartheid doctrines we appeal to you to use your considerable influence to reverse the decision . . . you must be aware that the closure of *The Rand Daily Mail* will have serious consequences for South Africa, both political and financial, and hand over the control of the country's media to the Nationalist government which you have always strenuously opposed."

I in turn felt I should show my concern by writing a letter to Harry Oppenheimer in view of my earlier political association with him, and the support I had from his father, Sir Ernest, in 1956 when I raised the £3 000 000 housing loan to clear Johannesburg's slums.

Harry Oppenheimer never acknowledged or replied to my letter of 25 March 1985, nor did the post office return it as undelivered. *The Rand Daily Mail* went out of existence and the one English-language newspaper that never feared the National Party disappeared off the South African opposition scene. By closing it, Oppenheimer, Waddell and others saved the struggling pro-Nat supporting morning newspaper *The Citizen* from extinction.

It was able to take over a large slice of *The Rand Daily Mail's* circulation and advertising revenue, and gave the Nationalist government a powerful daily voice in the largest urban concentration in South Africa.

In 1987, when Gordon Waddell left South Africa for good he admitted in an interview in *Leadership* (Vol 6, 1987, No 1) that he and others had erred in closing *The Rand Daily Mail*. He accepted a "degree of guilt" because the board of SAAN did not install new management in time to save *The Rand Daily Mail*. ". . . The problem lay with the management of the business as opposed to the editorial side. To the extent that I failed to carry that point of view, then I must have been guilty."

Looking back, it is clear that by closing *The Rand Daily Mail* the forces of South African liberalism had been dealt a damaging blow by some of its leading "liberal" businessmen, who were more concerned with the loss of profits, which they could afford, than in opposing apartheid, which in fact was making it difficult for them to continue their business activities. They appeared to give up the struggle by closing the *RDM* instead of carrying on the political battles that they themselves had fostered over many years and in which invested considerable funds.

Harry Oppenheimer, when he was a member of Parliament, and as a leading "liberal" financier, had a reputation for clear thinking. His public statements were always consistent in condemning the apartheid theorists and their impractical attempts to establish segregation in South Africa. As one of the most powerful men in the private sector, his action in handing over some important political and business responsibilities to Gordon Waddell, who to all intents and purposes was undoubtedly inexperienced in these affairs as a recent immigrant to South Africa, was a source of puzzlement to some of us, who had links with Oppenheimer through the Progressive movement.

Waddell inexplicably, in his short business and political career in South Africa, took part in decisions that led to the various mergers undertaken by the Progressive Party (despite the fact that Oppenheimer and many "old Progs" had spent many years in nurturing the Progressive Party) and in the needless destruction of its most loyal newspaper supporter, *The Rand Daily Mail*.

We can get some indication of Oppenheimer's thinking on Progressive Party affairs from Hackland's interview with him on 30 October 1978 at 44 Main Street.

Hackland: ". . . and in . . . policies other than constitutional were you involved?"

Oppenheimer: "No, not to any great extent. I mean I knew the people well and there was endless talk of politics, but I can't truthfully say I played a leading part in building up policy . . . I don't think I had a big influence . . . I did not feel, since I was not in Parliament, that I had to be responsible for everything the Progressive Party went for . . . I've been quite happy with the general trend of policy . . ."

Hackland: "Do you feel your influence in the Party has declined with its growth? In other words, basically since 1975?"

Oppenheimer: "Oh, yes, I think so. I don't think I'm as vital to the party, perhaps, as I used to be. And obviously the Party is bigger; I don't know them so well and I've got older. So I think that must be so."

Hackland: "How regularly are you consulted, or is your opinion canvassed on policy issues?"

Oppenheimer: "I see the leaders of the Party quite often. They are, you know, very kindly to me and they discuss policies with me . . . I've been very comfortable with this Party. Again, not agreeing with everything they do; naturally one doesn't . . ."

Oppenheimer (Later in the interview): "Well, I think it was thought in the early days to be very wild (the Progressive Party) . . . I mean of course one knew it wasn't . . . and I knew it was a very conservative policy otherwise I wouldn't have gone for it because I'm a conservative old body . . . I would say business thought it had no chance of success. And I also think they thought, quite wrongly, that it was long before its time . . ."

74

We founder-progressives must question what went wrong with us along the road to the new South Africa at a time when liberalism was most needed by the country. Was it intended that the liberal summit, for which we had striven since 1959 with all our idealism and visions of the future, would inexplicably be reached by the right wing National Party, the advocates and perpetrators of South Africa's scourge of racialism – apartheid – and not in the company of liberals?

It is indeed ironic that the original Progressive Party was no longer on the political scene when the dramatic changes for which it had struggled were announced in 1990; and that although there are two founder Progressives in Parliament, Eglin and De Beer, the party itself will never take part in the historic reconstruction of South Africa, for which it had visions in 1959, of keeping alive the liberal aims of true democracy.

To his credit, Colin Eglin did tell President De Klerk, during the 1991 debate on the president's speech, that "speaking as an old Progressive" he complimented De Klerk on where he was going and what he wanted to achieve for the new South Africa . . . because this was what the founding Progressives had aimed for from the start.

Eglin the survivor, speaking for himself, told the president that he would be watched and supported as long as he kept to "liberal and progressive principles" in the period of reconstruction.

To justify my criticism of the way the Progressive leadership had moved the party sideways since 1974, it is worth recalling what has happened since 1977 when Colin Eglin, De Beer and Waddell were on the merger trail. Eglin's merger with Schwarz's Reformists had disappointed many of the old Progressives.

Eglin and the leading Progressives were not concerned with the views of the "old" Progressives. As Eglin told Hackland, the "party had to become more broad-based."

Unfortunately the act of "broad-basing" meant that conservative-minded politicians were being admitted into the Progressive Party, which in time was to change the way the party was conducted, possibly to the detriment of its libral objectives. It could be said that this is where Eglin, who otherwise did a remarkable job in building up the Progressives, made tactical errors. "Broad-basing" the party meant being influenced by the conservative-minded politicians with whom he had allied himself and the party. This created potential conflicts in spite of more liberal policies.

After the 1974 electoral success, Eglin appointed Van Zyl Slabbert to head a policy review commission. In time, Slabbert's proposals were adopted and the PRP discarded the qualified franchise in favour of one person/one vote, among other advances in policy.

Eglin continued "broad-basing" the PRP by merging with a section of the dying United Party under Japie Basson to bcome the Progressive Federal Party. The Bassonites, as they were called, offered no philosophical or ideological basis for the merger. De Villiers Graaff was retiring and the Bassonites needed a political home. Among their number was Professor Nic Olivier (a former Nationalist) who became a valuable acquisition since he was a perceptive political scientist and research worker.

Other than Olivier the merger with the Bassonites merely resulted in further dilution of the progressive movement with MPs who were of the conservative mould, faced with the prospect that they had to carry out liberal policies which in the future could create problems for some or all of them.

It was obvious that this presented the party with a "conflict" situation where these MPs who were really not liberals in the progressive sense might in a crisis have to decide whether they move to the right or to the left. Most likely they would go to the right.

Trouble meanwhile was brewing for Colin Eglin. Little did he realise (though he may have been aware) that Gordon Waddell was no friend of his and from the time Waddell became an MP, he openly let it be known he wanted Eglin out of the leadership. When Eglin stumbled over the Don McHenry episode in Parliament, the kingmaker Waddell had Eglin deposed. The charismatic Van Zyl Slabbert became the new leader.

It did not take long for Slabbert to show his mettle when he dealt a short sharp blow expelling Japie Basson (then chairman of the Party's executive), who insisted as a senior PFP member that he was prepared to serve on the President's Council if asked to do so, against the Party's wishes.

This was the first evidence of serious dissent developing with the leader of the Bassonite faction that had been merged with the progressive movement – who could by no stretch of imagination have been considered a liberal in the progressive sense.

I am certain that Eglin must have been most unhappy that "broad-basing" the Progressive Party would have this kind of end result – but that was the risk when one merged with disaffected members of United Party, who, unlike the 1959 Progressives, were not liberals.

There was no comment from Oppenheimer behind the scenes, and in his interview with Hackland he explains why he remained silent and did not proffer public advice to the Progressives of the political dangers ahead when using mergers with non-liberals in order to enlarge the party who were by then in important positions in its hierarchy.

Waddell's career in Parliament ended in 1977 when he was recalled by Harry Oppenheimer to become head of Johannesburg Consolidated Investments, a major Oppenheimer company. Zach de Beer immediately went back to Parliament as MP for Parktown as Rene de Villiers had also resigned. But within two years De Beer resigned his seat and was back in the Anglo stable; he realised, no doubt, that any ambitions for leadership would come to nothing as long as Slabbert was there. He would have a long time to reconsider a new formula to return to Parliament in more favourable times, when he would finally retire from Anglo-American.

75

The Tri-Cameral Parliament was established in 1983 amidst tremendous opposition from most coloureds, who showed their displeasure by staying away from the polls. Coloured MPs were elected on the derisory turnouts of between three and ten per cent.

The Progressives, despite the fact that the Tri-Cameral Parliament only catered for whites, Indians and coloureds and excluded blacks entirely, decided to participate.

The multiracial chamber has had some positive benefits, in that it has been a limited forum in which whites, coloureds and Indians, (however restricted by the apartheid system), have been able to conduct some political dialogue about the country's problems. In particular, the coloureds and Indians have been able to gain experience in the parliamentary system, to understand how it works.

Dr Van Zyl Slabbert told me recently that while he was the PFP leader he had reached a point where he felt that the entire party should resign, fight an election with a policy of "no confidence" in the Tri-Cameral system unless it was reconstructed to include everyone – white, black coloured, Indian – and refuse to take their seats if the government failed to meet their demands.

He put this to some key members of the caucus, but met with no enthusiasm.

Slabbert is a realist and an academic democrat of the highest principles, and it was clear that he was unhappy with his role in Parliament. He realised that he was at the crossroads.

In February 1986 I was in the white House of Assembly, waiting for Van Zyl Slabbert, as leader of the PFP, to reply to the No Confidence Debate, when his twin sister Marcia, who was in the visitor's bay with me, whispered that Slabbert was going to resign that afternoon from Parliament.

I was astonished, I had lunched with him two days before, and although I was a friend of his, he had said nothing to me of his intentions.

Frederick Van Zyl Slabbert opened his reply by saying (from *Hansard*):

"What must the role of our opposition be in a complex and conflict-ridden society such as ours? Even now, with clarity of conviction, I can answer: An opposition must question the actions of government – which we have done.

"It must expose the contradictions and shortcomings of government – which we have done. It must protest against injustice and the erosion of civil liberties – which we have done. It must define alternatives to the policy dead-ends into which government leads us – which we have done . . .

"But there is another aspect of opposition which has a momentum and life of its own . . . that is, political leadership in opposition . . . This has to be judged on different grounds and the most important judge is the person himself. He has to decide when the tension between analysis and practice is no longer bearable to himself. In other words, he has to decide when is the right time to go. The magic moment for any political leader is to find the right time to go."

He then referred to the 1983 referendum, when the country voted for the Tri-Cameral Parliament in South Africa. The executive powers remained in the hands of President PW Botha and the white Parliament; the other two houses were effectively powerless.

He complained that no one in the government addressed the real problems in South Africa.

"I have made it my business to get to know this government and to try and understand its thinking. Given my position, I think I have explored every nook and cranny for possible leverage to promote the politics of negotiation . . .

"The circumstances in our country are simply too serious for us to bluff ourselves in the clubby atmosphere of Parliament, no matter how desperately a way out is needed . . . I am afraid this government does not understand the politics of negotiation or if they do they do not abide by them. Dismantling apartheid has nothing to do with negotiation.

"Apartheid is not up for negotiation. It has to go completely. What is up for negotiation is its alternative."

Van Zyl Slabbert went on:

"The Tri-Cameral Parliament is a hopelessly flawed and failed constitutional experiment. It does not begin to solve the problem of political domination, it compounds it. It has nothing to do with effective powersha-ring . . . I remain an incurable democrat. This motivates my involvement in politics and inspires my vision of the future. I do believe we can become a non-racial united South Africa where all its people can participate voluntar-ily in the governmental institutions of this land."

There was a silence in the House as MPs on both sides watched Van Zyl Slabbert sit down as his resignation statement made its impact. The Progressive Federal Party MPs appeared to be in a trance, despite the fact that Slabbert's speech was momentous and historic – equalling the important speeches made by Margaret Ballinger since I had been in Parliament. I know, from discussions with them afterwards, that the PFP MPs were not concerned with his historic analysis of the government's role and the Tri-Cameral edifice, but distraught that Slabbert had left them suddenly, without adequate notice.

It was terrible news for the Progressives. I am reliably informed, by Van Zyl Slabbert himself, that over the previous three months he had raised the matter with Helen Suzman, (who apparently never took him seriously), Colin Eglin and Harry Oppenheimer; he had told them that he was unhappy with his role as leader of the PFP and its participation in the Tri-Cameral Parliament. He assured me that at least one-third of the PFP MPs knew of his intentions.

I cannot recall a South African party leader who has resigned from Parliament under similar circumstances. I admired the frank and critical line Slabbert took, especially since it was done in the open, in Parliament, so that both the government and the opposition in Parliament, and the people outside should fully understand his reasons for his dramatic departure from the Tri-cameral parliament.

Peter Soal, the Democratic Party MP for Johannesburg North and one of his party's whips, told me in June 1991 that he learned purely by accident, two days before, that Slabbert was going to resign. Ken Owen, then the assistant editor of the *Sunday Times*, telephoned Soal and asked him if there was any truth in the rumour that Slabbert was going to resign from Parliament. Soal laughed it off and said it was groundless. Owen informed Soal that there had been a meeting at an address in Johannesburg at which, among others, certain members of the PFP Caucus were present, namely Andrew Savage, MP from Port Elizabeth; Pierre Cronje (Natal); Errol Moorcroft and Alex Boraine. Soal then decided that there must be some-thing in it, and in his inquisitive way began his own investigation. Boraine, perhaps inadvertently, then confirmed that it was true. Soal told Helen Suzman, who confronted Slabbert; he told her he was resigning. She had known for months that he was unhappy and had considered this step; according to Slabbert he had mentioned this before but she had ignored it.

At 1.45 pm that day, Slabbert called an urgent meeting of the PFP Caucus, where he broke the news. The MPs were flabbergasted, but there was no time to take any action, and they had to wait for it to be played out in the House when Slabbert would reply to the No Confidence debate for the last time as leader of the PFP.

In a state of shock, the PFP once more elected Colin Eglin to the leadership. I saw Colin later that day in his office, and he felt that he was being conned into taking the leadership again. He did not want it – he was decidedly unhappy about it.

But the PFP did not have any option; there was simply no one else of any stature to elect.

Colin Eglin did not last long in his second term. In the general election in 1987 the PFP did badly. Eglin, after talks with senior members, advised the Caucus that he was going to resign as leader and Zach de Beer was at long last elected leader of the PFP at the 1988 congress. However, there was a problem – De Beer did not have a seat in Parliament and it was obviously urgent that he should have a seat at the beginning of the 1989 Session not only as the Party's leader, but as leader of the PFP in the Tri-Cameral Parliament. Nic Olivier, the PFP research head, who was an indirectly elected MP resigned, and Zach de Beer became an MP until the 1989 election, when he once again was elected as MP for Parktown.

Zach de Beer was retiring from Anglo-American. He and others had evolved a plan to create a new party out of three disparate political movements, of which he hoped, in the end, to become the leader.

The first of these was of course the PFP, who had suffered serious losses in the 1987 elections. The second was a small group of MPs under Wynand Malan, a leading Nationalist who retained his Randburg seat in the election with the support of the PFP after dissenting from the National Party. He had been joined by two MPs who had defected from the Progressives, Peter Gastrow and Pierre Cronje, both from Natal. Malan and his colleagues were known as the National Democratic Movement.

The third element essential to the formation of the new party was a movement started by a former Nationalist, Denis Worrall, one of the architects of the Tri-Cameral constitution, and more recently South African ambassador in London. Worrall's group had no parliamentary representation, but acquired much publicity in the 1987 election when, with the help of the PFP and dissident Nationalists, he very nearly defeated Minister of Constitutional Development Chris Heunis, the Cape Leader of the National Party. Worrall did not have a viable party, but his showing in the election was impressive enough to get him invited to sup at Zach de Beer's table.

De Beer and his friends decided once more to "broad-base" the PFP by merging with these other groups, and perhaps attracting those Nationalists who were looking for a more acceptable home.

De Beer was backed in this manoeuvre by six former PFP MPs who had lost their seats in the 1987 election and who were keen to return to Parliament – perhaps they missed all the perks of the parliamentary "club": the free travel, the new car every four years, but most of all the pension. Who can tell?

With De Beer, they mistakenly believed that by bringing together, in one party, former Nationalists like Worrall, Wynand Malan (a born-again Christian) and others, a "centrist" Democratic Party would be a more palatable alternative to the nationalist-minded South African voter.

De Beer's proposals for this coming together were ludicrous. Here was an established party, with a thirty-year history, making coy overtures to three dissident MPs, Wynand Malan and his two cronies (who had previously defected from the PFP anyway), and Worrall's embryonic group that had little in its favour beyond a dodgy opinion poll which gave it a rating of eight per cent.

Even the government-supporting *The Citizen*, no friend of the Progressives, pointed out the inadvisability of this alliance, which would lead to the disappearance of the progressive movement and the struggle of the white liberals.

De Beer and his backers would not listen to advice or appeals. I met De Beer one morning in Johannesburg, by accident, and told him I did not approve of what he was doing to the Progressive movement.

He smiled and said: "We've always disagreed, haven't we, Boris?"

76

In January 1989, Parliament re-convened with 17 PFP MPs. The three component parts – PFP, Malan's Group and Worrall's menage – called separate congresses, dissolved themselves and were reconstituted as the Democratic Party, with a "troika" leadership of Zach de Beer as Parliamentary leader, Denis Worrall and Wynand Malan.

Unceremoniously, the Progressive Federal party was buried. There was no political wake, no speeches, no last supper. It was consigned to history's dust. Although the PFP was now a much-changed version of the original Progressive Party, it did have the benefit of a forward-looking progressive-liberal policy – but it was dealt the mortal blows by politicians who could in no way claim that they were the heirs of the Progressive founders in 1959. However immature we 1959 progressives may have been, we looked forward to a (distant) future, to a non-racial democratic South Africa in which we had played a formidable role in shaping.

But it was not to be.

The new party that was born immediately after the PFP was declared a lifeless corpse, was the ultimate achievement of Zach de Beer's political career, the Democratic Party. Fortunately, by a series of manoeuvres, it was able to take over the infrastructure of the late lamented PFP – the offices, secretariat and all its assets. The DP was in business.

For many old Progressives the Democratic Party does not have the moral force and political clout to influence liberal thinking in South Africa.

Today the Democrats are a new party that is in a political wilderness of its own construction, with no black support and with many former PFP supporters now elsewhere, perhaps in the ranks of the National Party, which has annexed the principles of the old Progressive Party. Members of the National Party openly state in Parliament that there is no longer a role for the Democratic Party.

At the present time the Democratic Party has a crisis of identity. Despite denials it is public knowledge that they are divided as to whether they should form an alliance with the Nationalists or to simply join the National Party; about one third of the members seem to want to join the ANC. The original Progs have not expressed any decision either way.

The DP's electoral history so far is not encouraging. In the general election of 1989 it managed to win 29 seats, losing the status, which the PFP had, of official Opposition, to the Conservative Party, who were returned with 39 seats. The important statistic is that the DP only obtained 20 per cent of the votes, similar to the PFP results in 1981. In that period the progressive movement remained static, and the DP did not win back one seat from the Nationalists, despite their declared intention to do so. The DP has a pact with the Nationalists in the Johannesburg City Council and is able to govern the city. It recently retained a seat in a by-election because of this pact.

The Democratic Party in Parliament ran into trouble in the 1990 budget debate, which was further evidence that the "broad-basting" of the movement has lead to conflicts between the "conservative-minded" politicians and the party's liberals.

Without any consultation with the Democratic leadership in Parliament, Harry Schwarz, its shadow finance minister compromised the party into voting for the government's annual budget, which was still the budget of the apartheid administration. No counter-action was taken by its leader Zach de Beer or any of the MPs present to denounce Schwarz's move, or dissociate themselves from his action. De Beer did not inform the Speaker that the party was voting against the budget provisions as he should have done, or even taken the drastic action of walking out of the House with his Democratic colleagues leaving Harry Schwarz to his own devices, and voting alone with the government.

Later in 1990, after this strange episode in Parliament, Harry Schwarz resigned to become South Africa's ambassador to Washington, essentially representing the Nationalist government. Schwarz was running true to form. In 1977 he had stated that he would do anything if it helped South Africa. Ambassador Harry Schwarz was always a great patriot.

In 1990, Zach de Beer finally realised his ambition to lead a political party in South Africa. He was elected sole leader of the Democratic Party after Wynand Malan announced his resignation from the party and from politics. Denis Worrall accepted that he was not going to become the leader and withdrew, after a spirited challenge.

It had been a long road for Zach de Beer; thirty-two years, and five political parties, starting from the old United Party, the Progressive Party, then the Progressive Reform Party, the Progressive Federal Party and finally now the Democratic Party. As the result of President De Klerk's statements in 1990 and 1991, it seems more than likely that the Democratic Party could disappear by its own hand, as did its ancient ancestor, the United Party.

The sad part of this saga is that although the progressive movement had undergone all the so-called "broad-based" changes that its leaders were seeking, what did change were the politicians who were brought in by the mergers, who were not liberals in the ideological sense. For various reasons, they were opponents of the Nationalists and apartheid, and they were individuals who wanted a political home – the Reformists, the Bassonites; they all wanted to be in a parliament, whether it represented only whites, or the fraudulent Tri-Cameral with MPs like the coloureds and Indians who sat in a "parliament" but who had no executive power whatsoever. Above all, they did not mind that the parliament to which they were elected did not have a single black man to represent the overwhelming majority of the people of South Africa.

There was no Progressive Party in the Chamber when President de Klerk made his historic announcement in February 1990 – to hear De Klerk claim for the National Party what had been Progressive Party policy for more than thirty years – a non-racial, democratic South Africa.

Dr Brian Hackland made a remarkable prediction at the end of his thesis in 1984. On the last page, looking to the future, he writes :

"By 1981 it had become clear that the government had accepted the Progressive Party's central tenet that repression on its own could not be effective in the long term in South Africa. While it was clear that any changes would be within the overall context of apartheid and would be designed to strengthen rather than dismantle the system, the ideological justifications of change were often couched in the rhetoric previously used by the Progressive Party.

"The threat, for the Progressives, was that they would come to be redundant if the National Party appeared to embark on the very programme advocated by the Progressive Party for the previous 21 years."

In 1990 President de Klerk announced his new policy for South Africa – and it "was the very programme advocated by the Progressive Party for the previous 21 years."

There is now no Progressive Party to become redundant – there are some Democrats who are facing the threat of final redundancy as they debate their future.

77

Before winding up my review of the Progressive movement, I cannot leave the subject without recording the views of both the leader of the United Party, Sir De Villiers Graaff, and his lieutenant Mr Douglas Mitchell of Natal, who spent so much of his time in politics scheming to get rid of liberal philosophy and liberals in the United Party. It is fortunate that Brian

Hackland was able to get the transcript of an interview between Terry Wilks (a political journalist with the *Daily News* whom I remember when I was in Parliament), and Douglas Mitchell, which speaks for itself about the United Party's "liberals" and the real attitude of the UP hierarchy towards them.

Brian Hackland's hitherto unpublished interview with Sir De Villiers took place in Cape Town on 5 August 1980.

Hackland: "And so the people who broke away, although apparently they didn't meet beforehand, knew who was likely to come with them?"

Graaff: "They still say they didn't meet? I wonder. You must read Douglas's book." [Douglas Mitchell]. " . . . And here was where the break came. These chaps were totally out of touch with the electorate."

About Jan Steytler and the 1959 breakaway, Graaff had this to say: "He was the Cape leader as well. Much against my will, mind you. I knew my Jan Steytler. He could talk nonsense by the hour . . . And good heavens, I remember the morning of his [Steytler's] divisional committee. The organiser and the secretary rang me up . . . what he didn't know and should have known was that about forty of the chaps on his divisional committee . . . were people who served with me in my regiment. And there was just no argument . . . (The secretary) said . . . What are your orders? I said: You chuck him out. And they chucked him out just like that.

"Zach de Beer and Colin Eglin were chairman and vice chair of the Cape Peninsula council . . . and down here, out of a hundred and fifty people, I think they got eleven votes . . . There was no popular support at all, and it was quite obvious that they would lose their seats although the English press nearly went mad trying to talk them into it . . ."

Hackland: "There was . . . that you were aware of, any conspiracy or plan to oust liberals or progressives from the Party?"

Graaff: "There was no such plan. There was no intention of ousting them, chucking them out or anything of the sort . . . it had been a good congress . . . they'd had their differences, had a good scrap, and some had won, some had lost . . . but there was no plan to get rid of them or anything of that kind at all. Nothing whatever . . ."

After discussing how he was helping and training Eglin and De Beer to take over one day, Graaff told Hackland: ". . . But they got this bee in their bonnet and then felt they would have forced the issue had it not been that they rushed in to see Harry Oppenheimer straight away and he promised them support. And when I was to see Harry Oppenheimer – we'd made a date to meet – he announced the night before that he supported the Progressives. What was the use of going to see him?"

Terry Wilks's interview with Douglas Mitchell is of an entirely different order. Mitchell was the leader of the United Party in Natal, a front-bencher and member of the UP Leader's Committee in 1959. Mitchell was the mover of the Land Resolution at the 1959 UP congress which was unacceptable to the progressive-liberals and which was the immediate cause of the break with the UP when they formed the Progressive Party. Wilks interviewed him over several days, 12-14 December 1974. This is extracted from Hackland's papers, and needs no comment.

Mitchell: "I was told the full story . . . This wasn't drafted [the Land Resolution] to get rid of them. I wouldn't have gone to that amount of trouble . . . But they were on the verge of expulsion. They didn't want to be expelled, not with disgrace, but to go out as martyrs, that was what they wanted . . . Then they'd go and form their own political party. Which is exactly what they did. And that is why they all . . . beat their breasts and patted their heads and said: We are the upholders of the great . . . in political life in South Africa. We are the greatest and the best, when it comes to upholding principles! They were conceived in disgrace and born in dishonour. That's your Progressive Party . . .

"It's not a political party. And knowing its origin . . . I followed it all day long . . . it has no future as a political party . . . And the time will come when its members will disintegrate because over-riding considerations will take their political loyalties from this issue . . . they can have their ephemeral successes based on the command of big moneybags . . . that doesn't worry me in the slightest . . .

"Why doesn't the United Party get stuck in, take off the gloves and wipe them out? The answer is . . . leave these do-gooders, social salvationists, who are on our left, because on your left you must have the political rubbish bin into which all the curious people with curious political ideas can be all safely packed away together, but it must be on the left of the United Party."

Wilks: "Yes, you never get Progs taking part in agricultural debates or . . ."

Mitchell: "They've got no policy for it . . ."

Wilks: "Yes, that's right. Or on education.

Mitchell: ". . . no policy on water affairs . . . no policy on land . . . on conservation, the environment . . . no policy on defence . . . they will deal with sporadic cases . . . of a man who's been, they feel, martyred for his religious beliefs in connection with his military duty . . ."

Wilks: "They were the big martyrs going out . . . these were the people feeding the press at congress with the stories because all that took place was in committee (the 1959 UP congress) . . . the press was not there, whether Afrikaans or English, to form independent judgements of how the thing developed. All the press were outside and then they got sent information by Helen Suzman. Boris Wilson was the one, the biggest culprit there."

Mitchell: "Yes. By Jove, Yes."

Wilks: "Yes. He was almost their sort of public relations officer."

Mitchell: "Bad little fellow . . . Married to whats-his-name's sister-. . . those two lawyer chaps, brothers in Maritzburg . . . Oh, dammit . . . Anyway, I knew her, the girl, that's right. Yes, he was a bad fellow. Very able."

Wilks: "Yes. Oh, yes."

Mitchell: "That slim face. Ferret type. Sure."

78

Looking back over nearly half a century as an active, liberal, anti-apartheid campaigner and as an observer of the South African political scene, what conclusions can be drawn from the role we liberals played in the turbulent 1940s, 1950s and 1960s, in our struggle against apartheid? When Nationalist protagonists were moving heaven and earth to establish it for ever – as they often arrogantly told the white and black people of South Africa, what did we do?

Dr Verwoerd proclaimed, many times, to South Africans that he and the National Party were in power because it was the Will of the Almighty.

When President De Klerk announced his radical changes in 1990, the Nationalists gave the impression that not only had they taken over the Progressive Party's original democratic policies of racial integration, but they were going to create a "new era" for South Africa, embracing all the egalitarian principles for which we liberals had fought so hard and so long.

To what extent was this total change of direction due to our years of struggle when we were derided by most white South Africans? We were years ahead of our time, often smeared as communists by our political opponents to the right of us. Was De Klerk's statement a cynical tactical move by the National Party, camouflaging a "hidden agenda" which would, in the course of time, unfold so that the white man in the near future could, through the new constitution, maintain his position of control in South Africa?

In February 1990, after President De Klerk's momentous announcement, I asked a leading Nationalist front-bench MP if there was a "hidden agenda" and whether the NP was sincere in the moves initiated by the party and the Broederbond, (still the think-tank of the National Party). He assured me that it was a genuine move and that the party had been at work for three years preparing the way, because it realised that it had no option but to come to terms with black South Africans or perish as a "volk" in the foreseeable future.

"Wait," he said, "until you see our draft proposals for the new constitution – you will then agree how serious our intentions are to create a new South Africa."

Some draft proposals have seen the light of day and although South Africa is assured that they are put forward for discussion by all the groups who will participate in the round table negotiations, one cannot rule out the possibilities of a "hidden agenda". The horrendous violence, the unrest, the allegations that there are groups in the government who are supplying arms to the Inkatha Freedom Party of Buthelezi, the fact that De Klerk has for a long time ignored the appeals from black organisations – the ANC and the PAC – and the human rights groups to investigate the underlying causes of the violence and destabilisation, all adds up to the possibilities that there are individuals in the National Party hierarchy who have other plans for the future, making it evident that the "hidden agenda" could be hidden even from De Klerk.

How else does one explain the rapid, overnight conversion from extreme right wing nationalist policies to a new egalitarian South Africa?

It is hard to accept that the white nationalist voter is ready to surrender white control and the survival package for which he has so long striven – the conservative movements don't encourage this interpretation – to become an unprotected minority under a black government.

Some commentators are already saying that the NP's draft proposals, which will seek to protect all minorities in a second chamber, are so hedged with blocking devices on every conceivable issue of "rights", that a coalition of the National Party, with some of the numerous fragmented and balkanised apartheid "tribal" units, and hundreds of conservative black local authorities and "conservative" black religious movements, including a majority of the Democratic Party, could create a front that would keep the white strategists of die volk in a "new era" of power for many years to come.

President de Klerk has made it quite clear that he will bring about such an alliance, and he is capable of doing it – we only have to look at the terms on which the coloureds and Indians were "bought" when the Tri-Cameral Parliament was established. Recently allegations by the Labour Party in June 1991 that the coloured MPs who joined the National Party amid a "campaign tantamount to bribery", have caused a definite rift in the Labour Party's relationship with the President.

Are liberals, progressives and others to the left of centre entitled at this stage to be optimistic that in the end there will be a just and balanced solution to South Africa's political problems?

It must be conceded that the change in direction taken by the Nationalists, however nebulous and hedged with "ifs" and "buts" is far better for South Africa than the disastrous road to apartheid, even though the Nationalists have signalled that they do not appear to have abandoned some white entrenchment, in one form or another, because of the checks and balances in the new constitutional proposals.

It is not only liberals who have to question future optimism. Every white person who remains in South Africa has to accept the fact that he or she lives on the continent of Africa with nearly 700 million black people, and that South Africa is still the "last bastion" of white domination which is fast disappearing. It is no longer possible for 5 million whites to keep alive a political system which ignores the existence today, politically, of 30 million blacks; a system which does not allow everyone, irrespective of colour, to have an equal right with every other person to a share in the fruits of their labour.

The great debate and political struggle is on between white and black. In this respect, what did our liberal movements achieve?

We must admit that the liberal movement made little impact on conservative white nationalists and most English-speaking whites. We liberals were always branded as enemies of the "volk" and linked with the "swart gevaar", as agitators and fellow-travellers of Marxist-Leninism, whatever these derogatory labels meant. One only has to consult the Afrikaans press or *Hansard* to realise what meagre influence we really had in the corridors of power.

We progressive-liberals were a divided lot, and most of us came from an established, affluent white society, created by our forefathers who, like most whites, misused the cheap labour of our black compatriots, giving little or nothing in return. History told us that white skins were better than black skins and we continued, despite our liberal views, to hold millions of blacks hostage to poverty and social deprivation.

White Nationalists, who realised that there was no place for them elsewhere in the world, unexpectedly had their chance to make their last ditch stand in 1948. They were in power and entrenched apartheid in the hope that it would persevere forever. We liberals were outnumbered. Our political messages, initially, were only heard by a small sector of English-speakers, while the rest of white South Africa was nurtured on the doctrine of race hatred and the need to keep white supremacists in power. We lost out too because the Afrikaner nationalist was not interested in our policies and principles. He had been frightened off by years of indoctrination and the fear of black domination and communism which, in his eyes, were practically synonymous.

The Progressive Party, when it opened its doors to black members, found that very few joined. Those who did were conservative blacks generally shunned by the black community. For years, some Progressive leaders were anti-ANC, falling for government propaganda that the ANC were "terrorists" in their liberation struggle. For a while the Progressive Party's vital connections with blacks were surprisingly with Buthelezi's conservative Inkatha movement during the attempts to establish the Indaba in Natal. Some of its MPs have kept up a dialogue with leaders of the independent and semi-independent Bantustans, but this has not got them very far.

Fortunately, Progressives were saved embarrassment from attempting to get further black support, which was in any case beyond their reach, by the Prohibition of Political Interference Act of 1968. This benevolent-sounding law effectively stopped all multiracial political parties at that time from existing. The Progressives decided that they had a role to play in the white parliament, while the Liberal Party disbanded.

The blacks themselves ignored white political parties and were not interested in the white struggle for power, because it was a struggle to determine which white group was to dominate. Blacks saw a different final solution. Blacks would either get power by negotiation with whites or by revolution. In recent years light began to dawn on a wide spectrum of white individuals and organisations that the road to a negotiated peace in South Africa was being charted by realists like Frederick van Zyl Slabbert, who having resigned from Parliament, established IDASA (Institute for a Democratic Alternative for South Africa) to bridge the communication gap between the black movements, like the African National Congress, and whites of all political shades of opinion who recognised the urgency of consultation across colour lines. This was totally absent in the South African political environment because of the apartheid system. Thus the first meeting was held outside South Africa in Dakar, as a tentative step to avoid the looming racial conflict; it has since mushroomed to the extent that there is today in South Africa a constant political dialogue between black and white, however tenuous and fragile it may at times seem to be.

Is this where we Progressive liberals failed as a formal group over the years? We were unable to take our message into the minds and hearts of blacks in South Africa – we kept to the white edges while the PFP sidetracked itself into the Tri-Cameral monstrosity which excluded blacks. It was inevitable that Progressive credibility declined as many coloured and Indian MPs were made into lackeys of the government.

Our South African brand of progressive liberalism also failed largely because most times we were long on principle and short on practise. We stood for the rights of man, but did not, or could not, do enough directly about men, women and children who were deprived of those rights, except to talk about them in the abstract in the cosy confines of our homes, our meeting-places and in the Nationalist-controlled political institutions – leaving practical action to extra-parliamentary organisations like the Black Sash, and to a few of our own MPs who came face-to-face with the realities of not being white in South Africa and living under apartheid's shackles.

Without doubt, most of us were so intimidated by the might of Verwoerd's all-embracing political system that we simply abdicated our responsibilities and retreated into our safe progressive liberal shelters.

The Nationalists startled South Africa in 1991 by their "confessions" in Parliament and elsewhere; they were hoping – without actually asking for it – for forgiveness, since one way or another they would like all those who were not white and had suffered under apartheid to forget these terrible sins of the apartheid years. This dimension of "repentance", of seeking forgiveness, is still unfolding.

But if we progressive liberals are frank, we must agree that it is not necessary to join in this communal breast-beating to acknowledge and admit where we went off course in our attempts to derail and destroy apartheid – and why we failed in those attempts.

When Van Zyl Slabbert made his historic resignation statement in Parliament in 1986, he knew then that to achieve real change one had to break out of the institutional Nationalist stranglehold, to create new lines of communication with the real leaders of black South Africa, like the African National Congress, who until recently were banned in South Africa and branded as terrorists. It was no longer of consequence to talk to the leaders of the Bantustans. Their political status amongst blacks was low.

79

Despite the claims of some liberal theorists and economists who opposed sanctions, in the final analysis it was the extent of the worldwide pressure over the previous ten years and the crippling effect of financial sanctions that brought the Nationalist government to its knees. The role of anti-sanctioneers like Helen Suzman and her parliamentary colleagues, Buthelezi and others, who were supported by the majority of financial and industrial leaders and the Nationalist government of South Africa, was ultimately futile.

The prospect of coping with the hundreds of thousands of blacks who in 1989 and 1990 thronged the stadiums and streets of South Africa in protest, the continuing internal violence, advancing economic collapse, the strength of black trade unions, the unacceptable cost to the white taxpayer of maintaining white and black armies fighting in Angola, the costs of destabilisation of Mozambique and Zimbabwe, and above all the cost of maintaining apartheid in South Africa was the burden the white man could no longer carry. The negotiating table was no longer a mirage in the bright South African sunshine; it could be reached.

The path ahead is tortuous. Since Mandela and other leaders have been released, Oliver Tambo and many exiled ANC members have returned to South Africa. The banned organisations are now taking part in political activity, making their presence felt. Much pre-negotiating ground has been covered in spite of the horrors of violence in the black areas and widespread political unrest in all sectors.

In the face of this terrible violence, can De Klerk and Mandela maintain a dialogue which will work its way through the political and social minefields?

Their aim is clear – they want to reach the negotiating table. This was emphasised to Raymond Louw and me at our meeting with the former President of the African National Congress, Oliver Tambo, in May 1991 at his home in London.

Tambo said the ANC was a democratic movement that would not go back to "guerrilla" warfare to achieve its aims. This was a thing of the past and no matter how long it took, "negotiation was the only weapon that would bring peace between black and white in South Africa." If the ANC were to find itself in a situation where it felt that it had to take up arms again, "it would put things back many, many years", and this was the last thing he or the ANC wanted. This view of negotiations was backed by Mandela in his opening address to the ANC's congress in South Africa on 2 July 1991 in Durban and amplified in his important interview with Stanley Uys in *The Star* (18 July 1991). Mandela made clear that the organisation had decided "to be flexible and conciliatory on key issues blocking the negotiating process."

Both De Klerk and Mandela lead divided constituencies. But what is emerging is that, although the ANC has called for a constituent assembly as a first step, the likelihood is that a multi-party conference will be held initially, and could be "closer than most people expect." (De Klerk, SABC-TV interview, 17 February 1991).

Who will participate in such a multi-party conference is still to be decided, but at this stage even Andries Treurnicht, leader of the Conservative Party, is indicating that the CP may well attend the conference to put its case against the new South Africa.

The next hesitant steps to the new South Africa after the multi-party conference are hazy. It is unlikely that President De Klerk will establish an interim government consisting of whites, blacks, coloureds and Indians. Fortunately for De Klerk, he will still have the mechanism and powers of the Tri-Cameral Constitution to "make transitional arrangements" arising out of a multi-party conference.

De Klerk suggested in his television interview (17 Feb), that he would take steps to consult white voters on the reform process in a referendum, as well as another with blacks.

What success he will have with white voters remains to be seen. The impression one has at this time is that the overwhelming majority of whites are politically indifferent – the average white man is not taking part in the current dialogue in the new South Africa, although by now he must at least be aware of some of the current developments.

Nelson Mandela, in an address to students at the University of the Witwatersrand in February 1991, made "an emphatic plea to ordinary South Africans to become involved in the process of creating democracy – a task which (should) not be left to the politicians alone . . . we do not see the resolution of our conflict happening without public activity." (*The Star*, 21 February 1991).

It is the political leaders who are participating – the majority of whites, at this stage unlike the demonstrating blacks, are keeping their views on the new South Africa close to their chests.

Some disturbing trends are emerging. The government has given permission for schools to be deregulated *vis-à-vis* admissions to schools that are at present racially segregated, leaving the decision to the parents' committees. The number of schools that have received permission to open to blacks is pitifully low, and even then there is a host of "qualifications" – proportions, school fees, maintaining standards; all the old white bogeys are still in place.

The Saturday Star (16 February 1991) featured a report "that Helen Suzman, former MP for Houghton, sternly reprimanded parents in her old constituency when she heard that Houghton Primary School would not be desegregated this year. 'Incredible,' she said. 'This is a sad blot on the liberal reputation of the Houghton constituency, which over all these years without reservation has voted for a policy of non-racialism.' "

Is this the shape of things to come?

In the 1991 debate on the State President's speech, it was evident to me that on all sides of the Tri-Cameral Parliament a new attitude had emerged against the ANC, which had taken the place of the old enemy, the swart gevaar, as the new black danger. No longer were ALL blacks the peril, but THIS political group of blacks. This has been so all year. It has reached the point where Nelson Mandela, in his speech at the 16 June commemorative rally reprimanded the South African press for "running our struggle . . . and our forthcoming conference in July. The ANC was certainly not in a shambles as has been implied by the newspapers and its leadership did not spend its time on deadly struggles for personal power."

Is this anti-ANC stance a symptom of hardening attitudes amongst whites, conservative coloureds and Indians? Is this a reaction to the repeated call by the ANC for a constituent assembly, which would give the ANC and its allies an overwhelming majority to govern the new South Africa, raising the centuries-old spectre of black domination, such as they now perceive in Zimbabwe?

While De Klerk can possibly reach a compromise on the future new South Africa with the black leaders and on their participation, he has an almost insurmountable task in changing ingrained white and black prejudices which have been reinforced by forty-three years of an official apartheid government. This is the hardest task of all.

Blacks too will have their problems of realignment; they will have to cope with Black Consciousness Movements and anti-whitism, a reaction to the white domination and repression, the denial of human rights and well-remembered white brutality towards blacks.

These deeply rooted elements may well be the final barriers to a peaceful new South Africa.

80

There are still some important questions that have to be answered.

Why has the Nationalist government been unable to stop the serious ethnic violence amongst blacks, which has escalated in the last few years and particularly in 1991? The government has at its disposal the formidable might and power of the Defence Force and the Police and should long ago have stopped the violence and investigated its root causes. It appears to have chosen not to do so. Why?

Are the reports which appear prominently in the British press under headlines like "SA MILITARY GIVES ARMS TO INKATHA" true? (*The Independent*, 11 June 1991). John Carlin, reporting from South Africa, wrote "the South African Defence Force (SADF) has deliberately fanned the township violence of recent months, including the funding and supplying of weapons to Mangosuthu Buthelezi's Inkatha Freedom Party as part of a comprehensive 'dirty tricks' strategy to ensure FW de Klerk's National Party remains in power after the end of apartheid."

It was followed a day later by a further prominently placed report quoting Defence Minister Magnus Malan: "You ask us what our aim is. I can answer that in one word – Victory. Victory at all costs . . . Victory in spite of all terror. Victory however long and hard the road may be. For without victory there is no survival." This had been issued as a statement in 1980.

Two days after Mandela's conciliatory statement on 18 July the bubble burst over the question of "secret funding" of Inkatha, which had surfaced in the British newspapers, and was constantly denied by the Nationalist government in South Africa.

The Weekly Mail (Johannesburg) on 19 July disclosed, in a front-page news report taken up by most of South Africa's newspapers and the news programmes of the South African Broadcasting Corporation, that it had uncovered evidence that the secret police had paid the Inkatha Freedom Party at least R250 000 of taxpayer's money for the purpose of organising rallies and other anti-ANC activities shortly after the release from prison of Nelson Mandela in 1990. One rally was the spark for an upsurge of civic violence now known as the "Maritzburg War" in which many people died.

The allegation of funding by the secret police was immediately denied by the Inkatha leader Mangosuthu Buthelezi. His denial however lacked credence when later the same day President de Klerk and Adriaan Vlok (Minister of Law and Order) admitted that "secret funding" had been part of the covert operation to fund organisations that opposed sanctions and violence.

In a dramatic interview on 25 July on SATV where he was questioned by the editor of the *Weekly Mail*, Anton Harber, the (then) Minister of Law and Order, Adriaan Vlok confirmed that in addition the South African Police had used the sum of R1,5 million of taxpayers' money to establish Inkatha's trade union movement UWUSA (United Workers of South Africa) to oppose Cosatu (Congress of South African Trade Unions) the country's largest trade union organisation. Soon after UWUSA was established it took part in industrial disputes which resulted in violence and deaths in Natal and Transvaal in 1986, 1989 and 1990.

In another SATV "Agenda" programme, "Pik" Botha, the Foreign Minister, when confronted by three newspaper editors about the money given to Inkatha, admitted that the police had given money from secret "slush funds" of taxpayers' money to various political organisations to fight sanctions and violence. With unseemly haste Inkatha refunded the R250 000 the following day.

Nelson Mandela's reaction was swift. The ANC and the government "were now clearly on a collision course" – he was doubtful that "a complete breakdown in relations could be avoided . . . we have said all along that the government is following a double agenda . . . while talking to us they were conducting a war against us," was his biting response.

A stormy ten days after the "Inkathagate" revelations and the world-wide criticism which followed, the pressures on President de Klerk began to tell as he must have realised that the credibility he had successfully established, and to which he was entitled, suddenly crumbled around him. The "slush" fund disclosures which involved some of his senior cabinet colleagues, Vlok, Malan and "Pik" Botha about possible misuse of taxpayers' moneyengulfed his rising international status.

He acted quicklyto re-establish confidence. On 30 July he announced a major cabinet reshuffle. Disappointingly however, despite clamour from both inside and outside South Africa to remove General Malan and Adriaan Vlok from the cabinet, he merely pushed them sideways into so-called "minor" cabinet posts, leading "Pik" Botha where he was in Foreign Affairs.

All the same influential cabinet players are still in office in the government albeit in different portfolios.

What has President de Klerk achieved by by his cabinet reshuffle? He does not appear to have removed the architects of the "hidden agenda" if there is one – they are still there, perhaps a little muted. Will not their presence in the cabinet give observers inside and outside South Africa the impression that, even if President de Klerk's explanations at his press conference on 30 July about covert operations, "slush funds" and use of taxpayers' money are acceptable, he will be seen as the political prisoner of the men in his cabinet who are still in ministerial office in the government?

Can President de Klerk convince South Africa and the international community that he will be fully in charge of the vital negotiations that lie ahead regarding the new South Africa?

As I write these final chapters, President de Klerk and his government are still facing a crisis and a serious problem of credibility, not only in South Africa but outside the country. The government appears to have been caught by the "hidden agenda" of some of its cabinet members in the midst of a great effort to get sanctions off its back, IMF loans reintroduced and the restoration of post-apartheid South Africa to a position of international respect.

President de Klerk is also faced with the possibility that the negotiations with the ANC may for the present be in jeopardy because of the "hidden agenda" or the "double agenda" which he denies but which has come to light. This may be the tip of a political iceberg.

I hope, however, that the faith that Nelson Mandela and the ANC have in negotiations (as Oliver Tambo told me was the only weapon that will bring peace between black and white) will ultimately allow this grave situation to resolve itself in the interests of South Africa.

There are still academics and politicians who do not believe that De Klerk and the Nationalists have a "hidden agenda". Van Zyl Slabbert, in *The Sunday Star* (16 June 1991), dismissed talk of the President having a hidden agenda, although those around him may. It is this last phrase which is the crux of the matter. "He can't afford one, there's too much at stake for him . . ." Slabbert goes on to say that when President de Klerk "bit the bullet with his historic speech he also sacrificed control of the agenda."

Nobody controls the agenda now, Slabbert believes. "It is unfolding, depending on the interaction between them. You have to look at the major players every day to find out what the agenda for the day is going to be."

I do not say that De Klerk himself has a "hidden agenda" – but De Klerk's vulnerability lies in the men around him; the Afrikaner volk as a whole who have been thoroughly indoctrinated over more than a lifetime with the notion that the fatherland is not to be surrendered at any price. This is reflected by Magnus Malan in his statement quoted above. In these days of complete uncertainty, when no one knows what the agenda is, might there not in fact be a "hidden agenda" operating without De Klerk's knowledge?

Is violence surviving, although Mandela and Buthelezi have signed an accord to end it, because it is an essential part of the white man's plan to destabilise the relationship between the ANC and Inkatha supporters in order to maintain a divide and rule policy in South Africa, and so to weaken the black participants in the negotiations?

It is not far-fetched to assume that the Nationalist apartheid movement cultivated thousands of black people in the past, who, for practical benefits gave support to the white apartheid strategists of the past, not only in South Africa but also in the "independent homelands".

Inter-racial violence was exported to the Transvaal black townships from the fighting fields of Natal – to Soweto, Thembisa, Sebokeng, Khatlehong, Kagiso and other places, with deaths resembling the worst of the fighting in Beirut, carried out in the most barbaric way by "faceless" people who were accused by opponents of the Nationalist government and the ANC of giving support to Buthelezi's Inkatha "warriors" with their shields and spears" to continue the fight against non-Inkatha Zulus.

A new element emerged in the townships around Johannesburg earlier in 1991 which appeared to originate in the single-sex hostels inhabited by spear-carrying Inkatha Zulus who carried out massacres of ANC supporters, forcing them to retaliate, while the police were accused of standing by or aiding Inkatha. As a result, negotiations between the ANC and the government were on the verge of collapse. Despite various appeals to the warring forces, to Buthelezi, De Klerk and Adriaan Vlok (the Minister of Law and Order), there was little sign that violence would cease.

The ANC refused to attend the multi-party conference called in Pretoria in May by President De Klerk on the grounds that he was not doing anything to stop the violence. All together, these factors as well as the government funding disclosed by *The Weekly Mail* seem to have as their goal the destabilisation of future constitutional negotiations, amid mounting civil chaos.

81

Where do the progressive liberals stand today?

Very few are left to join in the important decision-making around the negotiating table. None of the original Liberal Party of 1953 are taking part – many are dead. Of the Progressives, all the founding MPs have gone, or are on the sidelines, with the exception of Colin Eglin and Zach de Beer, who are in the Democratic Party.

We have to admit we were helpless to stop the Nationalists from wrecking democracy in South Africa, although Progressive Party MPs were able to do good work in fighting apartheid in and out of parliament. They embarrassed the government with thousands of questions, unearthing scandalous treatment of blacks; they exposed the harsh realities of the life of a black in South Africa. This made many white progessives feel that something was being done to help apartheid's victims. Did we stop the Nationalists from implementing their policies? Or was it, in the end, internal black defiance and the outside world with its years of sanctions and its package of constant pressures with an economically crippled white-governed South Africa which effectively forced the Nationalists to stop in their tracks?

The policies we progressive liberals had pursued for years, which the Nationalists had always spurned, and which we had failed to achieve in over forty-two years of active opposition – this is what the Nationalists, in their final act of survival, have turned to.

Is this our achievement?

We must ask ourselves: Is there still a role for the white liberal in black Africa? Or will South Africa follow patterns set in black countries to the north of us, where even white liberals have been forced to leave their African homes because the black majority is now in control and does not want the white man to play a significant part in their political and social economies, irrespective of his positive liberal beliefs?

In the same way that some Nationalists may have their "hidden agenda", blacks may let us go on believing that we white liberals have a role to play – but if and when they take power one day by controlling the civil service and take grip of the country's finances, will they do what the rest of black Africa has done – make whites expendable?

I was impressed with Oliver Tambo's answer during our private interview in May 1991. He said that the African National Congress could only succeed in government with white support and assistance. He indicated that the new infrastructure of the ANC would have room for white members on its highest bodies, and it is "rightly correct to live peacefully with each other to sort out things – man to man." I pointed out that people were fearful that the ANC would act as the Zimbabweans have done, and that the future for whites was therefore unsure – "we are different to the Zimbabweans," he reminded me.

Tambo has great hopes for the future. "Violence," he said, "must and will come to an end – man changes slowly – leave the old things, seek the new."

I was glad that Oliver Tambo, then the leader of the African National Congress, was optimistic about the future of South Africa.

I told him that I have serious reservations.

Even if in the next few years an equitable political settlement is achieved, both whites and blacks have to overcome the effects of years of indoctrination by the Nationalist Party who controlled the media, censored the books, installed Christian national education, laid waste all black education which is in crisis, segregated people, removed millions from their homes, fostered race hatred and fear – one can go on – all this will not vanish overnight, or even in a year or two. It may take years to overcome the mentally disabling effects of decades of indoctrination. While this state exists it may be very difficult to bring blacks and whites together in mutual understanding.

The Dutch Reformed Church and other allied religious movements have given a lead by declaring that their support for apartheid in the past was a sin. Earlier in 1991 black and white clergymen of various denominations stood shoulder to shoulder forgiving each other's past transgressions in upholding apartheid. Yet they have found when they put these declarations of unity to their white congregations, the laity rejected the religious consensus. This is one of the main dilemmas that will face all those who want to establish the new South Africa.

Will the ordinary, relatively affluent South African white, when it comes to the final, vital, decision, put his indelible stamp on the constitutional proposals in support of the white and black leaders in their negotiations, or will he withdraw from the brink because of the built-in prejudice of history?

Amongst blacks as well, the dying and dead bodies in the daily carnage indicates that white, and some black, leaders are still prepared to sacrifice thousands of human lives in the black versus black struggle, a human tragedy which has the effect of keeping the whites at present in power, to buy time to find yet another pathway to the promised white fatherland for which the Afrikaner and many of the English-speaking whites seem still to yearn.

Will the whites in South Africa, who by their own admission and actions are conservative in outlook, see this as their chance to struggle to the bitter end, to protect their privileged white status, forcing the blacks to rise up in final frustration and destroy the hopes for the "new era", that could leave South Africa dry, bare, arid and motherless as if it was the lonely unpopulated Kalahari desert?

EPILOGUE

I started this memoir with recollections of my father, who dominated so much of my early life, and it is appropriate that I finish with him.

There were the mysteries I never solved. Where did he come from? What was his real name? What were the real reasons why he was imprisoned in Siberia? Why did he not speak to his brother in New York for over thirty years? Was there some family dispute? What happened to him in Australia?

I have tried to give as full a picture of his character as I could; his poetry, his writing, his attempts to break away from the hard life at the Market, which fascinated me as a small boy.

I am still trying to solve these mysteries, and perhaps now that I have written this book I will in time find some answers.

In October 1990 I visited the Soviet Union, and while I was in Moscow decided to find the small village or town of Dubrovna, where my father claimed to have been born. No one in Moscow knew of such a place. It may have been destroyed in World War II.

I also took with me the Croxley duplicate book, which contained in its early pages the play *The Extremists*, which Father had dictated to me. At the back of the book were some of his writings in Russian, signed by him, which I hoped to have translated in Moscow.

This was impossible, because the Russian director of the Africa Institute, whom I had earlier met in London, was out of the country, and I did not know anyone else in Moscow.

I resigned myself to finding some one in London. On my way to Heathrow, on the wide-bodied Aeroflot airliner, an air hostess was serving drinks shortly after take-off at 11 am. As she came to my seat, she announced that mineral water and beer were free, but spirits had to be paid for.

I joked with her that drinks were free on other airlines. What was wrong with Aeroflot? The jest fell flat, and I settled for mineral water.

As I sipped the mineral water, I felt a tap on my shoulder, and turned to see a bottle of vodka being offered by a young Russian. In English, with a heavy Russian accent, he said:

"We heard you talk to the hostess. Please have some of our vodka."

"Oh, no," I said. "I was only joking. In any event it's too early for me."

"We are Russians," he said. "We drink vodka anytime. And this is a good time. You must have some with us."

I bowed to the inevitable and held out my glass, which still contained some of the mineral water. He was unimpressed.

"You need a new glass." He went over to the galley, fetched one and filled it with vodka.

As I raised my glass to him, I noticed that he was not alone; he had two companions, a man and a woman. They introduced themselves - Vladimir, who offered me vodka; Nikolai a young man with a drooping moustache; and the attractive Larissa. We all drank vodka.

They told me that they were on the way to London; a Soviet Trade delegation going to work with De Beers Diamond Corporation, which had recently concluded an agreement with the Russians.

The vodka flowed, and within an hour or so the bottle was empty. I must say that I never felt better in my life or spent a more interesting morning. It was a fitting end to my Moscow trip.

The vodka loosened inhibitions, and they told me all about themselves as we discussed politics, the future of Russia and whether Gorbachev would survive.

I volunteered that I was of Russian origin and that my name was Boris. We had another round of vodka on the strength of this felicitous information. I told them as much as I knew about my father, and then had a thought – why not ask these delightful Russians to read my father's Russian writing.

I produced the book and turned to the pages which my father had himself written. Perhaps they could tell me what it was; a history or autobiography or some hints about his origins or even his real name as there was a signature at the end of some pages.

My young friends looked at the text and discussed it rapidly amogst themselves.

"Sorry, Boris, but this is not Russian. Maybe Arabic. We can't read it."

I was astonished.

"Are you sure?"

"Of course," said Vladimir. "Did you say that your father was in a Siberian prison?"

"Yes." I was again surprised. "Why do you ask?"

"Well, many Russian Jews were sent to prison in Siberia, and they spoke Yiddish as well as Russian. Maybe your father has written this in the Yiddish language."

All these years I had assumed that Father had written in Russian, but this was a revelation. I thanked my Russian friends, and we exchanged addresses, as one does on these occasions.

Back in London, I asked my Israeli neighbour to look at my father's writings. He was fascinated as he began to translate. The Russians were right; my father had written in Yiddish.

My Israeli friend confirmed that my father had written poetry, signed in 1927, and there were the first few pages of a play about some people on board ship who argued about god and religion.

It rang a bell. It was in 1927 that my father had begun his dictation to me of his play. He must have realised that I could solve his language problem, when I showed him the verse I had written. That is how I came to be press-ganged into service as his scribe and how a very important part of my life began.

While we were discussing this interesting translation I received a letter from my only relation in the world from my father's side of the family, my cousin Ruth in New York.

She sent me a photostat of a pre-Hitler map of Russia from the records of the Russian Institute at Columbia University. It shows the town of Dubrovna near the River Dnieper. So the town did exist before World War II.

She also enclosed a report from the Nahum Goldmann Museum of the Jewish Diaspora in Jerusalem, which gave a history of the town and its inhabitants.

Dubrovna was a small town in Byelorussia. Jews were first mentioned there in 1685. There were 801 Jewish taxpayers in 1766. In the eighteenth century Dubrovna became a centre for the weaving of prayer shawls which were eventually exported to western Europe and America.

Dubrovna was also a centre for scribes of the Torah Scrolls, phylacteries and mezzuzot – who received permission to form a professional union in the early period of Soviet rule.

The manufacture of prayer shawls ceased in the 1920s. The population of Jews fell from 4 481 in 1847 to 3 105 in 1926, about 39 per cent of the total population of the town.

The shattering information was that the Jews in Dubrovna were murdered by the Germans and their Byelorussian collaborators at the end of 1941.

No wonder no one I met in Moscow, or the Russians on the Aeroflot aircraft, knew about Dubrovna. If there is anything left of the original town, it has been absorbed and renamed, with its history and its Jews buried in the soil of the Ukraine, and I may never meet the descendants of my father's family.

Ruth Tobin tells me that the last contact they had had with their relations in Dubrovna was in 1932, when an old friend who had emigrated to Australia went back to the town to visit family. She brought warm greetings from Ruth's parents' family, who were then still living in Dubrovna.

She has not heard from them since, and they were most probably victims in the 1941 slaughter. It does not, then, seem possible that any living trace of my father's past can be found.

My father's Yiddish writings have not yet been fully translated, nor his signature deciphered. My cousin Ruth is adamant that his name was Tobin. The Russian Embassy suggested to me that it was not a Russian name, but an adopted one.

Father's signature looks a lot like Samuel Wilson – something like "Sam Milsun". This again makes some kind of sense, because when my father arrived at Ellis Island in New York at the beginning of this century, the frustrated immigration officers admitting Russian emigres and refugees, who did not speak English, did themselves not speak any other exotic language.

Sometimes they short-circuited the process by giving a phonetic equivalent of the name - as they heard it - or something which was the closest "American" name to it.

Sam Milsun? Samuel Wilson? Or was it Samuel Tobin?

Who knows? Will I ever find out?

INDEX

Gottlieb, Gertrude, 164-6.
Graaff, Sir De Villiers, 204, 238,
   242-3, 245, 247, 250-1, 255, 260,
   261, 263, 267-8, 278, 281, 286,
   288-91, 295, 297, 299, 300-1,
   312-4, 316-9, 323, 330, 336-7,
   339-40,342-8, 349, 351, 357, 371,
   375, 386-7, 418-20, 424, 431,
   438-9.
Greenberg, Mr Justice, 75.
Greyshirts, 83, 85.
Groblersdal, 161.
Group Areas Act, 138, 295, 395, 407.

Hackland, Dr Brian, 416, 419, 420,
   423-5, 429, 430-2, 438-9.
Hall, Lester, 349.
Halliday, Dr, 96.
Hampson, Harry, 70.
Hansard, 171, 187, 248, 261, 289, 299,
   300, 301, 306, 308, 309, 316, 325,
   330, 331, 356, 372, 433, 443.
Harber, Anton, 448.
Harding, 375.
Harmel, Michael, 72.
Harrison, Laurie, 84, 109, 110.
Harvey, Richard, 174, 176, 179, 189,
   190, 204, 224.
Hawarden, Eleanor, 140, 145, 146.
Health Committee, 174, 175, 183,
   184, 185, 203, 206.
Hepple, Alex, 72, 132, 255.
Herstigte Nasionale Party (HNP),
   406,
Hertzog, Dr Albert, 279, 369, 382,
   404, 405, 408.
Hertzog, General JBM, 69, 73, 83,
   84, 259, 273, 344.
Heunis, Chris, 435.
"hidden agenda", 441, 449.
Higgerty, Jack, 240, 259, 278.
High Court of Parliament, 139, 196.
Hill & Everett, 62.
Hillbrow, 141, 142, 144, 195, 250.
Hitler, 14, 15, 33, 58, 59, 61, 69, 74,
   83, 84, 109.
Hodgson, Jack, 72.
Hofmeyr, JH (Jan), 132, 138, 146,
   163, 186, 266, 292.
Holland, Allan, 31.
Holmes, Dr Ivor, 176, 210, 211, 212,
   217, 219, 220, 222.
homosexuality, 54.
Horak, Don, 352.
Horak, HL, 197, 278.

Hospital (Hill) (constituency), 182,
   234, 235, 249, 259.
Hottentot's Holland, 255.
Houghton, 87, 155, 258, 410, 446.
House of Assembly, 194.
Housing Loan, 217, 220, 222-4, 226,
   228, 229, 231, 234, 247, 280, 284.
Huddleston, Father Trevor, 156, 164,
   177, 224, 311.
Huggins, Godfrey, 150.
Hughes, Gray, 321.

Ida, 26, 76.
IDASA (Institute for a Democratic
   Alternative for South Africa), 443.
Immorality Act, 137, 395.
Indaba, (Natal), 443.
Independent, The, 440.
Independent Newspapers & Journals
   (Pty) Ltd, 294.
Independent Ratepayers, 141.
Indians, 138, 432.
Indian National Congress, 138.
Indian Housing, 206.
Influx Control, 151, 323, 337, 357,
   367, 375, 376, 397.
Inkatha Freedom Party, 441, 447, 448,
   450.
"Inkathagate", 449.
Inkatha Movement, 443, 447.
International Court, 138.
International Monetary Fund, 425,
   449.
International Press Institute, 428.
Isaacson, 16.
Ismay, Hugh, 153.

Jabavu, 180, 184.
Jack, Mr, 24, 28.
Jankelowitz, Mr, 7.
Jeremiah, 34.
jewish, 15.
Jewish Board of Deputies, 326.
Jewish farmers, 328.
Jewish immigration, 73.
Johannesburg, 66, 68, 69, 75, 78, 396.
Johannesburg Chamber of Commerce,
   136, 141, 156-7, 165, 174, 177.
(------------) Non-European Affairs
   Committee, 136.
Johannesburg Festival Year, 211.
Johannesburg North, 427, 434.
Joubert Park, 199.
Judaism, 15.
Justice Vote, 303.
Kagiso, 450.

Medical Association, SA, 131, 139.
Medical & Dental Council, 123.
Medical School, 92, 94, 96-8, 101, 102, 122-5, 128, 181.
Mentz, (), 282, 283, 323, 324.
Mervis, Joel, 243, 292, 419.
Meyer, Eric, 18.
Meyer, Dr Piet, 369, 382.
Miller, Hymie, 176-7, 189, 203, 204, 212, 218, 220, 222, 223, 226, 228, 229, 231, 232, 233, 236, 237, 259, 282, 283, 284, 306.
Miller, Mrs, 24.
Milner, Lord, 236.
Milner Park, 22.
Mine Workers' Union, 131.
Mitchell, Douglas, 262, 270, 278, 295, 305, 316, 320, 339, 340, 343, 344, 346, 350, 354, 418, 424, 438, 439, 440.
Mitchell, Kathleen, 189, 204.
Mixed Marriages Act, 395.
Molteno, Donald, 352.
Moorcroft, Errol, 434.
Moore, Philip, 286, 314.
Morley, Graham, 65.
Moroka, 164, 180, 184, 210, 216, 217, 223.
Moroka (Emergency Camp) Advisory Board, 214.
Moscow, 453.
Mozambique, 396, 445.
Muller, Hilgard, 263.
Mussolini, 33, 61, 69, 83.

Nahum Goldman Museum of the Jewish Diaspora, 455.
Nancefield, 18, 213.
Natal, 28, 68, 407.
Natal Witness, The, 383.
National Democratic Movement, 435.
National General Practitioners Group, 183.
National Health Services Commission, 108, 122, 131.
Nationalists, 35, 83, 85, 86, 103, 129, 131, 132, 133, 134, 147, 148, 151, 157, 159, 161, 162, 171, 174, 185, 186, 188, 208, 215, 232, 234, 235, 236, 239, 243, 250, 251, 255, 358, 364, 368, 376, 416, 426, 435, 438, 441, 443.
Nationalist Government, 72, 206, 409, 429, 445, 451.
National Party, 18, 101, 128, 132, 172, 173, 196, 237, 258, 266, 387,

405, 406, 407, 430, 435, 436, 437, 441, 442, 452.
National Union of South African Students (NUSAS), 101, 116.
Native Advisory Boards, 220, 222, 310.
Native Affairs, 131, 178, 229.
Native Affairs Department, 210, 260.
Native Affairs Vote, 285, 286.
Native Chiefs, 312.
Native Commissioner's Court, 366, 396, 397.
Native Housing, 166, 175.
Native Law & Administration, 126.
Native locations, 99.
Native Policy, 125, 153, 155, 162, 163, 263, 268, 278, 279, 287, 301, 312, 317, 319, 342.
Native Representative(s), 87, 125, 266, 291, 297, 315, 317, 318, 337, 342, 376, 378, 385, 388, 410.
Native Representative Council, 125, 139, 152, 310.
Native Trust Land Act of 1936, 69.
Natives, 35.
Nazi (s), 14, 59, 74, 85, 96.
Neame, "Bunny", 292.
Nel, De Wet, 312, 314, 315, 326, 386.
New York, 110, 118, 453, 455.
Nicholas, HC, 41, 42.
night schools, 87.
Nikolas, Joe, 7, 12.
Nixon, Peter, 422.
Non-European Affair Committee (Department), 174, 175, 176, 178, 194, 203, 205, 206, 209, 212, 214, 215, 216, 218, 219, 223, 224, 226, 231, 232, 238, 275, 276, 282, 284, 309, 382, 414, 423.
Non-European Hospital (NEH), 98, 99, 101.
Non-European Winter Clothing Appeal & Financial Fund, 217.
Norgarb, Mrs Emily, 31.
Norwich Union, 52, 56.
Nutrition & Public Health, Conference, 94.
Nyanga, 378, 379, 381.

Observer, The, London, 132.
Observatory, 48.
Observatory Primary School, 6.
Odendaal, JH, 236, 248, 249.
Old Fort, 48.
Olivier, Prof Nic, 431, 435.
O'Meara, John, 41.

462

Uys, Stanley, 328, 329, 334, 340, 402, 445.

Vaal River, 67.
Van den Berg, MJ, 322.
Vanderbijl Park, 371, 373.
Van Deventer, Johan, 92.
Van Niekerk, GLH, 363.
Van Niekerk, Sannie, 320, 335.
Van Ryneveld, Clive, 266, 270, 346, 352.
Van Vuuren, PZJ, 171-3, 179, 188, 190, 201, 204, 215-6, 227, 262, 305, 309, 311, 333.
Van Wyk, Mr, 251, 252.
Vermaak, Mrs, 246.
Vermeulen, Piet, 417.
Verwoerd, HF, Dr, 138, 162, 164-6, 170, 171, 174, 177-8, 181, 186-7, 191-2, 194, 203-6, 208-9, 211, 213-5, 217-299, 231, 236-8, 243, 250, 253, 254, 255, 256, 260, 262, 263, 267, 268, 269, 273-7, 279, 280, 281, 283-6, 290, 291, 295, 297-9, 300, 309-15, 317, 318-9, 328, 330, 332, 335, 338, 340-1, 347, 355-6, 358, 359, 360-8, 370, 370-6, 378-89, 380, 382, 383, 384-6, 388-9, 395, 399, 400-7, 409, 412, 426, 441.
Very High Frequency Broadcasting (VHF), 369, 382.
Victoria Falls, 75.
Viking (radio), 64, 65, 69, 70, 79.
Viljoen, Dr Gerrit, 405.
"Vine, Owen," 290, 318.
Vlok, Adriaan, 448, 449, 450.
Voortrekkers, 35.
Von Moltke, Mr, 304.
Vorster, BJ, 273, 275, 282, 298, 299, 301, 412, 417, 418, 425.
Vrededorp, 206.
Vundla, 215, 216, 305, 309, 311.

Waddell, Gordon, 422, 424, 426, 427, 428, 429, 431, 432.
Wakkerstroom, 151.
Walker, Leslie, 159, 239, 242, 245, 251.
Wanderers Ground, 19.
War Communication Department, 102.
Warden, Lee, 262, 266, 285, 385.
Waring, Frank, 179, 269.
Warren, Miles, 320, 322.

War Veteran's Action Group, 139.
Wassenaar, Dr, 207, 235, 236.
Waterson, Sydney, 262, 344, 345, 346, 349.
Watson, Jack, 198, 199.
Watts, Hilda, 72.
Watts, James, Professor, 121, 126.
Weekly Mail, The, 448, 450.
Weinbren, Ben, 72, 73, 131, 132, 140, 147.
Weiner, Leslie, 91, 92, 96, 110.
Wentzel, Mr, 304.
Wessels, Bernardi, 423.
Western Area Removal Scheme, 164-7, 171, 172, 191-2, 311.
Western Native Township, 214.
White City, 180.
Whitehouse, Charles, 352, 353.
White River, 251.
"white supremacy", 186.
Whiting, Mr, 81, 85.
Wilks, Terry, 439, 440.
Williams, Hunt, 65.
Williams, Townley, 266, 345, 346.
Wilson, Adrian, 352, 408
Wilson, Boris (Benjamin, Benny), 6, 11, 16, 19, 28, 32, 37.
Wilson, Ethel, 3, 6, 23, 24, 25.
Wilson, Hannah, 1, 3, 15, 17, 26, 31, 32, 35, 36, 44, 52, 60, 62.
Wilson, Leon (Len), 3, 10, 13, 15, 18-9, 35-6, 52, 60, 77, 102, 244, 391.
Wilson, Max, 3, 10, 25, 26, 34, 60, 61, 76, 77, 78, 79, 102.
(----------) (alias Thomas Maxwell), 130.
(----------) (alias Desmond J Leaney), 130.
Wilson, Nigel, 352, 408.
Wilson, Pauline, 126, 127, 128, 142, 151, 259, 261, 272.
Wilson, Samuel, 3, 13, 37, 119, 456, (Sam Milsun) 455, 456.
Wilson, Sonya, 3, 37.
Wilson, Virginia, 352, 408.
Windhoek, 375.
"Winds of Change" Speech, 358.
Witwatersrand University (Wits), 35, 39.
Woods, Donald, 424.
"Woolfson, Benjamin", 307, 326, 330, 331, 333.
Women's Defence of the Constitution League, 198, 199, 200.
Worrall, Denis, 435, 436.